Human Resource Management

A Critical Text
(Second Edition)

Edited by John Storey
The Open University Business School

THOMSON

LEARNING ™

Australia • Canada • Mexico • Singapore • Spain • United Kingdom • United States

THOMSON

— ✳ —™

LEARNING

Human Resource Management

Copyright © 2001 John Storey

The Thomson Learning logo is a registered trademark used herein under licence.

For more information, contact Thomson Learning, Berkshire House, 168–173 High Holborn, London, WC1V 7 AA or visit us on the World Wide Web at: http://www.thomsonlearning.co.uk

British Library Cataloguing-in-Publication Data
A catalogue record for this book is available from the British Library

ISBN 1-86152-605-9

First edition published by Routledge 1995
Simultaneously published in the USA and Canada by Routledge
Reprinted by International Thomson Business Press 1996, 1997 and 1999

This edition published 2001 by Thomson Learning

Typeset by LaserScript Limited, Mitcham, Surrey
Printed in Great Britain by TJ International, Padstow, Cornwall

Contents

List of Figures

List of Tables

List of Contributors

David Ashton, Professor of Sociology, Centre for Labour Market Studies, University of Leicester.

Chris Brewster, Professor of International Human Resource Management, Cranfield School of Management.

Lee Dyer, Professor, Center for Advanced Studies, Cornell University.

Alan Felstead, Reader in Employment Studies, Centre for Labour Market Studies, University of Leicester.

David Guest, Professor of Organizational Psychology, King's College, University of London.

Paul Iles, Professor for HRD, Liverpool Business School, Liverpool John Moores University.

Susan E Jackson, Professor of Management, School of Management and Labor Relations, Rutgers University.

Ian Kessler, University Lecturer in Management Studies and Fellow in Human Resource Management, Said Business School and Templeton College, University of Oxford.

Thomas Kochan, Professor, Sloan School of Management, Massachusetts Institute of Technology.

Karen Legge, Professor of Organisational Behaviour, Warwick Business School, University of Warwick.

Mick Marchington, Professor of Human Resource Management, Manchester School of Management, UMIST.

John Purcell, Professor of Human Resource Management, School of Management, University of Bath.

Paul Quintas, Professor of Knowledge Management, Open University Business School.

Graeme Salaman, Professor of Organisation Studies, Open University Business School.

Hugh Scullion, Reader in International Management/Director, Executive MBA, University Business School, Nottingham.

Keith Sisson, Emeritus Professor of Industrial Relations, Warwick Business School, University of Warwick.

John Storey, Professor of Human Resource Management, Open University Business School.

Randall S Schuler, Professor of Human Resource Strategy and Director, Center for Global Strategic Human Resource Management, School of Management and Labor Relations, Rutgers University.

Diana Winstanley, Senior Lecturer in Human Resource Management, Imperial College Management School.

Jean Woodall, Professor of Human Resource Development, Kingston Business School.

Preface

The antecedents of this book stem from the publication in 1989 of *New Perspectives on Human Resource Management* – one of the first books on the subject outside the USA and one of the first world-wide to make a critical analysis of the subject. There then followed a fully re-written volume (under the title *Human Resource Management: A Critical Text*) published in 1995 which included a wider range of contributors and subjects. The present volume, a second edition, follows that path and it is, in turn, further extended in order to introduce and assess a number of new issues including, for example, the place of ethics in HRM; the management of joint ventures and alliances; and knowledge management.

Each of the other chapters which cover the central heartland issues and debates in HRM has been fully re-written by experts in their respective fields. As a result, the whole subject area is comprehensively addressed in a fully updated manner. As before, the volume is distinctive in that authors have provided authoritative overviews of their allotted topics while also introducing and weighing the significance of newly-available data. The objective is to provide a resource for students, policy makers and practitioners.

Why is this book sub-titled 'a critical text'? For three reasons. First, because all the chapters eschew the proselytizing so often encountered in 'managing people' books. The HRM phenomenon and its constituent elements are scrutinized very closely and its various meanings, implications, origins and stakeholders are subjected to detailed and searching analysis. Second, the text is 'critical' in the positive sense: the contributors offer new interpretations which ought to help in pushing the debate forward. Third, in many chapters there is also an element of stricture and critique. This centres on the gap between the rhetoric of humanistic values and the practices which often disavow and even mock the expression of these values.

The book would not have come to fruition without a great deal of co-operative effort. I am grateful above all to the 20 contributors who submitted such thoughtful and well-crafted material. The book has been a truly collegial effort. Acknowledgements are also due to Karen McCafferty at the Open University Business School who provided outstanding professional support, and to Jenny Clapham and Martha Abbott at Thomson Learning who helped to steer the project in a focused way. Finally, I am grateful as ever to the Open University Business School for offering such a stimulating and exciting environment.

John Storey

Part 1
Introduction

Human Resource Management Today: An Assessment

1

John Storey

It is hard to imagine that it is scarcely much more than a decade since the time when the term 'human resource management' (HRM) was rarely used – at least outside the USA. Yet nowadays the term is utterly familiar around the globe and hardly a week goes by without the publication of another book on the subject. When writing this chapter in the spring of 2000 I visited the Amazon.co.uk website in order to see what range of books was available on this subject. Remembering that just over a decade ago there were scarcely any books at all with this title it is staggering to find that there are 448 publications matching the title search 'human resources' and 394 titles with the fuller term 'human resource management'. There are now numerous textbooks, 'handbooks', encyclopaedias, encyclopaedic dictionaries, case-books, research monographs and critiques. Moreover, the idea of HRM, according to the book titles, seems to have colonized just about all industry and service sectors – most notably the 'hospitality industry', schools and further and higher education, health services, banks, the voluntary sector, government and the public sector, small and medium-sized enterprises (SMEs), and even the military. There are also versioned books on HRM for many different occupational specialists: the ones which caught my eye were those directed towards sport and recreation managers and the one for golf-course superintendents. Likewise, the territorial coverage is impressive: books can be found analysing HRM in Europe, Australia, the United States, India, and the Pacific Rim. In addition, there has been a welter of publications on international HRM, HRM in multinational corporations and various cross-national comparisons in HRM practices.

In addition to the books there are, of course, the journals, the conferences, the academic sub-groups, the practitioners and so on. And yet, as the phenomenon of HRM seems to flourish – at least at the conceptual level – it remains, and always has been from its earliest inception, highly controversial. There are numerous questions about its nature, its domain, its characteristics, its reach, its antecedents and its outcomes and impact. On each and all of these there is much disputation.

Newcomers entering the debate midstream must often wonder what is going on. There appears to be so much confusion and there are, even among many commentators, many points of misunderstanding. In part the confusion arises because authors and speakers seem sometimes to forget – or are perhaps simply unaware – of the situated origins of some of the issues and stances. HRM has been confidently declared by some as 'in crisis' and even 'dead'. A workshop series (sponsored somewhat ironically by the Institute of Personnel & Development (IPD)) pondered the 'HRM in Crisis?' theme and yet its contributors seemed perplexed as to the nature, source or character of this crisis (Sparrow and Marchington 1998). As the first contributor (Derek Torrington) was soon arguing: 'No crisis here' (1998: 32) – and most contributors to the volume, including the editors themselves, seemed to agree! In the same collection, David Guest undertook a search for a potential alternative 'orthodoxy' to HRM. Various candidates were considered – for example, the contract culture, flexibility, psychological contracts – none was found as a sufficiently viable contender.

In the introduction to the previous edition of this book (Storey 1995) it was noted that when HRM emerged on the scene in the late 1980s it was 'a fragile plant' but that within a short period there were many signs that it had taken a fairly secure hold. The update above seems to confirm this assessment. Major American contributions have been eagerly received within the UK – not least by the HR practitioners' main professional body The Chartered Institute of Personnel and Development (CIPD). Thus, Dave Ulrich's (1997) *Human Resource Champions* and Jeffrey Pfeffer's (1998) *The Human Equation* have both given a highly positive and uncritical fillip to the underlying propositions on HRM. Likewise, Mark Huselid of Rutgers University has been celebrated for providing statistical 'proof' of the performance outcomes of HRM policies and practices. Even the more critical texts such as Karen Legge's (1995) *Human Resource Management* have simply added fuel to the flames.

Moreover, developments in the wider literature on management, strategy and organizations have produced theories markedly in tune and supportive of the HRM thesis: for example, the Resource-based theory of the firm, the Learning Organization and more recently, Knowledge Management, are all major strands of thinking and research which lend weight to the idea of HRM. For example, resource-based theories suggest that sustainable competitive advantage stems from unique bundles of resources that competitors are unable, or find extremely hard, to imitate (Wernerfelt 1984; Barney 1991). Ironically, it has tended to be economists and others who have argued the case that human assets in particular can fulfil this criterion (Polanyi 1962; Lippman and Rumelt 1982; Teece 1982; Teece, Pisano *et al.* 1990).

In the context of all of the above indicators, 'crisis' is perhaps not the most appropriate descriptor and yet, as mentioned, there persist deep uncertainties and controversies. In this introductory chapter the purpose is to help chart a path through some of the undergrowth. The debate has become rather complicated and multi-stranded. It is necessary to return to fundamentals. Some of the debates are almost meaningless in the absence of an understanding of their origins. Those working in the field of employment management or the management of human resources (whether as academics or practitioners) ought to be able to make a special contribution to the furtherance of its understanding. As has been noted, while resource-based theory has 'extolled' the benefits of human assets, insights into the many difficult coping mechanisms required in order to realize this potential has to come from 'the organizational behaviour, organization theory and human resource management literature' (Coff 1997: 375). So far at least this contribution has arguably been lacking and insufficient.

But, in order to progress we need to be clear about the *different bases* of the continuing controversies. It can be suggested that these revolve largely around three different areas: first, the *meaning* of HRM, second, the *practice* of HRM and third, the *ethical standing* of HRM. As there is a separate chapter in this volume devoted to the third item, the focus here will be on just the first two controversies.

CONTROVERSIES ABOUT MEANING

Controversy in the area of meaning turns on the imprecision, variability, ambiguity and even contradictions which have been seen to imbue the construct. Noon (1992) asks whether HRM is 'a map, a model or a theory?' Keenoy (1990) refers to its 'brilliant ambiguity' and sees much of its resilience as stemming from this ambiguous character. For Keenoy and Anthony (1992) the whole point of HRM is to inspire – 'to explain it is to destroy it' (ibid.: 328). There is indeed much to the point that there is a degree of evangelism about HRM and associated management movements. In many of these cases the big ideas lose something when translated into detail.

Many critics have pointed to the contradictions and ambiguities inherent in the discourse about HRM. Keenoy suggests that these can only be resolved by accepting the metaphor of 'HRM as hologram' – i.e. a projected image which shifts and implicates the observer (Keenoy 1999). His 'holographic' conclusion is that HRM could be regarded as 'a collective noun for the multitude of concepts-and-methods devised (particularly post-1979) to manage and control the employment relationship' (p. 17). To a large extent this merely reflects how the term is already widely, indiscriminately and unhelpfully deployed. The troubled search for the essential unvarying meaning of HRM can become unnecessarily obsessive. Indeed, the postmodernist critique of 'management' has already made the point that all 'definitions' and conceptualizations of management/organizational approaches are socially constructed. This point has been neatly elaborated in relation to the whole concept of 'enterprise' by du Gay (1996).

The constructionist and postmodern perspective aside, the simple fact is that much of the confusion arises and persists because people using the term (and nowadays that seems to be just about everyone – practitioners, academics, consultants and critics alike) frequently do so while ignoring a key distinction that was made at the very beginning of the debate (Guest 1987; Storey 1987) – that is, HRM on the one hand as a *generic term* simply denoting *any approach to employment management* and on the other, HRM as *one specific and arguably minority form* of approach to employment management.

Now, when one tries to delineate the constituent elements of the specific approach there is certainly potential scope for controversy. But the main features are relatively clear and arguably no more prone to ambiguity, contradiction and uncertainty than any other managerial or social construct such as 'Total Quality Management', 'Partnership', 'Public Sector Broadcasting' or 'Social Class'. It is possible – and I would argue on balance more helpful than unhelpful – to conceive of HRM as one 'recipe' among many others (see Storey and Sisson 1993; Sisson and Storey 2000). The point to note is that there is a range of alternative ways to manage the employment relationship. Some of these ways are distinctive and some are indistinctive and piecemeal. One relatively distinctive approach among this range has been termed HRM. To describe an 'approach' or a 'recipe' one must be able to identify certain characteristic features. HRM as much as any managerial approach (arguably none of which is fully coherent, consistent and contradiction-free) has proceeded from a fairly basic set of interlinked propositions. There are relatively few outright attempts to offer a 'definition' but the one below gives the flavour (Storey 1995: 5).

> Human resource management is a distinctive approach to employment management which seeks to achieve competitive advantage through the strategic deployment of a highly committed and capable workforce using an array of cultural, structural and personnel techniques.

This can be seen as an encapsulation of a 'discursive formation'. Managers who seek to 'lead' and to 'change' do so to a large extent through the management of meaning. Exponents of HRM in its distinctive sense are usually alluding to the above formulation to one degree or another. In other words it is a characterization of one line of thinking. It is perhaps necessary to spell out what the above 'definition' does *not* mean. First, it does not mean that all management changes 'since 1979' are of this character (many initiatives over the past 20 years are patently diametrically opposite to this formulation). Second, it does not mean that workers exposed to HRM policies necessarily and unproblematically do become 'committed'. Third, it does not mean that all approaches to employment within the HRM mode necessarily in practice get every element in place. Even among the organizations broadly seeking to manage in this way there will typically be gaps and lapses. And of course there will be instances where the blatantly cynical use the language with little or no discernible reflection of this in their practice.

None of this should mean that it would be more helpful simply to stop talking about HRM. Some kind of label to indicate the set of characteristics that are going to be described would seem to be necessary. It might be, as Wood (1995) has suggested, that the term 'High Commitment Management' should now be preferred – at least it has the advantage of distinguishing between the generic people-management meaning and the more particular meaning.

HRM in the particular sense emerged on the scene as a historically-situated phenomenon. It was a response to new levels and types of competition which had eroded confidence in traditional formulae. To some extent it can be regarded also as an attempted articulation of an alternative to the Fordist-IR model of labour management which aimed to secure compliance through temporary truces based on negotiated settlements. The key elements of the 'new' alternative approach are summarized in Figure 1.1. As can be seen from this figure, HRM is an amalgam of description, prescription, and logical deduction. It describes the beliefs and assumptions of certain 'leading-edge' practitioners. (It is interesting to note that in the LBS study, the consortium of organizations seeking to discern best practice in HR self-styled themselves the 'Leading Edge Forum' (Gratton *et al.* 1999).) The 'recipe' prescribes certain priorities. And it deduces certain consequent actions which seem to follow from the series of propositions. The first element shown in the figure concerns beliefs and assumptions. The most fundamental of these is the idea that, essentially, it is the human resource among all the factors of production which really makes the difference. It is human capability and commitment which in the final analysis distinguishes successful organizations from the rest. (Interestingly, with the predominance of the 'resourced-based view' in strategic management theory this kind of proposition has arguably become the new orthodoxy.) It follows logically from this premise that the human resource ought to be treated with great care. It is a special resource requiring and deserving managerial time and attention. Moreover, the human resource ought to be nurtured as a valued asset, and not be regarded as an incidental cost. A further underlying belief is that the aim is not merely to seek

1. *Beliefs and assumptions*
   - That it is the human resource which gives competitive edge.
   - That the aim should be not mere compliance with rules, but employee commitment.
   - That therefore employees should, for example, be very carefully selected and developed.

2. *Strategic qualities*
   - Because of the above factors, HR decisions are of strategic importance.
   - Top management involvement is necessary.
   - HR policies should be integrated into the business strategy – stemming from it and even contributing to it.

3. *Critical role of managers*
   - Because HR practice is critical to the core activities of the business, it is too important to be left to personnel specialists alone.
   - Line managers are (or need to be) closely involved as both deliverers and drivers of the HR policies.
   - Much greater attention is paid to the management of managers themselves.

4. *Key levers*
   - Managing culture is more important than managing procedures and systems.
   - Integrated action on selection, communication, training, reward and development.
   - Restructuring and job redesign to allow devolved responsibility and empowerment.

Figure 1.1 The HRM model

compliance with rules and regulations from employees, but to strive for the much more ambitious objective of commitment.

The second main element in Figure 1.1 concerns *strategy*. The idea that HRM is a matter of strategic importance requiring the full attention of chief executives and senior management teams is seen as a further distinguishing characteristic. It stems, of course, from the first belief about sources of competitive advantage. This belief might lead, in turn, to the proposition that an HR director must have a place on the board in order to influence company policy-formulation at the highest level. But, as long as the chief executive and other senior members are attending to the strategic aspects of HRM the precise functional composition of the board might be regarded as a secondary matter. An associated assumption is that decisions about human resources policies should not stem from a set of *a priori* notions about good professional personnel practice, but should take their cue from an explicit alignment of the competitive environment, business strategy and HRM strategy. Some exponents of strategic HRM would even suggest that HRM policies should not only derive from the corporate plan, but should constructively feed into that plan.

The third element concerns the role of *line managers*. If human resources really are so critical for business success, then HRM is too important to be left to operational personnel specialists. Line managers are seen as crucial to the effective delivery of HRM policies: conducting team briefings, holding performance appraisal interviews, target setting, encouraging quality circles, managing performance-related pay, and so on.

In practice there is a further element to this. Much of the drive for HRM came in fact, not from personnel specialists, but from line and general managers (see the evidence in Storey 1992). In some instances, HRM-type policies were pushed through despite the reluctance of personnel professions (this point has, in the meantime, frequently been overlooked or forgotten). In these cases, personnel were still clinging to the rationale that they were the privileged mediators between labour and management and that they alone could gauge the feasibility and practicability of new initiatives. Such protestations were cast aside by a newly resurgent managerialism in the 1980s. To this extent at least, the emergence of HRM can be seen as ultimately associated with an upsurge in managerial confidence. For example, initiatives such as the quality movement (TQM) and more recently initiatives such as Knowledge Management have tended to arise from outside the HR/personnel specialist function – as has been well-noted for example in the latter case the main drive has come from information and communication technology specialists (ICT). So much is this the case that commentators have had to cajole personnel specialists to 'find their place' and role within this movement (e.g. Scarbrough *et al.* 1999).

There is a further strand to the idea of a critical role for managers. A great deal of HR activity and energy is directed at managers themselves, rather than shopfloor employees. A disproportionate amount of training and development activity and resources is consumed by management development. Where psychometric testing is used, this is more likely to be directed towards managers – both for selection and promotion purposes. Activity in the realms of target-setting performance management and career planning is again typically geared mainly towards managers. In other words, the panoply of HRM technology is seen in its fullest form in the management of managers.

The fourth distinguishing feature of HRM relates to the *key levers* used in its implementation. A notable element, at least in the early years, was a shift of emphasis away from personnel procedures and rules as the basis of good practice, in favour of a new accent on the management of 'culture'. This trend was remarkable. Just a few years ago, the idea of paying regard to something so intangible as 'organizational culture', still less spending senior management time in seeking to manage it, would have seemed implausible. Since then, such an aspiration seems to have found a critical place in virtually every senior executive's agenda. So central is this that the twin ideas of 'managing culture change' and moving towards HRM have often appeared to coincide and become one and the same project.

Corporate culture management has generated much excitement because it is perceived to offer a key to the unlocking of consensus, flexibility and commitment. These are self-evidently prized objectives. 'Consensus' suggests the achievement of a common set of values and beliefs. It promises an alternative to industrial conflict. Few managers can imagine all disagreements would disappear (even if this were deemed desirable, which is questionable) but many aspire to the securing of consensus about fundamental objectives and priorities. 'Flexibility' is the second prize. If the culture could be changed so as to remove restrictions on movement between erstwhile separate 'jobs', then productivity would be improved. There is, of course, concern that the idea of 'flexibility' is merely a substitute term for greater managerial control. 'Commitment', the third prize in culture change programmes, is seen as potentially carrying labour performance on to an even higher plane. Beyond a simple willingness to work flexibly, there would be an apparent endeavour to succeed. Committed employees would 'go the extra mile' in pursuit of customer service and organizational goals.

These three prizes are obviously highly desirable from an employer's perspective. But how can they be attained? 'Managing' organizational culture is a complex venture. It means altering fundamentally the whole set of ways in which things are routinely done and possibly even seeking a shift in patterns of attitudes, beliefs and values. An array of organizational development (OD) techniques (or 'interventions', as consultants in the OD tradition prefer to term them) is on offer for this purpose.

Apart from the categories represented in the figure it is important to note also that human resource management has two characteristic qualities which extend across the categories. It has been noted that HRM has both 'hard' and 'soft' dimensions. The hard aspect relates to the business-focused and calculative aspects of managing 'headcounts' in as 'rational' a way as any other factor of production. It emphasizes detached and coolly-rational planning. It stresses the 'resource' aspect in the title and this aspect finds its reflection, for example, in the use of psychological tests as a way of sorting and selecting for entry, promotion or exit. (It would thus eschew, for example, industrial relations rules and procedures such as 'last in first out' or seniority arrangements or arguably any other form of 'custom and practice.) The hard dimension finds its impetus and legitimation in a market-responsive mode of action. It reflects also the business-strategy focus often found in HRM accounts. By contrast, the 'soft' face of HRM traces its roots to the human-relations school and emphasizes communication, training and development, motivation, culture, values and involvement. It presages and echoes the resource-based model of the firm and suggests that competitive advantage can be gained by avoiding short-term cost-cutting in favour of a longer-term focus on building and sustaining capability and commitment.

In total, HRM, whatever else it might or might not be, is an influential and in many quarters highly persuasive narrative which helps to give some shape, direction and meaning to an otherwise complex world. Given the controversies, some observers are tempted to dismiss the phenomenon as 'mere rhetoric' – rather than recognize its more serious status, at the very least, as important rhetoric. Two points can usefully be borne in mind here. The frequently-made point that a few industrial relations academics have found new posts teaching HRM in Business Schools is true but relatively trivial. The power of the narrative goes well beyond that incidental. Take, for example, the central conclusion of Fortune Magazine's survey of 'The World's Most Admired Companies'. Summarizing the expressed views of CEOs it states 'the ability to attract and hold on to talented employees is the single most reliable predictor of overall excellence'. Or take just one of the many major management consultancy groups specializing in HR. The Hay Group is a major US-based global consultancy. Its central 'pitch' to its corporate clients world-wide is classic HRM. Its declaration is 'Hay Group – People Before Strategy'. They continue:

> Global competition, customer focus and the need for speed and flexibility have transformed the business equation. But to get the results you want you must still depend on your people to carry the day. You must select talented individuals; develop, motivate and reward them; and provide them with the organizational cultures and work processes that will allow them to succeed.
>
> (Hay Group Web Site, February 2000)

Corporate customers spend an awful lot of dollars as a result of such logic or narrative. Consultants aside, senior managers responsible in some way for making decisions affecting employment are expected to be able to articulate some coherent rationale for their stream of decisions. Some choose to adopt the HRM rhetoric. It becomes a question amenable to empirical testing, whether the sense-making and visioning are also accompanied by actual practice.

So much for the 'idealized' and narrated model. The question which may legitimately be asked next is whether any of this has actually been put into practice. This brings us to the second area of controversy surrounding HR referred to earlier: the question of take-up and, where adopted, the question of impact. But before moving to the 'evidence' it is worth reiterating the point that HRM is an important phenomenon in its own right even at the conceptual rhetorical level. It has been an important and influential discourse among practitioners. Even when the precise label 'HRM' is not used, the underlying narrative is often quite clear.

CONTROVERSIES ABOUT PRACTICE

The early debate about HRM was conducted largely in the absence of any data about actual practice. In recent years much more information both from large-scale surveys and from detailed case studies has become available. Here it is sufficient to note the broad thrust of the findings. The empirical data now available to us is of two kinds. The first relates to evidence about the extent of use of certain practices (sometimes referred to as 'diffusion'); the second concerns evidence about the impact and outcomes resulting from the implementation of these practices.

Evidence about practice

In general, empirical studies tend to find that there is fairly extensive use of the individual elements of HR practices (such as employee involvement, more careful attention to employee selection and to communication than heretofore) (Storey 1992; Cully *et al.* 1999; Millward *et al.* 2000; Guest 1997; Gratton *et al.* 1999). The extent, however, to which these practices are linked together into a meaningful strategic whole is much more contentious.

The Workplace Employee Relations Survey (Cully *et al.* 1999) offers some recent and representative information about the extent of use of a number of HR practices and it contains some information about the strategic location of HR. The survey found that two-thirds of all managers (68 per cent) said that the workplace had a formal strategic plan that included the issue of employee development (p. 57). A 'further indication of how human resource matters are incorporated into wider business plan' is the involvement of employee relations managers in the business planning. This was said to be widespread. Another indicator that was used was the attainment of Investors in People standard. Overall, just under one-third (32 per cent) of all workplaces were IiP accredited while a further 16 per cent had applied but had not been successful (p. 58). An indicator of the individualizing aspect of HRM practice was found in the extent of performance appraisal. Formal appraisals were reported in 79 per cent of all workplaces. This statistic of course does not mean a universal coverage of appraisal in these workplaces. Appraisal is more common among managerial ranks but, in workplaces where appraisals were conducted, a surprisingly high proportion – two-thirds – used them also for all their non-managerial staff.

A few academics have claimed to have demonstrated the strategic role played by senior HR/personnel specialists. For example, Torrington (1999) states that his research 'showed that the personnel function was involved in strategy to a significant extent' (p. 29). His table of data shows personnel chiefs claiming 'strategic involvement' in areas such as HR planning, recruitment and selection, training, management development, reward and so on. But few personnel specialists claimed strategic involvement in quality issues and work design. It should also be noted that the kind of 'strategic involvement' claimed was overwhelmingly that of developing strategy with line managers and not developing strategy alone. Additionally it should be noted that the informants were senior personnel specialists and it might be thought that they would be likely to claim some level of strategic influence. None the less, even among these informants only a handful 'were able to give any indication of anything like an integrated HR strategy' (p. 31). Over half the interviewees 'felt that they should be doing more in terms of strategy' (p. 31).

Similarly, Gennard and Kelly (1994) also draw upon interviews with personnel directors. Approximately one-third of those interviewed suggested that they recognized a difference between HRM and personnel management and a similar proportion said that their organizations had actually adopted in whole or in part an HRM approach. Those who did proselytize a difference tended to suggest that HRM, when compared with personnel, entails: more integrated involvement with the formulation of business strategies; greater co-ordination in the approach to devising people policies; is more proactive; and a higher priority for people-management policies than in the past (1994: 25). Taken as a whole these findings would seem to suggest some considerable evidence of some kind of changes occurring both in the conceptualization of the nature and place of people-management and apparently in its practice. None the less, Gennard and Kelly for their part conclude that because many of the personnel specialists *not actually adopting the HR label* were actually pursuing policies similar to those who had changed the label or were at least using the label in order to conceptualize the kind of changes taking place, then the notion of a difference was 'sterile'. This seems not to be a valid conclusion to draw. Moreover, reliance on personnel directors as a source of information about changes to HR practice and its strategic standing is also somewhat unreliable. As has been argued previously, many of the more significant changes to employment management have originated from outside the specialist function.

Using an in-depth, qualitative research method for a study of 15 mainstream British employing organizations, Storey (1992) found that the way in which managers were seeking to manage labour was indeed undergoing extensive and significant change. This change was evident in a number of ways. Notably, the drive was coming from sources and along paths which were not conventionally regarded as part of industrial relations proper. There had been little sign of outright 'industrial relations reform' of the old kind (following, for example, the nostrums of Flanders (1970), Donovan (1968) or McCarthy and Ellis (1973)). Rather, the recasting had come about as a result of redesigns in production systems, organizational restructuring, quality initiatives and 'culture campaigns'. Moreover, many of the new initiatives (such as a stronger emphasis on direct communication) were occurring in workplaces with established trade unions. HR and IR were operating relatively separately, there was a 'dualism' in the unfolding pattern of employment management. This point was validated in the subsequent analyses of the Workplace Industrial Relations Survey which confirmed that there was, in fact, greater likelihood of HR initiatives to be found in organizations with unions than in non-union settings. Notably, many of these initiatives had been devised, as well as driven and delivered, by non-personnel specialists.

To what extent did the important changes which were uncovered amount to evidence of a decisive shift to the human resource management model? This is a very moot point. It is worth quoting directly from the research report:

> The temptation is to seek to measure all change against this 'template'. And an associated danger is the reification of subtle and incomplete tendencies. Both of these divert attention away from extensive and far-reaching changes, which albeit not in themselves constituting HR, are nonetheless of profound significance in shifting the terrain of labour management relations. What seems to have been occurring in the British mainstream is a whole clutch of different, but not divergent, initiatives which range across specialist boundaries. Analyses which attempt to confine themselves within the ambit of conventional frameworks therefore risk a blindness with respect to the changing patterns which emerge from these.
>
> (Storey 1992: 264–5)

HRM is said to be fundamentally unitarist. This means that it supposedly has little tolerance for the multiple interest groups and the multiple expression of interests which trade unions and the proceduralist traditions make manifest (the early discussion by Foulkes (1980) did much to drive this idea). Yet the pattern of findings shown in Storey (1992) and in the WIRS surveys (see the analysis by Sisson 1993) revealed that HRM initiatives, contrary to expectations, were often found in unionized settings and that firms were pursuing a 'dualist' approach – i.e. broadly maintaining some measure of trade union relations while also initiating new HR initiatives outside of the collective framework. Trade union recognition and the appurtenances of union relations, such as collective bargaining, were being maintained. But running quite separately from all of this were the new initiatives discussed above. In some of the cases this dual dealing was even conducted by separate departments or units, and the communication between them was rudimentary and even hostile. To this extent, what can be said to have been revealed in British industrial relations was the coexistence of two traditions.

A different kind of point also deserves to be noted in relation to the idea of unitarism and the neglect of multiple interest groups. It has been increasingly argued in recent years that long-term, sustained, competitive advantage is only feasible when the various needs of different stakeholders are taken into account.

It is noteworthy also that while certain leading figures in the Institute of Personnel & Development have been very chary about using the term 'HRM', they none the less champion the ideas which underlie it. Thus, in an interview recorded as part of the Open University's MBA programme, the Director General of the CIPD, Geoff Armstrong, argued that while there were 'horses for courses' in employment approaches and no single one-best way, there were, none the less, in a competitive world increased advantages to giving 'a more strategic investment of management time and thinking and money into the development and creation of capacity through people, and more and more organizations are coming to that view'. There is 'a need to communicate widely, to identify the needed behaviours and competencies, and people need to be trusted and not just be compliant obey-ers of instructions, employers need to invest in their learning and their future employability so that they get self fulfilment – it's a new sort of psychological contract'. When asked what proportion of British organizations he thought were pursuing this new strategy he conceded that most were still preoccupied with cost-driven strategies (and that in so far as this meant getting the basic operations sorted out this was a necessary step), but that leading firms – and he instanced Cable & Wireless, BOC, and Tesco – were already pursuing such an agenda and were reaping the benefit. Similarly, this visionary change agenda is still being urged – see for example Ulrich's *Human Resource Champions: the Next Agenda for Adding Value and Delivering Results* (Ulrich 1997) and Laabs (2000) who argues that even in the USA, HR 'has come a long way' but has still a lot further to go if it is to complete the transformation from administrative support function to strategic business partner' (p. 52).

Evidence about performance impact and outcomes

There is a growing body of research which seeks to examine the impact, if any, of HRM policies and practices on organizational outcomes. The most notable studies are these which use large data sets and which interrogate the data using sophisticated statistical techniques. In general, the available studies appear to reveal impressive evidence of robust impacts and outcomes. The now classic studies in the United States include those by Huselid (1995), Becker and Gerhart (1996); Huselid *et al.* (1997); Ichniowski (1997), and Macduffie (1995). In Britain, the major studies include those by Patterson *et al.* (1997) and Guest (1997).

Debate to some extent has tended to polarize between the competing merits of best practice (universalistic prescription) models and the 'best fit' (contingency) models. But a third hypothesized relationship has been added by Delery and Doty (1996) who argue that in addition to these two there is also the 'configurational' perspectives. This last suggests that what matters is to find the 'themed' collection of HR practices which interact meaningfully together in order to meet the needs of particular situations. The proposition is that there are different 'bundles' which, for example, give varying emphases to, say, human capital formation through training and development. Thus, in total, it is possible to say that there are in fact three theories of the linkage between HRM and performance. The extent to which these three are compatible or incompatible is, as we shall see, somewhat open to question.

The studies testing the *universalistic thesis* (i.e. the hypothesis of a set of best practices in HRM) have been the most popular and the most well-supported. Empirical studies confirming this association include those reported by Huselid (1995), Huselid *et al.* (1997), Delaney and Huselid (1996). In the UK, researchers at the University of Sheffield Institute of Work Psychology have reported interim results from a ten-year study examining the influences upon company performance (Patterson *et al.* 1997). They find that when compared with a range of other factors (such as investment in R&D, a focus on quality or on business strategy) which one might expect to impact upon company performance, a concentration on people management practices has by far the most powerful impact. In addition, it should be noted that the WERS team found that 'workplaces with a high number of "new" management practices and employee involvement schemes were substantially more likely to report high productivity growth' (Cully and O'Reilly 1998: 25).

The *contingency/best fit thesis* has also found some support – for example Delery and Doty (1996) reveal a link between Miles and Snow's three types of business strategy and different approaches to HRM. The *configurational thesis* has also been supported (Delery and Doty 1996). The early work by Schuler and Jackson (1987) while primarily conceptual in nature has found some support in more recent empirical work (Schuler *et al*. 1989).

Overall, however, there have been relatively more studies of the 'universal best practice' model of HRM and the results of such studies have tended to be more consistently positive. We would seem to have come a long way since Lengnick-Hall and Lengnick-Hall (1988: 671) could observe that 'there is little empirical evidence to suggest that strategic HR directly influences organizational performance or competitive advantage'. In consequence of the new studies and their relative consistency in positive associations, Guest (1997: 263) argues that these more recent studies provide 'encouragement to those who have always advocated the case for a distinctive approach to the management of human resources'. He has also stated 'We can now say with increasing confidence that HRM works. But this is a skeletal finding and we need to put a lot of flesh on the bones' (Guest 1997: 274). Similar observations have been made by others, for example Huselid *et al*. (1997: 186) and it is one picked up again below. The important point to note is that simply because survey-based approaches do not reveal the whole picture (for example they are likely to provide little understanding of the actual processes involved) this is hardly a reason to dismiss them entirely.

Another kind of outcome, apart from profit and productivity, is the impact of HRM policies and practices on workers' responses. Using data from an annual survey conducted by the IPD, Guest (1999) points to the 'surprisingly positive' nature of the workers' verdict on HRM: 'A large proportion of the UK workforce have been on the receiving end of the kind of practices commonly associated with HRM. Furthermore, they like them. The more HR practices they are currently experiencing in their employment, the more satisfied they seem to be' (pp. 22–23).

Hesitations and reservations about the reliability and validity of such large-scale studies have of course been expressed. For example, it has been argued that 'the claim that the bundle of best practice HRM is universally applicable leads us into a utopian cul-de-sac' (Purcell 1999: 36). Questions can be asked about the precise content and comparability of the menus or 'bundles' being evaluated. It transpires that different studies, to a certain extent, use different ingredients in their lists. There are also concerns about the reliability of single-respondent box-tickers who report on behalf of whole organizations. Moreover, the meaningfulness of 'mere' correlations and other statistically-derived data in the absence of adequate theory is open to question.

However, even this list of problems is perhaps an insufficient basis on which to justify the dismissal of such forms of research. Similar statistical approaches are common practice in a whole range of sciences including, for example, epidemiology. The associations found in large-scale surveys while certainly not providing the whole answer or the whole picture are useful additions to the research effort.

But in what sense is it being suggested that HRM 'works'? Bottom-line financial performance is but one measure; progress in evaluating HRM outcomes might also look more widely across the 'scorecard'. Associated with this last point is the argument about sustainability. It may well be that a quick profit or rise in a company's share price can be achieved by short-term cost-cutting measures – including 'headcount reductions' – which have often been found to gain a favourable response from institutional investors. But this form of accountancy-led management may not deliver long-term growth or innovation. Investigations into longevity have also indicated the importance of human resource policies (Collins and Porras 1998).

We return now to the question as to whether the universalistic, contingency and configured approaches are necessarily incompatible. It would seem from the evidence that these can operate simultaneously. It is in one sense at least misleading to cast them in opposition to each other. The much-vaunted universalistic *versus* best-fit distinction misses the point that *both* could obtain. Thus, it may be that, more or less across the board, there is a tendency for organizations which practise 'people-focused' policies (for example taking recruitment and selection seriously, taking care to communicate objectives, targets and outcomes effectively, ensuring adequate training and development and so on) to gain some advantage from this. Insofar as this is the case, the results from the universalistic studies would reflect this. At the same time, it may also be the case that some particular groups of organizations because of their distinctive competitive positions could benefit disproportionately from such practices. Such instances would be picked up by the contingency and configuration studies. It is not surprising under these circumstances that some contributors defy classification under the universalist versus contingency/configurationist labels. Thus Schuler's work at times appears to endorse the universalist position (e.g. Huselid, Jackson and Schuler 1997), at other times his work is strongly geared to the contingency/configurationalist (e.g. Schuler and Jackson 1987). The same could be said for Guest's various studies (1997, 1999). And Arthur's (1994: 683) study of the effects of HRM/commitment policies versus control policies on manufacturing performance has notoriously been claimed by various camps. But his conclusions seem in the main to endorse the 'best practice' hypothesis, as he says 'these results support observations made by Walton (1985) and others concerning the effectiveness of commitment-type human resource systems' (at least within the context of the type of technological environment which he studied).

The point to remember is that large-scale surveys by their nature reflect characteristics of the population studied; attempts to extrapolate a prescription for an individual firm may be misconceived. An analogy might be found in the many studies in areas such as the health effects of cigarette smoking. Universalistic studies may well produce a finding that on the whole non-smoking and plenty of exercise is associated with a range of health indicators. Likewise, the results may be accentuated in particular sub-sets of the population (e.g. those who are pregnant). Thus the contingency of pregnancy and non-smoking may be statistically confirmed. Moreover, the configurationalists can also find endorsement when the combined effects of non-smoking, appropriate exercise and certain dietary choices are noted. In total, the various types of study can each have its contribution to make. None on its own is likely to be adequate but if well conducted in its own terms the research has the potential to be cumulative.

Summary

The mesmerizing spell of the one-best way formula or basket of high-commitment HR practices has influenced not only the statistical testers but has also influenced wider commentary about the validity and viability of the idea of HRM. In consequence, the 'failure' of HRM to 'diffuse' across economies has not only been noted but sometimes interpreted as tantamount to proof of failure of the concept *in toto*. The arrival of the recession of the early 1990s also came at a time when academics were trying to figure out the meaningfulness (as well as the meaning) of the new concept. Unsurprisingly, the counter-indicators such as the large lay-offs at that time, the publicity given to a number of zero-hour contract cases and the rise of the 'McJobs' gave huge cause for caution. But there are equally dangers in missing the significance of the growth sectors of various economies in our concern to remain alert to the low-paid, low-skilled and exploitative segments.

Thus, in India for example, huge growth has occurred in the electronic and computer software industries. The pool of highly educated workers has attracted numerous international companies such as Microsoft, Oracle and NTT. Nor are the local computer companies all foreign-owned and reliant on 'outsourced' routine tasks. The European software company, Baan, has headquartered its R&D operations in Bangalore and Novell has opened an R&D centre in Hyderabad. This multi-billion dollar industry pays its programmers ten times the average Indian income, has constructed campus-style working environments, and is installing employment practices which look very similar to the HR model. Likewise, in Ireland much economic progress has resulted from the planned investment on education and training and the partnership arrangement between government, trade unions and employers. Such instances should give pause for thought.

Clearly, HRM is no panacea; no set of employment policies ever will be. But, as a persuasive account (or narrative) of the logic underpinning choice in certain organizations and as an aspirational pathway for others, it is an idea worthy of examination.

CONTRIBUTIONS IN THIS VOLUME

As is perhaps evident from even this brief overview of research and commentary on human resource management, the domain remains lively, vibrant and contested. There are many new initiatives and analysis is struggling to keep pace in making sense of the changes and weighing their significance. The chapters which follow in this book offer a wealth of insights from leading analysts in their respective fields.

The chapters are organized into five parts. This first part of the book sets the scene with some overall reviews of the state and nature of HRM. The second part focuses on the key theme of strategy and the extent to which and the way in which HR's contribution might be interpreted as strategic – or not. The third part gets to grips with the key practice areas or the heartland activities of HRM. Thus there are chapters dealing with employee resourcing (including recruitment, selection, and career management); training and development; corporate culture and change management; the management of reward; and employee involvement. In part four the lens is widened to take in key themes in international and comparative practice. This means that the reader is exposed to the conduct of, and developments in, HR in some important territories such as Europe and the United States while, additionally, issues concerning the international management in the sense of cross-border management are tackled. The final part of the book looks to the future and assesses, for example, current developments in knowledge management.

Some readers may wish for a brief introduction to the content of each of the individual chapters. In Chapter 2 Karen Legge reviews and critiques the alleged relationship between high commitment management and high performance. She questions the conceptual and methodological soundness of the positivistic research conducted in pursuit of establishing a causal link between these 'variables'. In the course of this wide-ranging critique she mounts a robust defence of the stance taken by the 'critical writers'. An important though much neglected topic is the relationship between ethics and HRM. This is the focus of the analysis by Jean Woodall and Diana Winstanley in Chapter 3. A case could be made for suggesting either that HRM has a tendency towards the unethical or conversely that an ethical approach is integral to its nature. In this chapter a range of ethical frameworks is identified and their implications for HR policies and practices examined. Woodall and Winstanley make a strong case for a higher standard of 'ethical literacy' among HR academics and practitioners. In Chapter 4 John Purcell subjects the crucial idea of 'strategy' in human resource management to a rigorous re-examination. He argues that there is often a fundamental contradiction in the discussion of strategic HRM. This derives, he suggests, from the fact that a postulated 'best practice' set of HR policies cannot credibly be placed alongside the claim that HR needs to be 'integrated' with business strategy. As he points out, business strategies, by definition, vary and therefore, by implication, HR policies and practices would also have to vary if they are to remain integrated with that (changing) business strategy. In addition, Purcell points out further weaknesses in conventional understandings of strategic human resource management and he puts forward the case for a 'configurational' approach to the understanding of strategy in HRM.

One of the ongoing uncertainties and debates has been the extent to which the personnel management function might have changed in response to the influence of HRM. This is the topic addressed by Keith Sisson in Chapter 5. He steers a clear path through the extensive and often complex data which are now available. He argues that the personnel function is in far better shape than many commentators would have expected but that the nature of the contribution from these specialists has scope for improvement.

In Chapter 6 David Guest explores the changing links between industrial relations and human resource management while at the same time making a wide-ranging assessment of the whole span of 'employment management' options. This chapter deals with labour management strategy in its widest sense. Drawing on different surveys it also juxtaposes in an insightful way the findings about recent developments on employment strategies and their impacts.

Chapter 7 by Randall Schuler, Susan Jackson and John Storey takes a more detailed look at what is involved in the enactment of strategic human resource management. The chapter offers a framework for understanding HR's contribution to business strategy.

In Chapter 8, under the umbrella title of 'employee resourcing', Paul Iles tackles the core practice issues of recruitment, selection, assessment and career management. It encompasses the processes of sorting, sifting, tracking and locating of employees. In contrast to traditional textbook treatments of these topics, this chapter examines them critically within the context of wider organizational power relations.

Chapter 9 by David Ashton and Alan Felstead reveals and interprets the latest trends and issues in training and development. The chapter sets the analysis within a detailed and authoritative account of changes to national and organizational level contexts. It compares developments in Britain with those in other countries. With the marshalled data the authors are also in a privileged position to assess the meaningfulness of such concepts as the knowledge economy, lifelong learning and the learning organization.

In Chapter 10 Graeme Salaman subjects the highly influential idea of corporate culture change to a rigorous and critical examination. He sees 'enterprise' as the core theme of most corporate culture projects and he assesses the nature and ramifications of these attempts to manage meanings, subjectivity and identity.

Chapter 11 by Ian Kessler addresses the issue of pay and reward. There has been considerable debate about the role and consequences of contingent or performance-related pay and indeed about how such pay methods fit within HR approaches. Kessler carries this analysis further while additionally assessing reward systems in a much broader frame. The chapter is unusual in the way it offers a theoretical basis for future interpretations of pay and reward.

In Chapter 12 Mick Marchington explores the nature, extent and consequences of employee involvement (EI) initiatives. Marchington argues that while the number of workplaces which have introduced various EI arrangements has increased, the outcomes achieved to date have not been as impressive as might have been expected. Marchington suggests that much more could be gained from EI if managerial action in relation to it was embedded in a more rounded high commitment HRM strategy.

Chapter 13 by Chris Brewster places the range of issues discussed in preceding chapters into an international comparative context. In particular, this chapter makes a strong contribution towards the understanding of the nature of varying practices across the European countries. The analysis is important for both theory and practice in an age of increasing globalization.

In Chapter 14 Tom Kochan and Lee Dyer analyse the reasons for the comparatively slow progress in the 'transformation' of American employment practices. This is a far more sober assessment than is to be found in the celebrated account of *The Transformation of American Industrial Relations* (Kochan *et al.* 1986). The updated argument as developed in this volume fits well within the framework of arguments mounted earlier in this book. The shift from pragmatic and reactive employment management to the kind of sophisticated model offered by HRM cannot, they now maintain, be brought about across the economy by managers alone. Concerted action by other stakeholders and institutional support would also seem necessary if such a shift is to occur on a large scale.

Chapter 15 by Hugh Scullion moves us from comparative management to 'international human resource management' – that is, it tackles the HR problems and practices of firms operating in more than one country. Among other themes this includes the management of expatriates, the management of local (that is, host country) nationals, and the role of the corporate HR function in international firms. This chapter includes a wide-ranging critical review and assessment of this fast-developing field.

In Chapter 16 Randall Schuler continues and deepens the international management theme by analysing the HR issues which are at play in international joint ventures and alliances. These forms of cross-border arrangements are increasingly common and the HR aspects are recognized as vital to their success – and yet, to date, these aspects have been insufficiently understood. Schuler moves the analysis on significantly by providing new analytical frameworks as well as new empirical data.

One of the most influential, if not indeed *the* most influential, over-arching idea in recent years in the field of management and business has been that of 'knowledge management'. This is the subject of Chapter 17 authored by John Storey and Paul Quintas (the latter being the first person in the UK to be appointed to a Chair of Knowledge Management). Knowledge Management is a multi-disciplinary domain but the most dominant approach so far has been that deriving from an information and communication technology (ICT) perspective. In this chapter, Storey and Quintas outline the essential attributes of knowledge management and then they identify and discuss the main HRM issues which are relevant to its practice.

Finally, Chapter 18, 'Looking to the Future', revisits the debates raised at the start of this introductory chapter in the light of the contributions made by the intervening chapters and seeks to identify the most important emerging issues.

REFERENCES

Arthur, J.B. (1994) 'Effects of human resource systems on manufacturing performance and turnover', *Academy of Management Journal*, **37**(3): 670–87.

Barney, J. (1991) 'Firm resources and sustained competitive advantage', *Journal of Management* **17**(1): 99–120.

Becker, B. and Gerhart, B. (1996) 'The impact of human resource management on organizational performance: Progress and prospects', *Academy of Management Journal* **39**(4): 779–801.

Coff, R.W. (1997) 'Human assets and management dilemmas: coping with hazards on the road to resource-based theory', *Academy of Management Review* **22**(2): 374–402.

Collins, J.C. and Porras, J.I. (1988) *Built to Last: Successful Habits of Visionary Companies*, London: Random House.

Cully, M. and O'Reilly, A., Millward, N., Forth, J., Woodland, S., Dix, G. and Bryson, A. (1998) *The 1998 Workplace Employee Relations Survey, First Findings*, London: Department of Trade and Industry, HMSO.

Cully, M., Woodland, S., O'Reilly, A. and Dix, G. (1999) *Britain at Work: As Depicted by the 1998 Workplace Employee Relations Survey*. London: Routledge.

Delaney, J.T. and Huselid, M.A. (1996). 'The impact of human resource management practices on perceptions of organizational performance', *Academy of Management Journal* **39**(4): 949–69.

Delery, J. and Doty, D.H. (1996) 'Modes of theorizing in strategic human resource management: tests of universalistic, contingency and configurational performance predictions', *Academy of Management Journal* **39**(4): 802–35.

Donovan, Lord (1968) *Report of the Royal Commission on Trade Unions and Employers Associations*, London: HMSO.

du Gay, P. (1996) 'Making up managers: enterprise and the ethos of bureaucracy', in S.R. Clegg and G. Palmer (eds), *The Politics of Management Knowledge*, London: Sage.

Flander, A. (1970) *Managers and Unions: The Theory and Reform of Industrial Relations*, London: Faber.

Foulkes, F. (1980) *Personnel Policies in Large, Non-Union Companies*, Englewood Cliffs, NJ: Prentice Hall.

Gennard, J. and Kelly, J. (1994) 'Human resource management: the views of personnel directors', *Human Resource Management Journal* **5**(1): 15–32.

Gratton, L., Hope Valley, V., Stiles, P., Truss, C. (1999) *Strategic Human Resource Management*, Oxford: Oxford University Press.

Guest, D. (1987) 'Human resource management and industrial relations', *Journal of Management Studies*, **24**(5): 503–21.

Guest, D. (1997) 'Human resource management and performance: a review and a research agenda', *International Journal of Human Resource Management* **8**(3): 263–76.

Guest, D. (1999) 'Human resource management – the workers' verdict', *Human Resource Management Journal* **9**(4): 5–25.

Huselid, M. (1995) 'The impact of human resource management practices on turnover, productivity and corporate financial performance', *Academy of Management Journal* **38**(3): 635–72.

Huselid, M., Jackson, S., Schuler, R.S. (1997) 'Technical and strategic human resource management effectiveness as determinants of firm performance', *Academy of Management Journal* **40**(1): 171–88.

Ichniowski, C. and Shaw, K. (1997) 'The effects of HRM practices on productivity – a study of steel finishing lines', *American Economic Review*, **87**(3).

Keenoy, T. (1990) 'HRM: rhetoric, reality and contradiction', *International Journal of Human Resource Management*, **1**(3): 363–84.

Keenoy, T. (1999). 'HRM as hologram: a polemic', *Journal of Management Studies* **36**(1): 1–23.

Keenoy, T. and Anthony, P. (1992) 'HRM: metaphor, meaning and morality', in P. Blyton and P. Turnbull (eds), *Re-assessing Human Resource Management*, London: Sage.

Laabs, J. (2000) 'Strategic HR won't come easily', *Workforce* January: 52–56.

Legge, K. (1995) *Human Resource Management: Rhetorics and Realities*, Basingstoke: Macmillan.

Lengnick-Hall, C. and Lengnick-Hall, M. (1988) 'Strategic human resource management: a review of the literature and a proposed typology', *Academy of Management Review* **13**(3): 454–70.

Lippman, S.A. and Rumelt, R.P. (1982) 'Uncertain imitability: an analysis of interfirm differences in efficiency under competition', *The Bell Journal of Economics* **13**: 418–38.

McCarthy, W.E.J. and Ellis, N.D. (1973) *Management by Agreement*, London: Hutchinson.

Macduffie, J.P. (1995) 'Human resource bundles and manufacturing performance: organisational logic and flexible production systems in the world auto industry', *Industrial and Labor Relations Review* **48**(2): 197–221.

Millward, N., Bryson, A., Forth, J. (2000) *All Change at Work? British Employment Relations 1980–1998 as Portrayed by the Workplace Industrial Relations Survey Series*, London: Routledge.

Noon, M. (1992) 'HRM: A map, model or theory?', in P. Blyton and P. Turnbull (eds) *Reassessing Human Resource Management*, London: Sage.

Patterson, M.G., West, M.A. *et al.* (1997) *Impact of People Management Practices on Business Performance*, London, Institute of Personnel and Development.

Pfeffer, J. (1998) *The Human Equation: Building Profits by Putting People First*, Boston: Harvard Business School Press.

Polanyi, M. (1962) *Personal Knowledge: Towards a Post-critical Philosophy*, Chicago: University of Chicago Press.

Purcell, J. (1999) 'Best practice and best fit: chimera or cul-de-sac?' *Human Resource Management Journal*, **9**(3): 26–41

Scarbrough, H., Swan, J. and Preston, J. (1999) *Knowledge Management: a Literature Review*. London: IPD.

Schuler, R. and Jackson, S. (1987) 'Linking competitive strategies with human resource management practices', *Academy of Management Executive* **1**(3): 207–19.

Schuler, R.S., Jackson, S.E. and Rivero, J.C. (1989) 'Organizational characteristics as predictors of personnel policies', *Personnel Psychology*, **42**: 727–85.

Sisson, K. (1993) 'In Search of HRM', *British Journal of Industrial Relations*, **31**(2): 201–10.

Sisson, J. and Storey J. (2000) *The Realities of Human Resource Management*, Buckingham: Open University Press.

Sparrow, P. and Marchington, M. (eds) (1998) *Human Resource Management: The New Agenda*, London: Financial Times/Pitman Publishing.

Storey, J. (1987) 'Developments in the Management of Human Resources: An Interim Report', *Warwick Papers in Industrial Relations*, Coventry: University of Warwick. No. 17.

Storey, J. (1992) *Developments in the Management of Human Resources*, Oxford: Blackwell.

Storey, J. (ed.) (1995) *Human Resource Management: A Critical Text*, London: International Thompson.

Storey, J. and Sisson, K. (1993) *Managing Human Resources and Industrial Relations*, Buckingham: Open University Press.

Teece, D. (1982) 'Towards an economic theory of the multiproduct firm', *Journal of Economic Behavior and Organization* **3**: 38–63.

Teece, D., Pisano, G. *et al.* (1990) 'Firm capabilities, resources and the concept of strategy', *University of California Working Paper EAP–38*.

Torrington, D. (1999) 'Crisis and opportunity in HRM: the challenge for the personnel function', in P. Sparrow and M. Marchington (eds) *Human Resource Management: The New Agenda*, London: Financial Times/Pitman.

Ulrich, D. (1997) *Human Resource Champions: The Next Agenda for Adding Value and Delivering Results*, Boston: Harvard Business School Press.

Walton, R.E. (1985) 'From control to commitment in the workplace', *Harvard Business Review*, **63**(2): March–April.

Wernerfelt, B. (1984) 'A resource-based view of the firm', *Strategic Management Journal* **5**(2): 171–80.

Wood, S. and deMenezes, L. (1998) 'High commitment management in the UK: Evidence from the workplace industrial relations survey, and employers' manpower and skills practices survey', *Human Relations*, **51**(4): 485–515.

Silver Bullet or Spent Round? Assessing the Meaning of the 'High Commitment Management'/Performance Relationship

2

Karen Legge

INTRODUCTION

What we 'discover' or perceive about the material or social world is inevitably theory-laden (Heisenberg's Uncertainty Principle; Cicourel 1964; Popper 1959). This is clearly reflected in the titles of the two preceding volumes of this series, edited by John Storey, namely *New Perspectives on Human Resource Management* (1989) and *Human Resource Management: A Critical Text* (1995). It is the 'perspective' ('new' or 'critical') that informs each text which creates the picture of HRM that each provides, just as much as the supporting empirical data that is called forth by such perspectives (cf. Guest, 1989, 1995; Legge, 1989, 1995a; Purcell, 1989, 1995). Indeed, as Keenoy (1999: 14–15) remarks, in likening HRM to a hologram

> As with a hologram, HRM changes its appearance as we move around its image. Each shift of stance reveals another facet, a darker depth, a different contour. As a fluid holistic entity of apparently multiple identities and forms, it is not surprising that every time we look at it, it is slightly different. This is why, conceptually, HRMism appears to be a moving target, and why, empirically, it has no fixed (fixable) forms.

But what is the precise relationship between theory and empirical data? David Guest (1999: 8–9) has gone so far as to suggest that some of the so-called 'critical writers' on HRM (identified as Keenoy, Legge and Willmott) have been cavalier in their treatment of empirical data: 'there is a hint of slippage in the analysis to reflect a preferred interpretation'. In other words, Guest argues, the critical writers use empirical data to suit their own agendas (rather than their agendas being directed by the empirical world). He asserts that the gang of three use data selectively, on the one hand to suggest that 'soft' HRM is 'either not practised or is ineffective' and, on the other hand, to suggest that HRM is either 'hard', with implications for exploitation through labour intensification, downsizing and so on or, if 'soft', it engages in 'exploit(ing) workers through a subtle management of their mind-set by constructing for them a view of reality reflected in organisational culture'. Guest implies that the critical writers, on the basis of insufficient or biased data, make assertions and draw unwarranted inferences about workers' experience of HRM, accepting workers' veracity when they claim that it is exploitative (as in Garrahan and Stewart's (1992) Marxist interpretation of the working practices in the Nissan car plant at Sunderland) but claiming their 'false consciousness' when workers appear to like HRM. ('False consciousness', of course, is an unacceptable concept in the eyes of a positivist, being unfalsifiable.) With some justification, Guest argues that the critical writers' tendency to treat workers as cultural dupes is as, or even more exploitative, than that which such writers claim of HRM. All this, he concludes 'smacks of setting up a straw man, even of capitalising on the academic debate and, in terms of actor network theory, promoting it for one's own ends'.

Perhaps there is just a touch of projection here. The position taken by the so-called critical writers is quite explainable in terms of the different data sources used, which generate different, but by no means contradictory, interpretations. The assessment that HRM 'is not practised or ineffective' is derived largely from survey data, such as the Warwick Company Level Surveys and the last two iterations of WIRS/WERS. Indeed, data from the latest WERS survey (1998) has been interpreted by the researchers involved (Cully *et al.* 1999) (all of whom, it may be noted, appearing to adhere to the conventional employee relations pluralist theoretical position) as showing that only 14 per cent of the responding workplaces have 'soft' HRM fully in place (defined as eight plus out of fifteen 'high commitment management' practices) as opposed to 29 per cent which had three or less, 22 per cent of which, with three or less HCM practices and no unions, may be defined in Guest's own memorable phrase as constituting a 'black hole' (Guest 1995: 125). The assessment that HRM 'is not practised' does not seem unreasonable in the light of such evidence. The interpretation that HRM is, or can be, a major threat to workers is based largely on qualitative case-study data, where, certainly on the part of one of the critical writers, it has been explicitly recognized that the data (e.g. in relation to TQM and JIT) has been collected from a variety of theoretical perspectives (see, for example, Legge, 1995b: 224–34). In his interpretation of the critical writers' penchant for straw men, is not Guest indulging in similar behaviours? (I will, like Guest, impute motive later in this chapter!)

Putting Guest's criticisms aside for the moment, it must be recognized that he makes a valuable point in that we should always be conscious that data is collected and interpreted from a theoretical position. Willmott (1993) (cited in Guest 1999: 8) makes his own position *vis-à-vis* empirical data about cultural management explicit when he states

> In a post-empiricist era, Weber's appeal to 'facts' must of course be problematized: the modernist idea that opinions can be corrected by the compelling reality of facts is no longer plausible ... the role of the intellectual is not to correct opinion with fact, but rather, to participate in what Foucault (1984: 74) has termed 'a new politics of truth' in which the normativity of knowledge is more fully appreciated.

Likewise, Keenoy (1999: 15) is equally explicit about his position *vis-à-vis* the empirical reality:

It is not just that different frames of reference produce alternative accounts of the same phenomena – a process which privileges the observer(s) in the act of *interpreting* an apparently mute, solid and ordered facticity – but that each phenomena *may possess and can project a variety of mutually implicated identities* – a process which privileges the multiple 'entitiness' of phenomena (author's emphasis).

In comparison with these two writers, sympathetic to what has been termed 'the linguistic turn' (Reed 1992: 11), Guest identifies 'with those (of us) who maintain a foot in the modernist and positivist camp' (Guest 1999: 9). And what, might it be asked, are the present day concerns of HRM researchers, who, along with Guest, are of a modernist, positivistic persuasion? In a word, their project is the search for the Holy Grail of establishing a causal relationship between HRM and performance. And in this search some success is claimed, in particular that the more the so-called 'high commitment/performance' HRM practices are adopted, the better the performance (see, for example, the empirical studies by Arthur, Delery and Doty, Huselid and his colleagues, MacDuffie, Youndt and his colleagues and, of course, by David Guest, cited below).

The purpose of this chapter is to explore this endeavour and to pose some questions. In the light of the above, how conceptually and methodologically sound is this project, according to the tenets of positivism? If we were to find major short-comings here and the research delivering less than it promises, how do we account for its present popularity (see, for example, Arthur 1992, 1994; Becker and Gerhart 1996; Delaney and Huselid 1996; Delery and Doty 1996; Guest 1997; Guest and Hoque 1994; Huselid 1995; Huselid and Becker 1996; Huselid *et al*. 1997; Ichniowski *et al*. 1996; MacDuffie 1995; Purcell 1999; Youndt *et al*. 1996; Wright and Gardner 2000)? Are the proponents of this academic debate pursuing an agenda in their own interests, as the critical writers have been accused?

THEORIZING AND SPECIFYING HRM

In considering the relationship between HRM and performance, the three most basic questions are: how are we to conceptualize HRM, how are we to conceptualize performance and how are we to conceptualize the relationship between the two? For the testing of the relationship between HRM and performance, from a positivistic perspective, the first requirement is a theory-derived conceptualization of HRM and its precise specification as an independent variable.

Clearly positivists cannot work with the subtleties and sophistication of Keenoy's (1999: 16) approach, which, likening HRM to a hologram, regards it 'not as a concrete, coherent entity but as a series of mutually implicated phenomena which is/are in the process of becoming'. For a positivist, HRM must be a precisely specified variable, not a process. Process, in theory, pertains to the relationship between HRM and performance, not to HRM as a concept. That said, in treating HRM as a variable, positivists have not acted consistently, either at the level of theorizing or in terms of specifying the concept of HRM.

As Guest (1997) himself has pointed out, there is no consistency in the theorizing of HRM. Some commentators (e.g. Miles and Snow 1984; Hendry and Pettigrew 1990; Schuler and Jackson 1987) take what Guest terms a 'strategic' approach.

Because they are concerned with the relationship between external contingencies and HRM policy and practice (the 'external fit' approach), they implicitly treat HRM as the *dependent* variable, a 'third order' strategy very much dependent on the first order strategies about portfolio planning and the second order strategies about internal operating procedures (Purcell 1989). An assumption here is that if HRM 'fits' external contingencies/business strategy, 'better' performance will result (the contingency approach).

A second approach, resting on systems theory, is the 'descriptive' approach, taken by commentators such as Beer *et al.* (1985) that essentially identifies four broad elements of HRM policy and four key outcomes. Given the systems assumptions about interrelationships and feedback, in theory HRM, at different points in time, can act as both an *independent* and *dependent* variable. Two further problems here, by Guest's admission, are the theories' lack of specificity in delineating the variables involved and, being non-predictive and non-prescriptive, they 'provide no clear focus for any test of the relationship between HRM and performance' (Guest 1997: 265).

The third conceptualization of HRM lies in the normative theories, such as the 'mutuality' model of Walton (1985), Guest's (1987) own working of that model and Pfeffer's (1994) suggestion that there is an identifiable set of best HR practices that have universal, additive, positive effects on performance. Guest's own model argues that if an integrated set or 'bundle' (MacDuffie 1995) of HRM practices is applied in order to generate high commitment, quality and flexibility in the workforce, higher worker performance will result and this will have a positive effect on organizational performance, irrespective of external circumstances or business strategy. 'Unlike other approaches, this normative perspective argues that specific practices and specific HRM goals will always be superior' (Guest 1997: 265). Leaving aside for the moment whether it is legitimate to down-play the potential effects of business context on performance (an *intervening* variable, potentially moderating the effects of the independent variable, the bundle of 'high commitment' HRM practices), there is still lack of agreement about what should comprise the 'bundle' of practices and how they should be specified.

Useful though this categorization is, it is inconsistent with that of Delery and Doty (1996). While there is a good match between their categorization of traditional contingency theories and Guest's strategic theories of HRM, there is disagreement when it comes to classifying Guest's normative theories. While both would agree that Pfeffer's approach reflects a universalistic, best practices approach, they take a very different view as regards the integrated set or 'bundles' of best practice. Guest sees this as a universalistic theory (see above) while Delery and Doty (1996: 803–4) see it as a form of contingency theory. In other words, the 'bundles' of best practice theories are configurational, based on typologies of ideal types and the systems assumption of equifinality. As such, they are concerned with how the *pattern* of multiple independent variables is related to the dependent variable rather than how individual independent variables are related to the dependent variable (Pfeffer's approach). The theories are contingent in that they assume that organizations must develop an HR system that achieves internal consistency of the organization's HR policies and practices (horizontal 'fit') and a congruence of the HR system with other organizational characteristics, such as the firm's strategy (vertical 'fit') (see Arthur 1992; MacDuffie 1995). This sort of confusion is not conducive to the avowed positivistic goal of developing a cumulative body of knowledge anymore than is the lack of agreement about what 'high commitment/performance' practices should comprise and their appropriate specification.

To add to the confusion it should be noted that the universalistic and contingency approaches rest on very different and contradictory theoretical approaches. The universalistic approach is consistent with institutional theory and arguments about organizational isomorphism (DiMaggio and Powell 1983). In other words, the assumption here is that organizations that survive do so because they identify and implement the most effective 'best' policies and practices. As a result, successful organizations get to look more and more like each other. Contingency approaches, on the other hand, are consistent with resource-based theories that argue that sustained competitive advantage rests not on imitating so-called 'best practice', but on developing unique and non-imitable competences (Barney 1991).

Turning to the empirical research examining HRM and performance relationships, further confusions are evident. Here HRM is operationalized in terms of 'high commitment' (or in American terminology, 'high performance') work practices (e.g. presence of self-directed work teams, initial weeks of training per non-managerial employee/hours training per year after initial training, presence of contingent pay). However, as Becker and Gerhart (1996) point out, analysing five major studies of HRM/performance relationships (by Arthur 1994; Cutcher-Gershenfeld 1991; Huselid 1995; MacDuffie 1995; Kochan and Osterman 1994), there is little agreement about what practices should be included. Of the 27 practices included in these studies, not a single one is common to all five and there are only two (self-directed work teams and problem-solving groups/QCs) on which four studies agree, and two more (contingent pay and hours training per year after initial training) on which three studies agree. Of the 15 'high commitment' work practices identified in WERS (Workplace Employee Relations Survey) 1998 (Cully *et al.* 1999), only seven appear on the American list.

Similarly, even where there may be some measure of agreement on the inclusion of a particular 'high commitment/performance' working practice, there may be no agreement on its specifiication and measurement. Thus, although the concept of contingent pay is included in MacDuffie's (1995), Huselid's (1995) and Arthur's (1992) list of 'high performance' practices, each measures it differently. For example, Huselid uses the proportion of the workforce covered by profit sharing, gainsharing and merit pay, while Arthur uses the percentage of employment costs accounted for by bonus or incentive payments (Becker and Gerhart 1996: 793).

Further, there is sometimes disagreement about whether a practice is likely to be positively or negatively related to performance. For example, Arthur's (1994) high performance system specifies a low emphasis on contingent pay, whereas Huselid (1995) and MacDuffie (1995) place a strong emphasis on its presence. Again, Huselid (1995) and Pfeffer (1994) describe the presence of internal promotions and access to employee grievance procedures as indicative of a 'high performance' HRM system, while Arthur (1995) and Ichniowski *et al.* (1994) classify them as aspects of more rigid HRM systems, often associated with less productive, unionized workplaces.

Not only, then, is there a lack of agreement about what are the key 'high commitment/performance' practices, but little consensus on the appropriate level of specificity in operationalizing these concepts. As Wright and Gardner (2000) point out, in relation to pay, does one assess the presence or absence of contingent pay, or does one specify a variety of approaches for tying pay to performance (merit pay, bonuses, stock options, profit-related pay, commissions and so on)? One could also specify the range of different performance criteria to which pay could be tied, such as profits, share price growth, revenue growth, new product development, cost reductions, etc. The fact that most studies opt for the simple measure of presence/ absence is worrying as this tells us nothing about how effectively the practice is implemented. With reference to contingent pay, for example, Purcell (1999: 27) reminds us that 'Bowey and Thorpe (1986) found that it was not the type of pay system that affected the outcome but the use of consultation in the design phase – i.e. that process was more important than content'.

Leaving aside the issue of specification, questions have also been raised about the validity and reliability of measures of HR practices. Most of the American studies already cited involve large-scale postal surveys of 'single respondents answering quick questions', to quote John Purcell (1999: 28). Purcell questions whether one senior management respondent can possibly have knowledge of the whole firm and, also, of the desirability of questions 'that encourages the respondent to tick a box and not go to the file to find the answer'. Further, the use of single respondents grows more problematic the more complex and diversified the firm. It is especially suspect when the respondent is asked to make judgements on how the firm compares with others, particularly in relation to matters of performance (see below).

If there is a question mark over the validity of the data in these studies, their reliability (and, hence, generalizability) is also suspect. While most studies rely on single respondents (and, hence, issues of internal consistency dominate), a multiple respondent study by Gerhart et al. (forthcoming) (cited in Wright and Gardner 2000), designed to examine sources of variance in the measurement of HR practices, found 'frighteningly low' levels of overall reliability of HR practices measures. They noted that the statistic [rwg] commonly used in multiple respondent studies was inappropriate because it only assesses 'agreement' within one firm rather than 'reliability' across firms. However, although they found almost no inter-rater reliability for more 'objective' measures of HR practices, they report better inter-rater reliability on subjective measures (involving Likert-type scales) of the effectiveness of the HR function.

CONCEPTUALIZING AND MEASURING PERFORMANCE

As David Guest (1997) has identified (and in his own work has sought to rectify – see Guest 1999) the conceptualization of performance used in most of the American studies already referred to is extremely limited. Reflecting what appears to be a highly managerialist and unitarist outlook, as true children of capitalism (cf. Fukuyama 1989), the measures of performance selected are invariably those relating to financial performance and productivity. A study by Rogers and Wright (1998) (cited in Wright and Gardner 2000) reviewed 29 empirical studies containing 80 separate observations of an empirically tested link between HRM and organizational performance. They categorized the performance measures into HR (turnover being the only employee measure they found), organizational (e.g. productivity, quality, customer satisfaction), financial accounting (e.g. return on assets) and financial markets (e.g. Tobin's q – the difference between the market and book value of a firm's assets). They found that only three effect sizes were reported relating HR to human resource outcomes, but 34 relating to organizational, 24 to accounting and 19 to financial market outcomes. No sign here of the 'balanced scorecard' approach to performance advocated by David Guest (1997: 266) and to some extent achieved in Guest's (1999) own study of employee reactions to HRM and in the WERS (1998) survey, which tapped employee attitudes to work and their assessments of the climate of employee relations (Cully *et al.* 1999, Chapters 6, 8 and 12). The lack of American studies on employee outcomes seems misguided as all the theoretical rationales of how HR affects organizational performance rest on the assumption that it occurs *through* these employee outcomes. Hence one is forced to question the ability of these studies to test the theory – surely the object of positivistic research?

Apart from the very limited and questionable conceptualization of organizational performance and, with the exception of Guest (1997: 267), no recognition that these are but social constructions, there are problems with measurement. As Wright and Gardner (2000) point out, with the notable exception of Huselid's (1995) study, there is a tendency not to assess multiple performance measures in any single study. As a result, researchers are unable to examine the interrelationships among outcomes, although Huselid's study suggests these may be significant (at least some of the effect of HR practices on firm performance was mediated by the reduction in employee turnover). Problems such as these, though, pale into insignificance when compared to those associated with examining the *relationship* between HR and performance.

HRM AND PERFORMANCE: UNIVERSALISTIC 'BEST PRACTICE' OR CONTINGENCY 'BEST FIT'?

As already indicated, there is no agreed conceptualization of HRM ('strategic'? 'descriptive'? or 'prescriptive'?) or of the relationship between HRM and performance ('universalistic'? 'contingency'? or 'configurational'?). There is some consensus on performance measures generally used in practice (largely financial), but a recognition that these are inadequate as they ignore measures of employee outcomes on which improvements in organizational performance theoretically depend. These problems in establishing causal relationships are exacerbated by further difficulties.

Levels of analysis

A first issue is the practical one of trade-offs in selecting an appropriate level of analysis in testing HRM/performance relationships (Wright and Gardner 2000). Plant level studies (e.g. MacDuffie 1995; Youndt *et al.* 1996) have three strengths: the risk of variance in HR practices is minimized; the respondent(s) is likely to have first-hand knowledge of the HR practices – both espoused and in-use — increasing the validity of the responses; there is the potential of providing the most proximal measures of performance. The drawback is that research at this level may not allow assessing the 'fit' between HR practices and business strategy and there are the perennial issues of generalizability (see Purcell 1999: 31).

Organizational or business level studies are optimal for assessing relationships between HR practices and business strategy, but given that businesses often have multiple locations, categories of employee and jobs, as indicated earlier, precise assessments of HR practices become problematic, especially if the research design relies on just one senior management respondent.

The bulk of research linking HR practices and performance has been conducted at corporate level (see Wright and Gardner 2000) given the reliance on financial measures of performance, as it is at this level that much of the publicly available financial data exists. However, this exacerbates problems associated with the validity of single respondent assessments given the complexity of assessing HR practices over a range of businesses, the problem that there may be variance between the business strategies across businesses within some corporations (hence identifying *a* business strategy is likely to be problematic) and, because these studies cross industries, the difficulty in partialling out all of the industry effects.

At first sight, there may appear to be here just a methodological issue rather than a theoretical one (i.e. the researcher needs to be careful to match appropriately the research question with the level of analysis). However, what is worrying theoretically is that, if the majority of the research studies remains located at the corporate level, given the American obsession with measures of financial performance, this is not conducive to assessing the enacted aspects of employee behaviour that constitute the intervening variable in explaining the relationship between HR practices, operating and financial performance. It is difficult to see how such studies can *test* causal relationships, as opposed to making theory-derived inferences about the correlations they find.

This brings us to some major difficulties.

Causality

First, with some exceptions (see Becker and Gerhart 1996: 783), the majority of the American studies are cross sectional rather than longitudinal and, hence, as intimated above, while causality may be inferred from correlation, technically it is not tested. This gives rise to three possibilities. A causal relationship may exist in the direction inferred, i.e. HRM policies and practices give rise to positive outcomes. However, as Purcell (1999: 30) points out, even if this did exist, it might reflect no more than a temporary 'Hawthorne' effect in response to a change programme. (Of course it is possible, with the same direction of causality, that HRM, particularly 'hard' HRM, may give rise to negative outcomes, or as Guest and Hoque (1994) report, positive outcomes on organizational performance measures but negative outcomes on HR/ employee outcomes.) Or, reverse causality may exist. In other words, just to take the financial outcomes, as a firm becomes more profitable or its share price rises, it may invest in 'high commitment/performance' HRM practices, such as expenditure on training or profit sharing. As Wright and Gardner (2000) point out, this may be due to a belief that such practices will further increase performance, from a belief that they will reduce the risk of performance declines, or they might stem from a belief in the justice and efficacy of wealth distribution. However, it is the profits that generate HR practices rather than vice versa. A further possibility, identified by Wright and Gardner, is that the observed relationship between HR practices and performance may stem not from any true relationship (that is, 'true' from a positivistic perspective), but from the implicit theories of organizational survey respondents. Their argument on this later point is as follows.

Implicit performance theories (e.g. Brown and Perry 1994; Golden 1992; McCabe and Dutton 1993) suggest that respondents' implicit theories of relationships between variables of interest bias their responses to survey questions. So, for example, if a respondent has little detailed knowledge of the HR practices in her firm (highly likely if the firm is large, diverse and multi-sited), but knows that the firm is performing well in terms of productivity and profitability, she may infer that 'high performance' HR practices *must* exist, given this level of performance, based on the implicit theory that such practices are related to high performance. In their own study (Gardner, Wright and Gerhart 1999, cited in Wright and Gardner 2000) some support was found for implicit theories about the HR/performance relationship, in a simulated study. Gardner, Wright and Gerhart presented line managers, HR managers, MBAs and HR Masters students with scenarios of high and low performing firms and then had them estimate the use of HR practices in each firm. They report that all four groups estimated significantly greater usage of 'high performance' HR practices in high as opposed to low performing firms. This suggests that the observed relationship between measures of HR practices and firm performance may simply be an artefact of the implicit theories about their relationship held by respondents.

Processes

It is widely recognized, even by adherents to this research agenda and its associated positivistic research designs (e.g. Becker and Gerhart 1996; Guest 1997; Wright and Gardner 2000), that little has been done to unlock the 'black box' of the processes that link HRM (however conceptualized) with organizational performance (however conceptualized). But unless this is done, for example, by developing models that include theory-derived, key intervening variables, it is not possible to rule out unequivocally alternative causal models that explain empirical associations between HR practices and organizational outcomes (Becker and Gerhart 1996: 793; Purcell 1999: 29).

The question then becomes how many and what intervening variables should there be in the 'black box' (employee behaviour? employee skills? strategy implementation? operating performance?) (Becker *et al.* 1997; Becker and Huselid 1998) and how should these variables be specified? For example, 'operating performance' might be defined and measured in terms of customer satisfaction, customer retention, sales revenues, quality defects, scrap, downtime, productivity, labour costs; employee behaviours in terms of productivity, creativity and discretionary effort (Becker *et al.* 1997; Wright and Gardner 2000). Then there is the issue of distinguishing between espoused and actual HR practices and employee skills and behaviours (Wright and Snell 1998). And, as Wright and Gardner (2000) point out, the greater the number of intervening variables identified and the greater the level of specificity, the greater the multiplicative effect in determining the processes of a model, as the model building requires specification of the relationships between each of the specifications of the major intervening variables.

If this complexity is problematic when a universalistic approach to HR practices/ performance relationships is adopted, it becomes additionally so when a contingency or configurational approach is preferred. With contingency models of HRM/ performance relationship there are issues of causal ambiguity and path dependent contingencies that add up to idiosyncratic choices (Boxall 1992; Collis and Montgomery 1995; Purcell 1999). Causal ambiguity refers to the numerous and subtle interconnections between contingent factors that make each organization's experience, in a sense, unique. Path dependency recognizes the emergent nature of strategy and the dependence of policy choices on the organization's history and culture. Put the two together and the resultant idiosyncratic contingency suggests that each organization has to make choices of HR policy and practice based on its judgment not just of appropriateness to business and operational strategies but what 'suits' the history and culture of the organization, what 'feels' right (Purcell 1999: 35). Such potential complexity sits uneasily with the large-scale surveys and quantitative approaches of positivism.

TRAVELLING HOPEFULLY IN SEARCH OF THE HOLY GRAIL?

In fairness to researchers committed to the project of exploring HRM/performance relationships, as can be seen by my referencing, they are among the first and most trenchant critics of the limitations of the empirical studies in this area (see, for example, Becker and Gerhart 1996; Guest 1997; Huselid and Becker 1996; Purcell 1999; Wright and Gardner 2000). But, with the exception of Purcell (an employee relations pluralist empiricist, in my view, *not* a positivist) the response is to argue for the improvement of positivistic designs, not their abandonment. An issue on which there appears to be a wide measure of agreement is the need to open up the 'black box' of the processes that link HRM with organizational performance/outcomes.

Two British commentators, Guest and Purcell, from different perspectives, have made some useful suggestions here. David Guest (1997), by background a psychologist and, hence unsurprisingly, the more dyed-in-the-wool positivist, following MacDuffie (1995), suggests that expectancy theory might provide a theory of process to link HRM practices and performance as it links motivation and performance. Specifically, expectancy theory proposes that, at the individual level, high performance depends on high motivation, coupled with the necessary skills and abilities and appropriate role design and perception. Harking back to his early work (Guest 1987) Guest equates skills and abilities with quality, motivation with commitment and role structure and perception with flexibility. Hence, in terms of this debate, Guest suggests that HR practices designed to foster these HR outcomes (e.g. selection and training for skills and abilities/quality, contingent pay and internal promotion for motivation/commitment, employee involvement and job and team-working design for appropriate role perception and perception/flexibility) should facilitate high individual performance, which in turn is a contributory factor in high performance outcomes (e.g. high productivity, low absence and labour turnover), that should contribute (other things being equal) to financial outcomes. Building on these ideas, Guest (1999), in an empirical study of workers' reactions to 'high commitment' HRM policies (see Guest and Conway 1997), suggests that the psychological contract may be a key intervening variable in explaining the link between HR practices and employee outcomes such as job satisfaction, perceived job security and motivation. Furthermore, although Guest's research is cross sectional and, hence, raises the usual questions about causality, the inferred direction of his empirical findings is supported by a similar longitudinal study conducted by Patterson *et al.* (1997).

Nevertheless, Guest (1997) acknowledges the limitations of these models in terms of explaining organizational outcomes. While we may be able to measure the impact of HRM practices on *HRM* outcomes (quality, commitment and flexibility in Guest's terms) the measurable impact of HRM practices on *organizational* and *financial* outcomes is likely to become progressively weaker because of the wide range of potentially intervening variables. It is debatable whether such models can be developed due to their potential unmanageable complexity. Guest (1997) also admits that we need to have a theory about the circumstances under which human resources matter more and a theory about how much of the variance (between HR practices and performance) can be explained by the human factor. (Hence Becker and Gerhart's (1996: 790–1) call for more attention to be paid to size effects rather than to [often low levels of] statistical significance.) Purcell (1999), building on the work of Arthur (1992, 1994), has some interesting observations here.

First, Purcell (1999: 36–7), while more sympathetic to contingency than universalistic approaches, is essentially a pragmatic pluralist. He recognizes that, on the one hand, claims that the bundle of best practice HRM is universally applicable 'leads us into a utopian cul-de-sac', ignoring dual labour markets, contingent workers and business strategies that logically do not require 'high commitment' HR practices to achieve financial success. On the other, the search for a contingency model of HRM is a chimera, 'limited by the impossibility of modelling all the contingent variables, the difficulty of showing their interconnection, and the way in which changes in one variable have an impact on others, let alone the need to model idiosyncratic and path dependent contingencies'. The way forward, Purcell argues, is the analysis of how and when HR factors come into play in the management of strategic change. Purcell suggests that we should explore how organizations develop successful transition management, build unique sets of competencies and distinctive organizational routines and, in situations of 'leanness', with greater dependency on all core workers, develop inclusiveness and such workers' trust. The focus should be on

> appropriate HR architecture and the processes that contribute to organisational performance in the short and medium term, and which positively contribute to the achievement of organisational flexibility or longevity. This may well involve redrawing the boundaries of the firm and thinking about the way HRM can be a source of competitive disadvantage as well as advantage.
>
> (Purcell 1999: 38)

Note, while Guest and Purcell might not be a million miles away from each other in their concerns about the psychological contract and about when the human factor is more or less important, their approach to empirical research is different. Guest still seems concerned with establishing the measurable, linear causal relationships beloved of positivists. Indeed, the tenets of the experimental method seem to permeate his thinking as when he comments: 'To establish linkages, we also need longitudinal research designs, *ideally with some sort of interventions to alter HRM practices*' (Guest 1997: 274) (added emphasis). Purcell, on the other hand, while undeniably an empiricist, seems to be advocating a research agenda that calls for longitudinal, qualitative, in-depth case studies, where the focus is on uncovering idiosyncratic contingencies just as much as patterned regularities of behaviour.

SILVER BULLET OR SPENT ROUND? HOLY GRAIL OR GRAVY TRAIN?

As is evident from the foregoing analysis, much of the research on HR 'high commitment/performance' practices and organizational performance is at best confused and, at worst, conceptually and methodologically deeply flawed. With honourable exceptions, the lack of convincing modelling of the processes that might link HR practices and organizational outcomes, reflected in the inadequacy of performance measures, raises the question of why this issue and the associated positivistic research designs appear to be *the* fashionable project for high profile HRM research today. I can think of two explanations, one optimistic, the other less so.

The first explanation is that those wedded to this endeavour are both convinced of the importance of the research question (i.e. the impact of HRM policies and practices on organizational performance), of the appropriateness of neo-positivistic research designs for exploring the research question and of their ability to ultimately refine their research designs so as to overcome existing limitations. Of the importance of the research question there can be no doubt. *If* it could be convincingly demonstrated that certain HR practices or bundles of practices unequivocally lead to positive organizational performance outcomes and that the size of the effects far outweighs the cost of implementing such policies, one would indeed have found a silver bullet to aim at organizations performing poorly. A cynic might note that, in the UK, major protagonists of a positive 'high commitment' HR practices/performance relationship – Guest and Patterson, for example – are in receipt of grants to research this relationship from the Institute of Personnel and Development which has a direct professional and commercial interest in demonstrating such a link! Moreover, establishing the validity and generalizability of causal relationships is certainly claimed to be the *raison d'être* of neo-positivistic research designs (see, for example, the classic paper by Campbell 1969). Furthermore, leading protagonists of this research agenda have many suggestions about how to rectify some of the flaws and limitations of earlier research designs.

Thus there are advocates for an increasing focus on within-industry studies (in order to examine the idiosyncratic strategies and bases for competition that exist in specific industries), business level studies (in order to examine the fit between HR practices and strategy) and plant level studies (in order to examine the relationship between HR practices and employee outcomes) rather than on the prevalent corporate level studies (see, for example, Becker and Gerhart 1996; Wright and Gardner 2000). There are calls for developing more consistent and valid measures of HR practices, either by reducing complexity (focus on practices with regard to one job/one business/one site), or by using multiple respondents, (e.g. Becker and Gerhart 1996; Delery and Doty 1996; Wright and Gardner 2000) or by corroborating self-report measures 'with more objective indicators of strategic posture' (Youndt *et al.* 1996: 861). There is a general wish to see more longitudinal studies (e.g. Delery and Doty 1996; Guest 1997;Wright and Gardner 2000) and a recognition that a broader range of organizational outcomes, particularly employee outcomes, need to be built into research designs – the 'balanced score-card' approach (Becker and Gerhart 1996; Guest 1997; Wright and Gardner 2000). All call for the need to open up the black box of the processes that link HR practices to performance outcomes and some recognize the necessity of examining the differences between espoused and enacted HR practices via qualitative case studies (e.g. Purcell 1999; Wright and Gardner 2000).

What is interesting here is that although their language expresses the tenets of neo-positivism (see, for example, Becker and Gerhart's sub-headings in their 1996 paper: 'Developing a cumulative body of knowledge', 'Obtaining more robust and valid findings', 'Specification and measurement errors') the suggestions for improving the validity of the studies, not surprisingly given the complexity of the relationships involved, appear to involve some compromise with the positivistic value of generalizability. This presents us with something of a paradox. It is reported that the most widely tested and most strongly supported relationship 'either across industries or within a specific sector' is that where more 'high commitment/ performance' HR practices are used the better the organizational performance (see Guest 1997: 272). But, if this is both a valid finding *and* one of great apparent generalizability, why the call now to focus down the studies, even to the extent (admittedly among a minority) to admit a role for qualitative case studies? The only reason to sacrifice generalizability is in the interests of increased validity, so does this mean that confidence in the validity of this finding *and the neo-positivistic designs that produced it* is weaker than Guest's words might imply? Certainly, if one has confidence in this finding, why is it that 'high commitment/performance' policies are not more widely adopted (see Cully *et al.* 1999: 291; Purcell 1999: 36)? There seem to be some contradictions here.

A second explanation for the popularity of this research agenda is that it accords with the twenty-first century *zeitgeist* (cf. Grint 1994; Guest 1990) – that of an 'audit society' where surveillance in the interests of performativity forever broadens its scope and sharpens its focus (Lyon 1994). Thus while the so-called 'discipline' of the market place constitutes a form of surveillance in the private sector, government agencies increasingly monitor government-set performance standards in the public sector.

In Britain, university business schools are subject to both forms of surveillance. On the one hand, given ever-declining unit funding for universities from the state, business schools are treated as milch cows, subsidizing universities as a whole by attracting profitable MBA students whose high fees give them a right to demand high levels of 'customer care', particularly as satisfied alumni generate further business and endowments. Attracting and retaining such customers in a highly competitive market means branding one's product with seals of approval. Enter the surveillance of accreditation exercises – the UK AMBA, the American AACSB and the European EQUIS. On the other hand, as universities still receive public funding, they must be regularly monitored by public agencies to ensure the maintenance of standards, translated as 'value for money' (in spite of, or perhaps *because* of diminished state funding) and to decide eligibility for a particular share of available funding. Enter HEFCE and the dreaded Teaching Quality and Research Assessment exercises. The government Research Councils enter into the 'value for money' spirit of these activities, prioritizing research proposals that are 'relevant', i.e. promise economic pay-offs rather than solely contribute to knowledge. The outcomes of all these surveillance exercises are reflected in various widely publicized league tables (for example, the *Times Good Universities Guide* – following the model of the *Good Food Guide* no doubt? – and the *FT World Wide League Table of Business Schools*).

A common factor in these auditing activities is that to do well is to ensure better levels of funding than to do badly. And success in one area is supportive of success in others. Loyal alumni can endow Chairs that support research activity. Excellence in research is one factor that contributes to a high position in Business School league tables. A high position in Business School league tables is an effective recruitment device and an improving position allows the increase in fee per student that gives more surplus that could be devoted to more research.

So how does all this relate to the attraction of the HR practices/performance research agenda for British researchers in particular? First, there are clear practical pay-offs, if either the universalistic, contingency or configurational model can be demonstrated. Hence research designs that pursue this agenda are likely to be attractive to the UK research councils and attract funding. Second, in evaluating the quality of research, for example in both the HEFCE Research Assessment Exercise (1998) and in the *FT World Wide League Table of Business Schools* (2000), great weight is placed on papers published in refereed journals and, in particular, those published in the so-called 'A' rated journals. These are the top-rated journals according to their impact factor as assessed by the Social Science Citation Index. The top ten management journals in world rankings are all American and, generally speaking, pursue a managerialist, positivistic agenda. Indeed, a major protagonist for cumulative, positivistic research is no other than Jeffrey Pfeffer, a major player in the HR practices and performance debate (see, for example, his vitriolic debate with John van Maanen, an opposing social constructionist organization theorist) (Pfeffer 1993, 1995; van Maanen 1995a, b). If British researchers aspire to publish in these top-ranked journals, with all the benefits this confers, they must inevitably engage with the debates and paradigmatic positions that these journals support. Even if they prefer the easier (?) route of publishing in British or other European journals, the influence of the American journals is such that any academic that aspires to an international reputation has to engage with the 'American' debates unless they locate themselves firmly within the non-empiricist, critical, European tradition of the gang of three and eschew the American Academy of Management conference scene, except in the role of guerrilla fighters or lepers.

Whether one sees engagement in this research agenda as the worthy quest for a magic silver bullet or even as the search for the Holy Grail or whether one views the endeavour sceptically as getting on a gravy train that is likely only to yield a spent cartridge depends on the nature of one's theory-directed gaze. This is an issue that returns us to the questions of perspective as raised at the start of the chapter.

REFERENCES

Arthur, J.B. (1992) 'The link between business strategy and industrial relations systems in American steel minimills', *Industrial and Labor Relations Review*, **45**: 488–506.
Arthur, J.B. (1994) 'Effects of human resource systems on manufacturing performance and turnover', *Academy of Management Journal*, **37**: 670–87.
Barney, J. (1991) 'Firm resources and sustained competitive advantage' *Journal of Management*, **17**: 99–120.
Becker, B. and Gerhart, B. (1996) 'The impact of human resource management on organizational performance: progress and prospects', *Academy of Management Journal*, **39**(4): 779–801.
Becker, B.E. and Huselid, M.A. (1998) 'High performance work systems and firm performance: a synthesis of research and managerial implications', in Ferris, G.R. (ed.), *Research in Personnel and Human Resource Management, 16.* Greenwich, CT.: JAI Press, pp. 53–101.
Becker, B.E., Huselid, M.A., Pickus, P.S. and Spratt, M.F. (1997) 'HR as a source of shareholder value: research and recommendations', *Human Resource Management*, **36**(1): 39–47.
Beer, M., Spector, B., Lawrence, P.R., Quinn, Mills, D. and Walton, R.E. (1985) *Human Resource Management; A General Manager's Perspective*, Glencoe, Ill.: Free Press.
Bowey, A. and Thorpe, R. (1986) *Payment Systems and Productivity*, Basingstoke: Macmillan.
Boxall, P. (1992) 'Strategic human resource management: beginnings of a new theoretical sophistication?' *Human Resource Management Journal*, **2**(3): 60–78.
Brown, B. and Perry, S. (1994) 'Removing the financial performance halo from Fortune's "most admired companies"', *Academy of Management Review*, **37**(5): 1347–59.
Campbell, D. (1969) 'Reforms as experiments', *American Psychologist*, April: 228–42.
Cicourel, A.W. (1964) *Method and Measurement in Sociology*, Glencoe, Ill: Free Press.

Collis, D.J. and Montgomery, C.A. (1995) 'Competing on resources: strategy for the 1990s', *Harvard Business Review*, July/August: 118–28.

Cully, M., Woodland, S., O'Reilly, A. and Dix, G. (1999) *Britain at Work*, London: Routledge.

Cuthcher-Gershenfeld, J.C. (1991) 'The impact on economic performance of a transformation in workplace relations', *Indusrial and Labor Relations Review*, **44**: 241–60.

Delaney, J.T. and Huselid, M.A. (1996) 'The impact of human resource management practices on perceptions of organisational performance', *Academy of Management Journal*, **39**(4): 949–69.

Delery, J. and Doty, H. (1996) 'Models of theorizing in strategic human resource management: tests of universalistic, contingency, and configurational performance predictions', *Academy of Management Journal*, **39**(4): 802–35.

DiMaggio, P.J. and Powell, W.W. (1983) 'The iron cage revisited: institutional isomorphism and collective rationality in organizational fields', *American Sociological Review*, **48**: 147–60.

Foucault, M. (1984) 'Truth and power', in Rabinow, P. (ed.), *The Foucault Reader*, Harmondsworth: Penguin.

Fukuyama, F. (1989) *The End of History*, Glencoe, Ill.: Free Press.

Gardner, T.M., Wright, P.M. and Gerhart, B. (1999) 'The HR-firm performance relationship: can it be in the mind of the beholder?' Working Paper, Center for Advanced Human Resources Studies, Cornell University, Ithaca, NY.

Garrahan, P. and Stewart, P. (1992) *The Nissan Enigma*, London: Mansell.

Gerhart, B., Wright, P.M., McMahan, G.C. and Snell, S.A. (forthcoming). 'Measurement error in research in human resource decisions and firm performance: how much error is there and how does it influence effect size estimates?' *Personnel Psychology*.

Golden, B.R. (1992) 'The past is the past – or is it? The use of retrospective accounts as indicators of past strategy', *Academy of Management Journal*, **35**(4): 848–60.

Grint, K. (1994) 'Reengineering history: social resonances and business process reengineering', *Organization*, **1**(1): 179–201.

Guest, D.E. (1987) 'Human resource management and industrial relations', *Journal of Management Studies*, **24**(5): 503–21.

Guest, D.E. (1989) 'Human resource management: its implications for industrial relations and trade unions', in Storey, J. (ed.), *New Perspectives on Human Resource Management*, London: Routledge, pp. 41–55.

Guest, D.E. (1990) 'Human resource management and the American Dream', *Journal of Management Studies*, **27**(4): 378–97.

Guest, D.E. (1995) 'Human resource management, trade unions and industrial relations', in Storey, J. (ed.), *Human Resource Management: A Critical Text*, London: Routledge, pp. 110–41.

Guest, D.E. (1997) 'Human resource management and performance: a review and research agenda', *International Journal of Human Resource Management*, **8**(3): 263–290.

Guest, D.E. (1999) 'Human resource management – the workers' verdict', *Human Resource Management Journal*, **9**(3): 5–25.

Guest, D.E. and Conway, N. (1997) *Employee Motivation and the Psychological Contract*, London: IPD.

Guest, D.E. and Hoque, K. (1994) 'The good, the bad and the ugly: human resource management in new non-union establishments', *Human Resource Management Journal*, **5**(1): 1–14.

Hendry, C. and Pettigrew, A. (1990) 'Human resource management: an agenda for the 1990s', *International Journal of Human Resource Management*, **1**(1): 17–43.

Huselid, M.A. (1995) 'The impact of human resource management practices on turnover, productivity, and corporate financial performance', *Academy of Management Journal*, **38**: 635–72.

Huselid, M.A. and Becker, B.E. (1996) 'Methodological issues in cross-sectional and panel estimates of the human resource-performance link', *Industrial Relations*, **35**: 400–22.

Huselid, M.A., Jackson, S.E. and Schuler, R.S. (1997) 'Technical and strategic human resource management effectiveness as determinants of firm performance', *Academy of Management Journal*, **40**(1): 171–88.

Ichniowski, C., Kochan, T., Levin, D., Olson, C. and Strauss, G. (1996) 'What works at work: overview and assessment', *Industrial Relations*, **35**(3): 299–333.

Ichniowski, C., Shaw, K. and Prennushi, G. (1994) 'The impact of human resource management practices on productivity', Columbia Business School Working Paper 015, Columbia University, NY.

Keenoy, T. (1999) 'HRM as a hologram: a polemic', *Journal of Management Studies*, **36**(1): 1–23.

Kochan, T.A. and Osterman, P. (1994) *The Mutual Gains Enterprise: Forging a Winning Partnership Among Labor, Management, and Government*, Boston: Harvard Business School Press.

Legge, K. (1989) 'Human resource management: a critical analysis', in Storey, J. (ed.), *New Perspectives on Human Resource Management*, London: Routledge, pp. 19–40.

Legge, K. (1995a) 'HRM: rhetoric, reality and hidden agendas', in Storey, J. (ed.), *Human Resource Management: A Critical Text*, London: Routledge, pp. 33–59.

Legge, K. (1995b) *Human Resource Management, Rhetorics and Realities*, London: Macmillan.

Lyon, D. (1994) *The Electronic Eye*, Cambridge: Polity.

MacDuffie, J.P. (1995) 'Human resource bundles and manufacturing performance; organizational logic and flexible production systems in the world auto industry', *Industrial and Labor Relations Review*, **48**: 197–221.

McCabe, D.L. and Dutton, J.E. (1993) 'Making sense of the environment: the role of perceived effectiveness', *Human Relations*, **46**(5): 623–43.

Miles, R.E. and Snow, C.C. (1984) 'Designing strategic human resource systems', *Organizational Dynamics*, Summer: 36–52.

Patterson, M., West, M., Lawthom, R. and Nickell, S. (1997) *Impact of People Management Practices on Business Performance*, London: IPD.

Pfeffer, J. (1993) 'Barriers to the advance of organizational science: paradigm development as a dependent variable', *Academy of Management Review*, **18**(4): 599–620.

Pfeffer, J. (1994) *Competitive Advantage through People*, Boston: Harvard Business School Press.

Pfeffer, J. (1995) 'Mortality, reproducibility, and persistence of styles of theory', *Organization Science*, **6**(6): 681–86.

Popper, K. (1959) *The Logic of Scientific Discovery*, London: Hutchinson.

Purcell, J. (1989) 'The impact of corporate strategy on human resource management', in Storey, J. (ed.), *New Perspectives on Human Resource Management*, London: Routledge, pp. 67–91.

Purcell, J. (1995) 'Corporate strategy and its link with human resource management strategy', in Storey, J. (ed.), *Human Resource Management: A Critical Text*, London: Routledge, pp. 63–86.

Purcell, J. (1999) 'Best practice and best fit: chimera or cul-de-sac', *Human Resource Management Journal*, **9**(3): 26–41.

Reed, M. (1992) 'Introduction', in Reed, M. and Hughes, M. (eds), *Rethinking Organization*, London: Sage, pp. 1–16.

Rogers, E.W. and Wright, P.M. (1998) 'Measuring organizational performance in strategic human resource management: problems, prospects, and performance information markets', *Human Resource Management Review*, **8**: 311–31.

Schuler, R.S. and Jackson, S.E. (1987) 'Linking competitive strategies with human resource management practices', *Academy of Management Executive*, **1**(3): 209–13.

Storey, J. (1989) (ed.) *New Perspectives on Human Resource Management*, London: Routledge.

Storey, J. (1995) (ed.) *Human Resource Management: A Critical Text*, London: Routledge.

van Maanen, J. (1995a) 'Style as theory', *Organization Science*, **6**(1): 133–43.

van Maanen, J. (1995b) 'Fear and loathing in organization studies', *Organization Science*, **6**(6): 687–92.

Walton, R. (1985) 'From control to commitment in the workplace', *Harvard Business Review*, **63**(2): 77–85.

Willmott, H. (1993) '"Strength is ignorance, slavery is freedom": managing culture in modern organizations', *Journal of Management Studies*, **30**(4): 515–52.

Wright, P.M. and Gardner, T.M. (2000) 'Theoretical and empirical challenges in studying the HR practice-performance relationship'. Paper presented at the Special Workshop 'Strategic Human Resource Management', European Institute for Advanced Studies in Management, INSEAD, Fontainebleau, France, 30 March–1 April.

Wright, P.M. and Snell, S.A. (1998) 'Toward a unifying framework for exploring fit and flexibility in strategic human resource management', *Academy of Management Review*, **23**(4): 756–72.

Youndt, M.A., Snell, S.A., Dean, J.W. and Lepak, D.P. (1996), 'Human resource management, manufacturing strategy, and firm performance', *Academy of Management Journal*, **39**(4): 836–66.

The Place of Ethics in HRM   3

Jean Woodall and Diana Winstanley

INTRODUCTION

Until very recently, there has been little debate around the ethical basis of human resource policy and practice. Areas such as recruitment and selection, remuneration, performance management, and employee involvement would seem ripe for attention. Some recent academic work has debated the ethical basis of HRM as a concept and total practice (Legge 1997, 1998; Miller 1996a, 1996b), but apart from the development of ethical awareness among managers (Snell 1993; Maclagan 1998) and the ethical dimensions of the change management process (Mayon White 1994; McKendall 1993), the detail of HRM policy and practice has escaped ethical scrutiny. Furthermore, the discipline of business ethics is more preoccupied with the social responsibility of business in relations with clients, and the environment, and only touches upon employee interests as one of several stakeholders, or only to the extent that employees might suffer adverse impact to health and personal integrity as a consequence of their role in producing the organization's goods and services. That the way in which employees are managed within organizations may invite ethical scrutiny appears to have been overlooked. This disinclination to address ethical issues within HRM recently struck some leading authors in the field as 'a curiously undeveloped area of analysis' (Mabey, Salaman and Storey 1998: 15).

This chapter reflects on some of the issues arising out of recent developments. It seeks to go beyond either dissecting individual HR practices to identify whether they are moral, or debating whether the totality of HR is 'ethical'. Instead, it seeks to raise the level of ethical debate by adopting a multi-faceted approach using a variety of frameworks. Finally, it argues that raising ethical awareness and sensitivity is an important task for both HR academics and professionals. This chapter concludes by making a case for providing human resource professionals with an ethical 'armour', by suggesting how the exercise of ethical sensitivity and reasoning might become a legitimate reference point alongside the more prevalent recourse to arguments which seek to justify 'the business case', 'strategic fit', and/or 'best practice'. The argument to be advanced is that bringing an ethical dimension into HRM is not merely about pronouncing what is 'right' and 'wrong', nor about taking such statements at face value. Ethics is a critical and challenging tool. There are no universally agreed ethical frameworks, but this is not to offer an excuse for collapsing into moral relativism. Some ethical frameworks are more relevant to the study of HRM than others, and different situations require the exercise of ethical insight and flexibility in reasoning.

Above all, ethical decision making usually involves choices between alternatives, but rarely is the choice a straightforward one between right and wrong.

ETHICS AND EMPLOYEE WELL-BEING VERSUS STRATEGIC FIT AND BEST PRACTICE

On the whole, ethical issues have been of marginal significance to the unfolding debates around HRM. Any emphasis upon ethics and employee well-being within the HRM debate is therefore very contentious, and has become more so as organizations have struggled for survival in the last 20 or so years. So, it is not surprising that the ethical dimension of HR policy and practice has been almost ignored in recent texts on HRM, with the exception of the collections edited by Towers (1996), Mabey *et al.* (1997) and Mabey *et al.* (1998). The focus has been upon upon 'strategic fit' and 'best practice' models of HRM, and in high performance HR practices (Huselid 1995; Guest and Peccei 1994; Guest 1997, 1999; Purcell 1999; Tyson 1997a, 1997b; Tyson and Doherty 1999). However, there is enough argument to the contrary to suggest that employee well-being and ethical treatment are as justifiable a focus as 'strategic fit' and 'best practice'. After all, the Harvard analytical framework for HRM (Beer *et al.* 1984: 16) was one of the earlier models to suggest that as well as organizational well-being, HRM also had to concern itself with the promotion of individual and social well-being.

Even today, there is a strong case to support the argument that employee well-being and ethical treatment are as justifiable a focus as 'strategic fit' and 'best practice'. First, the 'enlightened self-interest' model of business suggests that a business will be more successful if it pays attention to ethics, as this will enhance its reputation with customers, and improve motivation among employees (for an example of the benefits of this, see Wilson 1997). Second, the 'business of business is business' argument is not a paramount, nor sufficiently persuasive one in not-for-profit organizations, including most of the public sector, social business, non-governmental organizations (NGOs) and the voluntary sector. Finally, there is a powerful argument that the wider economic system and ultimately the business organizations within it exist to serve human and societal needs rather than the opposite.

In this chapter we go even further to suggest that not only has the focus on 'best practice' and 'business case' HRM marginalized ethics, it has also subsumed and neutralized it through incorporating some of its language and manifestations in a diluted way, one example of which is in the participation and partnership literature discussed below. The question this poses is whether using business case arguments advances or diminishes the cause of ethical HRM.

THE ETHICAL DIMENSION IN THE EARLY HISTORY OF PERSONNEL PRACTICE AND ITS MARGINALIZATION WITHIN HRM

Welfare and employee health and well-being

At this point it is important to recollect that ethical concern took a central place in the earlier history of professional HRM. Its origins in personnel management and employee welfare date back to the formation of the Welfare Workers Association in 1913, a forerunner of the Chartered Institute of Personnel and Development, and even earlier with relation to the social reformers, philanthropists, and non-conformist religious groups that emerged during the course of the UK industrial revolution. Obviously the scope of professional personnel practice subsequently developed to cover other aspects including industrial relations, manpower planning and organization development, and most recently, contribution to and involvement in overall organizational corporate strategy. Despite concerns that the original welfare role of personnel professionals might compromise the status and strategic base of HRM, it has not been totally eclipsed. Yet, over time the notion of employee well-being has been reduced to a more specific set of practices confined around 'wellness' programmes and health screening, rather than extended to the wider experience an individual has of organizational life, including the demands of work roles, how their performance is managed, and the support and development they receive. There is abundant evidence that most of the causes of individual stress at work are due to the organization or insecurity of work itself (see Table 3.1 below), and over 30 per cent of employee sick leave in the UK is due to stress, anxiety or depression (Doherty and Tyson 2000). Contemporary concerns over long working hours reflect that after years of reductions in the average working week, for the first time this century, this trend has reversed.

If we look back over the last hundred years, we might see improvements in the welfare and position of employees, but this has not been based on steady progress. Concern with these issues peaked in the late 1960s and 1970s, but was followed by a deterioration in the 1980s and early 1990s. It could also be suggested that although many employees are better off in material terms than a hundred years ago, a new series of pressures have led to greater psychological ill-health with more stress, anxiety, insecurity and exhaustion from long hours of work. None the less, there are aspects of academic and professional HR practice that have sustained an ethical concern.

Job design and motivation

A concern with job design and employee motivation was indeed one of the means by which ethical treatment of employees and concern for their welfare were sustained well into the twentieth century. The influence of the Human Relations movement through the early work of Elton Mayo (1933), and the later work of Herzberg (1968) and Maslow (1970) and the Quality of Working Life movement in the 1970s, are all important illustrations of this. The focus upon work systems and job design to satisfy human motivational needs – and especially the need for autonomy, variety, skill

Table 3.1 The most highly rated causes of stress in the workplace

Time pressures and deadlines	60%
Work overload	54%
Threat of job losses	52%
Lack of communication and consultation	51%
Understaffing	46%

Source: C. Cooper/Trades Union Congress (1997) 'Crisis Talks', *Personnel Today*, October: 29–32.

development and self-actualization – were firmly on the management agenda in the 1960s and 1970s, but today only receive a glancing acknowledgment relative to the emphasis upon 'high performance' and 'high commitment' work systems linked to efficiency and effectiveness, rather than intrinsic job satisfaction.

Participation and involvement

Linked to the human relations literature is the industrial relations literature which has also highlighted participation and involvement issues, a key theme in contemporary partnership and stakeholder approaches mentioned below. In addition, some work focused on issues of power sharing and control, leading to a number of industrial democracy experiments in the 1960s, notably the Lucas Aerospace project. Some of this early industrial relations literature has raised the more general issue of social responsibility (Flanders 1970), a focus which largely became eclipsed in later work. Although there is some elaboration of different partnership models and approaches in contemporary human resource management (for example highlighting the differences between representative and direct participation, US integrationalist and UK mutual gains models) unitarist models have been in the ascendance. Thus there is less discussion of issues to do with pluralism, power differentials, and approaches that truly extend the type, scope and power of employee voice, and more on its impact on organizational performance (for example Sako 1998). Once again ethical issues become either marginalized or subsumed by business case arguments.

Organizational justice

An enduring academic and professional interest in ethical issues is present around the subject of organizational justice, in the exercise of both substantive and procedural justice. Interest in the former has been sustained by a concern with fairness and equal opportunity. Research into discrimination, particularly in the areas of recruitment, selection, remuneration and career development, has addressed issues of gender, marital status, race, and ethnicity, and more recently, age. Voluntary action on fairness and equal opportunity by organizations, individuals, and professional groups has included codes of professional practice, and training both within professional education, and subsequent professional updating. Equality legislation since the mid 1970s has been the bedrock for this and although there has been further legislation in this area, such as the Disability Discrimination Act 1995, in the 1990s the ethical agenda moved away from legislation supported approaches, towards more internal business case approaches to diversity management. The ethical principle moved from equality to freedom, although in practice many diversity approaches will also incorporate and build on the gains of equal opportunities programmes (for example see Cornelius and Gagnon 2000; Sen 1999).

Turning to procedural justice, this has always been a strong theme in both professional practice and academic research in industrial relations. Fair process as well as fair outcome have been an abiding concern in collective bargaining, remuneration, job evaluation and recruitment. However, once again, the changes brought about by HRM have led to a marginalization of these issues. This can be illustrated by reward management. Traditionally, 'good practice' highlighted the role of job evaluation as a basis for ensuring fairness and justice. More recently this has been discarded for an emphasis upon strategic focus, flexibility and individual and group performance.

Human resource professionals as 'ethical stewards

Finally, there has also been some interest in the role of the human resource specialist as a guardian of ethics, with the human resource function assuming the role of 'ethical stewardship' and ethical leadership. Most discussion of this has appeared sporadically within professional HRM journals. For example, some writers have stressed the HR manager's role in raising awareness about ethical issues, in promoting ethical behaviour, and in disseminating ethical practices more widely among line and project managers. Another ethical role for HR professionals involves communicating codes of ethical conduct, providing training in ethics, managing compliance and monitoring arrangements, and taking a lead in enforcement proceedings (see for example Arkin 1996; Pickard 1995; Johns 1995; Wehrmeyer 1996). Where ethical conduct is questioned, HR managers have traditionally overseen arrangements for the handling of discipline and grievances. For some (Connock and Johns 1995), the mantle of ethical leadership should not just be worn by HR managers alone: the responsibility should also be placed firmly on the shoulders of the whole senior management team and line managers. This is an argument that is very much in keeping with moves to get HRM enacted by a wider group of organizational stakeholders.

ETHICAL CONCERNS IN CONTEMPORARY HRM

Thus if ethical concern has been an enduring, but sporadic and low priority concern in the history of professional personnel practice and academic inquiry, then why does it require more attention now? The answer lies in the changes which have taken place in human resource management over the last two decades. In addition to 'strategic fit' and 'best practice', a number of themes do seem to preoccupy contemporary HRM. In particular, the preoccupation with flexibility, commitment, culture, quality and performance, raises a number of ethical issues.

'Flexibility' in variable pay systems or in the contract of employment, and 'high commitment' work practices raise ethical questions about practices as varied as 'presenteeism' and long working hours. An Institute of Management Survey in 1996 revealed that 84 per cent of managers reported that they worked in excess of their official hours, averaging 50–60 hours per week (Institute of Management 1996), a finding corroborated by other surveys (Simpson 2000). Such presenteeism arises out of an insecurity and fear of redundancy that induces people to stay at their desks longer in order to demonstrate visible commitment and gain an advantage over others. Simpson has shown how highly gendered such behaviour is, with detrimental effects on the advancement of women into senior management. While these practices affect managers on standard employment contracts, flexible employment contracts also now mean insecurity for nearly half the UK workforce, of which part-time employees form 31 per cent, the self-employed 13 per cent, and a growing army of temporary workers on short-term contracts supplying employees for the full range of jobs from nursing to further education, and call centre staff to computer programmers (Stanworth 2000). Finally, the gross inconsistencies around performance-related pay which places a substantial amount of earnings 'at risk' for the majority of employees, while disregarding company performance in the remuneration of senior executives and board members (Heery 2000), indicates that violations of organizational justice are at the heart of HRM.

Performance management systems based upon 'stretch' targets and close surveillance and control, place increasing emphasis upon processes for evaluating, grading, and classifying individuals (Winstanley 2000). In addition the growing use of psychological tests, not just for recruitment, but also to select people for redundancy based upon cultural fit, after organizational restructuring, raises questions of integrity and the inappropriate use of instruments that were designed to measure genuine occupational or job requirements (Baker and Cooper 2000). Furthermore, a desire to 'capture hearts and minds' in the service of corporate goals, has extended the focus of training and development activity beyond the mere acquisition of knowledge and skills into shaping values and attitudes, by means of new techniques of value and culture change (see Chapter 10 of this volume for a deeper exploration of this). While outdoor management development has gained a poor image for attention to the physical safety of participants, there is evidence that this is exaggerated, and reason to believe that it is practised with greater respect for the psychological safety of participants than many current techniques of value change such as Neuro-Linguistic Programming (Woodall and Douglas 2000).

None of these issues are merely issues of organizational justice. They also raise questions about the scope of employer duty of care, about individual rights to autonomy, privacy, dignity and self-esteem, and the boundaries between organizational demands and employee subjectivity. How might this ethical agenda best be addressed? There are two issues here. One concerns the nature of ethical inquiry and its relation to action. The other concerns the ethical frameworks to be employed.

THE NATURE OF ETHICAL ENQUIRY: THE CASE FOR ETHICAL SENSITIVITY AND REASONING

The professional and academic HRM community tend to have a different understanding of what 'ethical' concern means, compared with the community of business ethicists. For the former, the words 'ethical', 'moral', and 'good' are all synonyms denoting what is best practice. The concern is with action – doing something about a situation to bring it back into ethical equilibrium (for examples of this see Miller 1996a, 1996b; Arkin 1996; Pickard 1995; Johns 1995; Wehrmeyer 1996). In contrast, business ethicists focus on developing the ethical frameworks that may inform moral decision making (Donaldson 1989; Maclagan 1998; Beauchamp and Bowie 1983; Petrick and Quinn 1997). While morality is about adopting and justifying a stance on an issue or topic, ethics involves taking one step back in order to reflect on these underlying principles, decisions, and problems (see Figure 3.1).

So while HR professionals and academics might well be more inclined to investigate potential options for action – such as devising and upholding codes of practice, or establishing procedures for 'whistleblowing' and 'ethical ombudsmen', or introducing social auditing and staff charters, they might be less inclined to reflect upon the ethical principles guiding such actions, and the inevitable value conflict and dilemmas that arise. This is what is meant by 'ethical sensitivity' and 'ethical

> ***Ethics is the consideration and application of frameworks, values and principles for developing moral awareness and guiding behaviour and action.***
>
> At the individual level ethics guides individual judgement and conduct when faced with moral dilemmas and choices, whereas morals may reflect a more personal intuitive and unexamined stance which may operate out of an individual's awareness. At the collective level ethics represents common values enshrined in rules, and codes of practice for guiding behaviour, and which underpin professional and organizational life. Morality on the other hand is the customary values held about what is right and wrong which become embedded or fostered in a society or culture.

Figure 3.1 A definition of ethics

reasoning'. When embarking upon ethical reasoning, depending upon which ethical framework is used at the time, it is very easy to become swamped by a discussion of absolute versus relative values, and by the distinction between virtues, principles, rights and responsibilities. Is ethics about attitudes, values or behaviour? Is it a set of rules for correct conduct or a means for adopting a system of moral principles or virtues?

Inevitably moral disagreement and judgments are concerned with attitudes and feelings, not facts. Something that MacIntyre (1985) calls 'emotivism' comes unavoidably into play. Ethical statements, by their nature are subjective attempts to invoke agreement and adherence to one or other ethical framework, rather than objective statements of truth. Yet, this is not a licence for ethical relativism – a 'nobody's right, so anything goes' position. A distinction can be made between relativism and informed dissent based upon an awareness of and sensitivity to the plurality of ethical positions. Rather, it is important to be ethically aware of how an individual's own dispositions affect the choice of an ethical frame of reference. The ethical positions taken on a particular aspect of HR policy and practice are highly likely to differ between a chief executive, an HR professional, a line manager and the wider workforce. This can be illustrated by the issue of working hours for managerial and professional staff. A chief executive might take the position that unwillingness to work anything less than a 50-hour week is indicative of a lack of commitment, and that as 'the social responsibility of business is to make a profit', then there is no ethical justification for challenging this position. Conversely, a line manager might consider that the 'cost' of getting his/her staff to work long hours is justified by the 'benefit' of meeting the team's performance targets: the ends justify the means. An employee might consider the expectation of a 50-hour week to be exploitative and a violation of their employment rights. Finally, a human resource manager, mindful of the legal responsibilities around working hours and 'duty of care', plus the wider implications for stress in personal lives, might wish to adopt a middle position. However, appeals to a 'business case', the need for 'strategic fit', or 'best practice', will not resolve this dilemma. So, the issue becomes one of developing an ethical sensitivity around this issue and of adopting an appropriate form of ethical reasoning in resolving dilemma and debate.

Thus the ethical agenda for HRM becomes the development of ethical sensitivity and reasoning. Ethical sensitivity is the ability to reflect upon human resource management and be able to identify the ethical and moral dimensions and issues. Ethical reasoning is the ability to draw on relevant theory and frameworks to make more explicit the alternative interpretations and responses that could be made to inform decision making. This chapter now proceeds to illustrate this by introducing a variety of relevant ethical frameworks which can be used to analyse and understand the ethical dilemmas encountered in contemporary HRM.

ETHICAL FRAMEWORKS AND THEIR RELEVANCE TO HRM

The following discussion provides a resumé of the different ethical frameworks that can be applied to various aspects of HRM practice. The chapter has adopted a multi-faceted perspective departing from previous approaches which attempt to evaluate HRM policy and practice either in relation to a more restricted menu of theories such as deontological, utilitarian, or stakeholder theory (Legge 1997), or a rather eclectic assemblage of principles concerning 'systems, procedures and outcomes' (Miller 1996a, 1996b). It tries to avoid the traditional knots many ethicists get caught up in when counterbalancing universalism with relativism, or 'good in itself' versus consequentialist theories. The aim is to provide clear, non-technical outlines and examples. The main frameworks are summarized in Table 3.2, and are categorized as minimalist approaches, individual/humanist approaches, and interrelational approaches. It is not necessarily the case that these are mutually exclusive either/or choices of approach.

ETHICAL ARGUMENTS THAT UPHOLD A MINIMALIST POSITION

A managerialist position is based on the assumption that either individually or collectively, wider managerial interests must prevail over the claims of other specific interests, and that the status quo must be protected with minimal tolerance of change. This position is usually a minimalist one, justified by reference to a range of ethical arguments, including ethical egoism, utilitarianism and libertarian and contract-based approaches.

Ethical egoism is a minimalist ethical position based upon the Hobbesian assumption that 'the only valid standard of conduct is the obligation to promote one's own well-being above anyone else's' (Beauchamp and Bowie 1983: 18), an injunction to act upon the basis of maximizing self-interest: *the interests of employers and shareholders outweigh those of individual employees.*

This is not to imply that ethical egoists do not consider the interests of others when it suits them, and may well do so in order to fend off unpleasant consequences. This is not far from the position of Friedman (1962) and Sternberg (1994, 1997) that business works solely for the benefit of shareholders. In this model the ethical role of the HR professional would be limited to supporting the enlightened self-interest of the employer, rather than the rights of employees (unless, of course, not to do so would have an adverse impact upon organizational effectiveness). This is a very commonly used ethical argument in HR practice. It explains why organizations might at the same time have been concerned to offer high pay to 'millenium bug' computer programmers, while simultaneously placing them upon very insecure and stressful employment contracts, or even treating other work groups in an inferior manner. Ethical egoism often underpins so-called 'business case' arguments.

Table 3.2 Everyday ethical frameworks

General approach	Ethical framework	Main principles
Minimalist Positions	**Ethical Egoism**	*The interests of employers and shareholders outweigh those of individual employees*
	Model 1: Self-interest	Promote own interest above others
	Model 2: Enlightened Self-interest	Business case arguments suggesting need to take others into account
	Utilitarianism	*The ends justify the means – assess the consequences*
	Model 1: Act Utilitarianism	Assess how to maximize the greatest good for the greatest number
	Model 2: Rule Utilitarianism	Act in accordance with rules fashioned on utility
	Nozick – Libertarianism	*Liberty and freedom is all – action to limit this leads to unanticipated consequences*
	Model 1 – Nozick	Freedom for employer
	Model 2 – Sen's Freedom's for individuals	The fundamental principle of freedom is the individual capability 'to do things that a person has reason to value'
	Rawlsian Justice Theory	*It's a question of getting the balance right between freedom and quality. Inequalities should favour the most disadvantaged*
Individual and humanism Approaches	**Kantian Rights Based Ethics**	*There are fundamental rights that as human beings we are all entitled to*
	Universality	What is right for one is right for everyone
	Reversability	Do unto others as you would be done by
	Respect for persons	Treat people as ends in themselves, not merely as means to an end
	General Rights Based Approaches	*Individuals have rights to autonomy, privacy, dignity, respect, self-esteem, authenticity, etc.*
	Ethics of Care	*Dispassionate objectivity gets us nowhere. Subjectivity, particularity and empathy for each individual are important*
	Virtue Ethics	*Behave with integrity, enacting virtues and values in all that you do*
Inter-relational Ethics	**Communitarian Ethics**	*No person is an island – community is important*
	Stakeholding Ethics	*Everyone involved or affected should have a voice*
	Model 1 – Paternalist	Take each stakeholder's needs into account, actively find these out
	Model 2 – Pluralist	Actively involve stakeholders in decision-making
	Discourse Ethics	*It's not what you agree, but the way you agree it*

Utilitarianism is a teleological ethical framework (from the Greek 'telos' meaning the final purpose, issue or goal), in that it is primarily concerned with outcomes or consequences: *the ends justify the means – assess the consequences.*

It, too, is based upon ethical egoism, with the addition of an arithmetical basis to justify the reasoning. This is the 'moral calculus' of the nineteenth-century philosopher, Jeremy Bentham. In its commitment to maximize 'utility' two approaches can be distinguished: 'act' utilitarianism where the decision-maker needs to assess how the greatest good or utility could be achieved, and 'rule' utilitarianism where individual acts require adherence to rules which have been fashioned on utility. These are principles which have been used in a public policy context for distribution of benefits or allocation of scarce resources, but are seldom used in HRM practice. For example, electronic surveillance of teleworkers to detect and deter their 'abuse' of electronic mail, and to monitor work loads and work practices, could be justified in terms of the wider business benefit, but this may be at a significant and unknown cost to individual employees, as a result of stress, and anxiety induced by the invasion of personal privacy. Perhaps the most frequently encountered use is utility analysis of selection and assessment methods, or cost benefit analysis of training and development interventions, whereby all the costs of administering and delivering methods and interventions are weighed in terms of the outcomes for the organization and individuals. Yet, even in these cases, the managerialist perspective predominates, as the individual's 'utility' (right) in terms of privacy or fairness is contingent upon the benefits to all. HR professionals often resort to a crude form of utilitarian reasoning after the event, to justify action and inaction alike. Arguably, the current compulsion towards HR auditing with its focus upon outcomes arises from a desire for a post hoc rationalization of the utility of policies, for example, in training and development. However, the classical criticisms of utilitarianism always apply: the difficulty of predicting potential outcomes and the relative weights to be attributed to different individual utilities.

The Rawlsian theory of distributive justice is closely related to the moral calculus of utilitarianism, but with an attempt to allow individual interests greater weight in argument: *it's a question of getting the balance right between freedom and equality: inequalities should favour the most disadvantaged*. Rawls (1971) advocates two principles: first, that each individual has an equal right to basic liberty and second, that inequalities in distribution should be to the benefit of all, or to the extent that the least advantaged do not suffer further disadvantage. This contract-based model synthesizes a calculation of utility with three 'strong' ethical principles: fairness, equality and freedom, with the former having overriding priority. What is a very sophisticated model designed for application in the public policy realm, has indeed provoked much academic debate (Barry 1973; Miller 1976), but surprisingly little application. It has certainly not been used within either academic or professional HRM circles, although there is the potential for it to be used in complex pay and remuneration negotiations, for example with relation to the pioneering compensation philosophy of Ben and Jerry's ice-cream business in the USA, which reduced pay differentials between senior management and the shop floor to a ratio of 7:1 (Wilson 1997).

An alternative to the Rawlsian position in the arguments over the balance between liberty and equality, is that of Robert Nozick (1974), who would have argued that, far from protecting the rights of the least advantaged, it is more important and just to protect the right to liberty, an argument which could be deployed in support of an enterprise culture and freedom from the restraints of much HR legislation: *liberty and freedom is all, action to limit this leads to unanticipated consequences*.

One rationale for this is that any infringement of liberty leads to problems of unintended consequences. Thus taking the example of accelerating executive pay levels for the privatized industries, or the levels of runaway economic inequality in the US and UK, Nozick would argue that the ethical principle should be to support liberty, and not redistributive justice to impose greater equality. Another writer on freedom, Sen (1999) – and see also Cornelius and Gagnon (2000) – takes a different view, and suggests that the problem with traditional theories such as utilitarianism, libertarianism and Rawlsian ethics is that they all are flawed if individual freedoms are taken as important. As he sees it freedom is the individual capability 'to do the things that a person has reason to value'. In his conception, consequences therefore are important, as is freedom, but unlike Nozick, so are agency rights – e.g. rights which promote the 'free agency of for example women' to be transformers of their own lives. This also subtly shifts the notion of freedom away from that of the employer to that of the employee.

Egoism, utilitarianism and libertarianism are essentially frameworks of ethical reasoning that can be conveniently used by management to defend the status quo or a minimalist position. So, while it might be argued that introducing measures to achieve a family-friendly workplace might be advantageous to the overall experience of employment in an organization, and particularly helpful in attracting and retaining female 'human capital', these theories only justify action if the overall gain is deemed to outweigh the costs. These are also theories that rest upon the notion of the individual as the 'unencumbered self' (Sandel 1984), in that other claims and obligations they might have outside the immediate parameters of the 'moral calculus' are irrelevant. Again, this can be illustrated by looking at how those employees with dependent relatives are treated at work. Social convention relating to domestic role segregation and income differentials, means that more women than men are likely to take time off work to care for dependants. Yet, if each employee is to be treated as an 'unencumbered self', then there is no justification for taking such social factors into account when arranging work hours, managing performance and considering candidates for promotion.

HUMANISM AND ETHICAL FRAMEWORKS THAT ACKNOWLEDGE THE WORTH OF THE INDIVIDUAL

Humanism itself is not fashionable within academic HRM circles. The essentialism underlying the notion of the human subject is dismissed as an ideological delusion or cultural artefact by Critical Theorists, Post-Modernists, and Labour Process Theorists alike. The ascendancy of economic or cultural determinism over human agency has made it a 'fact' that cannot be challenged. Within HRM the *resource* rather than the *human* element prevails, as does *management* rather than *development.* Yet opponents of humanism often conflate the normative and the descriptive, framing the debate in a way that renders illegitimate any mention of human-centredness. However, while naive appeals to the sanctity of the human subject can be faulted, to represent this as totally delusional and as an ideological or cultural product, is to remove any possibility of ethical human agency, and open the doors to ethical agnosticism or relativism.

There are several frameworks that can be applied here. First of all there is a 'strong' ethical position that places individual interest at the centre of all ethical consideration, but in contrast with ethical egoism's concern to limit infringement on action to support the employer's interests, it is preoccupied with a positive assertion of basic rights for all: *there are fundamental rights that as human beings we are all entitled to.*

Most commonly, 'rights-based' ethical frameworks tend to draw upon two key concepts from the eighteenth-century German philosopher, Immanuel Kant: the two categorical imperatives. The first is to follow the principle that what is right for one person is right for everyone, and thus it is important to do unto others as you would be done by – the criteria of universality and reversability. The second is the principle of respect for persons whereby people should be treated as ends in themselves and never as means to an end.

This Kantian framework epitomizes 'deontological' approaches to business ethics. Deontology derives from the word 'deon' meaning duty in Greek, but this set of theories have come to mean much more than duty. They generally cover approaches that link ethics to things that are good in themselves, rather than in relation to 'telos' or goals. Kantian approaches propound a number of rights, usually embracing issues such as the fundamental right to life and safety, and the human rights of privacy, freedom of conscience, speech, and to hold private property. Rights-based frameworks continue to be relevant to HRM, particularly in areas such as selection interviewing (the right to privacy and confidentiality of personal information, particularly where it is not relevant to the job), occupational testing (such as the right to feedback), equal opportunities and diversity management (the right to be treated as the same, or the right to be given special treatment), flexible employment contracts and working time (the right to 'family-friendly' practices), 'whistleblowing' (the right to speak out about wrongdoing), staff charters (which may outline employee rights and responsibilities), and even employee development (the right to physical and psychological safety, such as in relation to outdoor training, or an organizational culture change). However, such rights-based approaches (although they certainly received considerable support 20 years ago), now receive short shrift among practising human resource professionals. Rather than being challenged on their own intellectual terrain, they are dismissed as 'impractical', and of a lesser legitimacy than the 'business case' arguments outlined above.

In focusing on individual and human aspects, human rights are just one angle. Another is to turn to human 'virtues', individual characteristics and disposition. These enjoin us to *behave with integrity enacting virtues and values in all that you do.*

Neither HR academics nor professionals have paid much attention to the resurgence of interest in virtue ethics, which has been led by the work of Alistair MacIntyre (1985) and Robert Solomon (1992, 1993). Perhaps the Aristotelian and medieval scholastic origins of the concept make it difficult to convey to a modern management audience. At its heart, the Aristotelian notion of virtue is as a disposition, meaning that it arises from a deep state of being, rather than a behaviour to be picked up and shed at will. Virtue in this view is therefore not something we do, but more a way of being. Virtues are practised because human beings are urged to 'lead a good life' aiming to achieve the optimum but not excess in all things. This all makes it difficult for virtue to be grafted on as a new set of HR practices, instead it would imply that it would need to underpin the organizational culture in a much more fundamental and pervasive way. This may even suggest that it would only be possible for organizations such as the Body Shop, the John Lewis Partnership, and the Co-operative Bank, whose virtues have become embedded in practices (though not necessarily uniformly nor consistently) and extolled in deeply held value sets, to aspire to virtue. It would be impossible for those organizations that adopt and shed their values with each new organizational change initiative to adopt this ethical stance.

What, however, are the virtues that an employer and employee would exhibit today? MacIntyre's (1985) list of the classical 'Homeric' virtues of fifth-century Athens (including excellence, courage, cunning, sense of shame in wrong-doing, honour, fidelity, and congruence) and of the classical 'Athenian' values (including the co-operative values that one might expect in a city-state such as justice, order, friendship, self-restraint and wisdom) may warrant debate today. Solomon (1992, 1993) draws upon Aristotelian accounts of virtue to present a contemporary view of virtues for business ethics. He identifies six: community, excellence, role identity, holism, integrity, judgment and sensitivity (Solomon 1993: 216). Many of us have similar lists (for example, Winstanley and Stoney (2000) identify humanistic ones of attachment and reciprocity, security, acceptance, congruence, self-actualization and meaningfulness). We suspect that to make this at all appealing to HR managers, the language of 'virtue' would need to be transmuted into 'values', but in so doing the concepts would be in danger of becoming changeable, ephemeral and superficial.

Virtue ethics is both appealing and frustrating. For example, integrity is a key issue for HR professionals (Pearson 1995) and appears in the debate around professional codes of practice in both the UK and USA (IPD 1995; AHRD 1999), but academic critics argue that it has been markedly absent in contemporary HRM (Legge 1995a, 1995b; Woodall 1996). Also, it is easy to generate laundry lists of competing virtues with little consensus about why they are included and to whom they apply (employers in general, HR specialists or employees). Ultimately, they need to be embedded in the contemporary social, economic, or political context, which brings us back to some of the other aforementioned ethical frameworks.

Much of the preceding debate rests upon intellectual reason – feelings, intuitions and senses are viewed as dysfunctional to ethical judgment and to be purged from ethical reasoning, but *dispassionate objectivity gets us nowhere. Subjectivity, particularity, and empathy for each individual are important.*

Gilligan (1982, 1987) has shown that more subjective and intuitive approaches to ethical problem solving are legitimate. Her reassertion of the role of feeling and empathy in ethical reasoning takes us back to a more humanistic basis for managing people. Unlike the formalistic theories of ethical egoism, utilitarianism, rights and justice, etc. she argues that moral judgments need to be sensitive to both the needs of the situation and other individuals. Being impartial makes it difficult to imagine oneself in the other's position, and thus adequately understand the other's perspective (Carse 1996: 86). For Gilligan, moral reasoning involves empathy and concern, emphasizing responsiveness and responsibility in our relations with others, where moral choices are made in relationship with others, not in isolation. An ethic of care is based on the assumption that detachment from self or others is morally problematic, since it breeds moral blindness, indifference and a failure to discern or respond to need.

Gilligan's approach arose out of research into the ethical reasoning processes used by women, whom she found to be more inclined to adopt the 'care' approach. Aside from the issues raised by the gendered nature of much ethical debate, the ethics of care has much relevance to human resource management. Its incorporation of a place for feeling and emotion in organizational life has resonance with the growing literature on 'emotion in organisation' (Fineman 1993) and the current revival of interest in personal development and interpersonal dynamics which draws upon humanistic psychology such as Rogerian counselling (Rogers 1967) and Gestalt (Clarkson 1998), with their emphasis upon empathy, acceptance, genuineness and congruence. What would an ethics of care look like in practice? It would change the emphasis of HR away from formal systems and rules and procedures, to decision-making on a more personal basis – for example with respect to working hours, it may mean a line manager allowing an individual time off for family responsibilities, or an HR manager enabling flexibility in working hours and offering job shares, part-time working, term-time working or a number of other atypical work contracts to parents wishing to fit in work and child-care.

There is always the danger that an ethic of care can become oppressive and degenerate into a dominant parent-child metaphorical relationship, where employers take responsibility for decision-making and safeguarding employee interests – paternalism again. The lack of empowerment, autonomy and openness that can result can be detrimental to employees and raise further ethical questions around emotional labour. However, Gilligan's ethics of care framework is very different from paternalist and welfarist models of HRM, and moves far away from viewing employees instrumentally as a human 'resource', incorporating more fully the notion of respect and empathy for the individual that is missing from many practices in contemporary performance management, training and development, health and safety and culture management (see for example Winstanley 2000). The humanistic values of empathy, acceptance, genuineness, congruence and unconditional positive regard are *very* different values from those that underpin HRM, and more importantly, best practice HRM. Contingent pay and highly developed performance management and reward systems, do not sit well with 'unconditional positive regard' (Winstanley 2000), and empathy is generally not a subject taught on MBA courses! Research suggesting a gap between rhetoric and practice (such as Legge 1995a) does not suggest there is a high level of genuineness and congruence evident in contemporary HRM.

There is also another critique of the 'subjective and intuitive' approach, which lays it vulnerable to the charge of 'sentimentality'. Would it really lead to a more humane workplace? There is much evidence to suggest that equal rights and discrimination legislation were brought in to promote more objective decision-making, for the very reason that subjective approaches could lead to discrimination, prejudice, favouritism and bias. The challenge here must be how to ensure the informal organization promotes the ethics of care model without these undesirable consequences.

INTERRELATIONAL ETHICS

The common theme in this group of approaches is that as well as taking individuals into consideration, there need to be mechanisms to underpin the interchange and dialogue that inevitably takes place when individuals come together. Therefore, as well as promoting individual voice, they focus on process issues and the interrelatedness of organizational life and the exchanges that take place as individuals interact.

The emphasis upon high commitment management and culture management enjoins the employee to identify very strongly with the objectives of the workplace. This is more than traditional paternalism, as it is asserting that the employing organization is a community of purpose (Warren 1998) to which all are bound. For individuals to be part of a community to which they have obligations as well as rights: *no person is an island – community is important.*

Recent debate around the notion of a community of purpose suggests that commitment to job security for employees is a basic condition for its effectiveness (Coupar and Stevens 1998; Monks 1998). In addition, communitarianism is a social philosophy that focuses upon the shared values of individuals within a community of purpose. This is a philosophy for life at the individual, group, organizational and societal level. Etzioni (1995) has been one of the most influential writers and campaigners on this subject, and suggests that the unbridled liberal defence of freedom is a fallacy: we are all members of overlapping communities and the workplace is one such community of purpose. Unlike stakeholding which espouses diversity of value and plurality of interests, communities of purpose emphasize shared values, belonging and inclusiveness.

What would an organization adopting a 'community of purpose' stance look like? It may adopt many of the Japanese practices of single status, single unionism, long-term employment, high investment in training and development, recruitment from school, and be based on behavioural compatibility, with teamwork, flexibility and high commitment. It may alternatively exhibit many of the features described for partnership companies – which the Industrial Participation Association describe as employment security, company flexibility, sharing of financial success with the workforce, the development of good communication and consultation, and representative and employee voice (IPA 1997). The kind of companies identified here include Welsh Water, Hyder, Blue Circle, United Distillers, Rover, Marks and Spencer, John Lewis (see Overell 1997), and also those companies linked with the Centre for Tomorrow's Company and the Committee of Inquiry for New Vision on Business, including BP, BT and NatWest. Guest and Peccei (1998) identify four different views of partnership (representative participation, direct participation, a US integrationalist perspective and a mutual gains model) and interestingly, the third of these links in very strongly to high commitment work practices, and the debate mentioned at the outset of this chapter, namely on best practice HR. This raises the issue of there being convergence on the one hand, with best practice, Japanese HRM, partnership practices and even learning organizations becoming one and the same (such as with Rover in the 1990s), but on the other hand some very different choices. Take, for example, the role of the unions: some 'communities of purpose' include unions and see their role as vital (such as Welsh Water, see IPA 1997, Overell 1997) and some do not (such as John Lewis, see Overell 1997).

As well as the variety of models for a 'community of purpose', there is another problem facing the adoption of this approach to HRM. While the appeal to mutuality is currently very strong on the part of employers, the overall balance of rights and responsibilities appears to be in their favour. This is illustrated in the way that new payment systems expect employees to assume more responsibility and risk, with variable pay, and in the persistence and extension of long-hours cultures for managers and professionals, despite European Union directives on working hours. Similarly, adverse business conditions can also disturb the commitment to a 'community of purpose' as in the cases of Rover and Marks and Spencer.

A problem with these arguments that stress 'community' and mutuality is that they focus upon achieving harmony and consensus. The danger is that all too often the equilibrium of a community of purpose can be disturbed by 'greedy' employers

(Coser 1974) concerned to push for more, be it by means of 'stretch' targets and variable pay or in their appetite to 'shape' employee values, beliefs, and corporate cultures (Woodall 1996 and Salaman Chapter 10 in this volume). Furthermore, a community of purpose is always in danger of becoming too paternalistic and narrow in its perspective, which might present problems for ensuring that values of diversity and difference are able to flourish and grow.

Human resource professionals have displayed a cautious enthusiasm for the concept of stakeholding: *everyone involved or affected should have a voice.*

Although it entered the popular literature on business strategy and management after the publication of Freeman's seminal text (1984), it has taken centre stage more recently by virtue of its widespread utilization in the political and public policy domains, where social inclusiveness is seen as an antidote to the rampant individualism of the Thatcherite era (see for example Hutton 1995; Kelly *et al.* 1997). However, there is some conceptual confusion. Stakeholding can refer both to the *process* of giving employee involvement in decision making and the meeting of employee needs or *outcomes*. Furthermore, this conceptual confusion becomes even greater when stakeholding is interpreted in terms of *inclusion and inclusiveness* (Winstanley and Stoney 1997).

In the employment arena, stakeholding has suggested an approach promoting greater involvement and employee voice in managerial decision-making, through a range of different consultation and participation methods. The debate over partnership and mutuality in the 'Fairness at Work' legislation has provoked a guarded response from employers. Employee rights must not be at the expense of the employer, and must be tempered by responsibility. While it is possible for organizations to implement a stakeholding approach, as illustrated by the Body Shop experiment with social auditing to gain feedback from employees as a basis for addressing their needs (Jackson and Sillanpaa 2000), a more moderate approach may be more suitable for other organizations (RSA 1995). Raising employee expectations without being able to sustain the resources to conduct social auditing, or time-consuming consultation and participation, is highly risky in terms of both retaining employee support and also maintaining profitability and effectiveness (Winstanley and Stoney 1997). It is also questionable as to whether stakeholding models can overcome some of the barriers encountered by firms operating within global markets, where economics has led firms to source from the Third World, and where it is very difficult to access the complex network in the supply chain, as was found to be the case when Marks and Spencer were accused in a TV programme of using child labour in Third World countries. Also, it is all too easy for approaches to involvement and participation based upon stakeholding to be used manipulatively and duplicitously by employers anxious to bind employees into a rhetoric of excellence and enterprise, for example where employee empowerment is introduced for cost-cutting reasons, but promoted on the basis of its involvement of staff in decision making (Ojeifo and Winstanley 1999). Finally, employee needs may compete against those of others: customers, suppliers, the local community, etc. and little work has been done on how to adjudicate between such rival claims.

A related but theoretically more complex approach to the same issues is to be found in discourse theory: *it's not what you agree, but the way that you agree it.*

Discourse ethics attempts to operationalize stakeholding by providing a framework for ethical decision-making and conflict management (French and Allbright 1998).

It draws upon the work of the Frankfurt School, and in particular, Karl-Otto Apel (1989) and Jurgen Habermas (1989, 1990) (for a useful overview see Kettner 1993). Although much of the work was developed in the context of public policy making and debate, it has much relevance as a means to identify methodologies for consensus decision-making among organizational stakeholders. Discourse ethics suggests that the role of ethicists is not to provide solutions to moral problems, but to provide a practical procedure that is both rational and consensus enhancing by means of which issues can be debated and discourse can take place. In the course of identifying processes through which decisions might be made, it asserts the moral requirement to include all those affected by the issue or decision in the discourse; that all have the ability to challenge and evaluate the assertions of others; that all are willing for their own stance to be open to questioning and to maintain openness and transparency of aims and goals, and finally that power differentials are neutralized in the course of debate (Kettner 1993: 34–5).

While this framework is based upon powerful reasoning, it is difficult to see how the conditions for rational discourse might be achieved between stakeholders. It could easily be applied to negotiations over pay differentials, dispute resolution and performance management, if only employers, managers, trade unions and so on, were willing to suspend their power position. However, this requires such a massive shift in employee relations culture and politics as to be inconceivable.

CONCLUSION

This chapter has provided a brief outline of the range of ethical frameworks that can be applied to HRM policy and practice. Some, such as rights-based theories, are easier to apply than others, such as discourse theory and the Rawlsian model of justice. Some have a strong intuitive appeal, such as stakeholding and communitarianism, but present difficulties in adjudicating between competing claims. A few theories might appear 'irrelevant' or too radical, such as virtue theory or the ethics of care, and yet others are inherently 'conservative' (such as ethical egoism, utilitarianism and Rawlsian justice theory). However, the point is that they can all be used to throw some light upon the practice of HRM. Ethical literacy among HR academics and professionals has a legitimate place in both analysis and practice, and is necessary for ethical sensitivity and reasoning. While the debate might continue as to whether the totality of the HRM 'model' is ethical, there is a strong case for arguing that many ethical frameworks and principles can be applied to this aspect of management. However, above all, the research agenda around HRM can no longer be confined to discussions of 'strategic fit', 'best practice', high performance and commitment. It needs to be refreshed by adopting a more human-centred perspective and by addressing the ethical dimension to HR policy and practice. We raised the question at the outset of this chapter, of whether performance and business case approaches to HRM help or hinder the consideration of ethics. Clearly for those adopting the minimalist ethical approaches in Table 3.2, the business case is fundamental to ethical inquiry. Although Cartesian logic pushes us into rhetorical positions of being in favour or against, the reality might be that it is not an either/or question. It might not be that we adopt a business case or human-centred position, but we draw on both. The restrictions placed by the 'best practice' literature, however, force us to consider only those areas where ethics contributes to the 'business case'.

In this chapter we have argued that there are ethical positions that may not always coincide with the 'business case' but which still need to be heard and with which HR specialists need to engage.

REFERENCES

Academy of Human Resource Development (AHRD) (1999) *Standards on Ethics and Integrity*, first edition, Baton Rouge, LA: AHRD.

Apel, K-O. (1989) 'Normative ethics and strategic rationality. The philosophical problem of political ethics', in R. Schurmann (ed.) *The Public Realm: Essays on discursive types in political philosophy*, New York: State of New York Press.

Arkin, A. (1996) 'Open business is good for business', *People Management*, 11th January: 24–7.

Baker, B. and Cooper, J. (2000) 'Occupational testing and psychometric instruments: an ethical perspective, in D. Winstanley and J. Woodall (eds) *Ethical Issues in Contemporary Human Resource Management*, Basingstoke: Macmillan.

Barry, B. (1973) *The Liberal Theory of Justice: a critical examination of the principal doctrines*, Oxford: Clarendon Press.

Beauchamp, T.L. and Bowie, N.E. (1983) *Ethical Theory and Business*, second edition, New Jersey: Prentice Hall.

Beer, M., Spector, B., Lawrence, P., Mills, Q., Walton, R. (1984) *Managing Human Assets*, New York: Free Press.

Carse, A. (1996) 'Facing up to moral perils: the virtues of care in bioethics'; in S. Gordon, P. Benner, and N. Noddings (eds) *Caregiving: readings in knowledge, practice, ethics, and politics*, Philadelphia: University of Pennsylvania Press.

Clarkson, P. (1998) *Gestalt Counselling in Action*, London: Sage.

Connock, S. and Johns, T. (1995) *Ethical Leadership*, London: Institute of Personnel and Development.

Cooper, C./TUC (1997) 'Crisis Talks', *Personnel Today*, October: 29–31.

Cornelius, N. and Gagnon, S. (2000) 'Exploring Diversity Management from an Ethical Perspective', paper presented at the Third Ethics and HRM Conference, Imperial College, January.

Coser, L.A. (1974) *Greedy Institutions: patterns of undivided commitment*, New York/London: Free Press/Collier Macmillan.

Coupar, W. and Stevens, B. (1998) 'Towards a new model of industrial partnership: beyond the HRM versus industrial relations argument' in P. Sparrow, and M. Marchington (eds) *Human Resource Management: The New Agenda*, London: Financial Times/Pitman Publishing.

Doherty, N. and Tyson, S. (2000) 'HRM and employee well-being; raising the ethical stakes', in D. Winstanley and J. Woodall (eds) *Ethical Issues in Contemporary Human Resource Management*, Basingstoke: Macmillan.

Donaldson, T. (1989) *Key Issues in Business Ethics*, London: Academic Press.

Etzioni, A. (1995) (ed.) *New Communitarian Thinking: Persons, Virtues, Institutions, and Communities*, Charlottesville and London: University of Virginia Press.

Fineman, S. (1993) *Emotion in Organizations*, Sage: London

Flanders, A. (1970) 'The Internal Social Responsibilities of Business', in *Management and Unions: the theory and reform of industrial relations*, London, Faber, pp. 129–154.

Freeman, E. (1984) *Strategic Management: A Stakeholder Approach*, London: Pitman.

French, W. and Allbright, D. (1998) 'Resolving a moral conflict through discourse', *Journal of Business Ethics*, vol. 17: 117–194.

Friedman, M. (1962) *Capitalism and Freedom*, Chicago; The University of Chicago Press.

Gilligan, C. (1982) *In a Different Voice: psychological theory and women's development*, Cambridge, MA: Harvard University Press.

Gilligan, C. (1987) 'Moral orientation and moral development', in E.F. Kittay and D.T. Meyers (eds) *Women and Moral Theory*, Totowa, NJ: Rowman and Littlefield.

Guest, D. (1997) 'Human resource management and performance: a review and research agenda', *International Journal of Human Resource Management*, 8(3): 263–276.

Guest, D. (1999) 'Human resource management – the workers' verdict', *Human Resource Management Journal*, 9(3): 5–25.

Guest, D. and Peccei, R. (1994) 'The nature and causes of effective human resource management', *British Journal of Industrial Relations*, 32(2): 219–42.

Guest, D. and Peccei, R. (1998) *The Partnership Company: benchmarks for the future*, London: IPA.

Habermas, J. (1989) *Moral Consciousness and Communicative Action*, Cambridge MA: MIT Press.

Habermas, J. (1990) 'Discourse ethics: notes on a programme of justification', in S. Benhabib, and F. Dallmayr (eds) *The Communicative Ethics Controversy*, Cambridge, MA: MIT Press.

Heery, E. (2000) 'The new pay: Risk and representation at work', in Winstanley, D. and Woodall, J. (eds) *Ethical Issues in Contemporary Human Resource Management*, Basingstoke: Macmillan.

Herzberg, F. (1968) 'One more time: how do you motivate employees?' *Harvard Business Review*, **46**(1): 53–62.

Huselid, M. (1995) 'The impact of human resource management practices on turnover, productivity, and corporate financial performance', *Academy of Management Journal*, **38**(3): 635–672.

Hutton, W. (1995) *The State We Are In*, London: Jonathan Cape/Random House.

Involvement and Participation Association – IPA (1997) *Towards Industrial Partnership: Putting it into practice*, London, IPA (No. 3 – Welsh Water).

Institute of Management (1996) *Are Managers Under Stress?: A Survey of Management Morale*, Corby: Institute of Management.

Institute of Personnel and Development (1995) *The IPD Code of Professional Conduct and Disciplinary Procedures*, London: IPD.

Jackson, C. and Sillanpaa, M. (2000) 'Conducting a social audit: lessons from the Body Shop Experience', in D. Winstanley and J. Woodall (eds) *Ethical Issues in Contemporary Human Resource Management*, Basingstoke: Macmillan.

Johns, T. (1995) 'Don't be afraid of the moral maze', *People Management*, **1**(20): 32–5.

Kelly, G., Kelly, D. and Gamble, A. (1997) (eds) *Stakeholder Capitalism*, Basingstoke: Macmillan.

Kettner, M. (1993) 'Scientific knowledge, discourse ethics, and consensus formation in the public domain', in E. Winkler and J. Coombs (eds) *Applied Ethics: A Reader*, Oxford: Blackwell.

Legge, K. (1995a) *Human Resource Management: Rhetorics and realities*, Basingstoke: Macmillan.

Legge, K. (1995b) 'HRM: rhetoric, reality and hidden agendas' in Storey, J. (ed.) *Human Resource Management: a critical text*, London: Routledge, chapter 2, pp. 33–62.

Legge, K. (1997) 'The morality of HRM' in C. Mabey, D. Skinner, T. Clark (eds) *Experiencing Human Resource Management*, London: Sage.

Legge, K. (1998) 'The morality of HRM' in C. Mabey, G. Salaman, and J. Storey (eds) *Strategic Human Resource Management: A Reader*, London: Sage/Open University Press.

Mabey, C., Clark, T. and Skinner, D. (eds) (1997) *Experiencing Human Resource Management*, London: Sage.

Mabey, C., Salaman, G. and Storey, J. (1998) *Strategic Human Resource Management: A Reader*, London: Sage/ Open University Business School.

MacIntyre, A. (1985) *After Virtue: a study in moral theory*, second edition, London: Duckworth.

McKendall, M. (1993) 'The tyranny of change: organization development revisited', *Journal of Business Ethics*, **12**: 93–104.

Maclagan, P. (1998) *Management and Morality*, London: Sage.

Maslow, A. (1970) *Motivation and Personality*, second edition, New York: Harper and Row.

Mayo, E. (1933) *The Human Problems of Industrial Civilisation*, New York: Macmillan.

Mayon-White, B. (1994) 'Focus on Business Change and Ethics. The ethics of change management: manipulation or participation?' *Business Ethics: a European Review*, **3**(4): 96–100.

Miller, D. (1976) *Social Justice*, Oxford: Clarendon Press.

Miller, P. (1996a) 'Strategy and the ethical management of human resources', *Human Resource Management Journal*, **6**(1): 5–18.

Miller, P. (1996b) 'Ethics, strategy, and human resource management: delivering value to the employee', in B. Towers (ed.) *The Handbook of Human Resource Management*, second edition, Oxford: Blackwell.

Monks, J. (1998) Trade unions, enterprise and the future', in P. Sparrow and M. Marchington (eds) *Human Resource Management: The New Agenda*, London: Financial Times/Pitman Publishing.

Nozick, R. (1974) *Anarchy, State and Utopia*, New York: Basic Books.

Ojeifo, E. and Winstanley D. (1999) 'Negotiated Reality: The Meaning of Empowerment' in Quinn, J. and Davies, P. (eds) *Ethics and Empowerment*, Basingstoke: Macmillan, pp. 271–299.

Pearson, G. (1995) *Integrity in Organisations: an alternative business ethic*, London: McGraw-Hill.

Overell, S. (1997) 'Harmonic motions', *People Management*, 11 September: 24–30

Petrick, J.A. and Quinn, J.F. (1997) *Management Ethics: integrity at work*, London: Sage.

Pickard, J. (1995) 'Prepare to make a moral judgment', *People Management*, **1**(9): 22–5.

Purcell, J. (1999) 'Best practice and best fit: chimera or cul-de-sac?' *Human Resource Management Journal*, **9**(3): 26–41.

Rawls, J. (1971) *A Theory of Justice*, Cambridge, MA: Harvard University Press.

Rogers, C. (1967) *On Becoming a Person: a therapist's view of psychotherapy*, London: Constable.

Royal Society of Arts (RSA) (1995) *Tomorrow's Company: the role of business in a changing world*, London: RSA (Centre for Tomorrow's Company).

Sako, M. (1998) 'The nature and Impact of Employee "voice" in the European Car Components Industry', *Human Resource Management Journal*, **8**(2): 5–13.

Sandel, M. (1984) 'The procedural republic and the unencumbered self', *Political Theory*, **12**: 81–96.

Sen, A. (1999) *Development as freedom*, Oxford: Oxford University Press.

Simpson, R. (2000) 'Presenteeism and the impact of long hours on managers, in D. Winstanley and J. Woodall (eds) *Ethical Issues in Contemporary Human Resource Management*, Basingstoke: Macmillan.

Snell, R.S. (1993) *Developing Skills for Ethical Management*, London: Chapman and Hall.

Solomon, R.C. (1992) *Ethics and Excellence: co-operation and integrity*, New York and Oxford: Oxford University Press.

Solomon, R.C. (1993) 'Corporate roles, personal virtues: an aristotelian approach to business ethics', in E. Winkler and J. Coombs (eds) *Applied Ethics: A Reader*, Oxford: Blackwell.

Stanworth, C. (2000) 'Flexible working patterns, in D. Winstanley and J. Woodall (eds) *Ethical Issues in Contemporary Human Resource Management*, Basingstoke: Macmillan.

Sternberg, E. (1997) 'The defects of stakeholder theory', *Corporate Governance: an international review*, **5**(1): 3–10.

Sternberg, E. (1994) *Just Business: Business Ethics in Action*, London: Little Brown and Warner Books.

Towers, B. (ed.) (1976) *Handbook of Human Resource Management*, Oxford: Blackwell.

Tyson, S. (1997a) 'Human resource strategy: a process for managing the contribution of HRM to organisational performance', *International Journal of HRM*, **8**(3): 277–290.

Tyson, S. (1998b) (ed.) *The Practice of Human Resource Strategy*, London: Pitman.

Tyson, S. and Doherty, N. (1999) *Human Resource Excellence Report*, London: FT/Cranfield School of Management.

Warren, R. (1998) 'Between contract and paternalism: HRM in the community of purpose', paper presented to the second UK Conference on Ethical Issues in Contemporary HRM, Kingston Business School, January.

Wehrmeyer, W. (1996) 'Green policies can help bear fruit', *People Management*, **2**(4): 38–40.

Wheeler, D. and Sillanpaa, M. (1997) *The Stakeholder Corporation: a blueprint for maximising stakeholder value*, London: Pitman.

Wilson, A. (1997) 'Business and its social responsibility', in P. Davies (ed.) *Current Issues in Business Ethics*, London: Routledge.

Winstanley, D. (2000) 'Conditions of worth and the performance management paradox', in D. Winstanley and J. Woodall (eds) *Ethical Issues in Contemporary Human Resource Management*, Basingstoke: Macmillan.

Winstanley, D. and Stoney, C. (1997) 'Stakeholder management: a critique and a defense', paper presented at the Fifteenth International Annual Labour Process Conference', 26–28th March, University of Edinburgh, Scotland.

Winstanley, D. and Stoney, C. (2000) 'Inclusion in the workplace? The stakeholder debate', in P. Askonsas and A. Stewart (eds) *Social Inclusion – Possibilities and Tensions*, Basingstoke: Macmillan.

Winstanley, D. and Woodall, J. (2000) (eds) *Ethical Issues in Contemporary Human Resource Management*, Basingstoke: Macmillan.

Woodall, J. (1996) Managing culture change: can it ever be ethical? *Personnel Review*, **25**(6): 26–40.

Woodall, J. and Douglas, D. (2000) 'Winning hearts and minds; ethical issues in Human Resource Development, in D. Winstanley and J. Woodall (eds) *Ethical Issues in Contemporary Human Resource Management*, Basingstoke: Macmillan.

Part 2
Strategic Issues

The Meaning of Strategy in Human Resource Management

4

John Purcell

SEARCHING FOR MEANING IN STRATEGIC HUMAN RESOURCE MANAGEMENT

In 1984 Harvard Business School adopted its first core course in HRM based on the book by Michael Beer and his colleagues, appropriately titled *Managing Human Assets*. This book contains an approach known universally as 'the Harvard Model' (see Boxall 1992 for an excellent discussion). The book was premised on the view that the problems of historical personnel management can only be solved:

> ... when general managers develop a viewpoint of how they wish to see employees involved in and developed by the enterprise, and of what HRM policies and practices might achieve these goals. Without either a central philosophy or a strategic view – which can be provided *only* by general managers – HRM is likely to remain a set of independent activities, each guided by its own practice tradition.
>
> (Beer *et al.* 1985) (emphasis added)

What was emerging was a view that successful companies would, and in a prescriptive sense should, actively seek the full utilization of employees' assets. These resided in the abilities and behaviour of employees and could only be released by and realized through types of autonomy or self-management, empowering employees to make decisions for themselves. In this way they would become more committed to the enterprise, its goals, values and strategies, as well as to each other and their immediate bosses. This would only happen if it were bolstered by a set of supportive and consistent HRM policies. Furthermore, argued Beer and his colleagues, this was not going to happen unless it had the support of strategic managers and their active involvement. In this sense HRM, unlike personnel management, is a strategic issue.

To say that HRM is a strategic issue which needs the attention of general managers who have the power, unlike personnel managers, it is implied, to get things done, does not make HRM itself strategic. The integration with strategy is central to all models of HRM and virtually all authors are agreed that this is *the* distinctive feature of HRM, compared with personnel. Guest (1987) for example argues for 'integration'. This means that human resource planning must become an integral component of the strategic planning process and must cohere with marketing, production, and finance strategies. Storey is clear on the need for the distinctive approach of HRM to be linked to strategy. Not only is there a need for HRM to be 'a matter of strategic importance requiring the full attention of chief executives and senior management teams ... (but also) decisions about human resource policies ... should take their cue from an explicit alignment of the competitive environment, business strategy and HRM strategy' (Storey 1992: 6,7).

The problem here is to define quite what is meant by 'strategy' and 'strategic decision making'. If 'importance' is not, itself, a sufficient criterion to identify a strategy either as an outcome (a decision) or a way of doing things (a process) then to say that HRM is strategic forces us to look closely at the various meanings of business and corporate strategy. Only then can we see if and when HRM is strategic. This is the purpose of this chapter.

In recent years the search for the strategy link has been overtaken by a hunt for the interconnection between HRM, especially high commitment management and its American variant, high performance work systems, and business success. The most notable proponent of a positive link is Huselid (1995). The assumption is that if a causally valid link is found (Purcell 1999) then HRM must be strategic, and should be recognized as such. What is less clear is how this link is established through company actions and policies in the people management area. This draws attention to the processes of strategy making inside the organization. Originally business strategy was seen more as an external, market-related, set of decisions designed to position the firm in an advantageous way compared with its competitors. Here, the work of Michael Porter (1980, 1985) was dominant. Early efforts to model internal HRM strategies with external positioning (for example Arthur 1994) had some success but were limited in value if only because the typologies used (differentiation or cost leadership) were crude. More recently business strategy researchers and theorists turned their attention to the internal attributes of successful firms looking at the growth, renewal and utilization of resources (most of which were human). This gave emphasis to learning, networks, cultures and organizational agility. Once strategy thinking begins to look at internal, firm-specific processes the strategic link with HRM is much easier to assert. If we can identify business strategy processes that take place in an organization, and ten approaches to strategy have been identified (Mintzberg *et al.* 1998), then we can become more precise on the meaning of 'integration' (Guest 1987) and 'explicit alignment' (Storey 1992) in the link with strategy.

STRATEGY AND THE BEST PRACTICE MODEL OF HRM

But first, unfortunately, we need briefly to divert from this central task to be clear what is meant by human resource management. Some authors use the pronoun 'it' when referring to HRM as though it has a precise meaning and can be clearly identified as a set of practices unified as a particular managerial approach to labour management, for example Grant and Oswick (1998). This approach is seen in the best practice model of HRM propounded most obviously by Pfeffer (1994, 1998) and his seven attributes or elements of HR best practice. If this definition of HRM as a set of practices is universally applicable then we can use 'it' as a shorthand since we all know what is meant. But if we do this the notion that HRM is linked to strategy becomes untenable. It is not possible for HRM to be both one set of practices and strategic.

Every firm cannot adopt the best practice model and simultaneously differentiate itself from its competitors, in just the same way that there is no one best marketing strategy for every firm. If marketing and production (or what we should call operations to cover the service sector) are different between firms how can one best HRM model 'cohere' with different strategies? If technology and information systems vary between firms in the same sector, as they often do, how can one approach to HRM fit with these different requirements? More centrally, if the jobs people do vary widely will management be likely to adopt one particular approach, that of HRM, and then link this to wider strategies?

The effect of defining HRM as a particular approach to labour management, and thus referring to HRM as an 'it' raises four substantial problems. First, no other function of management can be described or captured by the singular pronoun, 'it'. Personnel management is not an 'it', neither is marketing nor operations, nor business strategies. What is being covered by these terms are particular sets of activities: how people are managed in the organization; how the firm manages its relationship in the market and meets competition; how the means and methods of production or operations are organized to maximize efficiency and minimize costs. These are, at their best, value-adding activities, but, managed badly or out of kilter with other activities, can be value destroying. But they are activities, meaning a combination of policies, practices and processes which, in the long and short term influence the behaviour of individuals and the firm as an entity.

Second, we are faced with a particularly tricky problem if we define HRM as a particular process of management, as one set of activities and policies, and then say that the crucial defining characteristic of HRM is the link with strategy. How do we explain the relatively slow take-up of HRM? Many researchers, for example Osterman in the USA (1994) and Wood and Albanese (1995) and more recently WERS98 in the UK have noted the small number of workplaces adopting an integrated set of HRM practices, which, when taken together, is associated with improved economic performance. Industry and sector focused research confirms this, whether in the USA in the motor industry (Pil and MacDuffie 1996), the apparel or clothing industry (Dunlop and Weil 1996) or the steel industry (Arthur 1992; Ichniowski et al. 1997), or in the UK in hotels (Hoque 1999), greenfield sites in manufacturing (Guest and Hoque 1994), the health service (Guest and Peccei 1994) or more recently in manufacturing firms (Patterson et al. 1998) or aerospace companies (Thompson 1998, 2000). 'In short, although individual work practice innovations are quite common, *systems* of innovative practices are relatively exceptional' (Ichniowski et al. 1996). What is more, 'studies of longevity often find that the half-life of many innovations is short, suggesting their effectiveness is often less than managers had expected' (ibid.: 304). If it is argued that HRM is both strategic and a particular method (one best way) of managing employees, then it must mean that all the other firms are acting irrationally, or foolishly, and certainly not strategically in failing to adopt 'it', HRM. This is not credible. One is much more likely to find explanations of why firms do not adopt 'it', HRM, because it is not strategically sensible for them to do so. It may be that the constraints of strategies in technology, operations and markets, the behaviour of competitors, and their relationship with customers and suppliers, or the shareholders, make it too expensive or too difficult. This is known as the problem of diffusion and it degrades the analysis to suggest there is no link to strategy.

It also leads to a peculiar problem of what to call the labour polices of firms that do not have the 'it', HRM. Guest (1995) is left with the term 'black hole' to categorize firms with neither well-established collective relationships with their employees through trade unions, nor the adoption of the sophisticated bundle of HRM. The ACAS study of the South West Region of the UK (Tailby *et al.* 1997) found that 'black hole' type firms were the most prevalent. All of them employed people and all of them had the problem of deciding how best to manage all of the resources at their disposal, the human and the non-human ones. If our concern is about the way strategies for managing people at work are linked to, informed by, and at times influence other business strategies, then we need to paint on a wide canvas, covering all types of firms.

The third problem of the narrow definition of HRM as 'it' is that there can be confusion between whether we are looking at the behaviour of the organization as amalgam of the behaviours and policies of individual managers and functional areas, or whether our concern is primarily with the HR professionals, those with HRM (or personnel) in their job titles. In one sense this is easily disposed of since 'people strategies' inevitably involve line managers as well as specialists, and HRM strategies are deeply influenced by the wider strategies of the organization to do with the mission and markets, the way the firm is structured and the way HRM links with strategies in other functional areas. Purcell and Ahlstrand (1994) refer to HR strategies as 'third order' strategies, in the same way that other functional strategies are third order, flowing from, but also upwardly influencing, these wider corporate (i.e. covering the whole of the enterprise) and business unit strategies. Our concern has to be equally about the way work is organized and how this links to technology, operations and marketing, as about particular policies on team-working, or recruitment and reward, of communication and involvement. The latter may (but equally may not) be the responsibility of HR professionals, but these specialists can never, on their own and in isolation from other managers, determine the whole of HRM strategy since they are not in control of all of the factors. It has often been noted that HR professionals, like personnel managers before them, have highly ambiguous roles and need to thrive on ambiguity to survive and make a contribution (Gowler and Legge 1981). The distinction between personnel management and HRM to many practitioners is about the centrality of the role they play in the organization. It is nothing to do with a particular approach to labour management, one best set of practices. One of the respondents to Grant and Oswick's study of practitioners' views on HRM said:

> There is and always was a gradual evolution of personnel management. I see HRM as just the latest stage of this evolution. Personnel management is becoming a part of the overall business strategy and this is reflected in the use of the term HRM rather than the use of the term personnel management.
>
> (Grant and Oswick 1998: 185)

Here, perhaps, HRM is 'a rose by any other name'. Grant and Oswick categorize this manager's response as one of the atheists, who did not believe that HRM existed. This might be true if HRM is this narrow conception of a particular approach, our 'it'. If, however, we see HRM as a generic description that incorporates a whole range of practices and policies related to the management of people in every organization *but* as 'a part of the overall business strategy', as this manager put it, then we can make some progress. Another manager in the same research was reported as saying that 'my own view is that HRM joins the management of people and the business strategy together' (ibid: 187). That is the meaning adopted here, whatever the title of the function in a particular organization. It is often the case that personnel management has tended to be seen, by line managers especially, as an isolated activity that is in effect responsible for managing the supply of labour. The distinctive claim of HRM, in contrast, is the link with business strategies and in particular the way the link is established, and the two-way direction of influence. Business strategies inform what sort of HRM is appropriate, but HRM helps determine what types of business policies are possible and desirable.

A fourth, and probably the most serious 'real world' problem of defining HRM as a distinctive approach is that it excludes much of the actual strategic decisions that many organizations have taken in employment in the last two decades. These include 'downsizing' (major redundancy programmes), delayering (removing layers of management to create flatter organizations), outsourcing (a form of sub-contracting), a growing use of flexible and contingent labour (such as fixed-term contracts or agency staff), joint ventures and supply chain partnerships, divestment and acquisitions. These decisions, much to do with the size, shape and structure of the firm deeply influence people's jobs and have taken up much of the time of HR directors and have dominated board agendas. To exclude them from a consideration of HRM lacks credibility. What is more, the very firms which are engaged in these activities are often simultaneously the ones seeking to implement the sophisticated particular approach of HRM for some of their employees. To understand their strategic behaviour we need to look at the whole of their employment strategies since it is likely that one begets the other.

THE GENERIC APPROACH TO HRM: EXTERNALIZATION AND INTERNALIZATION

A much broader conception of human resource management (although he did not use the term) was initially proposed by Gospel in 1983 and fully developed in 1992. He proposed a threefold categorization of sub-processes of work relations, employment relations and industrial relations which were necessarily linked together to form a holistic approach to the management of the firm's human resources, or 'labour management', as he called it.

> **Work relations** covers the way work is organised and the deployment of workers around technologies and production processes.

> **Employment relations** deals with arrangements governing such aspects of employment as recruitment, training, job tenure and promotion, and the reward of workers.

> **Industrial relations** is concerned with the representational systems which may exist within an enterprise (and more generally involvement and participation).
>
> (Gospel 1992)

The great advantage of this conception of human resource management or labour management is that it goes beyond the traditional boundaries of personnel management to incorporate, under work relations, the jobs and tasks people perform and the way these are organized and influenced by operational management and the adoption of technologies. This is usually referred to as 'work organization'. The strategic possibilities are obvious. Designing an HR system under this schema would need to take account of, and itself influence, choices in operational and technology strategies, and these would be bound to be influenced by the way the firm seeks to trade in a given marketplace alongside competitors. In employment relations all forms of contracts, whether short-term and highly exploitative or long-term and secure are allowed for. In the same way choices or variety in industrial relations need to be made in the light of historical and environmental circumstances. The focus of strategic decisions in human resource management covering the three sub-areas is on management initiated processes and policies covering all possibilities and allowing for variety within the organization, say between managerial employees and contract cleaners.

This type of all-encompassing approach allows us to compare human resource management between firms and sectors and historically. In its generic meaning HRM is defined in a commonsensical way. Our focus is on management decisions and behaviours used, consciously or unconsciously, to control, influence and motivate those who provide work for the organization – the human resources. Strategy is about winning. The underlying assumption of strategic human resource management is managing people in such a way as to help the firm gain a competitive advantage over its competitors, or at the minimum to ensure that HRM as practised is not a source of competitive disadvantage, pulling the firm down. There are big choices to be made, and powerful forces at work to influence policy options.

Gospel shows how decisions in the three sub-processes of human resource management are deeply influenced by five factors. These are (1) the nature of the markets, both product and labour, that the firm trades in; (2) the structure or organization of the firm which to a greater or lesser extent mediates, or at times buffers, between HR decisions and the external market; (3) the nature of the managerial hierarchy in the firm, or what may be called the managerial division of labour between levels from top to bottom, and between functional specialisms; (4) the type of technology used and the way it is deployed; and (5) the extent to which management recognize and exercise choice in human resource management, as in other areas (Gospel, 1992: 6–8). The way management seeks to manage the human resource is a matter of choice, not something determined by markets and technology, but choice is not limitless, it is constrained. Far from there being one best way, human resource management strategies can and do vary considerably, certainly over a long time scale.

One of the most fundamental of all strategic choices concerns the boundary of the firm. What should be inside and what should be externalized? The assumption in institutional economics from Commons (1934) and Coase (1937) onwards is that choice is between the market external to the firm and the hierarchy or administrative mechanisms inside the firm. What informs choice is the relative cost of transactions, thus transactional cost analysis. The issue is one of how the firm chooses whom to employ, not in terms of individual attributes but what categories of jobs and job holders should be inside the company, and what is best left to outside individuals, firms or contractors. If the external market is relatively cheap to use in a transactional sense – because there is good market information, there is an ample supply of people, the tasks asked of them are easily defined and can be performed straightaway without company specific training and performance monitoring is easy – then there may be a preference to externalize some part of the firm and thus employment. There has been a huge growth in recent decades in *externalization*, for example outsourcing, joint ventures, franchise arrangements and the use of labour market intermediaries, the employment agencies, which supply labour to major firms often in large numbers (Purcell and Purcell 1999). While acquisitions have continued the trend of corporate growth, this has been accompanied by firms divesting from non-strategic areas which did not fit the portfolio. This has enabled them to focus on their core activities.

Internalization has also been given great emphasis in recent years. This is seen in the development of flexible production systems, or one stop shops in the service sectors usually requiring team working, multi-skilling and extensive training. The way work processes are designed to combine human and non-human resources together can become distinctive or unique, requiring insider knowledge that can never be bought from outside. This is particularly the case when 'lean' processes are adopted requiring high degrees of cooperation within and between production or service teams (Hutchinson *et al*. 1998). This is associated with the development of internal labour markets and emphasis on the management of relationships inside the place of work, whether through partnerships with trade unions, works councils or consultative committees and a whole array of direct forms of participation. Thus trends of both internalization and externalization have been clearly visible in many firms, especially the multinational companies in all sectors. These big decisions have profound implications for HRM.

STRATEGY AND STRATEGIC DECISION MAKING

If we are to categorize decisions on externalization and internalization as strategic, or indeed use the same epithet for particular approaches to the management of labour, we need to be clear about what is meant by the terms 'strategy' and 'strategic decision making'. This both helps define boundaries to the subject of strategic human resource management and helps us understand the approach different researchers have taken in looking at the contribution of HRM to business performance. The use of the word 'strategy' or 'strategic' is now so widespread that it has lost most of its original or useful meaning, yet we have to be very clear about what constitutes a strategy, and how we can distinguish a strategic decision from a non-strategic or operational decision. The founding fathers of HRM, such as Beer and his colleagues, proclaimed HRM as strategic because it was important and deserved the attention of general managers at a senior level. This might be true but importance is not a measure of strategy. Our concern is with strategic decisions both in the wider sense of business strategies and more narrowly in HRM.

Quinn's definition of strategy is particularly useful since it combines internal resources with external focus:

> A strategy is the pattern or plan that integrates an organisation's major goals, policies and action sequences into a cohesive whole. A well-formulated strategy helps marshal and allocate a organisation's resources into a unique and viable posture based on its relative internal competencies and shortcomings, anticipated changes in the environment, and contingent moves by intelligent opponents.
>
> (Quinn 1990, quoted in Grant 1998)

Some key attributes of strategies can be identified as follows:

- Strategy is either a plan or a pattern of action. The presumption that strategies are formal statements and should be written (as, for example, insisted on by the Investors in People [IiP] standard) is misplaced and far too restrictive.
- Action is in sequences. Thus to combine these two together, strategy can be 'emerging patterns of action' as Mintzberg (1979) puts it, which evolve over a period, part in trial and error but with a clear view of the outcome desired and planned for.
- Strategy is about co-ordinating or orchestrating resources in a unique way based around what the organization is good at – internal competencies, but also coping with what it is poor at – shortcomings. Co-ordination presupposes collaboration between functions, departments or individuals.
- Strategy is about future action based on forecasts, guesses and anticipated change both in the environment (political, economic, social and technological) and about what the competitors will do, or have done. In stable environments extrapolations from the past provide guides for the future. In turbulent and fast moving environments, as typified by the millennium age, discontinuities are more frequent making strategy more risky, yet more necessary.
- Strategy, a plan or a pattern of action, is about change, doing a co-ordinated set of things differently in the hope it will ensure organizational success, however defined.

This may seem fairly uncontroversial but the strategy field is subject to numerous disputes about focus and process, rationality and behaviour and about breadth and depth. In an attempt to integrate and synthesize the field Mintzberg, Ahlstrand and Lampel (1998: 9–15) suggest strategy can be

> *A plan*, or something equivalent – a direction, a guide or course of action
>
> *A pattern*, that is consistency in behaviour over time
>
> *A position*, namely the locating of particular products in particular markets
>
> *A perspective*, namely an organization's fundamental way of doing things
>
> *A ploy*, a specific "maneuver" intended to outwit an opponent or competitor.

This mixture of external focus (position and ploy) and internal attribute (pattern and perspective) is combined with a future orientation seen in the plan whether it be deliberate or emergent. The idea of 'strategic intent' (Hamel and Prahalad 1989) is helpful since this presupposes a sense of purpose, a vision of what to aim at even if it is very unclear how to get there.

> Few, if any strategies are purely deliberate, just as few are purely emergent. One means no learning, the other means no control. All real-world strategies need to mix these in some ways: to exercise control while fostering some learning. Strategies, in other words have to *form* as well as be *formulated*.
>
> (Mintzberg *et al.* 1998)

The mix of internal and external attributes to strategy also helps identify the three central forces in strategy formulation: environment, organization and leadership (ibid: 286).

Different authors have focused on particular aspects of business strategy and the strategy process in the last 50 or so years since its rise as a dominant feature of business studies. One of the most important divisions in thinking about and analysing strategy is between the rationalist 'design school', most notably seen in the work of Michael Porter and the 'process school', most closely associated with the work of Henry Mintzberg. In the design school priority is given to analytical techniques and to an assumption of rationality on the part of decision takers. Its primary focus is what strategy *should* the firm pursue. Its origins are found in industrial economics with emphasis placed on deductive theory building where theory leads to hypothesis generation (what is expected to happen if the theory holds true) to observation and testing often using statistical techniques based on quantitative data. This assumption of rationality and deductive theory building has been deeply influential on American research in HRM, with its emphasis on quantitative research methods to test hypotheses derived from earlier research. The process school emphasizes the 'crafting' of strategy with formulation and implementation being merged together, adjusted and revised with learning a key attribute. The primary foci here are what strategy *is* and how it is created. This relies more on an inductive approach and an emphasis on qualitative data. Induction starts with observations which lead to generalizable conclusions which are subsequently confirmed or denied by subsequent observations leading to reformulation of the general statements. This approach has been deeply influential in industrial relations scholarship in Europe and this inductive empirical tradition has flowed through into HRM research and analysis in the UK (for a fascinating discussion of the fall of inductive research in the USA see Kaufman 1993).

Quite different conclusions can be reached on HRM and strategy by using the two approaches. Grant (who favours the rationalist design school) summarizes well the differences between the two approaches in strategy thinking.

> The problem with the rationalist approach, as emphasised by Mintzberg's attack on strategic planning (Mintzberg 1994), is that the analysis is too narrow – it has tended to be overformalized and has emphasised quantitative over qualitative data. The danger with the Mintzberg approach is that by downplaying the role of systemic analysis and emphasising the role of intuition and vision, we move into a world of new-age mysticism in which there is no clear basis for reasoned choices and in which disorder threatens the progressive accumulation of knowledge.
>
> (Grant 1998)

This fear of disorder is revealing since it presupposes a world of control where management control is defined as to ensure that what ought to happen does happen. It is accepted that senior managers know what ought to happen, whereas Mintzberg and many others, including many in HRM, argue that this is impossible. Far from the process school 'threatening the progressive accumulation of knowledge' it does the reverse by placing great store on organizational learning. 'The notion that strategy is something that should happen way up there, far removed from the details of running an organization on a daily basis, is one of the greatest fallacies of conventional strategic management' (Mintzberg op. cit.).

In a recent book Mintzberg and his colleagues (1998) try to reconcile some of these differences. Looking across the whole field of strategy research and writing they identify ten schools grouped into three categories. The first category are prescriptive, setting out how strategy should be formulated, and are essentially focused on external actions with an assumption that the organization can be directed from the top, organizational members are acquiescent and implementation is non-problematic. The three schools in this group are:

Prescriptive strategy making

- The Design School   strategy formulation as a process of *conception*
- The Planning School   strategy formation as a *formal* process
- The Positioning School   strategy formation as an *analytical* process

This last school is best exemplified by the work of Michael Porter whose two early books on *Competitive Strategy* (1980) and *Competitive Advantage* (1985) have been most widely used in trying to match HRM with business strategies (for example in steel mini mills (Arthur 1994). There is something perverse in trying to make this connection since Porter himself dismisses HRM from any idea of strategy. Of the six points necessary for sustainable competitive advantage listed in a recent paper, the sixth was 'operational effectiveness as given' (Porter 1996: 74). Later he wrote that:

> ... if strategy is stretched to include employees and organizational arrangements, it becomes virtually everything a company does or consists of. Not only does this complicate matters, but it obscures the chain of causality that runs from competitive environment to position to activities to employee skills and organisation'.

> (Porter 1997: 162)

The subservient position of employees and organizational arrangements could not be clearer and the assumption of a one-way causal chain does not allow for any contribution of HRM beyond the pursuit of effectiveness.

The next group of strategy schools identified by Mintzberg and his colleagues take a more internal approach and are concerned with how strategies are made. There is a wide difference between the various schools and some are more relevant to HRM than others.

There are six schools in this group.

Strategy making as a process

- The Entrepreneurial School   strategy formation as *visionary* process
- The Cognitive School   strategy formation as a *mental* process
- The Learning School   strategy formation an *emergent* process
- The Power School   strategy formation as a process of *negotiation*
- The Cultural School   strategy formation as a *collective* process
- The Environmental School   strategy formation as a *reactive* process

The first two schools place emphasis on leaders and the top management team and how they think and act. This includes the way in which the organization is 'seen' by strategy makers: how far they value employees and the contribution HRM can make to strategy and change, whether a strength or a weakness, a cost or a source of advantage. The limits to strategic imagination are explained by some as an outcome of bounded rationality (Cyert and March 1963). Where there are limits to information sources, decision makers can only deal with a few factors at a time and in any case are prone to bias in interpretation of 'facts'. The effect of this has been described by Winkler (1974) as the 'view from Mount Olympus'. There is clear vision from the peak to the horizon (the market environment) but the slopes of the mountain (the organization) are shrouded in cloud. Others use systemic theories to explain how firms

> differ according to the social and economic systems in which they are embedded . . . . . In the systemic view, the norms that guide strategy derive not so much from the cognitive bounds of the human psyche as from the cultural views of the local society. The variables in the systemic perspective include class and professions, nations and states, families and gender.
>
> (Whittington 1993)

The appropriate homily for the cognitive school, say Mintzberg and colleagues (1998) is 'I'll see it when I believe it'. This rather neatly captures the often blinkered nature of the strategy process, especially when it comes to people management, and helps explain the problem of diffusion.

The next three schools of strategy pay much more attention to organizational factors that influence strategy formulation and have more resonance with HRM. This is particularly true of the Learning School. Not only is there an emphasis on the emergent process of strategy making but also attention is paid to strategy by doing and adapting. It focuses attention on all of the organization's members and allows for ideas and actions to be developed and deployed by middle mangers, sales people, administrative staff and shopfloor workers. 'In other words, informed individuals anywhere in an organisation can contribute to the strategy process' (Mintzberg *et al*. 1998: 178). This is dependent, of course, on the condition that they are given the opportunity and the resources to do so and understand the strategic intent of the organization. Hamel and Prahalad (1989) suggest that strategic intent is not simply focus and vision or ambition but

> also encompasses an active management process that includes: focusing the organisation's attention on the essence of winning; motivating people by communicating the value of the target; leaving room for individual and team contributions; sustaining enthusiasm by providing new operational definitions as circumstances change; and using intent consistently to guide resource allocations.
>
> (Hamel and Prahalad 1989: 68)

Words familiar to HRM such as commitment, empowerment, motivation, team work, communication, reward and learning sit neatly with this conception of strategy formulation. At the same time they provide a major challenge to the organization and its managers, especially on how to create the environment where resources can be orchestrated and learning takes place. I have heard this type of strategy making described as the 'little brain theory' where large numbers of small incremental improvements and changes take place, each contributing to 'winning'. The contrast is with the 'big brain theory' which emphasizes planning, deliberate action and the power of the top managers – like generals in command of battalions who in set piece battles 'command and control'.

If the learning school incorporates all organization members in an optimistic shared endeavour then the power school and the culture school indicate the difficulties in implementation. The power of vested interests, the fear of change and defensive behaviour all conspire to make it difficult, if not impossible, to formulate optimal strategies. Compromise is essential among stakeholders and action may be delayed until a crisis occurs. On the other hand what emerges may be more realistic and achievable and be built around alliances and relationships within and beyond the organization. Within HRM this is especially pertinent in working with trade unions and other forms of employee representation such as European Works Councils.

Culture has increasingly been seen as a source of competitive advantage and a key resource in the sense of the totality of the organization being seen as a 'social community' (Kogut and Zander 1996). This sense of community, binding organizational members together in a shared endeavour is seen as something which is hard to imitate and copy, and thus can provide one of the best barriers to competitive threat (or negatively can be a source or organizational rigidity). Thus some part of competitive strategy has focused on culture management, a process with strong connections with HRM. (For a good example of culture management as HR Strategy in a fast moving, knowledge-intensive firm see Grugulis *et al.* 2000.) This recognition that the internal strength of the firm may be the best source of sustained competitive advantage, especially when the external environment is turbulent has had a dramatic effect on strategy thinking. It led to the emergence of the so-called Resource Based View of strategy (RBV) and placed human resource management centre stage for the first time in strategy analysis (Boxall and Purcell 2000).

The last school in Mintzberg's group of six approaches of how strategies get made is the environmental school. At the extreme this asserts that there is little choice and that environmental factors or forces are central in the process. Either the organization responds to these forces or it dies. A focus on the environment in strategy making is, however, extremely helpful in HRM terms since it forces an analysis of the factors which limit or constrain choice, whether in the labour market, the values and beliefs that people bring to and expect from work, the laws and customs of societies or the ethical beliefs about employment. It is also useful in that it helps explain why organizations have a tendency to do the same thing. Why, for example, do call centres have a habit of engaging in extensive measurement and surveillance of employees, or City of London finance staff often work well in excess of the maximum 48-hour week? It is hard to explain this type of ingrained behaviour in terms of Porter's competitive strategy.

Institutional theory uses the term *institutional isomorphism* to suggest three reasons for people in organizations doing the same thing (Oliver 1997; Powell and Di Maggio 1991). It may be that organizations are coerced into doing certain things. For example since the mid 1980s the Treasury, as the holder of the purse strings for the public sector in Britain, has allowed employing authorities reliant on public finances to choose whatever payment system they want for their staff *provided* it is performance related! The latest battle is with the teachers over this issue. They certainly feel coerced. Another example is the way major customers place pressure on suppliers for types of HR practices to be adopted, or to reduce pay rates (Kinnie *et al.* 1999). Other explanations are that there is a process of miming or copying (mimetic isomorphism), following fashion or seeking, through bench marking, to do what the best companies do, even if the circumstances are different. HRM suffers especially from this tendency since there is a long tradition of best or good practice as exemplified by personnel management textbooks and by the best practice approach.

Normative isomorphism concerns the influence of professional expertise or norms of doing things in a certain way enshrined in the mystique of expertise through specialist consultants, technologists and lawyers. It is interesting to see in a new industry like call centres the technology tends to come from a very limited number of sources, the same consultants are often used and managers build their careers by moving from one centre to another, spreading the one best way approach as they go. The outcome is, in the main, a fairly standardized way of managing employees in 'the dark satanic mills of the late 20th century' as one journalist put it, even if it does not fit with the business strategies of the organization (Kinnie 2000).

The final group of strategy formation approaches, although Mintzberg *et al.* only list one school in this category, is concerned with the fit between the organization and its environment but also with strategic change.

Strategy as Fit

- The Configuration School   strategy formation as a process of *transformation*

This is effectively a combination of all the other schools but takes an historical perspective looking at the distinct stages or episodes of growth and stability. Six premises are suggested as characteristics of the configuration school.

1. Most of the time, an organization can be described in terms of some kind of stable configuration of its characteristics ...
2. These periods of stability are interrupted occasionally by some process of transformation – a quantum leap to another configuration.
3. These successive states of configuration and periods of transformation may order themselves over time into patterned sequences, for example describing life cycles of organizations.
4. The key to strategic management, therefore, is to sustain stability or at least adaptable change most of the time, but periodically to recognize the need for transformation and be able to manage that disruptive process without destroying the organization.
5. Accordingly, the process of strategy making can be one of conceptual designing or formal planning, systematic analysing or leadership visioning, co-operative politicking, focusing on individual cognition, collective socialization, or simple response to the forces of the environment ...
6. The resulting strategies take the form of plans or patterns, positions or perspectives, or else ploys, but ... each for its own time and matched to its own situation (Mintzberg *et al.* 1998).

In the strategic human resource management focus the configuration school draws attention to the three important areas. First, it suggests that strategies will vary during the life cycle of the organization, from business start-up to maturing and decline. This has been suggested by Kochan and Chalykoff (1987) and by Purcell (1989) and more broadly by Miles and Snow (1978). Second, configuration also means appropriateness to the sector. That is, the type of HRM appropriate for a consulting company which employs talented graduates and pushes them hard will be different from a hospital, as will a mail order company be different from a hotel chain. In Minzberg's terms the differences will be seen in different configurations of organizational structure and different ways in which power is distributed in the organization, seen for example in the role of middle management. At the minimum, finding the appropriate HRM system is the basic requirement, what may be termed 'table stakes' (Boxall and Purcell 2000). In order to be able to compete alongside the other competitors in the sector, the firm has to be able to meet industry standards if only to recruit and retain qualified people and meet customer expectations.

Third, configuration is about change or transformation. Whole sectors can change with the advent of new technologies or through deregulation, as in the finance sector, especially domestic banking and insurance. Here the growth of telephone banking, e-commerce and the entry of newcomers into the market has transformed years of stability into a period of hectic change and the fight for survival. In the process the 'table stakes' are challenged and replaced by a new set of ideas about appropriateness in HRM based on customer service, fast-moving consumer goods and retailing, all a far cry from the stability, order and hierarchy of the clearing banks of the 1970s. At such times the three key forces on strategy making of environment, organization and leadership become tangible. Strategy in HR, like in other areas, is about continuity and change, about appropriateness for the circumstances, but anticipating when the circumstances change. It is about taking strategic decisions.

STRATEGY AS IMPLEMENTATION

Strategic decisions have distinctive attributes which are especially pertinent for strategic HRM and help delineate it from operational or routine patterns of behaviour. Grant (1998: 14) says that strategic decisions have three characteristics:

- they are important;
- they involve a significant commitment of resources; and
- they are not easily reversible.

We can add, following Johnson (1987) that strategic decisions are taken in conditions of uncertainty. That is, there is a risk in that it is uncertain what will happen in the environment, or how competitors might react. This uncertainty is likely to be time related. There is often a lag between decision, action and effect, with costs often borne up front while the stream of benefits, it is hoped, will flow through later, but quite when is difficult to predict in more than hazy outline. This lag problem can be crucial and can deter strategic risk taking. If strategic decisions are big and risky, involve resource allocation, have an uncertain pay-back over a future period which is difficult to predict then, not surprisingly, they are likely to involve a coalition of executives from different functions and areas coming together to make the decisions and effect the implementation. It will also require a form of consensus from employees affected by the decision and contribution to its success. This is not just because of the scale of the decision but because the implementation of the decision will have implications for the co-ordination of resources in different parts of the business, both between functions and in hierarchical terms. Thus the requirement for integration across the organization is a hallmark of a strategic decision.

> 'A strategic decision and the implementation of strategy are likely to involve managers crossing boundaries within the firm in negotiating and coming to agreements with managers in different parts of the business ... [Furthermore, implementing major decisions is] likely to involve the persuasion and

organisation of people to change from what they are doing. Moreover, the expectation may be that they change towards something that is ill-defined, uncertain and unfamiliar. Not surprisingly the management of strategic change can be highly problematic.

(Johnson 1987: 5–6)

This explains in part, at least, why increasing attention is given to implementation strategies. 'In the absence of a consistent and useful strategy paradigm that they can use, managers appear to have embraced attention to 'implementation' as their saviour, more or less abandoning strategy as either unimportant or uninteresting' (Prahalad and Hamel 1994: 5). Implementation strategies like organizational learning strategies, power strategies, and resource-based or cultural strategies are areas where human resource management has much to offer. Just when HRM analysts discovered business strategies (often using outmoded definitions of strategy), so strategy thinking came to recognize HRM as a strategic issue linked to organizational performance.

The advantage of the configuration school of strategy is that it allows for adaptation after periods of stability and builds in explicitly a life-cycle approach to the growth and decline of the firm, or for metamorphosis. It also places emphasis on strategy implementation. This is where strategic HRM can play a major role. If the firm is seen as a repository of capabilities in which individual and social expertise is transformed into economically valuable products, as suggested by Kogut and Zander (1992) then 'by its tacitness and social complexity, a firm's stock of knowledge is an important determinant of its competitive advantage' (Hoskisson et al. 1999). And this changes over time and is created and deployed by human capital and human processes.

One example of this strategy implementation and configuration of resources can be taken from research in the UK Aerospace industry. This large-scale, time series study concluded that 'there is compelling evidence that investing in HR pays. Firms increasing their use of high performance HR practices between 1997 and 1999 recorded increases in value-added per employee ranging from 20 to 34 per cent' (Thompson 2000: 1). This is good news for the minority of firms who adopted high-performing practices. It is the link with other findings of the research that is especially revealing. First, rather than there being one set of practices in HR there was evidence of firms adapting HR practices to fit with their changing strategies and structures. Second, when HR was linked explicitly to the adoption of lean production techniques (classic implementation strategy) then the value added improvements were greater. Third, utilizing sophisticated HR practices was associated with much greater investment in capital equipment (ibid). That is HR was, or became, strategic in some firms (but only a minority) not because it was linked to the market position of the firms, as suggested by a Porterian view of strategy, but because it was integrated internally or operationally, with both production and capital investment strategies, and this emerged over time. Strategy coalitions between functional areas of marketing, operations, supply chain and finance become key features of successful HR strategy, in the same way as HR strategy is key to operations. This is clear in many of the classic sector studies on HRM and performance, for example MacDuffie (1995) in the auto industry, Dunlop and Weil (1996) in clothing, Youndt et al. (1996) in manufacturing and Ichniowski et al. (1997) in steel. Thus the configurational approach to strategy emphasizes internal and external decision making and allows for focus on implementation as a set of integrated strategic actions.

This was not always the case. In the early years of strategy theory 'implementation' was seen to be 'comprised of a series of sub-activities which are primarily administrative' (Andrews 1968 quoted in Hoskisson *et al.* 1999: 422). This downgrading made HRM a mere operational function. Not surprisingly, in the effort to become strategic many practitioners and academics sought to find the link between HRM and strategy as conceived by the positioning theorists, like Porter, who dominated thinking in the 1980s. Now once strategy is recast, moving from outside the firm to inside to look at resources, processes and behaviours, the strategic potential of HRM is much more easily defined and visible especially if a generic view of the subject is taken in the all-encompassing sense of 'people management', the term preferred by the professional institute for HR professionals, the CIPD.

CONCLUSION

Big strategies in HRM are most unlikely to come, *ex cathedra,* from the board as a fully formed, written strategy or planning paper. Strategy is much more intuitive and often only 'visible' after the event seen as 'emerging patterns of action'. This is especially the case where much of the strategy, as in HRM, is to do with internal implementation and performance strategies, not exclusively to do with external market ploys. The great divide in strategy thinking and analysis, which can be easily exaggerated, is between the 'design school' and the 'process school'. In the former, strategy is usually deliberate and built on an assumption of economic rationality. The tools of analysis are more quantitative than qualitative and the presumption is the need for a plan of action often concerned with market behaviour and with plans based on the identification of opportunities and threats. What happens inside the company is mere administration or operations.

The process school covers a variety of approaches within the general rubric of a concern with how strategies are made and what influences strategy formulation. This is much more a study of what actually happens with explanations coming from experience rather than deductive theory. A number of different approaches exist within the process school which have great relevance to strategic human resource management. One emphasizes the way organizations have to learn in order to adapt and take strategic discussions, with learning spread throughout the organization, not just restricted to a few senior executives (thus the interest in learning organization and knowledge management). Another uses the framework of power to understand the political process involved in making and implementing strategic decisions (thus the focus on whether organizations have, and should have, HR directors on the Board). This is closely linked to a view that emphasizes organizational culture, including the beliefs and values of top decision makers and their cognitive frameworks. This may explain why strategies often fail, or difficulties are reached in implementing strategic decisions, especially those that involve all or most members of the organization. At the same time the cultural roots of strategy making can be seen as a source of competitive advantage. In turbulent environments it may be that the manifest internal strengths and relatively few weaknesses of the firm may be a source of competitive advantage: i.e. the way people are managed including how they do their jobs and tasks can be a source of competitive advantage in the medium or long term. This is the basis of the resource-based view of strategy (RBV).

One of the problematic issues in strategy generally, and in SHRM particularly, is why organizations seem to have a habit of doing the same thing. This is explained through the lens of institutional isomorphism which looks at three isometric forces outside the organization in the environment. One is the tendency to copy, especially so-called best practice, without understanding why 'best practice' worked in the first place. Another is because there is little choice as organizations are coerced, maybe by the short termism in the capital market, or by major customers, into doing certain things (Kinnie *et al.* 1999) or, as is more often the case in HRM, not doing something – like, say, training. The third pressure for conformity is through the spread of ideas via professionals such as technologists, consultants and career managers, seen in the rise of HRM consultancies.

The implication of the 'design' school is that many things are possible, while the logic of the institutional theory or the environment school is that little can be done except swim with the tide of affairs. This is the half empty–half full glass problem writ large – there is both change and continuity, stability and discontinuity. The configuration approach to strategy allows for a longer time span to be taken. Strategies will vary depending whether the firm is a small start-up or a mature giant, and will differ between sectors so that the minimum required of an HR system, the so-called table stakes, will be markedly different between firms in different sectors and growth cycles. The configuration school also focuses on change. When is a new configuration needed and how can that best be managed? This focus on strategic decisions in bringing about change is especially important in HRM strategies since their concern is with the future, the unknown, thinking of and learning how to do things differently, undoing the way things have been done in the past and managing its implementation.

REFERENCES

Arthur, J.B. (1994) 'Effects of human resource systems on manufacturing performance and turnover', *Academy of Management Journal*, **37**(3): 670–87.

Arthurs, J.B. (1992) 'The link between business strategy and industrial relations systems in American steel minimills', *Industrial and Labour Relations Review*, **45**(3): 488–506.

Beer, M., Spector, B., Lawrence, P., Quin Mills, D. and Walton, R. (1985) *Human Resource Management: A General Manager's Perspective*, Glencoe, Illinois: Free Press.

Boxall, P. (1992) 'Strategic human resource management: beginnings of a new theoretical sophistication', *Human Resource Management Journal*, **2**(3): 60–79.

Boxall, P. and Purcell, J. (2000). 'Strategic human resource management: where have we come from and where should we be going?', *International Journal of Management Reviews*, **2**: 183–203.

Coase, R. (1937) 'The Nature of the Firm', *Economica* 4.

Commons, J. (1934) *Institutional Economics*, New York.

Cully, M., Woodland, S., O'Reilly, A. and Dix, G. (1999) *Britain at Work: as depicted by the 1998 Workplace Employee Relations Survey*, London: Routledge.

Cyert, R.M. and March, J.G. (1963) *A Behavioural Theory of the Firm*, Englewood Cliffs, NJ.: Prentice Hall.

Dunlop, J. and Weil, D. (1996) 'Diffusion and performance of modular production in the US apparel industry', *Industrial Relations*, **35**(4): 334–55.

Gospel, H.F. (1983) 'Management Structure and Strategies: An Introduction', in H.F. Gospel and C.R. Littler (eds) *Management Strategies and Industrial Relations*, London: Heinemann.

Gospel, H.F. (1992) *Markets, Firms and the Management of Labour in Modern Britain*, Cambridge: Cambridge University Press.

Gowler, D. and Legge, K. (1981) 'Groups that provide specialist services', in R. Payne and C. Cooper (eds) *Groups at Work*, London: Wiley.

Grant, R.M. (1998) *Contemporary Strategic Analysis*, third edition, Malden, MA: Blackwell.

Grant, D. and Oswick, C. (1998) 'Of believers, atheists and agnostics: practitioners' views on HRM', *Industrial Relations Journal*, **29**(3): 178–93.

Grant, R.M., Jammine, A.P. and Thomas, H. (1988) 'Diversity, diversification, and profitability among British manufacturing companies, 1972–84' *Academy of Management Journal*, **31**(4): 771–801.

Grugulis, I., Dundon, T. and Wilkinson, A. (2000) 'Cultural Control and the 'Culture Manager': Employment Practices in a Consultancy', *Work, Employment and Society*, **14**(1): 97–116.

Guest, D. (1987) 'Human resource management and industrial relations', *Journal of Management Studies*, **24**(5): 503–21.

Guest, D. (1995) 'Human Resource Management, Trade Unions and Industrial Relations', in J. Storey (ed.) *Human Resource Management: A Critical Text*, London: Routledge.

Guest, D. and Peccei, R. (1994) 'The Nature and Causes of Effective Human Resource Management', *British Journal of Industrial Relations*, **32**(2): 219–42.

Guest, D. and Hoque, K. (1994) 'The Good, the Bad and the Ugly: Employment Relations in the New Non-Union Workplaces', *Human Resource Management Journal*, **5**(1): 1–14.

Hamel, G. and Prahalad, C.K. (1989) 'Strategic Intent', *Harvard Business Review*: 63–76.

Hoque, K. (1999) 'New approaches to HRM in the UK hotel industry'. *Human Resources Management Journal*, **9**(2): 64–76.

Hoskisson, R.E., Hitt, M.A., Wan, W.P. and Yiu, D. (1999) 'Theory and research in strategic management: swings of a pendulum', *Journal of Management*, **25**(3): 417–56.

Huselid, M. (1995) 'The impact of human resource management practices on turnover, productivity and corporate financial performance', *Academy of Management Journal*, **38**(3): 635–70.

Hutchinson, S., Kinnie, N., Purcell, J., Collinson, M., Terry, M. and Scarbrough, H. (1998) *Getting Fit, Staying Fit, Developing Lean and Responsive Organisation*, London: Institute of Personnel and Development.

Ichniowski, C. and Shaw, K. (1995) 'Old Dogs and New Tricks: Determinants of the Adoption of Productivity-Enhancing Work Practices', in M. Bailey, P. Reiss and C. Winston (eds) *Brookings papers on Economic Activity*.

Ichniowski, C., Kochan, T.A., Levine, D., Olson, C. and Strauss, G. (1996) 'What Works at Work: Overview and Assessment', *Industrial Relations*, **35**(3): 299–333.

Ichniowski, C., Shaw, K. and Prennushi, G. (1997) 'The Effects of Human Resource Management Practices on Productivity: A Study of Steel Finishing Lines', *The American Economic Review*, **87**(3): 291–313.

Johnson, G. (1987) *Strategic Change and the Management Process*, Oxford: Blackwell.

Kaufman, B.E. (1993) *The Origins and Evolution of the Field of Industrial Relations in the United States*, Ithaca: ICR Press.

Kinnie, N. (2000) 'Explaining Call Centre Working', *People Management*, 8 June.

Kinnie, N., Purcell, J., Hutchinson, S., Terry, M. and Scarbrough, H. (1999) 'Employment Relations in SMEs: market-driven or customer-shaped?', *Employee Relations*, **21**(3): 218–35.

Kochan, T.A. and Chalykoff, J.B. (1987) 'Human Resource Management and Business Life Cycles: some preliminary propositions', in A. Kleingartner and C.S. Anderson (eds) *Human Resource Management in High Technology Firms*, Lexington, Mass: Lexington Books.

Kogut, B. and Zander, U. (1992) 'Knowledge of the firm, combinative capabilities, and the replication of technology', *Organizational Science*, **3**: 383–97.

Kogut, B. and Zander, U. (1996) 'What Firms Do? Coordination, Identity, and Learning', *Organization Science*, **7**(5): 502–18.

MacDuffie, J.P. (1995) 'Human resource bundles and manufacturing performance: organizational logic and flexible production systems in the world auto industry', *Industrial and Labour Relations Review*, **48**(2): 197–221.

Miles, R. and Snow, C. (1978) *Organizational Strategy, Structure and Process*, New York: McGraw-Hill.

Mintzberg, H. (1979) *The Structuring of Organisations*, Englewood Cliffs: Prentice Hall.

Mintzberg, H. (1994) 'The Rise and Fall of Strategic Planning', *Harvard Business Review* (Jan–Feb): 107–114.

Mintzberg, H., Ahlstrand, B. and Lampel, J. (1998) *Strategy Safari: A guided tour through the wilds of strategic management*, New York: The Free Press.

Oliver, C. (1997) 'Sustainable Competitive Advantage: Combining Institutional and Resource Based Views', *Strategic Management Journal*, **18**(9): 697–713.

Osterman, P. (1994) 'How Common is Workforce Transformation and Who Adopts It?', *Industrial and Labor Relations Review*, **47**(2): 173–88.

Patterson, M., West, M.A., Lawthorne, R. and Niskell, S. (1998) 'Impact of People Management Practices on Business Performance', *Issues in People Management No. 22*.

Pfeffer, J. (1994) *Competitive Advantage through People: Unleashing the Power of the Workforce*, Boston, USA: Harvard Business School Press.

Pfeffer, J. (1998) *The Human Equation: Building Profits By Putting People First*, Cambridge, Mass: Harvard Business School Press.

Pil, F.K. and MacDuffie, J.P. (1996) 'The adoption of high-involvement work practices', *Industrial Relations*, **35**(3): 423–55.

Porter, M.E. (1980) *Competitive Strategy*, New York: Free Press.

Porter, M.E. (1985) *Competitive Advantage*, New York: Free Press.

Porter, M.E. (1996) 'What is Strategy?', *Harvard Business Review*, (Nov–Dec): 61–78.

Porter, M.E. (1997) 'Response to letters to the editor', *Harvard Business Review*, March–April: 162–63.

Powell, W.W. and DiMaggio, P.J. (1991) *The New Institutionalism in Organisational Analysis*, Chicago: University of Chicago Press.

Prahalad, C.K. and Hamel, G. (1994) 'Strategy as a Field of Study: Why Search for a New Paradigm?', *Strategic Management Journal*, **15**: 5–16.

Purcell, J. (1989) 'The impact of corporate strategy on human resource management' in J. Storey (ed.) *New Perspectives on Human Resource Management*, London: Routledge.

Purcell, J. (1999) 'Best Practice and Best Fit: Chimera or cul-de-sac?', *Human Resource Management Journal*, **9**: 26–41.

Purcell, J. and Ahlstrand, B. (1994) *Human Resource Management in the Multi-Divisional Company*, Oxford: Oxford University Press.

Purcell, K. and Purcell, J. (1998) 'In-sourcing, outsourcing and the growth of contingent labour as evidence of flexible employment strategies', *European Journal of Work and Organizational Psychology*, **7**(1): 39–60.

Storey, J. (1992) *Developments in the Management of Human Resources: An analytical review*, Oxford: Blackwell.

Tailby, S., Pearson, E. and Sinclair, J. (1997) *Employee Relations in the South West: Workplace Survey*, Leicester: ACAS.

Thompson, M. (1998) 'HR and the bottom line: Jet Setters', *People Management*, **16** (April): 38–41.

Thompson, M. (2000) 'The Competitiveness Challenge: The UK Aerospace People Management Audit 2000 Final Report', London, SBAC.

Whittington, R. (1993) *What is Strategy and does it matter?*, London: Routledge.

Winkler, J.T. (1974) 'The Ghost at the Bargaining Table: Directors and Industrial Relations', *British Journal of Industrial Relations*, **12**(2): 191–212.

Wood, S. and Albanese, P. (1995) 'Can we speak of high commitment management on the shop floor?', *Journal of Management Studies*, **32**(2): 215–47.

Youndt, M.A., Snell, S.A., Dean, J.W. and Lepak, D.P. (1996) 'Human resource management, manufacturing strategy and firm performance', *Academy of Management Journal*, **39**(4): 836–66.

5 Human Resource Management and the Personnel Function – a case of partial impact?

Keith Sisson

INTRODUCTION: THE CHANGING FOCUS OF DEBATE

On the basis of the largely fragmentary survey evidence available at the time, this chapter in the previous edition (Sisson 1995) argued that the HRM phenomenon appeared to have had little or no impact on the personnel function in the UK in the 1980s and early 1990s. Hopes that HRM would lead to a more strategic approach to the management of human resources had been largely frustrated. There did not even appear to have been moves to adopt the new title, the number of specialist personnel managers with 'human resources' in their title turning out to be less than one per cent in 1990 (Millward *et al*. 1992: 29). Critically, there appeared to have been no increase in board level representation of personnel, even in the very large companies.

Equally, however, fears about a decline in the numbers and influence of personnel managers turned out to have been groundless, as did worries about the 'externalization' of the function. There had been, it is true, greater fragmentation or 'balkanization', but this mirrored developments in management more generally. Similarly, concerns about the implications of HRM for the values of the personnel profession had subsided, the number of young people prepared to submit themselves to the rigour of the IPM's examination scheme growing from strength to strength.

One explanation put forward for the relatively little impact was that, outside of a small number of mostly foreign-owned 'greenfield' workplaces, the UK had seen very little of HRM. Certainly it had seen very little of the people-centred 'soft version'. Admittedly, there had been what Storey (1992: 28) had referred to as the 'remarkable take-up by large British companies of initiatives in the style of "human resource management" model'. Yet many of the initiatives, as Storey's study confirmed, rarely added up to an integrated approach. Key ingredients such as single status and guarantees of employment security were noticeable by their absence. Also, paradoxical as it seemed, these practices were much more likely to be found in union rather than non-union workplaces.

It was even questioned whether there was much evidence of the 'hard' version of HRM. A great deal of what was going on, however it was labelled, was better understood in terms of 'hard' rather than the 'soft' version (see, for example, ACAS 1992, 1993; Millward *et al*. 1992: 364–5; Citizens' Advice Bureaux 1993). Yet, even in these cases, the notion of managers making strategic choices from a menu of options seemed far removed from reality. Certainly they were taking advantage of the political context to assert their control, but their use of it, and their response to business conditions, remained largely ad hoc and pragmatic.

A second explanation put forward was implicit in the profile of personnel managers presented in the chapter. Not only did personnel managers in the UK comprise an extremely heterogeneous group in terms of their activities. Using Tyson and Fell's (1986) categories, the great majority, above all in UK-owned organizations, were essentially 'clerks' or 'contract managers' rather than 'architects'. Their main activities involved relatively routine administration, which may have been critical for the day-to-day operation of the business, but was far removed from the grander notions of strategy, strategic choice and 'regime competition' that had become some of the defining characteristics of HRM. The chapter went on to ask whether it was possible to have HRM with a personnel management profile such as existed in the UK.

The remit for the present chapter is to update the portrait of the personnel function in the UK. The task is both easier and more difficult than the last time. The publication of the results of the fourth Work Employee Relations Survey (WERS) carried out in 1998 (Cully *et al.* 1999; Millward *et al.* 2000) provides us with a richer source of data about the personnel function than ever before. At the same time, however, making sense of such data is a major challenge. It is not just that there is an enormous amount of material to be digested. Much of it appears at first sight to be contradictory.

Complicating matters further, as Chapter 1 has pointed out, is that the debate has understandably moved on. For practitioners, as Torrington (1998) rightly reminds us, there is no dispute that the personnel function involves both operational and strategic dimensions. The major difference of opinion arises over the best way of delivering what is involved. At the risk of over-simplification, one view is that personnel specialists need to put some distance between themselves and the operational detail. 'Strategic role requires HR to take 'heretical' action' is the title of one recent report in *People Management* (John 1998). In it, US HR 'guru', Thomas Stewart, author of *Intellectual Capital: the New Wealth of Nations* (1998), is quoted as suggesting that 'a view is emerging that the strategic and bureaucratic paper-pusher roles can no longer co-exist – the only way to go is to tear the HR function apart, outsource and downsize it, and call it something else'.

Although there have been no comments as extreme as this in the UK, some organizations would appear to be edging towards this position. BP Chemicals (Industrial Relations Services 1997) and NAAFI (Industrial Relations Services 1999) are examples. A major restructuring of the specialist function has involved reductions in numbers, the devolution of operational responsibility to line managers and a considerable amount of outsourcing (which even extends to writing employee references in the latter case). In the words of Mike Nicolson, the HR Director of NAAFI,

> Previously, our personnel function was seen as providing administrative support and welfare-type services to the organization. It wasn't strategically focused. Our role now is to ask questions such as 'where is the business going?' and 'how can HR contribute to its success?' and then to provide answers.
>
> (quoted in Industrial Relations Services 1999)

The opposing view, which can be associated with such well-established figures as Torrington (1998) in the UK and Ulrich (1997) in the USA, is that personnel specialists are unlikely to be able to make a strategic contribution, unless they are able to demonstrate expertise in operational matters. The devolution of responsibilities and the outsourcing of service provision have their place, but not to the extent that the first group wants to go. Personnel specialists, in Ulrich's (1997: 253–4) words, need to pursue a 'multiple-role model' reflecting several metaphors: 'partner in strategy execution'; 'administrative expert'; 'employee champion'; and 'change agent'.

A related debate concerns the representation of the personnel function in the senior management team, which in the case of the large plc raises the issue of main board representation. The background is set by the research evidence from the Industrial Relations Research Unit's second company level industrial relations survey of 1992, suggesting that lack of board level representation was not just symbolic of the status of personnel issues. Companies with a main board personnel director were not only more likely to take personnel matters into account in strategic business decisions, but also have personnel policy committees and company-wide policies (for further details, see Sisson 1995: 98–9; Purcell 1995: 78–9). Torrington (1998: 32), on the basis of more recent survey and case study evidence, has suggested that 'formal positioning on the board, or lack of it, did not seem to make much difference to the extent of personnel's influence'. Personnel specialists often found ways around it by informal networking. Rather, what counted were more informal sources of 'corridor power'. (Interestingly, however, most non-board members aspired to this status and were fighting for it or expressing discontent about not having it.)

For many academics and policy makers, the 'conundrum', to use the WERS team's word (Cully *et al.* 1999: 295), is to understand why the so-called 'high commitment management' practices associated with HRM are not more widespread, given the growing body of 'compelling evidence' (ibid. 286) of their link with better performance. Here two main explanations have been put forward (see, for example, European Foundation, 1997: 2000). The first emphasizes process. Most of us, it can be argued, have considerably underestimated the problems in modernizing people management. It is not just a question of the considerable time and resources that are involved, both of which are so much at a premium, although these are fundamental. A major problem, as Pil and MacDuffie's (1996) review of the literature on innovation reminds us, is that there are costs associated with unlearning old practices and introducing new ones. In the circumstances, it is not surprising that many of the well-known cases of the introduction of new forms of people management turn out to be exceptional and tend to involve either 'green-field' operations or a crisis situation that forces the parties to shift from their traditional ways of working. Otherwise, there is a strong temptation for managers to prefer the incremental path to change, i.e. to try one or two elements and assess their impact before going further, even though this means forgoing the benefits of the integration associated with 'bundles' of complementary practices.

The second, and more uncomfortable, explanation puts the emphasis on choice and the scope that exists for managers to exercise choice. Like the first, it also starts with a questioning of conventional wisdom. It suggests that the 'transformation thesis', which has informed so much of our thinking in the area of people management and work organization more generally, is seriously flawed. In practice, competitive success based on the quality and up-skilling that HRM implies is only one of a number of strategies available to organizations. Others include seeking protected or monopoly markets, growth through take-over and joint venture, shifting operations overseas, cost cutting and new forms of 'Taylorism', most of which do not involve a change in people management.

Significantly, no less an authority than the *Bundesvereinigung der Deutschen Arbeitgebervbände* (the Confederation of German Employers' Organizations), which can hardly be accused of being an apostle of critical labour process theory, emphasizes the point. Arguably, the European Commission's 1997 Green Paper *Partnership for a new organisation of work* is one of the most balanced as well as clearest statements of the case for modernizing the approach to people management. The BDA none the less accuses the Commission of having a 'rather simplistic conception' of new work organization in that it assumes a general shift from a 'Tayloristic' system with a high division of labour towards a flexible team-based work process (see EIRO-online 1999). According to the BDA, there is 'no general turning away from "Taylorism"'. Indeed, after a period of widespread use of 'lean production concepts' in the early 1990s, the 'pendulum is currently swinging in the opposite direction' whereby many companies are reintroducing more 'Tayloristic' work concepts. The developments in work organization, the BDA goes on, are very different depending on the specific national, branch and company circumstances and particular market conditions. Context, in other words, is all-important.

Against this background, the next section seeks to re-profile the personnel function in the UK on the basis of the 1998 WERS data. As well as updating the details on the numbers and qualifications of personnel specialists, it focuses on the involvement of personnel specialists in operational and strategic matters and the organization of the personnel function in terms of its devolution, outsourcing and board level representation. The third section considers the variations on the major themes, emphasizing in particular the different patterns emerging depending on the size, sector, age and ownership of workplaces. The fourth and final section discusses the implications of the findings. It concludes that, while senior managers seemed to have accepted many of the underlying precepts of HRM, they continue to be unwilling or unable to take on board the 'high commitment management' model associated with it. Personnel practitioners, it is argued, need to stay on the campaigning trail, while policy makers have to recognize that much remains for them to do to improve the context for the effective management of people in the UK.

THE PERSONNEL FUNCTION RE-PROFILED

The personnel of personnel

In terms of numbers, qualifications and titles, the WERS data have some very positive messages. In the words of the WERS team (Millward *et al.* 2000: 80), 'One of the most significant changes is that the people responsible for managing employee relations in 1998 were quite different from those who were managing it at the beginning of the 1980s'. Perhaps the most important change, they suggest, has been the degree to which the responsibility for personnel management has shifted from general managers to personnel specialists and functional line managers. During the 1980s only around one sixth of managers responsible for employee relations were specialists, but by 1998 this had increased to nearly one quarter (23 per cent).

Significantly, too, with the exception of the larger workplaces, where the presence of a specialist was already nearly universal, this increase was across the board, regardless of sector, ownership and union recognition.

These personnel specialists are also much better qualified than they were. In 1980, just over half (52 per cent) of specialist managers said they had formal qualifications in personnel management or a closely related subject. By 1984 the proportion had grown to 57 per cent, where it remained in 1990. By 1998, however, it had increased to 72 per cent. Especially significant is that improved qualification is not something restricted to new entrants. The trend is also evident in the case of those with substantial experience. Indeed, the proportion of specialists with qualifications increases with the length of experience.

There has also been a considerable increase in the proportion of women within the ranks of employee relations management. Two fifths (39 per cent) of employee relations managers were women in 1990 compared with one eighth (12 per cent) in 1980. Moreover, women made up almost two thirds (63 per cent) of specialists in 1998 compared with one fifth in 1980 (19 per cent).

In 1998, female personnel specialists were just as likely to have qualifications as their male counterparts (44 per cent of women were qualified compared with 45 per cent of men), whereas in 1980 men were nearly twice as likely to be qualified as women. The experience and responsibilities of men and women were also comparable. Although men were still more likely to have responsibility for pay and conditions in 1998, there were no significant differences so far as responsibility for training and the handling of grievances were concerned. There had also been a reversal in position of presence in unionized workplaces. In 1980, the proportion of male and female specialists working in unionized workplaces was 62 per cent and 56 per cent respectively. In 1998, the proportions were 42 per cent and 45 per cent.

Especially noteworthy is the increase in the number or personnel specialists with 'human resources' in their job title. In 1990, one of the most commented on results was that less than one per cent of the total number of managers with personnel responsibilities had 'human resources' in their job title. By 1998, this had grown to seven per cent and accounted for nearly one third of specialists. Not only that. It is the increase in the number of 'human resource' managers that helps to account for the increase in the number of personnel specialists overall.

According to the further analysis of the WERS data undertaken by Hoque and Noon (1999), this signifies more than a change in title. 'Human resource' managers were more likely to hold a formal relevant qualification than were personnel managers. As will be discussed in more detail below, they were also more likely to be involved in the preparation of the strategic plan than personnel managers were.

A strategic as well as operating role?

One thing is clear. Personnel specialists are heavily involved in operational matters. Indeed, on the face of it, there appears to have been little change in the activities of personnel specialists in recent years. As Table 5.1 suggests, the proportions citing different job responsibilities are roughly the same in 1998 as they were in 1990 and 1984. The rank orders for each of the years are very similar as well.

Intriguingly, however, it appears that personnel specialists may be spending less time on these activities, raising questions about else they might be doing. Whereas in

Table 5.1 Job responsibilities of management respondent, by personnel specialist/non-specialist status, 1984 to 1998

	1984	1990	1998
	% of workplaces	% of workplaces	% of workplaces
Personnel specialists			
Handling grievances	94	93	96
Pay or conditions of employment	92	90	90
Recruitment or selection of employees	90	96	93
Staffing or manpower planning	86	83	81
Training of employees	78	71	78
Systems of payment	69	62	62
Non-specialists			
Handling grievances	83	87	91
Pay or conditions of employment	64	69	73
Recruitment or selection of employees	89	91	92
Staffing or manpower planning	85	84	90
Training of employees	83	82	88
Systems of payment	50	60	54

Base: All private sector workplaces with 25 or more employees.
Figures are weighted and based on responses from 781 specialists and 1,013 non-specialists (1984); 798 specialists and 899 non-specialists (1990); and 723 specialists and 1,017 non-specialists (1998).
Note: Excludes interviews not held at the workplace.
(Source: Cully *et al.* 1999: 226)

1984 they were spending on average 86 per cent of their time on these activities, by 1998 this had fallen to 69 per cent. Fewer personnel specialists, it seems, were spending *all* their time on these activities: only 17 per cent were doing so in 1998, which is down from 55 per cent in 1984.

One thing it is fair to conclude is that personnel specialists were spending more time on the collection and dissemination of information. Although the questions asked in 1990 and 1998 were slightly different, the WERS findings suggest that there has been an increase in the information being collected. Moreover, it is not just a question of an increase in individual items. The mean number of items for which information was collected rose by nearly one quarter from 3.0 to 3.7 (Cully *et al.* 1999: 227, Table 10.6).

As for the dissemination of information, there has been an increase in both the channels used to communicate with or consult employees and the amount of information given to them (Cully *et al.* 1999: 229, 231, Tables 10.7 and 10.8). Notable in the case of the channels used are the increases in the use of regular newsletters and regular meetings between management and employees, while in the case of the amount of information, it is the increase in the number providing details of investment plans that catches the eye. The one item to see a decline is staffing plans, which may be accounted for by the inclusion of '... before the implementation of any changes' in the wording of the question in 1998.

The WERS team's summary measure of information disclosure is also insightful. The proportion of workplaces where management gave little or no information to employees over the period 1984 to 1998 remained constant at around 16 per cent. The proportion where management provided information in the three areas rose progressively from 20 per cent to 36 per cent.

As the WERS team suggests, another possible explanation for the reduction in time that personnel specialists are spending on traditional activities is that they are engaged in the sort of strategic management decision-making associated with HRM. At first sight, the grounds for this possibility look good. More than two thirds (68 per cent) of respondents said the workplace had a formal strategic plan that covered, among other things, 'employee development'. In the great majority of these cases (83 per cent), the person responsible for employee relations was involved. Overall, 57 per cent of workplaces had a strategic plan covering 'employee development' to which there had been an input from the responsible personnel manager.

Less comforting are the findings in respect of workplaces with Investors in People (IiP) accreditation. As the WERS team reminds us, IiP is the national standard involving 23 indicators by which assessors judge the commitment, planning, action taken and systems of evaluation in place to meet training and development objectives. In total, scarcely one third (32 per cent) of workplaces were IiP accredited. A further 16 per cent had applied but had been unsuccessful and the remaining 53 per cent had never applied. Even in the case of workplaces that are part of a wider organization, the proportion with IiP accreditation only creeps up to two in five (39 per cent).

Combining the three indicators of the integration of personnel management into wider business strategy also produces interesting results. Two in five (40 per cent) of workplaces that are part of a wider organization had a strategic plan to which there had been an input from the responsible personnel manager and representative on the board of directors. Only over just one in five (21 per cent) reported having the three indicators, i.e. a strategic plan covering 'employee development' to which there had been an input from the responsible personnel manager, a personnel presence on the board of directors and IiP accreditation.

Another set of data bearing on the question comes from the incidence of what the authors of WERS suggest might be labelled 'high commitment management' practices. Table 5.2 suggests that there are some clear-cut associations here. In the words of the WERS team

> The differences are, for the most part, substantial and all are consistent. In each of the areas examined the practice was most likely to be found in workplaces covered by an integrated employee development plan and with access to a personnel specialist. They were least likely to be found in workplaces with neither.
>
> (Cully *et al*. 1999: 82)

The WERS team also go on to suggest that, although it is not possible to say each of the practices fit together, 'It is sufficient ... to demonstrate that these practices are not independent of either structure or strategy, and that there is evidence that a number of the practices consistent with a human resource management approach are well entrenched in many British workplaces' (Cully *et al*. 1999: 82).

Adding to the significance of these findings is that the multivariate analysis undertaken by the WERS team suggests the 'high commitment management' practices are associated with superior performance. In the words of the WERS team (Cully *et al*. 1999: 291), '"High commitment management practices" are associated

Table 5.2 Management practices, by presence of personnel specialist and integrated employee development plan

	Personnel specialist and integrated employee development plan	Personnel specialist only	No personnel specialist or integrated employee development plan	All workplaces
	% of workplaces	% of workplaces	% of workplaces	% of workplaces
Largest occupational group has/have:				
Temporary agency workers	19	18	14	18
Employees on fixed-term contracts	38	32	12	28
Personality tests	17	10	5	11
Performance tests	42	34	17	35
Formal off-the-job training for most employees	51	30	18	36
Profit-related pay*	24	14	5	15
Employee share ownership scheme*	12	10	1	6
Regular appraisals	69	61	31	58
Fully autonomous or semi-autonomous teams	44	33	14	34
Single status for managers and other employees	51	42	22	40
Guaranteed job security	20	14	1	13
Workplace has:				
Formal disciplinary and grievance procedure	97	95	64	88
Group-based team briefings with feedback	65	52	48	59
Most non-managerial employees participate in problem-solving groups	20	11	6	15
Two or more family friendly practices or special leave schemes	59	45	15	41

Base: All workplaces with 25 or more employees.
Figures are weighted and based on responses from between 1,835 and 1,889 managers.
* Profit-related pay and employee share ownership schemes are based on responses from 1,287 and 1,291 private sector managers respectively.
(Source: Cully *et al.* 1999: 81)

with better economic performance, better workplace well-being and a better climate of employment relations. . .'

Important though these findings are, there is a danger of ignoring the other key point to emerge from Table 5.2. The practices listed, it hardly needs emphasizing, are far from being revolutionary. Indeed, most personnel texts seem to assume them to be standard in today's workplace. Moreover, the figures also measure workplace *incidence* only and not *scope* of the practice, which can be important in establishing the type of team working, for example. Even in the 'best case' in the first column, where there is a personnel specialist and an integrated employee development plan, only six of the fifteen practices are practised in a majority of workplaces. In the 'worst case' in the third column (which is the majority), where there is no personnel specialist and no integrated employee development plan, only one of the fifteen practices is to be found in a majority of workplaces. Needless to say, this one, a formal disciplinary and grievance procedure, is hardly the epitome of a 'high commitment management' practice.

Perhaps even more telling, though, are the figures from the First Findings of WERS (Cully *et al*. 1998: 11) for the total number of practices being used in each workplace. Only one in seven (14 per cent) of workplaces had half or more of the practices in place. Only one in fifty (two per cent) had ten or more.

Details of the combinations or 'bundling' of practices in the First Findings of WERS are also illuminating. Training, team working and supervisor training appear to go together, as do individual performance pay, profit sharing and share ownership. Yet single status is associated with the first cluster but not the second, suggesting that direct participation and financial participation are seen as alternatives rather than complementary as might have been expected.

At first sight, there does not appear to be any substantial difference between personnel specialists who have adopted 'human resources' in their title and their peers in terms of the activities performed. The further analysis by Hoque and Noon (1999), however, suggests that more than a change in name is involved. As noted above, not only were human resource managers more likely to hold a formal related qualification than personnel managers were, but they were also more likely to be involved in the preparation of the strategic plan. Moreover, the strategic plan was more likely to emphasize employee development in establishments with a human resource manager rather than a personnel manager.

Organization

As the authors of WERS (Cully *et al*. 1999: 56) remark, the devolution of personnel management activities has been 'a consistent theme among those writing about HRM'. In the event, the data suggest things are more complicated than some commentators have suggested. Overall, nine out of ten workplaces had at least some supervisory employees with at least some 'people management' duties. Areas where supervisors were mostly responsible were training (86 per cent), health and safety (76 per cent), performance appraisals (66 per cent) and the handling of grievances (62 per cent). The areas where supervisors played a limited role were those related to pay: only 13 per cent of workplaces gave supervisors responsibility for either the pay or conditions of employment and even fewer (8 per cent) the remuneration system.

The WERS results also suggest that devolution does not necessarily equate to decision making authority. More than two thirds (70 per cent) said that supervisors could not make a final decision over any of three key issues – recruiting people to work for them, deciding pay increases and dismissing workers for unsatisfactory performance. Around a quarter (27 per cent) of workplaces with supervisors gave them the authority to make decisions on recruitment, but very few did so for dismissals and pay increases, where the proportions were 8 per cent and 3 per cent respectively.

Another relevant finding is that there is a low level of training of supervisors in people management skills. Thirty per cent of workplaces had never given supervisors training in these skills and a further 25 per cent had only given training to a few. This result is hardly to be expected if there had been extensive devolution.

In the case of our second concern, the outsourcing of personnel, the WERS data are indirect rather than direct. They certainly suggest an increase in the use of external advice, the proportion of workplaces involved rising from around a third to more than half between 1980 and 1998. As Table 5.3 suggests, especially noteworthy is the increase in the resort to government agencies such as ACAS and lawyers. The only source not to register an increase was employers' organizations.

For the most part, however, this development would appear to reflect eminently pragmatic considerations rather than a philosophical commitment to outsourcing. One is the decline in the number of support staff – WERS found that the number of managers with clerical support fell from 52 per cent to 44 per cent between 1990 and 1998. The other is the increasing complexity of the issues that have to be dealt with, notably in the light of the very considerable increase in the amount of legislation bearing on personnel management. Most importantly, it will be recalled from a previous section, there has been an increase in the number and qualifications of in-house personnel specialists.

Table 5.3 External sources of advice for employee relations managers, 1980, 1990 and 1998

	Cell percentages		
	1980	1990	1998
Sources of advice			
ACAS and other government agencies	10	12	23
Management consultants	4	6	16
External lawyers	1	16	32
External accountants	2	2	14
Employers' associations	12	6	10
Other professional bodies	*	1	19
Other answers	12	13	6
None of these	69	68	44
Weighted base	1,830	1,644	1,821
Unweighted base	1,868	1,697	1,740

Base: all establishments with 25 or more employees where the survey interview was conducted on site.
(Source: Millward et al. 2000: 73)

Less clear is whether the increase in the presence and qualification of workplace personnel specialists is to be related to the latest WERS findings in respect of the board level representation of the function. These suggest that there has been a further decline in board level representation in the private sector since 1990. In 1980, board level representation stood at 73 per cent. It increased to 76 per cent in 1984 before declining to 71 per cent in 1990. Between 1990 and 1998, it declined a further seven percentage points to stand at 64 per cent. The number of head offices employing personnel specialists also fell from nearly half (47 per cent) in 1990 to just over one third (36 per cent) in 1998.

The final piece of what is becoming an increasingly complicated jig-saw comes from the findings in respect of the degree of autonomy enjoyed by workplace personnel managers in multi-establishment organizations in areas that WERS labels 'operational matters'. The existence of policies on operational matters such as recruitment, performance appraisal, training, pay systems and pay and conditions of employment was widespread as was the need for workplace managers to follow them. For each of the nine issues, a majority of workplace managers had to follow policies set at a higher level in the organization. A summary measure of autonomy suggested that this was especially likely to be the case where there was a personnel specialist at a higher level. The chances of workplace personnel managers having to consult with a manager at a higher level in the organization where they did not have to follow policy were also much greater. The overall conclusion of Cully and his colleagues (1999: 59) is that 'The broad picture is . . . one of relatively well-developed structures for the management of employees, with control largely retained by personnel departments in the centre of the organisation'.

Also clear is that the degree of control exercised from the centre seems to have grown in the 1990s. Indeed, the WERS team talks of 'unequivocal evidence' of this happening. In both 1990 and 1998, respondents belonging to larger organizations were asked how decisions were made on three issues; the appointment of a senior manager, the recognition or derecognition of a trade union and the use of any financial or budgetary surplus. In each case, the proportions of workplace respondents saying that they were able to make such decisions declined over the period: from 39 per cent to 24 per cent for the appointment of a senior manager; from 31 per cent to 23 per cent for union recognition or derecognition; and from 34 per cent to 14 per cent for the use of financial surpluses.

Summary

Overall, therefore, in terms of numbers, qualifications and titles, the WERS data have some very positive messages. There have been notable increases in the number and qualifications of personnel specialists in the 1990s. The presence of one of these specialists is more likely to be associated with an integrated employee development plan and various 'high commitment management' practices such as regular off-the-job training, team working and single status. The increase in the number of personnel specialists also reflects a sevenfold increase in those among this group who have adopted the 'human resources' title. The presence of a specialist 'human resources' manager is even more likely to be associated with having an integrated employee development plan.

Even so, the number of workplaces with a personnel specialist remains less than one in four. There also appears to have been no great change in the activities of these specialists, although there are signs of an increasing involvement in the collection and dissemination of information. Few of the individual 'high commitment management' practices are found in a majority of workplaces. The number of workplaces with 'bundles' of them is extremely small, even though there is evidence that where they are present they are strongly associated with performance. Only a third of workplaces has IiP accreditation. Only two fifths of workplaces belonging to multiple organizations have a strategic plan covering 'employee development' to which there had been an input from the responsible personnel manager, a personnel presence on the board of directors and IiP accreditation.

At the same time, however, there is evidence that multi-establishment organizations have a raft of operational policies in areas such as recruitment and selection, pay and conditions, and union recognition and derecognition and that workplaces are required to follow them. Evidently, the headquarters of large multiple organizations do not lack the capacity to exert influence from the centre in personnel matters and they choose to do so to a considerable extent.

VARIATIONS ON THE THEMES

So far the concern has been with the general profile of personnel managers in the UK. The pattern differs from workplace to workplace and company to company. Such differences are not entirely random, however, and are critical to understanding what has really been happening to the personnel function in the 1990s.

Size

The results of the 1998 WERS suggest that the size of the workplace and/or the wider organization, as measured by the number of employees, is as critical a variable as it has been in previous surveys. Other things being equal, for example, workplaces with more than 500 employees were five times more likely to have a personnel specialist than those with 25–49 employees (Cully et al. 1999: 50, Table 4.1). Personnel specialists with 'human resources' in their title were also more likely in the larger workplaces, though it is interesting to note here that a higher proportion of specialist personnel managers in the workplaces with fewer than 50 employees (40 per cent) had adopted the title than for any other size group.

Similarly, the incidence of many of the 'high commitment management practices' appears to be associated with size. For example, larger workplaces were around twice as likely to have non-managerial employees involved in problem-solving groups, suggestion schemes and attitude surveys (Cully et al. 1999: 68, Table 4.6). As in the case of the presence of personnel specialists, stand-alone workplaces are also much less likely to have these practices than those that belong to larger organizations. Although they emphasize that it would very simplistic to conclude that the 'small business approach' to organizing work is totally unstructured, Cully and his colleagues (1999: 273) make the point that

> Organisational size and patterns of ownership proved to be clearly associated with incidence of formal structures and practices within small workplaces. Overall, small businesses – especially those with working owners – had a less formal approach than small multiples to the regulation of the employment

relationship. Compared to other small workplaces, they were less likely to have significant personnel expertise in-house, or the more sophisticated personnel systems such as performance appraisal, inventive payment systems, or family-friendly working practices. Combined with this – and especially when a working owner was present – these businesses tended to lack representative structures. Owner managers generally took the view that they were there to take decisions, and this was reflected in the way they ran their businesses.

Sector

A number of the key findings noted earlier also reflect the significance of the sector. For example, the great majority of workplaces in electricity/gas/water (97 per cent) and financial services (90 per cent) reported having a personnel specialist available at the workplace or higher levels. By contrast, only around a third of construction (32 per cent) and manufacturing (37 per cent) workplaces did so.

The representation of the personnel function on the board of directors in private sector organizations also differed significantly by sector. Perhaps most importantly, the decline in representation remarked on earlier was much greater in manufacturing than in services. In manufacturing, the proportion of workplaces with a main-board director was down from 73 per cent in 1980 to 44 per cent in 1998, whereas in services the decline was much more modest from 73 per cent in 1980 to 69 per cent in 1998 (Cully *et al.* 1999: 225).

It also seems that the capacity for strategic approach has been affected. Only one in ten (nine per cent) of manufacturing workplaces reported having a strategic plan encompassing employee development drawn up with the involvement of the manager responsible for employee relations, the representation of the personnel function on the board of directors and IiP accreditation. By contrast, almost half (47 per cent) of workplaces in financial services did so.

Changes in the composition of the work force by sector also lie behind the increasing feminization of personnel management that is one of the most marked changes of the 1990s. As Millward and his colleagues (2000: 60) confirm, the distribution of female personnel managers *within* sectors has not changed greatly over the two decades of the WERS investigations: they were under-represented in manufacturing and over-represented in private and public services in both 1980 and 1998. There has been a significant shift in the balance of employment *between* sectors, however, in particular a growth in private services and a decline in manufacturing. The effect of the growth in private sector services has been to create considerably more opportunities for female personnel managers.

'New', 'continuing' and 'departed' businesses

Especially relevant to understanding the increases in the proportion of workplaces having a personnel specialist is the contrast between businesses leaving and joining the sample (either because they had ceased/started trading or had reduced/increased employment below/above the size threshold). Put simply, the 'joiners', which are roughly equivalent to 'new' businesses, were much more likely to employ personnel specialists than the 'leavers', which for present purposes might better be described as 'departed' businesses. By contrast, there was very little change in the case of the 'continuing' workplaces, where about the same proportion had engaged a specialist by 1998 as had lost one. The new businesses among the 'joiners', along with 'continuing' businesses, were also much more likely than the 'departed' businesses to have personnel specialists with 'human resources' in their title.

The distinction between the three types of workplace is also important in accounting for the decline in specialist board level representation discussed in the previous section. In this case, however, the association is very different. The level of this representation remained constant in the workplaces of UK-based MNCs and rose in workplaces recognizing unions and belonging to larger organizations. By contrast, 'new' businesses, especially smaller local firms and those without union representation, were less likely to have board level representation than 'departed' businesses were.

Ownership

The significance of the difference between public and private ownership has already been touched on in a previous section. Other things being equal, public sector workplaces were more likely to employ personnel specialists than their private sector counterparts, although they were less likely to carry the 'human resources' designation. The responsibilities that these specialists were undertaking had also increased, leading the WERS team to suggest that their role had changed 'radically' in this sector. Especially noteworthy, reflecting moves to more local bargaining arrangements in public services, was the near doubling between 1990 and 1998 in the number of workplaces citing pay and conditions of employment among their responsibilities. 'High commitment management practices' were also more likely in the public sector than in the private sector, as was IiP accreditation.

Privatization also appears to be a factor in the growth in specialist human resource managers. This job title was 'particularly in evidence' in the electricity, gas and water supply industries. Indeed, it was in these industries that 'human resource' managers accounted for the majority of personnel specialists (61 per cent).

Foreign ownership is also significant in understanding many of the differences. Foreign-owned workplaces (51 per cent) were almost twice as likely to employ a personnel specialist as UK-owned ones (27 per cent). The personnel specialists in foreign-owned workplaces were also much more likely to include 'human resources' in their title. Human resource managers accounted for nearly two thirds of personnel specialists in foreign-owned workplaces (64 per cent) compared with around a quarter (26 per cent) in UK-owned ones.

Personnel specialists in North-American-owned workplaces, it seems, were especially prone to use the 'human resources' title. Subsequent analysis by Hoque and Noon (1999: 13–14) suggests that, whereas the label is confined to specialists in less than three per cent of UK-owned workplaces and seven per cent of European-owned ones, almost half (46 per cent) of their North-American-owned counterparts used it.

There has yet to be a detailed investigation of the wider significance of ownership for policies and practices. As indicated earlier, however, the analysis by Hoque and Noon does show a positive relationship between the use of the 'human resources' title and the adoption of a more strategic approach as measured by a greater emphasis on employee development in the strategic plan and greater personnel specialist involvement in its drawing up. In as much as foreign-owned workplaces displayed a stronger tendency than UK-owned ones to employ personnel specialists with the 'human resource' title, it is highly likely that further analysis will show that the contrast between UK and foreign-owned organizations is as 'striking' as Millward (1992: 33) and his colleagues said it was after the 1990 WIRS.

Summary

The general profile of personnel managers in the UK described earlier in the chapter differs from workplace to workplace and organization to organization. Especially relevant in helping to account for this diversity are the size of the workplace and/or the organization to which it belongs, the sector in which it operates, the age of the business (whether it is a 'new' or 'continuing' or 'departed' business) and its ownership. In a number of key respects, for example, the employment of personnel specialists, the indicators of a more strategic approach and the use of a number of 'high commitment management practices', changes in the structure of employment have been positive so far as personnel management developments are concerned. Many of the 'departed' businesses, it emerges, especially those in manufacturing, tended to be laggards in matters of personnel management practice, whereas many of the 'new' businesses show signs of taking heed of the advice to take managing people more seriously. There is one qualification to this optimistic picture, however. 'New businesses' were less likely to have board level representation of the personnel function than either the 'departed' or 'continuing' businesses. In the words of Millward and his colleagues (2000: 77), 'It is new workplaces, rather than established ones, which remained to be convinced of the value of board-level representation.'

DISCUSSION AND IMPLICATIONS

The picture that emerges from the WERS findings is somewhat confusing and presents us with a puzzle. At first sight, there is little evidence to suggest that the impact of HRM on the personnel function has been greater in the 1990s than it was in the 1980s. True, there has been an increase in the number of workplaces with personnel specialists with 'human resources' in their job title and it appears that this is more than just a change in name. Such people account for only seven per cent of managers responsible for employee relations, however, and one third of personnel specialists. It also emerges that there was a decline both in the number of personnel specialists at headquarters and in their board level representation in the 1990s. Furthermore, the development of a more strategic approach seems to be far from widespread and very few workplaces have the combinations of 'high commitment management' practices that have come to be associated with HRM.

Yet, at the same time, there is evidence of considerable development, which has also been more widely recognized, most notably by the Privy Council's granting of chartered status to the IPD. There has been a significant increase in the proportion of workplaces with specialist personnel managers. Approximately, one quarter of workplaces had such specialists in 1998, with three fifths of all workplaces having a personnel specialist available either at the workplace or at a higher level. Personnel specialists are also better qualified. Furthermore, there are signs of involvement in strategic as well as operational matters. In multi-establishment organizations especially, there are indications of a raft of policies. In the words of the authors of the fourth WERS report (Cully *et al.* 1999: 59)

> To summarise, the body of evidence examined thus far suggests that employee relations are generally an important aspect of management. Over half of all workplaces had an integrated development plan – one which encompasses employee development and was drawn up with the aid of an employee relations manager.

Even the finding that there is less autonomy in operational matters enjoyed by workplaces in organizations where there was a wider organizational structure to the personnel function has a positive side to it. It means, in the words of Cully and his colleagues (1999: 59) that there are 'relatively well developed structures for the management of employees'.

Two implications would seem to follow. One is that the personnel function in the UK appears to be developing the all-round operational and strategic competence that commentators like Ulrich and Torrington have been advocating. There is no great evidence, to put this another way, of the unloading of key responsibilities to either line managers or external agencies and an exclusive concern with the strategic dimension. The second is that the argument that the state of personnel function itself is a contributory factor in accounting for the absence of HRM can no longer be sustained. The personnel function in many organizations, it seems, has both the quality of people and the structures to deliver what senior managers ask of it.

In these circumstances, the most obvious explanation for the WERS findings is also probably the most reasonable. It is that HRM has had an impact on the personnel function in the UK, but that it has been partial. Put simply, senior managers seem to have accepted many of the underlying precepts of HRM as has the government. This is evidenced both in its pronouncements and in the granting of chartered status to the IPD. Thus, it is accepted that the management of people is important; that there needs to be greater coherence of personnel policies and their integration with business planning more generally; that management–employee relations are as important, if not more important, than management–trade union relations; and that personnel specialists need greater expertise. At the same time, however, senior managers have been unable or unwilling to take on board the more specific policy and practice prescriptions associated with HRM, in particular, the 'high commitment management' model rooted in extensive two-way communication, autonomous team working and an emphasis on training and learning.

This is where the two possible explanations for the WERS team's 'conundrum' discussed in the chapter's opening section come in. Many of the WERS findings are intelligible in terms of the 'process' explanation emphasizing the problems management has in modernizing employment relations in established 'brownfield' operations. Relevant here, for example, would seem to be the distinction between 'new', 'continuing' and 'departed' businesses. Other things being equal, many of the signs of change are to be found in 'new' businesses, including the increase in the presence of a specialist personnel manager (in particular those with the human resources designation), a strategic plan that is more likely to emphasize employee development and the greater likelihood of 'high commitment management' practices. By contrast, there are fewer signs of change in 'continuing' businesses, while the 'departed' businesses make their contribution by taking their poor personnel management practices with them.

The changes in the public sector and the privatized utilities also fit. In each case there have been fundamental changes in the financial and management structures. The effect, it would appear, is to have made it possible to develop a personnel function more in keeping with the requirements of increasingly decentralized operations.

Also compatible are the findings of Storey (1992) and others about the developments in the late 1980s/early 1990s. One of the distinguishing features of the changes in work organization such as 'just in time' and team working in many organizations was that they were driven by line managers rather than personnel specialists. The growth in the numbers and qualifications of personnel specialists in the 1990s, it can be argued, is to be seen as a lagged response, reflecting a growing appreciation of the people management implications of such developments that were so often ignored in the early phases of these initiatives.

Tempting though it is to leave matters on an optimistic note, it is important to point out that the broad thrust of the findings is also consistent with the 'choice' explanation. Arguably, most UK organizations in the 1990s have been in the business of restructuring. This has necessitated a much stronger personnel function and fairly tight control of operational matters from the centre in the case of the large multiple organizations, coupled with greater emphasis on the collection and dissemination of information. By the same token, it has not necessarily required the adoption of a more strategic approach (or having board level representation) and it certainly has not required the introduction of 'bundles' of 'high commitment management' practices, however compelling the evidence may be for the link with improved performance. In the words of Hunt (2000), 'Cuts in staff have placed it [the personnel function] in the role of decapitator rather than resource developer'.

Not to be forgotten either is that throughout the 1990s key features of the UK's business system continued to put a premium on cost minimization rather than investment in human resources:

- An overwhelming emphasis on shareholder value as the key business driver as opposed to the interests of other stakeholders.
- Institutional share ownership by investment trusts and pensions funds rather than banks which encourages a focus on short-term profitability as the key index of business performance rather than long-term market share or added value.
- Relative ease of take-over, which not only reinforces the pressure on short-term profitability to maintain share price, but also encourages expansion by acquisition and merger rather than by internal growth.
- A premium on 'financial engineering' as the core organizational competence and the domination of financial management, both in terms of personnel, activities and control systems, over other functions.

In these circumstances, as Legge (2000: 63) puts it in her own inimitable way,

> For low-cost producers, particularly operating in mature markets, investment in training, intensive communications and guarantees of job security may be seen as both unnecessary and undesirable. If behavioural compliance is sufficient, why go to the expense of trying to secure additional commitment.

Although, therefore, the personnel function at the end of the 1990s looks in much better shape than many of us would have predicted, there none the less remains considerable room for improvement. For personnel practitioners, following Legge (2000: 61) echoing Ulrich quoted earlier, it means staying on the campaign trail, not as champions of the workforce in the welfare sense, which is where the function began, but 'in the spirit of promoting and protecting a vital business resource'. For policy makers who are serious about promoting 'partnership', the 'knowledge economy' and so on, the implications of the state of personnel management are pretty clear-cut if uncomfortable. They will have to do much more than shout from the touch-line to bring about the necessary changes. This not only means using the financial and legal means at their disposal to establish standards and targets in key areas such as training and development, information and consultation, low pay and working time. More challengingly, it also means a serious review of some the features of the UK's corporate governance arrangements that are so inimical to investment in human capital.

REFERENCES

Advisory, Conciliation and Arbitration Service (ACAS) (1992) *Annual Report*, London: ACAS.

Advisory, Conciliation and Arbitration Service (ACAS) (1993) *Annual Report*, London: ACAS.

Citizens' Advice Bureaux (1993) *Job Insecurity*. London: Social Policy Section, Citizens' Advice Bureaux.

Cully, M., O'Reilly, A., Millward, N., Forth, J., Woodland, S., Dix, G. and Bryson, A. (1998) *The 1998 Workplace Employee Relations Survey. First Findings*, London: DTI.

Cully, M., Woodland, S., O'Reilly, A. and Dix, G. (1999) *Britain at Work*, London: Routledge.

European Foundation for the Improvement of Living and Working Conditions (1997) *New Forms of work organisation. Can Europe realise its potential? Results of a survey of direct employee participation in Europe*, Luxembourg: Office for the Official Publications of the European Communities.

European Foundation for the Improvement of Living and Working Conditions (2000) *The modernisation of work organisation – taking stock of the state of direct participation. Reflections on the findings of the EPOC project*, Luxembourg: Office for the Official Publications of the European Communities.

EIRO online (European Industrial Relations Observatory) (1999) Comparative supplement on national perceptions of, and the direction indicated by, the European Commission's Green Paper *Partnership for a New Organisation of Work*, European Foundation for the Improvement of Living and Working Conditions, Dublin.

Hoque, K and Noon, M. (1999) 'Counting angels: the personnel/human resource function in the UK. Evidence from the 1998 Workplace Employee Relations Survey'. Paper for British Universities' Industrial Relations Association conference, de Montfort University, 1–3 July.

Hunt, J. (2000) 'Human resources: Untapped resources', *The Financial Times*, 25 February: 14.

Industrial Relations Services (IRS) (1997) 'Benchmarking facilitates change and continuous improvement at BP Chemicals', *Employment Trends*, 630, April: 13–16.

Industrial Relations Services (IRS) (1998) 'The evolving HR function', *IRS Management Review*, Issue 10, July.

Industrial Relations Services (IRS) (1999) 'NAAFI looks to the future', *Employment Trends*, 678, April, 11–16.

John, G. (1998) 'Strategic role requires HR to take 'heretical' action', *People Management*, 10 December.

Legge, K. (2000) Personnel Management in the Lean Organisation', in S. Bach and K. Sisson (eds) *Personnel Management. A Comprehensive Guide to Theory and Practice*, Oxford: Blackwell.

Millward, N., Stevens, M., Smart, D and Hawes, W.R. (1992) *Workplace Industrial Relations in Transition: the ED/ESRC/PSI/ACAS Surveys*, Aldershot: Gower.

Millward, N., Forth, J. and Bryson, A. (2000) *All Change at Work*, London: Routledge.

Pil, F.K. and MacDuffie, J.P. (1996) 'The adoption of high-involvement work practices', *Industrial Relations*, 35(3): 423–55.

Purcell, J. (1995) 'The Impact of Corporate Strategy on Human Resource Management', in J. Storey (ed.) *New Perspectives on Human Resource Management*, Routledge: London.

Sisson, K. (1995) 'HRM and the Personnel Function', in J. Storey (ed.) *Human Resource Management: A Critical Text*, London: Routledge, pp. 87–109.

Storey, J. (1992) *Developments in the Management of Human Resources*, Oxford: Blackwell.

Torrington, D. (1998) 'Crisis and opportunity in HRM: the challenge for the personnel function', in P. Sparrow and M. Marchington (eds) *Human Resource Management The New Agenda*, Financial Times/Pitman: London.

Tyson, S. and Fell, A. (1986) *Evaluating the Personnel Function*, London: Hutchinson.

Ulrich, D. (1997) 'The changing nature of human resources: a model for multiple roles', in D. Ulrich, *Human Resource Champions*, Boston: Harvard University Press.

6 Industrial Relations and Human Resource Management

David Guest

INTRODUCTION

During the 1990s, there was some debate about whether human resource management could replace or at least accelerate the demise of traditional industrial relations. In the new millennium, it is increasingly clear that at a national level the Labour government is interested in neither. Indeed, as our first post-modern government (in the sense that the medium and the packaging are invariably the message) too often what matters most is the rhetoric rather than the substance. As a result, the field of employment relations is increasingly littered with positive words that soon become tarnished. 'New' industrial relations therefore appears to fit well with new Labour. Accommodated within it are encouraging concepts such as 'partnership', 'involvement' and 'fairness'. Beneath this rhetoric, and following the 'final settlement' (Undy 1999) of the Fairness at Work legislation and the sometimes grudging application of the European Social Chapter, it seems to have been very much 'business as before' reflected, for example, in debates about performance-related pay in the public sector and encouragement of employee share ownership in the private sector.

Trade unions, like industrial relations are 'old' and by implication bad. There is also an interesting ambiguity about human resource management. Many personnel managers have avoided the title because they feel it is too harsh, with its connotations of exploiting human resources (Hoque and Noon 1999). For the government, sensitive to presentation, this may serve as a caution. The IPD's preferred term, 'people management', may be just about acceptable but 'human resource management' can by now be considered 'old' and while some of the content can be embraced, the term may not fit comfortably within the government pantheon of positive terms. By implication, for new Labour, both industrial relations and HRM are 'old' concepts that do to fit well within the new millennium.

Nevertheless, the business of people management and employee relations has to be carried on in all organizations and for many workers these activities have an important bearing on their day-to-day working lives. Traditional concerns about the use and potential abuse of management power and the capacity of workers, collectively or individually, to counter this continue to be important. While the incidence of strikes and other high profile forms of industrial conflict are at an historically low level, this should not encourage a view that we are now a nation of satisfied, committed and productive workers or that industrial conflict is at an end.

We are perhaps fortunate in having a strong reality check in the form of the 1998 Workplace Employee Relations Survey (WERS). Among a number of novel features of this survey is a greater emphasis on human resource issues and information from employees about their satisfaction. So with the help of the rich body of information it provides, we are in a position to map the contemporary contours of both industrial relations and human resource management at the establishment level.

This chapter will therefore start with an analysis of the contemporary evidence about the practice of industrial relations and human resource management, drawing on WERS and other sources. It will do so within the conceptual framework used in the parallel chapter in the previous book in this series (Guest 1995). It will then explore in some detail two contemporary issues that have been identified by Bacon and Storey (2000) among others as the key 'new' issues in the 'new' industrial relations, namely partnership at work and the individualization of the employment relationship, reflected, *inter alia*, in the growing interest in the concept of the psychological contract. Partnership can be viewed as one possible route towards a new role for trade unions and collective interests; it has parallels in the USA in what is often termed a 'mutual gains' approach (Kochan and Osterman 1994). Individualism, in contrast, presents a real challenge to the collectivist and pluralist traditions within industrial relations. At the same time, it is often associated with the use of a distinctive approach to human resource management. Part of the analysis must therefore consider the relationship between individualism, human resource management and industrial relations institutions.

A FRAMEWORK OF THE ANALYSIS OF INDUSTRIAL RELATIONS AND HUMAN RESOURCE MANAGEMENT

In Guest (1995) it was suggested that a simple framework for considering the relationship between industrial relations and HRM would offer four main perspectives. We will use a slightly amended version of this framework again, as illustrated in Figure 6.1.

To develop these basic distinctions, we need some operationalization of the dimensions. Along the industrial relations dimension, an organization or workplace might be considered 'high' when there is a recognized trade union, together with worker representation and the presence of some sort of local negotiation and consultation activity. In a few cases, this might be institutionalized in the form of a partnership agreement while in others there may be a set of mutual commitments

		HRM Activity	
		High	**Low**
Industrial	**High**	Partnership	Traditional
Relations			Pluralism
Activity	**Low**	Individualism	Black
			Hole

Figure 6.1 Industrial Relations and Human Resource Management

reflected in a single union deal or single table bargaining; and in a few of the larger international companies there will be a senior level works council. At the other extreme, there will be workplaces with no form of collective representation.

Along the human resource management (HRM) dimension, a 'high' score would be reflected in the adoption of a large number of 'progressive' HR practices together with some attempt at strategic integration. At the other extreme, there will be workplaces with little systematic HR activity and no evidence that HR activities have been considered strategically. The term 'progressive' can be debated at length; for the present, we are interested in a set of what can be termed 'high commitment' or 'high performance' HR practices, noting in passing that these are not necessarily quite the same thing.

We can make the language slightly more contemporary by suggesting that organizations that recognize the legitimacy of industrial relations while also emphasizing HRM can be labelled mutual gains or partnership companies. Those that are low on industrial relations and therefore deny a pluralist stance can either emphasize a form of positive individualism of the sort found in softer versions of HRM or adopt an exploitative unitarism in which workers are simply viewed as another resource. Where there is little sign of progressive HR practice but a trade union presence and some form of collective activity, we have 'traditional pluralism'. Finally, we have workplaces with low levels of HR and no system of representation, the 'Bleak Houses' or, as we label them, the 'black holes'.

Interestingly, the 'new' industrial relations has tended to emphasize the left-hand side, where HRM is prominent. Debate generally has tended to neglect the right-hand side. We shall try in part to remedy this in the present chapter.

THE INDUSTRIAL RELATIONS DIMENSION

The picture from The 1998 Workplace Employee Relations Survey (WERS98)

The 1998 WERS data provide much the most comprehensive account of the state of employment relations at the end of the twentieth century and gives us a basis for beginning to locate establishments along the two dimensions. They make rather depressing reading for enthusiasts of traditional industrial relations and employee representation. Starting first with employee representation and closely related issues of union membership, in workplaces employing 25 or more people (and many now employ fewer than this) management estimates suggest that about 36 per cent of employees belong to a trade union. This is closely linked to size of workplace and organization, so it averages 23 per cent in workplaces with 25–49 workers and 48 per cent in those with over 500. It falls to 8 per cent of those in organizations with fewer than 100 workers and rises to 48 per cent in those with more than 10,000 workers. It is also strongly associated with sector, with 56 per cent in the public sector but only 26 per cent in the private sector belonging to a trade union. Turning the issue around, 47 per cent of workplaces have no union members while at the other extreme only 2 per cent have 100 per cent membership.

Union membership in a workplace does not in itself indicate industrial relations activity. However, it is generally a good guide; so 53 per cent of workplaces had union members and 45 per cent recognized a trade union for collective bargaining purposes. This leaves a number where there is union membership but no recognition, usually because the proportion of members is small. The 'non-recognition rate' is 16 per cent and a quarter of these workplaces have a union density of more than 10 per cent. The 'non-recognition rate' is much higher in the private sector, at 30 per cent than in the public sector where it is 3 per cent. This leads to a first general conclusion, aptly summarized by the WERS authors:

> It is fair to state that union recognition is predominantly a public sector phenomenon: two thirds of private sector workplaces were without a union presence, and only one in four recognised trade unions compared with more than nine in ten public sector workplaces.
>
> (Cully *et al*. 1999: 93)

Towers (1997) has drawn attention to what he terms the 'representation gap' whereby many workers have no independent opportunity for representation in their workplace. WERS98 highlights the extent of this gap, revealing that 60 per cent of all workplaces have no worker representatives. This includes 25 per cent where unions are recognized. In workplaces where there are no union members, management reports that 11 per cent have non-union representatives and this rises to 19 per cent of workplaces where union members are present but unions are not recognized for collective bargaining.

What we find, therefore, is a marked split between the public sector, where traditional industrial relations appears to have survived, albeit with some adaptations, and a private sector which, with the exception of a declining set of large establishments, is predominantly non-union and without worker representation. Even where there is union membership in the private sector, management is often disinclined to recognize the union. Indeed, management appears to be firmly in the driving seat, controlling the direction of employment relations. So what has happened to the traditional activities of collective bargaining and joint consultation? Again, the answers are not encouraging.

Collective bargaining is increasingly constrained, both in its organization and in its coverage. In workplaces where there is union recognition, 32 per cent in the private sector and 16 per cent in the public sector have a single union deal. Where there is more than one recognized trade union, single table bargaining is quite common, reported by 12 per cent in the private sector and 40 per cent in the public sector. This leaves just 17 per cent of unionized workplaces that had multiple union recognition and separate bargaining with each union.

Workplace negotiation is very restricted. WERS98 offered a list of nine conventional items including pay, payment systems, grievance handling, health and safety and training. There was no negotiation with union representatives over any of these nine issues in half the workplaces where trade unions were recognized. On average, union representatives negotiated on only 1.1 of the nine issues while non-union representatives negotiated over 0.9 issues.

If issues are not negotiated, are they instead covered in consultation? Only 34 per cent of public sector and 20 per cent of private sector workplaces had some sort of consultative committee (in some cases there may have been higher level consultative committees, for example at company level). The same set of nine issues listed for negotiation were presented again and the average number covered by consultative committees was 2.9 where union representatives were involved rising to 3.7 where non-union representatives were involved. No single issue was covered by more than a third of the committees. Management control of these consultative committees is indicated in a number of ways. Some fifty-one per cent of managers in the public sector and 29 per cent in the private sector, rated their consultative committees as highly influential. They were more likely to be rated highly influential where there were non-union representatives and particularly where these representatives were appointed by management rather than elected by workers. They were also rated more influential where they met more often; yet when the committees were made up of union representatives in highly unionized settings they tended to meet less often. In short, managers appear to rate committees as influential where they are able to exercise control over them. In other settings, the committees are more likely to be marginalized in the decision-making process.

The picture that emerges is one of limited traditional industrial relations institutions and activity, more particularly in the private sector, with employment relations in this sector largely controlled by management. There are therefore relatively few workplaces that would appear at the high end of an industrial relations continuum where that is defined in terms of a strong trade union presence with a representative worker voice channelled through negotiation and consultation with coverage of a wide range of issues. Such workplaces have largely disappeared from British industry. In one sense, this constrains our discussion of industrial relations and human resource management. However, it still leaves a set of questions about activities at other levels and more particularly at company level. It also leaves open the long-standing issue of the relationship between a trade union presence and human resource management. Finally, it raises questions about the complementarity of traditional industrial relations activities and human resource practices, an issue which can be considered under the umbrella concept of partnership at work.

HUMAN RESOURCE MANAGEMENT IN THE CONTEXT OF TRADE UNIONS: TOWARDS PARTNERSHIP

Unions may have given up their opposition to human resource management but they remain suspicious about it. As John Monks notes:

> In the wrong hands HRM becomes both a sharp weapon to prise workers apart from their union and a blunt instrument to bully workers.
>
> (Monks 1998: xiii)

This is, in effect, an argument for a union role ensuring that HRM is 'properly' applied. Clues to what this might mean in practice can be found in union statements endorsing partnership at work. The most widely understood set of principles can be found in the statements of the Involvement and Participation Association (IPA). They argue that partnership should be underpinned by four building blocks (IPA 1997):

- a recognition of the employees' desire for employment security and the company's need for maximum flexibility
- sharing success within the company both financially and in non-monetary ways
- informing and consulting staff and involving staff in discussions of issues both at the workplace and at company level
- providing the means for effective and independent representation of the people who work in the organization.

The attraction of partnership to the trade unions is that it is one of the few viable paths to a position where they might be valued by employers while retaining an independent workers' voice. The risk is that partnership becomes a device for management to incorporate unions, a new form of flexibility deal where 'responsible' trade unionism means that unions can never endorse industrial action. In an analysis for the IPA of the meaning and practice of partnership among its members, Guest and Peccei (1998) also suggest that partnership, despite its connotations of mutuality and mutual gains, may in practice be weighted towards the interests of the company. For example, perceptions of principles and the way they are put into practice indicate that it is the practices that appear to be to the advantage of the company, such as ensuring employee contribution rather than promoting employee welfare and rights that are most likely to be implemented. There is also evidence, even from those who might be expected to be at the leading edge of best practice, that levels of trust, and in particular management trust in trade unions, remain low in all but a few exceptional cases. Ironically, it is in those minority of cases where a high trust dynamic emerges that the benefits to the organization of partnership are most apparent.

As noted in the introduction, partnership is one of those warm words that can mean all things to all people. The IPA study suggests that in practice it is viewed as a combination of traditional employment relations, built around notions of direct and representative participation, and various aspects of human resource management. This makes it particularly appropriate for analysis in the context of this chapter. Also at a pragmatic level, without applying the label of partnership, we might expect to see it manifested in a combination of industrial relations and human resource activities. If we accept this, we can return to the WERS data and look again at what it tells us.

The first general finding from WERS98 is that HRM practices are strongly associated with a recognized union presence. Cully et al. (1999) give some emphasis to this in their report. At its simplest, there are more HR practices in place where there is a recognized trade union. They use a list of 15 practices and find that more than half are in place in 25 per cent of establishments that recognize a trade union but only 5 per cent of those that do not. They also find that management ratings of workplace performance are generally higher where there are both more HR practices and a recognized trade union. In other words, HRM and a union presence are potentially compatible and potentially beneficial. However, this does not imply any causal link since both are found in larger establishments and in the public rather than the private sector. Indeed in the private sector as a whole, there is no association between union recognition and having more than half the practices in place. Searching for evidence of 'the new industrial relations' in the private sector, Cully et al. found that

> only 4 per cent of recognised workplaces had a majority unionised workforce, where local representatives negotiated with management over some issues and where at least half of these high commitment management practices were in place.

> (Cully et al. 1999: 111)

Since, as we have already noted, only a quarter of private sector workplaces recognize a trade union, this leaves just one per cent of private sector workplaces where both traditional industrial relations and a reasonably extensive form of HRM are in place. On this basis, we can conclude that the new industrial relations and what we can label partnership-type activities, with or without the partnership label and an associated partnership agreement, have yet to establish even a small foothold in British industry. While there may be a few successful partnership cases, we must be cautious about talking them up and assuming they reflect a wider enthusiasm for partnership-type activities.

One of the interesting findings from WERS98 is the extent of the differences between the public and private sectors. These are discussed in some detail elsewhere (Guest *et al.* 2000) and specific findings will not be repeated here. However, on the basis of a standard count of HR practices, it appears that HRM has been more widely adopted in the public than in the private sector. Because many of the public sector HR practices have been agreed at national level, there is much less variation across the sector; and despite government attempts to introduce various features of performance management and, most controversially, performance-related pay, most are what might be described as worker-centred. For example, there are large gaps between the public and private sector in adoption of family-friendly policies, equal opportunities policies and off-the-job training. We might therefore expect to see some association between use of these practices and positive employee attitudes. Furthermore, the public sector appears to come closer to meeting the criteria of the 'new industrial relations' with its combination of well-established industrial relations procedures and a range of HR practices.

A regression analysis on the WERS data shows no link between use of these 'new industrial relations' practices and public sector employees' satisfaction and commitment. One possible explanation is a statistical one; since there is relatively little variation across the public sector in the use of these practices, there is too restricted a range on the 'independent variable'. Some support for this can be found from the analysis in the private sector, where use of a greater number of HR practices (though not necessarily the same ones as the public sector) is associated with higher satisfaction and commitment. From the perspective of the new industrial relations, there is more bad news in the analysis, since higher levels of trade union density are associated with lower levels of satisfaction and commitment. This association is found in both the public and private sectors. Taken as a whole, therefore, the data indicate that the new industrial relations, defined in terms that might be acceptable to trade unions, is almost non-existent in the private sector and does not appear to be associated with positive attitudes among employees in the public sector; in other words, where it is applied there is little evidence that it operates to the benefit of workers.

There are, of course, other versions of the new industrial relations. The one promoted by the previous Conservative governments gave much more emphasis to employee involvement. This is discussed much more fully in the chapter by Marchington (Chapter 12). For the present, to round off the analysis of WERS98, it is interesting to note that employee involvement appears to have a stronger and more positive influence than the more pluralist version that has been presented here. In the public sector, increased use of employee involvement, as measured on a range of indicators, is associated with higher levels of employee satisfaction and commitment. In the private sector, a more consultative climate has a similar result while increased employee involvement is associated with higher management ratings of labour productivity. What this indicates is that the informal climate of employee relations, which appears to be largely under management control and subject to management initiative is much more strongly associated with positive outcomes than the form of the new industrial relations that emphasizes mutuality between union and management.

Where, then, does this leave partnership? If WERS, without directly measuring partnership nevertheless offers no encouragement to it, can we glean any positive results from those organizations that have begun to move down the road to partnership? In embarking on even a cursory analysis, it is tempting to think back to the (much greater) impact of Peters and Waterman's (1984) *In Search of Excellence* and the subsequent critical analyses of what happened to some of the excellent companies. Rover's New Deal and Hyder's Partnership Agreement have been held up as models of best partnership practice while the companies experience performance problems, takeover and collapse. Kelly (1999) has argued strongly that partnership deals have done nothing either for companies or their employees; indeed the reverse might be the case. There is plenty of fuel to stoke the fires of those critical of partnership and what it can achieve.

Nothing in this analysis denies a potentially useful role for trade unions. One of the more telling findings concerns dismissals, which are one manifestation, albeit at the individual level and reflecting management initiative, of industrial conflict. Drawing again on the WERS98 data, dismissals per 100 employees ranged from 0.1 per cent in the highly unionized electricity, gas and water sector to 5.9 per cent in the hotels and restaurants sector which has one of the lowest levels of union organization of any sector.

Moving away from WERS, there are examples to illustrate the benefits of union involvement in certain areas of decision-making. One of the key areas associated with all variants of HRM is training. Green, Machin and Wilkinson (1996) have shown that a trade union presence is associated with more training in a workplace. Heyes and Stuart (1998) have taken this a step further and shown that the benefits are particularly marked where the union is not only present but also actively involved in decisions about training issues. Whether such activity can sensibly be described as partnership is open to question, but it does appear to go beyond the alternative adversarial approach.

Similar findings have been reported elsewhere. In the USA, Delaney and Huselid (1996) found that union pressure was associated with more training as well as with greater care in selection, internal promotions and more use of grievance procedures. In Australia, Deery and Iverson (1999), adopting a somewhat different perspective, showed how a positive industrial relations climate was associated with higher loyalty to the union and commitment to the organization and that this translated into higher productivity and lower absence, a kind of win/win situation for both company and union.

Returning to the UK experience, a few points are worth highlighting. First, despite a fair degree of hype, there are only around 30 to 40 partnership deals in the UK. A number of these have been born out of some sort of crisis and many depend on the enthusiasm of a very small group of key individuals, raising questions about their sustainability. From government down, there has been much more talk than action. The evidence from the IPA study (Guest and Peccei 1998), in line with some of the WERS findings for the private sector, suggests that the scope of partnership is largely determined by management and that where it has a positive impact on attitudes or performance it is largely attributable to the HR dimension rather than the industrial relations dimension. In one sense, partnership has become institutionalized both through its explicit advocacy in the Fairness at Work legislation (HMSO 1999) and through the government's Partnership Initiative (1999) to fund new partnership arrangements. It is therefore likely to be with us for some time, perhaps sufficient time to demonstrate its potential benefits more clearly.

For the trade unions, partnership is not necessarily the only game in town. It is still plausible to argue for a traditional strategy of pluralist confrontation in which the differences rather than the similarities between parties are highlighted (Heery 1998). This at least may focus more strongly on recruitment to the unions. But partnership is much the most attractive game to play. For the trade unions, and particularly the senior policy-makers within the TUC, it forms part of a coherent strategy for the future alongside campaigning for legislation and advocating closer ties with Europe and the European ethos of social partnership. Sceptics may doubt whether this will work. Undy (1999) has argued that *Fairness at Work*, now represented by the 1999 Industrial Relations Act, might best be viewed as a kind of final settlement of debts to the labour movement and no further labour legislation is envisaged. Although Britain has now signed up to the Social Chapter, closer economic ties with Europe appear no nearer. Evidence for the benefits of partnership, as this chapter has tried to show, is weak. This is not necessarily because partnership cannot work; it is more likely to be because what is labelled partnership often falls far short of the ideal. The IPA study did identify a few successful cases; and it also found that a majority of companies, even at what might be considered the leading edge of good partnership practice, still believe they have some way to go to become what they themselves would agree is a partnership company. It would appear that as far as partnership is concerned, the jury is still out.

Returning once more to WERS, it is clear that most managers prefer to deal with their employees directly rather than through a trade union. Most partnership deals to date may involve some variant of a works council or senior consultative committee; indeed the IPA study found that these were present in about 80 per cent of their members' organizations. But, as with the forms of representative participation developed many years ago, their impact on the shop floor is minimal (Heller *et al.* 1998). For employees, it is the HR practices that affect their daily lives and the risk is that even where there is some form of partnership agreement the trade union role recedes ever further into the background; the wasting or withering on the vine proceeds apace.

HRM AND THE GROWTH OF INDIVIDUALISM

One of the reasons why unions are valued, particularly among the professional, technical and white collar employees who now form an increasing proportion of their membership, is their ability to provide an individual service should it ever be needed. In particular, a union can provide support in the face of arbitrary treatment by management. However, this usually reflects workers' concerns at the individual level rather than a collective identity and it is just one aspect of a growing interest in individualism at work. Part of this can be attributed to the culture created by many years of Conservative government with its advocacy of an American form of market-based rugged entrepreneurial individualism. It also owes something to HRM with its core concept of commitment to the organization, reflected in individual–organization ties. This individual–organization linkage is preferred to the collective link represented by a trade union role. From a management perspective, the means to achieve individualism at work can vary quite considerably. In the USA, a distinction is sometimes drawn between a 'high' road and a 'low' road. Management may engage in sophisticated HRM to win the hearts and minds of employees and develop strong individual–organization linkages, the 'high' road; or it can pursue more aggressively anti-union policies designed to reduce any collective organization, weaken any opposition to management control and permit it to introduce tough, flexible performance management systems. In effect, therefore, the analysis of the growth of individualism at work can be considered in the context of the second dimension of high or low levels of HRM, albeit clouded a little by the form that the HRM takes, in a context where unions and collective activity are either absent or largely irrelevant.

Trends towards the individualization of the workplace can be studied from within a traditional industrial relations perspective. Brown and his colleagues (Brown *et al.* 1999), for example, have looked closely at the legal aspects of trade union recognition as one key feature of the context that can facilitate or constrain the growth of the individualization of the employment relationship, as well as charting the decline of collective representation. Bacon and Storey (2000) have presented a number of cases that demonstrate that while managers would generally prefer to operate in a union-free environment, low levels of trust in management's motives make this difficult to achieve. Crucially though, their cases also show that management is content to permit a union presence as long as managers are free to exert the level of control they desire. Unions, in other words, exist as empty shells. WERS98, as already noted, confirms a strong preference on the part of most managers to deal directly with workers rather than through a union or some other form of workers' representation and a general lack of sympathy with trade unions. In short, managers indicate a clear preference for the conduct of employee relations to be based on individual rather than collective arrangements. This leads on to the issue of what sort of arrangements they choose to put in place when they are more or less in control. There are three ways in which we will develop this analysis. One is to consider a little further the kind of human resource practices found in non-union workplaces. The second is to examine a particular feature of the individualization of the employment relationship, namely the use of fixed-term and temporary contracts; and the third is to consider the workers' response. For all of this, it can be argued that we need rather different analytic tools to those used in traditional industrial relations. Here we will make some use of the concept of the psychological contract, which, as a metaphor, captures some of the important features of the individualization of the workplace.

One of the key questions, therefore is – what do employment relations look like in contexts where there are no collective arrangements? It should be emphasized that this is now the norm in British workplaces, so it is an issue that justifies considerable attention. During the 1990s, a number of studies of employment relations and more particularly human resource practices in non-union settings were reported. These tended to confirm the choice between the high and low road, although in an earlier attempt to develop this distinction, Guest and Hoque (1996) identified four categories, the good, the bad, the ugly and the lucky firms. The 'good' were those deliberately pursuing the high road of progressive HR policies and practices to engender employee commitment; the 'lucky' were those who had implemented many of these practices not as part of any strategy but more to follow fashion. The 'bad' were those who had failed to introduce many of the high commitment HR practices, but more out of neglect or incompetence than any design while the 'ugly' were those who were deliberately avoiding HR practices, seeking to control the workforce through more coercive or regressive means.

In the context of a study of greenfield sites, it was possible to be fairly optimistic about the proportion of 'good' firms and the work of McLoughlin and Gourlay (1992) in the high technology sector tended to confirm this. However, Sisson (1993) in his analysis of the 1990 workplace industrial relations survey warned us of the large number of what he termed 'Bleak Houses' in a more representative sample, and WERS98 confirms this pattern. A straightforward analysis of the number of HR practices adopted in private sector workplaces shows that the typical uptake is very low. We have already noted that the public sector pattern is rather different and that a union presence is associated with more practices, largely because of the public sector effect. In other words, in non-union settings, where managers presumably have choice and control, a sizeable majority choose not to operate the kind of HR practices that are increasingly considered to benefit both organization and employees. This pattern is confirmed at the company level where the reported uptake of HR practices is equally low (Guest *et al.* 2000c). This suggests that as with partnership, we should not be beguiled by the cases of organizations that have attracted attention because of their apparently successful adoption of high commitment HR practices. They remain a minority. When they have a choice, most managers do not choose the high road of 'high commitment' HRM.

This leads on to the next two questions. What do they do instead and how do workers react? 'Flexibility' is one of the positive words in the management vocabulary and although it can take many forms and be closely associated with HRM, the form of flexibility most closely linked to the individualization of the employment relationship is the use of fixed-term and temporary contracts. These are now attracting considerable research attention.

Individual employment contracts, and more particularly fixed-term contracts, are an extreme form of individualism that are often associated with 'hard' HRM rather than the 'soft' or 'high commitment' version that may appear, at least on the surface, to be more employee-centred. Such contracts can usefully be seen within the wider debate on employment flexibility and it is important not to overstate their presence. There has been a slow but steady growth in the numbers in temporary employment including fixed-term contracts, but they still only affected 7 per cent of the working population in 1997, up from around 5 per cent in the 1980s (Tremlett and Collins 1999). Temporary contracts can reflect the kind of HRM about which John Monks has been understandably critical and it is not surprising to find that unions have generally been opposed to increased employment flexibility. Indeed, there is some evidence that a union presence is associated with lower levels of flexibility (Guest *et al.* 2000c). At the same time, there is little evidence that firms have adopted a strategic approach to flexibility along the lines of the flexible firm strategy that became widely discussed in the 1980s. Rather, the approach to the use of temporary employment is reactive and opportunistic. In this context, we should bear in mind that use of temporary employees is not a characteristically private sector phenomenon. The greatest use of temporary labour, mainly in the form of fixed-term contracts, is found in public administration, education and health. And although our stereotype may be of the seasonal worker, temporary workers are more likely to be managerial and more particularly professional workers. Nevertheless, if our assumptions are correct, then those on fixed-term contracts should be given less access to some of the employee-centred HR practices and feel less secure.

There is a small but growing amount of evidence about the experience of various forms of temporary employment. They, like other aspects of the individualization of the employment relationship can be usefully analysed within the context of the concept of the psychological contract. This term, first used in the 1960s, has come to be more widely used recently as a framework for the analysis of the impact of changes in employment on the individual (Rousseau 1995; Guest 1998). The key element of the psychological contract is that it is concerned with the often implicit expectations, obligations and promises that each side, individual and organization, is believed to have made about what each owes and expects to receive from the other. These transcend the formal employment contract and will often be implicit and unwritten but nevertheless quite powerful. They are reflected in notions such as a fair day's work for a fair day's pay and the idea of an organizational career. One of the reasons for interest in the concept is a widespread belief that the traditional psychological contract, reflected in these notions, has broken down. In a context of rapid change, violation of the psychological contract is almost inevitable and violation can have damaging consequences for both individual and organization. This is a familiar analysis but it is important to separate the rhetoric, which abounds in this area of work, from the reality, which is rather more prosaic.

One argument for using the psychological contract in the present context is that as the nature of employment relations changes, we need new concepts and tools to analyse it. A model of the psychological contract can provide a powerful analytic tool linking organization policy and practice to worker experience and reactions. The kind of model that might be used centres on the state of the psychological contract, defined in terms of core employment relations concepts such as fairness, trust and delivery of the deal. We can then explore the antecedents (organizational context, policy and practice) and consequences (employee attitudes and behaviour) along the lines set out in the model in Table 6.1. For example, we can explore how far a trade union presence helps to ensure a positive state of the psychological contract and whether more high commitment HR practices make a difference. We can also explore how far a positive psychological contract leads to benefits for individual and employer. There is now a growing body of UK data that helps to shed light on these questions.

In a series of annual surveys for the IPD (Guest *et al.* 1997; Guest and Conway 1998, 2000), we have been exploring the psychological contract and the state of the

Table 6.1 A model of the psychological contract

Antecedents	The 'State' of Psychological Contract	Consequences
Organization Climate	Fairness	Positive Employment Relations
Human Resource Practices	Trust	Job Satisfaction
Trade Union Membership	Delivery of 'The Deal'	Commitment
Individual Experiences		Motivation
Individual Expectations		

employment relationship among a random sample of the working population. This shows a consistent pattern of results from year to year. The findings about the state of the psychological contract show that a majority of workers consider it to be reasonably positive. For example, in 1998 66 per cent believe they are 'definitely' or 'probably' fairly rewarded for the amount of effort they put in, 82 per cent believe the organization has promised to ensure fair treatment by supervisors and managers and of these 67 per cent say the promise has 'always' or 'to a large extent' been kept; only 3 per cent say it has not. On the issue of careers, 60 per cent believe the organization has made some sort of promise about careers and of these 65 per cent say the promises have 'always' or 'to a large extent' been kept with only 3 per cent firmly dissenting; 32 per cent trust the organization 'a lot' and 45 per cent trust it 'somewhat' to keep its promises and commitment to employees. By and large these are positive results, although there is invariably a minority, rising to about a third of the workforce on some issues, who are less content with the state of their psychological contract.

We can identify what explains variations in the state of the psychological contract. Of course with cross-sectional results we need to be careful about inferring causality. However, in the context of the present discussion, much the most important factor associated with a more positive psychological contract is the use, as reported by workers rather than by management, of a larger number of high commitment HR practices (Guest 1999). Three other significant links are worth noting; a more positive state of the psychological contract is reported by those who experience direct participation and, unexpectedly, by those who work on fixed-term contracts. Trade unions members do not report a more or less positive psychological contract but they are likely to report the presence of more HR practices.

Moving on to some of the consequences, we can explore the link between the psychological contract and employment relations. The results show that there is a strong association between experience of more HR practices, a more positive psychological contract and a positive evaluation of employment relations in the workplace. Workers also feel that they have more scope for participation in relevant company decisions where there are more human resource practices, where there is scope for direct participation and where there is a better psychological contract. Finally, intention to quit is higher among those with a poor psychological contract, who report poor employment relations and who also have a lower level of commitment. Union membership is not significant. All these findings suggest that the psychological contract serves as an important core organizing variable, acting partly as an evaluation of company policy and practice. So we can see that use of HR practices has a direct effect on some outcomes but it is also strongly mediated by the psychological contract, suggesting that it is not only the practices but the way workers interpret them that matters.

In the 1998 IPD survey, with government legislation in the pipeline, particular attention was paid to the issue of fairness at work. Five items measured aspects of fairness at work and could be formed into a single measure constituting an overall measure of workers' perceptions of fairness. The question then arises as to which factors are most strongly associated with this measure of fairness. (Since this is a dimension of the state of the psychological contract, it could not be measured against the psychological contract.) The key factors significantly associated with fairness were the number of HR practices, higher income, fewer hours, being on a fixed-term contract and, towards the bottom of the list, not belonging to a trade union. In the context of our wider discussion, this confirms the importance of human resource practices and raises further troubling questions about the role of trade unions. By tradition they are strongly associated with fairness at work and will intercede where possible to tackle unfair treatment. But in this sample, which contained 36 per cent who were union members, the union is not perceived as being a positive influence. Of course it is possible to argue that people join trade unions because they are treated unfairly; but, as has been argued elsewhere (Guest and Conway 1999), the age and experience profiles indicate that few in the sample have recently joined a trade union, so this is not a plausible argument.

This raises more general questions about how workers perceive trade unions. Among trade union members in the same IPD survey, 26 per cent felt that they were more fairly treated because they belonged to a trade union while 3 per cent felt they were treated less fairly. However, this leaves 69 per cent who felt that union membership made no difference; by implication, other factors are more important. Among non-union members, 18 per cent felt they would be more fairly treated if they belonged to a trade union while 12 per cent thought they would be treated less fairly. Most of the remainder thought it would make no difference. Those who thought that belonging to a trade union might increase fairness were likely to work in services and to report fewer HR practices in place. In other words, where management neglects HR practices, workers are more likely to believe a trade union would help to promote fairness at work. There is some implication in this analysis of a substitution effect. Unions are associated with more HR practices but in the absence of HR practices, there is more likely to be a belief in the value of a trade union.

Returning to the issue of individualism, there are some interesting findings concerning fixed-term contracts. While these are traditionally considered to be to the disadvantage of workers, these surveys show that fixed-term contracts are associated with a more positive psychological contract and greater fairness of treatment. Supporting evidence comes from a parallel study concerned with contracts, motivation and innovation (Guest et al. 2000a). This shows that fixed-term contract workers have a more explicit, specific and bounded contract than permanent employees. In the jargon of the psychological contract, it is more transactional than relational. This provides their work with a reasonably clear focus and helps them to avoid a number of features of organizational culture that are increasingly making life uncomfortable for permanent employees. In particular, they are able to escape from the potential tyranny of 'organizational citizenship', the kind of cultural requirement to work long hours, to help out colleagues in difficulty and to promote the organization at all times. Citizenship behaviour can sometimes be described as careerist behaviour. However, the payoffs are uncertain and herein lies one of the problems of the psychological contract as it affects a number of permanent employees. They cannot afford to ignore these pressures to be good organizational citizens; but since they are ostensibly volunteering, they cannot really expect a pay-off. Promises of promotion and the like may be implied; but they may not be delivered. In a context of rapid change, this is made more likely by the potential departure of the manager who made the promises. One outcome is a perception of contract violation and reduced satisfaction and commitment.

This analysis raises the possibility that individualism in the workplace provides a new kind of power to some workers. In particular it does so for knowledge workers in high demand who have acquired the skills of career self-management and the capacity to maintain high 'employability'. In other words, they are putting into practice the rhetoric of the new career. They are taking control of their careers and their working lives by negotiating contracts which offer a much better balance between work and the rest of their lives and which free them from day-to-day aspects of exploitation by the organizational culture. Our study of media technicians (Guest *et al.* 2000a) found that they admitted to vigorously opposing the move to fixed-term contracts. Now, most can see huge advantages and few would go back to the old system. The more calculative hoard their skills and knowledge, creating the potential for a new adversarialism. Of course not all workers on fixed-term contracts are there by choice and it is too early to see a reversal of the laws of capitalism to the point where worker knowledge can exercise more local power than capital; but it does show that the kind of flexibility and individualism that has apparently been designed to help employers may end up offering more benefits to the contract workers. The use of the psychological contract as a framework within which to consider these issues provides us with a basis for understanding the individual impact of the new employment relations.

The final issue to return to is the use of HR practices. Recent evidence from national surveys of workplace and company level practice still shows a generally low take-up of HR practices. In non-union settings, managers do not choose to introduce the kind of progressive practices often shown to be associated with benefits to both company and employees. And confirming this last point, the evidence also convincingly shows that workers report a more positive psychological contract and are generally more satisfied, committed and motivated where there are more HR practices in place.

SOME CONCLUSIONS

This chapter has considered some developments in British industrial relations, drawing heavily on what Marginson (1998) has termed the 'survey tradition' in industrial relations research, and reported evidence to suggest that management is now in the driving seat in most organizations, more particularly in the private sector. By considering HRM *and* industrial relations, there is an implication that the unions and possibly other workers' representatives may be invited along for the ride. Management will certainly not trust them to do any driving. They may be invited into the front seat in a form of partnership to offer guidance and feedback on the way. They may help to ensure that management takes and stays on the 'high road'. However, most unions will be permitted, and sometimes seek no more than a back-seat driver role, offering occasional reactions but often ignored.

We have also considered HRM *or* industrial relations, and in particular considered the growing number of organizations and workplaces where there is no collective or representational activity of any sort. In these cases, it has been argued, we need new analytic tools with which to explore the employment relationship. One possibility which has some utility is the psychological contract. It captures elements of the individualization of the relationship and allows us to examine the impact of management policy and practice, including HRM, on employee attitudes and behaviour. Although the term can be defined in various ways, it has been suggested that in this context it can usefully be seen as a form of evaluation by workers of management policy and practice with particular reference to fairness, trust and delivery of promises. These are core issues that have always been implicit in the employment relationship.

One of the important and persistent findings from research is the low adoption of 'high commitment' or progressive human resource practices, particularly in the private sector. This is found in studies at both workplace and organization levels. Indeed the only hint of an exception is when employees themselves report on their experiences. However, this may be a function of the evaluative component built into some of these employee assessments; to take an extreme example, in one survey (Guest and Conway 1997) employees were asked whether there were 'sufficient opportunities for training and development' and 84 per cent said 'Yes'. They may judge 'sufficient' to be a very low level of training, reflecting the typically low value placed on training and development in British industry. They therefore report that appropriate training and development is in place, whereas questions directed to personnel managers about more objective indicators of training practice (about which workers could not reasonably be expected to be accurately aware) might reveal a very different picture. What the low take-up of practices means is that although much attention has been devoted to the impact of HRM on workers' attitudes and behaviour and on organizational performance, and the evidence on this tends to be positive, only a minority of organizations are reaping the potential benefits. On the HR dimension in our analysis, most organizations score low. It appears that although management may be in the driving seat, they are not behaving like sensible drivers. This gives unions an opportunity. Our analysis has shown that beliefs about the benefit of a union presence were higher where management had failed to introduce many HR practices; this may offer unions an opportunity. Doing so is likely to benefit workers by reducing arbitrary management and encouraging the introduction of more HR practices.

At the end of the day, however, we must recognize that many organizations, perhaps even a majority in the private sector, fall into a category variously labelled 'Bleak House' or the 'Black Hole' where there is a low level of HR and no union presence. An analysis of these types of workplace (Guest and Conway 1999) highlights two key points. First, they are not an undifferentiated mass. They contain a large number of quite small organizations where managers may behave as tyrants or may display benevolent paternalism. In the latter, scope for a form of informal and personal management has precluded any need for systematic application of HR practices or any felt need for representation. Indeed, Edwards (2000) in an analysis of responses by small firms to the minimum wage legislation, indicates that where relations are good, a form of collusion between management and workers may arise to circumvent the implementation of the minimum wage. It is interesting to note that the state of the psychological contract is consistently more positive in smaller organizations and workplaces. Yet, on average, those working in these 'black hole' organizations report a poorer psychological contract, lower satisfaction and commitment and much higher propensity to quit. In short, many are not very attractive places to work.

Our analysis at the outset can now be taken a little further by filling in the boxes in the simple model of HRM and industrial relations. It has been shown that the optimistic variant of the new industrial relations, the 'high/high' partnership organization or workplace is rare and, based on WERS, accounts for no more than one per cent of private sector workplaces in Britain. It is considerably higher in the public sector and may therefore account for up to 20 per cent of workplaces. However, there is no suggestion that partnership is widespread in the public sector or that these public sector workplaces reflect a form of sophisticated management. We have also shown, again based on survey evidence at workplace and organization level, that the HRM-oriented form of individualism applies in only a minority of workplaces. Optimistically, this might fall between 15 to 20 per cent. There are probably a similar number of workplaces where there is a union presence and low uptake of HRM. This leaves almost half of all organizations, and possibly a majority in the private sector that fall into the black hole.

What this implies is that management is not doing a very good job of managing its human resources. The popular cliché that 'people are our most important asset' is patently untrue; indeed in a recent survey of chief executives, this was more or less admitted (Guest *et al.* 2000c). There is therefore still a major challenge for trade unions. In most cases management will do what it can to keep them out. But where there is bad management, they will often be welcomed by employees. This is not on the basis of partnership but on the traditional grounds of providing representation and pressure for a better deal. Scope for partnership may come later, but that is a different game and it is an illusion on the part of government and others to believe that it is the only appropriate game in town. Management in too many organizations has failed to use its control to introduce the kind of human resource management that might be of benefit to both workers and the organization. They need pushing. There is still a strong case for some good, traditional but very necessary industrial relations.

REFERENCES

Bacon, N. and Storey, J. (2000) 'New employment strategies: Towards individualism or partnership', *British Journal of Industrial Relations*, **38**(3): 407–27.

Brown, W., Deakin, S. Hudson, M., Pratten, C. and Ryan, P. (1999) 'The implications of individualization for statutory trade union recognition'. Paper presented to BUIRA conference on the 1998 Workplace Employee Relations Survey, Cumberland Lodge, Windsor.

Cully, M. Woodland, S., O'Reilly, A. and Dix, G. (1999) *Britain at Work*, London: Routledge.

Delaney, J. and Huselid, M. (1996) 'The impact of human resource management practices on perceptions of organizational performance', *Academy of Management Journal*, **39**(4): 949–69.

Deery, S. and Iverson, R. (1999) 'The impact of industrial relations climate, organizational commitment, and union loyalty on organizational performance: a longitudinal analysis', *Proceedings of the 59th Academy of Management Conference*, Chicago, Ill.

Edwards, P. (2000). 'Small firms and the national minimum wage', *The Future of Work Bulletin*, No. 1: 1–3, Swindon: ESRC.

Green, F., Machin, S. and Wilkinson, D. (1996) 'Trade unions and training practices in British workplaces', *CEP Discussion Paper No. 278*, London: LSE Centre for Economic Performance.

Guest, D. (1995) 'Human resource management, trade unions and industrial relations', in J. Storey (ed.) *Human Resource Management: A Critical Text*, London: Routledge.

Guest, D. (1998) 'Is the psychological contract worth taking seriously?', *Journal of Organizational Behaviour*, **19**: 649–64.

Guest, D. (1999) 'Human resource management: The workers' verdict', *Human Resource Management Journal*, **9**(3): 5–25.

Guest, D. and Conway, N. (1998) *Fairness at Work and the Psychological Contract*, London: IPD.

Guest, D. and Conway, N. (1999) 'Peering into the black hole: The downside of the new employment relations in the UK', *British Journal of Industrial Relations*, **37**(3): 367–89.

Guest, D. and Conway, N. (2000) *Change at Work and the Psychological Contract*, London: IPD.

Guest, D. and Hoque, K. (1996) 'The impact of national ownership on human resource management practices and outcomes in UK greenfield sites', *Human Resource Management Journal*, **6**(4): 50–74.

Guest, D., Conway, N., Briner, R. and Dickmann, M. (1997) *The State of the Psychological Contract in Employment*, London: IPD.

Guest, D., Mackenzie Davey, K. and Patch, A. (2000a) 'The employment relationship, the psychological contract and knowledge management: Securing employees trust and contribution'. *Proceedings of the Knowledge Management: Concepts and Controversies Conference*, Warwick University, 9–10 February 2000.

Guest, D., Michie, J., Sheehan, M. and Conway, N. (2000b) *Employment Relations, HRM and Business Performance: An Analysis of the 1998 Workplace Employee Relations Survey*, London: IPD.

Guest, D., Michie, J., Sheehan, M., Metochi, M. and Conway, N. (2000c) *Human Resource Management and Performance: First Findings from the Future of Work Study*, London: IPD.

Guest, D. and Peccei, R. (1998) *The Partnership Company*, London: IPD.

HMSO (1998) *Fairness at Work*. Command No. 3968. Government White Paper, London: HMSO.

Heery, E. (1998) 'The relaunch of the Trades Union Congress', *British Journal of Industrial Relations*, **36**(3): 339–60.

Heller, F., Pusic, E., Strauss, G. and Wilpert, B. (1998) *Organizational Participation: Myth and Reality*, Oxford: OUP.

Heyes, J. and Stuart, M. (1998) 'Bargaining for skills: Trade unions and training at the workplace', *British Journal of Industrial Relations*, **36**(3): 459–67.

Hoque, K. and Noon, M. (1999) 'Counting angels: the personnel/human resource function in the UK. Evidence from the 1998 Workplace Employee Relations Survey'. Paper presented to the Dutch HRM Network Conference, Rotterdam, 19 November 1999.

Involvement and Participation Association (IPA) (1997) *Towards Industrial Partnership: New Ways of Working in British Companies*, London: IPA.

Kelly, J. (1999), 'British social partnership agreements: who wins, who loses?'. Paper presented to the LSE Industrial Relations Department Seminar, June 1999.

Kochan, T. and Osterman, P. (1994) *The Mutual Gains Enterprise*, Boston, Mass.: Harvard Business School Press.

Marginson, P. (1998) 'The survey tradition in British industrial relations research: an assessment of the contribution of large-scale workplace and enterprise surveys', *British Journal of Industrial Relations*, **36**(3): 361–88.

McLoughlin, I. and Gourlay, S. (1992) 'Enterprises without unions: The management of employee relations in non-union firms', *Journal of Management Studies*, **29**(5): 669–91.

Monks, J. (1998) 'Foreword', in C. Mabey, D. Skinner and T. Clark (eds), *Experiencing Human Resource Management*, London: Sage.

Peters, T. and Waterman, R. (1984) *In Search of Excellence*, New York: Harper and Row.

Rousseau, D. (1995) *Psychological Contracts in Organizations*, Thousand Oaks, CA: Sage.

Sisson, K. (1993) 'In search of HRM', *British Journal of Industrial Relations*, **31**(2): 201–10.

Towers, B. (1997) *The Representation Gap: Change and Reform in the British and American Workplace*, Oxford: Oxford University Press.

Tremlett, N. and Collins, D. (1999) *Temporary Employment in Britain*, London: DfEE Research Report RR100.

Undy, R. (1999), 'New Labour's 'Industrial Relations Settlement': The Third Way? Annual Review Article', *British Journal of Industrial Relations*, **37**(2): 315–36.

ACKNOWLEDGEMENT

Some of the material in this paper draws on work connected with an ESRC ROPA award (R022250141) 'Re-conceptualising the employment relationship: The case of the knowledge worker'. The Chartered Institute of Personnel and Development also provided funding to support the analysis of the Workplace Employee Relations Survey. Neil Conway and Adrian Patch assisted in the data analyses. I acknowledge the support of these organizations and individuals.

7 HRM and its Link with Strategic Management

Randall S. Schuler, Susan E. Jackson and John Storey

INTRODUCTION

The nature of the linkage between human resource management and business strategy has attracted considerable interest over a long period (Schuler and MacMillan 1984; Purcell 1989, 1995; Pfeffer 1998; Schuler and Jackson 1997; Storey 1992; Gratton, 1999, 2000). In this chapter we seek to move the debate forward by further developing the nature of HRM's strategic role and contribution.

One of the most dominant approaches during the last 20 years has been the attempt to build models that link human resources with broader aspects of the firm, for example the life cycle of the firm; its need for and ability to gain competitive advantage; or its type of competitive strategy. These discussions have been useful in expanding our awareness of the links between human resources management and strategic management and in offering insights into the rationale for the linkage. For example, the model that links human resource practices and competitive strategies is based on the rationale that particular employee *behaviours* are needed for each type of competitive strategy and these behaviours can be attained with different human resource practices.

Many models of strategic human resource management focus on some part of the implementation component of strategic management. Taken singly, however, they underestimate the impact of human resource management and underdescribe the rationale for this impact. What we would like to do in this chapter is offer a framework that both enlarges our perspective on the impact of human resource management and broadens the rationale for that impact. Consistent with the recent work in the field, we incorporate and build upon the work in strategic management. We also incorporate examples of human resource management activities that reflect this enlarged perspective of the impact of managing human resources. The chapter is divided into three major sections. The first section describes the activities of strategic management *formulation* and their HR implications. The second section describes the activities of strategy *implementation* and their HR implications. The third section describes some of the implications of strategic human resource management for the *roles and competencies* of HR professionals.

STRATEGIC MANAGEMENT COMPONENTS

While a great many models of human resource management have focused on some part of strategy implementation or execution, the impact of managing human resources is to be found in both *formulation and implementation* of strategy. This can be highlighted using Thompson and Strickland's (1998) framework of strategic management. In their framework there are five major activities of strategic management.

- Deciding what business the company will be in, forming a strategic vision, offering a set of values and a general strategy.
- Identifying strategic business issues and setting strategic objectives.
- Crafting strategic plans of action.
- Developing and implementing the strategic plans of action for functional units.
- Evaluating, revising and refocusing for the future.

These five activities can be roughly grouped into strategy formulation (the first three) and strategy implementation (the last two). The relationships between these activities and the implications for human resource management are illustrated in Figure 7.1.

Strategy formulation

As Figure 7.1 shows, strategy formulation activities can be further broken down into activities that focus on the firm as a whole (the boxes on the left) and activities specific to managing human resources (the boxes on the right). Furthermore, firm-based activities both determine HR strategy formulation and implementation activities and are partially affected by those activities (as shown by the dotted-line arrows). These linkages are described in more detail below.

Establishing the vision, mission, values and general strategy

A *vision* is management's view of the kind of company it is trying to create, and its intent to stake out a particular business position. At American Express, the vision is 'to become the world's most respected service brand'. And, Southwest Airline's vision is 'to be the airline of choice'. Each of these vision statements has an impact on managing human resources. Similarly, the success of each company in pursuit of its vision rests in part upon employees: for Southwest to be the airline of choice, employees (i.e. associates) have to be treated well enough to satisfy their customers.

A *mission* statement defines a company's business and provides a clear view of what the company is trying to accomplish for its customers. The mission of Merck Pharmaceuticals is to provide society with superior products and services – innovations and solutions that improve the quality of life and satisfy customer needs – to provide employees with meaningful work and advancement opportunities and investors with a superior rate of return. State Farm Insurance state that their mission is to:

- Provide quality insurance products.
- Offer friendly policyholder service.
- Settle claims fairly and quickly.
- Charge reasonable rates for insurance products.
- Maintain financial stability to fulfil commitment to policyholders.
- Uphold the State Farm marketing partnership.

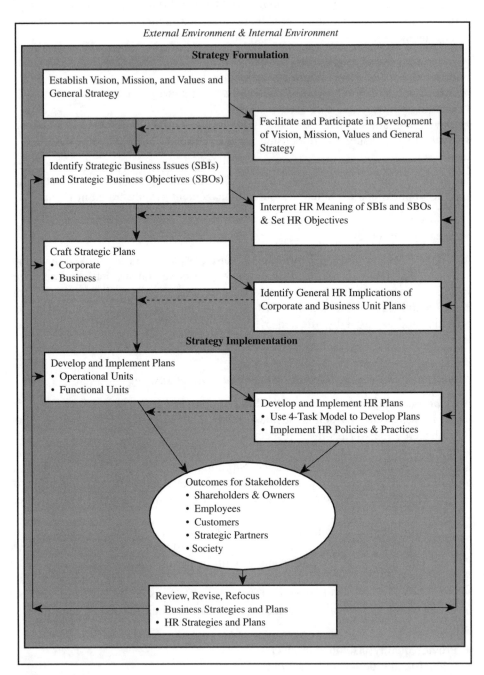

Figure 7.1 The strategic management process and its implications for human resource management

Each one of these mission statements, if it is to be enacted, requires a corresponding set of behaviours. These behavioural requirements, in turn, imply a distinctive set of human resource management practices.

Values are the strong enduring beliefs and tenets that the company holds dear – they help to define the company and differentiate it from other companies. The values of State Farm Insurance include:

- providing customers with the best possible service and value,
- building lasting relationships among customers, agents, employees and communities through respect, understanding and mutual trust,
- being financially strong, and
- keeping promises by always dealing fairly and with integrity.

These values have a direct impact on managing human resources. While similar to culture, values have a broader coverage, and are more enduring. According to Thompson and Strickland, developing the desired culture becomes an important activity in strategy implementation.

Statements of *general strategy* portray how the company plans to pursue its vision and mission. At American Express, their general strategy is to use both traditional and non-traditional distribution channels, to provide quality products supported by superior customer service. This enables American Express to build long-lasting relationships with customers and business partners.

Implications of the vision, mission, values and general strategy for HR

The organization's vision, mission, and values convey to employees answers to questions such as: Where are we going? Why are we going there? And how will we get there? The answers to these questions are of major importance when managing human resources. Consequently, the HR leader and staff need to be involved in the creation, maintenance and revision of the organization's vision, mission, values and general strategy. HR professionals can help ensure that other managers behave in ways that are consistent with the corporate vision, mission and values. They also can facilitate their inclusion in the identification and articulation of the strategic business issues and objectives.

Identifying strategic business issues and setting strategic business objectives

As shown in Figure 7.1, the second set of activities during strategic management formulation is the identification of strategic business issues (SBIs) and the setting of strategic business objectives (SBOs). During this phase of strategy formulation, the general strategy is further developed.

Strategic business issues are those issues, which if not resolved through effective strategic plans, will have significant negative consequences on the firm. Associated with strategic business issues are more specific, measurable objectives. Together, SBIs and SBOs focus the activities and energies of the firm. They also shape and define the strategic management tasks associated with strategy implementation.

Identifying strategic business issues and setting strategic business objectives involves deciding upon what is most important for the company to focus on consistent with the corporate vision, mission and general strategy. For example, at

American Express, the general strategy of providing quality products supported by superior customer service surfaces strategic issues such as the need to:

- become more globally competent;
- grow through successful acquisitions;
- become more innovative;
- enhance customer focus and solutions orientation.

An example of a strategic business objective associated with the need to become more innovative might be 'to develop ten new products per quarter during the next twelve months'. A strategic objective associated with becoming more globally competent and growing through successful acquisitions might be 'to acquire operations that support 20% growth in the Asia Pacific region within two years'.

Companies whose managers set objectives for each key strategic issue and then aggressively pursue actions calculated to achieve their performance targets typically outperform companies whose managers have good intentions, try hard and hope for success (Brews and Hunt 1999). This relationship was captured in the observation that 'You cannot manage what you cannot measure; and what gets measured gets done' (Bill Hewlett, Co-founder Hewlett-Packard). Typically strategic business objectives are the part of the strategic plan most often spelled out explicitly and communicated to managers and non-managers.

As shown in Figure 7.1, identifying and specifying strategic business issues and objectives is based upon the activities coming before. The specific SBIs and SBOs, however, reflect much more detail at the corporate and business unit levels than does the initial identification of a general strategy. The process of identifying the SBIs and SBOs is likely to highlight numerous implications for human resource management, as well as all functional areas in the company. These are then articulated even more during the process of strategy implementation.

Implications of SBOs and SBIs for HR

The SBOs and SBIs help focus attention on several important aspects of managing employees, including (a) the number of employees that will be needed as a consequence of anticipated growth, (b) new competencies and behaviors that will be required as a consequence of aspiring to provide higher quality customer service, and (c) higher levels of productivity needed as a consequence of identifying the reduction of operating costs as an objective. The precise way that HR responds to the requirements of SBIs and SBOs is determined during the development of HR plans. Before specific HR plans can be developed, however, corporate and business level plans must be developed.

Crafting strategic plans

The third activity required for strategic management formulation is the crafting of specific plans. This involves deciding how the vision, mission, values, general strategy, and the strategic issues and objectives are going to be achieved. According to Thompson and Strickland (1998), developing a strategic plan helps:

- Achieve strategic issues and objectives.
- Out-compete rivals.

- Achieve competitive advantage.
- Make strategic vision/mission a reality.
- Strengthen business in the marketplace.
- Address multiple stakeholders' needs.

Combining a vision, mission and statement of general strategy with strategic issues and objectives and a general strategy constitutes the essentials of a strategic plan. Typically, a good strategic plan is based on an analysis of the economy and industry in which the firm competes. It identifies sources of competitive advantage and the success factors that are critical to long-term effectiveness (Porter 1985). It analyses the existing and potential competition, assesses company strengths, weaknesses and core competencies. All of these are used as the basis for developing specific plans of actions intended to ensure the firm achieves its strategic objectives.

Making these activities a bit more complex is the reality that there are two levels of strategy formulation: corporate and business. 'Corporate strategy' concerns how a diversified company intends to establish business positions in different industries and the actions and approaches employed to improve the performance of the group of businesses the company has diversified into. Primary strategy-making concerns include the following:

- Ensuring the company is planning for the future.
- Building and managing a high-performing portfolio of business units (making acquisitions, strengthening existing business positions, divesting businesses that no longer fit into management's plans, entering into joint ventures and other strategic alliances).
- Capturing the synergy among related business units and turning it into competitive advantage.
- Establishing investment priorities and steering corporate resources into businesses with the most attractive opportunities.
- Reviewing/revising/unifying the major strategic approaches and moves proposed by business-unit managers.

'Business strategy' concerns the actions and the approaches crafted by management to produce successful performance in one specific line of business: the central business strategy issue is how to build a stronger long-term competitive position. Primary strategy-making concerns at the business level include:

- Interpreting changing market conditions.
- Devising moves and approaches to compete successfully and to secure a competitive advantage.
- Selecting competitive strategies.
- Forming responses to changing external conditions.
- Uniting the strategic initiatives of key functional departments.

Identifying the general HR implications of corporate and business unit plans

Once corporate and business level plans have been developed, the HR implications become more clear. For example, if corporate plans call for involvement in mergers and acquisitions, HR may need to develop the competencies needed for their involvement in 'soft' due diligence activities, in order to assess the compatibility of potential new partners in terms of corporate culture and specific HR policies and practices. If corporate plans call for improving the organization's learning capacity, HR may be called upon to help the various businesses learn from each other and derive more synergies from their common membership in the larger corporate entity. If corporate plans call for involvement in joint ventures, HR will need to become involved in all of the activities required to staff the new organization and ensure its success as a new organization (Schuler 2000).

Similarly, business unit plans are likely to have numerous implications for managing human resources. For businesses that are in industries undergoing rapid change, HR policies and practices may need to be continually adjusted to address changing industry and labour market conditions. For businesses that are moving from one life cycle stage into another (e.g. from rapid growth to mature, or from mature into decline), the focus of HR's activities also is likely to shift. For example, during the growth stage, the constant need for new talent focuses HR's attention on staffing and training, but as the business matures, attention is likely to shift to focus more on maximizing motivation and improving efficiencies.

Work linking human resource practices to the firm has often been rooted here, particularly in relationship to the competitive strategy selected. Porter's (1985) work applied to human resources by Schuler and Jackson (1987) and the work as applied to marketing by Treacy and Wiersma (1997), illustrates the direct impact on managing human resources through employee behaviours needed to implement the specific competitive strategy selected. Porter's work, however, also has implications for the strategy selection decision, i.e. if the existing human resource practices already elicit customer service behaviours, it may be more efficient to select a more competitive strategy of customer intimacy rather than switch to a product leadership strategy. Thus, Porter's model suggests that HR issues both flow from and partly determine a firm's approach to gaining competitive advantage at the level of business units.

Having described the three major sets of strategy formulation activities and their implications for HR, we move next to the activities involved in strategy implementation. At this point, the HR function begins to work through the specific implications of strategic decisions in much greater detail.

Strategy implementation

As Figure 7.1 shows, strategy implementation involves two sets of activities:

- developing and implementing strategic plans for functional units, and
- reviewing, revising, and refocusing for the future.

Developing and implementing strategic plans for functional units

Corporate and business-level plans provide the context within which plans are created for various functional activities, including marketing, human resources, research and development, manufacturing, finance, and so on. As illustrated in Figure 7.1, the development of specific HR plans occurs after HR has interpreted the meaning of each prior phase of strategy formulation. In this section we focus on crafting and implementing HR plans.

Developing and implementing HR plans

The HR implications of corporate and business plans are crystallized through the process of developing and implementing HR plans. The HR plans provide a blueprint to follow in order to fulfil the primary responsibilities of the HR function, which are: (1) ensuring that the organization has the appropriate number of people at the appropriate time and with an understanding of the vision, mission, values and strategy of the firm, and with an awareness and ability to pursue multiple opportunities in the firm; (2) ensuring that these people have the appropriate competencies to perform the jobs and roles in the organization; (3) ensuring that these people are performing their jobs and roles with the behaviours consistent with the organization and appropriate to the strategic business objectives; and (4) ensuring that these people are performing at the desired level of day-to-day productivity; are being attracted to the organization in sufficient numbers; and are willing to stay with the organization.

Using the Four-task Model to develop HR plans

The primary responsibilities of the human resource function constitute the core of the Four-Task Model of Human Resource Management. Stated more succinctly, the four main tasks of HR are:

- managing employee assignments and opportunities;
- managing employee competencies;
- managing employee behaviours;
- managing employee motivation.

These four main tasks are the *raison d'être* of human resource management. Together they provide the logic that guides the choice of specific human resource management policies and practices. Because the Four-task Model provides a framework for developing appropriate HR policies and practices, we describe it in some detail first.

MANAGING EMPLOYEE ASSIGNMENTS AND OPPORTUNITIES

Organizations need to have the right number of people at the right place at the right time. This classic adage of human resource planning is a fundamental component of 'employee assignments'. A critical part of the employee assignment task is deciding where to find the people needed, e.g. internally, externally, from the local area, or from other regions. Additionally, there is the decision of whether to outsource the recruitment and selection process. Helping employees make the transition into the organization is also included in this task. Employees entering the firm need to be aware of the vision, mission, values and general strategy of the organization. To fully utilize the competencies, behaviours and motivation levels of these employees, organizations need to provide opportunities for interaction, learning, sharing of knowledge and information, and the chance to work together effectively. Some of the questions that must be addressed to be effective in this task are:

- What number and type of employees are needed, with what qualifications?
- Where are they needed, and when?
- Where will they come from?

● What opportunities for growth, development, and rewards will attract them to the organization?

MANAGING EMPLOYEE COMPETENCIES

The second HR task is ensuring that individuals have the needed skills, knowledge and abilities to perform successfully. Systematic selection based upon job analyses linked with an organizational analysis, helps ensure that the appropriate skills, knowledge and abilities for all jobs and roles are known. Anticipating and planning for future jobs and organizational roles are also necessary to help ensure that employees in the future will be positioned (adequately trained) to have the appropriate competencies. Ensuring that the needed competencies are available requires answering questions such as:

● What competencies do employees have now?
● What new competencies will be needed in the future?
● What competencies will be less important in the future?
● Which specific employees need which specific competencies?
● Can/should needed competencies be purchased or developed?

MANAGING EMPLOYEE BEHAVIOURS

The third task is identifying and ensuring that employees exhibit the appropriate behaviours. Because behaviours often reflect attitudes, values and knowledge, this task requires understanding how these are related to specific behaviours. Increasingly, employee behaviours are seen as instrumental in fulfilling the needs of the firm, given its competitive strategy and the expectations of important stakeholders. For example, a customer-focused-solutions orientation may require employees to initiate discussion non-defensively, respond to questions, and offer further assistance. Working effectively in teams requires coordinating with others, and so on. Questions to be addressed for this task include:

● What behaviours does the organizational culture value?
● What behaviours are detrimental to the strategy and need to be eliminated or modified?
● How do employees' behaviours affect customers' buying patterns and satisfaction?

MANAGING EMPLOYEE MOTIVATION

There are three areas of interest when considering employee motivation:

1. The willingness to perform (effort). Substantial human resource staffing gains can be captured if employees are motivated to perform at a 90 per cent level of productivity, rather than, say, 75 per cent. Productivity improvements may require employees to work harder, longer, and/or smarter.
2. The willingness to stay with the firm when needed by the firm (retention). Retaining employees who possess the needed competencies, exhibit the

appropriate behaviours, and perform at high levels of productivity are critical to the success of the firm. Unplanned exits by these employees is thus uppermost for many firms. High retention rates enable firms to implement human resource policies and practices with a longer-term time horizon, e.g. career development, management development, and internal succession planning.

3. The willingness to work at the agreed upon time and place (reliability). Lower rates of absence permit an organization to enjoy more favourable staffing levels. Absences that can be anticipated, while still impacting staffing levels, may be less disruptive to offering high levels of customer service than unanticipated absenteeism. Overall worker productivity and compensation costs are also influenced by tardiness, almost as much as by absenteeism, particularly when unplanned. Tardiness immediately reduces the workforce, thus initiating action for temporary replacement, especially in a lean, efficient work system. Without such replacement, customer service is likely to be impaired, and even with a replacement, is likely to be compromised.

Thus, ensuring that employees meet the firm's motivational needs involves answering questions such as:

- How much more effort are employees willing and able to give?
- What is the optimal length of time for employees to stay with the firm?
- Can production costs or customer service be improved by reducing absence and tardiness?

HR policies and practices

HR policies and practices should be chosen to support the implementation of strategic business plans. In the context of the Four-task Model, HR policies and practices drive the actions required to fulfil the needs of the firm as specified by these plans and the strategic business issues and objectives associated with them. It is the linkage of HR policies and practices to the firm's strategic business objectives and plans that defines strategic human resource management and differentiates it from the older practice of personnel management (Schuler 1992). The major categories of HR policies and practices include:

- planning
- recruitment and selection
- training and development
- performance management
- compensation
- health and safety
- union–management relationships
- organizational change and design.

To be used effectively, the specific content of each of these policies and practices should be designed to address the four tasks of human resource management. The systematic consideration of the role each plays in achieving the four HR tasks ensures that policies and practices in all areas are both integrated with each other and linked with the firm's strategic business objectives and plans, in the context of the firm's vision, mission, values and general strategy.

To ensure that these policies and practices are implemented effectively, it is important to (a) explicitly articulate the assumptions being made when developing specific HR practices, and (b) specify the major challenges that need to be addressed in order to successfully implement the HR plans and state how these will be overcome. Table 7.1 illustrates some of the assumptions and challenges that might be associated with the design of just one HR practice – that of performance management. Listed in the table are specific actions that could be taken to ensure that the performance management practices address the Four Tasks for which HR is responsible. (A complete analysis would involve working through the assumptions

Table 7.1 Implementation issues: performance management

HR tasks	What HR actions?	Assumptions being made	Major challenges and actions
Employee Assignments and Opportunities	• Assess all aspects of current appraisal system • Utilize the job analysis to establish new performance criteria and standards that reflect process and results, both short term and long term	• All parts of the appraisal system influence an employees' performance • The success of appraisal systems depends upon lots of information	• Ensuring all parts are accounted for: being systematic and thorough in the assessment • Getting all the information: having a real partnership
Employee Competencies	• Performance appraisals need to be closely related to the new job design and analysis • Managers and employees will be trained to use the new appraisal • Appraisals may be designed for individual and team performance	• While motivation influences performance so does ability (P = f (AXM)) • The new KSAs required can be learned by most through training • Not all employees will be able to learn all new KSAs • Team performance is critical to success	• Ensuring that employees are capable and motivated: having line managers regard appraisal as a daily activity • Getting managers to use the new appraisals: establish rewards and punishments for their use • Ensuring people work in teams: appraise it
Employee Behaviours	• The new appraisal system will have to measure these behaviours • Tailor the appraisals to the job • Seek client input • Appraisals need to measure process and results	• Employees will exhibit the behaviours that are expected • Conflicts in the system may prevent employees from performing as expected • Process is as important as results	• Ensuring employees are aware: constant communication • Eliminating the problems in the system: analyse the system • Getting employees to be concerned with behaviours as well as results
Employee Motivation	• Develop extensive appraisal feedback • Appraisals will need to be done fairly • Valid appraisals need to be developed to identify how well employees are performing • Use appraisals for rewards and development	• Employees have a high need for where they stand and what's expected • 360 degree appraisal increases motivation and performance • Employees want fairness and due process • Employees are attracted to places that develop them	• Ensuring employees get feedback: appraise managers on giving feedback • Ensuring fairness: analyse the system for all possible causes of performance deficiencies • Getting managers to be fair and objective: train and reward them

and challenges associated with each of the four tasks for all of the other categories of policies and practices listed above.)

The example in Table 7.1 illustrates performance management issues for a firm that has identified 'developing a customer-focused, solutions-oriented' approach to doing business as a major strategic issue. Given this strategic issues, HR can probably anticipate the need for more performance data gathering and feedback. The change in needed employee competencies and behaviours will require new appraisal forms and processes. Managers will need new competencies to perform the appraisals. The HR department will have to facilitate 360° feedback. Recognizing that different jobs may require different behaviours, adaptable performance appraisal forms may be most useful to develop. Tying all the new appraisal forms to selection and compensation will help motivate employees to higher levels of productivity. Employees are more apt to remain with the company and outsiders will seek job applications. Appraisal will be instrumental in getting high levels of motivation, but it will likely need to be linked with compensation. Once employees have the ability to perform, they need evaluation, feedback and rewards to encourage them to actually use this ability to their highest level. The many specific HR actions affecting employee assignments, competencies, behaviours and motivation are outlined in Table 7.1.

Review, revise and refocus

The next activity of strategic management is reviewing the consequences of the strategy formulation and implementation process, evaluating the reactions of relevant stakeholders and deciding upon corrective actions or establishing new courses of action should the situation warrant (Kaplan and Norton 1996a and b; Marquardt 1997). Reviewing and evaluating require clear criteria against which to compare results. These criteria should reflect the results the firm hopes to achieve. The objective is not simply to evaluate whether plans have been carried out on schedule and within budget. Much more important is whether the actions taken have achieved the desired results. A complete review and evaluation consider all major stakeholders. Even if not formerly included in the evaluation processes, their voices are likely to be heard one way or the other. Figure 7.2 illustrates several key stakeholders and the concerns they are likely to have (Jackson and Schuler 2000).

The nature of the evaluation process regarding the attainment of the multiple stakeholder objectives is likely to be influenced by the nature of the strategic business objectives as well as characteristics of the internal and external environment (Jackson and Schuler 1990, 1995). The results of the evaluation process serve as input into decisions about how to revise the plans and may also alert managers to new strategic issues. Not surprisingly, human resource managers recognize that managing the change process – both individual change and organizational change – is one of their most significant tasks.

The success of new HR policies and practices needs to be systematically reviewed also, followed by revision and refocusing, if needed. This step in the strategic management process is essential for continuous learning and improvement. During this phase, HR analyses the reasons for any deficiencies in the organization's performances, as judged by each stakeholder group. Where deficiencies are found, the HR professionals must assess whether these are due to poor implementation of a good HR plan, or whether the original plan was itself flawed. Appropriate HR

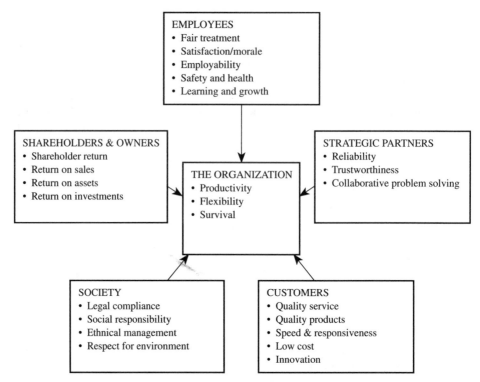

Figure 7.2 Organizational stakeholders and examples of their concerns

practices may be foiled by managers and subordinates who resist the changes needed. For example, managers may resist changing their leadership behaviours yet such changes may be essential to the successful implementation of new team-oriented HR practices and a culture of empowerment. Their subordinates may resist practices that require them to more actively evaluate and give feedback to their close colleagues and peers, fearing that this will disrupt friendships and create friction within the team.

Besides taking into account each of the relevant stakeholders, HR's review process must be sensitive to the dynamic nature of human reactions to change. On the one hand, early and frequent review can alert the organization to unanticipated disruptive reactions and enable early corrective action. On the other hand, however, it also is important to recognize that some deterioration in behaviour and performance is normal and to be expected immediately after major changes are implemented. Thus, it is incumbent upon HR to construct models that illustrate the changing consequences that can be expected over time in order to prevent incorrect evaluations and prevent premature revisions (Becker and Huselid 1998).

Clearly, the entire set of strategy formulation and strategy implementation activities required for HR to be a strategic player is both broad-ranging and quite complex. For HR professionals who are prepared to take on these challenges, these activities are exciting and rewarding. For many people working in this area, however, strategic human resource management requires developing some new competencies and adopting new attitudes of professionalism.

HR professionalism

The human resource department is the group formally established by an organization to help manage the organization's people as effectively as possible for the good of the employees, customers, the company, and society. HR professionals include external consultants and service providers with HR expertise. Co-ordinating the HR function is the responsibility of the HR leader. As suggested by our discussion of strategy formation and implementation processes, HR professionals need to be strategic players in order for organizations to effectively meet their key objectives and satisfy their major stakeholders.

By *strategic* we mean that HR activities should be systematically designed and intentionally linked to an analysis of the business and its context. In fact, the criticism of human resource management was not so much for the roles and responsibilities it was attempting to perform, as much as it was for the fact they were not connected to the day-to-day and long-term needs of the business. The current environment of the human resource profession calls for more than linking traditional activities with the business; it calls for doing more and different things, all of which are linked with the business and the concerns of all (Huselid, Jackson and Schuler 1997; Ulrich 1998). Examples of the various roles and responsibilities are shown in Table 7.2.

In the most competitive firms, HR professionals are becoming actively engaged throughout the entire process of strategy formulation and implementation. Compared to the past, when the personnel department served primarily administrative purposes, today HR professionals need a broader set of competencies. These include:

Table 7.2 Key roles and responsibilities for HR professionals

KEY ROLES	Responsibilities on the Job
Strategic Partner	• Shows concerns for multiple stakeholders, including employees, customers, shareholders and the society at large • Understands how money gets made, spent, and lost in a global context • Educates managers how the value of human resources and the consequences of managing people effectively (or ineffectively) impacts on the business
Innovator	• Helps the organization create an environment that supports continuous learning and creativity • Creates new approaches to managing people, and does not rely only on what others are doing
Collaborator	• Knows how to create win/win situations • Shares rather than competes • Works effectively across internal and external organizational boundaries
Change Facilitator	• Anticipates the need for change and prepares the organization for it • Thinks conceptually and articulates thoughts clearly • Execute changes in strategy • Energizes others to accept and embrace change

Business Competencies

- Industry knowledge
- Competitor understanding
- Financial understanding
- Global perspective/knowledge
- Strategic analysis
- Partner orientation
- Multiple stakeholder sensitivity.

Leadership Competencies

- Strategic visioning
- Managing cultural diversity
- Creator of learning culture
- Planning and decision-making skills
- Value shaper.

Change and Knowledge Management Competencies

- Network building
- Designing and working in flexible structures
- HR alignment
- Managing learning and knowledge transfer
- Consulting/Influencing
- Group/Process facilitation
- Organization development/effectiveness
- Managing large-scale change.

Professional/Technical Competencies

- Staffing
- Performance management
- Education/Development
- Remuneration/Reward systems
- Employee relations
- Employee communications
- Succession planning
- Union relations
- Safety/Health/Wellness
- Diversity management.

In addition to interpreting the meaning of business strategy for HR activities, the most effective HR professionals are able to conceptualize the role of effective human resource management in the organization and develop models to demonstrate their impact on outcomes about which managers care deeply. The Employee-Customer-Profit Chain model developed at Sears is an excellent example of the efficacy of models (Rucci, Kirn and Quinn 1998). The Four-task Model of Human Resource Management can facilitate this process by providing a framework for thinking through the role of human resource activities in achieving strategic objectives.

The competencies for HR professionals listed above are extensive. Can anyone really be expected to have all of these competencies? Alternatively, should anyone, particularly with the growing importance of managing human resources, be responsible for having all these competencies? Perhaps not. The evidence seems to suggest that increasingly human resource management responsibilities are shared, with activities being carried about through a partnership that includes line managers, HR professionals, employees, unions, customers, suppliers and outsourcers. While managing human resources today requires a substantial body of competencies, they are more likely to be found within a partnership, a team of colleagues, rather than within any one person, e.g. a human resource professional.

SUMMARY AND CONCLUSIONS

The field of human resource management has changed dramatically in recent years. Just as organizations have become more complex, dynamic, and fast-paced, so has the discipline of managing human resources. In addition, managing human resources has come to be seen as more important than ever. And in some, though by no means all organizations the human resource management function has responded to that challenge and as a consequence has made a real difference.

Fulfilling the importance of managing people in organizations is being done through linking human resource management with strategic management. In this chapter we have outlined how this linkage is articulated in organizations. Using Thompson and Strickland's five strategic management activities, we have suggested that human resource management can be linked with strategic management in both strategy implementation and strategy formulation tasks. Thus we have extended work done by others in the field of human resource management, particularly strategic human resource management, by offering a broader context in which activities associated with managing human resources can be linked with strategic management tasks. Figure 7.1 summarizes some of the implications for human resource management of the tasks of strategic management. These implications are presented to reflect bi-directionality, with human resource management concerns having an impact on strategic management tasks, as well as strategic management tasks having an impact on human resources activities.

Our discussion of the possible linkages between strategic management and human resource management is meant to just begin the conversation of how extensive the relationships are between these two disciplines. Following the five strategic management activities, we have shown how a variety of human resource activities and practices can be linked to both strategy formulation and strategy implementation. In doing this, we have also suggested that all human resource activities can be regarded as strategic – that is, all linked to the organization and the objectives of its multiple stakeholders. Finally, our discussion highlights the importance of a wide variety of competencies for required by HR professionals. Unless the HR leader and staff in an organization have the competencies needed to become effective partners in strategy formulation and implementation, the opportunities to create the linkages described in Figure 7.1 will be lost.

REFERENCES

Becker, B.E. and Huselid, M.A. (1998) 'High Performance Work System and Firm Performance: a Synthesis of Research and Managerial Implications', in G. Ferris (ed.) *Research in Personnel and Human Resource Management*, Greenwich, Conn.: JAI Press.

Brews, P.J. and Hunt, M.R. (1999) 'Learning to Plan and Planning to Learn: Resolving the Planning School/Learning School Debate', *Strategic Management Journal*, **20**: 889–913.

Gratton, L. (1999) *Human Resource Strategy*, London: Oxford University Press.

Gratton, L. (2000) *Living Strategy: Putting People at the Centre of Corporate Strategy*, London: FT Prentice Hall.

Huselid, M.A., Jackson, S.E. and Schuler, R.S. (1997) 'Technical and Strategic Human Resource Management Effectiveness as Determinants of Firm Performance', *Academy of Management Journal*, **40**: 171–88.

Jackson, S.E. and Schuler, R.S. (1990) 'Human Resource Planning: Challenges for Industrial/Organizational Psychologists', *American Psychologist*, **45**: 223–39.

Jackson, S.E. and Schuler, R.S. (1995) 'Understanding Human Resource Management in the Context of Organizations and their Environments', *Annual Review of Psychology*, **46**: 237–64.

Jackson, S.E. and Schuler, R.S. (2000) *Managing Human Resources: A Partnership Perspective*, Cincinnati, Ohio: South-Western Publishing.

Kaplan, R.S. and Norton, D.P. (Fall 1996a) 'Linking the Balanced Scorecard to Strategy', *California Management Review*, **39**: 53–79.

Kaplan, R.S. and Norton, D.P. (1996b) 'Using the Balanced Scorecard as a Strategic Management System,' *Harvard Business Review*, January–February: 75–85.

Marquardt, E.P. (1997) 'Aligning Strategy and Performance with the Balanced Scorecard', *ACA Journal*, Autumn: 18–27.

Pfeffer, J. (1998) *The Human Equation*, Boston: Harvard Business School Press.

Porter, M.E. (1985) *Competitive Advantage*, New York: Free Press.

Purcell, J. (1989) 'The Impact of Corporate Strategy on Human Resource Management', in J. Storey (ed.) *New Perspectives on Human Resource Management*, London: Routledge.

Purcell, J. (1995) 'Corporate Strategy and the Link with Human Resource Management', in J. Storey (ed.) *Human Resource Management: A Critical Text*, London: Routledge.

Rucci, A.J., Kirn, S.P. and Quinn, R.T. (1998) 'The Employee-Customer-Profit Chain at Sears', *Harvard Business Review*, March–April: 83–97.

Schuler, R.S. (1992) 'Strategic Human Resources Management: Linking the People with the Strategic Needs of the Business', *Organizational Dynamics*, Summer: 18–32.

Schuler, R.S. (2000) 'Human Resource Management Activities in International Joint Ventures', in J. Storey (ed.) *Human Resource Management: A Critical Text*, London: Thomson Learning.

Schuler, R.S. and Jackson, S.E. (1999) *Strategic Human Resource Management: A Reader*, London: Blackwell.

Schuler, R.S. and Jackson, S.E. (1987) 'Linking Competitive Strategies with Human Resource Management Practices', *Academy of Management Executive*, August: 207–19.

Schuler, R.S. and MacMillan, I.C. (1984) 'Gaining Competitive Advantage Through Human Resource Management Practices', *Human Resource Management*, **23**(3): 241–55.

Storey, J. (1992) *The Management of Human Resources*, Oxford: Blackwell.

Thompson, A.A. and Strickland, A.J. (1998) *Crafting and Implementing Strategy*, tenth edition. New York: McGraw Hill.

Treacy, M. and Wiersema, N. (1995) *The Discipline of Market Leaders*, Reading, MA: Addison-Wesley.

Ulrich, D. (1998) *Delivering Results: A New Mandate for Human Resource Professionals*, Boston: Harvard Business School Press.

Part 3
Key Practice Areas
of HRM

Employee Resourcing

Paul Iles

8

INTRODUCTION

Most treatments of employee resourcing (e.g. Taylor 1998: 1) see it as the core activity of generalist personnel and development work, involving 'effective hiring and firing, attracting the best candidates, reducing staff turnover and improving employee performance' and 'covering the range of methods and approaches used by employers in resourcing their organisations in such a way as to enable them to meet their key goals' (ibid.: 2). It involves the achievement of three fundamental activities: staffing, performance management and administration. Staffing objectives are concerned with ensuring that an organization is able to call on the services of sufficient numbers of staff to meet its objectives; it involves human resource planning (e.g. forecasting demand for employees and employee supply) and recruitment and selection (e.g. drawing up job descriptions and person specifications, recruiting and selecting new employees). Performance management is seen as concerned with managing absence and turnover, and monitoring and improving employee performance. 'Administration' is concerned with managing employment relationships in accordance with legal, ethical and professional principles. Taylor (ibid: 12), like many texts in this area, takes an avowedly practitioner perspective, with little emphasis on wider social perspectives or the interests of different stakeholders, and does not attempt to 'question the legitimacy of the employment relationship as it has developed in modern western society, excluding literature that takes a critical perspective on this and other issues'.

This chapter does not seek to cover what Taylor (1998) loosely terms 'administration', as this is an area which has not been the focus of much systematic theory and research. Texts in this area tend to offer advice, advocacy and prescription, or guidelines of 'best practice'. It does, however, cover aspects of performance management, but only those concerned with assessment and appraisal, rather than with setting development objectives, devising personal development plans, and introducing mentoring, coaching and counselling activities, all best viewed from the perspective of 'employee development' (see Chapter 9 in this volume) rather than 'employee resourcing'. It sees resourcing as essentially involving assessing, appraising, grading, tracking, sorting, sifting, and placing employees (and increasingly other kinds of workers) so as to make staffing and resourcing decisions. Since this is a core organizational process that occurs over time, it views 'career management' as a core resourcing activity, one often neglected in prescriptive accounts.

Often the study of employee resourcing has been left to occupational psychologists and personnel specialists alone, and has been insufficiently considered by organization theorists and organizational sociologists. (There are exceptions to this, e.g. Rose 1988; Hollway 1991; Silverman and Jones 1976; Salaman and Thompson 1978; Townley 1989, 1994; Windholf and Wood 1988.) This is unfortunate, particularly at a time when resourcing is increasingly seen as critical to managing large-scale processes of organizational change. Beaumont, for example, when arguing the 'enhanced potential importance' of the selection process, notes the role of *strategic selection*, wherein 'the design of a selection system supports the overall organisation strategy, the monitoring of the internal flow of personnel match emerging business strategies, and (there is) a need to match key executives to business strategies' (Beaumont 1993: 57). Yet despite the need for a fuller understanding of these processes, the bulk of existing social science and HR literature is concerned primarily and solely with assessing the efficiency of these processes, often in rather descriptive, prescriptive and atheoretical ways.

Yet such a concern does not exhaust the possible implications of these key organizational processes. They have a far wider significance, one of which is their role as the embodiment and operationalization of a form of expertise which critically defines the skills, values and qualities (or *competences*) required by modern forms of organization. Thus they both reveal and represent the form and direction of current forms of organizational change. These processes thus represent and reveal the working out of the play of power within organizations. In principle, and also in effect, contemporary processes of resourcing represent the moment when organizational restructuring meets and impacts on individuals, either as putative or actual employees. In so doing, they seek to define, understand, assess and place them in terms of organizationally-defined critical qualities. Resourcing is therefore the site of individual entry into – or rejection from – newly defined organizational roles. The issue therefore is not simply, or even perhaps primarily, one of efficiency or rationality, but of power: the capacity of, and the forms of knowledge and associated technologies through which organizations identify, define and assess individuals against structures of necessary competences or similar behavioural frameworks.

Townley (1989, 1994) has usefully noted that interest in more rigorous processes of resourcing can be seen not simply as related to a concern for more efficient staffing, but as, 'integral to what has been identified as HRM. The latter is understood as being characterized by an increasing emphasis placed on the attitudinal and behavioural characteristics of employees, factors which readily lend themselves to monitoring through selection and performance review' (Townley 1989: 92).

At a time when programmes of HRM inspired change encourage a focus on the 'organizational change lever' of employee resourcing, emphasizing the strategic significance of identifying and assessing key managerial and other competences to support structural change, it is imperative not only to describe what is happening in this area, but to understand its significance. As will be argued in the final section, it is necessary to get inside the structure of interrelated ideas, techniques and assumptions which comprise current models of resourcing and the qualities these schemes typically seek to identify, and to understand how they work to define the new employee and his/her necessary qualities.

More than this, the limitations of many psychological and personnel driven approaches to resourcing are that they are almost entirely, if understandably, concerned with improving the efficiency of the processes, and not with understanding their wider provenance and significance. They tend to focus on degrees of, and deviations from, scientific or technical or professional rationality; but they do not address the nature or implications of that rationality. Indeed, they are themselves part of the very discourse they describe, accepting the assumptions of the resourcing process and interested mainly in supplying technological improvements and evaluations. As Miller and Rose (1993) point out, this concern with efficiency and evaluation itself is an aspect of a particular conception of, and approach to, the 'government' of organizations. In the case of the subject matter of this chapter – employee resourcing – this process of *evaluation* occurs at a number of levels. First, it is absolutely fundamental to the processes of resourcing. Second, it is a key feature of the recent emphasis on identifying and assessing competences, which are often seen as a superior basis for managerial staffing. Third, the evaluation of evaluation processes (that is, the assessment of the validity of the assessment process) constitutes a major focus of much of the literature in the area, especially the psychometric literature concerned with the validity, reliability and utility of selection and assessment instruments.

The subject matter in this chapter therefore is the processes whereby modern organizations seek to recruit, select and deploy staff in a process of assessment, grading, sorting and sifting them in order to support the achievement of strategic objectives. The chapter has three purposes: to describe and explain developments and tendencies in employee resourcing; to relate these to prevalent directions of organizational change; and to address the ways in which these processes have been treated within the literature. The chapter does this by describing some major approaches to the understanding of these processes, from the psychometric to the strategic to the sociological. Although resourcing processes constitute its prime focus, the chapter seeks to do more than merely to offer an overview of current practice and issues in the field. The chapter is as interested in the ways in which these processes are understood and described as in how they are conducted. Crucially, it is interested in the inter-connections between the techniques of resourcing and the models which inform and explain these practices.

It will argue first, that recent changes in organizational systems and structures (of a sort often associated with the approach to organizational change known as Human Resource Management) are commonly associated with the search for recruits from within the organization, or outside it, with new attitudes, skills and experiences (or competences) as organizations make significant changes in their key capabilities. Current organizational emphasis on the systematic search, often *via* psychometric techniques, for individuals who display evidence of those competences is identified as critical to the newly defined performance of key managerial roles in particular, in furthering newly structured and focused organizations. This process reveals the nature of organizational change and the degree to which, and the manner in which, this change is centred round newly defined organizational employees. In the course of this discussion, a strategic framework for understanding employee resourcing is presented.

This discussion constitutes the first section. In the second section, some current trends in resourcing methods, with particular reference to human resource planning, recruitment, selection and assessment, performance management and career management, are discussed. In the third section, attention is focused on methods of identification and assessment of management competences, since this represents a major development in the constitution of the new manager in particular, and a major element in efforts to discover (or produce) individuals with the required managerial qualities. This section includes a discussion of job analysis as a process which underlies the identification of competences.

In section four a number of models of resourcing are considered. The first of these – the psychometric model – is fundamental to any understanding of the design of selection systems, selection methods and selection criteria, for it supplies their basic rationale. This is the approach which underpins 'scientific selection' (Hollway 1991; Rose 1985). The 'social process' model differs from this in focusing less on the individual as a set of stable qualities and rather more on selection itself as a process, wherein the individual him/herself is constructed. For example, one explanation of the often demonstrated high degree of validity of the assessment centre approach to identifying promotion potential may be that superior assessments are based on a recognition of the various qualities (not all formal or job-related) that are required for success in an organization; or that post-assessment centre judgements may be coloured by knowledge of the individual's performance in the assessment (Beaumont 1993); or that those who make assessments during the centre and those who make subsequent career or promotional judgements share similar organizational and managerial stereotypes.

One form of this social process approach simply notes the interplay between selection events, candidates' feelings and responses, and organizational outcomes, emphasizing the mutual adjustments and 'negotiations' that occur. A more radical form sees the 'candidate' and the selection decision as in various ways constructed by the process of selection and measurement. Thus assessment centres could be seen not as *discovering* potential, but as *defining and constructing* it.

The chapter concludes with some consideration of a radically different approach to the understanding of the resourcing process. The earlier models are in some way centred on a conception of the resourcing process in terms of its efficiency. The third approach eschews all concern with the *relevance* or *effectiveness* of the identified competence frameworks and those procedures which are designed to identify them, and instead offers a conception of these activities as part of a form of discourse of HRM which supports the process of government of the enterprise.

A STRATEGIC FRAMEWORK FOR UNDERSTANDING EMPLOYEE RESOURCING

In the late 1980s, as part of the move towards Human Resource Management, many organizations in North America and Europe began thinking of their resourcing processes as major levers to support strategic and cultural change. In part this was due to a growing conceptualization of strategic management as involving more than a search for product market-based competitive advantages. Underlying the development of specific products, with their limited life-cycles, was seen to be the acquisition and development of strategic skill pools, capabilities and core competencies. With the rise of skill-based competition (Klein *et al.* 1991), competitive advantage was increasingly seen as based on exploiting and developing the 'core competences' of the organization (Prahalad and Hamel 1990). Alongside this increased awareness of skill, capability and competence, and now increasingly knowledge, as keys to competitive advantage, and as major organizational assets and resources, has been the appreciation of the increased demands now being placed on managers and other key staff as a result of current organizational changes. Facing an increasingly difficult and demanding environment with increasing competitive pressures, many UK organisations took up a variety of HRM initiatives in order to encourage such apparently desirable qualities as initiative, pro-activity and entrepreneurialism (e.g. Storey and Sisson 1993).

As one way of delivering behaviours seen as necessary to support organizational strategies, resourcing initiatives have become increasingly important, alongside training and development, large scale cultural change, and total quality management and business re-engineering programmes. A particular focus has been on *management* as the key to organizational effectiveness, as it is the competency of managers that is seen to influence the return that an organization will secure from its investment in both human and material capital (e.g. Thomson *et al.* 2000). This concern has been most often expressed in the increasing emphasis given to managerial competences and to the need to identify the key managerial skills that underlie or underpin effective management performance. Once these underlying competences have been identified, recruitment and selection processes can then be installed to ensure that managers (and other staff) with the requisite skills and qualities are successfully attracted to the organization, assessed, placed in appropriate jobs or roles, and appraised, developed and rewarded against appropriate competency criteria (e.g. Boyatzis 1982; Bethell-Fox 1992).

This particular approach to resourcing will be considered in some detail later. At this point it is worth noting a number of examples of how UK organizations in the 1990s have revamped their resourcing strategies following strategic realignments and redefinitions of organizational mission and culture. New skills and competences required for managing in the new organization have often been specified, with people identified both externally and internally who display such qualities. Recruitment, selection and placement activities have then been undertaken to match such competence profiles with job demands and requirements.

In the personal financial services industry, increasing competition led to shifts in managerial roles from lenders and administrators to marketeers, sellers and entrepreneurs responsible for a wider range of products and services (Storey *et al.* 1999). Managerial jobs have become more outward looking, market-focused and team-orientated. Whilst technical competence has remained important, new commercial and managerial skills have become more central, requiring that such skills and qualities be more effectively identified, and more sophisticated techniques introduced to bring about improved linkages between business strategy, appraisal, staff development and recruitment and selection. Some companies recruit for specific basic entry-level technical jobs, and career paths are often viewed as needing to be more closely aligned with different business and product life-cycle needs (e.g. Gratton 1989; Robertson *et al.* 1991). Many banks also began to make extensive use of part-time and temporary staff in a search for both financial and numerical flexibility (Atkinson 1984), as well as instituting cultural and structural change programmes. These attempted to transform bureaucratic organizations stratified by grade and work roles, and hierarchically structured with narrow job tasks within cultures emphasizing deference, caution and loyalty to a paternalist employer into profit-centred, performance-orientated enterprises (e.g. Cressey and Jones 1992).

Since such a model 'demands quite different staff, with different qualities and outlooks' (ibid.: 70–71), it is hardly surprising that resourcing activities, including the assessment of internal staff for promotion, placement, transfer and development, loom large in many HRM initiatives. For example, many banks introduced large scale assessment programmes involving biodata, psychometric testing and assessment centres (Robertson *et al.* 1991).

In many manufacturing organizations, restructuring and job redesign have often demanded greater 'financial flexibility' and greater emphasis on multi-skilled teams working in flatter, delayered organizations. There has been a shift to promoting employee autonomy, self-monitoring and devolved decision making in less stable, more uncertain and more dynamic environments. This has led to greater emphasis on such skills and qualities as teamwork, openness, adaptability, broader vision, tolerance of ambiguity, self-confidence, a positive orientation to change, an ability to see multiple perspectives, a desire to improve, develop, and take on responsibility, and a wish to seek out and act on performance feedback. This has led to the greater use of structured interviews, work sample tests, self-assessment, assessment centres and psychometric tests.

Du Gay (1996) and du Gay and Salaman (1996) have analysed changes in the retail sector in the 1990s, but from a somewhat different perspective, one that we will develop in more depth later. Du Gay's main interest is in the way in which recent trends, such as increasing globalization, the feminization of the work force, the expansion of services and new modes of organizational conduct have blurred differences between production and consumption and the culturally ascribed identities of worker and consumer. This is partly because the relationship between service providers and consumers requires greater understanding of consumer needs and motivations. The modes of self-presentation and self-understanding required of people as consumers and employees are now little different. The growth of consumer culture, the perceived need to become 'close to the customer', and the stress within TQM in treating other employees as 'internal customers' mean that, increasingly, employees assume a 'customer' mindset, especially in retailing. In particular, there has been a greater emphasis on recruiting employees with strong interpersonal skills, such as empathy and communication skills, as well as on such entrepreneurial characteristics as managing budgets at all levels.

These developments have led to significant interest, by consultants and practitioners in particular, in the concept of 'emotional intelligence', mainly popularized by Goleman (1998). The argument is that emotional intelligence (EQ) is a more powerful predictor of leadership than IQ, which is seen as a threshold competence. Emotional intelligence is also seen in terms of emotional literacy or emotional competence, and is concerned with understanding one's own emotions and motivations and those of others. Despite practitioner and consultant enthusiasm, and the recent development of emotional intelligence questionnaires to assess EQ or EI, recent academic research has been considerably more cautious (e.g. Sternberg 1999; Planalp and Fitness 1999; Orloff 1999; Mayer 1999).

There have also been attempts to build strategic resourcing models, most urging greater linkage between HRM in general, and employee resourcing in particular, and corporate strategy (often adopting a rather naïve, apolitical, rational, conflict-free and unitarist view of strategy). Some attempt to relate resourcing activities to organizational structure, others to product life cycles or business life cycles, others to generic corporate strategies or product market strategies, such as cost-leadership, differentiation, quality or innovation strategies (e.g. Miles and Snow 1978; Porter 1985; Sonnenfeld and Peiperl 1988; Schuler and Jackson 1987). A 'matching' model is often implicit or explicit; as Williams and Dobson (1997: 319) put it, 'different strategies have different implications for the nature, role and importance of human resource management (HRM) and selection'. Resourcing practices are often seen as secondary processes, 'integrating' with business strategy in a rather reactive manner. However, more recent models, such as the resource-based view of strategy (e.g. Grant 1991; Kamoche 1996) offer more promise in developing more adequate strategic resourcing models.

Having outlined some of the ways British organizations in particular have attempted to respond to rapid environmental change by specifying the skills, qualities and competences required by employees and by introducing more sophisticated resourcing procedures, the chapter next reviews some recent trends in resourcing practice before critically examining general models of resourcing processes.

RECENT TRENDS IN RESOURCING PRACTICE

Human Resource Planning

In many prescriptive models of HRM, Human Resource Planning (HRP) is seen as the link between strategic business planning and strategic HRM. Especially relevant here is the recruitment and selection of specific numbers and types of employees and the specification of future job requirements and training needs so as to align them to strategic business plans. However, some authors use the term HRP to refer to essentially the same areas as the older terms 'manpower' or 'workforce' planning, but using a more modern, gender-neutral term (e.g. Taylor 1998). Others (e.g. Bramham 1994) see it as far wider, encompassing not just the 'hard' quantitative forecasting of labour supply and demand, but also embracing plans made across the whole range of HRM activity, including such apparently 'soft' issues as motivation, commitment and culture. The danger is that extending its use in this way tends to conflate HRP with HRM as a whole, and takes the specificity away from HRP as a discrete dimension of employee resourcing concerned with forecasting and assessing the extent to which the organization will meet its labour requirements (or perhaps increasingly its knowledge requirements, which may take the focus of HRP away from labour supply concerns to an interest in knowledge supply, and away from focusing on employees alone to emphasizing knowledge resources, chains and intermediaries).

The old 'manpower planning' sought to find ways of articulating organizational strategy through specific plans, with an emphasis on quantifiable data as a way of managing uncertainty. Just as business strategy and plans were expressed in numerical, measurable financial, marketing and production targets and objectives, for example, the manpower plan expressed personnel management's response, intended to ensure the necessary supply of people to meet set targets (e.g. Bratton and Gold 1999). In the rational model of manpower planning, three phases were identified: analysing manpower demand, predicting supply and designing the interaction between supply and demand to bridge the gap through acquiring, utilizing, retaining and reducing the organization's human resources. Drawing on operational research, employee resourcing was seen in terms of stocks and flows, with variables such as labour turnover, length of service, age distribution and promotion flows expressed in terms of statistical formulae, models and simulations in ways that only manpower analysts, rather than most line managers, could understand and use. Perhaps as a result, surveys in both the US (e.g. Nkomo 1988) and the UK (e.g. Pearson 1991; Cowling and Walters 1990) found little connection between strategic business planning and manpower planning, a failure to define or communicate business objectives to manpower planners, and a general lack of integration between the two planning activities. However, the planners themselves have tried to make their techniques more 'user friendly', assisted by the development of computerized human resource personnel information systems, able to help deal with such issues as tracking and forecasting absenteeism, retention and turnover. The emphasis has turned away from the rigidity of planning towards greater flexibility and towards viewing planning as a continuous process of diagnosis and action planning.

As with HRM in general, there have emerged 'hard' and 'soft' versions of HRP in the 1990s, (often in combination, as in the banking industry) as organizations adopt a variety of HRP practices in an opportunistic and pragmatic way (e.g. Storey *et al.* 1997). Often companies argue that the extent and rapidity of organizational and opportunistic environmental change – unstable business environments, globalization, the introduction of new technology, team-based working, outsourcing, the decline in the number of people on permanent contracts with defined jobs based on stable skill-sets and secure careers – has made planning, including human resource planning, problematic. Others argue that HRP is even more necessary in such circumstances, e.g. Bramham 1988: 7, who argues 'it is of course a paradox that as it becomes more difficult to predict and select, so it becomes more necessary to do so'. Others point to the inherently political nature of managerial decision-making interfering with rational planning, or the impossibility of accurately forecasting labour supply and demand based on past experience and past trends to predict future developments, or the role of 'discontinuities' in rendering planning of any kind redundant (e.g. Mintzberg 1994). HRP may thus impede the achievement of competitive advantage.

Recruitment strategies

Little systematic research has been done on the ways organizations go about actually attracting candidates to apply for jobs. A useful analysis of the attraction options open to organizations attempting to enhance their recruitment efforts is presented by Rynes and Barber (1990) – organizations can attempt to change their recruitment practices, change the inducements or incentives offered to applicants, or widen their recruitment net to target 'non-traditional' sources of applicants such as ethnic minorities, women returners and people with disabilities. Recruits seem very sensitive to such incentives as job titles, salaries and bonuses, especially when considering whether to accept a job offer. However, the actual channels or vehicles used to attract candidates also seem to influence what kinds of applicants are encouraged to apply and to persist in their application. The recruitment stage is the first phase of a process in which both applicant and organization send out signals, check if expectations have been met, make decisions on whether to go to the next stage and negotiate both legal and psychological contracts. Both parties to the relationship will attempt to influence each other's expectations through a process of mutual exchange and negotiation (Herriot 1989b). The kinds of recruitment literature sent out by organizations does seem to influence applicant intentions to apply, but informal sources of job information such as 'word of mouth' and referrals are generally seen by potential recruits as more specific and accurate sources of information than formal advertisements. These sources seem to attract employees who show longer tenure and lower turnover. This seems due to such applicants having lower (more realistic?) expectations and displaying less 'reality shock' when actually appointed (Iles and Robertson 1997). As a result, informal word of mouth recruiting is attractive to many employers, in addition to being seen as cheaper. Such recruits may also be more amenable to social control, due to the obligations felt to sponsors, such as relatives (Jenkins 1986). However, such informal recruiting practices may reduce diversity and encourage the recruiting of 'like by like', perhaps inhibiting creativity as well as ensuring that sections of the community currently under-represented in an organization's work force remain so, lacking access to the informal networks maintained by existing employees family and friends (Iles and Auluck 1991).

If organizations wish to recruit more people from currently under-represented groups, 'passive' adherence to formal procedures apparently accessible to all may not be enough. More 'targeted' recruitment practices aimed at particular sections of the community may be necessary, given the substantial evidence for continuing discrimination against women and black people for example on grounds unrelated to job performance. Such applicants may not, despite the prejudices of many employers, be less qualified or competent than traditional employees. It appears that such targeted recruitment initiatives can be effective in stimulating applications from the targeted group without deterring applicants from more traditional groups. However, such initiatives often require careful planning and attention to possible legal pitfalls. Considerable changes in other HRM areas such as induction, training and development, work practices and organizational culture may also be needed if organizations are not just to recruit but also to retain and develop such employees.

The recruitment *message* itself seems likely to affect applicant attraction. Glossy positive images may attract applicants, but may cause greater disillusionment and higher turnover later. More 'realistic' job previews, conveying less uniformly favourable messages, may attract fewer applicants, but recruit more committed employees as a result. Assessment centres and work samples may also provide 'realistic job previews' by giving a 'taste' of the job in question, allowing self-selection to take place if job requirements do not match applicant expectations. Site visits and opportunities to talk to potential colleagues may help in this respect also. Different messages may have different impacts on different groups; subsidized child care may attract parents, flexible schedules retired people.

The actual *behaviour* of recruiters also appears to affect applicants. Not only may women, for example, be put off from pursuing their application by 'offensive' questioning and comments, but the presence of women recruiters and managers on site visits and on interview panels may create more positive impressions. Applicants appear to respond well to recruiters who are seen as competent, informed, credible, and interpersonally skilled. Especially at the early stages of recruitment, these positive impressions of recruiters seem to influence applicants' willingness to take up job offers (Iles and Robertson 1997). 'Unprofessional' practices and long delays in response seem to put off applicants, as applicants seem to take these signals as an indication of how they will be treated if they take up the job offer. Applicants also seem to respond more positively towards recruiters demographically similar to themselves, important if the organization wishes to engage in 'targeted recruitment'.

Many organizations have increasingly 'externalized' recruitment activities, especially executive recruitment (Torrington and Mackay 1986). Recruitment consultancies in this area have grown rapidly, both for executive search (identifying candidates through direct personal contact) and for executive selection (identifying candidates through advertising and short listing). In both cases, the consultancy acts as an intermediary between the employer and the candidate. It seems as if companies use executive recruitment consultancies when they feel they lack in-house capabilities, when there is an advantage to having an outside opinion, when confidentiality is crucial, and when speed of recruitment is a priority. Executive recruitment consultancies do not often however appear to use more sophisticated techniques than references and interviews, though they may subcontract psychological testing (Clark and Clark 1990; Clark 1993).

The recruitment strategies used by organizations appear to interact with other HRM activities, especially other resourcing activities. Existing HRM practices for example may put a brake on innovative recruitment practices. Centralized HRM procedures may make localized recruitment policies less likely. Changes in recruitment practices may not be effective unless there are changes in other HRM policy areas. Targeting under-represented groups in recruitment, for example, may not be effective if selection criteria and practices remain unchanged, or if appraisal practices are left untouched, or if organizational cultures fail to positively value diversity and differences. Without such changes, such employees may feel marginalized, or even harassed, and may leave early. Similarly, recruiting higher-level, more qualified applicants may not be effective unless jobs are re-designed to give greater autonomy, significance and identity.

Recent developments in selection

In some ways research, especially meta-analytic research, in the 1990s has confirmed some of the traditional assertions concerning the validity of the classic selection instruments in predicting job performance (e.g. Salgado 1999). Ability tests (e.g. psychomotor, cognitive, physical), job knowledge tests, situational judgement tests, biodata and assessment centres have all been reported to show criterion related validities varying from medium (e.g. physical ability) to high (e.g. assessment centres, cognitive ability tests). More recent research has focused on personality tests, especially tests of specific personality dimensions such as conscientiousness or integrity. Personality measures have emerged as stronger predictors of job performance than was previously believed. A similar story emerges from the substantial studies into the employment interview, especially behavioural, structured interviews such as situational and behavioural description interviews. Again, these have now been accepted as sound predictors of job performance. These positive findings on the predictive validity of interviews (especially structured interviews), and personality tests, especially specific rather than general personality measures, overturn the conventional wisdom of the last 50 years. Such measures also appear to display validity generalization, in that European and North American studies show similar results across occupations and criteria.

With regard to personality, a consensus has been achieved with regard to the importance of the 'Big 5' personality dimensions, with recent questionnaires being developed around the dimensions of conscientiousness, emotional stability, neuroticism, agreeableness, and openness to experience.[1] Further developments have been to devise 'integrity' and 'customer service orientation' tests, usually associated with conscientiousness, agreeableness and emotional stability. Furnham (1994) for example, found that the Customer Service Questionnaire predicted job performance in Cathay Pacific. One conclusion from this research is that a composite of the Big Five dimensions taps the most important personality aspects of all occupations in industrialized countries (Salgado 1999).

With regard to the interview, it appears that structure moderates validity and is also associated with less adverse impact against minorities. However, structured interviews do not appear to be widely used in organizations, perhaps because they adversely affect other resourcing purposes of the interview, such as to recruit candidates, convey the central values of the organizational culture and enable better person–organization fit. This reminds us that the interview, like all assessment processes, is a social process of mutual decision-making, affected by impression – management, eye contact and the social skills of both parties, as well as by organizational prestige and job attractiveness (e.g. Herriot and Anderson 1997). Studies of the acceptance of utility analysis by managers are also revealing. Utility analysis has the objective of conveying the value, in a cost-benefit sense, of HRM systems, especially assessment systems, to managers – i.e. using the same 'business language' as marketing and finance. However, managers do not seem just to employ criteria of currency units to evaluate job performance, but use other criteria not usually represented in utility analysis, such as strategic needs, legal impact, diversity and the role of multiple decision-makers. Whyte and Latham (1997) have shown that managers were much more committed to HRM decisions when presented with validity information than with validity and utility information, even if an expert was used to induce positive attitudes to utility analysis[2]. Managers appeared negatively influenced by utility information, incredulous of utility estimates, and perhaps wary of 'selling' or 'coercive communication'.

Such findings have prompted researchers in the psychometric tradition to recognize that they need to broaden the focus of selection research. More attention has been given to theoretical aspects of predictor validity, as well as to advances in methodology. Greater attention has been given to job performance, with the recognition that job performance is multi-dimensional (e.g. contextual vs. task performance) and that job performance ratings – the usual performance criterion selected – need to be more thoroughly researched. This leads us into a discussion of another facet of employee resourcing, performance management.

Recent developments in performance management

Performance management is a topic that cuts across traditional HRM boundaries, as it also has implications for employee development. Here, however, we will focus on performance management as a dimension of employee resourcing and performance monitoring and review as part of the appraisal process. In many organizations, formal, systematic procedures are introduced to regularly assess employee performance, usually involving at a minimum an interview between a manager and employee, with documentation of recorded performance. Appraisal is often seen as aiding strategy formulation through providing information on employee skills and weaknesses, and strategy implementation by specifying what employees need to do to successfully implement a chosen strategy. It is also intended to help align training and development programmes to strategic needs, make placement or staffing decisions more effective and enhance performance.

Though the use of objectives in appraisal is common, there are criticisms of their use. They do not enable quantifiable comparisons between employees; they may encourage a focus on ends/results rather than means/processes; they may become out of date in changing environments; they may not encourage feedback on the how, rather than the what, of performance, so inhibiting development; and since individuals may lack control over their environments and other factors influencing performance beyond their control, objectives-based appraisal may seem arbitrary and unfair. More recently, competence or behaviour-based schemes have been introduced either to replace or to complement objectives-based schemes ('hybrid schemes'); competency frameworks are discussed in a later section. Other issues of relevance to the resourcing aspects of performance appraisal include relationships with organizational and national structure and culture (e.g. hierarchical, authoritarian cultures may not welcome peer or customer or subordinate assessments as much as the traditional top-down assessment of performance by a supervisor; matrix structures may find appraisees not committed to the process if some reporting lines are excluded from the process).

Sometimes the assessment of potential is recommended to be separated from the assessment of performance (e.g. by assessing career potential in an assessment centre, where participants are faced with facsimiles of tasks they have not had the opportunity to encounter in their current job). However, the assumptions behind most appraisal schemes (that staff are motivated by feedback, objective setting and payment linked to the assessment of performance) are not often examined. Unless the assessment is accurate and has credibility, the motivational power of the processes following from it, such as feedback, objective setting and pay for performance, is unlikely to be present. For Fletcher (1994), the traditional assessment orientated approach, comparing people and linking subsequent assessments with rewards, fails to deliver. Much work on performance rating fails to recognize that performance rating is a social process – employees typically work in groups; much of their work is not observed; evaluators have different, mixed motives for evaluating performance; rating decisions are embedded in a social context; rating processes are subjective; and social processes enter into all phases of the rating process, from attention through encoding through storage through integration through to rating itself. For example, supervisors seem to prefer to award positive ratings and show upward bias, giving more positive ratings than 'true' performance would merit, perhaps because they perceive negative events to follow from negative ratings, such as resentment, deteriorating working relationships, appeals, grievances, and legal and industrial action. Employees often appear to receive significantly higher ratings from appraisers of their own racial or ethnic group (e.g. Cox and Nkomo 1986), with black managers often being rated less positively on task and relationship dimensions of performance and seeming to have to face a more complex set of performance criteria, such as 'conforming' and 'fitting in'. White male manager limitations may be attributed to him alone, black female manager limitations may be attributed to limitations of the group as a whole. Task success or failure may be attributed differentially – to hard work or skill or ability for a white man, to luck, task ease or connections for a black woman (e.g. Heilman and Stopek 1985). Women may also be more likely to be given bland, innocuous feedback and see performance criteria as less fair, being evaluated in terms of thoroughness, honesty and dependability rather than in terms of intelligence, dynamism or energy, attributes more often valued in men (e.g. Bevan and Thompson 1991). Performance may also of course be impacted by harassment or bullying, resulting in negative performance ratings.

To counter such biases, found at all stages of the appraisal process, organizations are often recommended to use multiple raters, reviews of ratings from above the level of the manager, better appraisal training and more 'objective' approaches such as behaviourally-anchored rating scales or competence frameworks. Others argue that performance is not a knowable and observable objective reality, and so performance ratings can never be accurate representations of that reality.

Despite, or perhaps because of, its central role in most prescriptive models of HRM (e.g. Fombrun et al. 1984, who see appraisal information as leading to HRD activities and reward decisions and as inputs to employee resourcing decisions), appraisal remains contentious and unpopular. For Randell (1994), muddle and confusion still surrounds the theory and practice of appraisal, whilst Hartle (1997) argues that it has outlived its usefulness and should be dropped from the HRM canon. Others argue that 'performance management' offers appraisal 'the potential to reverse past trends, so that it is viewed less of a threat and a waste of time and more as the source of continuous dialogue between organisational members' (Bratton and Gold 1999: 214). These authors argue, following Barlow (1989), that appraisal is central to management control through its use in measuring and monitoring behaviour, and that this may be, despite a rhetoric of development, why appraisal is still contentious and problematic; as Barlow (1989: 500) says, 'institutionally elaborated systems of management appraisal and development are significant rhetorics in the apparatus of bureaucratic control'. For Townley (1994), appraisal is essential to enhance the 'manageability' of employees, with managers attracted to the idea of control in appraisal. The inherent tension between appraisal as a judgement and appraisal as facilitating development has been a constant theme in the literature, certainly since the classic studies of Meyer et al. (1965) in GE, which highlighted the way criticism had negative effects but praise little effect on performance, and showed how making career and salary decisions in appraisal impacted negatively on performance improvement. Appraisal tries to make the relationship between manager and employee rational, static and simple, whereas it is in reality ambiguous, dynamic and complex (Barlow 1989).

In addition to the problems discussed above, another line of criticism comes from TQM, which tends to regard the philosophy and principles of appraisal as ineffective and dangerous, reinforcing 'supervision' at the expense of 'leadership', demotivating staff, reducing pride in their work and encouraging adversarial relationships. This may be particularly true with the expansion of professional and knowledge workers; as Fletcher (1997: 149) points out, such workers value autonomy and independence, self-discipline, adherence to specialized standards and ethics, possess specialized knowledge skills and are often answerable to governing professional bodies, all of which conflict with the hierarchical authority, superior direction, administrative rules and procedures, organizationally-defined goals and standards, and emphasis on organizational position and organization loyalty characteristic of much appraisal. Perhaps for such reasons, many (except for organizational psychologists and HRM theorists!) have dropped the term 'appraisal' in favour of more collaborative, future oriented, developmental terms like 'Performance Review and Development', emphasizing links to HRD and career management.

Ouchi (1979: 843) has developed a contingency model of organizational control mechanisms which attempts to go beyond the descriptive or prescriptive approaches to appraisal that have dominated the literature. He distinguishes between the ability of organizations to measure either output or behaviour (i.e. ends and transformation processes), recognizing the dilemma organizations face between the desire to maintain control and the desire to foster development. If the organization has a high ability to measure outputs and a high knowledge of the transformation process (e.g. traditional manufacturing) it may base appraisal on behaviour or outputs. It may, however, only be able to appraise outputs, lacking knowledge of the transformation processes (e.g. sales); it may be able to observe behaviour, but not able to assess outputs, due to the group-based or long-term nature of the process (e.g. research); or it may have imperfect knowledge of the transformation process and poor ability to measure outputs (the 'clan' form, characterizing professionals and knowledge workers). This may lead to experimentation with other forms of appraisal, such as assessing inputs (e.g. knowledge and qualifications), using self-appraisal, peer appraisal, and customer appraisal – the kinds of 'multi source, multi rater' appraisal and feedback systems which are growing in popularity with the rise of team-based working, knowledge work and more autonomous work, including tele-working (Kettley 1997).

Fletcher and Baldry (1999) in their review of what they term 'multi source multi rater assessment systems' (MSMR) point out that whether such systems are oriented to development or are part of ongoing performance appraisal has considerable implications for their structure and likely outcomes. In the USA, MSMR systems seem often to be related to appraisal and reward, but this seems as yet less true of the UK, where the emphasis is on development. Such systems appear to have spread rapidly across both the private and public sectors in the UK, with a growing prescriptive literature on how to implement such systems, alongside little empirical basis or research guidance. In part, the move away from traditional top down assessments seems related to changes towards flatter structures, autonomous work units and wider supervisory spans of control. This may legitimize the involvement of subordinates and peers in appraisal, since such employees observe more and different managerial behaviours than is apparent to supervisors. With customer-facing roles in particular, greater autonomy and the use of new communications technology may mean that more and more employees will have little contact with immediate superiors, subordinates or peers, but enjoy increasing levels of direct contact with internal and external customers able to provide input on such dimensions of performance as timeliness and quality of service. There has been little research on customer ratings however, as compared to self, peer and subordinate appraisals.

A variety of factors seem to influence MSMR feedback, such as purpose (e.g. development vs. reward), confidentiality/anonymity of raters, choice of raters, frequency and timeliness of feedback, and how the feedback is provided, (e.g. averaging rater scores, reporting only to the individual target). In addition organizational factors such as hierarchical levels, organizational climates and leadership styles are important. Since conventional appraisal feedback often fails to motivate or improve performance, it would be interesting to assess whether 360 degree feedback is more effective, but much research still remains to be done. In the US, most studies show managers to be fairly positively disposed to the use of upward feedback for developmental, but not for administrative, purposes. In the UK, Redman and Matthews (1997) found managers ranging from enthusiastic to sceptical, with the majority being 'relatively indifferent'; such managers were also sceptical about its use to bring about change. Very little research, despite the apparent enthusiasm of organizations, has examined whether performance improves as a result of MSMR feedback, or generates development plans.

The 360 degree feedback/appraisal systems are often seen as systems more appropriate to flatter structures, teamwork, and greater involvement. For example, Gratton and Pearson (1994) showed that managers in a UK multinational often had empathy, delegation, giving recognition, feedback, and communication skills cited by subordinates and colleagues as development needs, despite company rhetoric about the importance of 'empowering' employees. Gratton and Pearson (1994: 103) argue that 'a complete appraisal of empowering behaviour can only be gained from a 360 degree feedback process, one which involves data collection from boss, peers and subordinates'. However, Fletcher, Baldry and Cunningham-Snell (1998) in a study of a pilot 360 degree feedback system in a major oil company found that it did not measure the competencies it purported to; it generated a massive level of redundancy so that only one construct was measured; and it did not correlate with other performance measures used in the organization. For Fletcher and Baldry (1999: 187) 'it seems reasonable to propose that they should be subject to some of the same checks in terms of the internal consistency, fairness and external criterion validity as are tests' – not something that is currently very apparent.

Recent developments in career management

Research and theory in career management in the late 1990s has moved from concerns with the individual (subjective, internal) career and with differences in managerial 'career anchors' (e.g. Schein 1978) towards changes in the labour market and in organizational career practices. A common theme has been that economic, cultural and organizational change has led to the decline of the 'standard' professional/managerial/white collar/skilled worker career, one involving employment security with one employer (though it was never a standard career for many women, casual or part-time workers). Instead of employment security, the focus is on 'employability', internal and external marketability and 'career resilience' (e.g. Waterman et al. 1994). Careers are increasingly seen as an individual responsibility, with organizations increasingly abandoning their career management responsibilities and no longer able to 'plan' a career for their employees. The concept of the 'psychological contract' has emerged to encapsulate these changes. This is defined by Robinson and Rousseau (1994: 246) as 'an individual's belief regarding the terms and conditions of a reciprocal exchange agreement between that focal person and another party'. It is often claimed that organizations have moved from offering more 'relational' to offering more 'transactional' contracts (more public, formal, short-term and specific).

Another line of argument suggests that careers have become more 'boundaryless', crossing product areas, technologies, functions, organizations, national boundaries, and other work environments (e.g. Arthur 1994; Hall and Mirvis 1995); others use terms like 'protean' or 'cellular' to describe emerging careers. Many commentators have suggested that in many cases organizations (e.g. banks) have shattered the old psychological contract, but failed to negotiate a new one (e.g. Herriot and Pemberton 1995, who identify potentially useful replacements in the form of the lifestyle, autonomy and development contracts, linking this line of argument back to career anchors).

However, there is much dispute about the extent and significance of these changes. Most would agree that careers are different from what they were, and perhaps need to be managed in different ways, by both individuals and organizations. Others go further, asking whether we can even talk of organizational careers, when the essence of the careers of the 1970s – security and promotion prospects – has all but disappeared; is it feasible to manage careers today? (Herriot 1995).

However, other commentators, perhaps paralleling the debate over the extent and significance of 'flexibility' (e.g. Atkinson 1984), point to survey evidence that the extent of job change and tenure is little different from what it used to be, that bureaucracy and hierarchy still persist, and that the traditional career is surprisingly alive and well; the career and traditional contract are not yet dead (e.g. Guest 1997; Guest and Conway 1997; Guest and Mackenzie Davey 1996).

What does appear to be the case is that careers are becoming more market driven, and that employee insecurity about jobs and careers remains, despite economic growth; what may be new is that this insecurity has spread to professional and managerial employees in the 1990s and that employees, feeling less loyal to their employers, are increasingly investing in life-long learning and updating skills. Certainly the surveys of MBA graduates reported in Thomson *et al.* (2000) paint a picture of a career-resilient group focused on taking responsibility for their development and careers and driven by a need to keep up to date and remain marketable. Yet MBA graduates are hardly representative of managers in general, let alone of employees; almost by definition one would expect such a group to show such characteristics.

Again, recent British work by Adamson *et al.* (1998) shows leading UK companies to use the rhetoric of employability and marketability in attracting recruits, rather than opportunities for advancement or progression. Again, however, it is unclear how typical this is, or how much the rhetoric is translated into practice. It does seem that many of the companies surveyed in Thomson *et al.* (2000) saw career development as an individual responsibility, engaged in little career or succession planning, used the external labour market extensively, appointed managers for a job, not a career, and did not expect them to remain for long. Yet again, many others did see career management as a shared responsibility, did engage in significant career and succession planning, did appoint for careers, did expect managers to stay for some time, and did make use of both the internal and external labour market. These differences appeared less determined by factors like size or sector, but more a matter of policy choice.

It may be that such differences are related to strategic choice; defenders may adopt a 'club' stance, adopting a 'make' strategy with extensive use of the internal labour market and relational contracts, and exhibiting a strong policy towards taking responsibility for career management. Prospectors may act as a 'baseball team', buying expertise from the external labour market, offering transactional, performance-related contracts and adopting a weak policy on career management, leaving career planning to individuals. Analysers may adopt an 'academy' approach, mixing the two styles identified above, but differentiating them in terms of core and peripheral workers, or strategic business units (Miles and Snow 1978; Sonnenfeld and Peiperl 1988; Thomson *et al.* 2000). It may also be that such strategic types attract, select and promote employees with different kinds of career anchors, and such choices are also related to organizational career management practices. Defenders may engage in rather basic, formal practices such as job postings and information on careers; analysers may be more likely to adopt active management and active planning practices such as mentoring and development centres; prospectors may be more likely to engage in multidirectional practices like 360 degree feedback (Baruch and Peiperl 2000; Thomson *et al.* 2000).

In addition to doubts over the extent and nature of career change, there are also doubts over the key concept of the 'psychological contract'. Is it entirely subjective and perceptual? How can it be a contract, if different parties hold different perceptions? How can 'the organization', composed of different stakeholders changing over time, be a party to the contract? And does the notion of 'violation', with its implications of broken promises, carry more explanatory power than 'unmet expectations'? (e.g. Arnold 1997). As with other areas of employee resourcing, like 360 degree feedback, there is much assertion and rhetoric, but little evidence or conceptual clarity.

ASSESSING AND IDENTIFYING OCCUPATIONAL AND MANAGERIAL COMPETENCES

A major issue in employee resourcing in recent years has been the process of identifying relevant qualities in existing staff and potential applicants that will enable an appropriate match to occur between person and job. These qualities have been variously described as skills, knowledge and other attributes (e.g. personality traits), but have increasingly been termed 'competences' (UK) or 'competencies' (US), concepts which we will examine in more detail shortly. The tool traditionally used to identify relevant attributes has been job analysis, regarded as a critical initial stage in the resourcing process. Job analysis can be categorized into task-orientated and person-orientated methodologies. Task-oriented analyses are often specific to a particular job and give little information on the skills or qualities needed to do the job adequately; these need to be inferred. Indeed, many staff, such as graduates, are often taken on not to do a specific job but to develop a career, often one involving frequent job changes. Recent developments in HRM practice such as flexibility, teamwork and multi-skilling also limit the usefulness of such task-oriented approaches. As a consequence, person-orientated approaches, such as the critical incident technique and repertory grid and behavioural event interviews, have grown in importance as a way of generating more directly the skills and behaviours needed to perform a job.

A principal aim of job analysis is to generate a job description and person specification. However, conventional job analysis tends to assume that there is such a target as 'the job', usually defined in terms of a stable collection of discrete tasks. It also assumes that the knowledge, skills and abilities identified as required for performance are for a job that currently exists. However, in the face of the variety of changes currently experienced by organizations (technological change, restructuring, globalization, the growth in a diverse workforce, rising numbers of mergers and acquisitions) such assumptions are unlikely to hold. In addition, many jobs are newly created, with no precedents to fall back on. Conventional job analysis procedures may therefore be historic and backward looking, rather than forward looking and strategic. One alternative is to try to carry out a strategic job analysis. Workshops may be held with key employees and other experts to identify future trends and their implications for future skills, involving such techniques as looking at best practice, examining other sectors, and scenario planning (Schneider and Konz 1989). For example, one UK-based accountancy firm wishing to move towards a more entrepreneurial, market-orientated 'managed business' attempted to identify the skills and qualities required by partners in the future as well as in the present. These included identifying selling opportunities, commercial awareness and persuasiveness. It then held development centres to assess partners against such criteria (Shackleton 1992).

Recent attempts to identify and assess the key skills and attributes needed by managers and other employees so as to make resourcing decisions have focused on the concept of occupational competences. This is characteristic of both American and British approaches, though there are some significant differences between the two approaches. Job competency in the American tradition has been defined as an underlying characteristic of a person which results in effective and/or superior performance in a job (Klemp 1980), and such competencies are derived through a person-orientated job analysis known as a 'behavioural event interview'. The aim has been to identify those characteristics that distinguish superior managerial performance, regarded as generic (though receiving different emphases depending on managerial level or sector). This research tradition (Boyatzis 1982) distinguishes between 'threshold' competencies, necessary as minimal requirements to do the job at all, and 'differentiators', seen as bringing about superior performance. One British example of an organization using the Boyatzis generic competency model for senior managers is Manchester Airport (Jackson 1989).

The dominant UK approach to occupational and managerial competences as embodied in the work of the National Council for Vocational Qualifications is somewhat different, being more geared to job performance in specific functions and to developing national standards of performance, expressed in terms of outputs rather than inputs. Occupational competence is defined as the ability to perform the activities within an occupation to the standards expected in employment. These standards are described in terms of elements of competence, performance criteria and range statements. The job analysis technique used, functional analysis, contrasts with the American approach in being task-oriented, seeking to identify the necessary roles, tasks and duties of the occupation, rather than the skills exhibited by successful role incumbents. There is however a parallel 'personal competence' model based on person-orientated critical incident and repertory grid techniques which resembles Boyatzis (1982) very closely.

There have been a number of criticisms made of competence models. One line of criticism is to point out the conceptual ambiguity underlying the term, since it sometimes seems to refer to behaviours or actions, sometimes to the abilities or characteristics underlying behaviour, and sometimes to the outcomes or results of actions. Sparrow and Bognanno (1993) for example distinguish between on the one hand 'competences', identified through functional analysis to indicate 'areas of competence' and generate standards (typified by the MCI approach); and on the other 'competencies', as behavioural repertoires brought to a role by effective or excellent performers (typified by Boyatzis 1982). They also identify a third type, namely, organization-specific competency models, such as core competences.

A second line of criticism has been to focus on the generic, 'off-the-shelf' nature of existing competency models. The argument is that particular sectors, industries and organizational cultures require much more organization-specific sets of competences, in part to ensure that employees can identify with the language of the model used. For example, Cadbury-Schweppes sought to define a 'language of competence' in order to 'find better ways of describing managers' and to help managers gain 'behavioural literacy' (Glaze 1989: 44). BP in the late 1980s also sought to identify key behaviours associated with effective management performance as a way of tapping into the corporate culture, involving key players and using the language of the organization (Greatrex and Philipps 1989). In attempting to implement the corporate strategy around an organization-specific, corporate-wide, competency-based model, BP encountered problems in transferring this Anglo-American model across a variety of national cultures. BP regarded the competences identified as generally capable of cross-cultural implementation, and as accurately capturing the shifts required in management behaviour. The behavioural anchors used to describe specific competences were, however, sometimes seen as 'culturally provocative' (Sparrow and Bognanno 1993: 55). Different countries were therefore encouraged to offer their own illustrations of how they might change behaviour, within the context of the broad competency framework.

A further criticism of many existing competency models is that they are often present or past focused, drawing on what has made for successful performance in the past rather than what makes for successful performance in the future. Whether generic or specific, competency models tend to be historic and retrospective in nature, rather than strategic and prospective. One response has been to try to identify 'competences for changing conditions', competences more suitable for dynamic, turbulent environments. For example, in the USA Schroder (1989) on the basis of observations of complex team simulations, attempted to identify 11 'high performance competencies', or observable skills resulting in high levels of performance in changing environments. Arguing that the Financial Services sector was now operating in such a turbulent environment, Cockerill (1989) contended that such competences could be reliably assessed by behavioural observations in the work place, as well as under simulated assessment centre conditions. The approach taken by BP was similar, in that it attempted to identify competences which 'enabled change to happen', whatever that change might prove to be (Sparrow and Bognanno 1993). Again, Morgan (1988) on the basis of workshops with a small number of Canadian managers attempted to describe 'managerial competences for a turbulent world', that is behaviours that will enable change to happen and help managers to 'ride the waves of change'. One danger in such a list is that the competences identified are often described in very abstract, generalized terms, very remote from observable behaviour, making it very difficult for assessors, and managers themselves, to discern how managers are expected to do these things well. Sparrow and Bognanno (1993) argue that in many cases organizations will want more specific, focused sets of strategic, future orientated competences – not so much 'competences for change' as 'changing competences', that is competences which are specific to particular organizational contexts, situations and environments. The relevance of particular competencies to the organization as a whole, or to a particular job or career stream, is seen to be subject to change, so competencies may well exhibit 'life cycles'. Some may be 'emerging', not particularly relevant at present, but of growing importance in the future. Others may be 'mature', becoming of less importance in the future due to strategic shifts, technological change or organization restructuring. Others may be transitional, relevant to an early stage such as a new venture, but perhaps less so as the organization matures. Others may be 'core', of enduring importance, underlying effective performance whatever the strategic direction taken by the organization. In consequence, competence profiles will therefore have a 'shelf life', though it is claimed that 'the more forward-looking the profile is, the longer its shelf life' (Sparrow and Bognanno 1993: 56). Recent trends in using competence frameworks in organizations appear to be: simplification (in language, number, processes); greater stress on technical/functional rather than behavioural competences; greater concern over their possibly inhibiting effects on change; and greater concern with line manager involvement, commitment and ownership of such frameworks.

An additional criticism of existing competence models is that they give insufficient emphasis to key managerial activities and skills like creativity, impact or sensitivity (termed 'soft' competences by Jacobs (1989)) which are hard to measure in any circumstances (though they are the kinds of qualities psychometric personality inventories are specifically designed to assess). However, despite these criticisms, it remains the case that many organizations still claim that competence approaches can help achieve a more strategically focused HRM, one described by Sparrow and Bognanno (1993) as exhibiting 'vertical integration' with business strategy and 'horizontal integration' across all the HRM policy and practice areas. Mabey and Iles (1993), using the terms 'internal' and 'external' integration, argue that competence approaches, by being couched in terms of actual behaviour and sensitive to the language used by line managers, can help achieve the 'external integration' of HR and business strategies, specifying individual behaviours that can clearly exemplify the direction taken by the new strategy or culture.

MODELS OF EMPLOYEE RESOURCING

The psychometric/objective model

Selection and assessment research and practice in the UK has been heavily influenced by the 'psychometric' model most fully developed in the United States. This model in a variety of forms is represented in most textbooks of HRM personnel management and organizational psychology as 'good professional practice', if not fully represented in actual selection practice. The model has its roots in British work on individual differences dating back to the early twentieth century, and even some work in the nineteenth century. This early work led to the development of psychometric and statistical techniques. Its paradigm status in work psychology and personnel management owes much to its application to mass vocational selection in the USA, in particular in both World Wars. Its principal focus is the 'job', conceived of as a set of discrete tasks. In this model, performance criteria are selected and individual 'attributes' of various kinds (knowledge, skills, abilities, etc.) are chosen as predictors of job performance. The attributes selected are then measured through a variety of procedures (tests, interviews, biodata, etc.). The assessment process is then validated, primarily in terms of criterion-related predictive validity (how well the predictor actually predicts job performance), usually expressed as a correlation coefficient. Other validity dimensions (e.g. construct and content validity) are also sometimes considered, especially by researchers. This model appears to value individualism (individual attributes are taken to predict individual performance), managerialism (the major criteria of performance are the achievement of organizational goals, as defined by top management) and utility (cost-benefit analysis of the monetary benefits conferred on organizations by using different selection procedures). Sometimes other concerns, such as bias or adverse impact on for example, women and minorities, are also taken into account. Recent developments in utility theory in assessing the benefits of investing in good selection practice are often attempted to give psychologists an equal say in the 'language of business' to other business professionals (Herriot 1993).

However, this model rests on a number of assumptions that are open to challenge. One is that by and large people do not change much – the characteristics they display before assessment remain quite stable, which is why prediction of job performance is possible. It also assumes that objective assessment of individual attributes is possible, and that this can be used to predict job performance. In addition, the assumption seems to be that job content also does not change much, and that job content primarily consists of specific sets of tasks which can be identified through job analysis. It also makes the assumption that job performance is measurable, though since 'objective' assessments of job performance are often hard to come by, supervisors' evaluations of performance are often used instead. Finally, the central assumption made is that the key purpose of assessment is the prediction of job performance.

Clearly, this model has a number of strengths. Individual differences in performance do seem to contribute significantly to differences in organizational performance, a contention underlying much of the growth in the HRM in recent years. However, many other factors also affect organizational performance. It also seems as if people do change as a result of job experiences. The kinds of attributes often assessed by psychologists – for example, locus of control, self-directedness, intellectual flexibility – seem to be affected by such work experiences as occupational success, racial discrimination, and the kinds of jobs one performs (e.g. Kohn and Schooler 1982; Iles and Robertson 1997).

A variety of factors have caused many researchers and practitioners, especially in Europe, to question aspects of this model. As organizations change, decentralize, restructure, get flatter and devolve accountability, the conception of the 'job' as a stable collection of discrete tasks has come under pressure. Multi-skilling, flexible specialization, and self-directed work teams have made this notion of a 'job' rather outdated, and these and other changes such as downsizing and the growth of 'portfolio careers' have changed our concepts of career success and career development. Knowledge and skill-based reward systems have also undermined the use of job evaluation and the role of the 'job' as the basis for reward. Self-directed work teams, matrix structures and notions of empowerment have challenged the traditional role of the supervisor and of supervisor evaluations. The increasingly diverse nature of the workforce has challenged some of the assumptions about the validity of assessment instruments. In addition, in Europe assessment has come to play a more strategic role in facilitating individual development and cultural and organizational change, rather than in selection alone (Iles 1992; Mabey and Iles

1993). Many of these changes have led to the rise of a more 'process' model of assessment in Western Europe, a model rooted in social psychology rather than in the psychology of individual differences (e.g. Herriot and Anderson 1997).

A more long-standing challenge to this paradigm of assessment has come from political and legal challenges to the fairness and validity of assessment and selection procedures. In the US in particular such challenges have come over groups with 'visible differences' such as race, age and gender. Similar concerns, especially with regard to gender, but less markedly with regard to age and race, have been manifest in recent years in much of Europe. Assessment instruments have increasingly been accused of exhibiting unfair and illegal discriminatory features, and the criterion of 'bias' or 'adverse impact' (defined as the degree to which a technique or procedure rejects a disproportionate number of applicants from one social group or screens out group members unfairly in ways that cannot be justified in terms of ability to do the job) has become an increasingly important 'evaluative standard' against which to judge selection procedures. In part this situation led to a drop in the use of psychometric tests in the 1970s; in part it stimulated research into 'validity generalization' to show that tests *were* in fact valid across situations. It also stimulated research into creating selection procedures which were as valid, if not more valid, than psychometric tests, but which generated less 'adverse impact'. Work samples, assessment centres and structured, criteria-related interviews all seemed to fit the bill in this respect. All of these procedures display a concern with a thorough job analysis to identify the criteria or competences held to constitute effective job performance, and a concern to 'sample' job content directly in the selection procedure itself in the form of simulations of some kind. This in itself marks an interesting departure from the traditional psychometric paradigm, with its concern to assess rather abstract and general 'signs' as predictors. Traditionally the predictor 'signs' (rather abstract personality traits or intellectual abilities) are quite remote from actual measures of job performance. In the 'sample' approach, predictor and criteria measures become as close as possible, both representing 'job performance' in some way. Such procedures not only seem less 'biased' than psychometric tests or traditional unstructured interviews; they also seem of similar or even higher validity (Robertson and Iles 1988). In recent years psychologists have also begun to question the 'geocentric' view of intelligence and job performance and conventional job knowledge tests, in favour of a focus on common sense, multiple intelligences and tacit knowledge (e.g. Sternberg 1999).

This whole area shows that the agenda for the psychometric-objective model has not in fact been set purely by neutral, scientific interests, but by political, social and legal pressures. More sophisticated critical adherents to the model (e.g. Hesketh and Robertson 1993) have called for a clearer conceptual appreciation of the relationships between and among predictors and criteria, and for a better understanding of measurement issues in selection. This position acknowledges that 'the selection literature has been atheoretical, with a primary focus on identifying approaches and techniques that have practical utility. Comparatively little emphasis has been placed on the development of conceptual frameworks for selection or on trying to understand why some procedures work and others not' (ibid.: 3). Their call is for developing a *process* model of selection that places it in a broader theoretical perspective of human abilities, personality, motivation and skill acquisition. Such a model also requires 'an examination of the task demands of environments and their interaction with individual psychological variables' (ibid.). The authors point out that research findings on assessment centres challenge the construct validity of what is being assessed. This question of what is being measured by these attempts to assess job competences is therefore unresolved, and the basis of the validity of such methods is uncertain (Hesketh and Robertson 1993). Herriot and Anderson (1997) also call for greater focus on processes, as well as a concern with impacts, development, decision-making, contracting, culture, job change, innovation, flexibility and team–organization fit if the psychometric paradigm is to overcome its roots in stable, bureaucratic organizations and its positivist, empiricist and managerialist assumptions.

This focus on process leads us to a discussion of an interactionist social process model of assessment and selection, one much more influenced by a European social and political agenda and one much more rooted in social rather than in differential psychology. Its concerns are less with differences, measurement, prediction and job performance than with relationships, attitudes, interaction, negotiation, identities and self-perceptions – distinctly social psychological concerns.

An emerging social process model

In one form, this approach focuses on issues of 'impact' and 'process', the selection process as a social process (e.g. Herriot 1989) and the impact of selection and assessment processes on candidates (e.g. Iles and Robertson 1989; Iles *et al.* 1989; Robertson *et al.* 1991; Fletcher 1991; de Witte *et al.* 1992). For example, Iles and Robertson (1989, 1997) have presented a theoretical model of selection and assessment processes on individuals, arguing that both the selection decision and candidates' attitudes to the selection process are likely to have effects on a variety of psychological processes, including organizational and career attitudes, self-efficacy, self-esteem and other psychological states. These are likely to lead to such behaviours as job, organization and career withdrawal or commitment. The impact of such processes is likely to be moderated by a variety of factors, such as candidate individual differences, prior information and explanation, features of the assessment process such as the quality, quantity and timing of any feedback, and contextual variables, such as the amount of organizational and social support provided to candidates. Partial support was provided for this model by empirical studies of development centres and assessment procedures in UK financial services organizations (Robertson *et al.* 1991). Other British studies have shown that assessment centre failure may lead to lower self-esteem and need for achievement (Fletcher 1991) and that development centre participation can affect career plans and attitudes (Iles *et al.* 1989).

This 'social process' model of assessment makes several assumptions which contrast with those underlying the US-based psychometric model (e.g. Herriot 1993). One is that people do change constantly in the course of their careers in organizations. This assumption underlies much of the British work on career and work-role transitions, as well as providing much of the impetus to action and work-based learning. Another assumption is that subjective self-perceptions are critical to work motivation and performance, and that these are influenced by assessment and selection procedures. The jobs people do increasingly involve interaction, negotiation and mutual influence, often taking place in multi-skilled, flexible, self-directed work teams. This emphasis on negotiation, interaction and mutual influence is perhaps one reason why European organizations continue to rely on the interview as the main selection method, as it opens up opportunities for a bilateral exchange of views, mutual decision making, and mutual negotiation. In addition, the recognition that assessment processes are social processes is particularly appropriate to the role of assessment in facilitating *development*, whether individual or organizational development, especially in the use of 'development centres' (e.g. Iles 1992).

Some American research into the impact of selection and assessment techniques has also looked to social psychology to examine assessment processes. One stream has examined the interview as a process of interaction, examining the role of such variables as non-verbal behaviour, age, disability, appearance, gender, race and physical attractiveness variables on interviewers' ratings, though often in acontextual, ahistorical ways such as employing students as 'interviewers' and using 'paper people' consisting of CVs, photographs, or brief taped transcripts of interviewers (e.g. Herriot 1987; Powell 1990; Heilman and Stopek 1985). British research in this tradition has been more likely to employ field studies, examining line managers' ratings and actual assessment centre results (e.g. Iles *et al.* 1989). In this particular study, a bank's assessment centre ratings were in general not related to ratings of appearance, physical attractiveness, or gender, in contrast to the results obtained in many American laboratory studies.

Other forms of this approach stress how actual selection processes deviate from the prescribed, idealized psychometric model. In some cases, researchers simply stress this divergence:

> recruitment practices are not as sophisticated as the professional model implies: that job descriptions are not widely used; that no explicit evaluation of methods is used (but) firms do have institutionalised methods of recruitment, however these recruitment procedures are normally a product of custom and practice.
>
> (Windholf and Wood 1988: 1)

In other cases, the researcher seeks to explain this discrepancy in terms of key organizational processes. Here, the focus is less on accounting for the gap between reality and rhetoric and more on understanding how the rhetoric is used to justify a decision made on grounds other than those cited. Salaman and Thompson (1978) for example, argued that the selection of British army officers reveals the use, in practice, of a set of values, understandings and assumptions among selecting officers, shared among them as part of their officer culture, which determine the outcome of selection choices, but which are masked by the deployment of, and by reference to, the formal procedures: 'These factors ensure that an inevitable residue of flexible *ad hoc* practices within the otherwise scientific selection process undermines the scientificity (objectivity and universalism) of the evaluations, while maintaining their "scientific" character' (ibid.: 303).

Another form of a social process perspective is far more radical. Unlike the psychometric approach, this focuses not on the rational properties of actions but on the processes whereby selection systems and decisions are presented as rational at all – how a decision is formulated so that it complies with and thus supports the impression of reasonableness. Thus the conventional approach to selection which seeks to assess the systematic status of a process or decision is replaced by an approach which looks at how selectors and others demonstrate, to themselves and others, that the process and decision were reasonable (Silverman and Jones 1973, 1976).

RESOURCING, KNOWLEDGE AND POWER

Perspectives on employee resourcing from strategic management, psychometric and social process perspectives can be compared in terms of how they see the purpose of assessment, their disciplinary base, preferred research methodologies, and view of the role of the assessor, assessee and instruments in the assessment process (e.g. Iles 1999: 141). Strategic management perspectives stress the strategic implementation role of resourcing, tend to rely on case studies and surveys, see assessors as strategic facilitators, assessees as strategic implementers and instruments as strategic change tools. Psychometric perspectives have stressed the prediction of job performance, validation studies, the assessor as an objective measure; the assessee as a passive object of measurement, and the instrument as a neutral measuring rod. The social process perspective tends to see assessment as part of an ongoing process of contract negotiation and renegotiation, the assessor as a partner, mentor or co-learner, the assessee as an active agent and mutual participant in contracting and the instrument as useful to facilitate dialogue. An alternative perspective, stemming from critical theory and sociology, takes a different view, seeing the purpose of assessment and resourcing as part of the government of organizations and the regulation of individuals, including their subjectivity. Often employing discourse analysis, it focuses on the role of the assessor as both regulator and judge/confessor, and the assessee as an object of power/knowledge as well as a self-regulating agent. The assessment instrument is seen as part of a technology of power and regulation. It is to this perspective that we next turn.

Employee resourcing can thus be seen not only in terms of its efficiency or reasonableness, nor even in terms of the ways in which reasonableness is contructed and displayed, but in terms of the relationships between these processes, the expertise on which they are based, and the practice of power within organizations. So far, the models discussed take efficiency as their primary concern and focus on ways of improving the efficiency of the processes, or seek to explain current developments in procedures and criteria in terms of changes in the nature of work organization – in particular, as Townley (1989) argues, in terms of 'the importance attached to increased individual discretion, and the implications this has for the administration of work' (ibid.: 102). Thus selection, and current developments in the identification of competences, may be regarded as elements in the 'government' of organizations. This approach addresses the ways in which power, knowledge and practice mutually support and reproduce each other. This is not simply to argue that practices and knowledge support power in an ideological or legitimating manner; it is instead to argue that power is that which traverses *all* practices, from the 'macro' to the 'micro', through which persons are ruled, mastered, held in check, administered, steered, guided, by means of which they are led by others or have come to direct or regulate their own actions (Rose 1990). In part this perspective stems from Foucault and his interest in the construction of knowledge and its relationship to power and 'technologies of power': disciplinary practices aimed at making behaviour visible, predictable, calculable and manageable (Townley 1994). Employee resourcing can thus be seen as essentially concerned with dividing, partitioning, ordering and ranking employees and candidates and imposing and maintaining organizational boundaries through hierarchical observation and normalizing judgement.

Power is inherent in knowledge itself, and in the techniques which that knowledge informs and justifies; for knowledge, as the analysis of competences and the assessment process reveals, plays a major role in constructing the individual manager as someone calculable, discussable and capable of being comprehended in the process of, and as the subject of, senior managerial interventions and decisions: the process of resourcing. The definition of competences may be based on structures of competence and the process of assessment may be based on psychometrically scrupulous testing instruments. These expertises are not simply the servants of power; they *are* power itself, having crucial significance for key decisions about selection, promotion, rejection, and for the characteristics which are defined – and accepted by all parties – as necessary and as properly constituting the new manager. Nor is this their only significance. What is also central to the importance of competence-based assessment is that it defines key selection qualities, and maintains the necessity and neutrality of these dimensions.

The processes of employee resourcing offer striking examples of major ways in which actions and judgements on candidates (internal in assessment, external in selection) which are critical for organizational restructuring and for individual experience are structured and made rational in terms of expert-derived systems and criteria.

Processes of resourcing reveal the interrelationships between knowledge and power, demonstrate the ubiquity of power/knowledge practices, and show the role of a form of organizational governmentality which allows the exercise of power through calculation, assessment and knowledge. Processes of resourcing, wherein individuals and employees are 'known' in terms of a set of qualities (competences), measured against these, and processed in terms of this assessment, are as revealing of organizations as they are of individuals.

To see the process of resourcing as elements of a discourse of HRM means regarding employee resourcing as an element of governmentality. Miller and Rose define discourse as

> a technology of thought, requiring attention to the particular technical devices of writing, listing, numbering and computing that render a realm into discourse as a knowable, calculable and administrable object. 'Knowing' an object in such a way that it can be governed is more than a purely speculative activity: it requires the invention of procedures of notation, ways of collecting and presenting statistics, the transportation of these to centres where calculation and judgements can be made.

(Miller and Rose 1993: 79)

This line of argument has been taken up in particular by researchers into call centres, where technology is used for the monitoring and surveillance of employees, subject to the 'gaze' of the supervisor. However, monitoring and feedback can also be used for developmental and customer service purposes, and call centres seem to differ widely in terms of their working conditions. Our concern here is somewhat different.

The identification of management competences and the technology of the assessment of these competences represents a remarkable instance of the 'knowing' and constituting of individuals and managers as managers. The discourse discussed here consists of a complex of intellectual, science-based conceptual frameworks (units of competence identified and distinguished through an elaborate research process, involving the opinions of managers themselves, then formulated into discrete 'real' and relevant elements of human action) being allied to a psychologically and psychometrically based technology for the identification and assessment and, crucially, measurement of individuals against the selected competences.

The 'knowing' and measurement of individuals in terms of frameworks of managerial competences is clearly an example of the exercise of organizational power – specifically, the power of HRM changes and their impact on individuals, as candidates or employees.

This analysis also holds for the assessment of competences. Townley, for example, argues that changes in selection processes and criteria, of the sort described earlier in this chapter, are associated with the emphasis, within HRM-style change, on

> the increased emphasis on 'flexibility' or the requirement for greater exercise of discretion. . . . The changes which have been associated with the introduction of selection and HRM generally, have been primarily associated with moves towards 'Japanisation' or 'flexibility' and the commitment to move away from 'bureaucratised' procedures.
>
> (Townley 1989: 106)

The approach suggested here differs somewhat in emphasis from that of Townley (1989, 1994). Townley seeks to make connections between structural (HRM) changes and developments within the resourcing process, arguing that developments in selection methods for example reflect and channel the organizational priorities or processes of HRM change. In a sense, her analysis therefore focuses on the rationality of these developments, albeit a rationality that is defined in terms of new organizational forms and dimensions of control. Here, however, we wish to draw attention not to the ways in which developments in resourcing processes support structural changes in practice, but to the ways in which processes of organizational change and developments in resourcing criteria and systems cohere and support each other as a set of related and mutually supportive ideas; a discourse of HRM which certainly impacts on employees and candidates and demonstrates the practice of power. The effectiveness of this however is defined by the discourse itself.

A further and closely related feature of such discourses is that they attend to, and define and constitute, the self – the subject. It is precisely by constituting, rather than opposing, the subjectivity of individuals that the power of organization, and indeed of human resource strategies, is exercised. The HRM discourse which defines managers and managerial competences, and which is represented in the human technology of the assessment centre, creates and shapes individuals as subjects – in this case, in terms of the constituent competences of the 'new' managers as 'required' by prevalent forms and directions of organizational change. Furthermore, the discourse of HRM also constructs a necessary and closed loop of causation: a conception of the environment which requires that organizations develop certain forms of business strategy, which in turn needs the support of certain organizational structures, cultures and personnel systems. These in turn require the new, competence-based manager. Thus we witness how, as Rose (1990) remarks, power works, not against, or in opposition to, the subject (the individual versus the State, private versus public, the organization against the employee, etc.) but through the construction, measurement, analysis and treatment of subjectivity – through the ways in which 'subjectivity has become an essential object and target for certain strategies, tactics and procedures of regulation' (ibid.: 15).

The frameworks and associated assessment procedures discussed in this chapter can be seen as offering a striking instance of the expert constitution of the self. Competences themselves are presented as real and deep underlying features of humans, *qua* managers. Further organizational progress (the 'career') is based upon evidence that an individual is able to offer that s/he has such competences. Frequently, disappointed and rejected candidates from the assessment process will be offered counselling or training in order to support them through the trauma of discovery not simply that they had failed a test, but that they had revealed a lack of key deep qualities. The focus of the discourse therefore is the topic on which, as argued here, it centres – the subjectivity of the individual, defined in terms of qualities and competences, and assessed against these and offered support to develop, or compensation and counselling for lacking these qualities. Efforts to define and measure managerial competences represent a paradigmatic example of a discourse within an organizational content. To regard these processes in this way helps to illuminate aspects and implications overlooked by more traditional discussions of the topic. Even resourcing procedures such as self-appraisal and 360 degree feedback, often seen as progressive, are mediated through such 'confessors' as mentors, consultants or coaches, who interpret, judge, punish, forgive and console, acting to actively construct identity and how individuals see themselves. Carter's (1996) study of an assessment centre showed that the feedback candidates received had important implications for how they constituted themselves as employees, how they viewed particular job roles, and how they viewed organizational change. Even those who felt the centre to be 'a game' internalized its judgements, welcomed its apparent openness and fairness, and accepted its symbolizing of a break with the past (from public sector electricity company to privatized utility). Du Gay (1996), and du Gay and Salaman (1996) extend this analysis to the ways assessment activities help reconstitute the nature and conduct of management and managers as proactive, self-regulating and entrepreneurial in a competitive market place. Managers are then charged with shaping and normalizing the behaviour of employees in similar directions, in part though competency frameworks and associated resourcing technologies. As du Gay *et al.* (1996: 278) put it, 'contemporary forms of organisational government are premised upon the mobilisation of the subjectivity of managers'.

In the context of this chapter, the most important element of HRM is that it serves as an overarching set of assumptions, techniques, data, frameworks, models and assessments which make sense of, and guide, the restructuring of organizations and management, within which employee resourcing occurs, contributes and makes sense.

NOTES

1 A major debate in personality theory has concerned the structure of personality and in particular how many broad traits are needed to provide a comprehensive description of personality (that is, tendencies to show consistencies in thought, feelings and action). Estimates, usually based on factor analysis or rational classification, range from 3 (neuroticism, extraversion and psychoticism, Eysenck 1975) to the 30 used in Saville and Holdsworth's well-known Occupational Personality Questionnaire (OPQ). The five factor structure, composed of broad domains of personality known as the Big 5, has emerged as the most replicable structure across measures, languages and life-spans. These 5 higher order trait domains are extraversion (outgoing, sociable, assertive), agreeableness (kind, trusting, warm), conscientiousness (organized, thorough, tidy), stability (calm, even-tempered) and openness to experience (imaginative, creative). A major advantage attributed to the Big 5 framework is that it can assimilate other structures; for example, extraversion and

stability are equivalent to Eysenck's extraversion and neuroticism, while psychoticism is a combination of low conscientiousness and low agreeableness.

2 The purpose of utility analysis is to report to HR and line managers, the utility, or financial benefit, of HR procedures, especially recruitment and selection procedures. The outcome is to assign a monetary value for the procedure. So, for example, though the costs of setting up and running assessment centres may seem high, the financial benefits of using them (for example in large organizations recruiting many staff and where job performance varies widely) can be shown by utility analysis to outweigh the costs through the selection of higher-performing candidates. However, existing utility models do not always take the political or strategic needs or the organization, the multi-dimensional nature of performance, and the multiple objectives of recruitment and selection into account.

REFERENCES

Adamson, S.J., Doherty, N. and Viney, C. (1998) 'The meaning of career revisited: Implications for theory and practice', *British Journal Of Management*, **9**(4): 251–60.

Alimo-Metcalfe, B. (1998) '360 Degree Feedback and Leadership Development', *International Journal of Selection and Assessment*, **6**(1): 35–44.

Arnold, J. (1997) *Managing Careers into the 21st Century*, London: Paul Chapman Publishing.

Arthur, M.B. (1994) 'The boundaryless career: A new perspective for organisational inquiry', *Journal of Organisational Behaviour*, **15**(4): 295–306.

Atkinson, J. (1984) 'Managing strategies for flexible organisations', *Personnel Management* **16**(8): 28–31.

Barlow, G. (1989) 'Deficiencies and the perpetration of power: Latest functions in management appraisal', *Journal of Management Studies*, **26**(5): 499–517.

Baruch, Y. and Peiperl, M.A. (2000) Career Management Practices: An Empirical Survey and Implications', *Human Resource Management*, forthcoming.

Beaumont, P. (1993) *Human Resource Management: Key Concepts and Skills*, London: Sage.

Bethell-Fox, C. (1992) *Identifying and Assessing Managerial Competences*, Milton Keynes: Open University.

Bevan and Thompson (1991) 'Performance Management at the Crossroads', *Personnel Management*, November: 36–39.

Boyatzis, R.E. (1982) *The Competent Manager: a Model for Effective Performance*, New York: John Wiley.

Bramham, P.J. (1988) *Practical Manpower Planning*, London: IPM.

Bramham, J. (1994) *Human Resource Planning*, London: IPM.

Bratton, J. and Gold, J. (1999) *Human Resource Management: Theory and Practice*, second edition, Basingtoke: Macmillan Press.

Carter, C. (1996) 'Rethinking the assessment centre: a technology of power', paper presented to British Academy of Management Conference, Birmingham, September.

Cascio, W.F. (1987) *Applied Psychology in Personnel Selection*, second edition, Englewood Cliffs, NJ: Prentice-Hall.

Clark, I. and Clark, T. (1990) 'Personnel management and the use of executive recruitment consultancies', *Human Resource Management Journal*, **1**(1): 46–62.

Clark, T. (1993) 'Selection methods used by executive search consultancies in four European countries: a survey and critique', *International Journal of Selection and Assessment*, **1**(1), January.

Cockerill, A.C. (1989) 'The kind of competence for rapid change', *Personnel Management*, **21**(9), September.

Cowling, A. and Walters, M. (1990) 'Manpower planning: where are we today?' *Personnel Review*, **19**(3): 3–8.

Cox, T. and Nkomo, S.C. (1986) 'Differential appraisal criteria based on race of the ratee', *Group and Organisational Studies*, **11**: 101–19.

Cressey, J. and Jones, B. (1992) *Banks and Cars in European Perspective*, Milton Keynes: Open University.

de Witte, K., van Laere, B. and Vervaecke, P. (1992) 'Assessment techniques: towards a new perspective?', paper presented to the workshop on psychological aspects of employment, Sofia, September.

du Gay, P., Salaman, G. and Rees, B. (1996) 'The conduct of management and the management of conduct: contemporary managerial discourse and the constitution of the 'competent' manager', *Journal of Management Studies*, **33**(3): 263–82.

du Gay, P. (1996) *Consumption and Identity at Work*, London: Sage.

du Gay, P. and Salaman, G. (1996) 'Making up Managers: Contemporary Managerial Discourse and the Constitution of the 'Competent' Manager'. Report to ESRC.

Eysenck, H. and Eysenck, M. (1975) *Personality and Individual Differences*, London: Plenum.

Fletcher, C. (1991) 'Candidates' reactions to assessment centres and their outcomes: a longitudinal study', *Journal of Occupational Psychology*, **64**: 117–27.

Fletcher, C. (1994) 'The effects of performance review in appraisal: evidence and application', in C. Mabey and P. Iles (eds) *Managing Learning*, London: Routledge/Open University Press.

Fletcher, C. (1997) 'Performance Appraisal in Context: organisational changes and their impact on practice', in N. Anderson and P. Herriot (eds) *International Handbook of Selection and Assessment*, Chichester: John Wiley.

Fletcher, C. and Baldry C. (1999) 'Multi source feedback systems: a research perspective', in C.L. Cooper and I.T. Robertson (eds) *International Review of Industrial and Organisational Psychology* 1999, **14**, Chichester: John Wiley, pp. 149–93.

Fletcher, C., Baldry, C. and Cunningham-Snell, N. (1998) 'The psychometric properties of 360 degree feedback: an empirical study and cautionary tale', *International Journal of Selection and Assessment*, **6**.

Fombrun, C., Tichy, N.M. and Devanna, M.A. (eds) 1984 *Strategic Human Resource Management*, New York: Wiley.

Foucault, M. (1979) *The Archaeology of Knowledge*, London: Routledge.

Furnham, A. (1994) 'The validity of the SHL customer service questionnaire', *International Journal of Selection and Assessment*, **2**(3): 157–65.

Glaze, A. (1989) 'Cadbury's dictionary of competence', *Personnel Management*, July: 44–8.

Goleman, D. (1998) *Emotional Intelligence*, London: Bloomsbury.

Grant, R.M. (1991) 'The resource-based theory of competitive advantage: implications for strategy formation', *California Management Review*, **33**(3): 114–35.

Gratton, L. (1989) 'Work of the manager', in P. Herriot (ed.) *Assessment and Selection in Organisations*, Chichester: John Wiley & Sons.

Gratton, L. and Pearson, J. (1994) 'Empowering Leaders: are they being developed?' in C. Mabey and P. Iles (eds) *Managing Learning*, London: Routledge/Open University Press.

Greatrex, T. and Phillips, P. (1989) 'Oiling the wheels of competence', *Personnel Management,* August: 36–9.

Guest, D. (1997) 'Human Resource Management and Performance: a review and research agenda', *International Journal of Human Resource Management*, **8**(3): 263–76.

Guest, D.E. and Conway, N. (1997) 'Employee motivation and the psychological contract', *Issues in People Management*, **21**, Wimbledon: IPD.

Guest, D. and Mackenzie Davey, K. (1996) 'Don't Write Off the Traditional Career', *People Management*, **2**(4) Feb.: 22–25.

Hall, P.J. and Mirvis, P.H. (1995) 'Careers as lifelong learning', in A. Howard (ed.) *The changing nature of work*, San Francisco: Jossey Bass.

Hartle, F. (1997) *Transforming the personnel management process*, London: Kogan Page.

Heilman and Stopek, M.H. (1985) 'Attractiveness and corporate success: different causal attributions for males and females', *Journal of Applied Psychology*, **70**: 379–88.

Herriot, P. (1987) 'The selection interview', in P.B. Warr (ed.) *Psychology at Work*, third edition, Harmondsworth: Penguin.

Herriot, P. (1989a) *Recruitment in the 1990s*, London: Institute of Personnel Management.

Herriot, P. (1989b) 'Selection as a social process', in J.M. Smith and I.T. Robertson (eds) *Advances in Selection and Assessment*, Chichester: John Wiley & Sons.

Herriot, P. (1993) 'A paradigm bursting at the seams', *Journal of Organisational Behaviour*, **5**: 23–6.

Herriot, P. (1995) 'The management of careers', in S. Tyson (ed.) *Strategic Projects for HRM*, London: IPD.

Herriot, P. and Pemberton, C. (1995) *New Deals*, Chichester: John Wiley.

Herriot, P. and Pemberton, C. (1996) 'Contracting Careers', *Human Relations*, **49**(6), 757–90.

Herriot, P. and Anderson, N. (1997) 'Selecting for change: how will personnel and selection psychology survive? In N. Anderson and P. Herriot (eds) *International Handbook of Selection and Assessment*, Chichester: John Wiley, pp. 1–38.

Hesketh, B. and Robertson, I. (1993) 'Validating personnel selection: a process model for research practice', *International Journal of Selection and Assessment*, **1**(1): 41–9.

Hollway, W. (1991) *Work Psychology and Organisational Behaviour*, London: Sage.

Iles, P.A. (1992) 'Centres of excellence? Assessment and development centres, managerial competences and human resources strategies', *British Journal of Management*, **3**(2): 79–90.

Iles, P.A. (1999) *Managing staff selection and assessment*, Buckingham: Open University Press.

Iles, P.A. and Auluck, R.K. (1991) 'The experience of black workers', in M. Davidson and J. Earnshaw (eds) *Vulnerable Workers: Psychological and Legal Issues*, Chichester: John Wiley.

Iles, P.A. and Forster, A. (1994) 'Collaborative development centres: the social process model in action?', *International Journal of Selection and Assessment*, **1**: 59–64.

Iles, P.A. and Mabey, C. (1993) 'Managerial career development techniques: effectiveness, acceptability and availability', *British Journal of Management*, **4**: 103–18.

Iles, P.A. and Robertson, I.T. (1997) 'The impact of selection procedures in candidates', in P. Herriot (ed.) *Assessment and Selection in Organisations*, Chichester: John Wiley & Sons.

Iles, P.A. and Robertson, I.T. (1989) 'The impacts of personnel selection techniques in candidates', in A. Anderson and P. Heriott (eds) *Handbook of Assessment and Selection in Organisations*, Chichester: John Wiley & Sons.

Iles, P.A., Mabey, C. and Robertson, I.T. (1990) 'HRM practices and employee commitment: possibilities, pitfalls and paradoxes', *British Journal of Management*, **1**: 147–57.

Iles, P.A., Robertson, I.T. and Rout, U. (1989) 'Assessment-based development centres', *Journal of Managerial Psychology*, 4 (3): 11–16.

Jackson, L. (1989) 'Turning airport managers into high-fliers', *Personnel Management*, October: 80–5.

Jacobs, R. (1989) 'Getting the measure of management competence' *Personnel Management*, June: 32–7.

Jenkins, R. (1986) *Racism and Recruitment: Managers, Organisations and Equal Opportunity in the Labour Market*, Cambridge: Cambridge University Press.

Kamoche, K. (1996) 'Human resources as a strategic asset: an evolutionary resource-based theory', *Journal of Management Studies*, 33(6): 757–85.

Keenoy, T. and Anthony, P. (1993) 'HRM: metaphor, meaning and morality', in P. Blyton and P. Turnbill (eds) *Reassessing Human Resource Management*, London: Sage.

Kettley, P. (1997) 'Personal feedback: cases in point', Report 326, IES: Brighton.

Klein, J.A., Edge, G.M. and Kass, T. (1991) 'Skill-based competition', *Journal of General Management*, 16(4): 1–15.

Klemp, O. (1980) 'The assessment of occupational competence', report to the National Institute of Education, Washington DC.

Kohn, M.L. and Schooler, C.C. (1982) 'Job conditions and personality: a longitudinal assessment of their reciprocal effects', *American Journal of Sociology*, 87: 1257–86.

Mabey, C. and Iles, P.A. (1993) 'The strategic integration of assessment and development practices: succession planning and new manager development', *Human Resource Management Journal*, 3(4): 16–34.

Mayer, J. (1999) 'Constructive thinking: The key to emotional intelligence', *Contemporary Psychology*, 44(6): 467–70.

Meyer, H.M., Kay, E. and French, J.R.P. (1965) 'Split roles in performance appraisal', *Harvard Business Review* 43, 123–9.

Miles, R.E. and Snow, C.C. (1978) *Organisational Strategy, Structure, and Process,* NY: McGraw-Hill.

Miller, P. and Rose, N. (1993) 'Governing economic life', in M. Gane and T. Johnson (eds) *Foucault's New Domains*, London: Routledge.

Mintzberg, H. (1994) *The Rise and Fall of Strategic Planning*, New York: Prentice Hall.

Morgan, G. (1988) *Riding the Waves of Change: Developing Managerial Competencies for a Turbulent World*, Oxford: Jossey Bass.

Nicholson, N. (1984) 'A theory of work-role transitions', *Administrative Science Quarterly*, 29: 172–91.

Nkomo, S.M. (1988) 'Strategic planning for human resources – let's get started', *Long Range Planning*, 21(1): 66–72.

Orloff, J. (1999) 'Emotional Intelligence', *Workforce*, 78(10): 16.

Ouchi, W. (1979) 'A conceptual framework for the design of organisational control mechanisms', *Management Science*, 25(9): 833–48.

Paddison, L. (1990) 'The targeted approach to recruitment', *Personnel Management*, November: 55–8.

Pearn, M. and Kandola, R.C. (1988) *Job Analysis*, London: Institute of Personnel Management.

Pearson, R. (1991) *The Human Resource*, Maidenhead: McGraw Hill.

Planalp, S. and Fitness, J. (1999) 'Thinking/feeling about social and personal relationships', *Journal of Social and Personal Relationships*, 16(6): 731–50.

Porter, M. (1985) *Competitive advantage: creating and sustaining superior performance*, New York: Free Press.

Powell, G.N. (1990) *Women and Men in Management*, second edition, Newbury Park: Sage.

Prahalad, K.K. and Hamel, G. (1990) 'The core comptencies of the corporation', *Harvard Business Review*, May–June: 79–91.

Randell, G. (1994) 'Employee appraisal', in K. Sisson (ed) *Personnel Management*, Oxford: Blackwells.

Redman, T. and Matthews, B.P. (1997) 'What do recruiters want in a public sector manager?, *Public Personnel Management*, 26(2): 245–56.

Robertson, I.T. and Iles, P.A. (1988) 'Approaches to management selection', in C.L. Cooper and I. Robertson (eds) *International Review of Industrial and Organisational Psychology*, Chichester: John Wiley & Sons Ltd.

Robertson, I.T., Iles, P.A., Gratton, L. and Sharpley, D. (1991) 'The psychological impact of selection procedures on candidates', *Human Relations*, 44(9): 963–82.

Robinson, P. and Rousseau, D. (1994) 'Violating the psychological contract: not the exception but the norm', *Journal of Organisational Behaviour*, 15, 245–59.

Rose, M. (1988) *Industrial Behaviour*, Harmondsworth: Penguin Books.

Rose, N. (1985) *The Psychological Complex*, London: Routledge & Kegan Paul.

Rose, N. (1990) 'Governing the soul', paper presented at conference on The Values of the Enterprise Culture, University of Lancaster, 1989.

Rynes, S.L. and Barber, A.E. (1990) 'Applicant attraction strategies: an organisational perspective', *Academy of Management Review*, 15(2): 286–310.

Salaman, G. and Thompson, K. (1978) 'Class culture and the persistence of an elite: the case of army officer selection', *The Sociological Review*, 26(2): 283–304.

Salgado, J.F. (1999) 'Personnel selection methods', in C.L. Cooper and I.T. Robertson (eds) *International Review of Industrial and Organisational Psychology* 1999, 14, Chichester: John Wiley, pp. 1–54.

Schein, E.H. (1978) *Career Dynamics: Matching Individual and Organisational Needs*, Reading, MA: Addison-Wesley.

Schneider, B. and Konz, A. (1989) 'Strategic job analysis', *Human Resource Management*, 28: 5–62.

Schroder, H.M. (1989) *Managerial Competence*, Iowa: Kendall/Hunt.

Schuler, R. and Jackson, S. (1987) 'Linking competitive strategies with Human Resource Management', *Academy of Management Executive*, **1**(3): 207–19.

Shackleton, V. (1992) 'Using a competency approach in a business change setting', in R. Boam and P. Sparrow (eds) *Focusing on Human Resources: a Competency-Based Approach,* London: McGraw-Hill.

Silverman, D. and Jones, J. (1973) 'Getting in: the managed accomplishment of 'correct' selection outcomes', in J. Child (ed.) *Man and Organisation*, London: Allen & Unwin.

Silverman, D. and Jones, J. (1976) *Organisational Work*, London: Collier Macmillan.

Sonnenfield, J.A. and Pieperl, M.A. (1988) 'Staffing policy as a strategic response: a typology of career systems', *Academy of Management Review*, **13**(4): 568–600.

Sparrow, P.R. and Bognanno, M. (1993) 'Competency requirement forecasting: issues for international selection and assessment', *International Journal of Selection and Assessment*, **1**(1): 50–8.

Sternberg, R.J. (1999) 'Successful intelligence: finding a balance', *Trends in Cognitive Sciences*, **3**(11): 426–32.

Storey, J. and Sisson, K. (1993*) Managing Human Resources and Industrial Relations*, Milton Keynes: Open University Press.

Storey, J., Cressey, P., Morny, T. and Wilkinson, A. (1997) 'Changing employment practices in UK banking: case studies', *Personnel Review*, **26**(1): 24–42.

Storey, J., Wilkinson, A., Cressey, P. and Morris T (1999) 'Employment Relations in UK Banking', in M. Regini, J. Kitay and M. Baethge (eds) *From Tellers to Sellers: Changing Employment Relations in Banks*, Cambridge, Mass.: MIT Press.

Taylor, S. (1998) *Employee Resourcing*, London: IPD.

Thomson, A., Mabey, C., Storey, J., Gray, C. and Iles, P.A. (2000) *Changing patterns of management development*, Oxford: Blackwell Publishers.

Torrington, D. and McKay, L. (1986) 'Will consultants take over the personnel function?', *Personnel Management*, February **4**: 34–7.

Townley, B. (1989) 'Selection and appraisal: reconstituting social relations', in J. Storey (ed.) *New Perspectives on Human Resource Management*, London: Routledge.

Townley, B. (1994) *Reframing Human Resource Management*, London: Sage.

Waterman, R.H., Waterman, J.A. and Collard, B.A. (1994) 'Toward a career-resilient workforce', *Harvard Business Review*, **72**(4): 87–95.

Whyte, G. and Latham, G. (1997) 'The futility of utility analysis revisited: when even an expert fails', *Personnel Psychology*, **50**: 601–10.

Williams, A.P.O. and Dobson, P. (1997) 'Personnel selection and corporate strategy', in N. Anderson and P. Herriot (eds) *International Selection and Assessment*, Chichester: Wiley.

Windholf, P. and Wood, S. (1988) *Recruitment and Selection in the Labour Market*, Aldershot: Avebury.

From Training to Lifelong Learning: the Birth of the Knowledge Society?

9

David Ashton and Alan Felstead

INTRODUCTION

Throughout the 1990s there has been a widespread consensus in national debates, both in the UK and elsewhere, that higher levels of training lead to greater productivity and thereby contribute to economic growth. Although a number of academics have sought to caution against this optimistic portrayal of the effects of training, this has done little to dent the faith that both politicians and political commentators have placed in the impact of training on the economy (see Green 1997 for a review). In some respects this belief has been reinforced by predictions about capitalism moving into a new phase of international or global competition, in which competitive advantage is seen to be derived from human as opposed to physical capital. This process of globalization is seen as virtually inevitable as new technology changes the parameters of competition, leading to the emergence of a knowledge-based economy. From the politician's perspective, once knowledge becomes the major source of competitive advantage then it is also important that the skill levels of the labour force are increased to enable workers to participate effectively in the process of production. In this scenario, learning becomes transformed from a one-off activity into a continuous process. At the level of government policies this is reflected in a spate of new of policies aimed at enhancing lifelong learning.

This belief in the efficacy of training has not been reflected to the same extent at the level of the company. Many companies continue to devote very few resources to the training and development of their employees. While some of the larger companies have pursued the principles of Human Resource Management (HRM) which we discussed in the previous edition of this chapter (Ashton and Felstead 1995), even this has started to change as the rhetoric of HRM has given way to a new discourse in the field of training and development, namely that of Human Resource Development (HRD). Training has now become HRD while the organizational forms which are seen to promote this are those of the High Performing Work Organization (HPWO). The old concern with integrating training and development with the business plan, instituting manpower planning and using formal and systematic methods of identifying training needs at all levels, which typified the good personnel practice, is now seen as an effective but somewhat dated approach, in which training is seen as a series of one-off activities, delivered as formal courses through designated training centres. The 'new' forms of HPWO operate on the principles of flat hierarchies, devolved responsibility for budgets and training, with training activities linked directly to performance improvement at the individual and organizational levels and taking the form of continuous learning with individual employees accepting responsibility for their own development (Guile and Fonda 1998; OECD 1999). Gone are the trainers as instructors and in their place we have learning consultants whose function is to provide advice on performance improvement at all levels and to act as support agents for the learning process in the workplace.

In some respects the new claims for the transformation of training are even more radical than those which were previously made for the impact of the principles of HRM. While under HRM, training as an auxiliary activity was linked to the business agenda and was driven by it, in the new HPWO training becomes transformed into learning, which itself is seen as one if not *the main source* of competitive advantage of the company. This places training at the very centre of the business strategy. In the last edition (Ashton and Felstead 1995), we took the level of commitment of a company towards investing in training as a measure of how far companies were adopting HRM principles and therefore changing their approach to the management of labour. Evidence then suggested that while some high profile employers had adopted forms of HRM the majority had not and were training only in response to externally-imposed forces such as government regulations and pressures from customers. The questions facing us in this new era of international competition is whether these new organizational forms, associated with high performance working are producing a radical transformation of training at the company level in the direction of continuous learning.

The debate on training and development has therefore matured and, to some extent, shifted since we wrote the chapter which appeared in the previous edition of this volume (Ashton and Felstead 1995). The current chapter reflects this change and has been substantially rewritten as a result. It begins by outlining some of the key institutional parameters within which these developments are set. This suggests that the UK has largely relied on a market-based approach to the delivery of training and acquisition of skills. The emphasis has been placed on employers and individuals in this process, and recent government initiatives indicate that it will continue to do so in the foreseeable future. Against such an historical background the chapter considers what has happened to training and skills in recent times. The evidence presented shows that, on average, training incidence has increased and that British workers have become more skilled. This prompts a number of research questions. What are the driving forces behind these developments? What role have employers played in this process and in particular, have employers taken up HRD as a conscious strategy? By drawing on recent research evidence, both in the UK and beyond, the penultimate section of the chapter offers some tentative answers which suggest that HRD is taking hold but only among a minority of UK employers. The chapter therefore concludes that radical changes will be needed in order for lifelong learning to become a reality for the majority of workers.

SETTING THE INSTITUTIONAL CONTEXT

The national training infrastructure provides more than merely a backdrop against which employers' training practices are located. Comparative research (Ashton and Green 1996) illustrates how national training infrastructures can influence both the level and amount of training undertaken by companies. In Britain the story has been of a minimalist training infrastructure emerging in the nineteenth century because the employers who pioneered the process of industrialization were able to compete successfully in national and international markets with a relatively low-skilled labour force. This was a society which industrialized without a national system of compulsory education to ensure minimal levels of literacy and numeracy. It was therefore left to employers, workers' organizations and individuals to provide the requisite skills.

The fragmented educational system of the nineteenth century supplied leadership skills through the private ('public') schools for a small elite, but for the masses, in so far as they attended schools, the main function of education was one of providing literacy and social control (Gardner 1984). Employers who expected to provide their own supply of skilled labour, looked to techniques such as on-the-job training, often organized through a system of sub-contracting (Littler 1982). In other instances, such as in construction, furniture manufacture, engineering and printing, employers used the remnants of the old medieval apprenticeship system to form a system of occupational labour markets. This provided a pool of skilled labour in the localities from which new employers could draw their labour force.

These occupational labour markets enabled the individuals who entered them the opportunity to acquire skills which they would then own and be able to transfer between employers. Access to these skills was controlled in some cases by employers, in others by unions or alternatively was jointly controlled. The costs of acquiring such skills were shared between the employer and the employee, while apprenticeship papers provided a nationally recognized form of skill certification. The result was a system of training which combined reliance on occupational labour markets with a minimal amount of firm specific on-the-job training. This produced a system of skill formation which was front-end loaded in that the training provided on entry to the labour market was expected to last for the rest of a person's working life. For a minority, apprenticeship training provided access to the lower levels of management. However, because the skilled workers monopolized a wide range of tasks, the majority of lesser skilled workers were denied the chance of obtaining a skill through on-the-job learning.

During the twentieth century, and especially after the Second World War, occupational labour markets were gradually undermined as the basis of skill acquisition for two reasons. First, the introduction of US management systems and (mass) production techniques gave management greater control over the production process at the expense of the skilled worker (Littler 1982). Second, the economic base of skilled work shrank with the decline of the manufacturing sector, while the growth occupations in the service sector were outside the control of unions. In the service sector, the absence of a strong union influence meant that management could exercise greater control over the skill formation process. The result was that companies came to exercise greater control over the amount and level of training activity. In a few cases they provided a substantial investment in training. However, many others chose to minimize such activity and buy in such skills as they needed. British employers who had been accustomed to producing low value-added goods, chose to compete on price not quality (Lazonick 1979, 1981; Elbaum and Wilkinson 1979; Zeitlin 1979).

In the aftermath of the Second World War, fear of falling behind foreign competitors did give rise to anxieties among politicians and some business leaders about the wisdom of relying exclusively on employers to provide an adequate level of skill for the nation as a whole. Previous government initiatives in the provision of training had been primarily directed at the unemployed. There was now an attempt to put pressure on recalcitrant employers to enhance the level of training they provided and thereby to share the costs of training more equitably between employers. This took the form of the 1964 Training Act and signalled a significant shift from a voluntaristic to an interventionist strategy. Intervention in the process of training took the form of Industrial Training Boards (ITBs) (Sheldrake and Vickerstaff 1987). The ITBs consisted of representatives of employers and unions and were charged with the task of monitoring the level and quality of training in the industry, and through the imposition of a levy on employers, equalizing the cost of training among employers while improving the quality. In many respects the ITBs were based on the concept of an occupational labour market, in which it is assumed that skills are transferable between firms and therefore all should carry an equal share in the costs of training. Nevertheless, they represented the first attempt on a national scale to close the low-skills route.

The ITBs lasted, in one form or another, for 20 years but were eventually disbanded for a combination of reasons. These included objections from many employers, ideological objections among government politicians to state intervention, but also they were disbanded because the changes identified above, namely the growth of mass production and later the decline of manufacturing industry, were undermining the use of occupational labour markets as a basis for skill formation (Sheldrake and Vickerstaff 1987; Senker 1992 and 1995). In the 1970s the industry-by-industry approach to encouraging training activities was replaced by the more highly centralized and direct strategy of the Manpower Services Commission (MSC). Established in the 1970s as a quasi-governmental corporatist body under the direction of employers, unions and the state, the MSC sought to establish a national system of vocational education and training, partially funded from the public purse (Ainley and Corney 1990). Some progress was made but the attempt by the MSC to use its programmes as a basis for a national system of training failed, primarily because the Thatcher government insisted on reverting to the traditional strategy of using training programmes to provide a cheap 'solution' to the problem of unemployment. Employers were being left to determine their own level of training activity and as the government started to look to the market to provide the solution to Britain's training problem, the MSC was dismantled, paving the way for subsequent government policy.

This period following the end of the Second World War also witnessed attempts to extend secondary education to the masses, through the introduction of first the tripartite system and in the 1960s the comprehensive schools. However, in spite of these and subsequent changes the majority of young people continued to reject the watered-down academic curriculum on offer and chose to leave school at the earliest date. Apart from an influx of young people into the more 'adult' atmosphere of the Colleges of Further Education in the 1970s and 1980s, this situation did not change significantly until the 1990s. However, as the apprenticeship system collapsed with the demise of occupational labour markets and with the proportion of unskilled jobs available declining in a context of high levels of unemployment, this created mounting pressure on young people to continue within the educational system in the hope of securing the credentials which would enable them to enter one of the higher level jobs (Ashton *et al.* 1990). Moreover, the expansion of educational opportunity following the Second World War meant that a larger proportion of the parents of children in the late 1980s had further education, thereby increasing the level of motivation among young people to prolong their education. The result has been a significant increase in the educational participation rates of young people since the late 1980s. The proportion of 16–18-year-olds in full-time education has risen from 33 per cent in 1987–88 to 55 per cent ten years later. Similarly, the numbers entering higher education have risen steeply over the same period. Most of this growth has been in degree courses, although the numbers registering for courses at sub-degree level has increased, albeit at a slower rate. The numbers graduating with a university degree expressed as a percentage of the 21-year-old cohort rose steadily from below 5 per cent in the 1950s and 1960s to around 15 per cent at the start of the 1990s. Since then it has doubled to around 30 per cent (DfEE 2000). Participation in part-time courses and mature student entry have also increased relatively quickly.

However, in spite of the improved participation rates of 16–18-year-olds in full-time post-compulsory education, the UK continues to lag behind its major international competitors.[1] In comparison with all the more developed countries, the UK lies at the foot of the league table despite the fact that the minimum school leaving age is lower in many of these countries. Among the Organisation for Economic Development and Co-operation (OECD) countries, it is only in comparison with the Czech Republic, Hungary and Mexico that the UK has higher participation rates among 18-year-olds (see Table 9.1).

The strength of the UK's education system lies in higher education. Here, the UK is among one of the world's leading nations. The rate of entry into higher education is high by international standards. The UK also has the highest first degree graduation rate in Europe as well as the highest graduation rate among those pursuing masters degrees (see Table 9.2). The indications are that the current government are keen to build on this comparative strength of the educational system, even at the expense of the development of work-based intermediate skills where the UK has been notoriously weak. Use of the educational system to deliver more and more of the country's skills has been advocated for several years by some authors (e.g. Soskice 1993). The fact that work-based training programmes such as Modern Apprenticeships have failed to deliver significant numbers of craft workers in recent years has underlined the political appeal of a mass higher education strategy (Middlemas 1999; *The Guardian* 28 September 1999).

However, cross-country comparisons of the qualification levels of the UK versus its international competitors continue to emphasize intermediate skills deficiencies. Among the most robust of these was one commissioned by the previous Conservative government (see DfEE and Cabinet Office 1996; Green and Steedman 1997; Steedman 1998). In that study equivalent intermediate qualifications were identified according to an evaluation of the standards of the relevant syllabuses, examination papers and assessment standards used. A benchmarking exercise was then conducted based on the equivalencies established. Using this method, just over one-third of the UK population of working age had any sort of intermediate qualification. In Germany, two-thirds of the population held an intermediate and in France about half were similarly qualified. About a third of both Singaporeans and Americans had intermediate level credentials, a proportion on a par with that found in the UK. However, the study also found that Singapore was rapidly moving away from the Anglo-Saxon bifurcated model – a high proportion of the workforce poorly qualified

Table 9.1 International comparisons of post-compulsory education[1] participation rates, OECD 1996

Country	Minimum Leaving Age	Percentage of Relevant Age Group[2]		
		Age 16	Age 17	Age 18
Australia	15	96	95	67
Austria	15	91	87	68
Belgium	18	100	98	86
Canada	16	91	80	68
Czech Republic	15	99	82	54
Denmark	16	93	82	74
Finland	16	93	92	83
France	16	96	92	84
Germany	18	97	93	85
Greece	14.5	81	64	63
Hungary	16	88	74	52
Iceland	15	88	77	69
Ireland	15	89	78	78
Italy	14	**	**	**
Japan	15	98	95	**
Korea	14	97	88	60
Luxembourg	15	81	79	**
Mexico	15	40	40	25
Netherlands	18	98	93	82
New Zealand	16	98	80	56
Norway	16	95	93	83
Poland	15	91	90	72
Portugal	14	77	72	55
Spain	16	83	76	65
Sweden	16	97	96	94
Switzerland	15	87	82	77
Turkey	14	**	**	**
United Kingdom	16	82	74	55
United States	17	86	82	58

Notes:
[1] This includes all education taking place in educational institutions. It therefore includes apprenticeships in countries which operate a dual system of workplace and college-based training such as Austria and Germany.
[2] Age participation rates are based on a full-time and part-time headcount.
** Not available.
Source: *DfEE (1998b: Table 7.6)*.

alongside a high proportion of degree-holders – to the Northern European model – high proportions with either intermediate credentials or degrees and a correspondingly low proportion who are poorly qualified. These results have been further substantiated by more recent work which draws from the International Adult Literacy Survey (IALS) and comparison of data collected according to the International

Table 9.2 International comparisons of participation rates in and graduation rates from higher education, OECD 1995

Country	Participation Rates		Graduation Rates[1]				
			Sub-Degree	First Degree		Higher Degree	
	Net Entry Rate[2]	Net Enrolment Rate[3]		Short	Long	Masters	PhD
Australia	**	30	**	34	x	12	1
Austria	26	14	5	x	10	*	1
Belgium	**	41	28	*	26	5	1
Canada	48	38	**	31	x	5	1
Czech Republic	**	16	6	2	11	x	*
Denmark	31	9	8	21	8	2	1
Finland	**	18	22	8	13	x	2
France	33	34	**	**	**	**	**
Germany	27	11	12	*	16	*	2
Greece	16	33	5	x	14	*	*
Hungary	40	12	*	18	x	4	*
Iceland	39	8	**	17	**	**	**
Ireland	27	27	14	10	10	10	1
Italy	**	**	7	1	11	*	2
Japan	**	**	29	23	x	2	*
Korea	**	34	16	23	x	3	1
Mexico	**	1	x	x	11	x	x
Netherlands	34	23	*	x	19	*	2
New Zealand	40	29	17	21	5	10	1
Norway	25	18	48	17	5	8	1
Portugal	**	18	6	2	13	1	1
Spain	**	26	2	10	14	*	1
Sweden	**	13	9	8	8	3	2
Switzerland	15	8	23	x	9	*	3
Turkey	16	10	3	8	**	1	*
United Kingdom	43	26	17	31	x	11	1
United States	52	35	22	32	x	12	1

Notes:
[1] Graduation Rates are calculated by dividing the annual flow of students qualifying by the average population of the theoretical graduation age group. The data are expressed as a percentage.
[2] Net Entry Rates are calculated by dividing the number of university-level entrants in a specified age group by the total population for that age group. The data are expressed as a percentage.
[3] Net Enrolment Rates are calculated by dividing the number of full-time and part-time students aged 18–21 by the population aged 18–21. The data are expressed as a percentage.
x Data included in another column.
* Not applicable.
** Not available.
Source: DfEE (1998a: Table 7.5).

Standard Classification of Education (ISCED) conventions (see Murray and Steedman 1998; Lloyd and Steedman 1999). In particular, the IALS analysis re-emphasizes the point that the UK and the US have similarly high proportions of the population with low levels of literacy compared to much lower proportions in Germany, Sweden and the Netherlands. The situation is reversed at the intermediate level, where the continental European countries outscore the UK and US by a considerable margin.

The institutions of government have made only rather weak and piecemeal attempts to correct this intermediate qualification deficiency from the demand side. While there have been many initiatives, schemes and programmes designed to cajole and exhort employers to provide more work-based training to workers at this level, this has rarely been enforced on employers – even under New Labour. While this is not the place to critique the many and various policies in this area over the last decade, a number of examples will serve to make the point.

Take the National Learning Targets. Initially introduced in 1991 at the behest of the Confederation of British Industry (CBI), they were intended to put Britain at least on a par with those of competitor countries. Following a period of consultation they were revised and updated in 1995, and then once more in 1998. However, they are focused on proportions of people qualified at particular levels. Originally, they focused on the employed population of various ages, but now they cover many more groups including school pupils and all those in the labour market (i.e. employed plus unemployed). Nevertheless, the targets have limited relevance to employers – in fact, only the target relating to Investors in People (IiP) directly focuses on organizations, but it has little force. The rest have an individual focus and are mainly used to judge providers' performance. The impact of the targets on employers is, by implication, limited. As Keep (1999) has recently noted, the majority of employers (73 per cent according to Spilsbury 1996) are unaware of the targets. In fact, only 18 employers bothered to respond to the recent consultation document outlining plans to revise the National Learning Targets; instead most of the 308 responses came from education and training suppliers (NACETT 1998: 11).

Despite occasional (if forlorn) cries for the reintroduction of some form of levy system, government policy – even under New Labour – continues to rely on the market-based solution with minimal intervention. Less than glowing evaluations of experiments with training levies overseas have further served to weaken the case of their reintroduction in Britain. Commentators such as Senker (1995) argue that the French levy system makes for an extravagant and inefficient use of training resources. Similar accusations have been levelled at the Australian Training Guarantee Act passed in 1990 (Noble 1997). The evidence here suggests that while employer spending on training per employee may have increased as a result of the levy (set at 1.5 per cent of payroll costs), the number of training hours to which they were exposed dropped.

A market-based approach is also evident in the institutional mechanisms through which government-funded training programmes are delivered. Despite a number of upheavals over the last decade this remains a consistent feature of these arrangements (Felstead and Unwin 1999). The most recent upheaval was the launch of a network of 82 Training and Enterprise Councils (TECs) in 1991.[2] They were established with the intention of being employer-led, locally-based and market-focused. On these grounds alone they encountered a barrage of criticism (e.g. Emmerich and Peck 1992; Jones

1999). In addition, the consequences the institutional architecture had for the type of trainee recruited, the nature of the course offered and the provider profile supported has been the subject of critical evaluation (for reviews see Felstead 1994, 1995 and 1998). The recent announcement in the *Learning to Succeed* White Paper (DfEE 1999) of the abolition of TECs and the Further Education Funding Council and the establishment of the Learning and Skills Council ushers in another chapter in the history of post-compulsory education. While its precise characteristics have yet to be announced, a heavy employer presence is likely, local involvement is assured and a market focus maintained (although reliance on output-related funding is likely be watered down).

Rather than acting on the demand side of skills, qualifications and training, most government initiatives over the last decade have tended to act on the supply side. The introduction of work-related qualifications in the form of National Vocational Qualifications (NVQs) and General National Vocational Qualifications (GNVQs), and the multitude of changes to government training schemes are among the most obvious. Furthermore, different parts of the supply side have been subject to reviews by policy-makers seeking improvements and modifications. The qualifications framework has been put under the spotlight in recent years with the simultaneous review of qualifications for 16–19 year olds by Dearing and Beaumont of the entire NVQ system (Dearing 1996; Beaumont 1996). Higher education, further education and the TEC system have also been put under public scrutiny (Dearing 1997; Kennedy 1997; House of Commons 1996; DfEE 1998c).

Despite being left to their own devices with regard to the skills of their workforces and the training they provide, we are still left with the question of what actually has happened to skills and training in recent times. In particular, how are employers responding, are they demanding more skills from their employees? Have they taken up the challenge from the government and started to embed Human Resource Development in their conscious decision-making procedures? Or is training and development still treated as a second or third order issue for British management?

CHARTING RECENT TRENDS AND DEVELOPMENTS

For some of the answers we turn to the training and skills data currently available. Since the first edition of this book (Storey 1995) there has been an upsurge of research interest in this aspect of labour market analysis; the terrain to be covered in the space of a single chapter has mushroomed accordingly. This section is therefore organized around some of the key questions which are driving the current debate and provide the macro context in which the chapter is set. Has training increased? How is training distributed? What is training designed to achieve? Are workers becoming more skilled?

Has training increased?

The most often reported statistic with respect to training volume relates to the proportion reported as undertaking training in a four-week period prior to interview for the Labour Force Survey (LFS). According to published figures this rose from 10.8 per cent of employees in 1986 to 15.6 per cent 12 years later (DfEE 1998b: Table 3.3). However, more detailed analysis suggests that this evidence presents an incomplete and misleading picture of trends in training activity. Subsequent LFS questions ask respondents about the length of training undertaken. For example, in 1985 26 per cent of those in training were on courses lasting less than one week (the shortest response option available), while the corresponding figure for 1994 was 45 per cent (see Felstead *et al.* 1999a). This is suggestive of a pattern of training activity in which training opportunities are being more thinly spread among a higher proportion of workers. Hence, training incidence is rising while training intensity is falling (this echoes the Australian experience outlined earlier).

A similar story can be told when examining patterns of training activity internationally. The Continuing Vocational Training Survey (CVTS) was carried out in 1994 and asked about the training offered by enterprises in 1993. Data were collected from the then 12 Member States of the EU. Country samples comprised a representative sample of enterprises with 10 or more employees. In total, around 50,000 enterprises took part. General guidelines for carrying out the survey were issued by Eurostat to ensure broad comparability. The results show that reliance on employee participation in Continuing Vocational Training (CVT) can be misleading. For example, both the UK and Ireland are above average trainers on this measure, while Greece and Portugal are below average. However, using the average length of CVT as the yardstick the picture is turned upside down – the UK and Ireland do relatively badly while Greece and Portugal do relatively well (European Commission 1997: 79, 97).

In addition, there is mounting evidence to suggest that LFS and CVTS-type questions offer a blunt measure of learning activity since much of it is informal and on-the-job (Eraut *et al.* 1998; Ashton 1998; Streeck 1989). It is therefore of little surprise that even simple (and crude) attempts to uncover this learning activity have proved relatively successful. For example, some research has shown that following up the traditional LFS question with a prompt card giving examples of training activities adds almost three percentage points to the proportion of respondents recording having had a training experience in the four weeks prior to interview. Further analysis shows that it is the less formal modes of training – 'instruction or training whilst performing your normal job', and 'teaching yourself from book/manual/video/cassette' – which are the least likely ones to be mentioned until the prompt card is shown (Felstead *et al.* 1997). This finding is consistent with the conclusions of Campanelli *et al.* (1994), who show that respondents often take a narrower view of the meaning of training than do either researchers or policy makers.

How is training distributed?

The short answer is unequally. Indeed, there is overwhelming evidence of persistent inequality between the 'haves' and the 'have nots'. The highly educated, for example, are significantly more likely to receive training than workers with lower qualifications. Similarly, training incidence is closely related to an individual's position in the wage distribution – the higher pay, the greater the likelihood of their being in receipt of training. Training also appears to be related to employer characteristics, such that working for a relatively small employer markedly reduces the likelihood of receiving training, as does working for an employer who does not recognize trade unions for collective bargaining (Machin and Wilkinson 1995). Other features of labour market flexibility such as temporary or part-time working similarly weaken an individual's chances of receiving training (Arulampalam and Booth 1998).

However, these findings may be the result of fewer hours spent in work or lower rates of job tenure (it is not clear from the econometrics whether these factors are taken into account). A similar story of disadvantage for these groups of workers can be repeated for training intensity (see Green 1999: Table 1).

A further twist to the pattern of disadvantage has also recently been revealed by labour market analysts (Machin and Wilkinson 1995; Arulampalam and Booth 1997; Green 1999). Their work suggests that training is concentrated among more or less the same group of recipients from period to period. So that those already privileged in the labour market – in terms of qualifications and pay, for example – are more likely to receive a *succession* of training episodes than those occupying less privileged positions. Hence, the distribution of training in Britain serves to accentuate rather than diminish patterns of labour market inequality.

What is training designed to achieve?

There is comparatively little on this important question. However, some attempts have been made to investigate it. For example, a postal survey of CBI members asked respondents to select up to three out of a possible seven training outcomes commonly mentioned in the literature as motivating employers' training activities. The results reveal striking variations according to occupation (Felstead *et al.* 1997). Enhanced problem-solving skills is high for managers (37 per cent) and associate professional employees (47 per cent), but is also a significant outcome for those who employ and train craft workers (33 per cent). For those dealing with customers, enhancing customer care is often reported as motivating training. As expected, a high proportion of clerical employers (74 per cent) report that training results in improved computing skills among their clerical staff. A slightly lower, but still high, proportion of associate professional employers (62 per cent) report likewise. Teamworking outcomes are consistently on the high side across all occupational groups.

Making workers more punctual or reliable, and getting them to work to deadlines, might not be regarded as a technical skill outcome. Nor would raised enthusiasm for the company be seen as a technical skill. Nevertheless making workers more punctual is a significant training outcome for those who train craft (24 per cent) and routine (22 per cent) staff. Increasing enthusiasm for corporate objectives is a strong outcome for those who train sales (35 per cent) and professional staff (41 per cent). These findings throw an interesting light on the common interpretation of the word 'training'. In much of the economic literature it is seen as involving an improvement in some particular well-defined competence. In fact, as is well known to the human resource specialist, it also involves massaging attitudes and behaviour, and particular training episodes can be designed exclusively to have that effect. As a result, further analysis of this data set has shown that employers may protect their investment in general training by including elements designed to raise employees' commitment to the organization and thereby minimize the extent to which job mobility is enhanced (Green *et al.* 2000b).

Are workers becoming more skilled?

There are now several data sets which seek to answer this perennial question. The earliest systematic survey data with which to assess the nature of skill change in

Britain was the Social Change and Economic Life Initiative (SCELI) (Gallie 1991). This data set was based on interviews with over 6,000 individuals in six different localities and was conducted in 1986. The survey asked respondents to compare their current job with what they were doing five years ago in terms of the level of skill required. Over the five-year period 52 per cent experienced an increase in the skills they required compared to only 9 per cent who saw their skills decline (Gallie 1991: Table 3). In other words, the commonest experience was that of upskilling.

According to the Employment in Britain Survey these trends appear to have continued well into the early 1990s (Gallie et al. 1998). Like the SCELI survey, the Employment in Britain Survey collected data from individuals aged between 20 and 60. This time, however, 3,855 employed individuals were interviewed across Britain between May and September 1992 (Gallie and White 1993: vii). More recently, the Skills Survey has extended the analysis to the late 1990s by collecting data on 2,467 employed individuals in 1997 (Ashton et al. 1999). This shows that while in 1986 52 per cent of jobs required some qualification, this figure had risen to 69 per cent by 1997. Another indicator that overall skill levels have been rising is shown by the amount of time individuals say it takes to train for the job they do. Some 22 per cent of respondents to SCELI in 1986 said that it took a long time (over two years) to train for their job. Of respondents answering the same question in the Skills Survey in 1997, 29 per cent said it took a long time to train for their job. The proportion saying that it took a short time (under three months) to train for their job fell from 66 per cent in 1986 (SCELI) to 57 per cent in 1997 (Skills Survey). A related question of how long respondents judged it took them to learn to do their jobs well, reveals a similar pattern. For example, the proportion who estimated that it took them less than one month fell from 27 per cent in 1986 to 21 per cent in 1997. Statistical tests reveal that all of these changes are significant (Felstead et al. 1999d; Green et al. 2000a).

However, there are winners and losers in this process. Among the winners are those who: switched from part-time to full-time work; remained in intermediate occupations; moved up the occupational hierarchy; were in the manufacturing or financial sectors; were among the better paid; and were employed in organizations with 'progressive' Human Resource Management (HRM) practices such as consultation procedures, appraisals systems and quality circles. The losers, on the other hand, include those who: switched from full-time to part-time work; were self-employed; remained in personal and protective service or sales occupations; were downwardly mobile; remained in the community-related industrial sector (e.g. sewage and refuse disposal, recreational activities, and health and beauty services); and were among the lowest paid in society. Skill change is, therefore, having a differential impact on different groups in society (Felstead et al. 1999b and 1999c).

EXAMINING COMPANY POLICY AND PRACTICE

Given that training incidence has increased and that workers have become more highly skilled, does this mean that UK employers have become more highly committed to training and development? In this section we aim to address more directly the question of whether employers have taken up Human Resource Development as a conscious strategy. Are issues of continuous employee development central to employers' labour management strategies or do they remain second or third order issues?

In the last edition, the only way in which we could then address the question of company training and development policies and practices was through the use of what Becherman *et al.* (1997) refer to as 'first-generation' questions. These are the questions about how much training companies did, which groups received it and how it had changed over the previous decade, questions which the previous section of this chapter has addressed and updated. However, if we are to answer the questions we set ourselves for this section, then we need to move on and ask 'second generation' questions, namely what drives training and what determines the various approaches which British employers take to their investment in training and development? Here we are fortunate in that research has started to make significant advances in understanding different approaches taken towards training, although much of the advance has come from studies of training in other countries.

How can employers' approaches to training and skills development be categorized?

At a theoretical level, following the work of Finegold and Soskice (1988), Ashton and Green (1996), Ashton *et al.* (1999) and Keep and Mayhew (1999), there is a growing awareness of the link between companies' product market strategies and the demand for skills. Companies operating in high value-added markets tend to generate a demand for higher levels of skill among their employees than those operating in low value-added markets. Therefore, we start by looking at the general characteristics of employers in the UK as this will provide clues about the level of skills they demand and may explain the findings referred to earlier, namely that in terms of educational levels, the UK labour market is characterized by a relatively low level of demand for intermediate skills. Is this because most UK firms operate in low value-added markets?

One of the main characteristics of the UK economy has been its domination by large, multi-product firms, usually organized along multi-divisional lines (Whittington 1993: 91) with the next tier down being characterized by a high proportion of single business organizations (Marginson *et al.* 1993). Using comparative European data Purcell (1995) argues that the UK has the largest concentration of large firms in Europe, although this may now be changing due to the restructuring and downsizing which has taken place over the last decade.

Given the influence of these large firms then their product market strategies are likely to play a large part in determining the demand for skills (Ashton and Green 1996; Keep and Mayhew 1999). Many of these, especially in the food, drink and tobacco industries, have relatively low-level technologies and are known to operate in relatively low value-added markets (Marginson 1994; Ackroyd and Proctor 1998). Moreover, foreign direct investment is taking the same route, with overseas investment being concentrated in labour intensive industries, presumably to take advantage of the UK's deregulated labour market to produce for the European market (Barrell and Pain 1997: 67). Similarly in parts of the service sector such as hotels and catering, competition is also still largely focused on price (Stern and Sommerlad 1999) suggesting that here as well, the structure of demand is primarily for low value-added goods and services (Keep and Mayhew 1999). The only exceptions are those industries such as pharmaceuticals, aerospace, chemicals and information technology, where UK employers are making substantial investments in R&D and where the emphasis is more on the delivery of quality differentiated products. All this suggests that the system of production in the UK is still largely wedded to Fordist production techniques and Taylorist forms of job design, although there are some limited areas of high value-added production.

How does this picture of a majority of firms operating in low value-added markets, with only a small proportion producing more quality products and services for high value-added markets, map against our knowledge of employers' strategies toward HRD and training? The answer is reasonably well. Latest research indicates that the UK has a small proportion of organizations which have adopted the principles of HRM and a smaller proportion still which have adopted HPWO practices. Below them are a group which have implemented some modern training and development practices. This suggests that some of these practices may be perfectly compatible with the some forms of low value-added production; for example, companies involved in the mass production of food which train their operatives well but only in narrowly defined tasks. However, there still exists a sizeable minority of organizations which treat training and development as third order issues with no coherent or systematic provision.

As we have seen above, the implementation of HRM principles results in training and development being integrated with the business plan, and therefore knowledge of the extent to which HRM has been implemented in UK organizations can help us start to provide answers to these questions with more precision. The results of the 1998 Workplace Employee Relations Survey (WERS) are helpful in this respect. Conducted in 1997/98 at 2,191 workplaces, WERS provides a nationally representative sample. Reporting the results of the initial analysis of the data, Cully *et al.* (1999) use three indices to measure the integration of HRM into the broader business strategy as a defining characteristic of HRM. These are: the incorporation of HR issues into the strategic plan, whether employee relations is covered at board level and whether the organization has achieved IiP. The researchers report that 68 per cent of all managers interviewed had a formal strategic plan and 56 per cent of workplaces had an integrated employee development plan. In the private sector 64 per cent of workplaces were part of a larger organization where someone at board level had an employee relations remit. Finally, 47 per cent of public sector workplaces and 26 per cent of private sector workplaces had achieved IiP. If we define an organization as having embedded the principles of HRM if it has all three characteristics then overall, one fifth of private sector organizations had all three elements, ranging from 9 per cent in manufacturing to 47 per cent in finance. However, if we broaden the definition to include all those with an integrated employee development plan then more than half of all establishments would be included. This suggests that employee development is taken seriously in more than half of all establishments. However, it still leaves the remaining 44 per cent treating training and development as second or third order priorities.

This may be a somewhat optimistic portrayal of reality in that policies determined by head office may not operate effectively at divisional or establishment level. Case study evidence reported by Rainbird (1994) from 21 public and private sector organizations suggests that while companies may preach the integration of training and development into their business strategies at the head office level, at the divisional level the situation may be somewhat different. She found that of the 21 companies, only one public sector and two high technology private sector organizations had succeeded in achieving a strategic and long-term approach to training in broad sections of the labour force.

Evaluations of IiP provide another source of information on the adoption of HRM in the form of a systematic approach to training. Achievement of IiP signifies that company HRD practices meet certain standards. Thus, those organizations which achieved IiP are far more likely to decide their training budget in relation to business plans. Alberga *et al.* (1996) report that employers involved in IiP are more likely to have a greater commitment to HR among their top management, to have integrated HR with business strategy, to have provided greater opportunities for continuous learning and to provide more effective evaluation of training than those who are not involved in the programme. In terms of training outcomes, Spilsbury *et al.* (1995) report that organizations with IiP deliver higher levels of training, especially among the lower level employees than non-IiP organizations.

However, a further word of caution is required with regard to this evidence as arguably all this good practice amounts to is a demonstration on the part of companies to produce a systematic analysis of training needs for all employees and to make appropriate provision. In the majority of companies this is likely to be in the form of formal courses delivering specific skills. The acquisition of IiP does not guarantee that the company is committed to continuous learning or the full development of all their employees' potential, only that they are providing training relevant for the performance of the present function of the organization.

We are now left with two outstanding problems in relation to our task of identifying the different approaches which employers adopt toward training and development. First, how many of these companies which may have some of the HRM principles in place have moved in the direction of the high performance work organizations we mentioned earlier, where continuous learning is part of the company culture? Second, at the other end of the spectrum, how many organizations exhibit little or no commitment to training and development? With regard to the latter, if we look beyond those committed to IiP this still leaves us with more than half of workplaces without such certification and 44 per cent outside even a broad definition of HRM. This suggests that many UK organizations are providing little if any systematic training for their employers.

The results of the EPOC (Employee Direct Participation in Organisational Change) survey enable us to start to identify how many organizations have moved in the direction of HPWOs. This is a nationally representative questionnaire survey conducted in ten European countries including the UK. The results of further analysis of this data are reported in the 1999 OECD *Employment Outlook*. The authors of that analysis found that on average, 15 per cent of European managers report initiatives undertaken in the last three years in favour of the introduction or extension of job-rotation, 27 per cent report the introduction or extension of teamworking, 33 per cent report greater involvement of lower level employees and 29 per cent the flattening of management structures. In the UK 13 per cent of managers report initiatives on job rotation, 33 per cent on teamworking, 48 per cent on greater involvement of lower level employees in decision making and 45 per cent report a flattening of management structures. Overall, these findings suggest the UK is on a par with other European countries in terms of the development of high performance work organizations.

While these appear impressive changes, if, as is the case here, our main concern is with the introduction of continuous learning within organizations, then this is only likely to occur in organizations where the flatter hierarchy leads to the devolution of responsibility to work groups or teams and where employees in these teams are involved in the problem solving process. As the work of Guile and Fonda (1998) suggests, it is only where this type of combination of work practices is in place that employees are continuously challenged to contribute toward organizational goals and where employee development becomes a continuous process. Unfortunately, the OECD (1999) do not provide a detailed breakdown by country of the combination of the four practices of job rotation, teamworking, devolved decision making and flattened management structures, and we are not therefore in a position to say what proportion of companies in the UK have taken all four initiatives. However, what the results do reveal is that for the ten European countries as a whole, only 1.9 per cent reported taking all four initiatives and only 8.5 per cent reported three. The adoption of more than three of these practices therefore appears to be somewhat limited.

The results of the 1999 IPD Training and Development Survey, a telephone survey of a representative sample of 800 establishments in the UK, provides further evidence of the distribution of HPWOs (IPD 1999). This survey contained information on a range of 13 high performance working practices ranging from the use of self-managed work teams to performance appraisal and multi-skilling. Further analysis revealed that these were to be found in five main combinations or clusters (Ashton *et al.* 2000). Approximately one-third of UK establishments do not make any use of these management practices; just under 50 per cent have mentoring and coaching practices, linked to performance appraisal and focused on the fine-tuning of individual skills; just under one-quarter have practices such as Total Quality Management (TQM) and Quality Circles and hence a focus on quality enhancement; almost 20 per cent have forms of multi-skilling and job rotation focused on the broadening of skills; and just over 10 per cent have introduced teamworking and self-managed work groups. However, when we combine the teamworking and self-managed work group initiatives with TQM and Quality Circles only 4.8 per cent report this combination, while if we include the multi-skilling/job rotation and the coaching and mentoring practices then only one per cent of organizations report all four combinations.

Taken together with the results of the EPOC survey, all this suggests that while the use of *specific practices* associated with high performing working organizations may be extensive among UK organizations, the kind of *combinations* which are likely to produce continuous learning in the workplace are still relatively rare. Thus, the picture we are left with is one of a very small proportion of organizations which are implementing clusters of HPWO practices, perhaps in the order of 5 per cent, and a larger group of companies (which includes this 5 per cent) which have implemented what may be recognizable as modern forms of HRM. Collectively this group represents something in the order of 20 per cent of organizations. A further 40 per cent of organizations have some form of training practice such as employee development plans, while for the remaining 40 per cent there is little or nothing in the form of modern or systematic training and development provision. Of course, these are only approximations based on the evidence of the WERS, EPOC and IPD surveys but they do provide some measure of the distribution of the different approaches UK employers adopt toward training and development. With this information we can now move toward answering the question concerning the reasons why employers adopt different policies.

Why do employers adopt different approaches to training and skills development?

Two studies from outside the UK have recently made important contributions to our knowledge of the reasons for differences in employers' approaches to training. Using a national survey of 1,760 enterprises in Australia and 42 case studies, Smith and Hyton (1999) found that training activity was triggered more by operational concerns such as the introduction of new technology or changes in working practices than it was by strategic issues. The same study found that the provision of training was mediated by a number of factors: enterprise size, the employee's occupation, industrial sector, senior management's commitment to training, and government policy. The importance of operational factors in triggering training events was also found in the UK IPD survey (IPD 1999).

Unfortunately, Smith and Hyton (1999) do not explore the ways in which these factors combine to structure the approach to training adopted by the employer. Here the work of Becherman and his colleagues (1997) in Canada has made an important contribution. They identify three general patterns which characterize the ways in which firms make decisions about training. The first is where reliance is placed on incidental learning and the firm decides not to make any formal investment in training. Although there is no formal decision to train, training nevertheless takes place through informal, incidental learning on-the-job. This approach to training was associated with an inward-looking business strategy, which, when combined with low labour turnover, means that both management and employees see no need for formal training. Where training takes place it is only in response to specific obligations, such as health and safety training or some other immediately compelling need. As we have seen, this is the case in about 40 per cent of UK establishments which have no systematic approach to training. In these establishments the results of the WERS survey indicate that training is only provided in one area – for example, in health and safety, which is found in 40 per cent of workplaces, in the operation of new equipment, found in 27 per cent of workplaces or in computing skills, found in 14 per cent of workplaces.

The second approach to training identified by Becherman et al. (1997) is event-triggered training. Here, formal training is only undertaken in response to specific events such as the introduction of new technology or work reorganization. Training is an episodic activity used to address a specific situation or problem but it is systematically delivered. This appears to be close to the approach we categorized above as characteristic of the 40 per cent of UK employers who have some form of 'modern' training in place.

The third approach is labelled 'commitment to a learning organization' referring to establishments where continuous learning has become a natural part of the business. Training tends to be institutionalized with a formal budget, a formal process of training needs assessment and an evaluation of outcomes. For Becherman et al. (1997) these include high-tech companies as well as some of those in the more traditional manufacturing and service sectors. The linking factor is the strongly-held belief among senior management that training, employee involvement, motivation, accountability and the ability to be self-managing are all critical and complementary ingredients of company success. They also suggest that this approach is linked to product and process innovation product market strategies. This is virtually identical to the approach identified above in the 20 per cent of UK establishments which have an HRM approach to training.

In summary, we can now see that what drives training depends on the approach of the company toward training. In traditional establishments it is largely external pressures. In those establishments with a more modern approach, characterized by a more systematic identification of training needs and training provision, it is the response to 'internal' changes such as new technology and new working practices *in addition* to external pressures. Frequently, it is associated with the use of a competence based approach to the analysis of training needs, typical of almost 50 per cent of UK establishments (IPD 1999). In those characterized by clusters of the new HPWO practices, learning is more continuous and built into the culture of the organization. Continuous individual and organizational learning is seen as crucial to enable the organization to adapt to its market and ensure survival. In these organizations the job of the trainer moves away from the delivery of formal courses in the direction of a learning consultant, identifying areas where performance improvements can be made and offering support to line managers and other employees to embed the process of learning in the workplace.

Recent research has also enabled us to start the process of identifying the reasons why employers should adopt one or other of these approaches toward the delivery of training and development. Here we find similar results from almost all the main surveys cited above, although it has to be remembered that we are not dealing here with tightly defined categories of organizations, merely those that tend to have a higher than average commitment to training. In general, there is a suggestion that HPWO are linked to product market strategies which focus on innovation and product differentiation (Becherman *et al.* 1997; Guile and Fonda 1998) and the existence of foreign competition (OECD 1999). More generally a high commitment to training, whether in HPWOs or those characterized by HRM practices, tends to be associated with the strong commitment of senior management to training and employee development (Becherman *et al.* 1997; Smith and Hayton 1998). Other factors identified by the EPOC and WERS surveys are: the size of the establishment or organization, the existence of recognized unions or other forms of worker representation and incentive compensation schemes, particularly profit sharing and pay linked to skill (OECD 1999). To these can be added the industrial sector and the structure of the personnel function (Cully *et al.* 1999).

Now that these different approaches have been identified, the next task is to identify the impact they have on the amount and type of training undertaken. Here we are now on strong ground. Using the results of the EPOC survey and reviewing the results of various other studies which have examined this question, the OECD report (1999) found a strong correlation between the presence of what it refers to as 'flexible' or 'high performance' work practices – that is, practices such as changes in the design of jobs toward greater complexity, higher skill levels and greater use of teamworking, increased delegation of responsibility and more effective communication – and training levels. Using data from the EPOC survey and other surveys in Australia and the US, the authors found that where these practices exist, firms are more likely to have a formal training programme and workers are more likely to receive training. In addition, they found that in Sweden the proportion of time spent in skill development is higher in workplaces with these practices in place than in those without. These findings are consistent with those of other researchers (e.g. Lund and Gjerding 1996; Osterman 1995; Lynch and Black 1998; Frazis *et al.* 1998). The finding that use of high performance work practices produces higher levels of training is hence a robust one.

It should be of no surprise that the use of these new practices tends to increase the level of skills of employees. Reviewing the literature in this area, the OECD (1999) cites the work of Cappelli and Rogovsky (1994). Their US study identifies three types of skills: foundation (basic reading and maths, communication and thinking, responsibility and management); interpersonal skills; and various workplace competencies. Cappelli (1996) also looked at skill requirements for production jobs and found – after controlling for capital intensity, R&D, the use of computers, education levels and the presence of a union – that TQM, teamworking and a flatter organization were associated to some extent with a greater likelihood of rising skill requirements. The OECD conclude that: 'Generally, the skills demanded in the groups employing the new practices more intensively are greater in all three areas, though the differences are not large' (OECD 1999: 207). Similar results are also emerging from various analyses of data collected by the Skills Survey. This comprises a nationally representative data set of almost 2,500 employed individuals in Britain interviewed in the early part of 1997. This shows that employees working for organizations with 'modern' high performance working practices are in higher skilled jobs than those in other organizations (Felstead *et al.* 1999b). Moreover, the 'new skills' of problem-solving, communication and teamworking are strongly correlated with the existence of 'new' management practices such as the use of Quality Circles, formal appraisal systems, the achievement of IiP and worker involvement in decision making (Ashton and Felstead 1998; Felstead and Ashton 2000).

It therefore appears that these new organizational forms are associated with a demand for higher levels of skills among employees and higher levels of training. What then of organizational performance? Do these new practices and skills pay off in terms of the bottom line? Here again, we now have fairly robust findings from a number of countries including the UK. Drawing on the work of a number of researchers (Becker and Huselid 1998; Delery and Doty 1996; Ichniowski *et al.* 1996; and Kling 1995), the OECD (1999) is satisfied to conclude that firms which employ practices such as multi-skilling, job rotation, teamworking, quality circles and worker involvement in decision making enjoy 'better financial performance and higher levels of productivity than those who do not . . . This beneficial effect is stronger when these practices are used in combination both with each other and with support from other human resource practices, such as training and appropriate compensation packages' (ibid: 182).

However, dissenting voices remain. For example, the studies by Coutrot (1996) in France fail to find such a connection. There are also methodological problems associated with the direction of causality in cross-sectional research. Despite this the longitudinal studies which exist suggest the direction of causality flows from the introduction of these practices to financial performance. Patterson *et al.*'s (1997) longitudinal study of 100 manufacturing companies in the UK, attribute 18 per cent of the variation in productivity and 19 per cent of the variation in company profitability to HRM practices. This makes HRM the most powerful predictor of changes in company performance, well ahead of other factors such as R&D, technology, quality and strategy. Similar, but less robust findings have come from the American Society for Training and Development (1999). All this suggests that it is not training per se that 'pays off' in terms of financial performance but training in association with 'high performance work practices'.

These findings inevitably raise the question of why all companies do not adopt these new practices. The answer may well lie in the fact that these practices may only be suitable for firms in differentiated high value-added product markets, where there is strong management commitment to employee development and also where the employees already possess a high level of skill. However, this is clearly an area where further research is required.

CONCLUSION

We are now in a position to answer some of the questions we have raised. The improvements in the skills base of the UK are in part a product of the efforts by previous governments to increase participation in higher education. However, some employers are also playing their part. Those with IiP and a formal commitment to training are now training all their staff, the unskilled as well as the skilled which explains why the process of upskilling has included many of the unskilled. The existence of a substantial group of UK employers committed to training may well help explain the increased incidence of training in the UK.

We have also established that there is a smaller group of organizations where there is a strong commitment to training and employee development which is a product of strategic HRM together with a small group of 'leading edge' or high performance work organizations which utilize the continuing development of employees' skills as a major source of their competitive advantage. In this respect a small group of employers have placed continuous employee development at the heart of business strategy. It is these two groups who are committed to training which is likely to account for the improvements we have noted in the frequency of training and the upskilling which has taken place.

However, a large group of UK employers are still not committed to training and development as a viable component of their business strategy. These are employers who only engage in formal training when they are forced, either by government legislation or customer requirements, for example, manufacturing firms which are obliged to obtain ISO 9000 before they can become suppliers to large retail firms (Felstead and Green 1994). For workers in these organizations notions of employee development never mind continuous learning remain a fantasy. Thus, when trying to make sense of trends in training and development in Britain we must stop thinking in terms of employers as a general category and differentiate between those who are committed to a systematic approach to training as opposed to the large minority who are not.

While we now have a more reliable 'map' of employers' approaches to training and development, this still leaves a number of questions to be resolved. While there remains some evidence for the proposition that the product market strategy generates the demand for skills, it is the nature of that link which is uncertain. The work of Becherman et al. (1997) in Canada suggests that while firms with high value-added products or services, operating in differentiated product markets, are more likely to have high performance working practices and invest in learning at work, not all companies in these markets do so. Neither are all companies operating in more conventional or traditional markets, such as the resource industries in Canada, characterized by more traditional or event-triggered approaches to training. Companies with a high commitment to training are also found in these traditional industries.

All this suggests that some of the most important factors responsible for the level of training offered by the firm stem from the characteristics of the organization. These characteristics include the use of high performance practices but also the commitment of senior managers to employee development. Thus, while the product market may be an important influence we just do not know whether it is more or less important than these other organizational characteristics in determining the type and level of training that takes place.

What we can be more certain about is that the prolonged use of market principles as the basis for government policy in this area has not created any radical change in the behaviour of employers or employees. Neither the policy of placing employers in control of the delivery of public training programmes at the local level nor the attempt to encourage individuals to accept more responsibility for their own training appears to have much of an impact. As for the much heralded move toward a knowledge-based economy built on lifelong learning, this appears to be as far away as ever, with few employers providing the appropriate conditions for continuous employee development and few occupational groups outside the professions showing much interest in lifelong learning. In sum, apart from the stimulus to training provided by IiP, changes in the institutional framework in the UK appear to have little impact on the prevailing pattern of training at the intermediate level and below.

Yet international comparisons such as those undertaken by the OECD (1999) and the ILO (1998) reveal significant differences between countries in both the level and pattern of training. This suggests that there are important differences in public policy which may be important in explaining these differences. Recent work is starting to further our understanding of these differences which go beyond calls for more direct government intervention to raise the level of training as, for example, through the use of training levies mentioned earlier.

In Germany the state has, over the years, forged links with the employers and unions to form a consensus over the level of training deemed necessary to support the economy. This consensus amounts to an agreement over the national institutional framework through which (apprenticeship) training is delivered. The state provides the theoretical input in the form of off-the-job training, with the employers providing the practical on-the-job experience and the unions agreeing to keep initial wages low to sustain the viability of the programme: all this being underwritten by legal agreements which specify the obligations of the various parties. The result is an institutionally dense environment which ensures the high levels of intermediate level training characteristic of the German system. This framework has been under siege from attempts by international agencies and multinationals striving to introduce more flexibility into the German labour market. So far, the basic components of the framework have remained intact and changes have only occurred in an incremental manner (Culpepper 1999).

The 'Tiger Economies' of South East Asia have also witnessed forms of state intervention in training which are now bearing fruit in terms of higher levels of skill formation. However, this represents a different form of intervention by the state. In countries such as Singapore, Taiwan and South Korea governments have attempted to move the economy in the direction of higher value-added forms of production through the effective use of an industrial policy. At the same time, they have co-ordinated the supply of skills with the changes in demand to reduce the likelihood of skill shortages and to systematically upskill the labour force. In this process they have used both education and public training programmes to increase the skills of all levels of worker to ensure that as the economy moved away from low value-added in the direction of higher value-added production, then the appropriate skills were in place. At the level of government they have devised new super-ministries to co-ordinate the decision making process and ensure that the needs of the economy take precedence over that of other interest groups when decisions about education and training are made (Ashton *et al.* 1999).

In conclusion, the improvements we have witnessed in the UK are no doubt a result of government investment in higher and further education, but elsewhere the impact of government actions has been limited. Meanwhile, a minority of employers are also making significant improvements in the delivery of training and continuous workplace learning. In this way, the use of the market as the guiding principle of public policy has resulted in incremental improvements to the system. Yet in spite of this, the UK shows no signs of catching up in its investment in training and development with its major competitors in Europe and every sign of falling behind its new industrial competitors from South East Asia. If there is to be a significant move in the direction of lifelong learning or a knowledge economy, then it will require far more radical changes to the institutional framework than is currently envisaged in the policy debates.

NOTES

1 Some data are collected for Britain, some for the UK; our use of terms in this section reflects this difference.
2 At the same time, 22 Local Enterprise Companies (LECs) covering Scotland were established. Since LECs have a much wider remit covering environmental, community and local economic development issues in addition to TEC-like responsibilities for the local implementation of national training and enterprise programmes, the discussion will focus on TECs.

REFERENCES

Ackroyd, S. and Proctor, S. (1998) 'British manufacturing organisation and workplace industrial relations: some attributes of the new flexible firm', *British Journal of Industrial Relations*, 6(2): 163–83.
Ainley, P. and Corney, M. (1990) *Training for the Future: The Rise and Fall of the Manpower Services Commission*, London: Cassell.
Alberga, T., Tyson, S. and Parsons, D. (1996) 'An evaluation of the Investors in People Standard', *Human Resource Management Journal*, 7(2): 47–60.
Amercian Society for Training and Development (1999) 'The State of the Industry Report', *Training and Development*, January: 23–33.
Arulampalam, W. and Booth, A.L. (1997) 'Who gets over the training hurdle? A study of the training experiences of young men and women in Britain', *Journal of Population Economics*, 10: 197–217.
Arulampalam, W. and Booth, A.L. (1998) 'Training and labour market flexibility: is there a trade-off?', *British Journal of Industrial Relations*, 36(4) December: 521–36.
Ashton, D. (1998) 'Skill formation: redirecting the research agenda', in F. Coffield (ed.) *Learning at Work*, Bristol: The Policy Press.
Ashton, D. and Felstead, A. (1995) 'Training and development', in J. Storey (ed.) *Human Resource Management: A Critical Text*, London: Routledge: 234–53.
Ashton, D. and Felstead, A. (1998) 'Organisational characteristics and skill formation: is there a link?', *University of Leicester Centre for Labour Market Studies Working Paper No. 22*, November.
Ashton, D. and Green, F. (1996) *Education, Training and the World Economy*, Cheltenham: Edward Elgar.
Ashton, D., Maguire, M. and Spilsbury, M. (1990) *Restructuring the Labour Market: The Implications for Youth*, London: Macmillan.

Ashton, D., Davies, B., Felstead, A. and Green, F. (1999) *Work Skills in Britain*, Oxford: ESRC Research Centre on Skills, Knowledge and Organisational Performance.

Ashton, D., Green, F., James, D. and Sung, J. (1999) *Education and Training for Development in East Asian Newly Industrialised Economies: The Political Economy of Skill Formation*, London: Routledge.

Ashton, D., Sung, J. and Powell, M. (2000) 'Work organisation, skills and training: the impact of high performance work practices on skill formation', *University of Leicester Centre for Labour Market Studies Working Paper*, forthcoming.

Barrell, R. and Pain, N. (1997) 'The growth of foreign direct investment in Europe', *National Institute Economic Review*, **2**: 63–75.

Beaumont, G. (1996) *Review of 100 NVQs and SVQs*, London: National Vocational Qualification Council.

Becherman, G., Leckie, N. and McMullen, K. (1997) *Developing Skills in the Canadian Workplace: The Results of the Ekos Workplace Training Survey*, Ottowa: Canadian Policy Research Networks Inc.

Becker, B.E. and Huselid, M.A. (1998) 'High performance work systems and firm performance: a synthesis of research and managerial implications', *Research in Personnel and Human Resources Management*, **16**: 53–101.

Campanelli, P., Thomas, R., Channell, L., McAulay, L. and Renouf, A. (1994) *Training: An Exploration of the Word and the Concept with an Analysis of the Implications for Survey Design*, Sheffield, Research Strategy Branch, Employment Department.

Cappelli, P. (1996) 'Technology and skill requirements: implications for establishment wage structures', *New England Economic Review*, May–June: 139–54.

Cappelli, P. and Rogovsky, N. (1994) 'New work systems and skill requirements', *International Labour Review*, **2**: 205–20.

Coutrot, T. (1996) 'Relations sociales et performance economique: une premiere analyse empirique du cas francais', *Travail et Emploi*, **66**: 39–58.

Cully, M., Woodland, S, O'Reilly, A. and Dix, G. (1999) *Britain at Work: As Depicted by the 1998 Workplace Employee Relations Survey*, London: Routledge.

Culpepper, P.D. (1999) 'The future of the high-skill equilibrium in Germany', *Oxford Review of Economic Policy*, **15**(1): 43–59.

Dearing, R. (1996) *Review of Qualifications for 16–19 Year Olds*, London: School Curriculum and Assessment Authority.

Dearing, R. (1997) *Review of Higher Education in the Learning Society*, London: School Curriculum and Assessment Authority.

Delery, J. and Doty, D. (1996) 'Modes of theorising in strategic Human Resource Management: tests of Universalistic, Contingency and configurational performance predictions', *Academy of Management Journal*, **4**: 802–35.

Department for Education and Employment (1998a) *Education and Training Statistics for the United Kingdom, 1997*, London: The Stationery Office.

Department for Education and Employment (DfEE) (1998b) *Education and Training Statistics for the United Kingdom, 1998*, London: The Stationery Office.

Department for Education and Employment (DfEE) (1998c) *TEC Review: A Consultation Paper*, London: DfEE.

Department for Education and Employment (DfEE) (1999) *Learning to Succeed: A New Framework for Post-16 Learning*, Cm 4392, London: The Stationery Office.

Department for Education and Employment (DfEE) (2000) *Skills for All: Research for the National Skills Taskforce*, London: DfEE.

Department for Education and Employment (DfEE) and Cabinet Office (1996) *The Skills Audit Report: A Report from an Interdepartmental Group*, Occasional Paper, London: HMSO.

Elbaum, B. and Wilkinson, F. (1979) 'Industrial relations and uneven development: a comparative study of the American and British steel industries', *CJE*, **3**(3): 275–303.

Elbaum, B., Lazonick, W., Wilkinson, F. and Zeitlin, J. (1979) 'The labour process, market structure and Marxist theory', *Cambridge Journal of Economics*, **3**(3), September: 227–30.

Emmerich, M. and Peck, J. (1992) *Reforming the TECs – Towards a New Training Strategy*, Manchester: Centre for Local Economic Strategies.

Eraut, M., Alderton, J., Cole, G. and Senker, P. (1998) 'Learning from other people at work', in F. Coffield (ed.) *Learning at Work*, Bristol: The Policy Press.

European Commission (1997) *Key Data on Vocational Training in the European Union*, Luxembourg: Office for the Official Publication of the European Communities.

Felstead, A. (1994) 'Funding government training schemes: mechanisms and consequences', *British Journal of Education and Work*, 7(3), September: 21–42.

Felstead, A. (1995) 'The gender implications of creating a training market: alleviating or reinforcing inequality of access?', in Humphries, J. and Rubery, J. (eds) *The Economics of Equal Opportunities*, Manchester: Equal Opportunities Commission.

Felstead, A. (1998) *Output-Related Funding in Vocational Education and Training – A Discussion Paper and Case Studies*, Luxembourg: Office for Official Publications of the European Communities.

Felstead, A. and Ashton, D. (2000) 'Tracing the link: organisational structures and skill demands', *Human Resource Management Journal*, **10**(3): 5–21.

Felstead, A. and Unwin, L. (1999) 'Funding systems and their impact on skills', *Department for Education and Employment Skills Task Force*, Research Paper No 11, London: DfEE.

Felstead, A. and Green, F. (1994) 'Training during the recession', *Work, Employment and Society*, **8**(2): 199–219.

Felstead, A., Green, F. and Mayhew, K. (1997) *Getting the Measure of Training: A Report on Training Statistics in Britain*, Leeds: Centre for Industrial Policy and Performance.

Felstead, A., Green, F. and Mayhew, K. (1999a) 'Britain's training statistics: a cautionary tale', *Work, Employment and Society*, **13**(1), March: 107–15.

Felstead, A., Ashton, D. and Green, F. (1999b) 'Justice for all? The pattern of skills in Britain', *University of Leicester Centre for Labour Market Studies Working Paper No 23*, May.

Felstead, A., Ashton, D. and Green, F. (1999c) 'Paying the price for flexibility? Training, skills and non-standard jobs in Britain', paper presented to the 'Skill, Training and Labour Market Flexibility Conference', School of Management, University of Newcastle, New South Wales, Australia, 25–26 November.

Felstead, A., Ashton, D., Burchell, B. and Green, F. (1999d) 'Skill trends in Britain: trajectories over the last decade', in F. Coffield (ed.) *Speaking Truth to Power*, The Policy Press: Bristol.

Finegold, D. and Soskice, D. (1988) 'The failure of British training: analysis and prescription', *Oxford Review of Economic Policy*, **4**(3): 21–53.

Frazis, H., Gittleman, M. and Joyce, M. (1998) 'Determinants of training: an analysis using both employer and employee characteristics', unpublished, February.

Gallie, D. (1991) 'Patterns of skill change: upskilling, deskilling or the polarisation of skills?', *Work, Employment and Society*, **5**(3), September: 319–51.

Gallie, D. and White, M. (1993) *Employee Commitment and the Skills Revolution*, London: PSI Publishing.

Gallie, D., White, M., Cheng, Y. and Tomlinson, M. (1998) *Restructuring the Employment Relationship*, Oxford: Oxford University Press.

Gardner, P. (1984) *The Lost Elementary Schools of Victorian England*, London: Croom Helm.

Green, A. and Steedman, H. (1997) *Into the Twenty First Century: An Assessment of British Skill Profiles and Prospects*, London: Centre for Economic Performance, London School of Economics.

Green, F. (1997) 'Review of information on the benefits of training for employers', *Department for Education and Employment Research Report, No 7*.

Green, F. (1999) 'Training the workers', in P. Gregg and J. Wadsworth (eds) *The State of Working Britain*, Manchester: Manchester University Press.

Green, F., Ashton, D., Burchell, B., Davies, B. and Felstead, A. (2000a) 'Are British workers getting more skilled?', in L. Borghans and A. de Grip (eds) *The Overeducated Worker? The Economics of Skill Utilization*, Cheltenham: Edward Elgar.

Green, F., Felstead, A., Mayhew, K. and Pack, A. (2000b) 'Training and labour mobility', *British Journal of Industrial Relations*, **38**(2), June: 261–75.

Guile, D. and Fonda, N. (1998) 'Performance management through capability', *Issues in People Management No. 25*, London: Institute of Personnel and Development.

House of Commons (1996) *The Work of the TECs, Report and Proceedings of the Committee*, House of Commons Session 1995–96, 6 February, HC 99, London: HMSO.

Ichniowski, C., Kochan, T.A., Levine, D., Olson, C. and Strauss, G. (1996) 'What works at work: overview and assessment', *Industrial Relations*, **35**(3): 299–333.

International Labour Office (ILO) (1998) *World Employment Report 1998–9: Employability in the Global Economy: How Training Matters*, Geneva: ILO.

Institute of Personnel and Development (IPD) (1999) *Training and Development in Britain: The first IPD Annual Report*, London: IPD.

Jones, M. (1999) *New Institutional Spaces – TECs and the Remaking of Economic Governance*, London: Jessica Kingsley.

Keep, E. (1999) 'Employer attitudes towards adult training', *Department for Education and Employment Skills Task Force Research Paper No 11*, London: DfEE.

Keep, E. and Mayhew, K. (1999) 'Knowledge, skills and competitiveness', *Oxford Review of Economic Policy*, **15**(1): 1–15.

Kennedy, H. (1997) *Learning Works: Widening Participation in Further Education*, Coventry: Further Education Funding Council.

Kling, J. (1995) 'High performance work systems and firm performance', *Monthly Labor Review*, May: 29–36.

Lazonick, W. (1979) 'Industrial relations and technical change: the case of the self-acting mule', *Cambridge Journal of Economics*, **3**(3) September: 231–62.

Lazonick, W. (1981) 'Production relations, labor productivity and choice of technique: British and US cotton spinning', *Journal of Economic History*, **41**(3): 491–516.

Lloyd, C. and Steedman, H. (1999) 'Intermediate level skills – how are they changing?', *Department for Education and Employment Skills Task Force Research Paper No 4*, London: DfEE.

Littler, C. (1982) *The Development of the Labour Process in Capitalist Societies*, London: Heinemann.

Lund, R. and Gjerding, A.N. (1996) 'The flexible company: innovation, work organisation and Human Resource Management', *Department of Business Studies, Aalborg University, DRUID Working Paper No. 96–17*.

Lynch, L.M. and Black, S.E. (1998) 'Beyond the incidence of employer-provided training', *Industrial and Labor Relations Review*, **1**: 280–308.

Machin, S. and Wilkinson, D. (1995) *Employee Training: Unequal Access and Economic Performance*, London: Institute for Public Policy Research.

Marginson, P. (1994) 'Multinational Britain: Employment and Work in an internationalised Economy', *Human Resource Management Journal*, **4**(4): 63–80.

Marginson, P., Armstrong, P., Edwards, P.K., Purcell, J. (1993) 'The control of industrial relations in a large company: initial analysis of the second company-level industrial relations survey', *Warwick Papers in Industrial Relations, No. 45*, Industrial Relations Research Unit, School of Industrial and Business Studies, University of Warwick.

Middlemas, J. (1999) 'Modern Apprenticeships: achievements so far', *Labour Market Trends*, **107**(9), September: 487–92.

Murray, A. and Steedman, H. (1998) 'Growing skills in Europe: the changing skills profiles of France, Germany, the Netherlands, Portugal, Sweden and the UK', *LSE Centre for Economic Performance Discussion Paper No 399*, July.

NACETT (1998) *Fast Forward for Skills: NACETT's Report on Future National Targets for Education and Training*, London: National Advisory Council for Education and Training Targets.

Noble, C. (1997) 'International comparisons of training policies', *Human Resource Management Journal*, **7**(1): 5–18.

OECD (1999) *Employment Outlook*, June, Paris: OECD

Osterman, P. (1995) 'Skill, training, and work organization in American establishments', *Industrial Relations*, **34**(2): 125–46.

Patterson, M.G., West, M.A., Lawthorn, R. and Nickell, S. (1997) *Impact of People Management Practices on Business Performance*, London: Institute of Personnel and Development.

Purcell, J. (1995) 'Corporate strategy and its link with human resource management strategy', in Storey, J. (ed.) *Human Resource Management: A Critical Text*, Oxford: Blackwell.

Rainbird, H. (1994) 'The changing role of the training function: a test for the integration of of human resource and business strategies', *Human Resource Management Journal*, **5**(1): 72–90.

Senker, P. (1992) *Industrial Training in a Cold Climate: An Assessment of Britain's Training Policies*, Aldershot: Avebury.

Senker, P. (1995) 'Training levies in four countries: implications for British industrial training policy', *EnTra Research Report RR105*, London: Engineering Training Authority.

Sheldrake, J. and Vickerstaff, S. (1987) *The History of Industrial Training in Britain*, Avebury: Gower.

Smith, A. and Hyton, G. (1999) 'What drives enterprise training? Evidence from Australia', *International Journal of Human Resource Management*, **10**(2): 251–72.

Soskice, D.W. (1993) 'Social skills from mass higher education: rethinking the company-based initial training paradigm', *Oxford Review of Economic Policy*, **9**(3), Autumn: 101–13.

Spilsbury, M. (1996) *Skill Needs in Britain*, High Wycombe: Public Attitude Surveys Ltd.

Spilsbury, M., Moralee, J., Hillage, J. and Frost, D. (1995) 'Evaluation of Investors in People in England and Wales', *Institute of Employment Studies Report No. 263*, Brighton: Institute of Manpower Studies.

Steedman, H. (1998) 'A decade of skill formation in Britain and Germany', *Journal of Education and Work*, **11**(1): 77–94.

Stern, E. and Sommerlad, E. (1999) 'Workplace learning, learning culture and performance', *Issues in People Management*, London: Institute of Personnel and Development.

Storey, J. (1995) (ed.) *Human Resource Management: A Critical Text*, London: Routledge.

Streeck, W. (1989) 'Skills and the limits of Neo-Liberalism: the enterprise of the future as the site for learning', *Work, Employment and Society*, **3**(1), March: 89–104.

Whittington, R. (1993) *What is Strategy and Does it Matter?*, London: Routledge.

Zeitlin, J. (1979) 'Craft control and the division of labour: engineers and compositors in Britain 1890–1930', *Cambridge Journal of Economics*, **3**(3), September: 263–74.

10 The Management of Corporate Culture Change

Graeme Salaman

Chandler was wrong. When he wrote he was right and for some time afterwards; but now we know he was wrong. Chandler maintained that the modern business enterprise replaced co-ordination through market mechanisms by co-ordination through organizational means – through organizational processes, functions and relationships. The invisible hand of market forces was replaced by the visible hand of management. Hierarchy replaced market (Chandler 1977). But he turned out to be wrong, for now the hand of management is most obvious in its *introduction* of market forces; and organizational relationships are increasingly co-terminous with, and difficult to distinguish from, managerially induced market forces. And with organizations restructured to become enterprising, the nature and attributes of the employee become critical.

This chapter is about current emphasis on market forces as principles of organizational structure and design, and crucially on the role of 'enterprise' within this paradigm. It argues that a distinctive reading of enterprise is the central feature of the recent concern of management writers and consultants with corporate culture. Despite the variations between different corporate culture projects, they retain an essential similarity: based on their concern to redefine the employee in terms of enterprise. Corporate culture has however been misunderstood and mistreated by those academic writers who confuse issues surrounding its intellectual integrity, research foundations and conceptual integrity with issues of its impact and organizational significance. Corporate culture is important because this term can be used to subsume a variety of organizational projects which seek to re-invent the manager and the employee as enterprising subjects. These attempts to 'make-up' the employee – some of which are described in this chapter – not only involve projects aimed at identifying, developing and assessing enterprising qualities (variously defined and formulated), they also locate responsibility for the development of these attributes with and within the individual. The employee now becomes responsible for being enterprising.

Such projects do not remain at the level of exhortation or symbolism – the much remarked on 'smoke and mirrors' so frequently dismissed by academic commentators. They are frequently supported by a range of actions, measures and processes which redefine the rules by which relationships and behaviour are defined and assessed.

Despite the diversity and differences of current projects to re-design organizations, most share a concern to *reconstitute the organization* – and its employees – in the name of, and in order to achieve, enterprise (Rose 1990; du Gay 1991; du Gay and Salaman 1992). Enterprise, unlike bureaucracy with which it is favourably contrasted (the two are defined entirely in terms of polar opposition and difference), of course requires radical organization change. The startling recent development of management consultancy and constantly changing consultancy projects not only depends upon a concern to develop enterprise at all levels within the organization, it is hardly possible to conceive of the extraordinary growth of consultancy without a prior commitment at organizational and societal levels, to the values of enterprise.

This focus on enterprise is clearly and directly related to the value placed on this quality in political regimes wherein 'the market' is seen as the necessary basis of efficient organizations, and where even within those public sector organizations that have not been privatized, surrogate market forces supported by various forms of benchmarking are employed as a morally cleansing force.

Enterprise is the cornerstone of corporate culture projects. The enterprising organization which is seen as essential to business success, liberates commitment and innovation and – at least potentially – simultaneously and flexibly aligns the employee with the customer and employer. It acts as a relay between organization and customer. But only so long as the employee embodies organizational values and priorities and takes responsibility for realizing these with customers. The organization can only be enterprising if the employee is enterprising; can only be customer-focused if the employee is customer-focused. But, unlike bureaucracy, the enterprising organization is not self evident; it tends to be defined simply in terms of non- or anti-bureaucratic qualities. The organizational forms which are necessary to develop employees' enterprise (and its associate qualities, flexibility, commitment, customer focus, commercial 'nous', etc. while retaining overall organizational co-ordination and control), remain uncertain (and possibly un-achievable). And so the organizational forms necessary to achieve this enterprising organization remain endlessly unclear and ambiguous: as each new design fails, it is replaced by another more promising alternative (Brunsson and Olsen 1993). The solution in this cycle of fads and panaceas (Gill and Whittle 1992; Keiser 1997) is to achieve enterprise through the individual employee; to reconstitute the employee in the form necessary to achieve the desired end: as a microcosmic enterprising organization.

Not all consultancy change packages are explicitly concerned with culture. But all such projects rely on a change in culture, at least in the sense that they depend on the very circumstances they seek to achieve: a change in the basic attitudes of employees. It is hard to think of any change programme, whether ostensibly focused on de-layering, quality, continuous improvement, re-engineering, team work, competences, etc., that is not concerned with seeking to engage with and define and change the attitudes and attributes of employees in the direction of increased enterprise.

Creating enterprising organizations means more than rejecting the classic canons of bureaucracy; it means more than ensuring a customer or market focus (more even than deciding what these would mean in structural terms). It means somehow translating a conception of the free-market system into an organizational reality. Most of all it means converting employees into economic agents: 'Restructuring organisational life in this sense involves 'making up new ways for people to be; it refers to the importance of individuals acquiring and exhibiting particular 'enterprising' capacities and dispositions' (du Gay 1996: 133). It means overturning and replacing the attributes associated with bureaucracy (obedience, detachment, professionalism, impersonality) with the virtues associated with, and required by, market-based organizational forms.

Corporate culture projects seek to achieve corporate enterprise by creating individuals who reflect, represent and implement organizational priorities in their attitudes and behaviour. They construct the individual in the form of the organization, achieving corporate enterprise through individual enterprise.

A similar but reverse process is also common: where the organization is defined in terms of the enterprising individual. This is the learning organization. The learning organization is defined as if it were an alert, responsive, adaptable, enterprising individual. Emphasis is placed on the desirable processes of growth, development, adaptation and learning that are seen to underlie healthy adaptive survival within a competitive milieu: '... the most successful corporations of the 1990s will be something called a learning organisation, a consumately adaptive organisation' (Fortune, quoted in Senge 1990: 8).

Learning and being enterprising are, at the organizational level, synonymous. The learning organization is one that is able to survive and thrive in complex, demanding and dynamic environments. The learning organization understands its environment, develops alert innovative responses, develops and retains relevant knowledge and consists of people who:

> ... exercise discretion, take initiatives, and assume a much greater responsibility for their own organisation and management. The need to remain open and flexible demands creative responses from every quarter, and many leading organisations recognise that human intelligence and the ability to unleash and direct that intelligence are critical resources.
>
> (Morgan 1958: 56)

The learning organization and corporate culture are two sides of the same coin: the currency of enterprise.

What this means is that current change programmes, however diverse, share a concern to reconstruct the organization in a non-bureaucratic, organic form in which the dysfunctional separation under bureaucracy of employees' cognition and commitment, reason and emotion is replaced by a restructuring of organizations according to free market rationality which requires the production of certain forms of conduct by all members of an organization.

I am arguing here not only for the importance of corporate culture projects, but for their centrality to current programmes of organizational change and to new ways of governing organizations. In so doing I am arguing for a wider sense of culture change than that normally employed. Conventionally, corporate culture is used to refer to programmes that are explicitly and centrally concerned to align employees' attitudes and beliefs with those of senior management: 'The strengthening of Corporate Cultures, it is claimed provides the key to securing 'unusual effort on the part of apparently ordinary employees'' (Peters and Waterman 1982: xvii). But, in reality, all current consultancy programmes, whatever their ostensible focus – job redesign, re-engineering, competences, devolved business units, etc. seek and rely on a major shift in employee attitudes.

Corporate culture as Thompson and McHugh point out, consists of the ways management attempts to manipulate and mobilize values, language, ritual and symbols in an effort to 'unlock the commitment and enthusiasm of employees' (Thompson and McHugh 1995: 198). The overriding concern is to change the way staff think, prioritize and behave.

The specific foci of corporate culture projects vary with their organizational location. But, whatever their variation they involve attempts to generate enterprise. Enterprise refers not only to attempts to construct employees as carriers of the organization's new customer-focused, commercially focused priorities, but also as people who accept these organizational values as their own and who define themselves in terms of their willingness, responsibility and ability to construct and reconstruct themselves successfully in terms of the changing requirements of their organization: in other words to market themselves. This redefinition of self and of personal value occurs within the context of organizational and personal marketability: 'The market driven necessity for cultural reconstruction' (Anthony 1994: 21).

The assertions of corporate culture theories are highly vulnerable. A number of criticisms have been mounted. In order to discuss these it is necessary to make some clarifications.

Corporate culture consists of a number of disparate elements. First there are the texts themselves produced by the notorious culture gurus – Peters and Waterman (1982), Deal and Kennedy (1982), Covey (1989), etc. These texts have been subjected to rigorous critique (see for example Guest 1990, 1992; Wood 1989; Ramsay 1996; Clark and Salaman 1998; Mabey, Salaman and Storey 1998; Meek 1992). These criticisms focus on deficiencies in the ways culture is theorized and conceptualized in these texts, and on their empirically-based research claims (when there are any). The conclusions from these critiques are in general highly negative: 'Most anthropologists would find the idea that leaders create culture preposterous: leaders do not create cultures' (Meek 1992: 198). An additional line of critique of these texts is that identified by du Gay: that corporate culture projects are 'merely ideological' – thus defining them as peripheral and insubstantial. But, as du Gay notes, it is precisely in their ideological character that much of the importance of corporate culture resides since enterprise-based corporate culture initiatives are an attempt to re-imagine and redefine not only the organization and the bases of relationships within the organization but to achieve a new conception of the employee. Corporate culture is thus '. . . a struggle for identities, an attempt to enable all sorts of people, from highest executive to lowliest shop-floor employee, to see themselves reflected in the emerging conception of the enterprising organisation and thus to come increasingly to identify with it' (du Gay 1991: 53–4).

There is, however, an important distinction between texts and projects. du Gay – and other commentators, notably David Knights and Hugh Willmott (Willmott 1993; Knights and Willmott 1987) – distinguishes corporate culture texts from corporate culture projects. Of course the former informs and legitimates the latter, but the academic deficiencies of the former do not necessarily vitiate the significance of practice. Many writers have noted the distinction not only between 'theory' and practice but between criticism of the theory and concern about the significance of the practices associated with it. There is a tension between two different charges. On the one hand the idea of corporate culture is held to distort and misuse the concept of culture. On the other hand it is seen as representing a powerful and significant force for change within organizations.

Discussion of corporate culture (and other consultancy-driven projects) is characterized by an obvious polarity. On the one hand are those critics who see corporate culture as significant and worrying. They recognize that corporate culture texts suggest glib and superficial analyses of organizational cultures, contain misconceived accounts of culture, poorly theorized analyses of organizational structure and functioning, inadequate understanding of the complexity and variety of organizational cultures and naïve accounts of leadership. Yet, as Anthony warns, none of these deficiencies should lead us to overlook the importance of culture to managers (Anthony, 1994: 96). Writers such as Alvesson (Alvesson 1987, 1989, 1991) and Willmott (*op. cit.*) argue for the significance of corporate culture projects as indications that management is 'trying to extend the sphere of instrumental action to rules governing emotions and the affective sphere' (Thompson and McHugh 1995: 215).

On the other hand are those writers who by implication at least, suggest that corporate culture projects are of little significance because of the deeply flawed analyses of organization or the grossly misused and impoverished notions of culture on which they are based (for example, Meek 1992). Some empirical accounts of corporate culture projects go some way to confirm these conclusions – certainly to the extent that such projects are unlikely to fulfil the expectations of managers or the fears of some commentators: compliance may be achieved but not commitment (for example, Ogbonna 1992a and 1992b; Ogbonna and Wilkinson 1988).

Much of the sociological critique of corporate culture addresses the quality of the analyses underpinning these projects. Some commentators define the role and responsibility of academics as exposing and attacking what is seen as untrue: '... the most important role for academic research is to expose and help to moderate the unproductive consequences of management fashions' (Ramsay 1996: 167). Guest, who has usefully summarized sociological responses to the burgeoning consultancy industry as a whole, confirms in a review of Peters and Waterman this tendency for critiques to fall into two major categories: 'those concerned with its methodological aspects of the study and those concerned with the analysis and argument' (Guest 1992: 8). In fact, however understandable academics' concern to critique consultancy ideas and associated projects at a common-sense level, this pre-occupation with the truth claims of corporate culture is not without its difficulties.

Sociologists are not usually primarily interested in others' ideas or associated practices because of, or to the extent that, they deviate from the sociologists' (or others') conviction of the truth or falsity of these ideas. Indeed it is a commitment of sociology that we treat social facts – including people's beliefs and practices however bizarre they may seem to us – *as things*, as realities, and that our interest in ideas is not limited to, and indeed should not even start with, the ideas we find congenial or true. 'Since our purpose', write Berger and Luckmann '... is a sociological analysis of the reality of everyday life, more precisely, of knowledge that guides conduct in everyday life, and we are only tangentially interested in how this reality may appear in various theoretical perspectives to intellectuals, we must begin by a clarification of that reality as it is available to the common sense of the ordinary members of society' (Berger and Luckmann 1966: 33).

The danger with focusing primarily on the deficient truth claims of corporate culture writings is that it confuses the assessment of truth with the analysis of the grounds, conditions and circumstances under which claims for truth are made, are disputed and are seen to be authoritative. It may also distract us from analysing the implications of the ideas and practices in question.

Inevitably questions about the bases of truth claims require awareness of and sensitivity to the ways of knowing and understanding which generate truth regimes within which particular sets of propositions can claim authority. A concern with explaining variations from these regimes risks overlooking, even implicitly supporting, that which should be the prime focus of enquiry: how and with what implications particular bodies of ideas gain currency and authority. The fact that a particular discourse establishes a dominance among managers is not a result of that discourse's correspondence with objective truth but because in one way or another it has managed to achieve the political dominance which establishes truth. Authority (truth) is precisely the quality for which different discourses compete. 'It is the outcome of the struggle between competing vocabularies that will decide what the truth of a particular matter will be; it is power relations rather than facts about reality which make things 'true'.' (du Gay 1996a: 45).

Some academics have found it hard to establish distance between themselves and these texts, partly because of course the texts lay claim to the traditional subject area of the academic – organizational analysis. This has led some commentators to focus on the status of these materials rather than on their role. But some writers who have criticized corporate culture writings for their inherent deficiencies, poor conceptualization, and so on, have also argued that these ideas and practices still merit attention. Wood (1989) for example, in an early review of Peters and Waterman and related others, notes that social scientists are likely to criticize them for their lack of interest in political issues. This point has also been forcibly stated by Knights and Willmott: '...organisational culture and symbolism has tended to abstract its subjects of study from the relations of power and domination that are both a condition and a consequence of the existence of culture and symbols in organisations' (1987: 41). The inadequate conceptualization of key terms in corporate culture writings – e.g. culture – has been criticized (Meek 1992). Their inadequate research base has been noted (see Guest 1992; Ramsay 1996). However, despite these failings, Wood – and others – cautions against rejecting these ideas because they fail our academic truth tests: they may well seem glib and shallow, but if they are important to senior managers they should be important to us (Wood 1989; du Gay 1996; Willmott 1993). Although 'The rise of both Excellence and Thatcherism has provoked derision and disdain from people who view themselves as representatives of a deep and authentic humanism', this response '... combines cultural elitism with a failure to understand the problem' (du Gay 1996: 58).

The solution to the polarization of analyses of corporate culture is thus to focus more on the significance of corporate culture in practice and less on the validity of its truth claims (an important example of this approach is Willmott 1993). Attention needs to shift from academic critique of texts – away from disputes about the status of these projects and their research and intellectual underpinnings. There is risk that such a focus distracts scholars from the broader point that culture change programmes seek to act as a relay whereby wider socio-political projects are translated into internal organizational projects. Although within the sociology of work the culture change literature's '... theoretical underpinnings have been criticised, empirical incidence debated, and internal contradictions exposed, *there has been little notice paid to the subjectivising aspects of the Excellence project, and their relationship to the polito-ethical objectives of Thatcherism*' (du Gay 1991: 47, my italics).

What, therefore, is the organizational significance of corporate culture and how can this duality between dismissing it as faddish and vacuous and recognizing its organizational significance be resolved or reduced?

What are the implications of corporate culture projects for power relationships within the organization, for management thinking and expertise, for the way management roles are defined and managers function, for the ways employees and organizations are made amenable and manageable? Despite the fluidity and fickleness and changeability of consultancy fads, they retain some core continuities: they confirm for example the right and responsibility of senior management to re-design the organization, and confirm that they have the necessary qualities to act to ensure the success of the firm. Whatever the nature of the detailed proposals and the theories on which they are built, consultancy interventions always confirm that senior executives *must* (because of environmental pressures for change and increased efficiency) initiate change and that they (with their consultants) are responsible for the survival of the organization.

The starting point of an analysis of the implications of corporate culture in projects of organizational change is the recognition that corporate culture constitutes not simply a series of ramshackle ideas but a discourse. To define it as a discourse means to recognize corporate culture as a 'technology of thought, requiring attention to the particular technical devices for writing, listing, numbering and computing that render a realm into discourse as a knowable, calculable and administrable subject' (Miller and Rose 1993: 79).

Corporate culture activities, regardless of their diversity or even of the quality of the research and analysis on which they are based, are significant because of the ways they reinforce a certain underlying governmentality. To focus on organizational governmentality is 'ask what authorities of various sorts wanted to happen, in relation to what problems defined how, in pursuit of what objectives, through what strategies and techniques' (du Gay 2000: 167). Corporate culture knowledge, whatever we may think of it, has established, and constantly re-establishes, authority: we should be more concerned with the power of these ideas and less with their truth.

One implication of this concern with the power/political implications of corporate culture projects is to raise the analysis of associated knowledge and expertise to a new importance: to consider it as potentially at least as part of the growth of management expertise that is linked to and part of processes of governmentality at the organizational level. If, as Terry Johnson notes, the characteristic outcome of power is not a relationship or process of domination but the probability that the normalized subject or employee will habitually obey – a compliance which in turn reinforces the legitimacy of power – then the various forms and bodies of knowledge which support these processes of self-regulation, the alignment of the personal and the organizational – become important. (This applies most obviously to those consultancy programmes which seek to define, 'make up', constitute, reveal, assess, describe, the employee: i.e. competence frameworks, 360 degree feedback systems, assessment centres and the like. But it also applies to other projects which require the participants to be willingly involved in and committed to programmes of improvement, teamwork, culture change, etc. thus to internalize the requirements of these programmes so that they becomes self-governing.)

Corporate culture projects' significance for the 'governmentality' of organizations concerns the 'shifting ambitions and concerns of all those social authorities that have sought to administer the lives of individuals and associations', and centres on the various constituents of governmentality – '...the diverse mechanisms through which the actions and judgements of persons and organisations have been linked to political objectives' (Miller and Rose 1993: 81). This is an alternative way of seeing and assessing the significance of these projects and ideas: not simply or even primarily as a cyclical series of faddish – and failing – panaceas, the significance of which is largely restricted to the insight their appeal offers into management anxieties and dependency. Corporate culture ideas and packages are important less for the detail and more for the way they supply and confirm a way of thinking about, knowing about, describing and assessing organizations and their component elements (structures, cultures, systems) and employees and their attributes (competences, values, attitudes,) and for 'rendering reality amenable to certain kinds of action' (Miller and Rose 1993: 81).

Central to the processes of organizational governmentality are the ordinary conventions and procedures and routines whereby organizations and employees are understood, analysed and discussed: ways of describing staff, ways of calculation, assessment, examination, ways of formulating and presenting data, and the professional specialisms built around these (Hollway 1991; du Gay and Salaman 1992). Many of these mechanisms play a role in shaping, normalizing and instrumentalizing the conduct, thought, decisions and aspirations of others in order to achieve the objectives of management (du Gay, Salaman and Rees 1996).

To define corporate cultures as a discourse implies not only that there are important connections between the nature of corporate culture as a structure and process of power (governmentality) within the enterprise and larger, socio-political discourses – e.g. enterprise – but also that corporate culture itself, as a set of ideas and practices is crucially implicated in power processes. Through discourse-based ways of knowing, the subject of the discourse – in this case the nature and attributes of the employee – is defined – and known. But there are other implications, equally important. One is to assert the power implications of this knowledge. Employees are not only known and defined, they are set around by practices which reflect and support this knowledge: '... the governance of the employee's soul becomes a more central element in the corporate strategies for gaining competitive advantage' (Willmott 1993: 517).

Fundamental to a view of knowledge in terms of its power implications or governmentality is that knowledge makes organizations and employees '... thinkable and calculable and amenable to deliberate and planful initiatives' (Miller and Rose 1993: 77). So regardless of the validity of corporate culture ideas, what senior executives think they know about organizations, environments, and the necessary characteristics of employees, the necessary rules for achieving improved performance, has a major bearing on how they seek to control, regulate, manipulate employees. Corporate culture certainly describes the world of organizations and the nature and role of employees within those organizations. But it is not merely descriptive: by describing organizations and employees it makes it easier and more legitimate and technically possible to try to change organizations and employees in certain ways.

A central feature of corporate culture as a discourse is that employees' subjectivity is no longer – if it ever was – an area of personal autonomy, freedom or choice but is an area that is subject to organizational power. Corporate culture not only addresses employees' subjectivity; it not only seeks to create and encourage the attributes and attitudes that are seen as necessary, it legitimizes these attempts; it establishes the right of managers to 'govern the soul'. But corporate culture consists of more than efforts simply to define or re-define the character of the employee, for this has been a concern of all management regimes. Corporate culture requires that employees' subjectivity becomes self-disciplining. 'In effect modern technologies of power subjugate by forcing individuals back on themselves so that they become tied to (their own) identity by conscience or self-knowledge' (Knights and Willmott 1989: 550; Foucault 1982: 212).

This is heady stuff. The polarization of the debate around corporate cultures generates two positions: one arguing that such projects are flawed and unrealistic, others arguing that they are significant as attempts to define the new employee in new regimes of governmentality. In this chapter I argue that the crucial significance of corporate culture projects lies in the way in which they articulate assumptions about and attempts to define the employee as part of larger programmes aimed at achieving enterprise within the organization and within employees. One way of advancing the debate is in an empirical way. Recent work by Rosenthal *et al.* has contributed in this way. This shows that in the research organization, a quality focused corporate culture project did have strong and positive effects on employees' view of work and of management but that this should not be seen as a 'totalising of management control' (Rosenthal *et al.* 1997: 500). The two cases that follow are also intended to contribute to our understanding of the implications of corporate culture projects for the process of governmentality within enterprising organizations.

The Health Trust

The Health Trust is a health care provision organization established by a government department but required to compete for the profitable provision of health care with other such organizations. It employs 1,800 people. Organizationally it consists of six functional departments: Medical, Operations, Finance, HR, IT, and Social Work. When the new CE took over in 1990 turnover was £17 million. By 1995 this was £40 million.

A new Chief Executive was determined that the Trust underwent fundamental change in order to enable it to compete and thrive within the NHS market. When the CE arrived the Trust was a 'sleepy hollow' where the management style was one of control and command, the culture was 'totally resistant to change, left wing and elitist'. The Trust was under intense pressure to change – deriving from the external 'market' and from the Chief Executive. Government changes had brought devolved budgets and this required considerably more management involvement. At ground level, employees (nurses, social workers, health visitors) are formed into independent multi-disciplinary teams. The new CE aspired to change the Trust to an organization where people: 'moved faster, were more flexible and less expensive'. The CE's aim was to 'stir things up so that perceptions are changed and people think differently'. His aim was to change behaviour. And to achieve this he wished to install and use newly developed competencies. These were to be used quite explicitly to break down traditional demarcations, destroy bureaucracy and change the organization's culture from a 'professionally driven service' to a 'customer driven service'. Competencies were developed to force the organization to focus on customers' needs, to satisfy those needs, to develop new ways of working (more flexible, integrated, more teamwork) and to do this within reduced budgets. The 'new manager' – developed through the new management competencies – is someone who understands the vision of the business and the strategies of the business and who achieves these through the people s/he manages – someone who internalizes and personifies – in his/her behaviour and attitudes – the sorts of behaviours that reflect the new organization, the new environment and the new culture.

The Chief Executive clearly and explicitly recognized this cultural element of the competence project.

> The kind of organization the staff want to work for can only come about if the individuals behave in the appropriate way. There are behaviours that must be consistent throughout the organization. We're no longer a public sector organization; jobs for life have gone. We've got to become an organization that can succeed competitively and these competencies are about the behaviours that we believe will enable us to succeed: the commercial behaviours; the marketing behaviours, the team building behaviours and the others.

The competencies are defined in the following terms: competence occurs when an individual has the combination of knowledge, skills, abilities, attitudes, values and personal style required to deliver effectively the purpose and responsibilities of their role within our organization. The process of competence application was as follows. First, a number of competencies were identified. These were then defined concretely and operationally at a number of grades or levels. These were in turn used to develop the competence profile of every role. Individual role incumbents were then profiled (by self, and manager) and the two standards – individual/role – compared. This would identify gaps and a development plan was drafted and agreed to fill these competence gaps. The benefits of this process to the Trust were explicit and clear. They were:

- To assist the Trust in ensuring that employees are meeting objectives – goals, standards, strategy.
- The clarification of roles for incumbents.
- An emphasis on performance and performance measurement.
- And contribute towards the identification and recognition of those employees who can most contribute to the new organization.

The CE saw a direct and critical link between the competence project and the achievement of a broad programme of culture change within the Trust. This had three aspects. First, the competencies themselves were seen as necessary for managers to expedite their newly empowered and autonomous (enterprising, non-bureaucratic) management roles. Second, the competencies were defined as those required for managers to operate successfully within a market-focused, competitive environment. Many of the competencies were simply individualized versions of the new qualities that the CE thought were essential for the success of the Trust as a whole – customer-focus, enterprise, quality, commercial awareness, etc. Third, the competencies required the individual managers to take responsibility for having, or developing, and displaying the competencies. The managers – like the new organization – had to be enterprising. They had to behave like mini organizations – scanning the environment, recognizing what was required of them, developing the necessary marketable products (or in this case, behaviours and attitudes). They had to be willing and able to recognize what was wanted of them and to change and market themselves.

Thus the competence project within the Trust not only carried the new values adopted and advocated by the CE, it also redefined the relationship between the employer and the manager in a way which reflected these values – i.e. away from secure employment, professional standards, loyalty (or, more negatively, bureaucracy, lack of customer-focus, etc.) and towards a more market-like relationship where managers were required to involve themselves in their own development in terms of the (new) organization's strategies and values.

Hotel International

Hotel International is an international hotel chain operating 160 hotels in 50 countries. Each night Hotel International sells about 50,000 rooms. The company's marketing strategy is aimed explicitly at the frequent international business traveller. The chain employs about 50,000 people.

The company bases its competitive strategy on achieving customer focus and customer satisfaction. Its senior managers are convinced that guest satisfaction is central to success. A general manager of one of its major hotels said: 'We strive very hard to get the whole organization focused on the customer and focused on providing the customer with a consistent and very high quality of service.'

HR specialists within Hotel International have given a great deal of thought to finding ways of ensuring that the many staff in many locations are committed to the senior managers' goals of high customer service quality.

The key to this was clearly and thoughtfully stated by the general manager of one of the North African hotels:

> People like to live a dream you know, and it is our duty to try to fulfil their dreams. The key is the human aspect of things. Technology can help a lot, but technology can be upsetting; the human service, the human element, soothes, and calms people. We have a job here to make people calm, to make them happier, and that a machine can't do – it aggravates people. So we have to make our guests feel as if they were a friend, that they're not a pawn in the world and that when they come to us they are recognized for what they are. We have to look after them and that's what I mean when I say that we are in the people business. It's the interaction between customer and client that counts. On this I have little direct influence at all. When you sit in the coffee shop and you're being served a cup of coffee I have no influence. I can make sure that the system functions: that the coffee's hot, that the china is clean, that the spoons are clean, that the table is clean and that the waiter serves the coffee properly and he himself looks neat and tidy – all that the system can arrange. But to give the smile, and to make the interaction right, that is much more than the system; that's a way of life. You can't force people to smile or to be happy, but you have somehow to create it.

But despite the relative complexity and difficulty of achieving 'the smile' – the human element – Hotel International in fact goes to considerable lengths to ensure that staff develop the appropriate attitudes and display the appropriate behaviour.

The first step in this process is the clear identification of what proper behaviour and quality interaction look like. This is achieved by a variety of methods. Mystery guests are employed to audit the quality of service and to identify shortfalls. The results are then reviewed by the teams responsible. Second, a thorough process of benchmarking is used to identify standards for each department and unit. A senior manager commented: 'We've worked out on a check that we could fail a guest in excess of 130 points during one visit.' Another technique is the use of committees of members of staff within each service or outlet which try to identify guests' expectations and how they can be met.

Once standards are identified, staff are thoroughly instructed in how these can be met – and exceeded. Training is critical here. Technical training is important; but it is not enough. The regional manager, Africa and Middle East remarked:

> I've seen people with less qualifications and with wonderful attitudes, who were appreciated much more than somebody who's highly qualified but doesn't have the right attitude. This is the service industry; it's the smile – it's the way you talk to people; it's the way you look at them; it's the way you welcome them.

Training therefore focuses on both technical and social – and interpersonal – elements: 'We obviously teach them what to do and how to do it; but we stress attitude and behaviour and the smile and how to talk to people – which is really what the guest remembers.'

And the HR specialists believe that even 'the smile' can be trained. A thorough 'customer care' programme breaks down a variety of key behaviours and routines into a series of minute operations or steps – for example, a guest arriving at the hotel reception to check in and to receive his/her room key. This activity is broken down – 'how to approach the guests, how to hand over the key to the guest, how to ask them to fill in the registration form – that's the real performance standard, and it gives them step by step what to do in order to achieve a proper interaction with the guest'.

But staff are also exposed to a widely publicized set of general standards or rules. In one major hotel these general standards are embodied in eleven golden rules of customer care. These rules, carried on a plastic card by all staff at all times, are an ambitious attempt to win the hearts and minds to the goal of customer care – exceeding the guests' expectations. These standards are communicated through induction and training. Each month a different rule is highlighted – on posters throughout the staff areas – for special attention.

This takes the form of a set of explicit and widely publicized rules or ideals. These rules are communicated energetically. Staff are encouraged – and rewarded – for showing compliance; those who fail to accept them are subject to remedial counselling support. The rules are associated with appraisal processes and rewards and are the focus of a special reward process whereby outstanding exemplars of the golden rules – who have been identified by guests or by mystery guests – are publicly rewarded every month.

The HR manager was clear about the objective of this project: 'This is something that develops our culture; all the training and development that we give our staff is very much reinforcing this message. And everything we have in place helps us as a business achieve our goals.'

CONCLUSION

These two cases reveal in an illustrative manner some of the ways in which corporate culture projects can contribute to processes of government within organizations. They help us move from general statements about discourse and governmentality to more specific and concrete examples of processes and relationships in corporate culture projects. They reveal the ways in which culture programmes are integrally implicated in larger programmes of organizational change, and reveal how different programmes of change depend upon and assume new regimes of the person.

These two cases suggest some of the ways in which corporate culture projects, despite their conceptual, theoretical and empirical limitations, seek to redefine the nature of employees and their relationships with their employers and indeed with their own attributes and behaviour. Neither of the projects illustrated in this chapter was ostensibly or primarily concerned with culture *per se*. One was concerned with competences and competence architectures; the other with a customer care programme. But it is clear that both were culture projects, in that both sought to 'unlock the commitment and enthusiasm of employees' (Thompson and McHugh 1995: 198). Furthermore, both were concerned with inculcating enterprise within employees: both change programmes aimed to make staff take responsibility for, and to be accountable for, achieving the goals of the organization. As the general manager of Hotel International noted, obedience is not enough: now identification is required: commitment and enterprise.

In both cases the subjectivity of employees is 'problematized', is made an object of management concern, or corporate significance, worthy of attention and requiring attention. This is a central feature, and something that distinguishes corporate culture. What is important is not simply how subjectivity is made problematic – i.e. the particular qualities that are defined as necessary – but the fact that it is problematized at all. As Rose asks: how and by whom are aspects of the human being defined as problematic, according to what systems of judgement and in relation to what concerns? (Rose 1995). In both cases the problematization of employees' subjectivity was directly and closely associated with projects of organizational change and with attempts to improve or ensure the achievement of enterprise, flexibility or customer focus.

The two cases illustrate how once employees' subjectivity is defined as problematic, management is defined as the authority that should, indeed must manage this subjectivity. Managers *qua* managers are accorded or claim the capacity to speak truthfully about employees, their nature and their problems (Rose 1995). This is one major way in which, as Townley has noted, management is defined in political terms, and management claims to define the nature of employee subjectivity are an example of the ways in which constitutive knowledge (of employees) and power connect (Townley 1993: 224). Managers' authority to engage in issues of employee subjectivity is based on the conviction not only that this 'soft' side of organization is a critical lever of organizational performance ('The guiding aim and abiding concern of Corporate Culture ... is to win the hearts and minds of employees' Peters and Waterman 1982: xvii), but also that differential levels of national economic performance are a consequence of cultural factors. Ouchi, for example, the author of the best-selling *Theory Z,* in his comparison of Japanese and American firms, explains American failure by the negative consequences of US bureaucratic work structures on workers' attitudes: 'involved workers are the key to productivity' (Ouchi 1981: 4).

The two cases also demonstrate how corporate culture not only defines management as legitimately concerned with subjectivity; it also defines them as competent in this area: as experts – or at least as potential experts on subjectivity. Managers' own competence becomes defined in terms of their ability to generate and engage with the 'self-fulfilling impulses' of employees (du Gay 1996: 26). Managers must now be able to enable employees to develop self knowledge and to connect personal objectives and personal development with corporate goals. The manager is central to the achievement of corporate culture, and this in itself requires new qualities and attributes (du Gay 1996: 21).

Corporate culture thus acts as a way of connecting ideologies of organization and management with individuals' behaviour. It is a method of *translation* of the organizational into the individual. Enterprise (i.e. flexibility, anti-bureaucracy, customer-focused) as necessary and desirable organizational (and indeed societal) qualities is translated into and achieved at the individual level through corporate culture projects. In both cases the culture projects were aimed at aligning organizational objectives and strategies with individual behaviours. The competences in the Health Trust and the values in the hotel chain involved the individualization of the qualities assumed by, or required by the organizational strategy.

Individual employees were defined in terms of competences and values as if they were themselves businesses or were running their businesses within the larger organizations. There were two aspects to this.

First, this means that they were required to be – or to become – entrepreneurial, dynamic, risk-taking, responsible, customer-focused, commercially sensitive, etc. They were required to display valued organizational qualities. Second, it means that employees were expected to take the organization's priorities (customer care in the case of Hotel International, flexibility and commercial focus in the Health Trust) as their own. To be responsible for achieving organizational priorities. Obedience, compliance are no longer enough. In the Health Trust the new manager is someone who takes responsibility for achieving – through his/her staff – the vision and strategies of the business. And in the hotel the employees are responsible for customer satisfaction – for 'the smile ... to make the interaction right'. And both these responsibilities will be unfulfilled if behaviour fails – often in very subtle ways – to communicate sincerity and commitment.

The two examples of corporate culture projects also illustrate the ways in which these projects supply a range of technologies: organizational mechanisms which have been developed often by expert advisers – consultants, engineers, occupational psychologists, IT specialists – to govern employees' subjectivity and direct it in certain directions. These technologies offer ways of describing employees, in terms of their nature, attitudes and attributes, with particular reference to subtle subjective aspects: demeanour, judgement, enthusiasm, compliance. They also enable the identification and measurement of these qualities, once identified. They supply theories which explain these attributes and offer methods to develop and direct them.

Finally, the cases confirm the central feature of corporate culture discourse: that individual employees are defined as responsible for being and becoming enterprising – for not only demonstrating the required qualities but for showing a willingness to develop and display the qualities. In both cases employees learned through a variety of organizational technologies ('feedback') about their 'strengths and weaknesses', their assessments, their profile. In both cases these data could be contrasted with formal requirements (established through competence standards, training standards, etc.). 'Enterprise', and 'commitment' to the qualities and behaviour necessary for customer-focus and commercial performance thus become central elements in self-knowledge, self-control and allegedly self-realization.

Finally the cases illustrate the role of corporate culture projects in organizational governmentality. Employers take responsibility for 'making up' employees in the face of environmental challenge and strategic necessity. Now employees are personally responsible for self-government – displaying the attributes the organization requires. Their nature and feelings and not simply their behaviour are now proper matters of organizational concern. And while they have no more control over the origin of corporate strategies (which are anyway defined as necessary adjustments to undeniable market or global forces) they are now responsible for strategy implementation.

REFERENCES

Alvesson, M. (1987) 'Organisations, Culture and Ideology', *International Studies of Management and Organisation*, **XVII** (3): 4–18.

Alvesson, M. (1989) 'The Cultural Perspective on Organisations: Instrumental values and basic features of culture', *Scandinavian Journal of Management*, **5**(2): 123–36.

Alvesson, M. (1991) 'Organisational Symbolism and Ideology', *Journal of Management Studies*, **28**(3): 207–25.

Anthony, P. (1994) *Managing Culture*, Buckingham: Open University Press.

Baxter, B. (1996) 'Consultancy Expertise: A Post-Modern Perspective', in H. Scarborough (ed.) *The Management of Expertise*, London: Macmillan: 66–92.

Berger, P.L. and Luckmann, T. (1966) *The Social Construction of Reality*, Allen Lane, London.

Bloomfield, B. and Vurdubakis, T. (1994) 'Re-presenting Technology: IT Consultancy reports as Textual Reality Constructs', *Sociology*, **28**: 455–77.

Brunsson, N. and Olsen, J. (1993) *The Reforming Organisation*, London: Routledge.

Chandler, A.D. (1977) *The Visible Hand: The Managerial Revolution in American Business*, Cambridge, MA: Harvard University Press.

Clark, T. and Salaman, G. (1998) 'Telling Tales: Management Gurus' Narratives and the Construction of Managerial Identity', *Journal of Management Studies*, **35**(2): 137–61.

Covey, S. (1989), *The Seven Habits of Highly Effective People*, New York: Simon and Schuster.

Deal, T.E. and Kennedy A.A. (1982; 1991) *Corporate Cultures*, Harmondsworth: Penguin.

du Gay, P. (1991) 'Enterprise Culture and the Ideology Of Excellence', *New Formations*, **13**: 45–62.

du Gay, P. (1996a) *Consumption and Identity at Work*, London: Sage.

du Gay, P. (1996b) 'Making Up Managers: Enterprise and the Ethos of Bureaucracy', in S. Clegg and G. Palmer (eds) *The Politics of Management Knowledge*, London: Sage: 19–35.

du Gay, P. (2000) 'Enterprise and its Futures: A response to Fournier and Grey', *Organisation*, **7**(1): 165–83.

du Gay, P. and Salaman, G. (1992) 'The Cult(ure) Of The Customer', *Journal of Management Studies*, **29**: 615–33.

du Gay, P., Salaman, G. and Rees, B. (1996) 'The Conduct of Management and the Management of Conduct: Contemporary Managerial Discourse and the Constitution of the "Competent" Manager', *Journal of Management Studies*, **33**: 263–82.

Fincham, R. (1999) 'The Consultant-Client Relationship: Critical Perspectives on The Management of Organisational Change', *Journal of Management Studies*, **36**: 335–52.

Foucault, M. (1980) *Power/Knowledge*, Brighton: Harvester.

Foucault, M. (1982) 'Their Subject and Power', in L. Dreyfus and P. Rabinow (eds) *Michel Foucault*, Brighton: Harvester.

Gill, J. and Whittle, S. (1992) 'Management By Panacea: Accounting for Transcience', *Journal of Management Studies*, **30**: 281–95.

Grint, K. (1994) 'Re-engineering History: Social Resonances and Business Process Re-engineering', *Organisation*, **1**: 179–201.

Guest, D. (1990) 'Human Resource Management and the American Dream', *Journal of Management Studies*, **27**: 377–97.

Guest, D. (1992) 'Right Enough To Be Dangerously Wrong', in G. Salaman (ed.) *Human Resource Strategies*, London: Sage: 1–19.

Hall, S. (1997) 'The Work of Representation', in S. Hall (ed.) *Representation: Cultural Representations and Signifying Practices*, London: Sage: 13–74.

Hollway, W. (1991) *Work Psychology and Organisational Behaviour*, London: Sage.

Huczynski, A. (1993) 'Explaining the Succession of Management Fads', *International Journal of Human Resource Management*, **4**: 443–63.

Jackson, B. (1996) 'Re-engineering The Sense of Self: The Manager and the Management Guru', *Journal of Management Studies*, **33**: 571–90.

Jackson, B.G. (1996) 'The Goose that Laid The Golden Egg? A Rhetorical Critique of Stephen Covey and the Effectiveness Movement', *Journal of Management Studies*, **35**(3): 353–77.

Jeffcutt, P. (1994) 'The Interpretation of Organisation: A contemporary Analysis and critique', *Journal of Management Studies*, **31:** 225–50.

Johnson, T. (1993) 'Expertise and the State', in M. Gane and T. Johnson (eds) *Foucault's New Domains*, London: Routledge: 139–52.

Keiser, A. (1997) 'Rhetoric and Myth in Management Fashion', *Organisation*, **4:** 49–74.

Knights, D. and Willmott, H.C. (1987) 'Organisational Culture as Management Strategy: A Critique and Illustration from the Financial Services Industry', *International Studies of Management and Organisation*, **17:** 40–63.

Mabey, C., Salaman, G. and Storey, J. (1998) *Human Resource Management*, Oxford: Blackwell.

Meek, L. (1992) 'Organisational Culture: Origins and Weaknesses', in G. Salaman (ed.) *Human Resource Strategies*, London: Sage: 192–212.

Miller, P. and Rose, N. (1993) 'Governing Economic Life', in M. Gane and T. Johnson (eds) *Foucault's New Domains*, London: Routledge: 75–105.

Morgan, G. (1988) *Riding the Waves of Change*, San Francisco: Jossey-Bass.

Ogbonna, E. (1992a) 'Managing Organisational Culture: Fantasy or Reality?', *Human Resource Management Journal*, **3**(2): 42–54.

Ogbonna, E. (1992b) 'Organisation Culture and Human Resource Management: Dilemmas and Contradictions', in Blyton, P. and Turnbull, P. (eds) *Reassessing Human Resource Management*, London: Sage.

Ogbonna, E. and Wilkinson, B. (1990) 'Corporate Strategy and Corporate Culture: The View from the Checkout', *Personnel Review*, **19**(4): 9–15.

Ouchi, W.G. (1981) *Theory Z: How American Business Can Meet The Japanese Challenge*, Reading, MA: Addison-Wesley.

Peters, T. and Waterman, R. (1982) *In Search of Excellence*, New York: Harper and Row.

Ramsay, H. (1996) 'Managing Sceptically: A Critique of Organisational Fashion', in S. Clegg and G. Palmer (eds) *The Politics of Management Knowledge*, London: Sage: 155–72.

Rose, N. (1990) *Governing the Soul*, London: Routledge.

Rose, N. (1995) 'Identity, Genealogy, History', in S. Hall and P. du Gay (eds) *Questions of Cultural Identity*, London: Sage.

Rosenthal, P., Hill, S. and Peccei, R. (1997) 'Checking Out Service: Evaluating Excellence, HRM and TQM in Retailing', *Work Employment and Society*, **11:** 481–503.

Senge, P. (1990) 'The Leader's New Work', *Sloan Management Review*, **32**(1): 7–23.

Thompson, P. and McHugh, D. (1995) *Work Organisation: A Critical Introduction*, Basingstoke: Macmillan.

Townley, B. (1992) 'In the Eye of the Gaze: The Constitutive Role of Performance Appraisal', in P. Barrar and G. Cooper (eds) *Managing Organisations in 1992*, London: Routledge.

Townley, B. (1993) 'Performance Appraisal and the Emergence of Management', *Journal of Management Studies*, **30:** 221–38.

Townley, B. (1995) '"Know Thyself": Self Awareness, Self Formation and Managing', *Organisation*, **2:** 271–89.

Townley, B. (1999) 'Practical Reason and Performance Appraisal', *Journal of Management Studies*, **36:** 287–306.

Willmott, H. (1993) 'Strength is Ignorance; Slavery is Freedom: Managing Culture in Modern Organisations', *Journal of Management Studies*, **30,** 515–52.

Wood, S. (1989) 'New Wave Management', *Work, Employment and Society*, **3,** 379–402.

11 Reward System Choices

Ian Kessler

INTRODUCTION

Given the enduring centrality of reward to the structure and operation of the employment relationship, it is hardly surprising that the way in which employees are compensated has remained central to discussion and research related to the notion of human resource management. Reward has invariably been key to conceptual and analytical human resource (HR) frameworks. It was the one policy area explicitly integral to both the Harvard (Beer *et al*. 1984) and Michigan models (Fombrun *et al*. 1984), while its identification as a key management lever (Storey 1992) in the pursuit of a range of HR and organizational goals, has encouraged interest in developing corporate pay and benefits practice. However, as these early models have evolved and debate on human resource management has coalesced around certain themes and issues, the consequence for our understanding of reward's contribution to the management of human resources has been somewhat uneven and uncertain.

These models and their treatment of pay have stimulated interest in various disciplines and frameworks, generating new and more varied insights and questions. Over the years, debate on reward has, of course, been heavily informed and structured by conceptual, analytical and theoretical frameworks from various disciplines. Reflecting the contrasting assumptions and preoccupations of these disciplines, the specific research questions raised and methods used have varied. Social or occupational psychology has perhaps been most to the fore with an interest in pay and motivation revolving around process and needs theories and concentrating very much on employee perceptions, attitudes and behaviours. However, more recent developments in economics and sociology have increasingly raised new issues about the nature and role of pay.

The emergence of organizational economics, as neo-classical assumptions governing firm behaviour have been relaxed, has given rise to an interest in pay as a control mechanism. Performance pay has been placed at the core of agency theory (Eisenhardt 1992) along with monitoring or surveillance as means of ensuring the alignment of principal–agent goals and actions. Transactions cost analysis has also been used to evaluate decision-making as it relates to pay practices (Walsh 1993). Thus different transaction costs have been seen to have markedly different implications for the use of different forms of pay supporting its use either as an internal or market based mechanism. The 'new institutional approach' within sociology has focused on the power of social and normative pressures to influence the character, incidence and diffusion of pay practices. Drawing on the strategy literature the resource-based view has also increasingly been used to assess pay's value in leveraging and supporting distinctive firm capabilities as the route to 'sustained competitive advantage'.

On the other hand, sensitivity to some of the complexities and subtleties associated with reward has often been lost. More specifically, an appreciation of the variety, complexity and sophistication associated with the design and operation of pay practices has sometimes fallen victim to an 'unholy alliance' between a specific and rather narrow set of research questions and a limited and particular set of research methodologies. In short, established HR models have commonly been mobilized to consider how human resource management can contribute to improved business performance through the use of quantitative, survey based research techniques. This methodological 'myopia' has encouraged a highly simplistic characterization of pay and indeed other HR practices and some remarkable distortions of theoretical frameworks which otherwise might be extremely powerful in explaining developments in reward management. Illustrative of this latter point is Gerhart et al.'s (1996) attempt to assess pay's contribution to business performance using the resource-based view of the firm, by reference to a few statistically testable variables. Given the emphasis placed by this view on social complexity and causal ambiguity as the route to 'sustained competitive advantage', such an approach seems at best highly questionable.

These problems might also be related to the fact that research on HR and business performance has tended to be data – rather than theory – driven. Despite stirrings of interest in new analytical and theoretical frameworks, these have not as yet been used extensively to generate research questions and structure research design. Richardson and Thompson (1999: 11), highlighting this point, cite Wright and McMahan's (1992) observation that the unsophisticated treatment of reward in mainstream HR models may well be related to the absence of a robust theoretical underpinning to the relationship between incentive pay and business performance. Such concerns imply a need to focus on *how* and *why* reward might contribute to business performance as means of highlighting the kind of statistical analysis required to establish meaningful relationships between variables.

The purpose of this chapter is to consider this doubled-edge treatment of reward which has seen the application of a wider range of analytical frameworks drawn from different disciplines to study it but at the same time some loss of sensitivity to the complexities associated with this policy area in mainstream human resource literature. It seeks to do this by considering the way in which reward has been dealt with by the conceptual and analytical models structuring and driving current deliberations on human resource management. Two models, highlighted elsewhere in this volume, will be drawn upon. One revolves around notions of high commitment, high involvement or high performance management (Wood 1999) seen in 'best' practice or universalistic terms. The other relates to a concern with contingency, fit or match.

Reward has been treated in two ways within the context of universalistic and contingency models. First, it has been included as part of an integrated and coherent general model of human resource management and while seen as a crucial sphere of policy and practice has been included along with such other important HR activities as recruitment, communication, involvement, work design and appraisal. Different forms of reward have routinely been presented as part of a high commitment bundle of practices while matching models have invariably linked reward to various contingencies. Second, compensation has been considered more directly through the lens of these different frameworks. Gerhart *et al.* (1996) for example examine new directions in compensation research by comparing the analytical value of the universalistic approach and the contingency model, while Wood (1996) specifically concentrates on pay within the context of high commitment management.

This chapter will address a number of issues. First, what kinds of questions do these different models raise about the nature and operation of pay systems? Second, to what extent has research systematically addressed these questions? Third, where research evidence is available to what degree does it provide support for the underlying assumptions and more explicit propositions about pay informing these models?

After a brief review of different types of reward and pay practice, the chapter is divided into two main parts. The first looks at pay and the universalistic model and the second considers pay and the contingency approach.

DEFINITIONS AND TYPES

Broadly defined, reward encapsulates one side of the coin that makes up the employment relationship. Thus, this relationship is often defined in terms of the 'effort-reward bargain' and Bloom and Milkovich (1992: 22) seek to capture this breadth by defining reward as a 'bundle of returns offered in exchange for a cluster of employee contributions'. In distinguishing between different types of reward a distinction is often made between *intrinsic reward*, internally driven and, for example, linked to work satisfaction, self actualization and pride in job or company, and *extrinsic rewards* associated more with monetary and non-monetary returns provided externally. This distinction has recently been subject to some re-conceptualization with a number of commentators distinguishing between tangible, transactional rewards and less tangible, relational rewards. Armstrong and Brown (2000), for instance, categorize rewards according to two dimensions: the nature of the reward (relational or transactional) and the basis of the reward (individual or communal). On this basis they equate relational-communal rewards with the working environment; relational-individual rewards with learning and development opportunities; individual-transactional rewards with pay; and communal-transactional rewards with non pay benefits such as pensions, holidays and 'perks'.

Within this agenda, the chapter focuses primarily on pay. None the less, the range of available compensatory returns listed above provides an important reminder that in discussing reward we are dealing with a set of related and perhaps complementary policies and practices. Indeed, the same to a lesser extent might be said about pay. Thus, the approach to pay adopted by any given organization will comprise a number of elements as reflected in different mechanisms and procedures designed to pursue various managerial objectives. In most organizations these elements emerge primarily in the form of pay structures and pay systems.

Pay structures are essentially designed to provide some internal ordering and hierarchy of jobs within a particular organization for the purpose of establishing differential rates of pay for that job or bundle of jobs as well as providing clear paths for career development and progression. The creation of such a structure, although closely related, is technically separate from the establishment of pay rates. It is usually pursued through the use of job evaluation, a mechanism employed to establish internal job worth through the systematic application of a set of rules and procedures to a given post rather than to the individual filling it.

Job evaluation may be used in a more or less formal and structured way. Non-analytical schemes such as job ranking and paired comparisons are relatively subjective but may be administratively viable in small and simple organizations. In larger and more complex organizations analytical schemes are more often used. They typically involve the identification of a set of factors, such as knowledge, responsibility and problem solving, against which different posts can be scored. The job scores, naturally representing the relative weighting of the organization's jobs, are then used as the basis for grades. While a specific occupation might form the basis for a single spot pay rate, it is more usual for a number of jobs of a similar weight to be included in a single grade and for such grades to allow for progression between minimum and maximum rate.

Pay systems are the mechanism driving this pay progression and more general pay uprating. In broad terms, such systems have tended to be founded on two basic and enduring principles: time and performance (Brown 1989). Time-based pay is structured and administered in a relatively simple and straightforward way. Employees are paid to work for stipulated periods of time with pay expressed by reference to these time periods as an hourly rate, weekly wage and annual salary.

The notion of pay for performance, in contrast, embraces a wide range of pay systems. These vary according to the unit of performance which, leaving aside Armstrong and Brown's slightly restricted interpretation, might be either the individual or the collective and in relation to the nature of performance, which might be either input or output based. These two dimensions provide the basis for Table 11.1 below, which sets out the main types of performance pay system. The individual-output systems tend to link pay to relatively tangible and quantifiable measures of employee performance – in the case of piecework, the unit of production or time saved against standard performance and with commissions, the sales achieved. In addition, performance-related pay has been narrowly defined for the purpose of this typology to identify a pay system which relates pay to concrete

Table 11.1 Pay systems: linking type of performance with unit of performance

	Unit of performance	
Type of performance	*Individual*	*Collective*
Output	Piecework	Measured Daywork
	Commission	Team Pay
	Individual Bonus	Profit Sharing
	Individual Performance-Related Pay (IPRP)	Gain Sharing
Input	Skills-Based Pay	Employee Share Ownership Schemes
	Merit Pay	
	Competence pay	

individual targets or objectives. It is distinguished from merit pay, the major individual-input scheme, which bases pay upon behavioural traits such as flexibility, co-operation and punctuality, which employees bring with them to the job. Skill-based pay can be seen in similar terms, rewarding employees for coming to their posts with certain physical and mental capacities or capabilities. More recently, this approach has evolved into competence based pay with its somewhat more structured and formalized approach to distinguishing and evaluating behaviours and abilities.

In general, collective-output schemes rely upon a geared relationship between pay and the performance of a work unit, whether this be the work group, the plant or the company. In other words, a stipulated level of performance defined at a predetermined level of group output, profit, sales or added value, leads in a mechanistic sense to given pay out-turn. In contrast to a number of the individual schemes, these systems rarely require an appraisal, although the pay-out may be linked to 'satisfactory' employee performance, and thus limit any need for managerial judgement. They do, however, vary markedly in their design. For example, a distinction can be made between approved profit-sharing schemes attracting tax benefits if structured in a particular way and non-approved schemes which while less tax efficient, can be organized in any way the company sees fit. Employee share ownership plans in contrast to other systems involve a transfer of ownership rather than just cash. ESOPs are based on capital being brought into the company, usually in the form of a bank loan, which is then used to buy shares for the employees and serviced by profits.

In any given organization, extrinsic rewards may, therefore, be seen to constitute a suite of practices covering pay systems, pay structure and non-monetary benefits. These practices, in turn, might be seen to take various forms and be designed in different ways. Attention now turns to the universal approach and the sensitivity it displays towards this variation and diversity.

Pay and the universal approach

Pay has been viewed in very different ways by the universal school depending on the form taken by the universal recipe and sometimes reflecting the tensions inherent within it. Wood's (1999) general characterization of these universal recipes in the guise of high commitment, high involvement and high performance models helps brings to the fore the contrasting positions held by pay. Thus, the downplaying of pay's significance in Lawler's (1986) high involvement model can be contrasted with its much more prominent (if sometimes contested and uncertain) position in high commitment and high performance approaches.

The high commitment and high performance approaches link pay and indeed other HR practices to employee attitudes and behaviours. As Wood (1999) notes, recent formulations of the high performance approach have placed particular emphasis on *behaviour*, suggesting that certain HR mechanisms have a particularly direct effect in this respect without the mediating influence of attitudinal re-structuring. Wood (1999) draws attention to Becker and Huselid's (1998) work on high-performance management, which appears to attach particular importance to contingent forms of compensation as a powerful technique for stimulating required behaviours in this unmediated way.

A tight definition of the high commitment approach would appear to give greater weight to pay's ability to influence employee attitudes, and more specifically its potential to generate organizational commitment. It is relatively silent on behaviours but the assumption must be that enhanced employee commitment feeds through to 'desired' behaviours, which then contribute to improved organizational performance. Certainly, the relationship between pay as well as other HR techniques and commitment has not always been treated in such a literal sense. As Wood (1999) notes, high commitment practices have sometimes been associated with high-profile companies, such as IBM and Hewlett Packard or simply identified as an alternative to Tayloristic mechanisms so clearly driven by notions of control. However, if a tight definition is adopted, the high commitment approach raises the following set of pay related questions: what types of payment systems and structures are viewed as contributing to attitudinal (re-) structuring? In what way might these pay systems and structures be deemed to encourage employee commitment? To what extent do these systems and structures actually stimulate employee commitment? How does any commitment generated in this way feed through to improved organizational performance via new forms of employee behaviour?

High commitment pay practices

Drawing on some of the major self-designated studies on high commitment management practices, it is clear from Table 11.2 that there are a number of differences in approach to the inclusion of pay practices. The first relates to the incidence and combination of collective and individual forms of performance pay. For many of the listed authors (Roach 1999; MacDuffie 1995; Wood, 1996; Walton 1985)

Table 11.2 Classification of authors and approaches

Author	High Commitment (Control/Cost Reduction) Pay Practices
Roach 1999	Individual PRP – incidence of merit-based performance pay Collective PRP – collective group-performance-based pay (employee share options, profit sharing, group bonus)
MacDuffie 1995	Contingent compensation: Corporate performance Plant performance Skills acquired
Wood 1996	Some merit element in pay
Arthurs 1992	Relatively high wages (relatively low wages) Stock ownership (incentive-based pay)
Walton 1985	Variable rewards to create equity and reinforce group achievement: profit and gain sharing (variable pay where feasible to provide individual incentive) Individual pay linked to skills and mastery (individual pay geared to job evaluation)
Cully *et al.* 1999	Profit Sharing and Employee Share Ownership Schemes
Pfeffer 1998	High pay contingent on organizational performance

high commitment compensation is seen to reside in some combination of collective and individual approaches. However, Arthurs (1992), Pfeffer (1998) and Cully *et al.* (1999) are more inclined to view this type of compensation in terms of collective reward alone. Second, the authors vary in the type of payment system that they associate with the high commitment approach. On the individual side, merit-based pay is most commonly cited, although emphasis is given by others to skill-based pay. Collective pay is defined by reference to various communal entities including the group, the plant and/or the corporation. Third, the authors differ in the attention given to pay structures and pay levels. In general, these dimensions of pay are overlooked. However, Arthurs and Pfeffer do include high wage levels as part of their high commitment pay package. Walton alone draws attention to pay structure by perhaps perversely (see below) including job evaluated pay as part of control strategy although others (including, for example, Wood) imply the significance of pay structure by including career progression on the basis of objective criteria in his range of practices.

Pay practices and the commitment rationale

With a few exceptions (Wood 1996) these authors do not provide a sophisticated discussion of, or justification for, the inclusion of particular pay practices. Indeed, Walton admits 'which (compensation) approach is really suitable to the commitment model is unclear' (1985: 82) and makes no meaningful attempt to explain why, for example, skill-based pay should encourage commitment to the organization rather than say the occupation or the job. This view is echoed by Wood (1996: 54) who notes with reference to the high commitment model, 'that there is not a clear consensus about the appropriate payment system'.

The uncertainty about what constitutes a high commitment pay practice may well reflect the fact that similar pay approaches can be compatible with markedly different corporate HR philosophies (Schuler 1992) or management styles and contextual circumstances (Kessler and Purcell 1995). In others words, any given pay practice can be used in very different ways and for markedly different purposes rather than necessarily being associated with any particular HR model or narrowly defined goal. The high commitment label is provided by academic researchers and may or may not reflect management intent. It is fundamentally misconceived to try to label any pay practice intrinsically high-commitment oriented.

Individual performance related pay

In reviewing the use of the different high commitment pay practices cited earlier, it is the status of individual performance related or merit pay that has stimulated the most heated debate. Wood (1996) sets its inclusion by Storey (1992) and Purcell (1993) in a commitment-oriented personnel approach against the views of others, such as Beer *et al.* (1985) who have seen it more as a hard, control-based technique. Indeed, Beer *et al.* have noted, 'by making pay contingent upon performance (as judged by management), management is signalling that it is they – not the individual – who are in control' (quoted in Pfeffer 1998: 113). However, as already noted, it is somewhat misguided to frame the debate in these terms. It is clear that a wide range of managerial goals have informed the use of IPRP as reflected in schemes designed in very different ways.

Certainly, the pursuit of employee commitment might be seen both directly and indirectly to underpin the use of certain IPRP schemes particularly given their inevitable focus on the individual. In a direct sense, such schemes are sometimes structured to 'lock' the employee into the organization through an association between the individual's pay-related objectives and broader corporate objectives. Less directly, such schemes in sometimes diluting union involvement in pay determination may well weaken employee commitment to the union and strengthen it to the organization as the source of any pay increase. More generally, IPRP as part of a broader individualization of the employment relationship sometimes accompanied by the use of related techniques, such as more direct forms of communication, might serve to undermine any sense of collective employee identity or solidarity and make workers more susceptible to other forms of loyalty. Although research suggests that organizations rarely use IPRP primarily as a means of undermining union influence (Thompson 1993), there have been high profile cases, such as British Rail in the early nineties, where the introduction of such a scheme was accompanied by the de-recognition of the unions. Indeed, Brown *et al.* (1998: 61) find that de-recognizing firms have moved further towards linking pay to individual performance than their unionized counterparts.

It is equally apparent, however, that other managerial goals play an important part in the use of IPRP. Such schemes have been used to address recruitment and retention problems by boosting the earnings opportunities of employees in tight labour markets. For instance, in Rolls Royce it was common practice for many years for the central pay mandate to encourage sites to allocate merit increases to employee groups in short supply. IPRP has also been seen as a more efficient use of the pay bill in targeting pay increases on those 'deserving' an increase rather than providing across the board increases. Thompson (1993) in his survey of almost 50 organizations found that around a third had introduced IPRP as a means of gaining tighter control of the pay bill.

On closer inspection, the doubts raised about IPRP as a high commitment technique often reside not so much in its intentions as in the way in which it is put into practice. As Hammer (1975) noted many years ago, 'It is not the merit pay theory that is defective. Rather, the history of the actual implementation of the theory is at fault'. Indeed, various employee attitude surveys have consistently shown that concerns reside less in the principle of pay for performance, which actually has fairly strong support (French and Marsden 1997), than in the way such schemes operate. The operational difficulties associated with IPRP are by now well rehearsed (Kessler and Purcell 1992; Kohn 1993) and do not require a further, detailed re-telling. In brief, these concerns relate to the three stages characterizing any IPRP scheme – the goal setting stage, the evaluation stage and the pay determination stage. The goal setting stage generates problems, which include difficulties in setting viable and meaningful targets for those in complex as well as those in more routine jobs. Moreover, the targets set are often based on what is easily measured rather than on what is important and can have perverse consequences, encouraging dysfunctional, while driving out desired, behaviours and attitudes. The evaluation stage raises concerns about subjectivity in appraisal, but as a judgmental process more fundamentally risks undermining the developmental purpose often informing the appraisal process in organizations. The final stage linking evaluation to pay runs up against the practical problem that the money available for such schemes is often extremely limited, certainly too small to have a powerful effect on employee orientations.

In general it has been assumed that these difficulties have negative consequences for employee attitudes and behaviours. There is some evidence to support this view with Marsden and Richardson's work (1994), based on an expectancy theory of motivation, highlighting employee concerns about the way in which IPRP has operated in the Inland Revenue. Drawing more widely on research in organizational studies, there may be grounds for suggesting that the difficulties associated with IPRP may affect commitment in a more direct sense. Thus, it might be argued that such problems encourage employee concerns about equity, procedural and distributive justice. There is fairly strong evidence to suggest that employees take remedial corrective action in terms of work inputs and outputs in response to perceived pay inequities. Moreover, Folger and Konovosky (1989) found a strong link between negative perceptions of procedural justice in pay terms and lower levels of organizational commitment. They also uncovered an association between employee trust in their supervisor and the procedural justice displayed by that line manager in determining pay. Thompson (1998) has also highlighted the importance of trust as mediating variable between employee views on reward and organizational commitment. Drawing on a psychological contract, he points to research highlighting the way in which unfulfilled employee expectations on reward may challenge employee trust in the organization and, in turn, their commitment to it. The emphasis placed on justice and trust as the basis for employee commitment makes it all the more surprising that high commitment researchers have not sought to include time-based pay, as an open and straightforward means of pay determination, and job evaluated pay structures, as a transparent means of establishing internal job worth, in their lists of practices.

Collective forms of performance pay

At first sight, the status of collective pay systems as a high-commitment practice is somewhat more obvious and less contestable than in the case of IPRP. This is particularly so in relation to profit and gain sharing as well as employee share ownership schemes, with employee reward being tied into various measures of organizational performance so inducing corporate loyalty and identification. The perceived importance of the link between profit sharing and share ownership schemes and employee commitment to the organization emerges in a number of different contexts. First, policy makers have consistently stressed this link and used it in part to justify the introduction of the approved schemes. As the Green Paper (1986: 2) on profit-related pay stated, 'PRP scheme should lead to a closer identification of employees with the companies in which they work'. Certainly company practice suggests that managers see the link as a crucial rationale for introducing these schemes. A survey of over 1,000 companies in the mid eighties found the most commonly cited reasons for implementing the various Inland Revenue approved schemes were 'to make employees feel they are part of the company and "to increase employees" sense of commitment to the company' (Smith 1986). Influential analytical and theoretical frameworks have also placed particular weight on the relationship between financial participation and commitment. Poole and Jenkins (1990), for example, see intrinsic and extrinsic commitment as the crucial, indeed sole, mediating variable between the selection of a profit-sharing scheme and the financial performance of the company.

Where the pursuit of employee commitment does represent a driving force behind the managerial use of these schemes, operational difficulties again emerge to weaken this effect. Perhaps the most significant of these is the 'line of sight' problem which suggests that even where pay is linked to profit, employees are unlikely to identify with the organization and behave accordingly given their limited influence over company financial performance. Given such broad and distanced pay-linked goals, 'free riding' is often commonly cited as another difficulty.

More fundamentally, and as in the case of IPRP, it is also evident that a range of managerial goals other than enhanced employee commitment underpin the use of these pay systems. Poutsma (1999), for example, distinguishes a range of such goals which influence the use of these forms of payment alongside employee commitment including flexibility of remuneration, gaining tax advantages, and as a defence against take-over. Pay flexibility, often in the guise of cost minimization in pay bill terms, is a particularly interesting justification for the use of profit sharing. Such flexibility highlights the way in which such schemes can just as plausibly be based on a management style oriented towards a 'harder' treatment of staff as they can on a management style reflecting concern with employee development or commitment. Weitzman (1984), presenting this pay flexibility rationale in a form which had considerable influence on Conservative governments in the mid eighties, stressed the way in which profit sharing ensured that wage determination was tied into the company's ability to pay and in so doing also provided an effective means of employment regulation. When profits were high the organization could clearly afford the pay rise, while when profits were low the absence of a pay increase ensured that jobs did not have to be sacrificed to finance it. Such a view of profit sharing was clearly about efficient pay bill management at both the micro and macro level. It had very little to do with employee commitment.

From pay to attitudinal, behavioural and organizational outcomes

The relationship between designated high commitment pay practices and assumed attitudinal and behavioural outcomes has been seen as somewhat problematic given the diverse managerial goals informing such schemes and the operational difficulties associated with them. None the less, it still remains legitimate to raise as an empirical issue whether such practices do in fact lead to attitudinal re-structuring in the form of enhanced employee organizational commitment and whether this follows through, in turn, to affect employee behaviour and organizational outcomes.

Research seeking to address these particular questions remains scarce (Milkovich 1991; Gerhart and Milkovich 1992; Brown and Armstrong 2000). This is not to deny research attempts to relate pay to outcomes. These have taken three main forms. First, and drawing mainly from applied psychology, there have been studies which have revealed links between pay satisfaction and certain behavioural outcomes such as absenteeism, turnover and quit rates. This work has usually been based on employee perceptions as they relate to the different facets distinguished in the Minnesota pay satisfaction questionnaire (Heneman and Schwab 1985): benefits, pay levels, pay increases and pay structure or administration rather than correlated with particular and tangible forms of pay practice.

Second, there has been research which has looked at the direct relationship between pay practices and organizational performance. This work, which has been fairly rare and not without methodological problems (Gehart and Milkovich 1992) has produced inconclusive results. Pearce *et al.*'s (1985) work on merit pay amongst managers in US Social Security administration found that it had no effect on organizational performance, while Gerhart and Milkovich (1990) using a larger and broader sample found that the greater use of bonuses for managers did have a positive effect on the company's rate of return on assets. There appears to be a stronger convergence of results as they relate to the effects of profit sharing schemes. Thus, Kruse and Weitzman (1990), in reviewing research in this area concluded that profit sharing did have a positive effect on productivity and company performance, although in much of this work the issue of cause and effect – whether such schemes lead to improved performance or whether such performance facilitates the use of such schemes – remains to be fully established.

The third type of research seeks to relate actual pay practices to outcomes in terms of employee attitudes and behaviours. It is this research which is clearly crucial in advancing the high commitment argument. As stressed, having identified which pay practices might lead to high employee commitment, the next step is to establish whether this is indeed the case. Again research of this kind is 'thin on the ground' and, when conducted, has not always produced consistent results. In the case of individual performance related pay, a recent IPD survey (Richardson 1999) suggested that managers view merit pay as having at best a modest effect on employee commitment. Over a half (53 per cent) indicated that there had been 'no change' in such commitment, exactly a third noting a 'small improvement' and only 8 per cent pointing to a 'large improvement'.

A more powerful piece of work, in that it sought to relate employee perceptions to the use of merit and incentive pay, conducted by Gallie *et al.* (1998) did, however, find that in certain circumstances such payment systems were associated with commitment. This study compared the impact of two control systems on organizational commitment, one based on technical control and consisting of practices such as short repetitive tasks and incentive pay and the other founded on performance management principles including individual appraisal, merit pay and internal career structures. It established that for employees in the commercial rather than the social sector, the performance management system was positively and significantly related to all three forms of commitment distinguished: flexibility, value and effort commitment. This finding is significant in number of respects. Certainly it establishes the 'golden link' between merit pay and organizational commitment assumed in the high commitment model. However, it is equally apparent that such a link may be related to merit pay's position with a bundle of perhaps supporting practices. Moreover it is a link limited in the study to employees in the commercial rather than the social sector. This suggests that such performance based control systems may be more appropriate to some types to workers rather than others, implying a degree of contingency at odds with this model's universalistic assumptions. As Gallie *et al.* note (1998: 251), it is possible that 'because of the different values which lead many people to enter the social sector, performance management systems tend to be less effective' in such contexts.

Research on profit sharing and employee share ownership schemes has tended to casts some doubt on a link with employee organizational commitment. While Bell and Hanson (1982) suggest a positive link, more robust work conducted by Dunn *et al.* (1991) using longitudinal data casts doubt on this finding. Indeed, Dunn *et al.*'s work confirms that of Gallie *et al.* (1998) which finds no relationship between profit sharing and any of the forms of commitment identified for employees in the commercial sector.

THE CONTINGENCY MODEL

Distinguishing pay contingencies

The relationship between pay practices and different contingencies might be viewed as taking two forms one of which remains within the high commitment framework and the other which moves beyond it. If contingency is about match, then the high commitment approach does contain elements of contingency. It suggests that the efficiency and effectiveness of high commitment pay practices in terms of their contribution to business performance, depends on internal fit with other HR practices and with production systems or job design. Gallie *et al.*'s (1998) performance management bundle might be seen as illustrative of this approach, while MacDuffie (1995) placed particular emphasis not only on HR fit but fit with production technologies as well. Others have taken this somewhat further in suggesting that apparent fit is not enough and that the 'success' of this bundle depends on them being embedded in and sensitive to specific circumstances and needs. The latter approach steps outside this framework in proposing that organizational 'success' does not necessarily depend on commitment enhancing pay practices. Indeed, it explicitly recognizes the range of goals that might be pursued by the same and different pay practices, suggesting the need to ensure some congruence between organizational circumstances, managerial aims and pay systems.

It is this latter approach which has generally been viewed in contingency terms. Yet, even within this perspective there have been differences of emphasis. As originally conceived (Lupton and Gowler 1969) and applied (Bowey *et al.* 1982) the contingency pay framework provided a comprehensive and sophisticated analytical map of the factors associated with organizational structure, design and operation which might affect the adoption of the different pay practices. Within the strategic human resource management literature, commentators have tended to take two approaches. The first and more established approach has placed an emphasis on what might be labelled a standard and relatively narrow set of contingencies. Thus Kochan and Barocci (1985) focus on the relationship between pay (along with other HR practices) and organizational life cycle; Fombrun *et al.* (1984) on the link with product diversity; and Schuler and Jackson (1987) on the associated competitive market strategies. This latter model has proved to be perhaps the most influential and suggests that pay practice might be expected to vary depending on whether the organization is pursuing a strategy based on innovation, cost or quality. These models share an emphasis on the alignment of pay practices with business strategies in a fairly mechanistic, market driven and top down manner.

Other more recent approaches founded on broader schools of thought from the field of organizational studies represent a return to an interest in the kind of more sophisticated relationship between a range of contingencies in explaining the link between pay and business originally highlighted by Lupton and Gowler (1969).

Two such approaches can be distinguished – the 'resource based' and the 'new institutional'. These approaches are founded on very different assumptions and as a consequence have contrasting implications for pay practice and business performance. They do, however, share an interest in the complex, and variously embedded 'web' of firm specific circumstances and needs which influence decision-making and in this sense might be viewed as being informed by some broad notion of contingency.

This section addresses the questions which follow on from the application of the fit approach in the mainstream strategic human resource management literature with its focus on a fairly limited set of contingencies and then from more recent work which has tended to view contingencies as a broader set of factors interacting in complex ways.

Contingency approach as business integration

The standard approach to contingencies established in the early SHRM literature suggests a degree of integration between pay practices and business strategy. This gives rise to a number of questions: to what extent and in what ways are pay practices integrated with business strategy? If they are integrated, does this contribute positively to organizational performance and if so how and why?

It is certainly the case that increasing attention has been given by commentators, practitioners and policy makers to greater integration between pay and business strategy. Indeed, the closer alignment between pay and business goals has been a central element of the 'New Pay' approach proselytized by Lawler (1995) and Schuster and Zingheim (1992) in the United States. As Gomez-Mejia (1993: 4) has noted:

> The emerging paradigm of the field is based on a strategic orientation where issues of internal equity and external equity are viewed as secondary to the firm's need to use pay as an essential integrating and signalling mechanism to achieve overarching business objectives.

It is an approach which has found an echo in the United Kingdom. Pritchard and Murliss (1992: 12), for example, state:

> For most organisations, pay is one of the most important items of cost, and in many of these it is the largest single cost item. Increasingly businesses are recognising the need to manage pay strategically.

However, evidence of such recognition or indeed any suggestion that it has been reflected in practice is at best patchy. In one of the few surveys which sought to evaluate the incidence and status of pay strategies, the Industrial Society (1997a) found that almost three quarters (73 per cent) of the 300 companies covered, did have a written pay strategy. Yet, under half (47 per cent) of these companies agreed that the pay strategy was efficiently linked to the HR strategy, with just over a half (57 per cent) feeling it met business needs effectively. The meaningful application of such strategies, particularly in terms of their effect on employee attitudes and behaviours, is further called into question by the finding that under half (49 per cent) of the survey organizations agreed that employees understood their company's reward policy.

More systematic attempts to relate pay practices to business strategies and contingencies have revealed some important connections. The most robust piece of work in this area has been conducted by Balkin and Gomez-Mejia (1987). They address a number of questions posed at the outset of this section by looking at the alignment between pay and specific organizational contingencies as well as whether such alignment has beneficial organizational consequences. They focus on the relationship between pay and product life cycle in a hi-tech and non-high-tech company comparison. There is some support (Balkin and Gomez-Mejia 1987) for the contingency view in that general incentive pay as a proportion of total compensation appears not only greater but more effective at the growth stage of the product cycle. Such effectiveness is found to be particularly effective at this stage for high-tech companies. Goold and Campbell's (1987) findings also provide backing for a contingencies view albeit with reference to a different set of contingencies. These researchers find a link between pay approaches and different company control strategies. Performance bonuses appear to be used more forcefully in more diverse businesses with a 'financial control' management style, than in more focused 'strategic controllers'. Such research is, however, fairly rare. It remains difficult to classify organizations according to the contingencies distinguished in the standard SHRM models within this school, let alone identify pay practices, which necessarily reflect them. As with high commitment pay, the varied managerial goals underpinning any given pay practice make it questionable to link it unambiguously to any contingency.

In the absence of this type of research, greater reliance has to be placed on illustrative examples of organizations, which have sought to relate pay to business strategies. As a clue to identifying such organizations and the circumstances stimulating this closer integration of pay and corporate strategy, a recent Towers Perrin survey (cited in Armstrong and Brown 2000) highlights the business priorities driving reward strategies and changes across a number of European companies. Amongst the most important were increasing and broadening employee competencies and skills, held as a priority by around a half (49 per cent), reinforcing 'corporate values and culture' viewed in these terms by just over a third (34 per cent) and creating a 'team based environment' noted by exactly a quarter. It may be worth briefly considering how and to what extent pay has been used to support each of these business priorities.

Pay practices have long been recognized as a powerful means of stimulating or reinforcing the process of organizational and cultural change. Indeed, there are a number of instances where pay has been used to send very strong messages about corporate values, beliefs and principles. First, pay has played an integral part in organizational responses to shifts in product market conditions. For example, in the late eighties and early nineties IPRP, in particular, was mobilized in the finance sector to support the perceived need for cultural change in response to deregulated product and more intense competition. As noted by the Abbey National HR Director:

> We needed a set of human resource strategies which would change the culture of the society into a more dynamic, commercially oriented, market and customer led and profit conscious organization ... It was considered essential to have reward systems in place which reinforced the performance and results oriented culture we wished to evolve.
>
> (Murphy 1989: 41)

Second, pay has been central to the creation of a new organizational identity, particularly in the wake of merger and acquisition. The recent acquisition of Bay by

Nortel was accompanied by the development of a new reward strategy with the goal of creating a 'truly unified company' given the very different histories and cultures of the two organizations (Westall 1999).

The use of pay to support the development of employee competences might also be seen as an important mechanism for stimulating organizational change. Competences shift the focus from *what* employees do in terms of individual targets under IPRP or particular tasks and activities under traditional job evaluated structures to *how* employees meet their responsibilities. In other words, competence-based pay involves linking rewards directly to particular and desired behaviours or personal characteristics. Naturally, this requires first identifying a set of relevant competences, sometimes linked to a given job family such as engineers or technicians, and then distinguishing criteria or standards, which allows some judgement in relation to competence acquisition. Such competences may be built into job evaluation so providing an additional dimension by which to assess jobs. Alternatively, they may be used directly to determine individual pay either by linking increases to the achievement of competences alone, as in Volkswagen, or by relating rises to competence as one of a number of criteria used for this purpose as in Bass and ICL (Industrial Society 1998).

As a further means of supporting organizational change, it is not surprising to find competence used in similar circumstances to those in which IPRP was used to stimulate and support culture change. Thus, the merger between Glaxo and Welcome was seen to provide an opportunity to introduce competence pay as a means of generating the behaviours required in the new company. Moreover, it is interesting to note that many of the companies using this type of pay such as the Royal Bank of Scotland, Scottish Equitable and Prudential Assurance, again can be found in the finance sector suggesting perhaps that it has taken the place of IPRP as a means of supporting responses to ongoing product market pressure and change.

The final business priority driving change in pay strategy, the creation of a team based environment, naturally directs attention to team pay. This type of pay has been presented by certain commentators as much more in tune with work and organization design than individual-based payment systems viewed as undermining collective and co-operative workplace behaviours. As Armstrong (1996: 22) has noted:

> The significant part that teamwork plays in achieving organisational success has directed attention towards how employee reward systems can contribute to team effectiveness. The focus is now shifting away from individual performance related pay which has conspicuously failed to deliver results in many instances, and towards team pay and other methods of rewarding the whole team.

Clearly the nature of team-based pay depends on the character of the team. Broadly defined the team equates with the collective as company or enterprise in our original typology of pay systems and covers profit and gain sharing schemes. However, the team as work group is also clearly central to this particular strategic priority related to new ways of working. For instance, the team based pay system recently introduced in the Coventry Building Society (Aitkins and Jackson 1999) was based upon its four main business areas – the branch network, the customer service centre, intermediary sales and marketing. Work units within each of these business areas share common performance measures for pay purposes. The performance of individual branches within the branch network is measured for pay purposes according to net retail receipts, mortgage advances and insurance sales. Other examples are available of organizations which have sought to introduce such team-based payment systems such as Ethicon, Norwich Union, Lloyds Bank and the Benefits Agency.

Yet despite these examples, what is particularly striking is the absence of a wider diffusion of team pay. An Industrial Society (1997b) survey found that in only 10 per cent of the organizations covered was pay related to team performance, a figure which confirmed earlier findings from a similar IPM survey, which indicated that only 11 per cent of white collar staff had team pay (1999). Indeed, the same limited diffusion is also apparent in relation to competency based pay. An Industrial Society (1998) survey of 344 organizations found only 5 per cent with 'pure' competency based pay systems, with a further 17 per cent indicating that competency was one component of the pay system. There are few signs of any underlying enthusiasm for such schemes. The same survey found that only 11 per cent of organizations were considering introducing a competence based scheme in the next 12 months, a figure very close to that suggested by a similar Industrial Relations Services (1995) survey.

It is difficult to avoid the conclusion that while the use of pay to encourage the development of employee competences and a team-based work environment are readily identifiable as business priorities, driving the formulation of new pay strategies, there is precious little evidence to suggest that such priorities are being translated into practice. It may well be that while competence and team-based pay have superficial attractions, being in tune with broader organizational developments and seen not least as a response to some of the weaknesses perceived as inherent in IPRP, they still remain difficult to put into practice. For instance, attention has been drawn to the difficulties associated with identifying and measuring meaningful competences (Sparrow 1996) as well as standards by which team performance might be judged (Market Tracking International 1996).

There may, however, be a more profound message to emerge from this absence of widespread diffusion which relates to the fundamental difficulties faced by organizations in seeking to change pay practices. As Arrowsmith and Sisson (1997: 67) conclude in their survey of developments in terms and conditions across a number of major industries '... organisations had made the simple and straightforward changes (to their pay systems). The next steps needed to put them into effect were of a different order of magnitude, making them especially daunting, and potentially involving costs in terms of employee commitment.' These difficulties might also be reflected in findings from a recent IPD study (1999) which suggested that while change in performance pay systems was taking place, it took the form more of fine-tuning than major overhaul. Around 40 per cent of the 434 organizations covered had modified their performance pay system but almost three quarters (71 per cent) of these suggested that the changes were only 'moderate' with only a third noting they were 'radical'.

The incremental and perhaps problematic nature of change in pay practice hinted at by these findings suggests a much more complex process of decision making in this sphere than that implied by any straightforward and mechanistic link between standard business contingencies and pay practices. Indeed such findings perhaps point to a dialectic between constraint and choice pursued by any given organisation suspended in a complex web of social, economic, political and historical factors likely to influence its pay approach. A number of approaches rooted to varying degrees in contingency have sought to address such complexity.

Contingency approach as complex process

In noting that the evolution of pay practices within any organization is affected by an array of factors, the notion of matching, so central to the contingency approach, is not being discarded. Rather, attention is being drawn to pay's fit or relationship with a wide array of influential factors and the complex interaction between them. Of course, the danger in extending the contingency approach to include such a variety of factors is that its explanatory value becomes diluted. Two theories, both interfacing with contingency theory albeit in different ways (Gerhart *et al.* 1996) help structure interest in this complex web of contingencies and provide more focused frameworks for analysis. The theories in question, resource-based theory and institutional theory, have been applied with varying degrees of directness and sophistication to pay practice. However, being based on very different assumptions, they raise distinctive sets of questions about the development of organizational approaches to pay. Both of these are dealt with below.

The resource-based view

As Oliver (1997) points out, the resource-based view is driven by the assumption of economic rationality, that is an organizational concern with efficiency, effectiveness and profitability or the pursuit of 'sustained competitive advantage'. The route to these ends is seen to lie in the firm's leveraging of distinctive resources and capabilities. This distinctiveness is seen to derive, in turn, from the use of such resources in socially complex, causally ambiguous and path dependent ways which makes them rare, not easily substitutable and difficult for competitors to imitate. Three sets of resources are typically identified: physical, organizational and human (Koch and McGrath 1996).

Pay might be seen as related to both human and organizational resources. Its relationship with human resources has tended to be in a supportive role. Thus interest has focused on whether pay can help generate and sustain employee know-how and skill. In this context pay has tended to be referred to in passing and as part of a range of HR mechanisms. Along with other such mechanisms particular payment systems have been seen as contributing to the generation of the firm's human capital pool through, for instance, skill formation. As Lado and Wilson (1994) note, 'the extent that human resource functions . . . . . (including) skill based pay constitute an investment in firm specific capital, they may be potent sources of sustained competitive advantage'. In addition, pay has been viewed as a means of retaining distinctive skills and capabilities within the firm, in other words acting as a resource mobility barrier (Mueller 1996). Forms of deferred compensation such as share option schemes have been seen as a means of encouraging the retention of key staff. Pay's supportive role in this sense has been highlighted by Cappelli and Crocker-Hefter (1996) in their comparison of HR approaches adopted by companies operating in the same product markets but competing on the basis of very different core competences. They compare the straight salary system and the absence of any sales commissions in Sears, competing on the basis of customer trust and sensitivity, with the highly incentivized pay system in Norstrom supporting its emphasis on fashion and encouraging impulse buying.

It is possible, however, to view pay as assuming a more significant role as an organizational resource. Organizational resources have been defined in different ways. Some have seen them residing in a distinctive organizational culture. Defined in this way, it has already been shown how pay might act as a powerful vehicle for the communication and enforcement of corporate values and beliefs. Such resources have also been defined in terms of distinctive systems, which might in their own right be the source of 'competitive advantage'. Gerhart et al. (1996), for example, stress that pay synergies derived from a particular fit between pay and other HR and organizational features may be a powerful means of leveraging distinctive employee capabilities. As they state, 'it is the extent of fit or synergies among the specific compensation plans and other organisational factors that creates value by attracting, motivating and retaining the appropriate employees' (1996: 147). It is this fit which remains crucial for it is the element which cannot easily be replicated by competitors. While the design of a pay programme is readily known or knowable, the way in which such programmes are integrated with other practices is often idiosyncratic and linked to company specific factors.

This notion of idiosyncratic bundling giving rise to pay synergies in a resource-based context raises some important pay related issues although the clarity with which they are presented or taken forward by Gerhart et al. is perhaps more debatable. It is unclear, for example, what is meant by a pay synergy. Attention is clearly being drawn to the organizational benefits that might be gained from matching different elements of the HR approach over and above the contribution those individual elements might provide. However, is it being suggested that pay has a privileged and particularly powerful position in this matching by virtue perhaps of its centrality to the employment relationship or are Gerhart et al. really just referring to HR synergies more generally? In fact, in searching for pay synergies the authors simply revert to fit between pay and crude corporate strategies along the lines previously discussed, concluding that 'there is little evidence either supporting or refuting the resource-based proposition that synergies contribute to sustained competitive advantage' (1996: 168).

Gerhart et al. also make little effort to explain exactly why pay is related to HR and organizational factors in a distinctive or idiosyncratic way. The emphasis is much more on seeking to describe particular configurations of HR practices which include pay and considering the interaction effects between them, concerns much more easily investigated through their survey techniques. This perhaps touches on the resource based interest in complexity as the source of competitive advantage but not so much on causal ambiguity and path dependence. Yet it is clear that if pay is to interact idiosyncratically with other HR practices and in so doing generate distinctiveness it becomes crucial to consider the historical development of pay systems.

The importance of evaluating complex interactions over time as a means of understanding how and why pay achieves idiosyncratic fit is illustrated by reference to a pay system which is often cited as a strategic resource, at Lincoln Electric, manufacturer of arc welding products. Although accounts of this system have tended to be celebratory and uncritical, a review of its development reveals how pay assumed its perceived status as a distinctive resource in number of ways. First, the company's approach to pay comprises a number of practices: a piecework system, shared profits, year-end bonuses and stock ownership options. These have been designed to address different types of attitude and behaviour, highlighting issues of fit not only between pay and other HR practices but also between different facets of pay. Second, Lincoln has developed a range of additional practices, which support this pay approach, including an employee advisory board, a suggestion scheme and job security. As has been noted, 'A host of other management practices at Lincoln Electric complement the compensation system to produce an atmosphere of trust and co-operation' (Chilton, 1993). Third, these pay practices have been established for many years reflecting and then supporting the company's founding philosophy. As a former chairman noted, 'We have always focused on rewarding individuals for their contributions. That was true 50 years ago and it is still true today' (Hodgetts 1997). The piecework system was introduced in 1914 and the year-end bonus in 1934. Fourth, these systems have been operated in company specific ways. For instance, it is an established feature of the Lincoln scheme that piecework rates are only adjusted when there is a capital improvement or an engineering modification, while if employees feel a new piecework standard is unfair, they can challenge it. Finally, and as already implied, these features have a positive feedback loop; trust in the scheme breeds trust, in turn, that management are not seeking to operate the scheme 'unfairly'.

As implied, methodological 'myopia' plays a large part in explaining Gerhart *et al.*'s failure to take greater account of complex interactions across time and space as a means of understanding how pay practices might become a source of distinctiveness and idiosyncratically embedded in a bundle of HR and organizational practices. The survey approach used is clearly ill-suited to dealing with firm specific complexity. However, there is also a tension at the heart of the resource-based view which casts some doubt on how notions of social complexity, causal ambiguity and path dependence are used in analysis. Thus, the assumption of economic rationality becomes somewhat problematic if these very factors are taken into account in explanation. How can economical rational decisions be made if cause and effect remain uncertain, if actors and systems interact in high complex ways, if organizations are driven by histories comprising countless internal battles, alliances and compromises? The institutional approach may provide an alternative and perhaps more satisfactory means of dealing with this uncertain and problematic process of decision making as it relates to pay.

New institutional theory

New institutional theory is essentially a cognitively driven approach, which views organizational actors as subject to a range of internal and external social as well as political pressures. These pressures encourage expected forms of behaviour and thus actors are seen as being motivated by a normative rather than an economic rationality (Oliver 1997). According to Oliver (1997: 698) social pressures in the form of norms, rules and beliefs are seen to operate at three different levels: the individual level reflected in the values of decision-makers; the firm level in terms of organizational culture and politics; and at the inter-firm level through regulatory pressures and industry-wide norms. Applied to developments in pay a number of questions emerge: what kinds of social pressures arise from these three levels to affect pay practice and how do these pressures affect the nature and pace of change in approaches to pay?

It is the focus on the firm and inter-firm level which raises some interesting insights into the evolution of pay systems and structures. Institutional theory clearly points to a new and powerful set of influences driving change in pay practice. However, these influences appear to point in different directions when considering the nature and to a lesser extent the pace of change. At the *inter-firm level*, the emphasis is primarily on pressures towards conformance. Thus organizations are seen as needing to establish legitimacy in the eyes of a range of external stakeholders as a means of procuring the resources necessary for their survival. These stakeholders will, in turn, be looking for organizations to conform to particular 'repertoires' and in so doing demonstrate adherence to accepted ways of behaving. DeMaggio and Powell (1983) suggest that pressures towards conformance or isomorphism can take three forms: coercive, normative and mimetic.

In pay terms, isomorphic pressures might be seen to emerge from a number of sources. Most obviously, coercive pressure might derive from legislative requirements recently reflected, for example, in national minimum wage standards. Financial relationships might also generate coercive pressure as the dependent body seeks to respond to the pay preferences of the funding body. In the civil service, for instance, it is clear that the Treasury's insistence on individual performance-related pay ensured compliance by executive agencies as a means of securing funding for their new pay systems. A less direct but equally revealing instance emerged in the university sector with attempts by the university employers to placate central government's preference for individual performance related pay. In an exchange of correspondence with an Oxford academic on the issue of performance pay, Howard Newby, then President of the Committee of Vice Chancellors and Principals of Universities in the UK stated, 'Such a movement (towards the adoption of performance pay) could help to persuade government that universities were determined to improve the performance of their institutions by giving staff incentives to contribute more' (Oxford AUT Newsletter, Jan 2000: 6). Although under-researched, it is also worth speculating whether such coercive pressure might be in evidence from key actors within the supply chain. Are suppliers in any way forced by major purchasers to pursue practices which might be viewed as impacting in desired ways on the production process?

Normative pressure might again take various forms. Certain industry norms about the best or most appropriate type of pay system might develop. Eisenhardt (1988), for example, notes the move from commission to salaries over the years as the accepted approach to paying employees in the US retail sector. She also highlights the power of pay traditions, finding a relationship between the age of a store and the type of payment system used. Thus, the older the store the more likely it was to have retained commission. Viewing this finding as a confirmation of institutional theory she suggests 'what may be happening is that a store is initially structured with a compensation type that reflects the institutional environment at the time of the founding. The compensation scheme then becomes legitimated over time within the store, and its continued use is rarely examined' (1988: 504).

In the broader UK industrial relations context, multi-employer collective bargaining might be seen to have traditionally been the source of normative pressure towards conformance. This form of bargaining provided an institutional structure for regulating pay determination in a substantive and procedural sense according to shared rules and norms across companies in the same industry. For many years such structures covered much of the British economy and, indeed, despite the decline in this form of bargaining it is interesting to note that it still appears to have some residual influence. Thus Arrowsmith and Sisson (1997) note that despite the demise of industry bargaining, engineering companies still continue to display similarities in pay terms, moving 'like ships in a convoy'.

Mimetic pressures might arise from the pay practices of influential others. Consultants clearly play a part in the replication of pay practices, while the same high-profile companies indulging in the use of new pay systems is regularly paraded at conferences and in personnel magazines. Industry networks may also provide a conduit for shared ideas. Pay clubs are indeed fairly common, organized on an industry-region basis. The absence of specialist skills might further encourage copying. Thus, when civil service executive agencies were forced to set up new pay systems and structures in a short period of time and with very little in-house personnel expertise it was not surprising that replication occurred. As noted by one of the civil unions monitoring agency pay approaches, 'In the form of "follow my leader" most new structures mimic those already introduced for higher grades and already introduced in early delegated areas' (PTC 1996: 5).

The implications of this inter-firm level of analysis for the pace of change is, however, somewhat less clear-cut and may indeed need to be empirically determined. Pressure towards conformance implies nothing about the speed of convergence. Isomorphic pressures may help explain quite rapid change in pay. Normative and mimetic pressures might be a useful way of explaining fashions and fads. These are sometimes pointed to in explaining developments in pay. For example, the popularity of IPRP in the late eighties was put down by some to fashion. As IDS noted at the time, 'Many organisations were vague and uncertain about what they were doing; some were swept away by the mood of the times' (IDS Focus, No.61, Dec. 1991: 6). Yet entrenched values and norms may well slow the pace of change in pay determination as illustrated by the work of Arrowsmith and Sisson (1997) as well as by the research of Eisenhardt (1988).

At the level of the firm, the tenets of institutional theory would appear to imply divergence rather than convergence in the nature of pay practice allied to an incremental and slow process of change. This combination of divergence and incrementalism derives from the normative power of company history, traditions and habits regulating attitudes and behaviour on pay as well as the high cognitive costs associated with a shift from established pay routines and systems. In other words, sensitivity to company specific features would suggest divergence in practice while the ongoing pull of the past and the costs associated with change would imply continuity. Certainly the normative power of history and its break on rapid change is well illustrated in pay terms by reference to Ahlstrand's (1990) description of productivity pay at Esso. He highlights how the use of productivity pay agreements in Esso over many years had lent them a symbolic importance in terms of enhancing managerial careers and sending messages that remedial managerial action was being taken in dealing with crisis, long after any meaningful link could be established between such agreements and the company's economic performance. In short, productivity pay retained a normative power despite the withering away of any economic rationale.

The application of new institutionalism to the study of pay practices remains potentially fruitful but as yet relatively under-explored. If this approach is to be used, however, two points may be worthy of consideration. First, the relationship between social and political pressures at different levels needs to be considered in greater detail, especially in light of the apparent tension between inter-firm influence tending towards conformance and intra-firm influence suggesting divergence in pay practice. While new institutional theory has tended to view the firm as relatively passive or reactive in the face of external pressures, a more dynamic relationship which sees a firm seeking to develop pay practices which reflect a more or less stable compromise between competing internal and external pressures may be more helpful (Oliver 1991). An example of this process at work is available in recent research on pay in the civil service (Gagnon and Kessler 1999), which revealed how certain executive agencies sought to trade off these competing pressures. These agencies sent signals in terms of broad principles and statements of intent to the Treasury that reflected their adherence to the principle of individual performance-related pay while developing pay schemes, which in terms of detailed design and operation, displayed elements of continuity with past civil service systems based on seniority and increases in the cost of living.

Second, the tendency to treat internal normative pressures such as firm habits, traditions and histories as tending towards inertia and incrementalism needs to be treated with care. While new institutionalism provides a plausible explanation for the slow pace of change in UK pay practices highlighted earlier, it is also important to note that organizations can react *against* their pasts sometimes in quite dramatic ways. If a company's past is interpreted as a more or less stable configuration of power relations between competing internal interest groups, a fundamental shift in these relations may lead to a quite profound change in practice as the newly formed group asserts its authority. The extent to which history can be a force both for conservatism and radical change is well illustrated by a comparison of pay developments in two companies, a privatized pharmaceutical company and a national newspaper (Kessler 1994). The former felt bound by its history to develop a 'weak' performance-related pay scheme, which bore many of the hallmarks of the old civil service approach. In contrast, a decline in union power in the newspaper company led management to react violently against past pay practices which had bolstered union interests and sought to force through a profound change in the approach to pay which established and supported their newly established prerogative.

SUMMARY AND CONCLUSION

At the outset it was suggested that the recent treatment of developments in pay practice by the two predominant strategic human resource management models – universalistic and contingency – had been somewhat uneven and uncertain. While new analytical frameworks were being brought to bear on pay under the auspices of these models, there appeared, at the same time, to be some loss of sensitivity to the complexities associated with the design, operation and effect of pay. This chapter sought to explore systematically pay's position within these two models by looking at the questions they raised and the extent to which research had addressed these questions and supported underlying assumptions and propositions.

The universalistic model, discussed primarily in terms of a high commitment approach, was seen to raise issues associated with the relationship between pay practices, attitudinal and, by implication, behavioural restructuring and organizational performance. A lack of consensus on the type of pay system encouraging such re-structuring was highlighted while evidence on the relationship between any of the suggested high commitment pay practices and the development of organizational commitment was seen as patchy. This lack of consensus was viewed as unsurprising given that any given pay system may well be used to pursue a range of managerial goals rather than necessarily being driven by a concern with employee commitment.

This perhaps suggests the need to display greater sensitivity to managerial intentions and contextual circumstances forming the backdrop to pay developments. Patchy evidence on the link between any given pay practice and attitudes as well as behaviours within the mainstream human resource management literature may well reflect a failure to draw upon well established frameworks, particularly from applied psychology. Marsden and Richardson's (1994) work represents an isolated but important step in this direction. Clearly there is more scope to apply, for instance, equity and expectancy frameworks to pay systems as means of assessing attitudinal and behavioural change.

Contingency theory viewed as stepping beyond the high-commitment approach in countenancing a fit between business goals and pay practices which did not necessarily rely on the latter's commitment enhancing properties, was seen to have emerged in two forms. The first raised questions about the link between pay practice and a number of stock organizational contingencies such as competitive strategy, corporate control mechanisms and stage of the 'life cycle'. While some evidence did provide support for the importance of certain contingencies, difficulties in distinguishing organizations according to such contingencies let alone deciding on the appropriate pay practice had limited the value of work in this area. In its place consideration was given to how pay could be used to pursue a number of stated business priorities – changing cultures, developing employee competences and encouraging a team-working environment.

While ways in which pay might further such priorities were readily available, more striking was the apparently low take-up of pay practices to further such ends. Indeed, the overwhelming impression was one of incremental change in approaches to pay. At certain points in their development organizations might seek to break away from their pasts but in general pay systems were seen to evolve and be subject to fine-tuning. It was suggested that the contingency approach in a second form was useful in understanding this situation. Thus frameworks were drawn upon which focused on a fit or match between pay and a much wider range of organizational circumstances and related to a greater array of corporate needs.

The frameworks in question, related to the resource based view of strategy and new institutionalism, shared a concern with complexity, ambiguity and history. They were, however, driven by different rationales. The resource based view, underpinned by assumptions of economic rationality with its interest in 'sustained competitive advantage', focused on how pay could be used to support distinctive human resource competence or how it could indeed become a resource in its own right in the form of a distinctive system. Where this approach had been applied, pay's contribution to business performance has been seen to derive from pay synergies linked to idiosyncratic fit or bundling of HR practices. As yet, however, little attempt has been made to explain how such bundles emerge and why pay might assume a particularly important place within them.

The institutitonal approach arguably dealt more plausibly with notions of complexity, ambiguity and history by recognizing their influence in a normative rather than an economic sense. Social and political pressures operating at the societal, corporate and individual levels were seen to exert a powerful influence on organizational developments in generating traditions, habits, rules, expectations, beliefs and values which actors felt they needed to meet. Applied to pay, this approach raises issues about the nature and source of these pressures at the different levels, how they impact and, given the approach's cognitive orientation, crucially how they were perceived and acted on by key organizational actors. This presents an exciting research agenda although as yet few attempts have been made to address it.

REFERENCES

Aitken, J. and Jackson, R. (1999) *Linking Pay to Team Performance at Coventry Building Society*, IRS Conference Presentation, London.

Ahlstrand, B. (1990) *The Quest for Productivity*, Cambridge: Cambridge University Press.

Armstrong, M. (1996) 'How Group Efforts Can Pay Dividends', *People Management*, 25 January: 22–27.

Armstrong, M. and Brown, D. (2000) *Paying For Contribution*, London: Kogan Page.

Arrowsmith, J. and Sisson, K. (1997) Pay and Working time: Towards Organisation Based Systems? Unpublished.

Arthurs, J. (1992) 'The Link between Business Strategy and Industrial Relations Systems in American Steel Mini Mills', *Industrial and Labour Relations Review*, **45**: 670–87.

Balkin, D. and Gomez-Mejia, L. (1987) 'Toward a Contingency Theory of Compensation strategy', *Strategic Management Journal*, **8**: 169–82.

Beer, M. Spector, B. Lawrence, P., Mills, D. and Walton, R. (1984) *Human Resources Management: A General Manager's Perspective*, New York: Free Press.

Becker, B. and Huselid, M. (1998) 'High Performance Work Systems and Firm Performance', in Ferris, G. (ed.) *Research in Personnel and Human Resource Management, Vol.16*, Stamford: JAI Press.

Bell, D. and Hanson, D. (1982) *Profit Sharing and Employee Share Holding Attitude Survey*, London: Industrial Participation Association.

Bloom, D.E. and Milkovich, G.T. (1992) 'Issues in Managerial Compensation Research', in C. Cooper and D. Rousseau (eds) *Trends in Organizational Behavior*, Chichester: John Wiley.

Bowey, A., Thorpe, R., Mitchell, F., Nicholls, E., Gosnold, D., Savery, L. and Hellier, P. (1982) *The Effects of Incentive Schemes*, Dept. of Employment Research Paper, No.36, London: DE.

Brown, W. (1989) 'Managing Remuneration', in K. Sisson (ed.) *Personnel Management in Britain*, Oxford: Blackwell.

Brown, I.D. and Armstrong, M. (2000) *Pay for Contribution*, London: Kogan Page.

Brown, W., Deakin, S., Hudson, M., Pratten, C and Ryan, P. (1998) *The Individualisation of Employment Contracts in Britain*, London: DTI.

Cappelli, P. and Crocker-Hefter, A. (1996) 'Distinctive Human Resources are Firms' Core Competencies', *Organizational Dynamics*, Winter: 7–22.

Cully, M., Woodland, S., O'Reilly, A. and Dix, G. (1999) *Britain at Work*, London: Routledge.

DeMaggio, P. and Powell, W. (1983) 'The Iron Cage Revisited: Institutional Isomorphism and Collective Rationality in Organizational Fields', *American Sociological Review*, **48**: 147–60.

Dunn, S., Richarson, R. and Dewe, P. (1991) 'The Impact of employee Share Ownership on Worker Attitudes', *Human Resource Management Journal*, **1**(1): 1–17.

Eisenhardt, K. (1988) 'Agency and Institutional Theory Explanations: The Case of Retail Sales Compensation', *Academy of Management Journal*, **31**(3): 488–511.

Eisenhardt, K. (1992) 'Agency theory: An Assessment and Review', *Academy of Management*, **14**: 57–74.

Folger, R. and Konovsky, M. (1989) 'Effects of Procedural and Distributive Justice on Reactions to Pay Rise Decisions', *Academy of Management Journal*, **30**: 110–25.

Fombrun, C., Tichy, N. and Devanna, M. (1984) *Strategic Human Resource Management*, New York: Wiley.

French, S. and Marsden, D. (1997) *Not Met: An Assessment of PRP in the Inland Revenue Five years On*, BUIRA Paper, Leicester.

Gagnon, S. and Kessler, I. (1999) *Pay and in Civil Service Executive Agencies*, BAM Conference, Manchester, September.

Gallie, D., White, M., Cheng, Y. and Tomlinson, M. (1998) *Restructuring the Employment Relationship*, Oxford: Oxford University Press.

Gerhart, B., Trevor, C. and Graham, M. (1996) 'New Directions in Compensation Research: Synergies, Risk, and Survival', *Research in Personnel and Human Resource Management*, **14**: 143–203.

Gerhart, B. and Milkovich, G. (1990) 'Organisational Differences in Managerial Compensation and Financial Performance', *Academy of Management Journal*, **33**(4): 663–91.

Gerhart, B. and Milkovich, G. (1992) 'Employee compensation: Research and Practice', in Dunnette, M. and Hough, L. (eds) *Handbook of Industrial and Organisational Psychology*, California: Consulting Psychology Press.

Gomes-Mejia, L. (1993) *Compensation, Organisation and Firm Performance*, San Francisco: South Western Publishers.

Goold, A. and Campbell, M. (1987) *Strategies and Styles*, Oxford: Blackwell Publishers.

Green Paper (1986) *Profit Related Pay*, 1986. Cmnd.9835, London: HMSO.

Hammer, W. (1975) 'How to ruin Motivation with Pay', *Compensation Review*, **7**(3): 17–27.

Heneman, G. and Schwab, D. (1985) 'Pay Satisfaction: Its multi-dimensional nature and measurement', *International Journal of Psychology*, **20**: 129–41.

Hodgetts, R. (1997) 'Discussing Incentive Compensation with Donald Hastings of Lincoln Electric', *Compensation and Benefits Review*, **29**(5): 60–66.

Industrial Relations Services (1995) 'Pay Prospects for 1995/96', *Pay and Benefits Bulletin*, **387**, November: 5–8.

Industrial Society (1997a) *Reward Strategies No. 31*, January, London: Industrial Society.

Industrial Society (1997b) *Pay Structures No. 39*, September, London: Industrial Society.

Industrial Society (1998) *Competency Pay No. 43*, January. London: Industrial Society.

IPD (1999) *Performance Pay*, London: IPD.

Kessler, I. and Purcell, J. (1992) 'Performance Related Pay – Objectives and Application', *Human Resource Management Journal*, **2**(3): 34–59.

Kessler, I. and Purcell, J. (1995) 'Individualism in Theory and Practice: Management Style and the Design of Pay System', in P. Edwards (ed.) *Industrial Relations, Theory and Practice in Britain*, Oxford: Blackwell Publishers.

Koch, M. and McGrath, R. (1996) 'Improving Labour productivity: HRM Policies Do Matter', *Strategic Management Journal*, **17**, 335–54.

Kohn, A. (1993) 'Why Incentive Plans Cannot Work', *Harvard Business Review*, Sept–Oct: 54–63.

Kochan, T. and Barocci, T. (eds) (1985) *Human Resource Management and Industrial Relations*, Boston: Little Brown.

Kruse, D. and Weitzman, M. (1990) 'Profit Sharing and Productivity', in Blinder, A. (ed.) *Pay for Productivity*, Washington: Brookings Institution.

Lado, A. and Wilson, M. (1994) 'Human Resource Systems and Sustained Competititve Advantage: A Competency Based Perspective', *Academy of Management Review*, **19**(4): 699–727.

Lawler, E. (1986) *High Involvement Management*, San Francisco: Jossey Bass.

Lawler, E. (1995) 'The New Pay: A Strategic Approach', *Compensation and Benefits Review*, July: 14–20.

Lupton, T. and Gowler, D. (1969) *Selecting a Wage Payment System*, Research Paper III, London: Engineering Employers' Federation.

MacDuffie, J. (1995) 'Human Resource Bundles and Manufacturing Performance', *Industrial and Labour Relations Review*, **48**(2): 197–221.

Market Tracking International (1996) *Reward Strategies*, London: Haymarket Business Publications.

Marsden, D. and Richardson, R. (1994) 'Performance Pay? The Effects of Merit Pay on Motivation in the Public Services', *British Journal of Industrial Relations*, **32**(2): 243–61.

Mueller, F. (1996) 'Human Resources as Strategic Assets: An Evolutionary Resource Based Theory', *Journal of Management Studies*, **6**, 7575–785.

Murphy, T. (1989) 'Pay for Performance: An instrument for Strategy', *Long Range Planning*, **22**(4): 40–5.

Milkovich, G. (1991) *Pay for Performance*, National Research Council, Washington: National Academic Press.

Oliver, C. (1991) 'Strategic Responses to Institutional Processes', *Academy of Management Review*, **16**: 145–79.

Oliver, C. (1997) 'Sustaining Competitive Advantage: Combining Institutional and Resource Based Views', *Strategic Management Journal*, **18**(9): 697–713.

Pearce, J., Stephenson, W. and Perry, J. (1985) 'Managerial Compensation Based on Organisational Performance: A Time Series Analysis', *Academy of Management Journal*, **28**: 262–78.

Pfeffer, J. (1998) *The Human Equation*, Boston: Harvard Business School Press.

Poole, M. and Jenkins, G. (1990) *The Impact of Economic Democracy*, London: Routledge.

Poutsma, E. (1999) *Recent Developments in Financial Participation within the EU*, Dublin: European Foundation for the Improvement of Living and Working Conditions.

PTC (1996) *Whatever Happened to National Civil Service Pay*. Research Brief 1, November, London: PTC.

Pritchard, D. and Murliss, H. (1992) *Jobs, Roles and People*, London: Nicholas Brealey.

Purcell, J. (1993) 'The End of Institutional Industrial Relations', *Political Quarterly*, **64**(1): 6–23.

Richarson, R. (1999) *Contingent Pay in the UK*, London: IPD.

Richardson, R. and Thompson, M. (1999) *The Impact of People Management on Business Performance: A Literature Review*, London: IPD.

Roach, W. (1999) 'In Search of Commitment Oriented Human Resource Management Practices and Conditions that Sustain Them', *Journal of Management Studies*, **36**(5): 653–71.

Schuler, R. (1992) 'Strategic Human Resource Management: Linking People with the needs of the Business', *Organisational Dynamics*, **22**: 19–32.

Schuler, R. and Jackson, S. (1987) 'Linking Competitive Strategies with Human Resource Management Practices', *Academy of Management Review*, **1**(3): 129–213.

Schuster, J. and Zingheim, P. (1992) *The New Pay*, New York: Lexington Books.

Smith, G. (1986) 'Profit Sharing and Employee Share Ownership in Britain', *Employment Gazette*, September: 125–42.

Sparrow, P. (1996) 'Too Good to be true?' *People Management*, 5 December: 22–29.

Storey, J. (1992) *Developments on the Management of Human Resources*, Oxford: Blackwell Publishers.

Thompson, M. (1993) *Pay and Performance: The Employee Experience*, Institute of Manpower Studies, Report 258, Brighton: IMS.

Thompson, M. (1998) 'Trust and Reward', in S. Perkins and J. Sandringham (eds) *Trust, Motivation and Commitment*, London: SRRC.

Walsh, J. (1993) 'Internalization Versus Decentralization: An Analysis of Recent Developments in Pay Bargaining', *British Journal of Industrial Relations*, 31(3): 409–32.

Walton, R. (1985) 'From Control to Commitment', *Harvard Business Review*, March–April: 77–84.

Weitzman, M. (1984) *The Share Economy – Conquering Stagflation*, Boston: Harvard University Press.

Westall, D. (1999) *Reward Strategies at Nortel*, IRS Strategy Reward Conference, 4–5 Oct. London.

Wood, S. (1996) 'High Commitment Management and Payment Systems', *Journal of Management Studies*, 33(1): 53–77.

Wood, S. (1999) 'Human Resource Management and Performance', *International Journal of Management Reviews*, 1(4): 367–413.

Wright, P. and McMahan, G. (1992) 'Theoretical Perspectives for Strategic Human Resource Management', *Journal of Management Studies*, 18(2): 295–320.

FURTHER READING

Armstrong, M. and Murlis, H. (1991) *Reward Management*, London: Kogan Page.

Brown, W. and Walsh, J. (1994) 'Managing Pay in Britain', in K. Sisson (ed.) *Personnel Management in Britain*, Oxford: Blackwell.

Chilton, K. (1993) 'Lincoln Electric's Incentive System: Can it be Transferred?' *Compensation and Benefits Review*, 25(6): 21–27.

Huselid, M. (1995) 'The Impact of Human Resource Management Practices on Turnover, Productivity and Corporate Financial Performance', *Academy of Management Journal*, 38(3): 635–72.

Kessler, I. (1994) 'Performance Related Pay: Contrasting Approaches', *Industrial Relations Journal*, 25(2): 22–35.

Mahoney, T. (1989) 'Multiple Pay Contingencies: Strategic Design of Compensation', *Human Resource Management*, 28(3): 337–47.

Mahoney, T. (1983) 'Approaches to the Definition of Comparable Worth', *Academy of Management Review*, 8(1): 14–22.

Management Pay Review (1996) 'Linking Pay to Competencies', *Incomes Data Service*, August, 11–14.

Millward, N., Stevens, M., Smart, D. and Hawes, W. (1992) *Workplace Industrial Relations in Transition*, Aldershot: Dartmouth.

Thompson, M. (1995) *Team Working and Pay*, Institute of Manpower Studies, Report 281, Brighton: IMS.

12 Employee Involvement at Work

Mick Marchington

INTRODUCTION

Employee Involvement (EI) now appears to be regarded as a central component in the bundle of practices associated with high commitment or 'soft' human resource management (HRM). Many academic discussions of HRM refer to EI, either as an explicit element of management policy and practice, or implicitly as a potential contributor to the achievement of higher levels of employee commitment through investments in human capital (see, for example, Marchington and Wilkinson 1996; Patterson *et al.* 1997; Pfeffer 1998; Wood 1999). Similarly, terms such as empowerment, autonomy, teamworking and open book management are peppered throughout the popular literature which publicizes and celebrates the latest initiatives in HRM (Case 1998; Foy 1994; Wilkinson 1998).

It will be apparent from earlier chapters in this book, however, as well as from several other collections of readings on the subject (see, for example, Legge 1995; Mabey Salaman and Storey 1999; Storey 1995) that much depends on the version of HRM which is under consideration. If HRM is conceived in terms of its 'hard' variant, where the major issue is how well the management of human resources is integrated with other elements of business strategy, then the place of EI is far from assured. In some of these situations, EI may not be seen as important by senior managers, given an emphasis on tight cost control, deskilled jobs, and a lack of investment in training. In others, EI may be little more than a one-way communications channel designed merely to convey the latest news in an attempt to convince employees of the logic behind management's decision. In these cases, if EI is practised, it is likely to take a rather diluted and marginal form, and contribute little to engendering employee commitment or improving organizational performance.

In contrast, if HRM is defined in terms of its 'soft' or high commitment variant, the emphasis shifts – at least in theory – to the management of 'resourceful humans', and to assumptions that employees represent an important asset to the organization and a potential source of competitive advantage. In these situations, which are often characterized by organizations whose products are marketed on the basis of quality rather than price, EI may take a variety of forms and be present in a multiplicity of different practices such as: frequent, open and two-way communications; concerted attempts to involve employees in resolving work-based problems; developments in task-based participation, teamworking and self-managed teams; share ownership and profit sharing. The analysis of EI which follows in subsequent sections of this chapter is based around the concept of 'soft' HRM rather than its 'hard' version, although in reality, shades of both may exist in parallel at the same organization (with different groups of workers), as well as in relation to the same employees (Truss *et al.* 1997).

Even where 'soft' or high commitment HRM is espoused as a policy goal by senior management and in the public relations literature of their organizations, this does not guarantee that EI will actually be put into effect at the workplace level, or that it will have much of an impact on employees or their organizations. As with other aspects of management and human resource strategy, there is often a sizeable gap between the espoused policy and the concrete practices at establishment level or below (Mabey *et al.* 1998; Marchington and Wilkinson 1996). In addition, even though it is claimed that EI is likely to make a positive contribution to organizations, it is difficult to determine its precise impact on employee and management attitudes, or to evaluate the relationship between EI and performance.

While it may now be common to argue that direct EI, as part of the bundle of HR practices, is connected with high levels of employee commitment and organizational performance, this is predicated upon a series of assumptions, none of which can be taken for granted. These assumptions are: that line managers are committed to EI and are willing and able to make it operate effectively in the workplace; that EI has a positive effect on employee attitudes, which leads to changes in work behaviour that feed through to higher levels of productivity and effectiveness; and that employees will acquiesce with management decisions to the extent that trade unions are marginalized at the workplace or are removed altogether (Marchington 1995). If none or only some of these assumptions are achieved, the impact of EI – and with it, one key element of HRM – is much reduced. In short, rather than assuming that EI will operate automatically as part of a high-commitment human resource strategy, it is argued here that the translation of EI from broad management policy to specific workplace practice, let alone employee commitment and performance, is beset with problems. This is the central theme of this chapter.

There are five main sections to the chapter. First, there is a discussion of the major differences between EI and industrial democracy, and an analysis of the nature and extensiveness of EI alongside brief descriptions of its principal forms. Second, the depth of line-management support for direct EI is analysed, as is the degree to which managers and supervisors are sufficiently trained and rewarded to make involvement work in practice. Third, there is an evaluation of the impact of EI upon employee attitudes and performance, and some consideration of the major methodological problems connected with assessing this. Fourth, the chapter moves on briefly to analyse the relationship between EI and workplace trade unionism, and in particular address the question of whether unions are being marginalized by EI, either by design or as a consequence of new initiatives. Finally, a few general conclusions are drawn. It should be noted that the focus of this chapter is on direct EI and that issues dealing with representative participation and union–management partnerships are addressed more fully by David Guest in Chapter 6.

THE NATURE AND EXTENT OF DIRECT EMPLOYEE INVOLVEMENT IN BRITAIN

EI entered the vocabulary both of practitioners and academics during the early part of the 1980s, not just in Britain but also elsewhere (see, for example, Cotton 1993;

Lansbury and Davis 1996; Sisson 1997). It represents a concerted attempt by employers to find participative ways in which to manage their staff by investing in human capital, and for the most part – with the support of successive governments and employers' organizations – it appears to have replaced earlier variants such as workers' participation and industrial democracy.

EI is a term which is redolent of employer initiatives. Its aims are those which support the achievement of management's goals, either directly in relation to performance improvements and competitive advantage, or indirectly through higher levels of employee commitment, satisfaction and identification with their employer. The decision about whether or not to 'involve' employees rests with managers who are able to define and limit the terms under which direct EI can take place, and in so doing further individualize employment relations (Sisson 1993). EI is established very much at management's discretion, resting almost exclusively on a voluntary, as opposed to a statutory base. The only exceptions relate to the obligation on larger private sector companies to include a statement in their annual report and to various pieces of legislation incorporated from Europe. Direct EI has repeatedly been extolled by governments of differing political persuasions as preferable to company-wide arrangements based on union representation. Of course, EI does offer opportunities for employees to gain – in terms of information, influence, and reward – but only in so far as this is to management's advantage as well. Without doubt, working life under a 'soft' HRM regime may be more pleasant than working in a 'bleak house' or 'black hole' organization (Guest 1999), but much depends on how management puts EI into effect.

Industrial democracy, on the other hand, commences from the standpoint that employees ought to have the opportunity to become involved in decision-making at work, in much the same way as political democracy refers to their rights as citizens (see, for example, Blumberg 1968; Heller *et al.* 1998; Pateman 1970; Poole 1986). It is an explicit form of power-sharing between employers and employees, usually through worker/union representatives, which has been practised for years throughout much of mainland Europe by means of worker director and works council arrangements. Perhaps the difference is most easily captured by the point that EI starts from the assumption that managers might see the advantage of *allowing* employees to become involved, whereas industrial democracy has its source in the *right* of the governed to exercise some control over those in authority. As suggested in the previous section, EI is the term which fits more easily with 'soft' or high commitment HRM, given its managerialist and neo-unitarist underpinnings, and its ethos of common and shared interests.

The growth in EI since 1980 can be estimated from data available through the successive Workplace Industrial Relations Surveys (Daniel and Millward 1983; Millward and Stevens 1986; Millward *et al.* 1992) and the 1998 Workplace Employee Relations Survey (Cully *et al.* 1999). From these, it is clear that direct EI has become considerably more extensive over this period, both in general as an element of HRM and in relation to specific forms of EI. The most recent survey (Cully *et al.* 1998) indicated that four of the top five 'new management practices and EI schemes' were forms of direct EI: these were teamworking (present in 65 per cent of all workplaces employing 25 or more staff), team briefing (61 per cent), staff attitude surveys in the last five years (45 per cent) and problem-solving groups (42 per cent). Profit-sharing schemes and employee share ownership schemes for non-managerial employees were present at 30 per cent and 15 per cent of these establishments respectively. (It should be noted that during this period there was also a decline in the extensiveness of joint consultative machinery from about 34 per cent of workplaces in 1980 to 29 per cent in 1998 (Cully *et al.* 1999).) This picture of growth in direct EI is reinforced by case study and anecdotal evidence, although it should be recalled that EI varies quite significantly in terms of its form, level, degree and scope (Marchington 1992). For simplicity, however, direct EI can be examined under four separate categories.

Downward communications

The first category is downward communications from managers to employees, the principal purpose of which is to inform and 'educate' staff so that they are more likely to accept management plans. It is the most dilute form of EI considered here in the sense that it does not challenge the existing status quo, and indeed should be an aspect of 'good' management practice in any event. The category includes practices such as briefing groups/team briefing and other regular structured techniques for passing information down the management chain – such as emails, informal and non-routinized communications between supervisors and their staff, formal written media such as employee reports, house journals or company newsletters, and videos which are used to convey standard messages to employees about the organization's annual financial performance or to publicize some new initiative.

Most studies seem to indicate that these forms of direct EI are among the most popular in Britain at the moment, and indeed systematic use of the management chain and team briefing were shown to be extremely popular in the WERS survey, with well over half of the workplaces in the main sample making use of them. Indeed, even in small businesses and workplaces, there was a substantial use of direct EI (Cully *et al.* 1999). In larger workplaces (25 or more employees), it is clear that the range of information which is now communicated to staff has grown over the last 20 years, especially in relation to investment plans and, to some extent, financial information. The survey by IRS (1999) lends support to the view that downward communications practices are widespread, especially company journals (found in 92 per cent of the organizations surveyed), team briefing (86 per cent) and email communications (82 per cent). On the other hand, it is clear that the nature of downward communications – in terms of the type of information released, the regularity of meetings and the commitment by management to EI – can vary significantly between organizations even though the same name may be used to describe these practices. This will be analysed more fully in a subsequent section of this chapter.

Upward problem-solving

The second category of direct EI is upward problem-solving, which is designed to tap into employee knowledge and opinion, either at an individual level or through small groups. These sorts of practice have several objectives, such as to increase the stock of ideas within an organization, to encourage co-operative relations at work, and to legitimize change. These practices are predicated on the assumption that employees are recognized as *a* (if not *the*) major source of competitive advantage for organizations, a source whose ideas have been ignored in the past or who have been told that 'they are not paid to think'. The best known of these EI practices are quality circles (despite often masquerading under a different name nowadays), suggestion schemes, attitude surveys and total quality management/customer care programmes. These are the sorts of practices which correspond well with the contemporary notion of regarding employees as assets and knowledge workers whose skills need to be harnessed in order to enhance competitive advantage.

As with downward communications, these practices are visible – at least formally – in many organizations. For example, the WERS 1998 survey (Cully *et al.* 1999) showed that attitude surveys were the most ex___ ___ form of upward problem solving found in organizations (45 per cent ___ ___ ___ laces employing 25 or more) and nearly three-quarters of ___ ___ ore were employed. Suggestion schemes and prob___ ___ ___ ss common, at 33 per cent and 38 per ___ ___ ___ nce in larger workplaces and org___ ___ kplaces operated all three of the___ ___ d problem solving was most app___ ___ . The IRS survey reported simil___ ___ ___ how much more common these ___ ___ rent sets of questions, but most c ___ ___ xtensive.

Task-ba___ ___

The third ___ ___ ___ and teamworking, in which emp___ ___ ___ ge and type of tasks undertaken ___ ___ ___ ce are horizontal job redesign (a ___ ___ ___ ___ vel), job enrichment and vertical role ___ ___ ___ rained to undertake tasks at a different, usua___ ___ ___ when they take on some managerial and supervisory du___ ___ ___ king (where the workgroup may ultimately organize the whole job). ___ ___ ___ ally, this represents the most far-reaching form of direct EI considered in this chapter, in terms of centrality to work processes and the level and scope of subject matter which may be controlled by employees. Indeed, it could extend to working without direct supervision, recruiting and disciplining fellow team members, and organizing work allocation and even methods (Marchington 2000).

While previously put forward as a counter to alienation at work, these practices are now sometimes viewed as making an important contribution to the achievement of competitive advantage (Walton 1985). Rather than seeing higher productivity as only achievable through increased de-skilling, the contrary argument – that expanded jobs, teamworking and empowerment are the keys to organizational success – now finds rather greater favour. It is apparent from WERS that teamworking is now practised in a large number of workplaces (65 per cent), although when this is actually deconstructed it appears that most examples are relatively weak in actual practice: the survey found that autonomous work groups, where team members have responsibility for the product or service, jointly decide how work is to be done and appoint their own team leaders, can be found in just three per cent of workplaces (Cully *et al.* 1999). It is rather more difficult to estimate the extent of task-based participation, given the lack of representative data, but it is important to note that these are not new inventions of the last decade; see, for example, the quality of working life experiments in the 1960s and 1970s (Kelly 1982; Knights *et al.* 1985).

Handwritten note:

Direct Employee Involvement
- o Downward Communication
- o Upward problem solving
- o Task based participations
  (teamworking)
- o Financial Involvement

Financial involvement

The final category of direct EI examined here is financial involvement, encompassing schemes designed to link part (or occasionally all) of an individual's rewards to the success of the unit or enterprise as a whole. These take a variety of forms in practice, including simple profit-sharing schemes and employee share ownership systems, which have been assisted substantially by legislation in Britain (Pendleton 1997; Poole 1989). ESOPs (employee share ownership plans) are seen in Britain (Pendleton *et al*. 1995; Wilkinson *et al*. 1994), but have long been much more extensive in the USA (Cotton 1993). Although the objectives for financial involvement are similar in many respects to those already discussed (e.g. educating employees about the performance of the organization and its commercial environment), there is also an assumption that employees with a financial stake in the overall success of the unit/ enterprise are more likely to work harder for its ultimate success. Of course, much depends upon whether employees also identify such a link, and how much control they have over the performance of the unit concerned. In the case of employee share ownership arrangements, the most popular of these schemes, this is negligible in financial terms (Pendleton *et al*. 1998).

Once again, we can turn to WERS for current data on the extensiveness of financial involvement in Britain. This shows the influence of legal and financial incentives on the likelihood that such schemes are adopted at workplace level. Profit-related pay operated in about half of all private sector workplaces which employed 25 or more in 1998, and the vast majority of these schemes were registered with the Inland Revenue, thus being eligible for tax relief (Cully *et al*. 1999). There was also an increasing take-up of this scheme in the public sector (for example, in universities) in the late 1990s before the tax benefits were withdrawn from 2000 onwards. Share ownership schemes open to all employees existed in about a quarter of these workplaces, with deferred profit sharing schemes in a small number. In total, 52 per cent of workplaces operated with at least one form of financial participation, with the largest workplaces and organizations being most likely to have them (Cully *et al*. 1999). Share ownership schemes were much more prevalent in 1998 than they had been about twenty years earlier, though in fact less popular than in 1990, whilst profit sharing had continued to become more extensive since the 1980s.

Summary

It is apparent, therefore, that a range of schemes exists for promoting EI, and that even in formal terms these can vary quite markedly. Some are based upon the direct involvement of employees, while others (which are addressed elsewhere in this book) are predicated upon the principle that individual employees are involved through their representatives. Some are concerned primarily with downward communications, whereas others are based upon employees contributing ideas and helping to solve work-related problems. Some are holistic, relating to extensions to the individual's job or new methods of organizing work, while others are more tangential and only require 'involvement' for brief periods on a regular or infrequent basis. Some schemes are designed to link directly part or all of an individual's pay to the performance of a unit or enterprise, whereas the majority relate to practices for which employees receive no financial reward for their involvement. On the other hand, despite the differences, other features are common to all the forms of direct EI considered here: managers are the prime instigators and implementers of new initiatives; employees are assumed to be keen on greater involvement, whatever form it takes; EI is expected to contribute towards the promotion of a common interest between managers and non-managerial employees; and increased levels of employee commitment to the organization and improvements in performance or/productivity are anticipated from EI.

THE ROLE OF MANAGERS IN PROMOTING EI

Managers at all levels in the organizational hierarchy are required to play a crucial role in the development and maintenance of direct EI, whichever form it takes in practice. There are, however, a number of critical points at which managerial actions or inactions can reduce the impact of schemes or cause them to function in ways which were not intended by their architects. For example, there may be incomplete coverage of a particular form of EI across an organization, which means that sizeable numbers of employees fail to be 'involved' in the manner prescribed by specialists at corporate headquarters. Equally, different EI techniques may contradict and conflict with one another (or with elements of HRM or organizational policy) rather than being integrated and set up to work in conjunction with each other. This is a problem particularly if there has been a tendency to adopt a short-termist, faddish and fashion-oriented approach to new initiatives. Moreover, supervisors and first-line managers may not share the commitment of their senior colleagues to EI, and be dubious about its benefits for the organization or for themselves. Finally, shop floor managers may not have the skills and attributes needed to operate direct EI face-to-face with their teams, perhaps because they feel uncomfortable in such situations or have never been adequately trained by their organizations. Each of these is now addressed in turn.

Incomplete coverage and lack of diffusion

Much of the case study evidence indicates that there are often significant gaps between formal policy statements and senior management beliefs and assumptions on the one hand, and the reality of EI at workplace level. A cursory examination of a company statement on employee involvement contained in the annual report might suggest a hive of activity, a judgement which may bear little resemblance to what happens at the workplace or appear unrecognizable to the participants themselves. This is clearly illustrated by examples relating to quality circle coverage, which indicate that only a minority of employees are actually members of circles at any time. For example, in a longitudinal study of a carpet manufacturer in the Midlands, it was found that the proportion of workers in membership of quality circles never exceeded 10 per cent, and some groups (such as the highly unionized weavers) still refused to 'buy in' to the concept a decade after it had first been launched (Ackers *et al.* 1992). Even though staff may actually be present at a problem-solving group, this is not to say that they will actually contribute to discussions or take the meeting seriously. Employees may find it much more desirable to attend a meeting which takes them away from stressful work situations, without the slightest interest in what is being considered; attendance cannot be assumed to imply commitment. Similarly with financial involvement, it is clear that many employees take advantage of share ownership schemes in order to reap monetary rewards, but soon sell their shares if they can get a better price for them or if they need cash urgently.

Given the 'voluntary' nature of quality circles and share ownership schemes, incomplete coverage may not be surprising (or even problematic), but there are also examples where team briefing sessions or team meetings fail to be held at regular and scheduled intervals. Perhaps team briefings are held infrequently, or no longer meet, while in some cases they might never have met since the scheme was introduced, despite the belief of the senior manager who was its instigator and champion (Marchington *et al.* 1992). In other cases, schemes are launched in a blaze of publicity, only to fall foul of a range of operational difficulties such as: tight production or customer service schedules which make it problematic to arrange sessions at certain times of the week or year; shift-workers who are away from the workplace for several days at a time; employees on part-time contracts who are not scheduled to work at times when briefings are held; or a workforce which is dispersed throughout the community or the country. The IRS survey (1999) quoted above suggests that this is a major issue and of the 43 organizations which responded to its questionnaire, just 11 stated that attendance at briefings was compulsory.

Competing initiatives and contradictory rationales

Even if EI schemes do cover the majority of employees in an organization, there are often problems in their introduction and implementation, as well as in their integration with existing EI schemes and other HR practices. In larger establishments, for example, it would not be unusual for seven or eight different EI practices to operate at the same time, covering the range of forms which were outlined earlier in this chapter. Some of these (especially in the area of representative participation such as joint consultative committees) may have been in existence for many years, whereas others (especially problem-solving groups) are more likely to be products of the last few years. On some occasions, these will have been introduced in a phased and planned manner and attempts will have been made to ensure that there is at least some complementarity between these different practices. In many other cases, however, recent initiatives owe rather more to fads and fashions, as well as moves by different departments to be seen as contributing to corporate success (Marchington *et al.* 1993). This multiplicity of EI arrangements can result in different practices competing with each other, and in some instances flatly contradicting the aims and objectives of other initiatives. For example, there may be major tensions between a suggestion scheme which pays for employee ideas and a TQM initiative in which employees are expected to undertake continuous improvement as part of their normal duties. As McCabe (1996) notes in his study of TQM at a British manufacturing company, power and departmental politics within organizations can heavily influence the outcome of any initiative, leading to failures and/or inconsistencies in their application.

It is possible to chart the dynamics of EI over time by representing each initiative as a 'wave' which portrays its growth and decline, its ebb and flow, in comparison with other initiatives. The waves metaphor is useful as it illustrates graphically the way that different initiatives achieve different levels of prominence and centrality within organizations, not only in relation to each other but also in relation to HR processes in general and to wider corporate concerns. The prominence and centrality of EI varies between organizations as well, influenced by managerial actions (and inactions) as well as by the power and influence of different departments and senior managers. In one organization, for example, the institutions of representative participation may have survived intact – though perhaps with lessened centrality – for more than 20 or 30 years, whereas in others they may have been jettisoned during the 1980s or 1990s in favour of direct EI, only to return in recent years as part of the wave of interest in and development of partnership schemes (Guest and Peccei 1998; Marchington 1998; Monks 1998). In others, a whole host of direct EI practices (such as team briefing, employee reports, problem-solving groups, suggestion schemes, task-based participation, profit sharing and employee share ownership) may have operated alongside each other for most of the past 20 years, perhaps varying in centrality and importance depending on the circumstances. In yet others, a faddish approach may have characterized the organization's approach to EI, with no particular scheme lasting for more than a few years as interest wanes soon after the new initiative has been implemented and attention turns to the next 'panacea' offered up by the management gurus.

In addition, the fact that direct EI – in particular, as it rarely relies on expert technical knowledge for its application – can be defined in such a way as to fall within the province of different departments increases the likelihood of competing initiatives and potentially contradictory rationales. New EI practices may even be introduced at the same time, with little or no co-ordination across the organization concerned. Plainly, this is more marked for different forms of EI, and it is possible that the motives which underpin and sustain representative participation or financial involvement may be philosophically and practically at odds with those which lead to the implementation of teamworking or TQM. However, problems can still arise with schemes which are similar in form, but are driven by different departments; for example, a system for internal communications championed by an HR department may have quite a different character to one which is promoted by a sales or public relations team. These notions of champions, 'impression management' and interdepartmental rivalries have been developed in more detail in Marchington *et al.* (1993).

It is not suggested that contradictory messages are confined solely to EI schemes, and it can be seen more widely in relation to other management plans and policies which have implications for employees. For example, a new teamworking initiative may be introduced, perhaps quite genuinely, with promises of empowerment and greater autonomy only to founder if employees find other aspects of their work are more tightly controlled and overseen (Marchington 2000). As Sewell and Wilkinson (1992: 112) conclude, on the basis of a case study of TQM in a manufacturing company:

> On the one hand, the rhetoric of HRM preaches commitment based on trust, a culture based on equality and a unity of goals backed up by practical measures which try to minimise differences ... On the other hand, they (the employees) are subjected to the closest scrutiny which is used to distinguish them from their peers on matters of the minutest detail.

Lack of commitment by first-line managers

EI schemes can also fail due to splits and discontinuities between different levels in the organizational hierarchy. Supervisors and first-line managers often react negatively to initiatives which they consider to be the brainchild of some young, new recruit on the promotional fast-track and feel that they are forced to comply with practices which they had no role in designing (Heller *et al*. 1998). It is dangerous for senior managers to assume that first-line managers readily identify with the organization for which they work and share their own views about the desirability of EI. The language of teamworking and empowerment, for example, while potentially attractive to more senior managers, can appear highly threatening and problematic to their more junior colleagues whose authority has often been built on technical expertise and the restriction of information flows to the shop floor. Similarly, expectations that first-line managers should operate as 'coaches' rather than 'cops' can be seen by supervisors as being at odds with their own common sense versions of what workers are 'really' like. In other words, rather than viewing EI as beneficial to the organization, supervisors may reinterpret it as 'soft' management and as 'long-haired idealists in corporate headquarters' doing nothing more than pander to shop floor employees (Wilkinson *et al*. 1993). This is partly because supervisors see themselves as much closer to the people for whom they are responsible, rather than being a part of management, a feeling which may intensify as their own job security is lessened and promotion opportunities are reduced. They are often cynical about the value of EI and TQM (Yong and Wilkinson 1999) and fearful about the implications of initiatives such as teamworking for their own jobs, especially when one of the supposed benefits is that it can eliminate the need for layers of management (Heller *et al*. 1998; Pfeffer 1998; Marchington and Grugulis 2000). Observers have suggested that supervisors are estranged from managerial goals and values (Scase and Goffee 1989), and the highly mobile career paths of EI champions merely serve to convince them that their own contribution is not particularly valued by organizations.

Practical reasons for failing to implement EI effectively

Even if supervisors do share the same values as their senior management colleagues, EI may still fail to be implemented fully in line with expectations for rather more practical reasons. First, supervisors and front-line managers already suffer from work overload in many organizations, and find it difficult to set aside time to communicate or consult with their subordinates. This is particularly pronounced in situations where supervisors are not explicitly rewarded for developing EI, and their performance is judged against key performance indicators and production or service criteria (e.g. number of items manufactured or queue lengths) which, on the surface at least, seem to be at odds with what can be gained from an EI programme. Although a company's mission statement may state, for example, that empowerment, teamworking and respect for employees are key objectives, supervisors soon become aware that production or service considerations assume priority in the event of conflicting priorities.

Second, given the desire by most organizations to implement new EI initiatives with a minimum of delay, supervisors often receive no more than a rudimentary level of training on how to operate schemes. Little or no time is devoted to ensuring that they understand and accept the principles which underlie EI, nor to training them in how to manage specific EI practices – such as how to brief a team effectively or seek suggestions from a quality circle. The IRS survey (1999), for example, indicated that less than half of the organizations sampled provided specific training for supervisors in how to run briefing groups. Yet it is acknowledged that the direct experience which employees have of any management initiative, EI included, has a major impact upon their attitudes and behaviour.

The evidence presented in this section clearly illustrates the sort of issues which are routinely encountered as managers grapple with the problem of how to operate direct EI, and which can lead to failures in the conversion of policy into practice. Given, as suggested above, that managers are central to the effective functioning of EI and HRM, this must necessarily limit its potential impact on employee commitment and performance. Although a number of the problems which have been identified could well be alleviated by the provision of more effective training or other adjustments to HR practice, there remain more deep-seated concerns which cannot be addressed so easily, in particular relating to supervisory commitment and inter-functional rivalries within management. Having said this, the recent IRS survey (1999) did suggest that, while the problem had not disappeared, managers at all levels now seemed to present less of an obstacle to EI than they had in the early 1990s.

THE IMPACT OF EI ON EMPLOYEE ATTITUDES AND PERFORMANCE

It has been noted already that employees are the principal target of EI schemes, and it might be assumed that EI should therefore have an impact upon their attitudes and performance. Analysis of employee responses in the Marchington *et al.* (1992) survey revealed that EI has a mildly favourable impact on employee attitudes, or perhaps more accurately it could be suggested that the existence or promise of EI is associated with more positive employee attitudes. There are less data available on the links between attitudes and behaviour, however, or between EI and employees' commitment to work and their employing organization. The whole area is bedevilled with a range of methodological problems, as we see below. But, it is also suggested here that attitudes to work and to EI need to be placed firmly within the relevant organizational and commercial context, and that employee responses to EI may act as a conduit for more general feelings of support for their employer or for anxieties about future employment security and job prospects.

Employee interest in EI

There is a general consensus from surveys conducted over the past 30 years (see, for example, Allen *et al.* 1991; Baddon *et al.* 1989; Dewe *et al.* 1988; Hespe and Wall 1976; Marchington 1980; Marchington *et al.* 1994; Ramsay 1976; Rees 1998) that employees are attracted to the idea of being involved at work and to the concept of involvement and participation; indeed, it would be remarkable if they were not, given the alternative is to wish for autocratic and non-communicative management styles! In principle, employees are keen to have more say within their establishments and to find out more about actions which are likely to impact upon their own jobs and activities at work. There are variations on the basis of factors such as personality and demographic characteristics according to the surveys, but nevertheless the common view is that employees are not satisfied with employers acting without some effort to keep them informed. The view expressed by Gallie and White (1993: 44) a number of years ago still seems accurate:

participation is of fundamental importance for employee attitudes to the organisations for which they work. It is strongly related to the way they respond to changes in work organisation and with their perception of the quality of the overall relationship between management and employees.

But there are limits to this desire for greater involvement, and certainly the attitude surveys suggest that employees are not searching for workers' control, or even for joint decision-making powers with management. Employees – in general – are dubious about styles of leadership which merely inform them about decisions *after* they have been taken, and seem to favour something in between a 'sells' style and a consultative approach; in other words, the implication is that employees like to have the opportunity to find out why (certain) decisions have been made, plus the potential to influence those which are felt to be within their own domain and about which they feel able to contribute ideas.

Employees appear keen to see schemes in their own place of work continue, whatever the specific EI practice in question. For example, nearly 90 per cent of respondents to the Marchington *et al.* (1992: 35–7) survey indicated that they wished team briefing to continue at their place of work, while for quality circles the figure was 80 per cent, and for employee share ownership/profit sharing it was about 85 per cent of all those with experiences of these practices. Proponents of EI should treat this figure with some caution, however, because some of the reasons for wanting particular schemes to continue suggest apathy and a calculated instrumentalism (quotes such as 'it's better than working', 'gives me half an hour off work', 'like a cash windfall' being typical employee responses) rather than high levels of commitment to the organization.

Employee attitudes and commitment

Some observers claim that EI leads to higher levels of employee commitment to or identification with employing organizations, and improved levels of corporate or business unit performance. Apart from the study by Patterson *et al.* (1997) in Britain – which was actually wider than just EI – many of the claims have been based on surveys in the USA where high commitment management has been pioneered by management gurus who argue that American companies have fallen behind the Japanese largely because of a failure to 'involve' their staff. In summarizing this literature, Cotton (1993: 232) suggests that practices such as gain-sharing and self-directed work teams have a strong effect on employee attitudes, that job enrichment and quality of work life have an intermediate effect, while quality circles and representative participation have a weak effect on employees. At Japanese companies in Britain – where team briefing typically takes place daily – it is more likely that employees feel that it has impacted on their attitudes and commitment to the organization (see, for example, Marchington *et al.* 1994), although there are doubts about whether or not this is seen as desirable or intrusive (Delbridge 1998).

Other researchers are sceptical about the possible impact of EI on attitudes, and more especially on employee commitment and performance. Kelly and Kelly (1991: 43–4) conclude their review of research into new industrial relations practices in Britain by saying that, although employees may be induced to think positively about EI schemes, 'there is little or no evidence to suggest that these practices have altered workers' largely negative views of management in general and of union–management relations'. Guest (1992) argues that there are problems in specifying precisely what is meant by commitment and how it is measured, which are not helped by the fact that people hold multiple commitments to groups as diverse as management, fellow workers, union, occupation, department, plant, or employer. A recent review of dual commitment (Snape et al. 2000) confirms this picture by drawing on data from surveys in a number of countries. Given the limited amount of time for which most employees are asked to be 'involved' by management, especially if it is 'bolted-on' to existing practices, it would be foolhardy to suggest that EI is capable of changing attitudes and behaviour, without more fundamental adjustments to the entire employment relationship.

It has already been mentioned that team briefing and upward problem-solving are two of the most widespread of all EI techniques, with employees particularly keen on seeing these continue in workplaces where they currently exist. Despite this, employees do not think that briefing, for example, has a great impact on employment relations or on their attitudes to work. Although many more respondents to the Marchington et al. (1992) study felt that things had improved rather than worsened, the vast majority reckoned that there had been little or no change, following the introduction of team briefing, on their understanding of management decisions, the quality of upward communications and openness, or on their commitment to the organization. Indeed, in the case of commitment, over three-quarters of respondents indicated that there had been 'no change'. In a sense, such low figures may not be surprising, given that, for most employees, briefing constitutes such a small proportion of their working lives (about 30 minutes a month, typically). Even if such a system works very well, therefore, its impact is only likely to be minor, compared with other aspects of the employment relationship, and we have seen already that in many cases problems within management render it markedly less effective. Cotton (1993: 87) makes this point starkly and effectively in relation to quality circles, although it could relate equally well to forms of downward communication: 'at most these (quality circle) programmes operate for one hour per week, with the remaining 39 hours unchanged. Why should changes in 2.5% of a person's job have a major impact?'

The material on employee share ownership and profit sharing also indicates that the impact on employee attitudes is generally minimal and in most cases these forms of financial involvement are marginal to working life. A study by McGrath (1999) of two organizations suggested that share ownership made little or no difference to employee commitment, loyalty or job performance for the simple reason that employee shareholders felt they had no influence over the level of profits or the distribution of rewards. Keef (1998) found that employees were only interested in share ownership because of the possible financial gains it might bring, and that the impact was limited because shares produced rewards which were low in comparison with their salaries. Even in situations where employees hold a significant level of shares, such as in employee-owned firms, the impact is still less than might be expected. In Pendleton et al.'s (1998) study of four bus companies, less than a third of the employees felt that share ownership had resulted in positive gains while many more felt that little had changed. However, those employees who 'feel' like owners – those with higher levels of shareholding and perceptions of participation – did appear to have higher levels of commitment and satisfaction with their organization.

It might be expected that employees who are involved in teamworking would display higher levels of satisfaction and commitment given that this represents one of the more extensive forms of direct EI available – although, as was suggested above, much depends on the version of teamworking which is experienced. A number of studies have indicated that employees in team situations tend to be more satisfied and motivated than those who are working under more traditional regimes (Edwards and Wright 1998; Geary 1993; Wilkinson *et al.* 1997). Even if it is acknowledged that teamworking involves harder work, it is regularly reported that this also offers the opportunity for more satisfying and fulfilling work (McArdle *et al.* 1995; Scott 1994). Yet, for a variety of reasons, there are considerable doubts as to whether teamworking actually leads to greater levels of employee control over work processes. These include: technical limits on the extent to which work can be redesigned meaningfully; failures by managers to implement teamworking properly; high levels of disinterest on the part of employees themselves; and inherent contradictions in the concept itself as workers learn to control themselves rather than be controlled by management. This last gives rise to the concept of 'concertive control' (Barker 1993). This represents a shift in the locus of control, all the more dangerous because employees become incarcerated in a new 'iron cage' whose bars are almost invisible to those involved. This leads people such as Sinclair (1992) to write about the 'tyranny of the team ideology'. The paradox here is that some analysts see the more extensive forms of EI as more dangerous than the 'dilute' forms precisely because they have the potential to entrap employees into doing managers' work for them as it tends to be seen as more satisfying than repeatedly undertaking boring jobs.

Organizational characteristics, EI and performance

There is little doubt that the impact of EI can vary significantly between organizations, even in those which operate with the same set of practices. In a number of the case studies conducted by Marchington *et al.* (1994), employees were very positive about EI, feeling that although it had been introduced by management for business-related reasons it had also served to increase employee satisfaction. In each of these 'positive' cases, nearly all respondents reported that the company was 'a good one to work for' and they displayed high levels of commitment to and satisfaction with their employer. In other organizations, employees were particularly negative about EI and employee relations, viewing management with some hostility and displaying an overwhelmingly instrumental attachment to work. Management's reasons for introducing EI were often seen as little more than attempts at work intensification, employees generally reported that EI had worsened in recent few years, and very few felt that specific EI practices had led to any improvements at work. A recent investigation by Frobel (1999) of teamworking in a chemical company confirmed that organizational context, and through that job satisfaction, was the most important factor in explaining employee evaluations of the effectiveness of this form of EI. It should be noted in passing, however, that McNabb and Whitfield (1999) found no association between the level of product market competition which organizations face and the *presence/absence* of EI schemes; they were not able to test for any link with employee views.

Differences in the views of employees appear to have little to do with the type or range of EI schemes practised at these organizations, but rather more can be

246 Key practice areas of HRM

explained by the way in which management responds to competitive pressures. It is suggested that in cases where there have been redundancies in recent times and future prospects look bleak to employees, EI practices and management are also seen in a predominantly negative light. Because most EI schemes are predicated upon a greater awareness of competitive pressures, it is hardly surprising that employees should refer to this knowledge when evaluating EI schemes. Regular bouts of 'bad news' conveyed through team briefing, for example, can result in employees having negative assessments of the briefing system itself. Similarly, a series of poor profit announcements may start to lead to conclusions that the employee share ownership scheme is not particularly good. Equally, a failure to take up ideas submitted through a quality circle programme, perhaps due to lack of money, can lead to criticisms of management and the circles themselves. In other words, negative evaluations of EI may be a barometer for more deep-seated anxieties about current and future prospects, while positive attitudes towards EI may be symptomatic of a 'feel good' factor about work and their employer.

Methodological limitations

There are a number of reasons why the results from employee attitude surveys should be treated with caution (Hyman and Mason 1995). First, there is the problem of bench-marking and determining the best date at which to start making 'before and after' comparisons; in the case of the former, should this be at the time the new scheme was introduced, or at some time before – when preparations were under way? In relation to the latter, because attitudes can vary considerably over time, as well as in response to specific events (such as redundancy announcements or pay claims), this makes comparisons problematic. Second, as we have seen above, it is extremely difficult in non-laboratory research to control for the influence of factors other than EI on attitudes and behaviour in order to isolate the relationship between just two variables. For example, claims that a new form of EI has led to reductions in labour turnover have to be assessed against the potentially greater influence of factors such as the rate of unemployment, the number of job vacancies locally, or the structure of pay differentials. Also, given that most large organizations operate with several EI practices at the same time, it is virtually impossible to evaluate the impact of any one of these on employee attitudes and behaviour. Third, many organizations do not measure performance with sufficient precision to enable any correlations to be made, nor do they keep comprehensive and systematic data on absence levels or labour turnover. In most cases, therefore, analysts are reliant on management assessments of the perceived linkage between EI and behaviour at work, and the belief, as Lawler *et al.* (1992: 62) found, 'that EI is a viable way to increase organizational performance'. Finally, as suggested above, contrary to claims that EI can lead to cultural change and increased employee commitment to the organization, it could be argued that EI is as much affected by the prevailing organizational culture as it is a source of change; that is, the direction of causality of this relationship could be in the opposite direction to that claimed by some of its proponents.

In summary, there seems to be little doubt that employees like the idea of EI, and the vast majority certainly prefer the prospect of more participative styles of supervision than more oppressive regimes of discipline and control. However, despite the appeal of EI in general terms, the evidence suggests that it has only had a limited impact upon employee attitudes and commitment, and even less on behaviour and performance. To some extent, this can be explained by the problems which managers face in initiating and sustaining EI at the workplace, but it may also be unrealistic to expect 'partial involvement' – that is, schemes which are bolted on to existing frameworks of employment relations in an unsystematic way – to bring about a transformation in employee attitudes and behaviour.

THE RELATIONSHIP BETWEEN EI AND TRADE UNION ORGANIZATION

The relationship between direct EI and trade unions is complex, although this has not prevented some observers viewing the two as being in direct competition with each other. A variety of outcomes is possible however, ranging from compatibility or synergy between EI and trade unions on the one hand, through to tension and competition between management and union representatives to secure influence over work. Alternatively, the relationship may be relatively unaffected, with direct EI and trade unions co-existing because they are seen to operate in quite separate zones. Much depends upon the objectives for EI which are pursued both by management and unions, as well as on existing patterns of employment relations at the workplace and in the organization more widely. McNabb and Whitfield (1999: 131), in their analysis of the WIRS3 data, also find differences at an aggregate level depending on the type of EI scheme being pursued. Their results indicate that

> the presence of a recognised union at the establishment is positively associated with the introduction of upward problem-solving schemes but negatively associated with the incidence of financial participation at the establishment. Unions appear to have no significant influence on the introduction of downward communications.

There was also no evidence that the presence of strong unions at the workplace constrained the introduction of EI.

Competition between unions and direct EI practices

There are 'a priori' reasons why direct EI may be seen to pose a threat and lead to the marginalization of unions at the workplace. Kumar (1995: 40), for example, argues that new management initiatives (including direct EI) which seek to increase efficiency and flexibility 'pose serious challenges to unions, threatening their traditional role of defending and advancing worker rights' and have the potential to seriously harm them. Beale (1994: 120) suggests that 'EI programmes provide an alternative source of information, ideas and interpretation of workplace experiences, an alternative to that provided by the union'. Kelly (1988: 265) summarizes the point succinctly: 'by linking elements of workers' pay to company performance, providing information about company performance, and encouraging workers to contribute their own ideas for its improvement, the hope is that conflicts of interest can be weakened. Clearly, schemes of this kind, if successful, would pose a considerable threat to the role and possibly to the very existence of trade unions'. There are certainly examples of this taking place where managers introduce a barrage of direct communications – such as briefing or videos – aimed directly at employees with the objective of reducing their dependence on the unions as the main transmitter of information, and making it more difficult for union representatives to challenge management's interpretation of issues (Wilkinson *et al.* 1997). Around a third of the IRS (1999) sample of companies felt that EI had weakened the unions at their organizations.

There are also examples where employers have not implemented EI with the *explicit* aim of undermining unions, although a consequence of managerial action has been to marginalize the union. A more open approach to employment relations which includes a package of direct EI practices can help to reduce distrust and cause employees to identify more with their employer, and hence diminish the role of the union. This may only be temporary if employers are unable to sustain product market success and maintain high wages and benefits. In situations where unions lack membership or recognition, it is possible that a substitution effect takes place in that direct EI fills in the gaps otherwise occupied by trade unions. To be successful, direct EI in these circumstances needs to be linked with superior terms and conditions, and not all employers are able to offer this. In addition, it needs to be recalled that, on the whole, non-union firms are less likely to use HRM and EI practices than are unionized workplaces (Cully *et al.* 1999).

A somewhat more textured and nuanced analysis of the relationship between EI (in this case teamworking) and union organization is provided by Martinez Lucio *et al.* (2000) in their research at Royal Mail. They argue against simplistic notions of unions being displaced by EI because this ignores the fact that unions are not passive recipients of new management practices but actively engage with managers in accommodating EI, perhaps by resisting some aspects and adapting to others. Nevertheless, the situation at Royal Mail was characterized by tension in that teamworking represented a challenge to the purpose and role of unions and to the ordering principles of the traditional workplace, buttressed to a large extent by an employer who was using legislation as a key element in its wider industrial relations strategy (ibid.: 275). Similar issues are evident from a study in the steel industry by Bacon and Blyton (2000) who found that conflict was associated with teamworking primarily because it failed to improve substantive terms and conditions for those union members who were covered by such arrangements, and indeed certain groups of workers actually lost out. This throws up the possibility that unions can delay the introduction of EI or alter its character in situations where there is sufficient collective cohesion to mobilize worker resistance.

Management–union complementarity

There are also situations where a degree of complementarity can exist between union organization and at least some EI practices. In the study by Marchington *et al.* (1992), this occurred at about half of the unionized workplaces, although it should be noted that the links tended to be stronger in relation to representative participation than it was for direct EI. In one of the chemical firms studied, part of the process of change included a wide-ranging involvement exercise in which senior managers made extensive efforts to maintain good working relations with the senior stewards, and not to alienate them by introducing changes without union support. The senior stewards were aware of the potential dangers of being 'incorporated' into management, but saw their involvement in the change programme as essential for the future well-being of their members and the company (Wilkinson *et al.* 1993). This was also apparent in a number of firms which operated TQM and upward problem-solving practices, but here it was also clear that union representatives ensured that their support for EI also led to improvements in working conditions and other HR practices; amongst other things, this helped to enhance their standing with union members (Wilkinson *et al.* 1997).

The surge of interest in partnership deals between employers and trade unions since the late 1990s also demonstrates how representative participation can operate alongside direct EI. Indeed, many of these agreements make explicit reference to a whole range of direct EI practices in addition to the provision of closer union–management relations at establishment or organization level. This is evidenced in the agreements at Welsh Water, Tesco and Barclays Bank, for example, and in the benchmarks for the Partnership Company (Guest and Peccei 1998). The issue of partnership is addressed in the companion chapter by David Guest in this volume. It is also interesting to note that, across Europe, trade union representatives have typically been involved in the introduction of direct EI in companies, and that in Britain (along with France and Spain) worker representatives had high levels of involvement in such discussions (Gill and Krieger 1999: 585).

A further scenario is where direct EI and unions run in parallel, with no obvious or overt relationship between them in what might be referred to as a 'dual' approach to the management of employment (Sisson 1993). In these cases, union representatives may take an agnostic view of schemes such as team briefing, seeing them as largely irrelevant to the union's role and unlikely to affect collective bargaining structure. Indeed, it is difficult for stewards to argue against direct EI if this is introduced in order to improve communications up or down the organizational hierarchy, largely because problems relating to breakdowns in information flow are regularly pointed out as a major concern by employees and unions in attitude surveys.

CONCLUSIONS

Successive Workplace Industrial/Employee Relations Surveys (Millward *et al.* 1992; Cully *et al.* 1999) have confirmed that EI has become more extensive across British employing organizations over the last 20 years. It is now a prominent feature of the employment relations landscape, at least in terms of the number of organizations which appear to practise one or more forms of direct EI – such as downward communications, upward problem-solving, task-based participation and teamworking, and financial involvement. As we have stated already, EI has the potential to make a significant impact at workplace level and enhance employee commitment to organizational goals.

As this chapter has illustrated, however, organizational reality is often much more mundane. Many employers have tended to adopt a faddish approach to EI which has resulted in conflicting and sometimes contradictory forms being practised within the same organization, and it is rare for there to be a well-planned and co-ordinated strategy for the development of EI as part of a broader HR strategy, which is itself firmly integrated into corporate objectives. Moreover, line managers have often lacked the enthusiasm and commitment which is expected from them if EI is to work in practice, partly because the supposed benefits are not actually advantageous to managers themselves. In addition, many employers have committed insufficient time and resources to training supervisors to deliver EI at the workplace. Given that some forms of EI are predicated upon the adoption of new styles of management ('from cops to coaches', for example), this omission can have severe consequences for the effectiveness of EI and HRM.

It is also clear that the impact of EI upon employees has not been great, although it is fair to say that responses have been mildly favourable in most cases, and management styles which incorporate direct EI are considerably more attractive than their autocratic alternatives. Such a cautious conclusion might well disappoint the proponents of EI, but perhaps little more could be expected given the minor impact which EI has on most employees' lives. In terms of time alone, most employees who are 'involved' in team briefings, for example, find that this takes up well under half of one per cent of their working time. For the most part, as well, their 'involvement' in this form of EI tends to be passive, and often it constitutes little more than listening to information which is not seen as of prime importance to them. Teams offer more in terms of ongoing involvement, but it is clear from the WERS data and from case study evidence that only rarely do these comply with the processes which characterize autonomous group working. These shortcomings have also meant that the supposed threat of EI to unions has been much less serious than some have feared, and in quite a number of cases direct EI has worked alongside existing union channels. In short, although it is theoretically possible for EI to promote substantial changes in employment relations, this is dependent upon a number of connections being made – especially by line managers – and in the majority of cases these connections are missed.

Although a realist would caution against expecting too much from direct EI, such a person would also urge employers to devote more energy to increasing the amount of real 'involvement' in employing organizations and to ensuring that line managers are provided with a greater range of skills to make EI work effectively. It could be argued that the haphazard, uneven and piecemeal way in which EI is introduced into most employing organizations does not provide a fair indication of what it could achieve under the long-term and systematic adoption of a high commitment HRM strategy. Whether most British employers have the inclination or the time to develop such a strategy remains a question for future research.

REFERENCES

Ackers, P., Marchington, M., Wilkinson, A. and Goodman, J. (1992) 'The Long and Winding Road; Tracking Employee Involvement at Brown's Woven Carpets', *Employee Relations*, **14**(3): 56–70.

Allen, C., Cunningham, I. and McArdle, L. (1991) *Employee Participation and Involvement into the Nineties*, Stockton-on-Tees: Jim Conway Foundation.

Bacon, N. and Blyton, P. (2000) 'The Diffusion of Teamworking and New Working Practices: What Role do Industrial Relation Factors Play?', in S. Procter and F. Mueller (eds) *Teamworking*, Basingstoke: Macmillan. pp. 244–61.

Baddon, L., Hunter, L., Hyman, J., Leopold, J. and Ramsay, H. (1989) *People's Capitalism?*, London: Routledge.

Barker, J. (1993) 'Tightening the Iron Cage: Concertive Control in Self-Managing Teams', *Administrative Science Quarterly*, **38**: 408–37.

Beale, D. (1994) *Driven by Nissan? A Critical Guide to New Management Techniques*, London: Lawrence and Wishart.

Blumberg, P. (1968) *Industrial Democracy; The Sociology of Participation*, London: Constable.

Case, J. (1998) *The Open-Book Management Experience*, London: Nicholas Brealey Publishing.

Cotton, J. (1993) *Employee Involvement; Methods for Improving Performance and Work Attitudes*, Newbury Park, CA: Sage.

Cully, M., O'Reilly, A., Millward, N., Forth, J., Woodland, S., Dix, G. and Bryson, A. (1998) *The 1998 Workplace Employee Relations Survey: First Findings*, Department of Trade and Industry, London: HMSO.

Cully, M., Woodland, S., O'Reilly, A. and Dix, G. (1999) *Britain at Work: As Depicted by the 1998 Workplace Employee Relations Survey*, London: Routledge.

Daniel, W. and Millward, N. (1983) *Workplace Industrial Relations in Britain*, London: Heinemann.

Delbridge, R. (1998) *Life on the Line in Contemporary Manufacturing: The Workplace Experience of Lean Production and the 'Japanese' Model*, Oxford: Oxford University Press.

Dewe, P., Dunn, S. and Richardson, R. (1988) 'Employee Share Option Schemes; Why Workers are Attracted to Them', *British Journal of Industrial Relations*, **26**(1): 1–21.

Edwards, P. and Wright, M. (1998) 'Human Resource Management and Commitment: A Case Study of Teamworking', in P. Sparrow and M. Marchington (eds) *Human Resource Management: The New Agenda*, London: Pitman, pp. 272–85.

Foy, N. (1994) *Empowering People at Work*, London: Gower.

Frobel, P. (1999) *'Analysing Factors for Team Effectiveness'*, Unpublished MSc dissertation, UMIST.

Gallie, D. and White, M. (1993) *Employee Commitment and the Skills Revolution*, London: PSI Publications.

Geary, J. (1993) 'New Forms of Work Organisation and Employee Involvement in Two Case Study Sites: Plural, Mixed and Protean', *Economic and Industrial Democracy*, **14**: 511–34.

Gill, C. and Krieger, H. (1999) 'Direct and Representative Participation in Europe: Recent Evidence', *The International Journal of Human Resource Management*, **10**(4): 572–91.

Guest, D. (1992) 'Employee Commitment and Control', in J. Hartley and G. Stephenson (eds) *Employment Relations: The Psychology of Influence and Control at Work*, Oxford: Blackwell Publishers.

Guest, D. (1999) 'Human Resource Management: The Workers' Verdict', *Human Resource Management Journal*, **9**(3): 5–25.

Guest, D. and Peccei, R. (1998) *The Partnership Company: Benchmarks for the Future*, London: Involvement and Participation Association.

Heller, F., Pusic, E., Strauss, G. and Wilpert, B. (1998) *Organisational Participation: Myth and Reality*, Oxford: Oxford University Press.

Hespe, G. and Wall, T. (1976) 'The Demand for Participation Among Employees', *Human Relations*, **29**(5): 471–505.

Hyman, J. and Mason, B. (1995) *Managing Employee Involvement and Participation*, London: Sage.

Industrial Relations Services (IRS) (1999) 'Trends in Employee Involvement', *IRS Employment Trends*, **683**: 6–16.

Keef, S. (1998) 'The Causal Association Between Employee Share Ownership and Attitudes: A Study Based on the Long Framework', *British Journal of Industrial Relations*, **36**(1): 73–82.

Kelly, J. (1982) *Scientific Management, Job Redesign and Work Performance*, London: Academic Press.

Kelly, J. (1988) *Trade Unions and Socialist Politics*, London: Varso.

Kelly, J. and Kelly, C. (1991) '"Them and Us": Social Psychology and the "New Industrial Relations"', *British Journal of Industrial Relations*, **29**(1): 25–48.

Knights, D., Willmott, H. and Collinson, D. (eds) (1985) *Job Redesign*, Aldershot: Gower.

Kumar, P. (1995) 'Canadian Labour's Response to Work Reorganisation', *Economic and Industrial Democracy*, **16**(1): 39–78.

Lansbury, R. and Davis, E. (eds) (1996) *Managing Together: Consultation and Participation in the Workplace*, Melbourne: Longman.

Lawler, E., Mohrman, S. and Ledford, G. (1992) *Employee Involvement and Total Quality Management*, San Francisco, CA: Jossey-Bass.

Legge, K. (1995) *Human Resource Management: Rhetorics and Realities*, Basingstoke: Macmillan.

Mabey, C., Skinner, D. and Clark, T. (eds) (1998) *Experiencing Human Resource Management*, London: Sage.

Mabey, C., Salaman, G. and Storey, J. (1999) *Human Resource Management: A Strategic Introduction*, Oxford: Blackwell Publishers.

Marchington, M. (1980) *Responses to Participation at Work*, Farnborough: Gower.

Marchington, M. (1992) *Managing the Team: A Guide to Employee Involvement in Practice*, Oxford: Blackwell.

Marchington, M. (1995) 'Employee Relations', in S. Tyson (ed.) *Strategic Prospects for Human Resource Management*, London: IPD, pp. 81–111.

Marchington, M. (1998) 'Partnership in Context: Towards a European Model?', in P. Sparrow and M. Marchington (eds) *Human Resource Management: The New Agenda*, London: Pitman, pp. 208–25.

Marchington, M. (2000) 'Teamworking and Employee Involvement: Terminology, Evaluation and Context', in S. Procter and F. Mueller (eds) *Teamworking*, Basingstoke: Macmillan, pp. 60–80.

Marchington, M., Goodman, J., Wilkinson, A. and Ackers, P. (1992) *Recent Developments in Employee Involvement*, Employment Department Research Series, No. 1, London: HMSO.

Marchington, M., Wilkinson, A., Ackers, P. and Goodman, J. (1993) 'The Influence of Managerial Relations on Waves of Employee Involvement', *British Journal of Industrial Relations*, **31**(4): 553–76.

Marchington, M., Wilkinson, A., Ackers, P. and Goodman, J. (1994) 'Understanding the Meaning of Participation: Views from the Workplace', *Human Relations*, **47**(8): 867–94.

Marchington, M. and Wilkinson, A. (1996) *Core Personnel and Development*, London: Institute of Personnel and Development.

Marchington, M. and Grugulis, I. (2000) 'Best Practice Human Resource Management: Perfect Opportunity or Dangerous Illusion?', *The International Journal of Human Resource Management*, (forthcoming).

Martinez Lucio, M., Jenkins, S. and Noon, M. (2000) 'Management Strategy, Union Identity and Oppositionalism: Teamwork in the Royal Mail', in S. Procter and F. Mueller (eds) *Teamworking*, Basingstoke: Macmillan, pp. 262–79.

McArdle, L., Rowlinson, M., Procter, S., Hassard, J. and Forrester, P. (1995) 'Total Quality Management and Participation: Employee Empowerment or the Enhancement of Exploitation?', in A. Wilkinson and H. Willmott (eds) *Making Quality Critical: New Perspectives on Organisational Change*, London: Routledge, pp. 156–72.

McCabe, D. (1996) 'The Best Laid Schemes o' TQM: Strategy, Politics and Power', *New Technology, Work and Employment*, **11**(1): 28–38.

McGrath, S. (1999) 'Attitudes to Employee Share Schemes', unpublished MSc documentation, UMIST.

McNabb, R. and Whitfield, M. (1999) 'The Distribution of Employee Participation Schemes at the Workplace', *The International Journal of Human Resource Management*, **10**(1): 122–36.

Millward, N. and Stevens, M. (1986) *British Workplace Industrial Relations, 1980–1984*, Aldershot: Gower.

Millward, N., Stevens, M., Smart, D. and Hawes, W. (1992) *Workplace Industrial Relations in Transition*, Aldershot: Dartmouth.

Monks, J. (1998) 'Trade Unions, Enterprise and the Future', in P. Sparrow and M. Marchington (eds) *Human Resource Management: The New Agenda*, London: Pitman, pp. 171–79.

Pateman, C. (1970) *Participation and Democratic Theory*, Cambridge: Cambridge University Press.

Patterson, M., West, M., Lawthorn, R. and Nickell, S. (1997) *The Impact of People Management Practices on Business Performance*, London: Institute of Personnel and Development.

Pendleton, A. (1997) 'Stakeholders as Shareholders: The Role of Employee Share Ownership', in G. Kelly, D. Kelly and A. Gamble (eds) *Stakeholder Capitalism*, Basingstoke: Macmillan.

Pendleton, A., McDonald, J., Robinson, A. and Wilson, N. (1995) 'The Impact of Employee Share Ownership Plans on Employee Participation and Industrial Democracy', *Human Resource Management Journal*, **5**(4): 44–60.

Pendleton, A., Wilson, N. and Wright, M. (1998) 'The Perception and Effects of Share Ownership: Empirical Evidence from Employee Buy-Outs', *British Journal of Industrial Relations*, **36**(3): 99–123.

Pfeffer, J. (1998) *The Human Equation: Building Profits by Putting People First*, Boston: Harvard Business School Press.

Poole, M. (1986) *Towards a New Industrial Democracy; Workers' Participation in Industry*, London: Routledge.

Poole, M. (1989) *The Origins of Economic Democracy: Profit Sharing and Employee Shareholding Schemes*, London: Routledge.

Ramsay, H. (1976) 'Participation: The Shop Floor View', *British Journal of Industrial Relations*, **14**(2): 128–41.

Rees, C. (1998) 'Empowerment Through Quality Management: Employee Accounts from Inside a Bank, a Hotel and Two Factories', in C. Mabey, D. Skinner and T. Clark (eds) *Experiencing Human Resource Management*, London: Sage, pp. 33–53.

Scase, R. and Goffee, R. (1989) *Reluctant Managers; Their Work and Lifestyles*, London: Unwin Hyman.

Scott, A. (1994) *Willing Slaves? British Workers under Human Resource Management*, Cambridge: Cambridge University Press.

Sewell, G. and Wilkinson, B. (1992) 'Empowerment or Emasculation? Shop Floor Surveillance in a Total Quality Organisation', in P. Blyton and P. Turnbull (eds) *Reassessing Human Resource Management*, London: Sage.

Sinclair, A. (1992) 'The Tyranny of a Team Ideology', *Organisation Studies*, **13**(4): 611–26.

Sisson, K. (1993) 'In Search of HRM', *British Journal of Industrial Relations*, **31**(2): 201–10.

Sisson, K. (1997) *New Forms of Work Organisation: Can Europe Realise its Potential?*, Dublin, European Foundation for the Improvement of Living and Working Conditions.

Snape, E., Redman, T. and Chan, A.W. (2000) 'Commitment to the Union: A Survey of Research and the Implications for Industrial Relations and Trade Unions', *International Journal of Management Reviews*, **2**(3) pp. 205–30.

Storey, J. (ed.) (1995) *Human Resource Management: A Critical Text*, London: Routledge.

Truss, C., Gratton, L., Hope-Hailey, V., McGovern, P. and Styles, P. (1997) 'Soft and Hard Models of Human Resource Management: A Reappraisal', *Journal of Management Studies*, **34**(1): 53–73.

Walton, R. (1985) 'From Control to Commitment in the Workplace', *Harvard Business Review*, **63**(2): 77–85.

Wilkinson, A. (1998) 'Empowerment: Theory and Practice', *Personnel Review*, **27**(1): 40–56.

Wilkinson, A., Godfrey, G. and Marchington, M. (1997) 'Bouquets, Brickbats and Blinkers: Total Quality Management and Employee Involvement in Practice', *Organisation Studies*, **18**(5): 799–819.

Wilkinson, A., Marchington, M., Ackers, P. and Goodman, J. (1993) 'Refashioning Industrial Relations: The Experiences of a Chemical Company in the 1980s', *Personnel Review*, **22**(2): 22–38.

Wilkinson, A., Marchington, M., Ackers, P. and Goodman, J. (1994) 'ESOPs Fables – A Tale of a Machine Tool Company', *The International Journal of Human Resource Management*, **5**(1): 121–43.

Wood, S. (1999) 'Human Resource Management and Performance', *International Journal of Management Reviews*, **1**(4): 367–414.

Yong, J. and Wilkinson, A. (1999) 'The State of Total Quality Management: A Review', *The International Journal of Human Resource Management*, **10**(1): 137–61.

Part 4
International HRM

HRM: The Comparative Dimension 13

Chris Brewster

INTRODUCTION

Human Resource Management (HRM) is universal. Every organization has to utilize and, hence, in some way, to manage, human resources. Two of the classic texts identified four areas (employee influence, human resource flow, reward systems, work systems, in Beer *et al.* 1985) or a five-step cycle (selection, performance, appraisal, rewards and development, in Fombrun *et al.* 1984), which they imply can be used to analyse HRM in any organization anywhere in the world. However, HRM practices vary across the world. This chapter focuses on the extent to which approaches to HRM differ, or whether regional forms of HRM, for example, in the Asia Pacific region, Europe or the US can be identified; or whether HRM varies country by country. Are the models converging and, if so, towards which model? The US case is particularly important, given the power of the US version of HRM. Are countries in the increasingly unified Europe developing a distinctive and converging pattern of HRM? Or are there identifiable differences in the way they manage human resources?

Some of the old cinemas, with what was then high-tech, wrap-around screens, used to show a sequence that started with a bird's-eye view of a small child. Then, through the use of telephoto lenses merging with satellite pictures, the camera slowly pulled back so that the child lost a little definition and became first one of a group of children and then gradually disappeared, as the group became part of a street scene. The camera continued to pull back to reveal the street to be successively part of a suburb, a city, a conurbation, a country, a continent, and eventually an invisible dot on the planet Earth. Each picture is in itself accurate: each helps us to understand some things better whilst blurring others.

This chapter uses this extended focus-pulling as an analogy for examining the differences in the way human resource management (HRM) is practised in different countries. The focus of much of the research and analysis of HRM, particularly in the UK, has been at work-place level. There is also a strong tradition comparing HRM in organizations of different size, sector or ownership within one country. At the other extreme, there are commentators who state, or imply, that their analysis is universal. This chapter adopts a mid-focus position, concentrating upon comparative HRM: the differences between countries. The main area of focus is comparisons within Europe, but occasionally the focus will pull back to compare HRM in the European continent with that in other parts of the world. As with the cinema metaphor, this picture is no more nor less accurate than the others: it just helps us to understand some things more clearly.

This chapter addresses this issue, first, by exploring two of the many different paradigms through which HRM is viewed: the universal and the contextual. It argues that in practice there is sufficient variation between countries to make a contextual approach relevant. It uses new research data to explore three central issues which show significant differences around the world: flexible working patterns, communications and the nature of the HR function. Finally, some conclusions are drawn about the importance of different levels of analysis in the study of HRM and the issue of convergence.

THE UNIVERSALIST AND CONTEXTUAL PARADIGMS IN HRM

Things are done differently in different countries. This includes differences in the way human resource management is conceptualized; the research traditions through which it is explored; and the way HRM is conducted. In conceptual and research terms two different (ideal type) paradigms might be classified as the *universalist* and the *contextual* (Brewster 1999a; 1999b). The notion of paradigm is used here in Kuhn's (1970) sense as an accepted model or theory, and with the corollary that different researchers may be using competing models or theories. This notion of paradigms has been applied to HRM elsewhere (Delery and Doti 1996; Wright and McMahan 1992).

There will, of course, be other paradigms. Many of these will, like the two ideal types explored in more detail in this chapter, have originated in particular geographical areas; though like them they will have adherents now in many countries. Thus, there is a strong Latin paradigm of research into HRM which, building on the French sociological and Marxist traditions and the focus on Roman law, is concerned with the establishment of large-scale concepts, societal level and political interactions and the nature and detail of the law. There are different approaches to the notion of HRM in Japan – and so on. For our purposes here, the universalist and contextual paradigms will serve as good examples, building as they do on the significant US and northern European traditions.

It is to some degree the difference between these paradigms, lack of awareness of them, and the tendency for commentators to drift from one to another, which has led to the confusion about the very nature of HRM as a field of study pointed out by many of its leading figures (e.g. Conrad and Pieper 1990; Guest 1992; Singh 1992; Storey 1992a; Boxall 1993; Dyer and Kochan 1995; Storey 1995).

The *universalist paradigm*, which is dominant in the United States of America, but is widely used elsewhere, is essentially a nomothetic social science approach: using evidence to test generalizations of an abstract and law-like character. As in other related areas of the social sciences, the universalist paradigm tends to seek convergence. This paradigm assumes that the purpose of the study of our area of the social sciences, HRM, and in particular strategic human resource management (SHRM) (see e.g. Tichy, Fombrun and Devanna 1982; Fombrun, Tichy and Devanna 1984; Ulrich 1987; Wright and Snell 1991; Wright and McMahan 1992), is to improve the way that human resources are managed strategically within organizations. The ultimate aim of this work is to improve organizational performance, as judged by its impact on the organization's declared corporate strategy (Tichy, Fombrun and Devanna 1982; Huselid 1995), the customer (Ulrich 1989) or shareholders (Huselid 1995; Becker and Gerhart 1996; Becker *et al.* 1997). Further, it is implicit that this objective will apply in all cases. Thus, the widely cited definition by Wright and McMahan states that SHRM is 'the pattern of planned human resource deployments and activities intended to enable a firm to achieve its goals' (1992: 298). The value of this paradigm lies in the simplicity of focus, the coalescing of research around this shared objective and the clear relationship with the demands of industry. The disadvantages lie in the ignoring of other potential focuses, the resultant narrowness of the research objectives, and the ignoring of other levels and other stakeholders in the outcomes of SHRM (Guest 1990; Poole 1990; Pieper 1990; Bournois 1991; Legge 1995; Brewster 1995b; Kochan 1999).

Arguably, there is greater coherence in the US in what constitutes 'good' HRM: a coalescing of views around the concept of 'high performance work systems'. These have been characterized by the US Department of Labor (1993) as having certain clear characteristics:

- careful and extensive systems for recruitment, selection and training;
- formal systems for sharing information with the individuals who work in the organization;
- clear job design;
- local level participation procedures;
- monitoring of attitudes;
- performance appraisals;
- properly functioning grievance procedures; and
- promotion and compensation schemes that provide for the recognition and financial rewarding of high performing members of the workforce.

It would appear that, whilst there have been many other attempts to develop such lists (see for example Storey 1992a; 1995), and they all differ to some degree, the Department of Labor list can be taken as an exemplar of the universalist paradigm: few US researchers in HRM would find very much to argue with in this list though they are likely to label their studies as SHRM. Both researchers and practitioners in other countries, however, find such a list contrary to experience and even to what they would conceive of as good practice. Thus, they might argue for sharing information with representative bodies such as trade unions or works councils, for flexible work boundaries, for group reward systems. And they might argue that attitude monitoring, appraisal systems, etc. are culturally inappropriate.

Common to this debate is the assumption that SHRM is concerned with the aims and actions of management within the organization. Perhaps in a country like the USA which has as an avowed aim of most politicians the objective of 'freeing business from outside interference', it makes sense to develop a vision of human resource management which takes as its scope the policies and practices of management. (Though here too it is worth pointing out, so that the argument is not misunderstood, that there are American commentators who do not accept this limitation on their analysis.)

Methodologically, research based on this vision of HRM is deductive: to generate carefully designed questions which can lead to proof or disproof, the elements of which can be measured in such a way that the question itself can be subjected to the mechanism of testing and prediction. Built into this paradigm is the assumption that research is not 'rigorous' unless it is drawn from existing literature and theory, focused around a tightly designed question which can be proved or disproved to be correct, and contains a structure of testing that can lead on to prediction. The research base is mostly centred on a small number of private sector 'leading edge' exemplars of 'good practice', often large multinationals, generally from the manufacturing or even specifically the high tech sector.

The *contextual paradigm* by contrast is idiographic, searching for an overall understanding of what is contextually unique and why. In our topic area, it is focused on understanding what is different between and within HRM in various contexts and what the antecedents of those differences are. Hence, the research mechanisms used are inductive. Here, theory is drawn from an accumulation of data collected or gathered in a less directed (or constrained) manner than would be the case under the universalist paradigm. Research traditions are different: focused less upon testing and prediction and more upon the collection of evidence. There is an assumption that if things are important they should be studied, even if testable prediction is not possible or the resultant data are complex and unclear. The policies and practices of the 'leading edge' companies (something of a value-laden term in itself) which are the focus of much HRM research and literature in the USA are of less interest to contextualists than identifying the way labour markets work and what the more typical organizations are doing

Amongst most researchers working in this paradigm, it is the explanations that matter – any link to firm performance is secondary. It is assumed that HRM can apply to societies, governments or regions as well as to firms. At the level of the organization (not 'firm' – public sector organizations are also included) the organization's objectives and strategy are not necessarily assumed to be 'good' either for the organization or for society. There are plenty of examples where this is clearly not the case. Nor, in this paradigm, is there any assumption that the interests of everyone in the organization will be the same; or any expectation that an organization will have a strategy that people within the organization will 'buy in to'. The assumption is that not only will the employees and the unions have a different perspective to the management team (Kochan *et al.* 1986; Barbash 1987; Keenoy 1990; Storey 1992a; Purcell and Ahlstrand 1994; Turner and Morley 1995), but that even within the management team there may be different interests and views (Hyman 1987; Kochan *et al.* 1986; Koch and McGrath 1996). These, and the resultant impact on HRM, are issues for empirical study. As a contributor to explanation, this paradigm emphasizes external factors as well as the actions of the management within an organization. Thus it explores the importance of such factors as culture, ownership structures, labour markets, the role of the state and trade union organization as aspects of the subject rather than external influences upon it. The scope of HRM goes beyond the organization to reflect the reality of the role of many HR departments, particularly in Europe: for example, in lobbying about and adjusting to Government actions, in dealing with such issues as equal opportunities legislation or with trade unions and tripartite institutions.

This paradigm is widespread in the UK and Ireland, Australia and New Zealand and in many of the northern European countries, and has some adherents in North America. Furthermore, if one were to judge by the journals and newsletters put out by the HR societies and consultancies, HR practitioners in the United States are interested in many of the same legislative and labour market issues as those elsewhere. This seems to apply particularly to the US public sector where, perhaps, the pressures of compliance are greatest. Interestingly, there are increasing calls from North Americans for a contextual paradigm or, to be precise, approaches which have considerable resonance with this paradigm, to be used in the USA (see, for example, Dyer 1985; Schuler and Jackson 1987; Dyer and Kochan 1995; Kochan 1999).

Outside the US, much of the research is located squarely in the contextual paradigm, concerned to develop a critique of the relationship between owners and/or managers and the employees and the society in which the organizations operate. There is less likelihood of the researchers assuming that the purposes of the power-holders in the organization are unchallengeable and that the role of research is to identify how their HRM contributes to those purposes. The universalist model has been subjected to significant critique in Europe, particularly. Looking at the UK, Guest sees 'signs that . . . the American model is losing its appeal as attention focuses to a greater extent on developments in Europe' (Guest 1990: 377); the same author is elsewhere sceptical of the feasibility of transferring the model to Britain. The point was also noted in Germany: 'an international comparison of HR practices clearly indicates that the basic functions of HR management are given different weights in different countries and that they are carried out differently' (Gaugler 1988: 26); and 'a single universal model of HRM does not exist' (Pieper 1990: 11). Critiques have also come from France (e.g. Bournois 1991). European authors have argued that 'we are in culturally different contexts' and, that 'rather than copy solutions which result from other cultural traditions, we should consider the state of mind that presided in the search for responses adapted to the culture' (Albert 1989: 75 translation in Brewster and Bournois 1991).

Many of the seminal management and even HRM texts are written as if the analysis applies at all levels: what Rose (1991) has called 'false universalism'. The early management theorists were generally clear that practice would converge towards the most efficient and therefore, they argued, the US, model (Burnham 1941; Drucker 1950; Harbison and Myers 1959; Kerr *et al.* 1960; Galbraith 1967). More recently, the convergence thesis has received support from transaction cost economics which also contends that at any one point of time there exists a best solution to organizing labour (Williamson 1975, 1985). 'Most transaction cost theorists argue that there is one best organizational form for firms that have similar or identical transaction costs' (Hollingsworth and Boyer, 1997: 34).

Many of these texts are produced in one country and base their work on a small number of by now well-known cases. As long as they are read by specialists in the relevant country with interests in these kinds of organizations, this may not be too much of a problem. But the world, and especially the academic world in our subject, is becoming ever more international. This is a major problem in relation to the US literature. The cultural hegemony of US teaching, publishing and the US journals mean that these texts are often utilized by other readers. US-based literature searches, now all done on computer, of course, fail to note any writing outside the universalist tradition. For analysts and practitioners elsewhere, and with interests in different sectors, countries and so on, many of these descriptions and prescriptions fail to meet their reality. It is not that either paradigm is necessarily correct or more instructive than others, but that the level and focus needs to be specified to make the analysis meaningful (Brewster 1999a).

This chapter is based on the belief that we have increasingly to take an international and comparative view of these issues. There is a growing internationalization in the business field. This holds true not only for the large multinationals in the private sector, but also for smaller employers and for organizations in the public sector. Through the emergence of large trading blocs like the European Union, this trend has been accelerated. Hence, an increased knowledge about the specifics of management across borders (Bartlett and Goshal 1989), including the availability of comparative knowledge of how management issues are handled in various countries, has become a prominent issue for the social scientists as it has become a key issue for all kinds of managers.

At the most general level, while the empirical data on national cultural differences is limited (Hofstede 1980, 1991; Laurent 1983; Tayeb 1988; Adler 1997; Trompenaars 1993), it does demonstrate considerable diversity. Cultural differences are reflected in legislation. The existence of institutional differences has long been recognized (Child 1981; Boyacigiller and Adler 1991; Rosenzweig and Singh 1991). In particular, patterns of ownership vary (Brewster 1993). Public ownership has decreased to some extent in many European countries in recent years, but it is still far more widespread than in the United States. And private sector ownership may not mean the same thing. In many of the southern European countries particularly, ownership of even major companies remains in the hands of single families. In Germany, as a different example, most major companies are owned largely by a tight network of a small number of substantial banks. Their interlocking shareholdings and close involvement in the management of these corporations mean less pressure to produce short-term profits and a positive disincentive to drive competitors out of the market-place (Randlesome 1993).

The general management discussion is beginning to be reflected in the specific field of comparative HRM (Boxall 1995; Brewster and Tyson 1991; Hollinshead and Leat 1995; Brewster, Mayrhofer and Morley 2000). In this respect, HRM is catching up with another aspect of the study of employment relationships, the study of industrial relations, which has long recognized the importance of international differences (see, for example, Due *et al.* 1991; Hyman 1994; Poole 1986; Stephans 1990; Przeworski and Spague 1986; Visser 1992; Bean and Holden 1992; Locke *et al.* 1995). Human resource management is increasingly acknowledged to be one of the areas where organizations are most likely to maintain a 'national flavour' (Adler 1997; Schuler and Huber 1993; Rozenzweig and Nohria 1994; Brewster 2000) and is the point at which business and national cultures have the sharpest interface.

Firmly based in the contextual paradigm, this comparative chapter examines three areas where differences in HRM between countries are apparent. These are communications, the role of the HR function and, in the next section, the nature of work.

THE CHANGING NATURE OF WORK

Flexibility in labour patterns is now widely accepted as a critical issue in HRM. This is an area bedevilled with terminological problems. The term 'flexibility' is the one most commonly used in Europe. The European Commission prefers the term 'atypical working' and some trade unionists talk about 'vulnerable work'. Certain aspects of this subject are referred to as 'contingent working' in the USA. Arguably, all of these terms are to a degree inaccurate and certainly all the terms come with their own metaphorical baggage.

Whatever the terminology, the assumption has been made that, with the amount of employment legislation and the embeddedness of the trade unions in the EU, the European workforce is highly inflexible and that this is linked to high levels of unemployment in some European states (see European Commission 1995). The evidence shows that this is wrong. Research conducted by the Cranet network[1], comparing organizations at national level across Europe (Brewster *et al.* 1997b; Brewster 1998; Mayne *et al.* 2000) is consistent with the national labour market statistics (European Commission, various dates), and workplace level data (Cully *et al.* 1999) in showing extensive and growing use of flexible working across Europe. Furthermore, some of these forms of flexibility (temporary employment and self-employment) are more widespread in Europe than in the US, and in others (part-time work) the US has about a median position on a ranking with the European countries (Standing 1997). Japan has a different pattern of flexible working to either of these territories, with considerable part-time working and temporary working, though less evidence of increases in these forms than elsewhere.

The Cranet data shows that despite differences within countries between sectors, particularly, flexible working practices are growing in both extent and coverage everywhere. This is so in nearly all countries in Europe, in Japan and Australasia, in all sectors, in organizations both large and small, and whatever the form or origin of ownership. 'Atypical' work patterns or contracts, such as temporary, casual, fixed-term, home-based and annual hours contracts, are on the increase nearly everywhere, despite differing legal, cultural and labour traditions (Mayne *et al.* 2000).

Rather than making use of a full range of the potential flexible working arrangements, most organizations still rely mainly on part-time or temporary employment. Throughout the last decade, at least four out of ten organizations increased part-time or temporary employment. Fixed-term employment, much more a public sector practice, has also become more widespread. However, organizations where these forms of flexibility cover a majority of workers continue to be in a clear minority. The survey suggests a flexibility learning curve: the increase in the use of flexible contracts tends to be significantly higher among those organizations (already) making comparatively high use of such contracts (Mayne *et al.* 2000).

The trends may be common, but practice is not. Between countries, and between organizations within countries, there are clear preferences for different kinds of flexibility (see Figure 13.1 for an example). No country or organization makes extensive use of the full range of flexible working patterns and contracts. Flexibility is dependent upon a complex, interlocking web of national culture, history, institutions, trade union approaches and strength, governmental approaches (including legislation) and managerial tradition (Tregaskis and Brewster 2000). Despite the hopes of some European politicians, there is no simple correlation between flexibility and employment or training provision. The data does suggest that flexible workers get less training, but it does not appear to be linked with job creation; some kinds of flexibility in some countries can be linked to employment creation or diminution, but there is no overall pattern.

Thus, in Spain there is a high level of short-term employment with low levels of part-time work. Countries such as Austria, the Netherlands, Sweden and the UK have a third or more of organizations with over five per cent of the workforce on temporary contracts. Others, including both EU and non-EU states, have far fewer whilst the UK, Sweden, Denmark and Ireland also have an even distribution, but with a higher emphasis being placed on temporary workers and to a lesser degree fixed-term contracts.

These differences correlate with differences in the institutional environment of these countries (Ruiz-Quintanilla and Claes 1996; De Grip *et al.* 1997; Tregaskis and

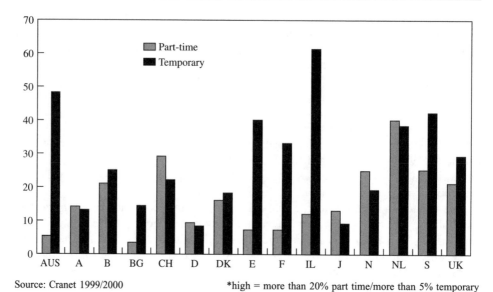

Source: Cranet 1999/2000   *high = more than 20% part time/more than 5% temporary

Figure 13.1 Percentage of organizations with high levels of part-time and temporary work*

Brewster 2000). Similarly, analyses of the extent of flexible working in Japan need to take into account the Japanese practice of restricting employment for women of more than 'marriageable' age.

The overall effect is to change the nature of the work relationship. There is now only just around a half of the European working population, for example, with permanent, full-time employment contracts. So many people now work part-time, or on a temporary contract, or as self-employed, or on the myriad other forms of work pattern, that the change in extent is developing into a change in kind. This will have extensive effects, also, beyond the world of work in areas such as finance and the housing market (mortgages and bank loans are not easy to come by for those on these flexible contracts); tax (many people are working but not earning enough to pay taxes); and demands on government resources (Brewster *et al.* 1997b).

Changes in the labour market which increase the amount of short-term and variable employment packages, or even the forms of getting work done through non-employment options such as subcontracting or consultancy are arguably at least moving the situation in the developed countries back towards the practices of the past – and of the current undeveloped world. However, you cannot step into the same river twice: and flexible working practices now operate in a very different environment than those of the past (MacShane and Brewster 1999). Although the trends are similar, there are still very different situations, assumptions and practices occurring in the different countries.

COMMUNICATIONS

Effective communication is a requirement for all organizations and vital for those looking for commitment from workers to the objectives of the enterprise. It could be argued that at the organization level, effective communication is at the heart of effective human resource management. Yet there is less clarity on what are the most effective form and content of communication for these purposes: and whether that varies by country. The US Department of Labor (1993) approach, as we have seen, emphasizes individual communication as the key; whilst the European approach has tended to emphasize collective communication. There has been a tendency to associate the concept of HRM with the individualization of communication and a move away from, or even antagonism towards, the concept of industrial relations (IR) – communication and consultation which is collective and particularly that which is trade-union based. As has been argued elsewhere (Brewster 1995a; 1995b), this non-union implication sits uneasily with the history and circumstances of Europe. Trade unionism remains widespread and important in Europe and furthermore Europe has extensive, legally backed, systems of employee communication. In some countries in Europe the establishment of workers' councils is required by law. These arrangements give considerable (legally-backed) power to the employee representatives and, unlike consultation in the US for example, they tend to supplement rather than supplant the union position. In relatively highly unionized countries it is unsurprising that many of the representatives of the workforce are, in practice, trade union officials. In Germany, as one instance, four-fifths of them are union representatives. The balance between individual and collective communication is a matter for empirical investigation (see Figure 13.2).

In fact, there has been an increase in all forms of communication: through representative bodies (trade unions or works councils), as well as through direct verbal communication and by direct written communication. The latter two channels have expanded considerably. To a degree, increases in direct communication to employees can be explained by the development of technology: word processors and mail-merge systems have opened up the possibility of sending 'individual' letters to all employees. Electronic and computerized mail is now firmly part of the canon of

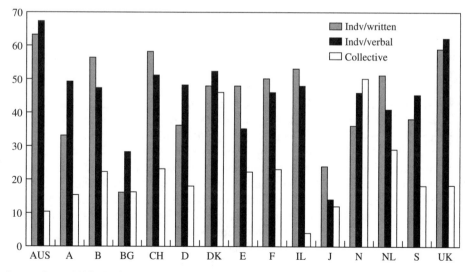

Source: Cranet 1996–1999/2000

Figure 13.2 Increases in individual and collective top-down communication (% of organizations)

downward communication, expanding enormously in the last three years of the twentieth century and continuing to do so. In no country does the proportion of organizations *de*creasing direct forms of communication amount to more than a tiny percentage, except for Japan, where 13 per cent and 14 per cent of organizations have reduced verbal and written communications. In the case of communications through representative organizations, the proportion decreasing communications through this channel are higher but still generally below one in ten. The exceptions are Sweden (12 per cent); the sample Central European country, Bulgaria (16 per cent – and other CEE countries show a similar pattern); and Australia, which is the only country where organizations decreasing their use of the representative communications channel is higher than the proportion increasing use.

As an overall summary, there is a widespread move to increase the amount of communication to employees, through any available channel or mechanism. The data shows that the various forms of communication are being seen as complementary rather than as alternatives. There is little evidence here of the replacement of representative communication by individualized communication. There is clear evidence, however, of the considerable moves that have been made by employers in many countries to expand the degree of information given to the workforce. The move appears to be unconnected with any legal requirements. And, this provision of information to the workforce still includes a substantial number of organizations who are expanding their use of the formalized employee representation or trade union channels.

When upward communication is examined, the two most common means in Europe, by a considerable margin, are through immediate line management – and through the trade union or works council channel. The evidence tends to support the analyses of those (e.g. Maurice *et al.* 1986; Hollingsworth and Boyer 1997) who focus on the presence or absence within countries of communitarian infrastructures that manifest themselves in the form of strong social bonds, trust, reciprocity and co-operation among economic actors.

There are clear differences between countries, with more communication being apparent in, broadly, the richer countries and less in, for example, the Southern European countries. In addition, increases in communication, both up and down, appear to be larger in the countries which are doing most (Mayrhofer *et al.* 2000). So far from convergence, there appears to be expanding divergence here.

Access to financial and strategic information is clearly hierarchical. The higher your position in the organization the more likely you are to be regularly briefed about the financial performance of the organization or its strategic plans. While the hierarchy still persists, the information gap appears to have narrowed during the 1990s as an increasing number of organizations make sure that their administrative staff know about the organization's plans and performance. Unionized organizations are more likely than non-union ones to provide such information. There are noticeable average 'slopes' in the distribution of this information with, again, the slope being most gentle in the Nordic countries (i.e. lower level staff receive more information) and steepest in the Southern European countries.

The fact that this communication continues to utilize staff representative bodies, as well as going directly to employees, indicates that the objective is transfer of information. The assumption appears to be that passing, or hearing, a message through several channels increases its chances of being received. This inevitably reduces the importance of the union channel. However, the evidence suggests that, compared to their US counterparts, employers in Europe and Japan, at least, are not using individual communication to replace trade union channels; rather, they are using as many forms of communication as they have at their disposal.

THE ROLE OF THE HR FUNCTION

Most commentators argue that human resource management has become more important to organizations in the last decades. This is because since human resources and the knowledge and skills they incorporate are difficult to replicate, they offer the opportunity of obtaining sustained competitive advantage for the organization, at a time when traditional ways of obtaining competitive advantage become ever easier to copy. Based on this argument we might have expected to see the influence of the human resource function on corporate decision increasing over time. Arguably, where the human resource function is represented at the key decision-making forums of the organization, and closely involved in strategic decision-making, awareness of the problems or opportunities that effective HRM might provide will be raised. Strategic decision-making in increasingly knowledge-reliant organizations will be improved. Evidence on three issues is instructive. These are: the position of HRM within the organization; the role of line management; and the extent of outsourcing of HRM.

HR membership of the Board is an obvious way to recognize the importance of HRM in corporate strategy decisions. The Cranet research data (Brewster and Bournois 1991; Brewster, Larsen and Mayrhofer 1997, 1999) show considerable stability over time, and considerable variation between countries. France, Spain, Sweden and Japan, for example, consistently report seven or eight out of ten organizations having an HR director on the board (or equivalent), while in the Central and Eastern European countries and Israel the figures are much lower (see Figure 13.3). Many other European countries, including the UK and Germany, and also Australia show a little less than half of the organizations with HR departments directly represented at the top decision-making level. The position of the Netherlands and Germany is interesting. These are countries where employees have rights to have representatives at the supervisory Board level; representation from the HR department tends to be lower. Presumably the employee representatives ensure that the HR implications of corporate strategy decisions are taken into account. Germany is a particularly interesting case, as one of the few countries where HR representation on the Board has increased notably over the rounds of the study, as human resource issues become more critical for these organizations and the function itself becomes less administrative. For the UK, although the 1998 WERS survey in the UK is not addressed to senior HR specialists at the organizational level, the estimates from the workplaces indicate a similar pattern (Cully et al. 1999).

When it becomes a question – perhaps the key question – of HR influence on corporate strategy, there is more uniformity: in most countries the personnel departments are involved from the outset in strategy formulation in around half the organizations.

The debate about the growing role of line managers in strategic (and indeed in operational) HRM is widespread in Europe. How should HR responsibilities be shared with line managers? In Europe the trend is clear: to give line managers more responsibility for the management of their staff and to reduce the extent to which

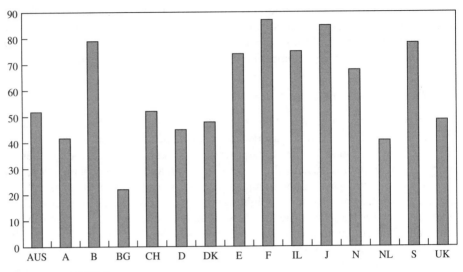

Source: Cranet 1999/2000

Figure 13.3 HR representation at Board level, or equivalent (% of organizations)

human resources departments control or restrict line management autonomy in this area (Brewster and Hoogendoorn 1992; Brewster and Soderstrom 1994; Brewster, Larsen and Mayrhofer 1997). This has created problems, with both personnel specialists and line managers unhappy about the way things are moving (Brewster and Hutchinson 1994). The trend towards increased line management authority in this area, however, remains undeniable.

Issues concerning the assignment of personnel tasks to line management vary widely. This has been the subject of more discussion in the UK than anywhere else in Europe. In fact, however, Britain is one of the countries where senior personnel specialists consistently report that primary responsibility for a range of personnel issues is least likely to be given to or shared with line managers. On a range of personnel issues it is the Italians who are most likely to lodge responsibility with the personnel department; the British come next. This stands in sharp contrast to the Danes, for example, who, on all issues, tend to give much greater responsibility to line managers. Furthermore, when asked about changes in responsibility, about half the European countries have been increasing line management responsibility faster than the UK.

Organizations have become smaller over a decade of downsizing; new technology has been introduced; and 'overhead' departments have been under pressure to prove themselves. One result has been an increase in the use of external providers. In the UK, for example, at the end of the 1990s almost all HR departments make use of external providers. As one example, 33 per cent of the HR departments use external providers to deal with 'pay and benefits'. The data also indicate that the use of external providers has increased over time. All this might imply that human resource departments would become smaller. However, the size of the HR departments relative to the total size of the organization has hardly changed in the last decade. In 1999 and 1995, one HR staff member supported every 76 employees, whereas in

1992 one HR staff member supported every 74 employees (van Ommeren and Brewster 2000).

The clear and unequivocal evidence presents a picture of remarkable stability in the size and influence of HR departments across Europe. Despite the increasing recognition of the importance of the effective management of human resources, the function has not improved its representation on the Board, nor its levels of influence. There have not been noticeable strides in sharing the HR role with line managers or in productivity. HR departments in Scandinavia were, and remain, more influential than those elsewhere; in southern Europe they remain as administrative as they were.

A few years ago, one perceptive commentator made the point that the rhetoric of the integration of the HR specialist function at the Board level and its position of influence has outpaced the reality (Legge 1995). The evidence from the Cranet survey confirms that. HR departments in general are not 'leaner and meaner', or more likely to be represented at the key decision-making forums, or more influential. In fact, despite the rhetoric, the influence of the HR function at the senior levels of the organization has barely changed over the last ten years.

CONCLUSION: SIMILAR TRENDS? DIFFERENT PRACTICES?

The evidence takes us back to the questions with which the chapter started. A key question in comparative HRM is that of convergence: what Locke *et al.* (1995: 159) have described as an 'old debate'. Are there differences between countries, are these being reduced as the pressures to conform become stronger and, if so, what are they converging towards? A US model of HRM, as policies of deregulation and decontrol spread from the US to Europe, might be one possibility (Locke *et al.* 1995). Another, reflecting the ongoing economic and political integration of European Union countries, is a convergence towards a distinctly European practice (Due *et al.* 1991). The answers are, inevitably, complex. And those looking to defend one position or another can easily find evidence to support their case.

Thus, there do seem to be trends (an increase in flexibility; a greater role for individualized communication; more line management responsibility for HRM) which are common in most of the developed areas of the world. However, there are clear regional differences between, say, the patterns of contingent employment, anti-unionism and the role of the HR department in the USA, Europe and Japan. And, going back to the focus-pulling analogy, within Europe different sub-regional patterns can be distinguished. Due *et al.* (1991) distinguish between countries, such as the UK, Ireland and the Nordic countries in which the state has a limited role in industrial relations and Roman-Germanic countries, such as France, Spain, Germany, Italy, Belgium, Greece and the Netherlands, in which the state functions as an actor with a central role in industrial relations. An analysis of pay systems found evidence of 'three clusters: a Latin cluster [which includes Spain, Italy, France]; a central European cluster ... and a Nordic cluster' (Filella 1991: 14). A study based on the Cranet data found that flexible working patterns tend to group countries into clusters which contain countries which are institutionally similar in terms of their labour markets even though they have little in common in terms of cultural characteristics (Tregaskis and Brewster 2000). This discussion of sub-regional developments in HRM should not pass without a small but significant detour to mention the 'test-bed' situation of the former Communist states of Central and Eastern Europe (CEE). Our research into these countries (Brewster 1992; Koubek and Brewster 1995; Hegewisch *et al*. 1996; Hegewisch 1997) indicates that whilst all of them have moved significantly away from the old models, the rate of change has been very different: the greater explanatory power of the contextual paradigm in such cases at least is manifest.

Below the sub-regional level there is clearly in existence a set of broad, relatively inert distinctions between the various national contexts of personnel management within Europe which make convergence to a European model of HRM problematic. The idiosyncratic national institutional settings are so variable that no common model is likely to emerge for the foreseeable future.

Our discussion of the issues of convergence and divergence in national patterns of HRM is, therefore, equivocal and perhaps needs more careful nuance than has been the case hitherto. HRM varies by country, sector and size of organization; by subjects within the generic topic of HRM; and by the nature of the organization (life-stage; governance; market, etc.). There is a related need to examine the balance between the extent to which foreign organizations bring new practices into a country compared to the extent to which they adjust to local practices. And we need to separate out policy from practice. Overall, however, the internationally comparative dimension of HRM is one that is demanding ever more attention from practitioners as they strive to cope with globalization: researchers are increasingly paying comparative HRM the same attention.

NOTES

1 The Cranet survey of policy and practice is an international research project conducted by a university or business school in each of 34 countries. The survey is conducted every three or four years, with increasing numbers of countries each year. There have been four separate rounds of the survey spanning over a decade. Between 6000 and 8000 responses from the senior HR practitioner in their organization have been collected each round, covering a broadly representative range of organizations from all sectors (see Brewster *et al*. 1996, 2000).

REFERENCES

Adler, N.J. (1997) *International Dimensions of Organisational Behavior*, third edition, Cincinnati: South-Western Publishing.

Albert, F.J. (1989) *Les ressources humaines, atout stratégique*, Paris: *Editions L'harmattan*: 75.

Barbash, J. (1987) 'Like nature, industrial relations abhors a vacuum: the case of the union-free strategy', *Industrial Relations*, **42**(1): 168–78.

Bartlett, C.A. and Goshal, S. (1989) *Managing Across Borders; The Transnational Solution*, London: Century Business.

Bean, R. and Holden, L. (1992) 'Cross National Differences in Trade Union Membership in OECD Countries', *Industrial Relations Journal*, **23**(1): 52–9.

Becker, B., Huselid M., Pickus, P. and Spratt, M. (1997) 'HR as a source of shareholder value: research and recommendations', *Human Resource Management*, **36**(1): 39–47.

Becker, B. and Gerhart, B. (1996) 'The impact of human resource practices on organisational performance: Progress and prospects', *Academy of Management Journal*, **39**: 779–801.

Beer, M., Lawrence, P.R., Mills, Q.N. and Walton, R.E. (1985*) Human Resource Management*, New York: Free Press.

Bournois, F (1991) 'Gestion des RH en Europe: données comparées', *Revue Française de Gestion*, mars-avril-mai: 68–83.

Boxall, P. (1993) 'The significance of human resource management: a reconsideration of the evidence', *International Journal of Human Resource Management*, **4**(3): 645–664.

Boxall, P. (1995) 'Building the theory of comparative HRM' *Human Resource Management Journal*, **5**(5): 5–17.

Boyacigiller, N.A. and Adler, N.J. (1991) 'The parochial dinosaur: organization science in a global context', *Academy of Management Review*, **16**(2): 262–90.

Brewster, C. (2000) 'Human Resource Practices in Multinational Enterprises', in Gannon, M.J. and Newman, K.L. (eds) *Handbook of Cross-Cultural Management*, Oxford: Blackwell (forthcoming).

Brewster, C. (1999a) 'Different Paradigms in Strategic HRM: Questions Raised By Comparative Research', in Wright, P.M., Dyer, L.D., Boudrea, J.W. and Milkovich, G.T. (eds) *Research in Personnel and Human Resources Management*, Supplement 4, Stamford: Jai Press Inc.

Brewster, C. (1999b) 'Strategic Human Resource Management: The Value of Different Paradigms', *Management International Review*, Special Issue 1999/3, **39**: 45–64.

Brewster, C. (1995a) 'Towards a European Model of HRM', *Journal of International Business Studies*, **26**(1): 1–21.

Brewster, C. (1995b) 'Human Resource Management: The European Dimension', in J. Storey (ed.), *Human Resource Management: A Critical Text*, London: Routledge.

Brewster, C. (1992) 'Starting Again: Industrial Relations in Czechoslovakia', *International Journal of Human Resource Management*, **3**(3): 555–74.

Brewster, C. (1993) 'Developing a "European" model of human resource management', *International Journal of Human Resource Management*, **4**(4): 76–84.

Brewster, C. and Bournois, F. (1991) 'A European Perspective on Human Resource Management', *Personnel Review*, **20**(6): 4–13.

Brewster, C., Communal, C., Farndale, E., Hegewisch, A., Johnson, G. and Van Ommeren, J. (2000) 'HR Healthcheck: Developments in HRM in the UK and the rest of Europe', *Management Research in Practice Series*, Financial Times, Prentice Hall.

Brewster, C. and Hoogendoorn, J. (1992) 'Human Resource Aspects of Decentralisation and Devolution', *Personnel Review*, **21**(1): 4–11.

Brewster, C. and Hutchinson, S. (1994) 'Flexibility at Work in Europe', report prepared for European Association of Personnel Management, December.

Brewster, C. and Soderstrom, M. (1994) 'Human resources and line management; the controversy and the evidence', in C. Brewster and A. Hegewisch (eds) *Policy and Practice in European Human Resource Management: the Evidence and Analysis from the Price Waterhouse Cranfield Survey*, London: Routledge.

Brewster, C. and Tyson, S. (1991) *International Comparisons in Human Resource Management'*, London: Pitman.

Brewster, C., Larsen, H. and Mayrhofer, W. (1999) 'Human Resource Management: A Strategic Approach', in C. Brewster and H. Larsen, *Human Resource Management in Northern Europe*, Oxford: Blackwell.

Brewster, C., Larsen, H.H. and Mayrhofer, W. (1997a) 'Integration and Assignment: A Paradox in Human Resource Management', *Journal of International Management*, **3**(1): 1–23.

Brewster, C., Mayne, L., Valverde, M. and Kabst, R. (1997b) 'Flexibility in European Labour Markets? The evidence renewed', *Employee Relations*, **19**(6): 509–18.

Brewster, C., Mayrhofer, W. and Morley, M. (2000) *New Challenges for European Human Resource Management*, London: Macmillan.

Brewster, C., Tregaskis, O., Hegewisch, A. and Mayne, L. (1996) 'Comparative Research in Human Resource Management: a review and example', *International Journal of Human Resource Management*, **1**: 585–604.

Burnham, J. (1941) *The Managerial Revolution*, New York: John Day.

Child, J.D. (1981) 'Culture, contingency and capitalism in the cross-national study of organizations', in L.L. Cummings and B.N. Straw (eds) *Research in Organizational Behaviour vol 3*, Greenwich Conn: JAI Publishers.

Conrad, P. and Pieper, R. (1990) 'HRM in the Federal Republic of Germany', in R. Pieper (ed.) *Human Resource Management: An International Comparison*, Berlin: Walter de Gruyter.

Cully, M. Woodland, S., O'Reilly, A. and Dix, G. (1999) *Britain at Work*, London: Routledge.

DeGrip, A., Hoevenberg, J. and Willems, E. (1997) 'Atypical employment in the European Union', *International Labour Review*, **136**(1): 49–72.

Delery, J. and Doti, H. (1996) 'Modes of theorising in strategic human resource management: tests of universalistic, contingency and configurational performance', *Academy of Management Journal*, **39**: 802–35.

Drucker, P. (1950) *The New Society: The Anatomy of the Industrial Order*, New York: Harper.

Due, J., Madsen, J.S. and Jensen, C.S. (1991) 'The Social Dimension: Convergence or Diversification of IR in the Single European Market?', *Industrial Relations Journal*, **22**(2): 85–102.

Dyer, L. (1985) 'Strategic Human Resources Management and Planning', in K.M. Rowland and G.R. Ferris (eds) *Research In Personnel And Human Resources Management Vol. 3*, Stamford: JAI Press.

Dyer, L. and Kochan, T. (1995) 'Is there a new HRM? Contemporary Evidence and Future Directions', in Downie, B., Kumar, P. and Coates, M.L. (eds) *Managing Human Resources in the 1990s and Beyond: Is the Workplace Being Transformed?* Kingston, Ontario: Industrial Relations Centre Press, Queen's University.

European Commission (1995) *Employment in Europe*, Luxembourg: Employment and Social Affairs Directorate.

European Commission (1996) *Employment in Europe*, Luxembourg: Employment and Social Affairs Directorate.

Filella, J. (1991) 'Is there a Latin model in the management of human resources?', *Personnel Review*, **20**(6): 15–24.

Fombrun, C.J., Tichy, N. and Devanna, M.A. (1984) *Strategic Human Resource Management*, New York: John Wiley.

Galbraith, J.K. (1967) *The New Industrial State*, London: Hamish Hamilton.

Gaugler, E. (1988) 'HR Management: An International Comparison', *Personnel*, August: 24–30.

Guest, D. (1990) 'Human resource management and the American dream', *Journal of Management Studies*, **27**(4): 377–97.

Guest, D. (1992) 'Right enough to be dangerously wrong: an analysis of In Search of Excellence', in G. Salaman (ed.) *Human Resource Strategies*, London: Sage.

Harbison, F. and Myers, C.A. (1959) *Management in the Industrial World: An international analysis*, New York: McGraw Hill.

Hegewisch, A. (1997) 'Labour market flexibility in Central and Eastern Europe', *Flexible Working Briefing*, **15** (July 18th): 8–10.

Hegewisch, A., Brewster, C. and Koubek, J. (1996) 'Different Roads: changes in industrial and employee relations in the Czech Republic and East Germany since 1989', *Industrial Relations Journal*, **27**(1): 50–65.

Hofstede, G. (1980) *Cultures Consequences: international differences in work-related values*, Beverley Hills: Sage.

Hofstede, G. (1991) *Cultures and Organizations: Software of the Mind*, London: McGraw-Hill.

Hollinshead, G. and Leat, M. (1995) *Human Resource Management: An International and Comparative Perspective*, London: Pitman.

Hollingsworth, J.R. and Boyer, R. (1997) 'Coordination of Economic Actors and Social Systems of Production', in J.R. Hollingsworth and R. Boyer (eds) *Contemporary Capitalism*, Cambridge: Cambridge University Press.

Huselid, M. (1995) 'The impact of human resource management practices on turnover, productivity and corporate financial performance', *Academy of Management Journal*, **38**: 635–72.

Hyman, R. (1987) 'Strategy or structure? Capital, labour and control', *Work, Employment and Society*, **1**(1): 25–55.

Hyman, R. (1994) 'Industrial Relations in Western Europe: An Era of Ambiguity?', *Industrial Relations*, **33**(1): 1–24.

Keenoy, T. (1990) 'HRM: A Case Of The Wolf In Sheep's Clothing', *Personnel Review*, **19**(2): 3–9.

Kerr, C., Dunlop, J.T., Harbison, F. and Meyers, C. (1960) *Industrialism and Industrial Man*, Cambridge: Harvard University Press.

Koch, M.J. and McGrath, R.G. (1996) 'Improving labor productivity: human resource management policies do matter', *Strategic Management Journal*, **17**: 335–54.

Kochan, T., Locke, R. and Priore, M. (eds) (1995) *Employment Relations in a Changing World Economy*, Cambridge, Mass: MIT Press.

Kochan, T. (1999) 'Beyond Myopia: Human Resources and the Changing Social Contract', in P.M. Wright, L.D. Dyer, J.W. Boudrea and G.T. Milkovich (eds) *Research in Personnel and Human Resources Management*, Supplement 4, Stamford: Jai Press Inc.

Kochan, T., Katz, H. and McKersie, R. (1986) *The Transformation of American Industrial Relations*, New York: Basic Books.

Koubek, J. and Brewster, C. (1995) 'Human Resource Management in Turbulent Times: the Czech case', *International Journal of Human Resource Management*, **6**(2): 223–48.

Kuhn, T. (1970) *The Structure of Scientific Revolutions*, Chicago: University of Chicago Press.

Laurent, A. (1983) 'The Cultural Diversity of Western Conceptions of Management' *International Studies of Management and Organisation*, **XIII**(1–2), Spring Summer: 75–96.

Legge, K. (1995) 'HRM: rhetoric, reality and hidden agendas', in J. Storey (ed.) *Human Resource Management: a critical text*, London: Routledge.

Locke, R., Piore, M. and Kochan, T. (1995) 'Introduction', in R. Locke, T. Kochan and M. Piore (eds), *Employment Relations in a Changing World Economy*, Cambridge, MIT Press.

MacShane, D. and Brewster, C. (1999) *Making Flexibility Work*, London: Fabian Society.

Maurice, M., Sellier, F. and Silvestre, J. (1986) *The Social Foundations of Industrial Power*, Cambridge, Mass: The MIT Press.

Mayne, L., Tregaskis, O. and Brewster, C. (2000) 'A comparative analysis of the link between flexibility and HRM stragegy', in C.J. Brewster, W. Mayrhofer and M. Morley (eds) *New Challenges for European Human Resource Management*, Basingstoke: Macmillan.

Mayrhofer, W., Brewster, C. and Morley, M. (2000) 'Communication, consultation and the HRM debate', in C.J. Brewster, W. Mayrhofer and M. Morley (eds) *New Challenges for European Human Resource Management*, Basingstoke: Macmillan.

Pieper, R. (ed.) (1990) *Human Resource Management: An International Comparison*, Berlin: Walter de Gruyter.

Poole, M. (1986) *Industrial Relations – Origins and Patterns of National Diversity*, London: RKP.

Poole, M. (1990) 'Human Resource Management in an International Perspective', *International Journal of Human Resource Management*, **1**(1): 1–15.

Przeworski, A. and Spague, J. (1986) *Paper Stones: A History of Editorial Socialism*, Chicago: University of Chicago Press.

Purcell, J. and Ahlstrand, B. (1994) *Human Resource Management in the Multi-Divisional Firm*, Oxford: OUP.

Randlesome, C. (1993) *Business Cultures in Europe*, Oxford: Butterworth-Heinemann.

Rose, M.J. (1991) 'Comparing forms of comparative analysis', *Political Studies*, **39**, 446–62.

Rozenzweig, P.M. and Singh, J.V. (1991) 'Organisational environments and the multinational enterprise', *Academy of Management Review*, **16** (2): 340–61.

Rosenzweig, P.M. and Nohria, N. (1994) 'Influences on Human Resource Management Practices in Multinational Corporations', *Journal of International Business Studies*, **25**(2): 229–52.

Ruiz-Quintanilla S.A. and Claes, R. (1996) 'Determinants of underemployment of young adults: a multicountry study', *Industrial and Labour Relations Review*, **49**(3): 424–39.

Schuler, R.S. and Huber, C.H. (1993) *Personnel and Human Resource Management*, fifth edition, Minneapolis/ St. Paul: West Publishing Company.

Schuler, R.S. and Jackson, S.E. (1987) 'Linking Competitive Strategies with Human Resource Management Practices', *Academy of Management Executive*, **1**(207): 424–39.

Singh, R. (1992) 'Human resource management: a sceptical look' in B. Towers, (ed.) *Handbook of Human Resource Management*, Oxford: Blackwell Publishers.

Standing G. (1997) 'Globalisation, labour flexibility and insecurity: the era of market regulation', *European Journal of Industrial Relations*, **3**(1): 7–37.

Stephans, J. (1990) 'Explaining Cross-National Differences in Union Strength in Bargaining and Welfare', paper read to the XII World Congress of Sociology, Madrid, July 9–13.

Storey, J. (1992a) *Developments in the Management of Human Resources*, Oxford: Blackwell Publishers.

Storey, J. (1992b) 'HRM in Action: the truth is out at last', *Personnel Management*, April: 28–31.

Storey, J. (1995) *Human Resource Management: A Critical Text*, London: Routledge.

Tayeb, M. (1988) *Organisations and National Culture*, London: Sage Publications.

Tichy, N., Fombrun, C.J. and Devanna, M.A. (1982) 'Strategic human resource management', *Sloan Management Review*, **23**(2): 47–60.

Tregaskis, O. and Brewster, C. (2000) 'Adaptive, reactive and inclusive organisational approaches to workforce flexibility in Europe', *Comportamento Organizacional e Gestão*, (forthcoming).

Trompenaars, F. (1993), *Riding the Waves of Culture*, London: Economist Books.

Turner, T. and Morley, M. (1995) *Industrial Relations & the New Order: Case Studies in Conflict & Co-Operation*, Dublin: Oak Tree Press.

Ulrich, D. (1987) 'Organisational capability as competitive advantage: Human resource professionals as strategic partners', *Human Resource Planning*, **10**: 169–84.

Ulrich, D. (1989) 'Tie the corporate knot: Gaining complete customer commitment', *Sloan Management Review*, Summer: 19–28.

US Department of Labor (1993) *High Performance Work Practices and Firm Performance*, Washington DC: US Government Printing Office.

Van Ommeren, J. and Brewster, C. (2000) 'The determinants of the number of HR staff in organisations: theory and empirical evidence', *Academy of Management Journal* (forthcoming).

Visser, J. (1992) 'The Netherlands: the end of an era and the end of a system', in A. Ferner and R. Hyman (eds) *Industrial Relations in the New Europe*, Oxford: Blackwell Publishers.

Williamson, O. (1975) *Markets and Hierarchies: Analysis and Antitrust Implications*, New York: Free Press.

Williamson, O. (1985) *The Economic Institutions of Capitalism*, New York: Free Press.

Wright, P.M. and McMahan, G.C. (1992) 'Theoretical Perspectives for Strategic Human Resource Management', *Journal of Management*, **18**(2): 295–320.

Wright, P.M. and Snell, S.A. (1991) 'Toward an Integrative View of Strategic Human Resource Management', *Human Resource Management Review*, **1**: 203–25.

14 HRM: an American View

Thomas Kochan and Lee Dyer

HUMAN RESOURCE MANAGEMENT AND NATIONAL COMPETITIVENESS

Can the United States maintain its traditional position of economic leadership and one of the world's highest standards of living in the face of increasing global competition? Concerned observers cite the following negative trends: lagging rates of productivity growth, non-competitive product quality in key industries, structural inflexibilities, and declining real wage levels and flat family earnings (Carnavale 1991). Further, they offer a plethora of proposed solutions, covering both broad public policies and practices.

The latter often call upon organizations to do a better job of developing and utilizing their human resources (Cyert and Mowery 1986; Marshall 1987; Walton 1987; Dertouzos *et al.* 1989). Newly industrializing economies such as Mexico, Brazil, and some of the Asian countries compete in world markets with wages that range from 10 to 30 per cent of those paid in more advanced countries such as Japan, Germany, and the US. For companies in the more advanced countries to compete in world markets without lowering wages and living standards requires not only ever-increasing levels of productivity, but also finding other sources of competitive advantage, such as high product quality, product differentiation, innovation, and speed to market.

However, competing on these grounds often requires major organizational transformations in human resource policies and practices. This is especially the case for US firms, which have grown up under the legacy of scientific management and industrial engineering principles that emphasize the separation of decision-making from doing and narrow divisions of labour and functional specialization. It is also true for unionized firms that have long done business under the 'New Deal' model of labour relations, which emphasizes job control, unionism and the separation of managerial prerogatives from worker and union rights.

The past decade has witnessed an explosion of interest in human resource management and the growth of new academic journals, professional societies, and industry–university research and educational partnerships. All of these share the view that human resource issues should and, given the increased awareness of their importance, shall be elevated to new levels of influence within corporate decision-making and national policy-making. In the US, these expectations and arguments have been voiced before, in some cases way before (Slichter 1919; Douglas 1919). None the less, even today we find that the human resource function within many

American corporations remains weak and relatively low in influence, relative to other managerial functions such as finance, marketing and manufacturing (Kochan and Osterman 1991). Moreover, despite the outpouring of academic writing on 'strategic human resource management', little progress has been made in developing systematic theory or empirical evidence on the conditions under which human resources are elevated to a position where the firm sees and treats these issues as a source of competitive advantage. Nor is there much research that actually tests the effects of different strategies on the competitive position of the firm.

Countless national competitiveness commissions and at least three national commissions sponsored by current or former US Secretaries of Labour have documented the need for the country, as well as individual firms, to invest more in human resources and encourage the development of workplace innovations to fully utilize employee talents once developed. But, so far, these clarion calls have often fallen on either deaf or hostile ears. Corporate managements, for reasons we will document below, have not been particularly enthusiastic, and responses from labour leaders have been mixed. Many of the recommended practices have been pioneered in non-union firms and some union leaders see them as inherently anti-union in nature. Yet the economic pressures of the 1980s led to a certain amount of joint union–management experimentation, and these experiences have produced a cadre of local and, to a lesser extent, national union leaders who are advocates. As yet, however, no clear vision or strategy on these issues has been articulated by the labour movement. And, finally, there has been virtually no action on the part of national policy-makers to create either the environment or the substantive policies needed to encourage or require either firms or unions to act more forcefully in this regard.

Why does the rhetoric so far outstrip the reality? One (although certainly not the only) answer is that theorists and researchers have cast their models of human resource management and related policy issues too narrowly. Specifically, they have relied too heavily on top management and human resource managers within corporations to drive the necessary transformation. Too little consideration has been given to the organizational and institutional contexts in which firms formulate and implement their human resource strategies and policies. Moreover, the literature has tended to treat each firm as an independent actor whereas, as we argue below, it is now clear that the practices of individual firms are influenced not only by their own business strategies, technologies, and structures, but also by the practices of other firms in their product and labour markets, as well as by the activities of their suppliers and customers, of trade unions, and of public policy-makers (Dyer and Holder 1988). Thus, we see the need to bring labour and government back into our theories and models of human resource management policy and practice. To do this we need to integrate recent works from human resource management with research from industrial relations, political economy, and internal labour markets. In this chapter we turn to that task.

GENERIC PRINCIPLES OF MUTUAL COMMITMENT FIRMS

Many terms have been used to describe firms that seek to treat human resources as a source of competitive advantage and to do so in a manner that preserves high standards of living: 'high involvement' (Walton 1985), 'excellent' (Peters and Waterman 1982), 'best practice' (Dertouzos et al. 1989), 'transformed' (Kochan et al.

1986), and 'high involvement' (Lawler 1986). We will use the term 'mutual commitment' (Walton 1985). We prefer this term since, as will be evident below, we believe that achieving and sustaining this approach requires the strong support of multiple stakeholders in an organization and in the broader economy and society in which the organization is embedded.

Figure 14.1 summarizes a set of generic principles that characterize the 'mutual commitment' approach. It is important to realize that these are broad principles which are operationalized in quite different forms across countries and firms. Therefore, they do not translate into a universal set of 'best practices', but rather stand as broad guidelines to be implemented in ways that conform to particular cultural or organizational realities. Further, much work remains to be done to test the validity of these principles, and to assess the interrelationships among the principles, practices and important societal, organizational and individual outcomes in different settings.

Figure 14.1 organizes the principles according to the three-tiered institutional framework presented in Kochan *et al.* (1986). At the highest level of the firm, first, it is essential that business strategies should not be built around low costs, and especially not around low wages, salaries, and benefit levels, but rather around such sources of competitive advantage as affordable quality, innovation, flexibility, speed, and customer service (Carnavale 1991). Second, key decision-makers must be guided by a set of values and traditions – often referred to as organizational culture – that views employees as valued stakeholders in the organization, not as mere cogs in the machine. Within any given business strategy and strategic context, top managers have significant discretion in human resource matters; values and traditions often dictate how, and how wisely, this discretion is used. Finally, at the strategy and policy-making level it is necessary that there be one or more mechanisms for giving voice to employee and human resource interests in strategy formulation and organizational

---

Strategic Level

Supportive Business Strategies
Top Management Value Commitment
Effective Voice for HR in Strategy Making and Governance

Functional (Human Resource Policy) Level

Staffing Based on Employment Stabilization
Investment in Training and Development
Contingent Compensation that Reinforces Cooperation, Participation and Contribution

Workplace Level

Selection Based on High Standards
Broad Task Design and Teamwork
Employee Involvement in Problem-Solving
Climate of Cooperation and Trust

Figure 14.1 Principles guiding mutual commitment firms

governance processes. One possibility is the use of planning mechanisms to ensure that human resource issues receive their just due in the formulation of business strategies (Dyer 1983; Schuler and Jackson 1987). In other contexts, informal labour–management information-sharing and consultation might be used. In still others it might be more formal forms of worker representation in corporate governance structures (e.g. labour leaders on the board of directors, works councils).

Moving down to the human resource policy level, we suggest three additional principles that are important for achieving comparative advantage from human resources. First, staffing policies must be designed and managed in such a way that they reinforce the principle of employment security and thus promote the commitment, flexibility, and loyalty of employees. This does not imply guarantees of lifetime employment, but it does imply that the first instinct in good times and bad should be to build and protect the firm's investment in human resources, rather than to indiscriminately add and cut people in knee-jerk responses to short-term fluctuations in business conditions (Dyer *et al.* 1985). Closely related is the matter of training and development. Clearly, firms that seek competitive advantage through human resources must make the necessary investment to ensure that their workforces have the appropriate skills and training, not only to meet short-term job requirements, but also to anticipate changing job requirements over time. That is, they – and their employees – must be prepared to adopt the concept of lifelong learning.

The third critical principle at the human resource policy level concerns compensation. Basic compensation levels must be adequate to attract and retain a committed, cooperative and involved workforce, and the compensation structure must be seen as being internally equitable by employees at various levels in different functions. Over and above competitive basic compensation levels and structures would be variable, or contingent, compensation schemes (e.g. bonus plans) designed to reinforce desired forms of quality, flexibility and the like, as well as to provide the firm with a means of controlling its labour costs in tough times without reverting to layoffs.

Finally, we move to the level of day-to-day interactions of employees with their environment, supervision, and jobs. Here we see several principles as critical. Clearly, in selection, high standards must be set regarding the level of skill, training and educational preparation required of new recruits. The ability to learn and the willingness to continue to learn over the course of one's career becomes an extremely important personal attribute for employees in mutual commitment firms. Second, the education and skills preparation of employees must be fully utilized on the job. This requires job and career structures that eschew narrow, Tayloristic job assignments in favour of flexible work organization that features expanded jobs and the free-flowing movement of employees across tasks and functional boundaries.

A third principle at the workplace level deals with opportunities for employees and/or their representatives to engage in problem-solving and decision-making in matters which involve their jobs and the conditions surrounding their jobs – what Lawler (1988) refers to as job involvement. The fourth and final workplace principle relates to the quality of relationships between employees, their representatives, and managers. A high-conflict/low-trust relationship (Fox 1974) is seen as incompatible with the task of building and maintaining mutual commitment. This does not mean that all conflicts between employees and employers wither away. Indeed we continue to assume that conflicting interests are a natural part of the employment relationship, but that these conflicts cannot be so all-encompassing that they push out the potential for effective problem-solving and negotiations. Instead they must be resolved efficiently and in a fashion that maintains the parties' commitment and capacities for pursuing joint gains.

Obviously the above set of principles constitutes a caricature of actual organizations. No organization is expected to meet all of these principles perfectly or through the same set of practices. None the less, in the broadest sense it is postulated that when these principles are properly operationalized they will come together in the form of an integrated system that, other things being equal, will produce globally competitive business results as well as globally competitive standards of living for employees.

The preceding principles have been presented as if firms have total discretion over the choice of their human resource strategies, and as if each firm's choice is independent of the strategies followed by other firms. But neither of these premises is the case. External factors, particularly the role of the trade unions, the State (government policy) and, in some countries, industry associations all influence and/or constrain the range of choices open to decision-makers. Moreover, individual firms are heavily influenced by the strategies followed by others in their product and labour markets, supplier and customer networks, and industries. Thus, a critical factor is the rate and depth at which the concepts underlying these principles are diffused across different institutions and institutional decision-makers, as well as across various firms and industries.

EXTENT OF DIFFUSION OF MUTUAL COMMITMENT PRINCIPLES

Unfortunately no single data base currently exists that allows us to estimate precisely how widespread the principles reviewed above are in US organizations today. It is probably fair to say that very few organizations have yet embraced the full set of principles in a coherent fashion. Clearly, however, the past decade has been a time of great experimentation with various of these principles, to the point that it is probably fair to say that most large and perhaps even a majority of relatively small firms have experimented with one or more of them at one time or another.

Supportive competitive strategies

We believe that one of the most powerful determinants and reinforcing forces for a mutual commitment human resources strategy lies in the nature of competitive business strategies. Clearly, many US firms recognize this as well. In some ways, however, large US firms suffer from the legacies of their prior successes in taking advantage of the vast size of the US markets. For this reason, they have experienced more difficulty adapting to export markets and the flexible production and differentiated competitive strategies needed to support mutual commitment human resource strategies (Carnavale 1991; Piore and Sabel 1984).

In the clothing industry, for example, despite the obvious difficulty of competing with imports from low-wage countries, American manufacturers and unions have made only limited progress in abandoning their traditional individual piecework and related mass production strategies in favour of practices that would give them advantages in time to market and quick response to changing customer preferences

(National Clothing Industry Labor Management Committee 1991). As a result, imports are taking a greater share of the market both at the low-price points where mass production continues to dominate, and at the high-price points where styling, fashion, and variability in tastes matter most.

In the US airline industry, the low-cost strategies of Continental and Eastern Airlines served to limit the success of the high-growth and service differentiation strategies of firms such as American and Delta Airlines, in the first decade following industry deregulation (Kochan and McKersie 1991). Thus, while low-cost strategies are difficult to sustain over the long run, especially when faced with competition from abroad, a significant number of American firms continue to give priority to this strategy and thereby slow the pace of innovations in human resource practices.

Managerial values and organizational culture

As noted earlier, we continue to see top executive and line management support as a necessary condition for introducing and sustaining the types of human resource strategies described in Figure 14.1. Yet there is little in the history of American management, or in the behaviour of American management currently, to suggest that management alone, left to its own devices, will produce the transformations in organizational practice needed to sustain and diffuse the delineated human resource principles. While some, perhaps even many, top executives share supportive values, they are buffeted by equally strong countervailing pressures that call for quick action taken to bolster the short-term interests of major shareholders.

Consider, for example, the following description of the dominant managerial strategies of the 1980s, offered by the top human resource executive at General Electric, one of the firms often cited as symbolizing exemplary practices:

> Economic power in the Eighties – the power to launch and sustain the dynamic processes of restructuring and globalization – has been concentrated especially in the hands of the larger companies, along with the financiers and raiders who alternatively [*sic*] support or attack them. If the Eighties was a new Age of the Entrepreneur – and small business did in fact account for most of the new job creation in the United States – it was Corporate America that accounted for most of the economic disruption and competitive improvement; it took out people, layers and costs while rearranging portfolios and switching industries.
> ... Across the decade in the US alone, there was over a trillion dollars of merger and acquisition activity. Ten million manufacturing jobs were eliminated or shifted to the growing service sector. Deals were cut and alliances forged around America and around the world.
>
> From where the shots were called was well-known. Restructuring and globalization did not emerge from employee suggestion boxes; they erupted from executive suites. ...
>
> So competitive rigor – imposed by companies in their employer roles and demonstrated by their restructuring and globalizing moves – was widely accepted because its rationale was widely understood. Given this climate – along with a political environment of relative deregulation – companies in the Eighties could focus more on portfolios than on people; fire more than hire; invest more in machines than in skills.

> The obvious reality of tough competitive facts inspired fear in employees and gave employers the power to act. Shuttered factories and fired neighbors is restructuring without subtlety: people could see the damage and feel the pain.
>
> (Doyle 1989: 1–2)

This, then, is perhaps the dominant political environment of corporate decision-making and governance that must be taken into account in building theoretical and action models in the human resource management arena.

Human resources in business strategy formulation

Clearly, very few if any inroads have been made into top-level business strategy formulation by either informal or formal forms of employee representation; the European experience remains distinctively European (Kochan *et al.* 1986). Some progress has been made in bringing human resource considerations into business strategy sessions through the integration of formal planning processes – exactly how much progress, however, it is difficult to say. Recent surveys suggest that at least some level of integration has been achieved by between 20 per cent and 45 per cent of medium-sized and large firms (Burack 1986; Nkomo 1986). More intensive case studies support these figures, but call into question the depth of the integration in many cases (Buller 1988; Craft 1988). Functionally, some progressive human resource departments are striving to adopt a so-called business partner role, which puts them in a position to interject human resource considerations in ongoing business decision-making (Dyer and Holder 1988). But, again, while the trend is in the right direction, at this juncture the development is probably neither very widespread nor particularly deep.

Employment security

Diffusion of the practices needed to demonstrate a commitment to employment continuity is particularly limited in the US (Dyer *et al.* 1985). Massive lay-offs became commonplace during the 1980s, affecting not only blue-collar and clerical employees, but also traditionally immune professional and managerial employees as well.

During this time, even firms that had garnered reputations over the years for eschewing lay-offs – Eastman Kodak and Digital Equipment Corporation, for example – gave up the practice (Foulkes and Whitman 1985). Many of these firms strove to handle their employment reductions in ways that smoothed the effects on both employees and survivors – by providing severance pay and outplacement services, for example. In general, however, employee cutbacks have been so severe and handled so badly that there appears to be widespread agreement among employers and employees that there has to be a better way. Whether these attitudes will eventually translate into a more systematic management of staffing levels and processes, however, remains to be seen.

Training and development

US firms spend huge sums on training and development (some estimates put the number at $30–40 billion per year). Still, in per capita terms the amount spent pales in comparison with the amounts spent by the US's most formidable international competitors (Kochan and Osterman 1991). For example, MacDuffie and Kochan (1991) found that US car-makers do less training than their Japanese and European counterparts, in part because US work systems demand fewer skills and in part because the US lacks national policies and infrastructures that support or require such firm-level investment.

Compensation

Current rhetoric clearly supports the use of variable, or contingent, compensation schemes at all levels of employment (such practices are already reasonably widespread among executives and upper-level managers). Arguments supporting these schemes, however, are as often couched in labour cost terms as in motivational terms which, of course, exposes employees, even relatively low-paid ones, to a downside risk on their earnings, a perspective that is hardly consistent with the philosophy of mutual commitment. At any rate, variable, or contingent, compensation is still another area where rhetoric seems to have outstripped reality by a fairly wide margin. Surveys show that such pay plans, including profit-sharing, gain-sharing, and group incentives, tend to be in effect in no more than one-fifth of medium-sized and large firms (Conference Board 1990; O'Dell 1987). Further, many of these plans are experimental, having been instituted only within the last five years, and they often affect only relatively small numbers of employees.

Selection standards and flexible work organizations

Some argue that selection standards in US firms are rising in response to technological and work design trends that are upskilling jobs. Others argue (or complain bitterly) that they are lowering, in response to shortages of qualified employees. In fact, there probably is some of both going on. Certainly, the desirability of moving to more flexible, and hence more demanding, forms of work organization is a shibboleth among many management writers in the US. In practice, however, the legacy of Taylorism and job control unionism (narrow job classifications, tightly circumscribed seniority and wage rules, and carefully guarded managerial and supervisory prerogatives) serves as a severe constraint on diffusion. Not surprisingly, the most highly visible and widespread use of work teams and other flexible forms of work organization has been found in new or 'greenfield' plants that are relatively free from these historical traditions (Walton 1980). In existing settings, some corporations have used the incentive of capital investments in new products or technology, and thus in job retention, to encourage (or require) local plant managers and, where present, union leaders, to reform their work systems. Chrysler, for example, took this approach in negotiating 'Modern Operating Agreements' (MOAs) in six of its facilities in the late 1980s (Lovel et al. 1991). Yet even the Chrysler experience repeats that which Walton (1985) and others have well documented, namely that such experiments seem to have some staying power, but that they generally fail to spread to other units within the firm. As such, they become experimental islands in a sea of traditional practices. Interestingly, the use of flexible work systems seems to be gaining faster acceptance among plant managers, local union leaders, and employees than among higher-level managers and national union leaders, whose support will clearly be required for diffusion to take hold.

To cite one example, Digital Equipment Corporation recently announced that it planned to close the two plants in its organization that had, by its own account, gone further than any others in committing to and implementing flexible, team-based work systems. One of these was a greenfield site specifically designed as an experimental plant from which others were expected to learn, and the other was an existing facility that invested heavily in the changeover and which won a number of awards from Digital management for its 'manufacturing excellence'. Both fell victim to top management decisions to move production to other facilities in a corporate downsizing move. We dwell on this case not to single out Digital, since in many ways this company has gone further than most others down the path of mutual commitment (Kochan *et al.* 1986). Rather, we use the case simply to illustrate the dependence of many workplace innovations on higher-level corporate decision-making. Ultimately, those within the management structure advocating manufacturing innovations lost the political debate to finance specialists who could demonstrate the logistical savings that would accrue from moving the products produced in these facilities to other locations.

Employee participation

There has probably been more experimentation with employee participation, or involvement, in workplace problem-solving and decision-making than with any other of the mutual commitment principles. A survey conducted in the mid-1980s showed that more than half of firms with 1,000 or more employees had implemented some version of quality circles or other employee participation programmes (Alper *et al.* 1985). More recent reports, although less well documented, suggest that the pace of experimentation may have quickened since that time. Even friendly observers, however, have noted that many of these participatory efforts encounter the same sorts of difficulties as do workplace innovations (with which they are, in fact, often linked), thus making them difficult to sustain, let alone diffuse (Lawler and Mohrman 1985; Drago 1988).

Low-conflict, high-trust environment

Measures of conflict in the workplace are difficult, if not impossible, to come by. Surveys of employee attitudes, however, including trust levels, are commonplace. While isolated companies continue privately to report stable (or in some cases even improving) employee attitudes, the overall pattern suggests a general erosion among virtually all employee groups. The decline is particularly sharp in measures of employee trust in management and in their companies generally (Fisher 1991; Gordon 1990; Hay Group 1991; Kanter and Mirvis 1989). Here there is diffusion; alas, the direction is directly counter to the principles of mutual commitment.

AN ALTERNATIVE CHANGE MODEL AND SOME PROPOSITIONS

Formal models of organizational change are not well developed with respect to human resource management issues. Implicit in the US literature on strategic human resource management, however, are two general propositions. First, that human resource policies and practices need to be matched to firms' competitive business strategies. And second, that change occurs when top executives and/or key line managers take sufficient interest in human resource issues to give them, and their professional human resource staffs, positions of high priority. These propositions reflect a fundamental weakness of human resource management theories: a myopic viewpoint which fails to look beyond the boundary of the individual firm.

Some years ago we (Kochan and Dyer 1976) noted the limitations of this view when applied to joint efforts to introduce and manage change in union–management relations. At that time we argued for a change model that recognized the diversity of stakeholder interests and the role of structural bases of power that affect such change efforts. In a similar vein, Kochan and Cappelli (1984), Jacoby (1985) and Baron *et al.* (1986) have emphasized the importance of external forces – union growth, government policy interventions, tight labour markets and/or crises such as the two World Wars – as predictors of innovation in human resource management practice.

Others have emphasized the importance of the politics of corporate decision-making (Pettigrew and Whipp 1991; Thomas 1992). Support for investment in or consideration of human resource policies is generally sought within broader contests for financial and other resources. The outcomes of these political contests depend heavily on the extent to which advocates can couch their arguments in the prevailing rationales or decision routines used in capital budgeting (e.g. payback periods, rates of return, cost savings, and headcount reductions). This political view can be extended to incorporate broader issues of corporate governance. Doyle's previously quoted description of the US approach to corporate restructuring notes that the speed of adjustment is often a function of the relative power and pressures exerted by shareholders or of takeover threats. In this view, support for human resource initiatives involves a contest not only among functional units within the firm (e.g. human resources and finance), but also among the interests of employees, shareholders, and other stakeholders.

In the precursor to this volume (Storey 1989), Purcell noted that the trend toward divisional or profit centre ('M-form') organizational structures also serves as a constraint on the elevation of human resources to levels of strategic importance. In these structures human resource decisions tend to be decentralized to the divisional level. This reduces the likely effects of overall corporate value systems and policies, and increases the probability that decision horizons will be short-term.

Two recent international studies reinforce the importance of developing models that extend beyond the boundaries of individual firms. Both Walton (1987) and Cole (1989) stress the importance of national and industry-level infrastructures for supporting the diffusion of innovations in human resource practices across national economies; both cite the lack of such infrastructures as a reason why the US lags in this respect.

Thus, a stronger model of change that considers internal political and external institutional and policy variables is required if we are to understand and effectively promote the diffusion of human resource innovations across the American economy. While we do not pretend to have a well-developed and tested model in hand at this point, the following key propositions for testing can be offered in the interest of developing such a model:

Proposition 1 The capacity of any individual firm to initiate and sustain human resource innovations is constrained by the extent to which these innovations are similarly adopted by other firms in its product and labour markets and customer and supplier networks.

The nub of this proposition is that no firm can transform its human resource practices alone. Human resource innovations are likely to suffer from what is called a 'market failures' problem (Levine and Tyson 1990). That is, while all firms and the macroeconomy would be better off if they all invested in human resource innovations, any particular firm will fail to capture the benefits of such investments if others fail to follow suit. This is most clearly seen in the area of investments in training. Leading firms, such as Motorola, IBM, Ford, and General Motors, that invest a great deal in training and development run the risk of losing these investments because their employees can attract a wage premium from firms that prefer to skim the labour market. This, in turn, reduces their incentives to invest to below the level that would prevail if all firms were developing their own internal labour markets.

The importance of suppliers and customers participating in human resource innovations can clearly be seen in the context of total quality management efforts. Final assemblers can realize the full pay-off of such efforts only if their suppliers meet corresponding quality standards. Thus, it is not surprising that such companies, and particularly Japanese plants operating in the US, have demanded that their suppliers develop parallel quality improvement programmes in order to become or to remain preferred suppliers. Obviously, the reverse logic applies to customers. In one study of car suppliers, for example, Gillett (1992) found that the extent of innovations in internal management systems varied directly with the expectations of the firms' customers. Change was quickest in coming and most far-reaching among those supplying Japanese customers, who not only demanded them, but also facilitated their implementation. It was slowest and least extensive among those supplying divisions of American firms that were themselves less committed to similar innovations.

While a number of leading firms are now demanding higher quality from their suppliers, or are being required to provide it to their customers, so far their reach has been rather limited and narrowly focused. The general weakness of industry associations in the US, along with the reluctance of firms to intervene in the human resource and labour-management relations affairs of their suppliers and customers, suggests that this avenue of change will have an important but limited impact. This, however, is a promising avenue for empirical research. It will be interesting to see, for example, if the pressures on suppliers, and of customers, produces a sustained and broad commitment to total quality, and whether this will carry over into areas of human resource management that face less direct, market-driven, across-firm pressure.

Proposition 2 Top and line management commitment is a desirable, but unlikely and generally insufficient condition for transforming human resource practices.

Virtually every article written on human resource innovations contains the obligatory final paragraph asserting the necessity for top management support for successful implementation. Yet, as previously noted, these managers are under many competing pressures from inside and outside the firm, and there is no reason to believe that employee and human resource considerations will tend to prevail in their strategic decision-making and day-to-day actions. While some chief executives, particularly the founders of such major companies as Polaroid, IBM, Digital Equipment, and Hewlett Packard, are well known for values that have long supported human resource innovations, such is not the case in most US firms, where less visionary CEOs have risen through the ranks of finance, marketing, manufacturing, or law, with little or no formal exposure to the human resource function or need to demonstrate human resource management skills.

US firms tend to promote and transfer managers rapidly, which also limits the power of managerial values as a driver of human resource innovations. Such rapid movement provides little incentive or opportunity for managers to develop the personal trust and commitment necessary to support such innovations. Under such circumstances, managers are likely to view investment in human resources as short-term costs that will at best produce pay-offs for their successors. A study of innovations at a number of Chrysler plants found that the average tenure of a plant manager was under two years, and that each time the manager turned over, the process of change was noticeably showed (Lovell *et al.* 1991).

The vast majority of top American executives believe that unions are unnecessary and undesirable in their firms (but perhaps not in the broader society). This evaluation is often translated into a high priority for union avoidance and/or containment. This, of course, limits the options for human resource professionals within such firms, since they must be careful to try to achieve desired innovations without the active involvement of union officials or, if a firm is non-unionized, to introduce innovations in ways that avoid creating the collective equivalent of a union.

In brief, the values of top executives and line managers are an important source of support that needs to be garnered. But reliance on a strategy of expecting these values to develop naturally is likely to continue to create islands of innovation that do not diffuse or that are not sustained. Thus, legal, structural, or personal bases of power that elevate the influence of employee and human resource policy interests will need to supplement and reinforce the values and commitment of top executives and line managers.

> *Proposition 3* Human resource innovations require a coalitional, multiple stakeholder change model.

If human resource professionals are in a relatively weak position in managerial hierarchies, and their more powerful line managers and top executives are only sporadic allies in the innovation process, a broader base of support and power will be needed to sustain innovations. The lessons of the historical models cited above suggest that these broader stakeholders include government regulatory agencies, employee and/or trade union representatives, and industry and/or professional associations. Historically, most democratic societies have relied on the pressure of unions to discipline and motivate management to upgrade human resource standards and practices. Continued decline in trade union membership in the US not only weakens this potential source of pressure, it creates a cycle of mistrust and adversarial tensions that limits the capacity of union leaders to work cooperatively with management on innovative programmes. Union leaders instead come to feel threatened and, in turn, define their primary challenge as a fight for survival and legitimacy. Thus, a cycle of low trust and high conflict gets perpetuated in a way that drives out opportunities for jointly sponsored innovative activities. Reversing this cycle would go a long way toward the diffusion of the mutual commitment principles noted above.

Similarly, to subvert the 'market features' effect noted above, government policy-makers will also need to be enlisted as part of a coalition supporting human resource innovations. This, in turn, requires a significant shift in the behaviour, and perhaps the mindset, of human resource management professionals who generally endorse voluntary industry efforts over government policies that would require or mandate innovative practices. This commitment to voluntarism is rooted both in an ideological predisposition to protect the prerogatives and autonomy of individual firms, and a recognition of the enormous diversity of the American economy. Yet herein lies a paradox. As long as these values and considerations dominate the politics of human resource management professionals, the diffusion, sustainability, and impact of the very principles they espouse are likely to remain quite limited.

> *Proposition 4*   Human resource professionals need to be open to learning from international sources. Transferring innovations across national borders and organizational boundaries offers the best opportunities for achieving broad, non-incremental change in human resource practices.

One important lesson brought home forcefully by Japanese direct investment in the US is that American managers perhaps have more to learn about human resource management from foreign competitors than they have to offer. The US car industry is perhaps the most visible example of this. Since the mid-1980s the most productive and highest quality car manufacturing plants in the US have been those that are Japanese-owned and -managed (Krafcik 1988). The New United Motors Manufacturing Inc (NUMMI) facility, jointly owned by General Motors and Toyota, but managed by the latter, has received the most attention because it achieved bench-mark levels of productivity and quality with an American workforce and union and with less technological investment than exists in most American-owned and -managed plants in the US. The dominant lesson from this case is that there is much value in a holistic approach to human resource management that is integrated with the dominant production system and which emphasizes the mutual commitment principles previously noted (Shimada and MacDuffie 1986).

Indeed, the human resource approaches introduced in NUMMI and other Japanese firms represent fundamental changes that cut across all three levels of the framework introduced in Figure 14.1. In some instances, US car companies are attempting to achieve similar systemic changes in their facilities and in new organizations such as GM's Saturn Division. Thus, the visible presence and high level of performance achieved with a human resource management system fundamentally different to that of comparable American facilities has been an extremely powerful spur to transforming practices across this industry.

The lessons offered to the US by other countries are not limited to Japan. Recently, policy-makers and academics (and an increasing number of union leaders) have become interested in the German apprenticeship and training system, as well as German-style works councils. Because these institutions require greater government and joint labour–business–government interaction and consensus, however, they have received only limited attention and support to date from the general business community and human resource managers and professionals.

Proposition 5 Documenting the effects of human resource policies on economic outcomes of interest to managers and employees is critical to sustaining support for these innovations. Learning networks that involve all the diverse stakeholders with an interest in these innovations can then speed the transfer, acceptance, and use of this knowledge in other settings.

NUMMI came to serve as an important spur to innovation in the automobile industry because word of its economic performance levels spread so quickly. More recently, MacDuffie and Krafcik (1989) have shown that the positive performance effects of the NUMMI approach generalizes to other facilities as well. As a result, the virtues of this approach are becoming even more widely accepted throughout the world car industry. Unfortunately, this is all too rare an example. Few human resource practices or interrelated systems of practices are evaluated in as systematic and convincing a fashion as has been the case in the car industry.

This approach was possible because the industry's major stakeholders accepted standard performance bench-marks (hours per car for productivity and number of defects per car and/or number of customer complaints per car for quality) and then cooperated with university researchers to collect, analyse, and publish the results of across-plant and across-firm comparisons (without revealing the identity of individual plants or firms). This type of learning network stands as a model of what is needed to accelerate the process of knowledge generation and innovation diffusion.

SUMMARY AND CONCLUSION

In summary, we believe that the type of change model that is necessary to support diffusion of human resource innovations has four main elements. First, it starts with a clear model of the generic principles or requirements that must be met. Second, it casts its vision internationally to discover world-class bench-marks. Third, it engages a broad coalition of human resource and labour advocates within and outside the firm in a network that works together to promote and diffuse innovations. Fourth, it then provides the analytic data required to evaluate and disseminate the economic effects of the innovations. With the strength of this broad base of support and harder evidence for the effects of the innovations, informed government representatives can then contribute by providing the national or macro-level infrastructure and policies needed to go from micro-firm specific islands of innovation to changes of sufficient scope and magnitude to make a difference in national competitiveness and standards of living. If this is done, the field of human resource management will have achieved its own transformation from the traditional image of personnel administration to a truly strategic orientation and contribution. If, on the other hand, events fail to move in these directions, the voices of human resource managers and professionals in many firms are destined to remain buried deep within the managerial hierarchy pleading for, but only sporadically receiving, the support and commitment of their more powerful managerial brethren.

Obviously, this view requires a substantial investment in high-quality research to identify promising human resource innovations and evaluate their effects on organizational and individual outcomes of interest to multiple stakeholders. Presupposed is a broadened perspective of the relevant stakeholders to include not only top managers (and maybe stockholders), but also various types of employees, labour leaders and purveyors of public policies. Also presupposed is a multi-national – or global – view, as well as a corresponding willingness to learn from the lessons of other countries. All this may represent a particularly radical departure for US scholars.

There is no assumption here that prevailing sentiments extolling the virtues of various forms of human resource innovations and the new-found influence of today's human resource managers represent either reality or inevitability. To achieve global competitiveness and satisfactory standards of living will require broadened perspectives of human resource systems, the development of more realistic models of organizational change, and a mountain of convincing evidence. Absent these, and the prevailing rhetoric cannot help but fall on deaf eyes.

REFERENCES

Alper, W.S., Pfau, B. and Sirota, D. (1985) 'The 1985 national survey of employee attitudes executive report', sponsored by *Business Week* and Sirota and Alper Associates, September.

Baron, J.N., Dobbin, F.R. and Jennings, P.D. (1986) 'War and peace: the evolution of modern personnel administration in US industry', *American Journal of Sociology*, **92**: 350–84.

Buller, P.F. (1988) 'Successful partnerships: HR and strategic planning at eight top firms', *Organizational Dynamics*, autumn: 27–43.

Burack, E. (1986) 'Corporate business and human resource planning practices: strategic issues and concerns', *Organizational Dynamics*, summer: 73–86.

Carnavale, A.P. (1991) *America and the New Economy*, Washington, DC: The American Society for Training and Development.

Cole, R.E. (1989) *Strategies for Learning*, Berkeley, CA: University of California Press.

Conference Board (The) (1990) 'Variable pay: new performance rewards', *Bulletin* No. 246.

Craft, J.A. (1988) 'Human resource planning and strategy', in L. Dyer (ed.) *Human Resource Management: Evolving Roles and Responsibilities*, Washington: Bureau of National Affairs.

Cyert, R.M. and Mowery, D.C. (eds) (1986) *Technology and Employment*, Washington, DC: National Academy Press.

Dertouzos, M., Solow, R. and Lester, R. (1989) *Made in America*, Cambridge, MA: MIT Press.

Douglas, P. (1919) 'Plant administration of labour', *Journal of Political Economy*, **27**, July: 544–60.

Doyle, F.P. (1989) 'The global human resource challenge for the nineties', paper delivered to the World Management Congress, New York, September 23.

Drago, R. (1988) 'Quality circle survival: an explanatory analysis', *Industrial Relations*, **27**(3).

Dyer, L. (1983) 'Bringing human resources into the strategy formulation process', *Human Resource Management*, **22**(3): 257–71.

Dyler, L. and Holder, G. (1988) 'A strategic perspective on human resource management', in L. Dyer (ed.) *Human Resource Management: Evolving Roles and Responsibilities*, Washington, DC: Bureau of National Affairs Books.

Dyler, L., Foltman, F. and Milkovich, G. (1985) 'Contemporary employment stabilization practices', in T.A. Kochan and T.A. Barocci (eds) *Human Resource Management and Industrial Relations*, Boston, MA: Little Brown.

Fisher, A.B. (1991) 'Morale crisis', *Fortune* November, **18**: 70–82.

Foulkes, F. and Whitman, A. (1985) 'Market strategies to maintain full employment', *Harvard Business Review*, July–August: 4–7.

Fox, A. (1974) *Beyond Contract: Trust and Authority Relations in Industry*, London: Macmillan.

Gillet, F. (1992) 'Supplier–customer relationships: case studies in the auto parts industry', MS thesis, MIT.

Gordon, J. (1990) 'Who killed corporate loyalty?', *Training* March: 25–32.

Hay Group (The) (1991) 1991–92 Hay Employee Attitudes Study, Hay.

Jacoby, S. (1985) *Employing Bureaucracies*, New York: Columbia University Press.

Kanter, D. and Mirvis, P. (1989) *The Cynical Americans: Living and Working in an Age of Discontent and Disillusion*, San Francisco, CA: Jossey Bass.

Kochan, T.A. and Cappelli, P. (1983) 'The transformation of the industrial relations and personnel function', in P. Osterman (ed.) *Internal Labor Markets*, Cambridge, MA: MIT Press.

Kochan, T.A. and Dyer, L. (1976) 'A model of organizational change in the context of union–management relations', *Journal of Applied Behavioral Science*, **12**: 58–78.

Kochan, T.A. and McKersie, R.B. (1991) 'Human resources, organizational governance, and public policy: lessons from a decade of experimentation', in T.A. Kochan and M. Useem (eds) *Transforming Organizations*, New York: Oxford University Press.

Kochan, T.A. and Osterman, P. (1991) 'Human resource development and utilization: is there too little in the US?', paper prepared for the Time Horizons Project of the Council on competitiveness, MIT.

Kochan, T.A., Katz, H.C. and McKersie, R. (1986) *The Transformation of American Industrial Relations*, New York: Basic Books.

Kochan, T.A., Osterman, P. and MacDuffie, J.P. (1988) 'Employment security at DEC: sustaining values amid environmental change', *Human Resource Management Journal*, Fall.

Krafcik, J.F. (1988) 'World class manufacturing: an international comparison of automobile assembly plant performance', *Sloan Management Review*, **30**: 41–52.

Lawler, E.E. III (1988) 'Choosng an involvement strategy', *The Academy of Management Executive*, **2**(3): 197–204.

Lawler, E.E. III (1986) *High Involvement Management*, San Francisco, CA: Jossey Bass.

Lawler, E.E. III and Mohrman, S.A. (1985) 'Quality circles after the fad', *Harvard Business Week*, **63**: 65–71.

Levine, D.I. and Tyson, L.D.'A. (1990) 'Participation, productivity, and the firm's environment', in A.S. Blinder (ed.) *Paying for Productivity*, Washington, DC: The Brookings Institution.

Lovell, M. *et al.* (1991) *Chrysler and the UAW: Modern Operating Agreements*, report to the US Department of Labor Bureau of Labor Management Relations and Cooperative Programs, Washington, DC.

MacDuffie, J.P. and Kochan, T.A. (1991) 'Determinants of training: a cross national comparison in the auto industry', paper presented at the 1991 meetings of the Academy of Management, August.

MacDuffie, J.P. and Krafcik, J.F. (1989) 'Flexible production systems and manufacturing peformance: the role of human resources and technology', paper delivered at Annual Meeting of the Academy of Management, Washington, DC, August 16.

Marshall, R. (1987) *Unheard Voices*, New York: Basic Books.

National Clothing Industry Labor Management Committee (1991) *A Strategy for Innovation*, New York: National Clothing Industry Labor Management Committee.

Nkomo, S. (1986) 'The theory and practice of HR planning: the gap still remains', *Personnel Administrator*, August: 71–84.

O'Dell, C. (1987) 'People, performance, and pay', American Productivity Center.

Peters, T. and Waterman, Jr., R.H. (1982) *In Search of Excellence*, New York: Harper & Row.

Pettigrew, A. and Whipp, R. (1991) *Managing Change for Strategic Success*, Oxford: Blackwell.

Piore, M. and Sabel, C. (1984) *The Second Industrial Divide*, New York: Basic Books.

Purcell, J. (1989) 'The impact of corporate strategy on human resource management', in J. Storey (ed.) *New Perspectives on Human Resource Management*, London: Routledge.

Schuler, R.S. and Jackson, S.E. (1987) 'Linking competitive strategies and human resource management practices', *Academy of Management Executive*, August: 207–19.

Shimada, H. and MacDuffie, J.P. (1986) 'Industrial relations and "humanware": Japanese investments in automobile manufacturing in the United States', working paper, Sloan School of Management, MIT.

Slichter, S. (1919) 'The management of labor', *Journal of Political Economy*, **27**: 813–39.

Storey, J. (ed.) (1989) *New Perspectives on Human Resource Management*, London: Routledge.

Thomas, R.J. (1992) *What Machines Can't Do: Organizational Politics and Technological Change*, Berkeley, CA: University of California Press.

Walton, R.E. (1980) 'Establishing and maintaining high commitment work systems', in Kimberley, J.R. and Miles, M. (eds) *The Organizational Life Cycle*, San Francisco, CA: Jossey-Bass.

Walton, R.E. (1985) 'Toward a strategy of eliciting employee commitment based on policies of mutuality', in R.E. Walton and P.R. Lawrence (eds) *HRM Trends and Challenges*, Boston, MA: Harvard Business School Press.

Walton, R.E. (1987) *Innovating to Compete*, San Franciso, CA: Jossey-Bass.

15 International Human Resource Management

Hugh Scullion

INTRODUCTION

There is no consensus about what the term International Human Resource Management (IHRM) covers although most studies in the area have traditionally focused on the area of expatriation (Brewster and Harris 1999). IHRM has been defined as 'the HRM issues and problems arising from the internationalization of business, and the HRM strategies, policies and practices which firms pursue in response to the internationalization process' (Scullion 1995: 352). The advantage of such a definition is that it covers a far broader spectrum than the management of expatriates and involves the world-wide management of people (Dowling *et al.* 1999). Also it highlights that IHRM is a separate field of study from comparative employment relations which seeks to examine the ways in which different countries handle similar employment relations issues and focuses on the extent of convergence or divergence between the different patterns of institutional behaviour in various countries (Bamber and Lansbury 1998).

A decade and a half ago, IHRM was described by one leading authority as a field in the infancy stage of development (Laurent 1986). The majority of research on multinational companies focused on highly visible strategies and activities such as international business strategies, international production and international marketing (Ondrack 1985). IHRM was one of the least studied areas in international business (Brewster 1991). In particular, the area of IHRM had received relatively little attention in terms of detailed empirical research – especially in relation to firms that have their headquarters outside North America. Indeed the bulk of research in this field has been conducted by American researchers from an American rather than an international perspective (Boyacigiller and Adler 1991). Also it has been argued that much of the earlier research on International HRM is still open to the criticisms of Schollhammer (1975) as being (1) descriptive and lacking in analytical rigour; (2) ad hoc and expedient in research planning and design; (3) self-centred in the sense that existing research literature is largely ignored; and (4) lacking a sustained research effort to develop case material (Brewster and Scullion 1997). Kochan *et al.* (1992) suggested that the IHRM literature suffered from the same conceptual and normative limitations characteristic of much domestic personnel management research. Research in IHRM had not proved to be very helpful in identifying the HR policies of international companies and this state of affairs reflected the predominant bias in most of the literature towards idealized prescriptive models with little real data about actual practices in real contexts.

More recently, it has been argued that the rapid pace of internationalization and globalization has led to a more strategic role for HRM as well as leading to changes in the content of HRM (Pucik 1992), and the need for a systematic approach to studying International HRM is increasingly being recognized. Schuler *et al.* (1993) developed an integrative framework to bring together the strategic and international elements of international HRM, which has been revised and further developed by De Cieri and Dowling (1999). Welch (1994) has also presented an integrated model which identifies the main determinants of International HRM policy and practice. There has been rapid development of the field of international HRM over the past decade (Black *et al.* 1999; Dowling *et al.* 1999), including the development of more sophisticated theoretical work in the area. One significant indicator of the growing importance of IHRM is the rapidly growing body of empirical research on the IHRM policies and practices of MNCs taking place outside North America (Brewster and Harris 1999). Also the increasing number of specialist international conferences and symposiums on IHRM reflects the growing recognition being given to this area by managers, consultants and researchers.

This chapter aims to critically assess developments in the area of international HRM over the last decade; to examine the key changes that are taking place in some important areas of international HRM; and to use that as a basis for proposing a new research agenda for the future. The focus of this chapter is on the links between international strategy and IHRM. There are three main sections in the chapter each of which examines a critical area in international HRM. The first, strategic management and IHRM, examines the role of the corporate HR function in the international firm, control mechanisms in the international firm and learning in the international firm. The second is international staffing, the area which continues to enjoy the majority of research attention in IHRM. The third is International Management Development. The important area of HR issues in international joint ventures and alliances is covered in depth by Schuler in Chapter 16.

First, the reasons for the rapid growth of interest in international HRM over the last decade will be outlined.

(a) International companies have increased in number and significance in recent years linked with the rapid growth of internationalization and global competition. This reflects the growing importance of international economic activity in general and results in the increased mobility of human resources (Young and Hamill 1992; Dicken 1998).

(b) There is growing recognition that the success of global business depends most importantly on the quality of a multinational's human resources and on how effectively these critical resources are managed and developed (Stroh and Caliguri 1998). Indeed, the effective management of human resources is increasingly being recognized as a major determinant of success or failure in international business, where the quality of management, in particular, seems to be a critical success factor (Black *et al.* 1999).

(c) The costs of poor performance or failure in international assignments are high, both in human and financial terms. Research suggests that the indirect costs of failure in international business such as loss of market share and damage to overseas customer relations in the foreign market may be particularly costly (Dowling and Schuler 1990).

(d) Recent research suggests that shortages of 'international managers' are constraining corporate efforts to expand abroad and that the successful implementation of global strategies may be constrained by an inadequate supply of international managers (Caligiuri and Cascio 1998; Scullion 1994).

(e) The rapid growth of internationalization of the small and medium-sized enterprise (SME) in recent years means that international HRM issues are becoming increasingly significant in a far wider range of organizations than the traditional giant multinationals (UN 1993; Mulhern 1995). The limited research on international HRM in international SME firms suggests they face very different problems to larger organizations and that models of IHRM which are based on large international firms may not be appropriate to smaller organizations (Scullion 1999).

(f) There is evidence that the performance of managers on international assignments continues to be a problem for many companies who continue to underestimate the complex nature of the HRM problems and issues arising from the internationalization of business (Caligiuri and Stroh 1995; Brewster and Harris 1999), and growing evidence to suggest that for companies new to the international arena, business failures may often be linked to poor management of human resources (Forster and Johnsen 1996).

(g) Recent research on international companies has revealed a movement away from more traditional hierarchical organizational structures towards the network organization where greater decentralization is facilitated by the development of networks of personal relationships that work through horizontal communication channels (Bartlett and Ghoshal 1990; Forsgren 1990). It is argued that HR plays a key role in network organizations and that personal networks and informal communication are important means of control (Marschan, Welch and Welch 1997).

(h) There is growing evidence that in a rapidly globalizing environment, many international companies have less difficulty determining which strategies to pursue than how to implement them and that a firm may find it difficult to adapt its control structures to the imperatives of globalization (Bartlett and Ghoshal 1998). It has been argued that the success of any global or transnational strategy has less to do with structural innovations than developing an often radically different organizational culture (Bartlett and Ghoshal 1998), which suggests that HR strategy plays a more significant role in implementation and control in the international firm.

Finally, in the next decade it has been argued that the international business environment will be characterized by greater turbulence and complexity, new economic alignments, new sources of competition, the rapid growth of the emerging markets, globalization and fragmentation of markets, the growth of SME internationalization, the emergence of new regional trading blocs and new forms of international alliances which involve competitive as well as co-operative collaboration (Parker 1998) which suggests that the challenges for international HRM will become perhaps even more demanding in the future.

While the majority of international HRM research continues to focus on providing guidance and advice to firms on how to select, develop and manage expatriate managers (Kochan et al. 1992), there is a growing literature which seeks to contribute to a better understanding of the relationship between international strategy and HRM (De Cieri and Dowling 1999; Schuler *et al*. 1993; Dowling *et al*. 1999; Hendry 1994). It has been argued that the fundamental strategic problem for top managers in international firms is balancing the economic need for integration with the social, cultural and political pressures for local responsiveness (Bartlett and Ghoshal 1989, 1999; Prahalad and Doz 1987). The underlying challenge is that, while the nature of global business calls for consistency in the management of people, cultural diversity requires adaptation and differentiation (Laurent 1986). These realities involve a balance between centralized control of HRM strategy and responsiveness to local circumstances (Kamoche 1996).

STRATEGIC MANAGEMENT AND IHRM

There is a growing stream of research which argues that at the international level the firm's strategic choices impose constraints or limits on the range of international HRM options (De Cieri and Dowling 1999). The argument is that there should be distinct differences in international HRM policy and practice in multi-domestic and transnational or globally integrated firms (Kobrin 1992; Schuler *et al*. 1993). Recent empirical research reported below examines the role of the corporate HR function in different types of international firm (Scullion and Starkey 2000). Other researchers link international HRM staffing policy and practice to strategy (Edstrom and Lorange 1997; Scullion 1996) while others suggest linkages between the product life cycle stage/international strategy and HRM policy and practice (Adler and Ghadar 1990; Milliman *et al*. 1991). Increasingly the central issue for MNCs is not to identify the best IHRM policy per se but rather to find the best fit for the firm's strategy, structure and HRM approach. While global strategy is a significant determinant of IHRM policy and practice, it has been argued that international human resources are a strategic resource which should affect strategy formulation as well as its implementation (Harvey 1997).

De Cieri and Dowling (1999) identify a stream of research that has been termed 'strategic international human resource management' (SIHRM). It examines the HRM issues and activities that result from, and impact on, the strategic activities and international concerns of multinationals. Schuler *et al*. (1993: 720) define SIHRM as:

> human resource management issues, functions and policies and practices that result from the strategic activities of multinational enterprises and that impact the international concerns and goals of those enterprise.

The SIHRM models draw on new theoretical work in both strategic management and HRM including institutional theory and the resource based view of the firm and partly due to developments in this area it has been argued that theory building in IHRM has advanced to a second phase (Dowling *et al*. 1999). However, while De Cieri and Dowling (1999) accept that the emergence of SIHRM as an area of study has been a useful development, they suggest it may be more useful to think in terms of strategic HRM in multinationals which allows a more balanced view to be taken of the similarities and differences between international and domestic HRM. De Cieri and Dowling (1999) develop a revised framework of strategic HRM in multinational firms which highlights that IHRM activities are influenced by both endogenous and exogenous factors. This research draws on the emerging body of strategic HRM literature that examines the relationships between endogenous characteristics, SHRM strategy and competitive advantage (Becker and Gerhart 1996; Dyer and Reeves 1995). Some empirical research has suggested that international firms will gain competitive advantage by using strategic HRM practices to support business objectives (Kobrin 1994), while other researchers point to the need for more empirical research on the nature of the relationship between strategic HRM policies and performance in international firms (Harzing 1999).

The role of corporate HR in the international firm

The roles and functions of corporate headquarters has received much research attention (Goold and Campbell 1987; Foss 1997); however, little attention has been paid to the role of the corporate HR function, particularly in the context of the international firm. Earlier research on the issue of board level representation by personnel directors in the UK and in Europe indicated a relatively weak position of personnel in the corporate office (Winkler 1974; Miller 1987). Marginson *et al.* (1993) revealed that there was a main board director in 30 per cent of UK companies. However, a survey of European companies found that the HR function is represented at board level in 49 per cent of organizations employing more than 200 employees (Brewster 1994). There has also been considerable research on the issue of HR managers' involvement in strategic decision making. The British evidence from the first and second company-level industrial relations surveys suggests that HR involvement in strategic decisions is patchy and mostly concerned with implementation rather than formulation of strategy (Marginson *et al.* 1988, 1993). Brewster's (1994) survey of European companies reported that around 50 per cent of HR managers across Europe felt that they were proactively engaged in the development of corporate strategy and that considerable variation existed across Europe on this issue.

Some US studies highlight the limited influence of HR managers on corporate strategy (Swiercz and Spencer 1992), while other studies suggest a more influential role for top HR executives (Tsui and Gomez-Mejia 1988). Similarly, while it has been argued that the status of HR managers has risen due to the perception that its contribution to business performance has increased (Ferris *et al.* 1991), other US studies suggest that the HR function remains low in influence relative to other major functions (Kochan and Osterman 1991). Few would argue, however, with the view of Hunt and Boxall (1998: 770): 'While there is some divergence of opinion, the dominant view in the international literature is that HR specialists, senior or otherwise, are not typically key players in the development of corporate strategy.'

The role of corporate HR: the UK debate

In the mid 1980s Purcell, on the basis of case study evidence, argued that there had been a considerable downgrading of the corporate personnel department (Purcell 1985; Purcell and Gray 1986). However, research undertaken on the largest 100 private sector employers in the UK indicated that the tendency for corporate personnel departments to be downgraded was far from universal and showed that some corporations in very different sectors of the economy had large corporate personnel departments undertaking a wide range of activities while others had a much smaller team of corporate personnel executives with a more limited role (Sisson and Scullion 1985). Purcell and Ahlstrand (1994), on the other hand, argued that the overall shift to decentralization of key activities has meant that corporate HR managers were playing more of a monitoring and control function and they questioned the justification for the continued existence of the corporate HR department.

In these studies, however, the links between the growing internationalization of the companies and the new corporate HR roles were not explored. This is surprising for a number of reasons: First, British capital is more globally oriented than that of any other major advanced economy (Edwards *et al.* 1996). British companies are unusual in the extent to which their assets are located overseas rather than at home (Marginson 1994). Second, in the 1990s there was a significant increase in the pace of internationalization of UK companies (Dicken 1998). Third, British firms are well known for their short-term focus and lack of attention to training and management development (Storey and Sisson 1993). An important question here is to what extent does this tradition constrain the ability of British multinationals to develop an international cadre of managers (Edwards *et al.* 1996)?

The corporate HR function and internationalization

Contrary to Purcell and Alhstrand's (1994) conclusion 'that a modern role for the corporate personnel role in British companies had yet to be fully discovered', a recent empirical study of 30 UK MNCs identified an emerging agenda for corporate HR in international firms which focuses on senior management development, succession planning, and developing a cadre of international managers and is conceptualized as a strategic concern with developing the core competences of the organization (Scullion and Starkey 2000). This built on earlier work which identified managing senior managers as a key role for the Corporate HR function (Sisson and Scullion 1985; Marginson *et al.* 1988, 1993; Hendry 1990; Storey, Edwards and Sisson 1997).

Three distinctive groups of companies were identified by the Scullion and Starkey (2000) study: centralized HR companies, decentralized HR companies and transition HR companies.

Centralized HR companies

The first group comprised ten centralized HR companies (six global companies and four international financial service companies), all of which had large, well-resourced corporate HR departments which exercised centralized control over the careers and mobility of senior management positions world-wide, including expatriate transfers which reflected the need for a high degree of co-ordination and control in these companies. Centralized control was reinforced by group-wide appraisal and job evaluation and through the rewards system for senior managers which increasingly aligned rewards with longer-term global business strategy (Tilghman 1994; Pennings 1993; Bradley *et al.* 1988).

In the global firms, international assignments increasingly became central to the organizational and career development process (Pascale 1990) and the management development function role of the corporate HR function became increasingly important for host country nationals, third country nationals and for high potential staff (Scullion and Starkey 2000). The global firms tended to utililize much further than the decentralized firms the practice of inpatriation, i.e. developing host country nationals or third country nationals through developmental transfers to corporate HQ (Harvey *et al.* 1999c). In the global firms the identification and development of high potential staff world-wide was a key challenge for corporate HR (Stroh and Caligiuri 1998; Harvey *et al.* 1999a, 1999b). These firms also established comprehensive career planning systems and the greater degree of central support for international management development reflected an increasingly strategic role for the corporate HR function.

Decentralized companies

The second group comprised 16 companies including 11 manufacturing multinationals and 5 service multinationals. These companies tended to have only one or two corporate HR executives who undertook a more limited range of activities than their counterparts in the first group reflecting the logic of the decentralization. However, two-thirds of the decentralized companies reported an increased influence of corporate HR over the management of top management and senior expatriates in the previous five years. In the highly decentralized international businesses this centralized control was strictly limited to senior managers and co-ordination of international transfers of managers was more problematic than in the global companies due to greater tensions between the short-term needs of the operating companies and the long-term strategic management development needs of the business. Yet increasingly corporate HR had recently used informal and subtle management processes to introduce a degree of corporate integration into the decentralized firm (Scullion and Starkey 2000). Similarly, central control over expatriates had been established relatively recently in a number of the firms reflecting a shift away from the excesses of the highly decentralized approach which was fashionable in the late 1980s (Storey *et al.* 1997).

Transition HR companies

The third group comprised four highly internationalized, well-established international companies, all of which had medium-sized corporate HR departments staffed by a relatively small group of corporate HR executives. Management development and the management of the careers and mobility of expatriates and senior managers was under stronger centralized control than in the decentralized companies. The centre could use subtle and informal methods which achieved a higher degree of central control than that suggested by the formal structures without compromising the internal consistency of their decentralized control system. The influence of the corporate HR function over the management of senior expatriates and the development of high potential managers in the subsidiary companies had grown considerably in these companies reflecting the switch towards a less decentralized approach in the early to mid 1990s. This supports the findings of recent research which suggests that recentralization is a significant new trend (Arkin 1999).

This discussion suggests that the role of the corporate HR function varies considerably in different types of international firms. Many organizations operate with a global and centralized HRM strategy for top managers and high potential executives, and a polycentric and decentralized one for all their other employees, suggesting that in practice many firms operate with a dual system where corporate HR manages a core of senior staff and key personnel while the rest of lower level management and staff are managed at the subsidiary level (Scullion and Starkey 2000).

Control mechanisms in the international firm

The problems of control in any diversified, multi-divisional firm are exacerbated in the multinational where operations are dispersed over considerable geographic and cultural distances and the environment is complex and heterogeneous (Baliga and Jaeger 1984). Edstrom and Galbraith (1977) suggest three modes of control in the MNE: (1) personal or direct control; (2) bureaucratic control which relies on recording and reporting, and (3) control by socialization where the 'functional behaviours and rules for determining them were learned and internalised by individuals thereby obviating the need for procedures, hierarchical communication and surveillance'. Edstrom and Galbraith (1977) argue that control through centralization is impossible in the large organization. In the multinational context, bureaucratic control involves transferring home country nationals and expatriates who remain 'the agent of the centre in the periphery' (Kobrin 1992).

Dowling *et al.* Schuler (1999) suggest a twofold taxonomy: output control which involves monitoring through data and cultural control which tends to be behavioural and subjective ... 'social interaction, personnel transfers, and the socialisation of employees to direct and control subsidiary performance'. It has been argued, however, that control modes may change as the firm's strategy evolves over time. During the early ethnocentric stage of a firm's international involvement home country expatriates exercise tight control. As strategy becomes polycentric, there is a marked decline in the number of expatriates abroad and their function shifts to communicate and co-ordination of strategic objectives. Finally, with globalization and evolution of a geocentric strategy there is a need for a broad range of executives with international experience (Adler and Bartholomew 1992).

Recent research on MNCs has revealed a movement away from more traditional organizational structures towards network organizations (Bartlett and Ghoshal 1990). Earlier studies of headquarter–subsidiary relationships tended to stress the flows from headquarters to subsidiary, examining the relationships mainly in the context of control and co-ordination. However, for many relatively internationalized firms this approach has significant limitations as the former periphery of subsidiaries can develop into significant centres for investments, key activities and influence (Dowling *et al.* 1999), and it is more realistic to regard some MNCs as loosely coupled political systems rather than tightly bonded, homogeneous, hierarchically controlled systems (Forsgren 1990). In respect of these developments Bartlett and Ghoshal (1990) have developed the notion of the MNC as an interorganizational system – a network of exchange relationships among different organizational units including external organizations (e.g. host governments, customers, suppliers,) as well as HQ and national subsidiaries.

The management of network MNCs is complex (Forsgren 1989) and personal networks and informal communication are important means of control in this type of multinational (Marschan, Welch and Welch 1997). Research suggests that MNCs can exert centralized control through the use of expatriates who may be trusted to implement corporate policies and procedures, and becomes a de facto centralizing control mechanism. Since network relationships are built and maintained through personal contact, staffing decisions are crucial to the effective management of the linkages that the various subsidiaries have established (Doz and Hamel 1998).

Finally, there is growing evidence that for many international firms the problems associated with the implementation of international strategy are now paramount (Bartlett and Ghoshal 1998). In the global firm, bureaucratic and output-based control which relies on monitoring and recording data becomes less important than control through socialization which requires more frequent transfers of personnel and integration of expatriates into the local culture. For example, informal controls become more important as management tasks become more uncertain and unstructured, as is likely to be the case with cross-national mergers (Marschan, Welch and Welch 1997). In this context, as structural forms of control defer to culturally based social control, the HR strategy emerges as the primary device for strategic implementation and control in the global/transnational firm (Scullion and Starkey 2000).

International HRM and learning

The strategic management literature suggests that learning, knowledge acquisition and adaptation are important potential sources of competitive advantage in international firms (Grant and Spender 1996; Prahalad and Hamel 1990; Kamoche 1997). A recent study identifies the issue of 'learning how to learn' as a key source of competitive advantage (Inkpen and Crossan 1995). Further, it has been suggested that Japanese firms are more adept than Western firms at maximizing learning opportunities (Hedlund and Nonaka 1993). Recent research suggests that corporate HR should attempt to meet the key strategic challenge of learning how to learn and seize the opportunity to add value to the organization through effectively supporting the organization's strategic learning objectives (Scullion and Starkey 2000). Many US organizations have recently created a position called chief learning officer (CLO) who is responsible for developing the human talent of the organization on a world-wide scale and for developing a global learning environment (Stroh and Caligiuri 1988). The creation of a global learning environment is at the same time a major challenge and a major opportunity for IHRM managers. The major challenge is to determine how best a learning environment can be developed in each country and to find the most effective ways of transferring learning across different national units. Pucik (1988: 93) argued that 'the transformation of the HR system to support the process of organizational learning is the key strategic task facing the HR function in firms engaged in international cooperative ventures'. Pucik (1992) further argued that global organizational learning is driven by teamwork across borders, acceptance of risk and the willingness to invest in new initiatives. It has been argued that this learning can be accelerated by the creation of a common strategic vision and that a willingness to tap into the potential of local managers increases employee involvement and commitment and creates greater opportunities for learning (Cyr and Schneider 1996).

Hamel (1991) argued that collaboration may provide an opportunity for one partner to internalize the skills of the other and suggests that the strategic agenda for the HRM function in firms involved in international alliances should be centred around the process of learning. In the context of competitive collaboration the competitive advantage of the firm can only be protected through the organization's ability to accumulate invisible assets through organizational learning. Given the importance of knowledge acquisition and skill building within international alliances (Hamel 1991), it has been argued that the transformation of the HR system to support the process of organizational learning is the key strategic task currently facing the HR function in many multinationals (Pucik 1988).

Scullion and Starkey (2000) argue that a major challenge for corporate HR is to make a vital contribution to support the strategic learning mission of the organization and to establish the HR function as a full strategic business partner. They suggest that the most exciting new territory for HRM specialists is the stewardship of core competence and organizational learning and argue that the HRM function needs to demonstrate how it contributes to an environment in which learning can flourish and how HRM policies and practices contribute to the learning of new skills, behaviours, and attitudes which support the strategic objectives of the organization.

INTERNATIONAL STAFFING

In IHRM research the topic of international staffing policies often occupies an important place, with considerable attention paid to the selection criteria for managers and on models to use in the staffing process. However, executive nationality policies in foreign subsidiaries usually emerge as the key issue in international staffing (Harzing 1999). Much of this research stems from concern about the high direct and indirect costs of making poor staffing decisions (Brewster 1991).

Executive nationality staffing policies

The research on executive nationality staffing policies indicates that a multinational company can choose from four options: (1) ethnocentric, (2) polycentric, (3) geocentric, (4) regio-centric (Heenan and Perlmutter 1979; Dowling *et al.* 1999). An ethnocentric approach to staffing results in all key positions at headquarters and subsidiaries in a multinational company being filled by parent country nationals. Many organizations have traditionally relied on parent country nationals for staffing top management positions abroad for a number of reasons: (1) their technical and business expertise; (2) ability to transfer the headquarters culture to the foreign operation; (3) political understanding of the headquarters organization; (4) effective communication between headquarters and the subsidiary; (5) the perceived lack of qualified host country nationals (HCNs), (6) the perceived greater ability of the PCNs to transfer know-how from the parent to the subsidiary; and (7) as a means of social control over the subsidiary (Harzing 1999). In this approach the primary function of expatriates has been as a control mechanism and secondarily, to provide managerial expertise, management development and to qualify expatriates for progression into senior management (Harvey 1999a). Researchers have, however, identified a number of major problems with an ethnocentric approach: (1) parent country nationals continue to experience difficulties adjusting to international assignments; (2) this approach to staffing limits the promotion opportunities of local managers which may lead to low morale and increased turnover; (3) parent country nationals are not always sensitive to the needs and expectations of their host country subordinates; (4) expatriates are very expensive in relation to host country nationals and often cost three or four times normal salary (Dowling *et al.* 1999; Black *et al.* 1999). Finally, researchers have long assumed that management expertise and knowledge to develop effective global management strategies originate within the parent organization. However, there is growing evidence that subsidiaries can play an important role in the creation and maintenance of global competitive advantage (Birkinshaw and Morrison 1998) suggesting the importance of alternative management pools for overseas subsidiary management staffing (Harvey *et al.* 1999b).

A polycentric staffing policy is one where host country nationals are recruited to manage subsidiaries in their own country and parent country nationals occupy key positions in corporate headquarters. A number of advantages to this approach have been identified (Hamill 1999; Dowling *et al.* 1999): (1) It eliminates language barriers and the adjustment problems of expatriates and their families. (2) Employing HCNs allows the possibility of a lower profile in the host country. (3) A polycentric approach allows continuity of management within the host country. (4) The employment of HCNs is generally less expensive. (5) Finally, this approach enhances the morale and career opportunities of local staff.

The literature also identifies a number of disadvantages which may be associated with a polycentric policy (e.g. Dowling *et al.* 1999; Scullion 1995). The major difficulty is that of achieving effective communication between HCN managers at subsidiary level and the PCN managers at corporate headquarters. A second problem with the polycentric approach is the difficulties in exercising effective control over the subsidiaries that arise when a multinational firm becomes a loose federation of independent national units with weak links to corporate headquarters. A third problem with this approach concerns the career paths of HCN and PCN managers as both have very limited opportunities to gain experience abroad outside of their own country. This lack of international experience is a liability in an increasingly competitive international environment (Scullion 1999).

In the geocentric approach the best people are sought for key jobs throughout the organization, regardless of nationality. This approach has two main advantages. First, it enables a multinational firm to develop a pool of senior international managers and second, it reduces the tendency of national identification of managers with subsidiary units of the organization (Kobrin 1992; Black *et al.* 1999). Three main problems have been identified in implementing a geocentric staffing approach (Dowling *et al.* 1999). First, it is increasingly the case that many host countries use their immigration laws to require the employment of local nationals (HCNs) where possible. Second, a geocentric policy can be difficult to implement because of increased training, compensation and relocation costs. Third, the successful implementation of a geocentric staffing policy requires a highly centralized control of the staffing process and the reduced autonomy of subsidiary management may be resented (Scullion 1996).

Regional approaches to international staffing are likely to grow in importance given that cross-border regional integration strategies are of increasing significance for multinational firms reflecting the development of major regional trading blocs (Segal-Horn and Faulkner 1999). However, it has been suggested that the choices by MNCs between stronger global structures and cross-border regional integration are sometimes influenced more by the interests of local divisional managers than by the

MNCs approach to strategic international expansion (Forsgren 1995). In the regional approach, host country managers may be transferred between the countries of a region (e.g. Europe) to regional headquarters but there is limited mobility of managers outside the region. One advantage of this approach is that HCN managers have the opportunity to influence decisions and compete for jobs at the regional level. In addition, it has been argued that the development of a regional approach can help the MNC through the evolution from an ethnocentric or polycentric approach towards a geocentric approach (Morrison, Roth and Ricks 1991). On the other hand, the disadvantages of the regional approach are that it can lead to identification with regional rather than global objectives and may limit the development of a global approach (Segal Horn and Faulkner 1999), and while career paths for local managers are improved at the regional level there are few opportunities for progression at parent headquarters level (Dowling *et al.* 1999).

The literature taking a more strategic approach on the issue of nationality of subsidiary managers has emphasized the need for some multinationals to have a global strategy with the flexibility to shift resources among units (Bonache and Fernandez 1999). A global strategy which requires that staffing decisions be centralized at corporate headquarters means trade-offs for the MNC (Evans *et al.* 1989a). First, there is less flexibility in adapting to local markets. Second, when a firm pursues a global strategy, it frequently emphasizes the organizational culture world-wide which may lead to conflict between national culture and corporate culture and limit consistency in the implementation of international HRM within the firm (Laurent 1986).

Comparative international staffing policies

The empirical research on trends in international staffing policies and practices reveals a significant contrast between European and US firms (Tung 1981, 1982, 1987; Brewster and Burnois 1991; Mayrhofer 1992). For example, the findings of an empirical study on UK MCNs highlighted considerable differences between UK and American experience in the early 1990s. The majority of UK firms continued to rely heavily on expatriates to run and control their overseas operations (Scullion 1994), which raises serious questions about the ability and commitment of some British MNCs to identify and develop host country managers in their foreign operations (Hailey 1999). In contrast Kobrin suggested that the tendency of US MNCs to reduce the number of expatriates had gone too far by the late 1980s and argued that US MNCs could face major strategic management control problems where managers identified with local units rather than with global corporate objectives (Kobrin 1988: 68–73). Researchers have argued that the basic assumptions connected with international staffing in US MNCs only partly apply to Europe and suggest caution regarding an uncritical and unmodified adaptation of concepts derived in the North American context (Mayrhofer and Brewster 1996).

Much of the early research on international staffing was largely descriptive, prescriptive and lacking in analytical rigour. Brewster and Scullion's (1997) critique indicates that staffing policies are often developed in isolation from other expatriation policies and fail to connect expatriate selection to the company's international strategy. More recently, however, research has shifted towards considering staffing questions in a more strategic context. In an effort to consider the range of possible headquarters–subsidiary relationships, researchers are suggesting more 'variety' (Bonache and Fernandez 1999) in approaches to staffing and other IHRM activities. In certain subsidiaries, for example, an ethnocentric approach may be appropriate, in others, a polycentric approach may work better. Rather than adhering to a particular policy, researchers are urging MNCs to consider global strategy as well as local conditions in determining appropriate staffing approaches (Scullion 1997). Drawing on the theoretical notions of the resource based view Bonache and Fernandez (1999) have attempted to explain the strategic dimension of expatriate selection. This work clarifies the linkage between expatriates and competitive advantage by highlighting the importance of the transfer of tacit knowledge to new markets. It also identifies the need to pay attention to the international transfer of teams and not just individual managers, which conflicts with the dominant trend in the expatriation literature.

Harzing's (1999) study highlights the importance of country specific factors and reports large differences between European countries in international staffing practices. In her study Japan and Germany were at one extreme with a high level of expatriate presence (and high direct expatriate control) while the USA and the UK were at the opposite extreme. This would support the findings in Wolf's (1994) study which indicated that German MNCs had the largest number of PCNs in the managing director position and is also consistent with the study of Kopp (1994) which shows that Japanese companies employ the largest number of PCNs in their subsidiaries. Harzing's findings on US MNCs are consistent with the earlier work of Kobrin (1988) who argued that US MNCs were progressively reducing the numbers of expatriates due to high costs and high expatriate failure rate, but are inconsistent with more recent research which suggests that the most common pattern among the majority of US MNCs is an increasing use of expatriates (ORC 1996). Harzing's findings are also at odds with recent work on British and Japanese MNCs. In the former case, Scullion (1994) shows that while half of British MNCs had developed policies to use HCNs to run foreign operations, in practice they continued to rely heavily on expariates to run their foreign operations. Similarly, Harzing's (1999) findings on Japanese MNCs would reinforce the conventional wisdom which holds that Japanese firms use large numbers of expatriates and are reluctant to allow HCNs a significant role in subsidiary management or to advance into regional or corporate level management. However, recent research on a large sample of Japanese subsidiaries challenges the notion that Japanese firms are unwilling to reduce their use of expatriates, and indicates that the number of Japanese expatriates is declining and has been for some time (Beamish and Inkpen 1998). Two main reasons are offered to explain this significant trend. First, the rapid increase in the number of Japanese subsidiaries has made it impossible to use expatriates at the same level as in the past. Second, Japanese firms are beginning to recognize the importance of empowering local managers (Beamish and Inkpen 1988) and are moving away from the overdependence on parent country national managers which had been described as the 'Achilles heel' of Japanese MNCs (Bartlett and Yoshihara 1988).

Some researchers have also paid attention to the country of location of the subsidiary, the industry and the country of origin of headquarters and it has been argued that the strongest and most direct type of expatriate control is found when all three factors work in the same direction (Harzing 1999). For example, it has been argued that direct expatriate control is particularly strong in the Far Eastern or Latin American subsidiaries of Japanese and German MNCs operating in the automobile or electronic industries, and much less important in the subsidiaries of US, French and British MNCs located in Scandinavian or Anglo-Saxon countries and operating in the food or paper industry (Harzing 1999). These findings support earlier research (Boyacigiller 1990; Wolf 1994) which found a higher level of parent country nationals when cultural distance was higher. These findings are also consistent with the earlier work of Tung (1981, 1982) who found that subsidiaries in Asian countries employed the largest percentage of parent country nationals, closely followed by subsidiaries in Latin American countries while subsidiaries in Europe and the USA employed a relatively larger amount of host country nationals in top positions. Harzing's (1999) study confirmed that subsidiary characteristics such as size, age, entry mode and function also have an impact on the level of expatriate presence in subsidiaries. More expatriates were found in young, large and underperforming subsidiaries while expatriate presence was lower in acquisitions than in greenfields (Hamill 1989).

INTERNATIONAL MANAGEMENT DEVELOPMENT

Due to pressures arising from intensified global competition some MNCs have attempted to increase the cost-effectiveness of their expatriates by paying more attention to the preparation and training for the international assignment (Harris and Brewster 1999). The high cost of expatriate failure is a further reason for companies undertaking development programmes for expatriates (Dowling *et al.* 1999).

Two problems make training and development for international assignments more complex than for domestic assignments. First, since the stress associated with a foreign assignment falls on all family members the issue of training programmes for the spouse and family need to be addressed (Linehan 1999). Second, the growing significance of repatriation problems for many MNCs (Black *et al.* 1998; Scullion 1994) highlights the failure by international firms to develop training programmes to facilitate re-entry of expatriate executives into the domestic organization. Comparative studies of MNC training practices found that US MNCs tend to use pre-departure training programmes much less frequently than European and Japanese firms (Tung 1982; Brewster 1991). A study of British MNCs reported that over 60 per cent of firms provided some predeparture training for some expatriate assignments (Scullion 1994), while US research suggests that only around 30 per cent of US managers destined for international assignments receive cross-cultural training (Black 1988; Black and Mendenhall 1990) mainly because top management generally does not believe the training is necessary or effective (Black *et al.* 1999). McEnery and DesHarnais (1990) estimated that more than half of US companies operating abroad provided no form of predeparture preparation.

Recent research on European MNCs (Price Waterhouse survey, 1997–98) showed that cultural awareness training is still the most common form of pre-departure training but it continues to be offered more on a voluntary basis rather than a compulsory one. Only 13 per cent of the firms surveyed always provided their expatriates with cultural training, though almost 50 per cent provided cultural briefings for 'difficult' assignments compared with 21 per cent in their 1995 survey. The evidence suggests that other forms of preparation – briefings, shadowing, look-see visits – are more frequent than formal training programmes and may be more cost effective (Brewster and Scullion 1997). One recent trend is that MNCs are extending their pre-departure training programmes to include the spouse/partner and children, reflecting the growing awareness of the link between expatriate performance and family adjustment (Harvey 1998).

Several models of training and development for expatriate managers have been developed including contingency models which consider the task, the individual and the environment before deciding the depth of training required (Tung 1981; Mendenhall and Oddou 1985; and Mendenhall, Dunbar and Oddou 1990). More recently, researchers have developed an integrated framework for pre-departure training which will allow organizations to tailor pre-departure programmes to the needs of each individual expatriate, taking into account both job and individual variables, together with assessment of existing levels of competence (Harris and Brewster 1999). A more tailored approach could become more important in the future given that traditional expatriate assignments are becoming less significant and that expatriate training needs are rapidly changing (Brewster and Scullion 1997). Also, it has been argued that due to the expected growth in female expatriation companies will need to re-evaluate the training and cross-cultural briefing sessions provided for female expatriates because the focus of most cultural training programmes centres on the experiences of male expatriates (Linehan and Scullion 2001; Forster 1999b). Meanwhile other researchers have questioned why companies often assume that cross-cultural training should take place only before the international transfer and they highlight the need for training and development throughout the assignment (Baumgarten 1995). However, the evidence suggests that in practice expatriate training programme design and practice is still largely done informally, with little regard to findings in the research literature (Black et al. 1999). Finally it is argued that the development of international managers in the future will involve more frequent cross-border job swaps, short assignments or assignments to multi-cultural project teams reflecting the further decline of the traditional expatriate assignment (Forster, 2000; Brewster and Scullion 1997).

International development for host country nationals and third country nationals

There is growing recognition that the probability of a global organization developing a competitive advantage will be reduced without an adequate supply of qualified managers, yet shortages of 'international managers' is becoming an increasing problem for international firms (Bartlett and Ghoshal 1999; Gregerson et al 1998). This is in large part due to failures to effectively recruit, retain and develop host country managers (Harvey et al. 1999c). A number of factors make the recruitment of host country managers more difficult and costly compared to recruiting in the home country. These include the following: lack of knowledge of local labour markets; ignorance of the local education system and the status of qualifications; language and cultural problems at interviews; and trying to transfer recruitment methods which work well at home to foreign countries (Scullion 1994).

Many MNCs have devoted most of their management development efforts to their parent country national managers and have tended to neglect the training and development needs of their host country national managers (Shaeffer 1989). Researchers have identified a number of important lessons for MNCs which are seeking to provide management development for such managers. First is the need to avoid the mistake of simply exporting parent-country training and development programmes to other countries (Dowling *et al.* 1999). Second, the management development programmes need to be linked to the strategic situation in each country as well as the overall strategy of the firm (Scullion and Brewster 1998). Third, and most importantly, is the need to utilize much further the practice of inpatriation – which has been defined as the selective process of transferring host country nationals and/or third country nationals into the domestic organization of the MNC on a permanent or semi-permanent basis (Harvey *et al.* 1999a). Inpatriate managers have been seen as firm-level strategic resources that increase the global competitiveness of the organization and as 'linking pins' between the organization's headquarters and foreign subsidiaries (Harvey and Buckley 1997). It has been argued that this type of international transfer exposes host country nationals to the headquarters' corporate culture and facilitates their developing a corporate perspective which encourages the development of global teams (Oddou and Kerr 1993). More recently it has been argued that the main advantage of inpatriation lies in its ability to facilitate competitive advantage through an increased emphasis on developing multiple strategic objectives through multiculturalism, which it is suggested will be increasingly important in the future to meet the demands of the growing emerging markets (Harvey *et al.* 1999b). Several studies have identified the need for a closer study of the barriers to bringing foreign nationals to head office. For example, relocating dual-career couples is becoming a world-wide issue for many multinational firms (Harvey 1998) and there is growing recognition that some cultures are less mobile and less willing to move (Brewster and Scullion 1997). The type of incentive and compensation packages for those 'hard-to-move' high potentials will also be an important dimension in a company's ability to bring people to the corporate office (Bonache and Fernandez 1997). Recently researchers have argued that strategic flexibility is necessary in international compensation and developed a strategic flexibility model of international compensation (Sparrow 1999) which they suggest will help MNCs cope with the increasing complexities they face in international compensation (Bradley *et al.* 1999). Finally, there have been few studies examining the performance appraisal of host country employees. One recent empirical study using research evidence from MNCs operating in China reported that while western MNCs have mainly implemented standardized appraisal practices for their local managers in China, there is a need for western MNCs to make some adjustments to their appraisal practices, and particularly the style of communication in appraisal discussions, in the Chinese context (Lindholm *et al.* 1999). This study also highlights the need for further research which directly investigates the experiences and perceptions of appraisal from the point of view of the host country employees (as most studies mainly deal with expatriate experiences of appraisal) and calls for comparative studies of MNC performance appraisal practices in different host countries.

Strategies for internationalizing managers

Researchers have identified a number of principal strategies used by firms to internationalize management (Evans 1992). First, companies are increasingly sending young high potential managers on international assignments, partly for developmental purposes (Scullion 1997; Black and Gregerson 1999). This was in sharp contrast to the earlier practice when many MNCs relied on developing a cadre of career expatriates who moved from one international position to the next (Brewster 1991). Second, there is a more general trend to give international experience to a wider range of managers and not just to a relatively small group of expatriates. Increasing numbers of international firms were also using short-term developmental assignments in order to develop larger pools of employees with international experience (Black et al. 1999). Third, there has been a rapid growth in the importance of external recruitment to fill management positions abroad (Brewster and Harris 1999), which represented a significant change for many MNCs who had relied mainly on internal recruitment for expatriate positions (Scullion 1994). Fourth, increasing numbers of companies are seeking to sell themselves more effectively to graduates through various types of marketing designed to highlight the international dimension of their activities and some British MNCs have widened their source of graduate recruitment to include some continental European countries (Brewster and Scullion 1997). Fifth, there is growing recognition of the importance of developing effective international management development programmes to help secure an adequate supply of senior international managers (Black et al. 1999; Gregerson et al. 1998). Sixth, the growth of inpatriation can provide a complementary source of global managers and it has been argued that there has been an emerging shift from emphasis on expatriation to an emphasis on inpatriation in the strategic staffing practices of MNCs (Harvey et al. 1999d).

Women in international management

As global competition intensifies, competition for global leaders to manage overseas operations will steadily intensify and MNCs must develop new ways to identify, attract, develop and retain international executive talent (Gregerson et al. 1998). The creativity and resourcefulness in finding an ample number of qualified managers who can manage across cultures effectively becomes the strategic challenge of IHRM managers (Harvey et al. 1999b). Yet, the evidence suggests that the number of female global assignees is proportionately low in relation to the overall size of the qualified labour pool. In North America less than 14 per cent of global assignees are women compared to the 45 per cent of women in management generally (Caligiuri et al. 1999) and the figures for Australia (Hede and O'Brien 1996) and Europe are considerably lower (Linehan et al. 2000a). Linehan and Scullion (2000) found that while organizations may be prepared to promote women through their domestic management hierarchy, few women are given opportunities to expand their career horizons through access to international careers.

The lack of willingness to recruit and develop women as international managers is worrying as recent research conducted on the outcome of women's global assignments has indicated that female expatriates are generally successful in their global assignments (Caligiuri and Tung 1999; Caligiuri et al. 1999) and that in many ways women are well suited to international team management (Harris 1995). Recent research has highlighted company support (e.g. cross-cultural training and relocation assistance, assistance with finding suitable schools) and support from the spouse as key components in female expatriates' 'success', and suggests that senior women expatriates may have more positive experiences on international assignments than their junior counterparts (Caligiuri et al. 1999; Linehan et al. 2000b). Recent research suggests that in the international context a mentoring relationship is even more important than in domestic management; however, there are not enough women in senior international managerial positions to act as mentors for other women and finding a suitable mentor may be problematic (Linehan 1999). An important informal barrier for women in international management is the lack of networking facilities. Linehan and Scullion (2001) suggest that the exclusion of females from male networking groups perpetuates the more exclusively male customs, traditions and negative attitudes towards female international managers and they identify the detrimental effects of these covert barriers which include blocked promotion, blocked career development, discrimination, occupational stress and lower salaries. They also suggested that corporate or organizational barriers are especially embedded in the managerial processes of traditional industries, with the newer, faster-moving industries such as the electronics, software and e-commerce sectors affording women greater opportunity in career progression.

Repatriation

The second area which impacts on the supply of international managers is the failure by many companies to adequately address repatriation problems. The repatriation of managers has been identified as the major IHRM problem for multinational companies in the UK and North America (Black *et al.* 1999; Scullion 1993; Forster 2000). For many UK MNCs this problem had become more acute in recent years because, for many companies, expansion of foreign operations had taken place at the same time as the rationalization of UK operations and a key problem for many companies was finding suitable posts for repatriates (Forster 1999b). From the repatriate perspective other problems associated with re-integrating into the UK are loss of status, loss of autonomy, loss of career direction and a feeling that international experience is undervalued by the company (Johnston 1991; Scullion 1994).

There is growing recognition that where companies are seen to deal unsympathetically with the problems faced by expatriates on re-entry, especially concerns about losing out on opportunities at home, managers will be more reluctant to accept the offer of international assignments (Scullion and Brewster 1998). Research in North America indicates that 20 per cent of all managers who complete foreign assignments wish to leave their company on return and retention of expatriate managers was also a growing problem for many MNCs (Adler 1986; Black 1999). Yet, while it is widely accepted that the costs of expatriate turnover are considerable (Dowling *et al.* 1999), many firms have not developed formal repatriation policies and programmes to assist managers and their families with repatriation difficulties or introduced mentor systems designed to assist the career progression of the expatriate manager (Stroh *et al.* 1998). Recent research indicated that managing repatriation was more problematic in the decentralized companies due to the weaker influence of the Corporate HR function and the less well developed career and succession planning systems (Scullion and Starkey 2000). Also, there is a dearth of research on the repatriation of female executives presumably because of their relative scarcity (Linehan and Scullion 2000). In practice, many firms continue to adopt an ad hoc sink or swim attitude towards both employees and their families and many expatriate managers continue to experience the repatriation process as falling far short of expectations (Stroh *et al.* 1998). Research suggests that repatriation should be regarded as an integral part of the process of expatriation (Forster 2000) which would involve a fundamental re-examination of the expatriate pyschological contract (Guzzo *et al.* 1994).

Barriers to international mobility

The number of expatriates MNCs are sending on international assignments is increasing steadily and will increase further in the future; however, the availability of people who are willing to accept global assignments is not increasing at the same rate (Caligiuri and Cascio 1998) and research shows that finding enough of the right people with the requisite skills for global assignments is one of the greatest IHRM concerns of MNCs (Stroh and Caligiuri 1998).

Studies of UK MNCs indicated that international mobility was becoming more problematic in many firms due to several factors including continued rationalization in the UK which created uncertainties regarding re-entry, the growing unwillingness to disrupt the education of children, the growing importance of quality of life considerations and finally, continued uncertainty regarding international terrorism and political unrest (Scullion 1994; Forster and Johnsen 1996). A survey of expatriate managers indicated that 67 per cent of respondents felt that their spouse's reluctance to give up their own career was a major constraint to their international relocation (Barham and Devine 1991) More generally, concerns about dual-career problems and disruption to children's education are seen as major barriers to future international mobility by many companies in many different countries (Pierce and Delahaye 1996; Harvey, 1998). In the past, working spouses were less common, generally female and were prepared to follow their partners' career transfers. More frequently, now, however, spouses must also leave a job or career in order to follow their partner to a foreign country. It has been argued that corporate relocation policies should reflect the increase in diversity of the workforce including the growth of dual-career couples (Harvey 1997). The growing significance of the dual-career problem can be illustrated by two developments. First, increasingly more and more women have or seek careers and not just jobs. For many it would be impossible to continue their careers in a foreign country (Shaffer and Harrison 1998). Increasingly, international mobility is limited by the dual-career factor which also poses restrictions on the career development plans of multinationals. Second, there is some evidence to suggest that families are less willing to disrupt personal and social lives than was the case in the past (Barham and Devine 1991).

A recent study which addresses the dual-career paradigm of the expatriation process proposes that a multi-stage global mentoring programme could help to provide effective socialization of expatriates and could facilitate adjustment during the overseas assignment. It is argued that the need for mentors may be particularly acute for expatriate dual-career couples where the international relocation has a significant impact on the trailing spouse (Harvey *et al.* 1999c). Mentoring is seen to demonstrate a recognition and concern by the parent organization of the need for the expatriated couple to re-establish a new balance in the new culture by recognizing the links between work and non-work life spheres during an international assignment. However, it is recognized that, in practice, mentoring is an under-utilized instrument to improve expatriate adjustment (ibid.).

CONCLUSION

Few scholars and practictioners would regard IHRM as a scientific field still in the infancy stage of development. It can be argued that considerable progress has been made over the last decade given the relatively recent emergence of the discipline. Not only has there been a growing awareness of the importance of HRM in the global arena and a greater understanding of the international dimensions of HRM (Dowling *et al.* 1999), there has been considerable progress towards developing theoretical models of IHRM (De Cieri and Dowling 1999). The trend over recent years has been to extend the linkage of HRM with business strategy from the domestic into the international arena and there is growing recognition that IHRM must be linked to the strategic evolution of the firm (Scullion 1996; Ferner 1994). Also, while the vast majority of research in this area still involves US MNCs, there is a growing body of solid empirical research in Europe and elsewhere which highlights in some depth the major IHRM issues and challenges which firms face as they undergo the internationalization process and charts the IHRM strategies, policies and practices firms pursue in response to globalization (Brewster and Harris 1999). This is an important development as studies suggest that there are major differences between US, Asian and European firms with regard to IHRM policies (Peterson *et al.* 1996; Dowling *et al.* 1999). While much of the recent research is less descriptive and more analytical than earlier work in the field, it still has an operational and practical orientation rather than a strategic orientation (Harzing 1999; Ferner 1997) and detailed case comparisons which are conducive to theory building are still relatively rare (Welch 1994). Further, empirical studies which integrate IHRM with the international corporate strategy of the firm are still difficult to find as are studies considering the integration of the various IHRM practices (Harzing 1999).

More recently some researchers have developed conceptual frameworks of strategic IHRM (Milliman *et al.* 1991; Schuler *et al.* 1993; Welch 1994; Taylor *et al.* 1996; De Cieri and Dowling 1999). These models draw on theoretical work both in strategy and HRM which highlights that IHRM activities are influenced by both endogenous and exogenous factors and suggest that MNCs will gain competitive advantage by using strategic HRM practices to support business objectives. However, there has been little research undertaken to empirically test the relationship between international strategy and IHRM, and there is a clear need for more empirical research on the nature of the relationship between strategic HRM policies and performance in international firms (Harzing 1999).

This chapter has also identified some elements which seek to contribute towards the establishment of a new research agenda in IHRM. While most IHRM studies have identified common IHRM issues and problems facing MNCs as they undergo the internationalization process, little progress has been made in developing multi-cultural, multi-country, multi-disciplinary research teams (Teagarden *et al.* 1995). The staffing of foreign operations also remains a critical issue in IHRM (Dowling *et al.* 1999) and in this area there is an urgent need for more large scale empirical international comparative work. Also, given the growth in importance of regional international business strategies, more attention should be paid to the growth of regional staffing policies which are also becoming more significant (Segal-Horn and Faulkner 1999). There is also an urgent need for more research on the recruitment, retention, development and management of host country national managers which this chapter has identified as a key challenge for MNCs, and particularly research which examines the experiences and perception of IHRM practices from the point of view of host country nationals. There is also a need for comparative studies of MNC IHRM practices as experienced by HCNs in different host countries. The problem of international mobility has been identified as a key factor determining the international capability of a firm and further research is needed both on the motivations for accepting international assignments and the barriers to international mobility. In this context there is a particular need for further work on the complex issues surrounding dual-career issues, lifestyle changes and the role of the spouse or partner.

This chapter has also identified the need for further research on the formal and informal barriers facing women who seek careers in international management and suggests that work on mentoring and networking for female international managers could be particularly fruitful. The changing nature of expatriation and the need for new models of expatriation have also been identified as areas for further research, particularly as dual-career, family and quality of life considerations and other factors are contributing to the decline of traditional patterns of expatriation. It was also suggested that IHRM in SME international organizations requires further research. The role of the corporate HR function in the international firm has been relatively neglected and requires further work, particularly in relation to the creation of a global learning environment and the most effective ways of transferring learning across different national units. Finally, there is a need for further empirical work on repatriation, particularly on the strategies and training approaches companies can develop to more effectively prepare expatriates for coming home. IHRM researchers should also seek to address a number of the criticisms of IHRM research made over the last decade which have not yet been fully answered. In particular Kochan *et al.*'s (1992) critique that IHRM research should be built round a broader set of questions which should consider the lessons and outcomes for all stakeholders and not just multinational firms and their managers is still valid. Also IHRM research is still open to the criticism that it fails to deal adequately with the management of managers as employees and it has been argued that an analytical perspective is needed which is capable of treating managers as employees and which enables researchers to be more sensitive to the dynamics of the management process in the MNCs (Edwards *et al.* 1993).

This chapter has suggested that international HRM must be linked to the international strategy of the firm and that its changing forms must be understood in relation to the strategic evolution of the international business firm. It has attempted to highlight some of the most important IHRM challenges and issues which firms face during the process of internationalization and globalization. Recent research suggests that international management development and, in particular, developing global leaders is a first priority in the management of international human resources in the global firm (Black and Gregerson 1999). In this context the growing role of the corporate HR function in the global firm regarding the management of senior managers can be linked to three trends which increase the need for corporate integration. First, the globalization of a wide range of industries. Second, the increasing degree of interdependence in some industries. Third, the need for increased flexibility in the deployment of resources (Scullion and Starkey 2000).

REFERENCES

Adler, N.J. and Bartholomew, S. (1992) 'Managing Globally Competent People', *Academy of Management Executive*, **6**: 52–64.

Adler, N. (1986) 'Women in Management Worldwide', *International Studies of Management and Organization*, **16**: 3–32.

Adler, N.J. and Ghadar, F. (1990) 'Strategic Human Resource Management: a Global Perspective', in R. Pieper, *Human Resource Management: an International Comparison*, Berlin: Walter de Gruyter.

Arkin, A. (1999) 'Return to Centre', *People Management*, 6 May: 34–41.

Baliga, B.R. and Jaeger, M.A. (1984) 'Multinational Corporations: Control Systems and Delegation Issues', *Journal of International Business Studies*, **3**(1): 25–40.

Bamber, G. and Lansbury, R.D. (eds) (1998) *International and Comparative Employment Relations*, London: Sage Publications.

Barham, K. and Devine, M. (1991) *The Quest for the International Manager: A Survey of Global Human Resource Strategies*, The Economist Intelligence Unit, London.

Bartlett, C and Ghoshal, S. (1999) *Managing Across Borders: The Transnational Solution, second edition*, London: Random House.

Bartlett, C.A. and Ghoshal, S. (1990) 'The Multinational Organization as an Interorganizational Network', *Academy of Management Review*, **16**(2): 262–90.

Bartlett, C. and Ghoshal, S. (1989) *Managing Across Borders: The Transnational Solution*, London: Hutchinson.

Bartlett, C.A. and Yoshihara, H. (1992) 'New Challenges for Japanese Multinationals: Is Organizational Adaptation Their Achilles Heel?', in V. Pucik N. Tichy and K. Barnett (eds) *Globalising Management: Creating and Leading the Competitive Organization*, London: John Wiley.

Baumgarten, K. (1995) 'The Training and Development of Staff for International Assignments', in A. Harzing and J. Van Ruyssevldt (eds) *International Human Resource Management*, London: Sage.

Birkinshaw, J. and Morrison, A. (1998) 'Building Firm Specific Advantage in Multinational Corporations: the Role of Subsidiary Initiative', *Strategic Management Journal*, **19**: 221–41.

Beamish, P.W. and Inkpen, A. (1998) 'Japanese Firms and the Decline of the Japanese Expatriate', *Journal of World Business*, **33**(1): 35–50.

Becker, B. and Gerhart, B. (1996) 'The Impact of Human Resource Management on Organizational Performance: Progress and Prospects', *Academy of Management Journal*, **39**(4): 779–801.

Black, J.S. and Mendenhall, M. (1990) 'Cross Cultural Training Effectiveness: A Review and a Theoretical Framework for Future Research', *Academy of Management Review*, **15**(1): 113–36.

Black, J.S. and Gregerson, H.B. (1999). 'The Right Way to Manage Expats', *Harvard Business Review*, March/April: 52–63.

Black, J.S., Gregerson, H.B., Mendenhall, M.E. and Stroh, L.K. (1999) *Globalizing People Through International Assignments*, Reading, MA: Addison-Wesley.

Bonache, J. and Fernandez, Z. (1999) 'Strategic Staffing in Multinational Companies: a Resource Based Approach', in Brewster, C. and Harris, H. (eds) *International HRM: Contemporary Issues in Europe*, Routledge: London.

Boyacigiller, N. (1990) 'The Role of Expatriates in the Management of Interdependence, Complexity and Risk in Multinational Corporations', *Journal of International Business Studies*, **21**(3): 357–81.

Boyacigiller, N. and Adler, N. (1991) 'The Parochial Dinosaur: Organizational Science in a Global Context', *Academy of Management Review*, **16**(2): 262–90.

Bradley, P., Hendry, C. and Perkins, S. (1999) 'Global or Multi – Local? The Significance of International Values in Reward Strategy', in C. Brewster and H. Harris (eds) *International HRM: Contemporary Issues in Europe*, London: Routledge.

Brewster, C. (1991) *The Management of Expatriates*, London: Kogan Page.

Brewster, C. (1994) 'The Integration of Human Resource Management and Corporate Strategy', in C. Brewster, and A. Hegewisch (eds) *Policy and Practice in European Human Resource Management: the Evidence and Analysis from the Price Waterhouse Cranfield Survey*, London: Routledge.

Brewster, C. and Burnois, F. (1991) 'A European Perspective on Human Resource Management', *Personnel Review*, **20**(6): 4–13.

Brewster, C. and Harris, H. (eds) (1999) *International HRM: Contemporary Issues in Europe*, Routledge: London.

Brewster, C. and Scullion, H. (1997) 'A Review and an Agenda for Expatriate HRM', *Human Resource Management Journal*, **7**(3): 32–41.

Caligiuri, P.M. and Stroh, L.K. (1995) 'Multinational Corporation Management Strategies and International Human Resource Management Practices: Bringing IHRM to the Bottom Line', *International Journal of Human Resource Mangement*, **6**(3): 494–507.

Caligiuri, P.M. and Cascio, W. (1998) 'Can We Send Her There?: Maximising the Success of Western Women on Global Assignments', *Journal of World Business*, **33**(4): 394–416.

Caligiuri, P.M. and Tung, R. (1999) 'Comparing the Success of Male and Female Expatriates from a US Based Company', *International Journal of Human Resource Management*, **10**(5): 763–782.

Caligiuri, P.M. Joshi, A. and Lazarova, M. (1999) 'Factors Influencing the Adjustment of Women on Global Assignments', *International Journal of Human Resource Management*, **10**(2): 163–79.

Cyr, D.R. and Schneider, S.C. (1996) 'Implications for Learning: Human Resource Management in East-West Joint Ventures', *Organization Studies*, **17**(2): 207–26.

D'Aveni, R.A. (1995) *Hyper Competitive Rivalries: Competing in Highly Dynamic Environments*, New York: The Free Press.

De Cieri, H. and Dowling, P.J. (1999) 'Strategic Human Resource Management in Multinational Enterprises: Theoretical and Empirical Developments', in P.M. Wright, L.D. Dyer, J.W. Boudreau, and G.T. Milkovich (eds) *Research in Personnel and Human Resources Management: Strategic Human Resources Management in the Twenty-First Century*, Supplement 4, Stamford, CT: JAI Press.

Dicken, P. (1998) *Global Shift: Transforming the World Economy*, third edition, London: Paul Chapman Publishing.

Dowling, P.J. and Schuler, R.S. (1990) *International Dimensions of Human Resource Management*, Boston, MA: PWA Kent.

Dowling, P.J., Welch, D.E. and Schuler, R.S. (1999) *International Human Resource Management: Managing People in an International Context*, third edition, Cincinatti, OH: South Western College Publishing, ITP.

Doz, Y. and Prahalad, C.K. (1986) 'Controlled Variety: A Challenge for Human Resource Management in the MNC', *Human Resource Management*, **25**(1): 55–71.

Doz, Y. and Hamel, G. (1988) *Alliance Advantage: The Art of Creating Value through Partnering*, Boston MA: Boston Harvard Business School Press.

Dyer, L. and Reeves, T. (1995) 'Human Resource Strategies and Firm Performance: What Do We Know and Where Do We Need to Go?', *International Journal of Human Resource Management*, **6**: 656–70.

Edstrom, A. and Galbraith, J. (1977) 'Transfer of Managers as a Coordination and Control Strategy in Multinational Organizations', *Administrative Science Quarterly*, **22**: 248–63.

Edwards, P.K., Ferner, A. and Sisson, K. (1993) 'People and the Process of Management in the Multinational Company: A Review and Some Illustrations', *Warwick Papers in Industrial Relations*, Number 43 July 1993, University of Warwick.

Edwards, P., Ferner, A. and Sisson, K. (1996) 'The Conditions for International Human Resource Management', *International Journal of Human Resource Management*, **7**(1): 20–40.

Evans, P.A.L. (1992) 'Developing Leaders and Managing Development', *European Management Journal*, **10**(1): 1–9.

Ferner, A (1994) 'Multinational Companies and Human Resource Management: an Overview of Research Issues', *Human Resource Management Journal*, **4**(3): 79–102.

Ferner, A (1997) 'Country of Origin Effects and Human Resource Management in Multinational Companies', *Human Resource Management Journal*, **7**(1): 19–37.

Ferris, G., Russ, G., Albanese, R. and Martocchio, J. (1991) 'Personnel/Human Resources Management, Unionization, and Strategy Determinants of Organizational Performance', *Human Resource Planning*, **32**(3): 215–27.

Festing, A. (1996) *Strategisches Internationales Personalmanagement*, Munchen und Mering: Rainer Hamp Verlag.

Forsgren, M. (1990) 'Managing the International Multi-Centred Firm: Case Studies From Sweden', *European Management Journal*, **8**(2): 261–67.

Forsgren, M. (1989) *Managing the Internationalization Process*, London: Routledge.

Forster, N. and Johnsen, M. (1996) 'Expatriate Management Policies in UK Companies New to the International Scene', *International Journal of Human Resource Management*, **7**(1): 177–205.

Forster, N (1999a) 'Another Glass Ceiling?: The Experiences of Women Expatriates on International Assignments', *Gender, Work and Organization*, **6**(2): 79–91.

Forster, N. (1999b) *Managing Expatriate Staff for Strategic Advantage: Getting the Best out of Staff on International Assignments*, London: Pearson Education/Financial Times Publications.

Forster, N. (2000) 'The Myth of the International Manager', *International Journal of Human Resource Management*, **1**: 126–42.

Foss, N.J. (1997) 'On the Rationales of Corporate Headquarters', *Industrial and Corporate Change*, **6**(2): 313–37.

Goold, M. and Campbell, A. (1987) *Strategies and Styles: The Role of the Centre in Managing Diversified Corporations*, Oxford: Basil Blackwell.

Grant, R.M. (1991) 'The Resource Based Theory of Competitive Advantage: Implications for Strategic Formulation', *California Management Review*, **33**(3): 14–35.

Grant, R.M. and Spender, J.C. (1996) 'Knowledge and the Firm: an Overview', *Strategic Management Journal*, **17**, Special Issue, December/Winter: 5–12.

Gregersen, H., Morrison, A. and Black, J.S. (1998) 'Developing Leaders for the Global Frontiers', *Sloan Management Review*, Fall: 21–32.

Guzzo, R.A., Noonan, K.A. and Elron, E. (1994) 'Expatriate Managers and the Psychological Contract', *Journal of Applied Psychology*, **79**(4): 617–26.

Hailey, J. (1999) 'Localisation as an Ethical Response to Internationalisation', in C. Brewster, and H. Harris, H. (eds) *International HRM: Contemporary Issues in Europe*, London: Routledge.

Hamel, G. (1991) 'Competition for Competence and Inter-Partner Learning with International Strategic Alliances', *Strategic Management Journal*, **12**: 83- 103.

Hamill, J. (1989) 'Expatriate Policies in British Multinationals', *Journal of General Management*, **14**(4): 18–31.

Harris, H. (1995) 'Women's Role in International Management', in A.W.K Harzing and J. Van Ruysseveldt (eds) *International Human Resource Management*, London: Sage.

Harris, H. and Brewster, C. (1999) 'An Integrative Framework for Pre-Departure Preparation', in C. Brewster and H. Harris (eds) *International HRM: Contemporary Issues in Europe*, London: Routledge.

Harvey, M.G. (1989), 'Repatriation of Corporate Executives: An Empirical Study', *Journal of International Business Studies*, Spring: 131–44.

Harvey, M. (1997) 'Inpatriation Training: the Next Challenge for International Human Resource Management', *International Journal of Human Resource Management*, **21**(3): 393–428.

Harvey, M. (1998) 'Dual-Career Couples During International Relocation: the Trailing Spouse', *International Journal of Human Resource Management*, **9**(2): 309–31.

Harvey, M. and Buckley, M. (1997) 'Managing Inpatriates: Building a Global Core Competency', *Journal of World Business*, **32**(1): 35–52.

Harvey, M., Novicevic, M.M. and Speier, C. (1999a) 'Inpatriate Managers: How to Increase the Probability of Success', *Human Resource Management Review*, **9**(1): 51–82.

Harvey, M., Speier, C. and Novicevic M.M. (1999b) 'The Impact of the Emerging Markets on Staffing the Global Organization', *Journal of International Management*, Fall, **5**(3): 167–186.

Harvey, M., Buckley, R., Novicevic, M.M. and Wiese, D. (1999c) 'Mentoring Dual Career Expatriates: a Sense-Making and Sense-Giving Social Support Process', *International Journal of Human Resource Management*, **10**(5): 808–27.

Harvey, M., Speier, C. and Novicevic, M.M. (1999d) 'The Role of Inpatriation in Global Staffing', *International Journal of Human Resource Management*, **10**(3): 459–76.

Harzing, A.W.K. (1999) *Managing the Multinationals: an International Study of Control Mechanisms*, Cheltenham: Edward Elgar.

Hede, A. and O'Brien, E. (1996) 'Affirmative Action in the Australian Private Sector: A Longitudinal Analysis', *International Review of Women and Leadership*, **2**: 15–29.

Hedlund, G and Nonaka, I. (1993) 'Models of Knowledge Management in the West and Japan', in P. Lorange, B. Chakravarthy, J. Roos, and A. Van de Ven (eds) *Implementing Strategic Processes: Change, Learning, and Co-operation*, Oxford: Blackwell: 117–44.

Heenan, D.A. and Perlmutter, H.V. (1974) 'How multinational should your top managers be?' *Harvard Business Review*, Nov–Dec: 121–32.

Hendry, C. (1990) 'The Corporate Management of Human Resources Under Conditions of Decentralization', *British Journal of Management*, **1**: 91–103.

Hendry, C. (1994) *Human Resource Strategies for International Growth*, London: Routledge.

Hunt, J and Boxall, P. (1998) 'Are Top Human Resource Specialists Strategic Partners? Self Perceptions of a Corporate Elite', *International Journal of Human Resource Management*, **9**(5): 767–81.

Inkpen, A.C. and Crossan M.M. (1995) 'Believing is Seeing: Joint Ventures and Organization Learning', *Journal of Management Studies*, **32**(5): 595–618.

Johnston, J. (1991) 'An Empirical Study of the Repatriation of Managers in UK Multinationals', *Human Resource Management Journal*, **1**(4): 102–108.

Kamoche, K (1996) 'The Integration-Differentiation Puzzle: A Resource-Capability View of the Firm', *International Journal of Human Resource Management*, **7**(1): 230–44.

Kamoche, K. (1997) 'Knowledge Creation and Learning in the International Firm', *International Journal of Human Resource Management*, **8**(3): 213–25.

Kobrin, S.J. (1988) 'Expatriate Reduction and Strategic Control in American Multinational Corporations', *Human Resource Management*, **27**(1): 63–71.

Kobrin, S.J. (1992) 'Multinational Strategy and International Human Resource Management Policy', unpublished paper, Wharton School, University of Pennsylvania.

Kobrin, S.J. (1994) 'Is There a Relationship Between a Geocentric Mindset and Multinational Strategy?', *Journal of International Business Studies*, **25**(3), third quarter: 493–511.

Kochan, T., Batt, R. and Dyer, L. (1992) 'International Human Resource Studies: a Framework for Future Research', in D. Lewin *et al.* (eds) *Research Frontiers in Industrial Relations and Human Resources*, Madison, WI: Industrial Relations Research Association.

Kochan, T. and Osterman, P. (1991) 'Human Resource Development and Utilization: Is There Too Little in the US?', *Time Horizons Project of the Council on Competitiveness*, Boston: MIT.

Kopp, R. (1994) 'International Human Resource Policies and Practices in Japanese, European and United States Multinationals', *Human Resource Management*, **33**(4): 581–99.

Laurent, A. (1986) 'The Cross-Cultural Puzzle of International Human Resource Management', *Human Resource Management*, **25**(1): 91–103.

Lindholm, N., Tahvanainen, M and Bjorkman, I. (1999) 'Performance Appraisal of Host Country Employees: Western MNEs in China', in C. Brewster, and H. Harris (eds) *International HRM: Contemporary issues in Europe*, London: Routledge.

Linehan, M (1999) *Senior Female International Managers*, Aldershot: Ashgate Publishing Company.

Linehan, M. and Scullion, H. (2000) 'The Repatriation of Female Executives in Europe: an Empirical Study'. Forthcoming.

Linehan, M., Scullion, H. and Walsh, J. (2000a) 'Understanding the Barriers to Women's Participation in International Management', *European Business Review*, Issue 6, October (in press).

Linehan, M. and Scullion, H. (2001) Challenges for Female International Managers: Evidence from Europe, *Journal of Managerial Psychology*, **16** (in press).

Marginson, P. (1994) 'Multinational Britain: Employment and Work in an Internationalised Economy', *Human Resource Management Journal*, **4**(4): 63–80.

Marginson, P., Edwards, P., Martin, R., Purcell, J. and Sisson, K. (1988) *Beyond the Workplace: Managing Industrial Relations in the Multi-Establishment Enterprise*, Oxford: Blackwell Publishers.

Marginson, P., Armstrong, P., Purcell, J. and Hubbard, N. (1993) 'The Control of Industrial Relations in Large Companies: an Initial Analysis of the Second Company Level Industrial Relations Survey', *Warwick papers in Industrial Relations*, no. 25, Coventry: IRRU, University of Warwick.

Marschan, R., Welch., D and Welch, L. (1997) 'Control in Less Hierarchical Multinationals: the Role of Personal Networks and Informal Communication', *International Business Review*, **5**(2): 137–50.

Mayrhofer W. and Brewster, C. (1996) 'In Praise of Ethnocentricity: Expatriate Policies in European Multinationals', *International Executive*, **38**(6): 749–78.

McEnery, J. and DesHarnais, G. (1990) 'Culture Shock', *Training and Development Journal*, April: 43–47.

Mendenhall, M. and Oddou, G. (1985) 'The Dimensions of Expatriate Acculturation: A Review', *Academy of Management Review*, **10**: 39–47.

Mendenhall, M.E., Dunbar, E. and Oddou, G. (1987) 'Expatriate Selection, Training and Career Pathing: A Review and a Critique', *Human Resource Planning*, **26**(3): 331–45.

Milliman, J., Von Glinow, M. and Nathan, B. (1991) 'Organizational Life Cycles and Strategic International Human Resource Management in Multinational Companies: Implications for Congruence Theory', *Academy of Management Review*, **16**: 318–39.

Miller, P. (1987) 'Strategic Human Resource Management: Distinction, Definition, Recognition', *Journal of Management Studies*, **24**(4): 347–62.

Morrison, A.K., Roth, K. and Ricks, D. (1991) 'Globalization versus Regionalisation: Which Way for the Multinational', *Organizational Dynamics*, Winter: 17–29.

Mulhern, A. (1995) 'The SME Sector in Europe: A Broad Perspective', *Journal of Small Business Management*, **30**(3): 83–87.

Oddou, G. and Kerr, C.B. (1993) 'European MNC Strategies for Internationalizing Managers: Current and Future Trends', in P.S. Kirkbride and B. Shaw (eds) *Proceedings of the Third Conference on International Personnel and Human Resource Management, vol. 1.*

Ondrack, D. (1985) 'International Human Resource Management in European and North American Firms', *International Studies of Management and Organization*, **15**(1): 6–32.

Organization Resources Counselors (ORC) (1996) *Worldwide Survey of International Assignment Policies and Practices*, New York: Organization Resource Counselors.

Parker, B. (1998) *Globalization and Business Practice: Managing Across Borders*, London: Sage Publications.

Pascale, R.T. (1990) *Managing on the Edge: How Successful Companies Use Conflict to Stay Ahead*, New York: Viking.

Pennings, A. (1993) 'Executive Reward Systems: A Cross-National Comparison', *Journal of Management Studies*, **30**(2): 261–80.

Peterson, R.B., Sargent, J., Napier, N.K., Shim, W.S. (1996) 'Corporate Expatriate HRM Policies, Internationalization, and Performance in the World's Largest MNCs', *Management International Review*, **36**(3): 215–30.

Pierce, J. and Delahaye, B.L. (1996) 'Human Resource Management Implications of Dual Career Couples', *International Journal of Human Resource Management*, **7**(4): 905–21.

Prahalad, C.K. and Hamel, G. (1990) 'The Core Competence of the Organization', *Harvard Business Review*, May–June: 79–91.

Prahalad, C.K. and Hamel, G. (1994) *Competing For the Future*, Boston, MA.: Harvard Business School Press.

Price Waterhouse (1997–98*) International Assignments: European Policy and Practice*, Price Waterhouse Europe.

Pucik, V. (1988) 'Strategic Alliances, Organizational Learning, and Competitive Advantage: The HRM Agenda', *Human Resource Management*, **27**(1): 77–93.

Pucik, V. (1992) 'Globalization and Human Resource Management', in V. Pucik, N. Tichy and C.K. Barnett (eds) *Globalizing Management*, New York: John Wiley and Son.

Punnett, B.J. (1997) 'Towards Effective Management of Expatriate Spouses', *Journal of World Business*, **32**(3): 243–57.

Purcell, J (1985) 'Is Anybody Listening to the Corporate Personnel Department', *Personnel Management*, September.

Purcell, J. and Ahlstrand, B. (1994*) Human Resource Management in the Multi-Divisional Company*, Oxford: Oxford University Press.

Purcell, J. and Gray, A. (1986) 'Corporate Personnel Departments and the Management of Industrial Relations: Two Case Studies in Ambiguity', *Journal of Management Studies*, **23**(2): 205–23.

Schuler, R.S., Dowling, P.J. and De Cieri, H. (1993) 'An Integrative Framework of Strategic International Human Resource Management', *International Journal of Human Resource Management*, **4**(4): 717–64.

Schuler, R.S. (1992) 'Strategic Human Resources Management: Linking the People With the Strategic Needs of the Business', *Organizational Dynamics*, **6**(4): 18–31.

Scullion, H. (1992) 'Strategic Recruitment and Development of the International Manager: Some European Considerations', *Human Resource Management Journal*, **3**(1): 57–69.

Scullion, H. (1993) 'Creating International Managers: Recruitment and Developing Issues', in P. Kirkbride (ed.) *Human Resource Management in Europe*, London: Routledge.

Scullion, H. (1994) 'Staffing Policies and Strategic Control in British Multinationals', *International Studies of Management and Organization*, **24**(3): 18–35.

Scullion, H. (1995) 'International Human Resource Management', in J. Storey (ed.) *Human Resource Management: A Critical Text*, London: Routledge: 352–82.

Scullion, H. (1996) 'Staffing Policy and Practice in an International Food and Drink Company', in J. Storey (ed.) *Blackwell Case Studies in Human Resource and Change Management*, Oxford: Blackwell.

Scullion, H. (1997) 'The Key Challenges for International HRM in the 21st Century', *Association of European Personnel Managers Handbook*, Institute of Personnel and Development.

Scullion, H. (1999) 'International HRM in Medium Sized Multinationals: Some Evidence From Ireland', in C. Brewster and H. Harris (eds) *International HRM: Contemporary Issues in Europe*, London: Routledge.

Scullion, H. and Brewster, C. (1998) 'Current Trends in European Expatriation', *Management Development Journal of Singapore*, **8**(1): 45–55.

Scullion, H. and Starkey, K. (2000) 'The Changing Role of the the the Corporate Human Resource Function in the International Firm', *International Journal of Human Resource Management* **11**(6): 1–21.

Shaeffer, R (1989) 'Managing International Business Growth and International Management Development', *Human Resource Planning*, March: 29–36.

Sisson, K. and Scullion, H. (1985) 'Putting the Corporate Personnel Department in its Place', *Personnel Management*, December: 36–39.

Sparrow, P.R. (1999) 'International Reward Systems: To Converge or not to Converge?', in C. Brewster and H. Harris (eds) *International HRM: Contemporary Issues in Europe*, London: Routledge.

Storey, J. and Sisson, K. (1993) *Managing Human Resources and Industrial Relations*, Milton Keynes: Open University Press.

Storey, J., Edwards, P. and Sisson, K. (1997) *Managers in the Making: Careers, Development and Control in Corporate Britain and Japan*, London: Sage Publications.

Stroh, L and Caligiuri, P.M. (1998) 'Increasing Global Competitiveness through Effective People Management', *Journal of World Business*, **33**(1): 1–16.

Stroh, L. and Caligiuri, P.M. (1988) 'Strategic Human Resources: a New Source for Competitive Advantage in the Global Arena', *International Journal of Human Resource Management*, **9**: 1–17.

Stroh, L., Gregerson, H.B. and Black, J.S. (1998) 'Closing the Gap: Expectations Versus Reality Among Repatriates', *Journal of World Business*, **33**(2): 111–24.

Swiercz, P and Spencer, B. (1992) 'HRM and Sustainable Competitive Advantage: Lessons from Delta Airlines', *Human Resource Planning*, **15**(2): 35–46.

Taylor, S., Beechler, S., Napier, N. (1996) 'Towards an Integrative Model of Strategic International Human Resource Management', *Academy of Management Review*, **21**(4): 959–85.

Teagarden, M., Von Glinow, M.A., Bowen, D., Frayne, C.A., Nason, S., Huo, Y.P., Milliman, J., Arras, M.A., Butler, M.C., Geringer, J.M., Kim, N.H., Scullion, H., Lowe, K.B. and Drost, E.A. (1995) 'Towards Building a Theory of Comparative Management Research Methodology: an Idiographic Case Study of the Best International Human Resource Management Project', *Academy of Management Journal*, **38**(5): 1261–287.

Tilghman, T. (1994) 'Beyond the Balance Sheet: Developing Alternative Approaches to International Compensation', *ACA Journal*, Summer: 36–49.

Tsui, A. and Gomez-Mejia, L. (1988) 'Evaluating Human Resource Effectiveness', in L. Dyer (ed.) *Human Resource Management: Evolving Roles and Responsibilities*, Washington, DC: BNA.

Tung, R.L. (1981) 'Selection and Training of Personnel for Overseas Assignments', *Columbia Journal of World Business*, **16**(1): 68–78.

Tung, R.L. (1982) 'Selection and Training Procedures of U.S., European and Japanese Multinationals', *California Management Review*, **25**(1): 57–71.

United Nations (UN) (1993) *Small and Medium Sized Transnational Corporations: Role, Impact and Policy Implications*, New York: UN Publications.

Welch, D. (1994) 'Determinants of International Human Resource Management Approaches and Activities: A Suggested Framework', *Journal of Management Studies*, **31**(2): 139–64.

Winkler, J. (1974) 'The Ghost at the Bargaining Table: Directors and Industrial Relations', *British Journal of Industrial Relations*, **12**(2): 191–212.

Young, S. and Hamill, J. (1992) *Europe and the Multinationals*, Aldershot: Gower.

16 HR Issues in International Joint Ventures and Alliances

Randall S. Schuler

Partnerships, alliances and joint ventures are becoming increasingly common. They can take many forms: technical exchange and cross-licensing, co-production, sale and distribution ties, joint product development programmes, or creation of joint venture firms with equity distributed among the partners, either domestically or internationally. The focus in this chapter is on joint ventures – and international ventures in particular. Although international joint ventures (IJVs) are particularly difficult to manage, it appears that as the necessity for rapid response becomes greater, as business risks and costs increase, and competition becomes more severe, firms are relying on them with increasing frequency (Schuler 2001; Hopkins 1999; Doz and Hamel 1998; Sparks 1999). While some IJVs are short-term in nature, others aim for longer term synergies and benefits between partners (Pucik 1988; Cyr 1995; Sparks 1999).

Although there is no single agreed-on definition of an IJV, a typical definition is:

> A separate legal organizational entity representing the partial holdings of two or more parent firms, in which the headquarters of at least one is located outside the country of operation of the joint venture. This entity is subject to the joint control of its parent firms, each of which is economically and legally independent of the other.
>
> (Shenkar and Zeira 1987)

Using an IJV as a mode of international business operation is not new. But economic growth in the past decade of global competition, coupled with shifts in trade dominance and the emergence of new markets, has contributed to a recent increase in the use of IJVs (Cyr 1995). According to Peter Drucker, IJVs are likely to grow in importance:

> You will see a good deal of joint ventures, of strategic alliances, of cross-holdings across borders. Not because of cost, but because of information. Economists don't accept it, but it is one of the oldest experiences, that you cannot maintain market standing in a developed market unless you are in it as a producer. As an exporter, you will be out sooner or later, because you have to be in the market to have the information.
>
> (Drucker 1989).

While the concept of the IJV may imply co-operation and partnership between two firms, it may not always be the case (Sparks 1999; Child and Faulkner 1998):

The change from competitive to collaborative strategies is often merely a tactical adjustment aimed at specific market conditions. Many of these new partnerships should be viewed as a hidden substitute of market competition, not its dissipation. The objective is similar: attaining the position of global market leadership through internalization of key value-added competencies. The potential competitive relationship between partners distinguishes strategic alliances that involve competitive collaboration from more traditional cooperative ventures.

(Pucik 1988: 78)

Pucik suggests that the implications between international joint ventures that are motivated by co-operation are different from those motivated by competition:

In a truly cooperative relationship the underlying assumption is the feasibility (and desirability) of long-term win/win outcomes. In the partnerships that involve competitive collaboration, the strategic intent of achieving dominance makes the long-term win/win outcome highly unlikely.

(ibid.: 79)

IJVs can differ according to the resources they are attempting to leverage. On the one hand, they may be leveraging visible resources including land, equipment, labour, money or patents. On the other hand they may be leveraging invisible resources, especially competencies such as management and organizational skill, knowledge of the market or technological capability. These assets are typically unseen and embodied in people within the organization. These assets, however, represent a tacit knowledge that may be difficult to understand and only copied by others over a long period of time.

Regardless of the motivation for the IJV or the resources involved, firms can structure their relationship so that they are bringing together either different structural or functional specializations that complement each other, e.g. production and marketing functions, or similar structural or organizational characteristics that build upon or add shared value, e.g. two banks combining their financial assets to build a greater asset base to enter new markets (Slocum and Lei 1993). A recent case study of a joint venture located in The Netherlands between a US firm (Davidson) and a UK firm (Marley), provides an illustration of the functional specializations that complement each other:

Located in Europe, Marley gave Davidson knowledge of the market. Far more than this, it gave them functional fit and personal contacts. While Marley understood the marketplace, Davidson had expertise in manufacturing and administrative systems. Thus, while Davidson supplied the technology and the systems, Marley supplied knowledge of the markets and the contacts needed to get the IJV built.

(Schuler *et al.* 1991: 53)

Thus IJVs can be differentiated in terms of: (a) co-operative vs. competitive motivations; (b) source of leverage: visible, physical resources vs. invisible resources such as competencies; and (c) the nature of their structure, functional specialization versus shared value-added. The IJVs between partners with competitive motives attempting to leverage competencies and using a functional specialization structure appear to be the most challenging (Pucik 1988; Slocum and Lei 1993). Here the relationship tends to be more unstable: one partner wants to gain at the expense of the other and the methods of defending against a partner's attacks on the other partner's competencies are problematic. The major source of instability and potential gain to one partner is *learning capacity*:

> The asymmetric appropriation of invisible benefits – such as the acquisition of product or market know-how for use outside of the partnership framework, or even to support a competitive strategy targeted at the partner – cannot be easily protected. The asymmetry results from the internal dynamics of the strategic alliance. Benefits are appropriated asymmetrically due to differences in the *organizational learning capacity* of the partners. The shifts in relative power in a competitive partnership are related to the speed at which the partners can learn from each other. Not providing a firm strategy for the control of invisible assets in the partnership, and delegating responsibility for them to operating managers concerned with short-term results, is a sure formula for failure.
>
> (Pucik 1988: 81)

Not surprisingly then, firms considering IJVs have become more concerned about learning, and the capacity for learning as reasons for forming an IJV with another firm. But, of course, this still remains just one reason among many (Child and Faulkner 1998).

REASONS FOR FORMING AN IJV

International joint ventures have become a major form of entry into global markets. Harrigan (1986) argued that since a joint venture draws on the strengths of its owners, it should possess superior competitive abilities that allow its sponsors to enjoy synergies. If the venture's owners cannot cope with the demands of managing the joint venture successfully, Harrigan advised the owners to use non-equity forms of co-operation such as cross-marketing and/or cross-production, licensing, and research-and-development consortia. Some companies shun joint ventures, preferring 100 per cent ownership to the drawbacks of loss of control and profits that can accompany shared ownership. However, many firms, regardless of previous international experience, are increasingly entering into IJV arrangements. The most common reasons cited in the literature include the desire to gain knowledge; host government insistence; to gain rapid market entry; increased economics of scale; and to spread risk.

Of these, the reason that appears to be increasingly important is the first which involves learning, knowledge, sharing and transferring. According to Lei, Slocum and Pitts (1997: 203)

> Alliances have emerged as organization designs that enable organizations to deal with the increasing complexity of building and learning new sources of competitive advantage to compete in the global economy. In principle, all strategic alliances may be thought of as coalignments between two or more firms in which the partners seek to learn and acquire from each other products, skills, technologies, and knowledge that are not available to other competitors.

While firms can learn *from* the other partner, e.g. knowledge about its products, skill, technologies, and even the process of forming and maintaining an IJV, they can also learn *about* the other partner, e.g. its culture, management style, goals and values. While both are important, they are important for different reasons as described later. In addition:

> Goals and expectations between the parents and between the parents and the joint venture are bound to change over time. This necessitates a process in which the partners build relationships and establish channels for communication in order that they may continue to learn about each other.
>
> (Cyr 1995: 173)

Learning, of course, can vary dramatically from one situation to another. Some organizations may not support or emphasize its importance while others make learning a priority. Some may engage in ventures in which the knowledge and competencies match those of the other partner (compatibility), while some may engage in ventures in which the knowledge and competencies add to or build upon those of the partner (complementarity). And some organizations are more able to absorb new knowledge and learn from it (absorptive capacity). Some are more willing and able to share and transfer this knowledge and learning with other units.

The literature highlights the variation in the types of knowledge that organizations can learn from or about. Categorizing broadly, knowledge can be explicit (transparent and recordable) or tacit (personalized and slowly diffused through interactions). Tacit knowledge can be further categorized at the individual and collective levels. All of these have implications for human resource management (Lei, Slocum and Pitts 1997). The literature also highlights the variation in the levels of learning. As Cohen and Levinthal (1990) stated, the cognitive structures of individuals provide the basis for organizational learning. Certainly learning occurs at the individual, group and organizational levels.

This implies that behaviours and styles of managers in organizations have a significant impact on the ability and willingness of a firm to learn. For example, learning requires managers to be open and willing to suspend their need for control. McGill, Slocum and Lei (1992) suggest that learning-oriented managers need to demonstrate cultural awareness and 'humility' which respects the values and customs of others: 'cultural-functional narrowness and/or ethnocentricity results in an educated incapacity that reduces the ability of organizations and managers to learn' (ibid.: 11). Learning can be facilitated by flexibility and a willingness to take risks. Human resource management policies and practices can play a role supporting this knowledge flow, sharing and transfer, e.g. by supporting and rewarding risk taking and flexibility (Cyr 1995; Lei, Slocum and Pitts; 1997; Pucik 1988).

While firms and individuals need the ability and willingness to learn as they enter into the IJV formation process, they also need to be receptive to learning and willing to be transparent so that others may learn as well. Thus both partners need to have similar qualities that support learning if the partnership is to have a longer-term success. Because learning capability can quickly lead to attaining competitive advantage, asymmetry in learning capability can soon lead to partnership instability and dissolution. Although potentially providing a short-term success for one partner, it may also preclude future beneficial IJV partnerships from even being established (Hamel 1991). Thus while IJV partnerships can produce significant advantages, these can be maximized more effectively in the context of a longer-term, co-operative relationship between the partners.

Thus learning is critical to today's IJVs, and this begins with the very nature of the design of joint ventures. Learning also continues as the parents learn more about each other and more from each other. This continues with the parents learning from the IJV itself, which they in turn can use for other units and other joint ventures. Knowledge, learning, sharing and transfer can be seen permeating several levels or stages of the international joint venture process. Consequently, human resource issues and activities permeate several stages of the IJV process and, thus are quite important to IJVs.

IMPORTANCE OF HRM IN IJVS

Analysed within the multiple stakeholder perspective, human resource management has a significant impact on the organization itself, its survival and profitability, the customers, the suppliers, the societal context, and the employees. More specifically, human resource management can impact on the organization (productivity, profits and survival), on the employees (fair treatment, satisfaction and employability) and customers and investors.

In the context of the IJV, human resource management has the potential to be even more important: its impact is on several organizations, not just one, and in several societal contexts, not just one (Dowling *et al.* 1999). Within the IJV context there are a multitude of organizational issues that are, at the same time, human resource issues. Broadly presented, they can be categorized by organizational level and individual/group level. The organizational/human resource issues in each of the two levels are shown below in Exhibit 16.1.

EXHIBIT 16.1

Categories of Organizational/HR issues in IJVs

Organizational Level:

- Parent-to-Parent Relationships.
- Parent-to-IJV Relationships.
- IJV-Environmental Context Relationship.
- Parent characteristics.

Individual/Group Level:

- Employees learning and sharing relevant knowledge.
- Employees having the competencies for the IJV.
- Employees engaging in the appropriate behaviours and attitudes.
- Employees with the needed levels of motivation for performance and for commitment to the organizations.
- Individuals being attracted to join the IJV.

At the organizational level the HR issues involve parent-to-parent relationships such as seeking and selecting; building trust and co-operation; and learning about each other and from each other. The parent-to-IJV relationship HR issues include the design of the appropriate structural relationship, for example the degree of control vs. autonomy, methods of integration, the assignment of managers and non-managers to the IJV, and the management and transfer of learning and knowledge. The IJV–environmental context relationship involves issues such as the identification of the relevant stakeholders and their objectives; and acquiring knowledge of the relevant laws, social system, language, tradition and labour market. The parent characteristics category raises issues such issues as the values, vision, culture, practices, structure and strategy that will enable the parent to learn from the IJV itself and the other parent, in other words, organizational capability. Developing and utilizing an organizational-level capability has become more important as competitive partners engage in IJVs.

There are several organizational/HR issues at the individual/group level in IJVs. These involve: learning, sharing, and transferring of knowledge to enable the other employees and team to learn and grow; competencies (knowledge, skills, abilities, personality and habits) to perform the organizational roles; behaviours, actions and attitudes that are consistent with needs of the business, customers and colleagues; motivation and commitment and so on. Virtually all of the issues listed in Exhibit 16.1 are significant in the IJV process and involve and depend upon human resource management.

IJV failure rates (up to 50–70 per cent) are high; they reflect the difficulty of establishing a successful IJV. The reasons for failure include: partners not clarifying each other's goals and objectives, the negotiating teams' lack of JV experience, and the lack of a realistic feasibility study. IJV failure rates also reflect the difficulty of implementing and developing a joint venture. For example, one partner learns faster than the other thus reducing partner dependency, partners cannot get along or managers from different partners within the venture cannot work together.

IJV failure can also be associated with how well either parent is able to benefit from the JV itself. The difficulties include the inability and/or unwillingness of the parent to learn from the JV, or lack of appropriate organizational structure, managerial roles and leadership (Harbison 1996).

Thus IJV success or failure can occur at several places making it easy to claim success prematurely. The criteria for defining success or failure depend on the parent companies' expectations and motives for establishing the joint venture. 'Joint ventures can be deemed successful in spite of poor financial performance, and conversely, they can be considered unsuccessful in spite of good financial performance' (Schaan 1988). For example, financial performance may take second place to profits from management fees or royalties from technology transfer. With the emphasis on learning in the current literature, criteria for success are increasingly seen in the longer-term perspective and from the viewpoints of multiple stakeholders.

Regardless of how failure rates are measured or determined, many of the underlying causes are traceable to human resource management. The results indicating the success rates of joint ventures support Harbison's (1996) findings. American joint ventures have a much higher failure rate than European and Asian joint ventures. While these relative success rates are not due entirely to differences in joint venture competencies, they do suggest that improvement in joint venture competences might increase joint venture success rates.

The HR activities included here relate to, are associated with, and impact the organizational level and the individual/group level human resource issues shown in Exhibit 16.1. These include policies and practices associated with environmental analysis, organizational structure, design, strategy, values, mission and culture, human resource planning, job design and job analysis, recruitment, selection and orientation and so on (Pucik 1988; Cyr 1995).

The relationships of HR policies and practices with the IJV process are developed through an analysis of the HR implications associated with the organizational/HR issues identified in Exhibit 16.1. These issues and implications are further categorized as they unfold in the IJV process in stages with the HR implications for specific HR activities.

FOUR STAGE MODEL OF IJVS

As noted earlier, the organizational and human resource issues in IJVs are clearly very extensive. They can, however, be categorized as falling into several stages as shown in Table 16.1.

The organizational/HR issues in each stage of the IJV process are numerous as illustrated in Table 16.2. The HR implications for each stage are also shown in Table 16.2.

Stage 1 – Formation: the partnership

Potential partners in an IJV need to separately determine their purposes for using an IJV as part of their business strategy. As noted earlier, several reasons have been

Table 16.1 Four stage model of international joint ventures organizational/HR issues

Stage 1 – Formation: the partnership
- a. Identifying the reasons for forming the IJV
- b. Planning for the utilization of its potential benefits
- c. Selecting a manager for new business development
- d. Finding potential partners
- e. Selecting a likely partner(s)
- f. Resolving critical issues and building trust/co-operation
- g. Negotiating the arrangement

Stage 2 – Development: the IJV itself
- h. Locating the IJV and dealing with the local community
- i. Establishing the right management structure
- j. Getting the right senior manager

Stage 3 – Implementation: the IJV itself
- k. Establishing the vision, mission, values, strategy and structure
- l. Developing the HR policies and practices
- m. Staffing and managing the employees

Stage 4 – Advancement: the IJV and beyond
- n. Learning from partner (each other)
- o. Transferring the new knowledge to the parents
- p. Transferring the new knowledge to other locations

© Randall S. Schuler, Rutgers University.

Table 16.2 HR implications in the four stages of the IJV process

Organizational/HR issues	HR implications
Stage 1 – Formation • Identifying reasons • Planning for utilization • Selecting dedicated manager • Finding potential partners • Selecting likely partners • Resolving critical issues • Negotiating the arrangement	• The more important learning is the greater the role for HRM • Knowledge needs to be managed • Systematic selection is essential • Cast a wide net in partner search • Be thorough for compatibility • Ensure extensive communications • More skilled negotiators are more effective • Integrative strategies for learning
Stage 2 – Development • Locating the IJV • Establishing the right structure • Getting the right senior managers	• Concerns of multiple sets of stakeholders need to considered for long-term viability and acceptance • The structure will impact the learning and knowledge management processes. These are impacted by the quality of IJV managers • Recruiting selecting and managing senior staff can make or break the IJV
Stage 3 – Implementation • Establishing the vision, mission, values, the strategy and structure • Developing HR policies and practices • Staffing and managing the employees	• These will provide meaning and direction to the IJV and employees • These will impact what is learned and shared • Need to design policies and practices with local–global considerations • The people will make the place
Stage 4 – Advancement and Beyond • Learning from the partner • Transferring the new knowledge to the parents • Transferring the new knowledge to other locations	• Partners need to have the capacity to learn from each other • HR systems need to be established to support knowledge flow to the parent and learning by the parent • Sharing through the parent is critical

© Randall S. Schuler, Rutgers University

identified. Knowledge and learning acquisition plays a role in all major categories of reasons. Thus all potential partners will have an interest in facilitating the learning process to acquire the desired or needed knowledge.

The reasons of potential partners for forming an IJV can be complementarity or compatibility. That is, they can match those of the other firm (compatibility) *or* provide a firm something that it needs but does not have (complementarity) in either visible or invisible resources. Many people suggest that IJVs are more likely to succeed in learning something if they have complementarity.

Their success is also more likely to depend upon having *absorptive capacity*. From an IJV perspective, absorptive capacity constitutes capabilities which affect a firm's ability to learn and which make them effective repositories of embedded knowledge. The firm's ability to monitor, process, integrate and deploy new flows of knowledge will depend, among other things, on its ability to link this knowledge to its existing knowledge base. As Hamel (1991) notes, a firm must already have knowledge and understanding in a given area if it is to learn from its venture partner in that area. Shenkar and Li (1999) found support for the importance of absorptive capacity in seeking a partner for an IJV. Furthermore, they also found that partners are more likely to search for partners with complementary knowledge, e.g. a managerial skill base complemented by a technological or marketing skill base. Shenkar and Li (1999) also found that partners tend to see that IJVs are the preferred way to gain tacit or embedded knowledge, particularly management skills or intangibles (Pucik 1988). More explicit knowledge such as marketing and technological may be equally learned by other forms of alliances as by IJVs (Pucik 1988).

When trust building, learning, communicating, and selecting are so critical to IJV success, they need to be planned. Early planning in joint ventures is especially important in order that differences in cultural and management styles between the parents and the venture are considered. Without planning the likelihood of reaping the gains from the IJV is diminished. Differences in partners on such qualities as culture, managerial styles, intentions, absorptive capacity, objectives of the IJV and even the role of the HR department can be part of an HR plan that includes an audit of these qualities.

In the context of the multiple stakeholder framework, HR planning can also include an analysis of such external factors as labour market conditions, nature of legal and cultural conditions, and political and economic conditions in the country or countries of the potential partner and the IJV itself.

A key step is the selection of the manager for new business development. These managers are the linkages between the two parents and the linkages with the JV itself. Although the CEO may spot IJV opportunities, it is the manager for new business development within an organization who is responsible for making the IJV happen. In this capacity, this manager is likely to interact with a counterpart in the other parent. Together these two may begin the activities remaining in stage 1. Thus they set the stage to link with the IJV itself. Consequently, the selection of this person is critical in the entire IJV process. The more knowledge and experience this individual has, particularly in IJVs, the more likely the IJV will be a success. Consequently, CEOs like Jack Welch of General Electric think that the selection of these managers is one of their most important responsibilities. But so also the organization will be more dependent upon this individual, so there will be a need to develop the incentives to increase the likelihood of the individual remaining with the company.

Partner selection determines an IJV's mix of skills, knowledge, and resources, its operating policies and procedures, and its vulnerability to indigenous conditions, structures, and institutional changes. In a dynamic, complex, or hostile environment, the importance of local partner selection to IJV success is magnified because the right partner can spur the IJV's adaptability, strategy-environment configuration, and uncertainty reduction (Luo 1998).

Luo (1998) suggests that local partner selection should be based upon three sets of criteria: financial attributes, organizational and strategic and that the likelihood of IJV success increases with a fit on these three sets of criteria. These fits are hypothesized to ensure cash-flow related concerns, co-operation and trust between partners, and an efficient operation. For organizations engaged in opportunistic, short-term behaviour, however, partner selection may be based on a lack of fit on some of Luo's criteria. For example, selecting a partner with limited absorptive capacity may help ensure that one's competitive advantage is maintained and that one's learning is enhanced. Such a situation, however, is likely to lead to distrust, control and IJV failure in the long term.

The very nature of joint ventures contributes to their failure: they are a difficult and complex form of enterprise and many companies initiate IJVs without fully recognizing and addressing the major issues they are likely to confront. Success requires adept handling of three key issues: control, trust and conflict.

Control, along with trust and learning, is one of the most important and most studied topics in the IJV literature. Control is defined as a purposeful and goal-oriented activity that influences the acquisition, interpretation and dissemination of information within an organizational setting. This definition highlights the information/knowledge qualities of IJVs.

Inkpen and Currall (1999), building on the discussions of bargaining power and learning asymmetry, suggest that as long as partners learn at equal rates from the IJV process *or* partners engage in forbearance behaviour, the need for control diminishes and trust increases. Inkpen and Currall provide an important clarification in their description of the relationship between control and trust. Learning *about* an IJV partner provides the basis for increased trust, as trust here becomes the vehicle by which knowledge is transferred. However, learning *from* an IJV partner provides the basis for increased bargaining power which reduces dependence upon the teaching partner. If the learning partner engages in opportunistic behaviour the relationship becomes unstable and may lead to greater efforts to control by the teaching partner which diminishes trust. Control issues in an IJV between two parents often arise in making decisions about sources of raw materials, product design, quality standards and production process among other factors.

Who actually controls the operation can depend on who is responsible for the day-to-day management of the IJV. Ownership distribution may matter less than how operating control and participation in decision-making actually is apportioned (Harrigan 1986). For a parent with minority ownership, for example, the right to appoint key personnel can be used as a control mechanism. Control can be achieved by appointing managers loyal to the parent company and its organizational ethos (Killing 1983). Of course, loyalty to the parent cannot be guaranteed: 'The ability to appoint the joint venture general manager increases the chances that the parent's interests will be observed, but it is no guarantee that the joint venture general manager will always accommodate that parent's preferences' (Schaan 1988: 14).

Top managers, however, will be expected to make decisions that deal with the simultaneous demands of the parents and their employees in the enterprise. At times, such decisions will by necessity meet the demands of some parties better than those of other parties. If the partners do not anticipate such decisions, they may fail to build in control mechanisms to protect their interests. Weak control also can result if parent-company managers spend too little time on the IJV, responding to problems only on an *ad hoc* basis. Finally, control-related failures are likely to occur if control practices are not re-evaluated and modified in response to changing circumstances.

A key issue is that of trust. Inkpen and Currall (1999) define trust as a reliance on another partner under a condition of risk. Four dimensions of trust include communication and information exchange; task co-ordination; informal agreements;

and surveillance and monitoring which indicate the absence of trust. Trust is positive because it strengthens interorganizational ties, speeds contract negotiations and reduces transactions costs. Trust is not only a control concept in the IJV relationship, but a dynamic and potentially unstable one as well.

Learning and trust are positively related while trust and the use of informal and formal controls are negatively related. Since learning is a critical component of IJV longevity, establishing mechanisms to ensure that trust increases benefits the relationship between IJV partners. Thus a partner needs to reduce the likelihood of engaging in opportunistic behaviour when the balance of power shifts in its favour. Partners need to resist the 'race to learn' at differential rates because this will shift the balance of power and the focus of dependencies.

Because joint ventures are inherently unstable relationships, they require a delicate set of organizational and management processes to create trust and the ongoing capacity to collaborate. This means that senior executives must be involved in designing management processes that provide effective ways to handle joint strategy formulation, create structural linkages, provide adequate day-to-day co-ordination and communication, and establish a win/win culture. It is also important that senior executives establish mechanisms to manage conflict.

Differences in such parent qualities as relative power, levels of commitment, experience with IJVs, goals, size, location of parents, and cultural similarity can lead to conflict. Many misunderstanding and problems in IJVs are rooted in managerial differences. Differing approaches to managerial style are one area that can create problems. For example, one party may favour a participative managerial style while the other may believe in a more autocratic style of management. Another area that can be problematic is acceptance of risk-taking when one parent is prepared to take more risks than the other. Such differences often make the process of decision-making slow and frustrating. The resulting conflict can be dysfunctional, if not destructive.

Differing levels of commitment from the two parents provide yet another source of difficulty. The commitment of each partner reflects the project's importance to the partner. When an imbalance exists, the more-committed partner may feel frustrated by the other partner's apparent lack of concern; or the less-committed partner may feel frustrated by demands and time pressures exerted by the other more-committed partner. The level of commitment by parties to the IJV can contribute to conflict and even to success or failure.

In resolving conflicts, it has been found that a problem solving strategy seems to be more effective than strategies involving compromise, force, or legalisms. They also found that parents with more experience in IJVs with each other tended to codify few understandings and rather relied on their knowledge of/and trust in each other. With experience, the IJV parents get to know each other better and develop ways of resolving differences.

Not surprisingly, the quality of IJV contract negotiations during the IJV formation can have an impact upon three consequences of importance: IJV formation satisfaction; IJV process performance; and IJV overall performance (Luo 1999; Lei, Slocum and Pitts 1997). Central to the quality of the contract negotiations are the bargaining processes and strategies used by each of the partners.

For partners interested in learning, approaching the negotiations with a problem-solving strategy would appear to be effective. The need for this strategy to be carried out by the negotiators would therefore be important. Establishing trust and mutual understanding, perhaps through previous experience, would aid in establishing the culture for the problem-solving strategy. Here HR activities can play an instrumental role. They can as well in the selection of the negotiator.

The characteristics of the contract negotiator(s) can also have an impact on the success of the IJV. These characteristics include cultural similarities, personality and skills, and loyalty. Selecting on these characteristics and ensuring that they are supported and rewarded are important human resource management contributions.

Stage 2 – Development: the IJV itself

Once the IJV process has been formed, there are several important activities that must be addressed in its development. These include for example designing the appropriate structure and staffing the IJV Top Team.

Two aspects of structure are particularly important: one is the extent to which the IJV will be able to make its own decisions, adapt to the local environment, and operate on its own; and the second is the methods or processes by which the IJV will be attached or integrated into the parent(s) in order to provide a transfer of knowledge, learning and other resources. There are many decisions for which autonomy may be given or withheld, by the parents *vis-à-vis* the IJV, for example, general administration, exploration expertise, R&D and so on.

How to balance the competing logics of integration versus responsiveness, or standardization versus localization can be viewed as a question of autonomy, specifically, whether to provide autonomy to the IJV itself or for the parents to retain it. Concerns here are for the IJV itself to be locally effective and the parents to be globally effective, and for the IJV and the parents to be able to develop their absorptive capacity so learning can be facilitated. Arguments for autonomy over these and other decisions relate to issues of dissimilar operating environments, lack of industry knowledge by parents or where the managing director of the IJV has a personal stake in the venture.

Arguments against providing autonomy would include the need for global co-ordination, hierarchical nature of the parents requires a control structure over the IJV system, prevention of the IJV from becoming too strong to control.

If the design grants a great deal of autonomy to the IJV, then the parents confront the question of how to integrate the IJV with the parents in order to provide the parents the opportunity to learn and transfer information and knowledge from the IJV, and yet enable the IJV to be effective locally. Such information and knowledge flow can be facilitated by formal methods such as detailed documents of conduct, and agreed upon exchanges of specific information; and/or by informal means such as the selection processes used by the IJV and/or personnel transfers and assignments between the IJV and the parents. Used in combination, the formal and informal methods may facilitate the transfer of both explicit and tacit knowledge.

With the information and knowledge flowing in both directions, absorptive capacity in the partners and the IJV may be increased, thus furthering the success of all three members of the IJV process. This would then provide the IJV process the appropriate structure. That is, the appropriate structure is where the parents provide the appropriate autonomy to the JV that enables the JV to develop the absorptive capacity to benefit from the parents and be effective locally.

The selection of the various members of the IJV is an important process in itself, and in combination with the design of the appropriate structure. Together these activities highlight the interdependence of individual and organizational capabilities and characteristics for the IJV to be locally effective and for the parents to be globally effective and have information and knowledge transfer occurring in order to build absorptive capacity. Without developing a learning (absorptive) capability in the IJV itself, the IJV process will become unstable. Just as distrust will develop between partners who are asymmetric in learning, so will it develop between the IJV itself and the parents. The impact will be a greater desire by the IJV for independence from the parents, thereby reducing the parent's global effectiveness and opportunity for learning.

Thus this process of selection in getting the top team is critical. To facilitate the objectives of the partnership and the IJV, the managing director and the HR manager may need to be sourced locally, and with criteria agreed upon by both parents. Both, however, may need to be acquainted with the parents (Schuler *et al.* 1992; Schuler and van Sluijs 1992).

When both parents are interested in the IJV and want it to succeed, they get involved in all the early key decisions. Under these conditions, the board of directors is likely to be composed equally of representatives of the parents and the IJV (internal and external to these entities). The chief operating officer, if not the managing director, may be selected from the source providing the most experience with the operation of the IJV.

Stage 3 – Implementation: the IJV itself

The implementation stage of the IJV process involves establishing the vision, mission, values, culture, strategy and structure; developing the human resource policies and practices of the IJV. By establishing vision and values the IJV begins to provide cohesion, meaning and direction.

The vision, mission, values, strategy and structure need to support, encourage and reward learning and the sharing of knowledge. They also need to support the other needs of the business, the needs of the parents and the needs of the other multiple stakeholders. With a high quality top management team in the IJV, the vision, mission, values, strategy and structure are more likely to be crafted to fit the local needs as well as those of the parents. At this point, it is clearly not in the interest of the IJV to ignore the linkages with the parents. For the parents, willingness to trust the IJV top management team to act in their interests and at the same time the interests of the IJV is critical.

The entire set of the HR policies and practices needs to be created for the IJV. The factors that these practices need to reflect include the IJV's vision, mission and culture; the labour market; and the need for global integration with parent(s) such as for knowledge transfer. As shown in Table 16.3, acceptable human resource policies and practice may vary substantially based upon the cultural dimensions of the countries (Hofstede 1993).

Who actually develops the HR policies and practices can range from one of the parents to the IJV exclusively. The more that the development is left with the IJV, the greater likelihood that the practices will be effective for local adaptation, but not as effective for global integration and learning transfer.

Table 16.3 Likely HR policies and practices in different cultural dimensions

HR Practices	Power Distance		Individualism	
	Low	High	Low	High
Staffing	Select for career progression Joint placement and career decisions	Select for specific job and level Boss places and plans employees' careers	Selection for team players and ... Willingness to contribute to firm	Selection for individual contributions and Desire to develop own career
Appraising	Joint problem solving Personal initiative in planning execution 360° feedback	Assign goals One-way communication	Not focused on task accomplishment as much as group membership and loyalty	Individual task accomplishments Set personal goals
Compensating	Employee participation and involvement in reward techniques Profit-sharing; gain-sharing	No employee participation Status distinctions accepted	Group-based contingent rewards Non-economic rewards that satisfy recognition needs	Individual-based contingent rewards Individual praise & recognition
Training & Leadership	Skills for advancement	Skills for present job Direction	Skill improvement to contribute to organization Group skills Consideration	Skill improvement for self improvement Autonomy
Work Design	Provides freedom, discretion and participation	Job structure, feedback and direction by boss	Facilitates work design that includes: Teamwork, Task significance, Feedback from others	Use of Task Identity, Autonomy, Feedback from job

HR Practices	Uncertainty Avoidance		Masculinity	
	Low	High	Low	High
Staffing	No job descriptions General career guidelines	Clear job descriptions Clear career paths Specific rules and policies	Fit into group Fit with organization	Take personal responsibility Ability to do job
Appraising	Set of difficult and specific goals which involve high risk-taking	Set easy goals with low risk raking	Use social benefit, quality of work life and equality	Job tasks & goals Work action plans Performance feedback
Compensating	Link pay to performance External equity Flexibility Broad banding	Limited use of performance-based (at risk) pay Predictability pay consistency	Use of social benefits, quality of work life, non-zero sum, job security	Use performance-pay Competitive pay, promotion and recognition
Training & Leadership	General application Participative; General directions	Task specific Structure; direction	Develop social skills	Develop task skills Initiating structure
Work Design	Challenge Job enrichment; personal intrinsic gain	Simple job design Limited scope of responsibility Enable group interaction	Job context important Colleagues, security and safety	Job content important Challenge, task accomplishment

© Randall S. Schuler, Rutgers University

Each partner may place differing priorities on the joint venture; therefore, a partner may assign relatively weak management resources to the venture. To be successful, the assigned managerial resources should have not only relevant capabilities and be of adequate quality, but the overall blend of these managerial resources should reflect a balance of the interests of both parents and of the IJV. These managerial assignments should reflect equal quality, particularly on the attribute of absorptive capacity, to help ensure an equal capacity to learn and transfer knowledge to the parents. Balance should also be evident in the number and importance of the managerial assignments made by both parents. This balance should also reflect the input and views of the IJV's top management team.

Because these assignments could be perceived as attempts to control the IJV (Pucik 1988), it could be argued that the IJV's top management should have the final say in the staffing of any positions within the IJV itself. Where trust needs are high, however, and the parents have the needed competencies, the parents may be able to dictate initial and temporary staffing needs. In the Davidson–Marley IJV case, because of the skills of the two partners, Davidson supplied the human resources relevant to the manufacturing systems and the administrative systems. Marley actually built the plant, but Davidson designed the interior of the facility to fit their technology. In addition, Davidson already assigned three design engineers from its facility in the US to be expatriates in Europe. These engineers worked with 14 contract designers recruited in Europe to design the component that was to be manufactured in the plant. Marley located a sales manager in The Netherlands, and supplied sales and marketing support to the company. These were all temporary managerial assignments that were removed once the facility was up and running and the local personnel were trained.

Deciding how to evaluate IJV managers is another major challenge. It has been claimed that several joint ventures have failed because of inappropriate staffing. Myopic, biased parent organizations may make poor selection decisions, or they may be tempted to use the IJV to off-load surplus. Performance evaluation of the top management team, therefore, is important.

Parents and the IJV need to be sensitive to the potential need for dual loyalties. For short-term expatriate assignments the potential may be moot, but for longer term expatriates, parents may have to expect, even desire, to have their employees develop dual loyalties. Dual loyalties may help facilitate the transfer and sharing of knowledge, because the employees can be trusted by the parents and the IJV itself. For Davidson and Marley, the assignments of design engineers and the controller were primarily for start-up purposes. These employees' loyalties remained with Davidson because of the explicitly temporary nature of their assignments.

It has been reported that more than 50 per cent of expatriates felt their overseas assignments were either immaterial or detrimental to their careers (Schuler, Dowling, Jackson and De Cieri 1991) – a finding which indicates potential motivational problems any IJV may encounter. The motivation of executives assigned to an IJV can be enhanced by the creation of a clear linkage between the assignment and an assignee's future career. Some assurance of job security may be needed to offset perceived risks. As with any overseas assignment, assignment to a joint venture may make the manager's future career appear uncertain. If the parent company has not thought through this issue, this uncertainty may be justified. Thus, parent organizations should offer career planning to counter the ambiguity and risks associated with an IJV assignment, and to limit the potential for unsatisfying repatriation experiences.

Apart from career-path disturbances, the assignment to an IJV post usually requires relocation to a foreign country with all the disruption to family and social life that such a posting entails. Benefits packages must be designed to maintain the economic and social lifestyle of the manager so that the individual does not lose through the IJV assignment.

Success of the IJV rests upon getting the right people, at the right place at the right time. Cyr (1995) summarizes the staffing situation for all IJV positions by pointing to the need for extensive screening procedures for employees at all levels; exchange of staff from the parents who are strong contributors with appropriate skill sets (versus 'deadwood' that the parent firms wanted to relocate); allocation of sufficient numbers of staff to the joint venture to maximize the benefits of continuous improvement through high employee involvement; along with issues concerning hiring, staffing and development.

Stage 4 – Advancement: the IJV and beyond

As the IJV becomes established, the partners' relationship continues to evolve. In Doz and Hamel's (1998) view, learning and adjustment by the partners are the key to alliance longevity and the avoidance of premature dissolution. If partners learn at unequal rates, the relationship can be inherently and inevitably dynamic. As partner A's learning surpasses partner B's, the bargaining power of partner A increases. At this stage, partner A can engage in opportunistic, self-interested behaviour or engage in forbearance. As partner B sees partner A engaging in forbearance, partner B's need for control decreases and the level of trust between the two partners grows. If partner A engages in opportunistic behaviour, partner B attempts to increase control, and thereby the level of trust diminishes (Inkpen and Currall 1999). Thus, when both partners trust each other, learning can continue.

Without learning symmetry in the partner relationship, the need for behaviour that may lead to greater control, diminished trust and a renegotiating of the arrangement increases. As trust diminishes IJV monitoring and control costs increase and there is greater reliance on formal controls rather than informal controls. But as partners learn more *about* and *from* each other, trust increases, partners are less protective of their knowledge, and new opportunities for greater learning are created (Inkpen and Currall 1999).

Consequently, partners need to establish conditions to: (a) reduce the possibilities of differential learning; (b) increase the likelihood of forbearance behaviour when differential learning occurs; and (c) increase the levels of trust in and knowledge of each other. While certainly influenced in the first stage activities of partner selection, these conditions can be further influenced by human resource management activities in this stage. Partners may jointly assess their learning capabilities and their overall goals of the IJV process; and partners may continue to ensure that formal and informal communication channels remain open and are used frequently.

Partners may also include successful management of the IJV process in managerial performance appraisal, compensation and development (Pucik 1988; Cyr 1995). They may also jointly assess their belief systems and assumptions. The more the partners are able to discard their own belief systems and assumptions, and revise if necessary, the more likely that there will be useful learning from the knowledge transferred. This is not always easy to do.

It is one thing for partners to share knowledge and learn from each other, and quite another for a parent to learn from the IJV itself. Topics of learning symmetry, trust and control may play out differently, and perhaps with a greater degree of complexity. In the scenario with the IJV itself, partner A can learn from and about partner B, and the IJV itself. For the sake of learning symmetry, partner A may want to ensure partner B also learns from the IJV itself. Thus, the need to set up mechanisms to transfer new knowledge from the IJV to both parents is essential although this may be more difficult with one local and one foreign parent.

Parents, however, may still find that building trust with the IJV itself is important. Without trust, the IJV may try to avoid transferring learning and knowledge to the parent. What is transferred instead is merely information. This may be more likely as the IJV grows and establishes its own identity and seeks independence from the parents. Notable American firms doing well at transferring knowledge from the IJV to the parent use two different techniques. Corning, one of the largest users of joint ventures, transfers learning through communication, largely oral communication. Their culture supports this process. Hewlett-Packard, by contrast, uses a disciplined, written approach. While different, both companies are long-experienced veterans of joint venture learning and knowledge sharing. The mechanisms for knowledge and information transfer that can be used include top management support, staff rotation and training, and rewards.

Essentially, parents and the joint venture need the right people who are willing and able to learn trust and transfer/share knowledge between them. And they need to have communication systems that are as complex as the IJV process itself. There is also scope to transfer learning to other units in the parents' organizations. Managers will need to be encouraged to behave in ways that facilitate learning and knowledge transfer, e.g. co-operative, team-oriented behaviours. To continue to get these needed behaviours, reward systems need to be aligned with those behaviours. Thus, there are both organizational level and individual/group level implications in transferring learning and knowledge of other locations.

IMPLICATIONS FOR HR MANAGERS AND HR DEPARTMENTS

Pucik (1988) and Cyr (1995) have devoted considerable attention to the role of the HR manager and the HR department in the organizations seeking to establish or consider alliances, particularly IJVs with a focus on learning. When discussing IJVs in particular, there is the additional need to consider the HR manager and department of the IJV itself. This adds complexity above and beyond most other forms of alliances not involving the creation of a unique and separate legal entity.

Pucik (1988) describes ten sets of activities for the HR department:

1. *Getting involved early.* The human resource department should be involved in the formation of the strategic alliance from the early planning stages. In a dialogue with the appropriate line departments, HR staff should assume responsibility for the development of a thorough organizational learning strategy.

2. *Building learning into the partnership agreement.* In order to maintain a long-term symmetry in the distribution of benefits from the partnership, both parties have to learn simultaneously. The process of parallel learning can and should be made explicit.

3. *Communicating strategic intent.* As a part of its responsibility for corporate communications, HR should co-operate with operational managers to assure that the strategic intent with respect to the partnership is adequately communicated to the employees. Training programmes should be developed to prepare managers to deal effectively with the ambiguity and complexity of strategic alliances.

4. *Maintaining HR input into the partnership.* The control of the HR department in joint ventures should not be bargained away, as it is within the boundaries of such an entity that much of the learning occurs.

5. *Staffing to learn.* The accumulation of invisible assets should be the key principle guiding the staffing strategy. Staffing and development plans should be established to cover the existing blind spots. Such an approach may require a considerable investment in the development of core competencies within the parent firm through a carefully calibrated transfer policy.

6. *Setting up learning-driven career plans.* From an individual perspective, effective learning and transfer of competencies span the entire career. While cross-cultural learning is most effective during the early career stages, functional learning and its effective application may require considerable business experience.

7. *Using training to stimulate the learning process.* Three kinds of training activities can create a better climate for learning. First, in internal training, managers should be made aware of the subtleties involved in managing collaboration and competition at the same time. Second, open communication and trust within the partnership is essential for the smooth transfer of know-how. Finally, any training programme geared to the acquisition of a specific competence should be, in principle, reciprocal. This diminishes the incentives for opportunistic behaviour.

8. *Responsibility for learning should be specified.* In order to create a climate receptive to learning, a specific responsibility for learning should be written into business plans for managers transferred into the IJV as well as those in the parent.

9. *Rewarding learning activities.* Management behaviour that encourages organizational learning, such as sharing and diffusion of critical information, should be explicitly recognized and rewarded.

10. *Monitor the HR practices of your partner.* Throughout the duration of the relationship, attention should be given to the partner's HR activities. Beginning with an HR audit prior to the establishment of the partnership, much insight can be gained from the continuous monitoring of the partner's staffing and training activities and practices for learning. (Adapted from Pucik 1988: 89–91).

For the HR department to perform all these activities effectively, it needs to have a very special leader. The leader not only must be knowledgeable in HR activities but also must be well-versed in topics such as mergers and acquisitions, productivity, and IJV efforts. He or she must be familiar with the needs of the business and able to work side by side with line management as a partner and with HR managers on other areas. Being part of the management team shapes the meaning of the HR leader's key roles, as described in Table 16.4.

To play these roles, the HR leader in a highly competitive environment where alliances and IJVs exist needs the competencies shown in Figure 16.1.

In addition to these three clusters of competencies that are particularly relevant in the context of IJVs, there are several that are regarded as basic technical and professional competencies (Cyr 1995; Ulrich 1998; Jackson and Schuler 2000). Lorange (1986) argued that IJVs must have their own, strong, fully-fledged HR department. The three major roles of the IJV's HR department are: (1) to assign and motivate people via job skills, compatibility of styles, and communication compatibility, (2) to manage human resources strategically; and (3) to ensure that learning is being created, shared and transferred so that the IJV is seen as a vehicle to produce not only financial rewards, but also managerial capabilities that can be used later in other strategic settings. To the extent an IJV is staffed with temporary managerial assignees, transferring people to an IJV every two years may not result in strategic continuity of management.

In addition to the three major HR roles, the new IJV will have to establish its own set of human resource practices, policies and procedures. Thus, the HR leader needs to possess many of the same competencies of the HR leader in the parent firms.

Table 16.4 The key roles for the HR leader in the parent of IJVs

Key roles	What is expected on the job
Partnership	Shows concern for multiple sets of stakeholders
	Understands how money gets made, lost and spent in a global context
	Knows the market and how IJVs can fit the business
	Works effectively with other HR leaders
Change Facilitator	Can execute change in strategy
	Can get others to work with partners
	Can think conceptually and articulate thoughts
	Is able to get others to change from competitor to partner
Strategy Implementor	Has the ability to build commitment and trust
	Responds to needs of several organizations
	Recognizes the importance of teamwork across organizations
Strategic Thinking	Is capable of educating line manager about trust and learning
	Knows the plan of top executives and can influence partner selection
	Is involved in the formulation of IJV strategies
	Can create structures and cultures for learning
Innovator	Sees the talent needed for executing IJV strategies
	Can adapt to changes in the stages of the IJV process
Collaborator	Knows how to work with partners to create a win-win situation
	Sees the wisdom of sharing over competing
	Works with IJV itself to insure its success

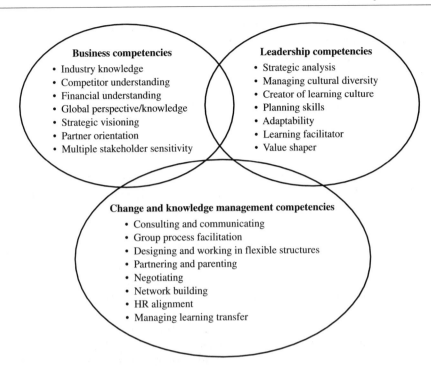

Figure 16.1 The three sets of HR competences for international joint ventures

The HR leader in the IJV needs to fulfil many of the roles shown in Figure 16.1 for the HR leader of the parents of the IJV. In addition, the HR leader in the IJV needs to play the dual role of working with and understanding the IJV and at the same time both parents. Competencies in negotiation, communications and tolerance are critical in this additional role. The HR leader also needs to manage the process of gaining independence from the parents. As part of a high-quality top management team, the HR leader will see the desire for greater control of the IJV by the local management team. Yet while other senior managers may want total succession, the HR leader must forebear this desire for the sake of continued learning and sharing with and from the parents. The IJV grows up to become an adult capable of interacting as an equal, but not totally separate, partner. Competencies in negotiations, humility, multi-loyalties, flexibility, change, persuasion and learning are critical in this process of managing the desire to become independent.

CONCLUSION

IJVs are an important organizational form and will continue to be so. Yet while there are many advantage to organizations using IJVs, there are also numerous challenges. These challenges appear insurmountable for many companies, as evidenced by the rate of failure in many international joint ventures. Based on the discussion in this chapter, many of these challenges are not associated with just one aspect of IJVs. Rather they are associated with many aspects of the IJV process.

The IJV process can be thought of as flowing through four stages: formation, establishment, implementation and advancement. While treated separately here, each stage is vitally dependent upon the other. Viewed from the perspective of human resource management, all stages are united by a variety of human resource issues and activities. Identifying and addressing these issues and activities takes a great deal of systematic investigation. Failure to do so may contribute to, if not outright result in, failure of the IJV. Nevertheless, it is possible that such failure is more common than one would estimate based upon the importance of human resource management in IJV. According to Cyr (1995: 21):

> Although HRM is recognized as important and deserving of attention, the amount of time spent on HR issues in international ventures remains small: 'of the 100 to 5,000 hours typically involved in creating IJVs, only about 4% of the time has been spent resolving human resource issue'.

Cyr (1995), Pucik (1988) and others suggest, however, that the lack of involvement in human resource issues and activities in IJVs is not due to a lack of recognition of their importance, but rather because as Cyr (1995: 21) has noted, 'Previous information related to the development and implementation of HRM practice in international joint ventures is very limited'.

One purpose of this chapter has been to bring together as much previous information as possible from as many areas as possible as they relate to human resource management in the IJV process. In addition to using the four stage model to help organize this information, the contemporary emphasis on the learning and knowledge perspectives of IJVs was used. Certainly as we move forward there are many ways in which the HR department and HR leadership can be involved. Their involvement is certainly strategic and highly important to organizations and HR and to the potential success of IJVs.

REFERENCES

Child, J. and Faulkner, D. (1998) *Strategies of Cooperation*, Oxford: Oxford University Press.

Cohen, W.M. and Levinthal, D.A. (1990) 'Absorptive Capacity: A New perspective on Learning and Innovations', *Administrative Science Quarterly*, **35**: 128–52.

Cyr, D.J. (1995) *The Human Resource Challenge Of International Joint Ventures*, Westport: Quorum Books.

Doz, Y.L. and Hamel, G. (1998) *Alliance Advantage: The Art of Creating Value Through Partnering*, Boston: Harvard Business School Press.

Drucker, P.F. (1989) *The New Realities*, New York: Harper & Row.

Hamel, G. (1991) 'Competition for Competence and Inter-Partner Learning Within International Strategic Alliances', *Strategic Management Journal*, **12** (special issue): 83–104

Harbison, J.R. (1996) *Strategic Alliances: Gaining a Competitive Advantage*, New York: The Conference Board.

Harrigan, K.R. (1986) *Managing for Joint Venture Success*, Boston: Lexington.

Hofstede, G. (1993) 'Cultural Constraints In Management Theories', *Academy of Management Executive*, **71**(1): 81–93.

Hopkins, H.D. (1999) 'Cross-Border Mergers and Acquisitions: Global and Regional Perspectives', *Journal of International Management*, **5**(3): 207–19.

Inkpen, A.C. and Currall, S. (1997) 'International Joint Venture Trust: An Empirical Examination', in P.W. Beamish, J.P. Killing (eds) *Cooperative Strategies: North American Perspectives*, San Francisco: New Lexington Press: 308–34.

Jackson S.E. and Schuler R.S. (2000) *Managing Human Resources: A Partnership Perspective*, seventh edition, Cincinnati, Ohio: South-Western Publishing.

Killing, J.P. (1983) *Strategies for Joint Venture Success*, New York: Praeger Publishers.

Lei, D., Slocum, J.W. Jr. and Pitts, R.A. (1997) 'Building Cooperative Advantage: Managing Strategic Alliances To Promote Organizational Learning', *Journal of World Business*, **32**(3): 202–23.

Lorange, P. (1986) 'Human Resource Management in Multinational Cooperative Ventures', *Human Resource Management*, **25**: 133–48.

Luo, Y. (1999) 'Toward A Conceptual Framework Of International Joint Venture Negotiations', *Journal of International Management*, **5**: 141–65.

Luo, Y. (1998) 'Joint Venture Success in China: How Should We Select A Good Partner', *Journal of World Business*, **33**(2): 145–66.

McGill, M., Slocum, J.W. and Lei, D. (1992) 'Management Practices in Learning Organizations', *Organizational Dynamics*, Summer: 5–17.

Pucik, V. (1988) 'Strategic Alliances, Organizational Learning and Competitive Advantage: The HRM Agenda', *Human Resource Management*, **27**(1): 77–93.

Schaan, J.L. (1988) 'How to Control A Joint Venture Even As A Minority Partner', *Journal of General Management*, **14**(1): 4–16.

Schuler R.S. (2001) 'Human Resource Management Issues and Activities in International Joint Ventures', *International Journal of Human Resource Management*, **12**(1): 1–35.

Schuler R.S., van Sluijs E. (1992) 'Davidson-Marley BV: Establishing and Operating An International Joint Venture', *European Management Journal*, **10**(4): 28–37.

Schuler, R.S., Dowling, P.J. and DeCieri, H. (1992) 'The Formation of an International Joint Venture: Marley Automotive Components Ltd.', *European Management Journal*, September: 304–309.

Schuler, R.S., Dowling, P.J., Jackson, S.E. and DeGieri, H. (1991) 'The Formation of an International Joint Venture', *Human Resource Planning*, **14**: 51–60.

Shenkar, O. and Zeira, Y. (1987) 'Human Resource Management In International Joint Ventures: Direction For Research', *Academy of Management Review*, **12**(3): 546–57.

Shenkar, O. and Li, J. (1999) 'Knowledge Search in International Cooperative Ventures,' *Organizational Science*, **10**(2): 34–44.

Slocum, J.W. and Lei, D. (1993) 'Designing Global Stategic Alliances: Integrating Cultural and Economic Factors', in G.P. Huber and W.H. Glick (eds) *Organizational Change and Redesign: Ideas and Insights for Improving Performance*, New York: Oxford University Press: 295–322.

Sparks, D. (1999) 'Partners', *Business Week*, October 5: 106.

Ulrich, D. (1998) *Delivering Results: A New Mandate for Human Resource Professionals*, Boston: Harvard Business School Press.

Part 5
Future Prospects

Knowledge Management and HRM 17

John Storey and Paul Quintas

INTRODUCTION

'Knowledge management' has become one of the most significant developments – if not indeed *the* most significant development – in management and organization theory in recent years. It is increasingly claimed that knowledge is 'the most important factor in economic life' (Stewart 1997: 2). Likewise, Prusack (1997: ix) contends, 'a firm's competitive advantage depends more than anything on its knowledge, or, to be slightly more specific, on what it knows, how it uses what it knows, and how fast it can know something new'. Current management literature is replete with like-minded claims.

The knowledge perspective offers what appears to be a new set of insights into the theory of the firm (for an examination of that aspect see Spender 1996) while at the same time, at the macro level, new claims are being made about a fundamental shift to an entirely new form of economy – the 'knowledge economy'. Although knowledge in varying degrees has obviously always had some part to play in human economic and productive endeavour from time immemorial, the 'new' claim is that, under current conditions, knowledge has come to assume the prime role among the various factors of production (such as land, labour, physical resources and capital) and that these other factors have been eclipsed in their significance by the power of knowledge and its criticality. As we shall see below, this perspective is not quite as new as many current protagonists would have us believe, but this lineage does not negate the fact that only recently has the issue of *knowledge* entered mainstream management discourse and there are now numerous examples of organizations which have launched, self-consciously and explicitly, elaborate 'knowledge management initiatives' – not always with complete success (Storey and Barnett 2000).

Knowledge management as a phenomenon is constituted by multiple sub-perspectives and approaches – information management and organizational learning are two of the most important of these. In the burgeoning conference circuit and specialist journals, as well as in many organizations, the knowledge management territory is being disputed by two main factions – information technology and human resources, with the former significantly dominating the public debate. From an economics perspective the concept of 'intellectual capital' is closely allied – and for some the latter would be the term of choice. This concept in turn is associated with the notion of 'human capital' and from there one can see the connection with human capital accounting which in the history of HR has not proved in practice to live up to its original promise. But proponents of the new knowledge perspective would claim that 'knowledge management' has much more to offer and that it carries fundamental and far-reaching implications for all aspects of organizational management. Crucially, however, in the context of this present volume, our principle concern is the interrelationship between knowledge management and human resource management. The central purpose of this chapter is to examine that relationship and explore its implications.

The chapter is organized into three parts. The first takes a closer look at the key themes, characteristics and research evidence concerning knowledge management. Given that background, the second part explores the idea of 'knowledge work' and 'knowledge workers' and seeks to clarify the HR management issues, problems and priorities which would seem to arise when knowledge becomes a primary organizational concern. The third examines the HR practices which would seem to best fit this kind of situation.

THE IDEA OF KNOWLEDGE MANAGEMENT

Current interest follows a long history of attention to knowledge from economic and organizational perspectives. In the late nineteenth century, using language that is surprisingly familiar in the current climate, Alfred Marshall observed that 'Capital consists in a great part of knowledge and organization ... Knowledge is our most powerful engine of production' (Marshall 1890). This line of reasoning is widely echoed today, as for example in the writings of Tom Stewart (1997: x) who similarly observes: 'Intellectual capital is intellectual material – knowledge, information, intellectual property, experience – that can be put to use to create wealth. It is collective brainpower. [...] Knowledge and information – not just scientific knowledge, but news, advice, entertainment, communication, service – have become the economy's primary raw materials and its most important products'.

Stewart's account is typical of the many attempts to describe the contemporary importance of knowledge: it emphasizes the *intangibility* of 'knowledge assets' – or 'intellectual capital'. These ideas have evoked a receptive response from some influential industrialists. To a large extent the importance of 'knowledge management' derives from the fact that many practitioners respond to it as if it were important. At the same time there are hints that the knowledge-based proposition carries some difficulties for managers. While senior managers alert to the potential of knowledge management may not have explicated the full range of problems, they have revealed an awareness of some of them. In particular, the difficulties of first detecting and then managing knowledge assets have been well noted. Thus, for example, the CEO of Texas Instruments, Jerry Junkins, has declared 'If TI only knew what TI knows' and Lew Platt, chairman of Hewlett Packard has stated 'I wish we knew what we know at HP' (cited in O'Dell and Grayson 1998: 154). As we will see later in this chapter, these are only some of the difficulties which are faced by those who seek to 'manage knowledge'.

It is important at this stage also to acknowledge that the scope and content of the field described by the phrase 'knowledge management' is in a state of being defined. Although a number of themes are emerging as a result of general consensus on their significance, there are still many interpretations of the boundaries and content of this new area. We should recognize that interest is converging on this field from a number of different perspectives, disciplines and practical concerns. Management perspectives include information management, communications organizational learning, strategic management, change management, human resource management, management of innovation, economics and the measurement and management of intangible assets. Very often the proponents of any one particular view only see their part of the larger picture. Amongst the many perspectives, ironically, there is a tendency for the *information technology* focus to dominate much of the writings and conference proceedings. This is ironic, of course, because most (though perhaps not all) information technology developments are concerned with data and information rather than knowledge. As Spender (1996) has pointed out, there is little point in introducing such a complex concept as knowledge into management discourse if we are not to take seriously the characteristics of knowledge.

A more comprehensive approach stems from the strategic management arena, focused on the *resources and capabilities* framework for explaining and predicting the superior performance of some organizations above others. Whereas previous economics-derived thinking emphasized resources as static bundles of assets, the notion of 'capabilities' (or 'core competencies') introduces a dynamic aspect to thinking about resources, including human resources (Scarbrough 1998). Key capabilities include the ability to generate, access and add value to resources. Unlike most of the economics derived approaches, the resources and capabilities approach emphasizes the advantage created by internal capabilities:

> Resources are inputs into the production process – they are the basic units of analysis. ... But, on their own, few resources are productive. Productive activity requires the co-operation and co-ordination of teams of resources. A capability is the capacity for a team of resources to perform some task or activity. While resources are the source of a firm's capabilities, capabilities are the main source of its competitive advantage.
>
> (Grant 1991: 118–19)

Resources may be internal or external to the organization, requiring the existence of capabilities to build and maintain the internal resources, and capabilities to manage and secure cross-boundary access to external resources. The vast majority of tangible resources are available to all organizations, at a price, but organizational capability is likely to be unique and intangible:

> Since the origin of all tangible resources lies outside the firm, it follows that competitive advantage is more likely to arise from the intangible firm-specific knowledge which enables it to add value to the incoming factors of production in a relatively unique manner.
>
> (Spender 1996: 46)

Creating core competences or capabilities means creating competitive advantages which could not be replicated in the way that most traditional resources can be replicated. Core capabilities to create new knowledge or to transform and share existing knowledge are likely to rely heavily on tacit or implicit knowledge. This makes them difficult to manage, as well as making them hard to copy. This point is illustrated by the CEO of Chaparral Steel, who claims he can 'tour competitors through the plant, show them "almost everything and we will be giving away nothing because they can't take it home with them"' (Leonard Barton 1995: 7). Similarly, Nonaka observes that 'it is extremely difficult for people to share each others' thinking processes' (Nonaka 1994: 19).

Baumard (1999) has usefully distinguished between knowledge that is currently tacit but might be articulated, such as the kinds of reflections surfaced in a post-project review, and that knowledge which is inherently tacit and incommunicable, such as the knowledge that underlies the ability to make intuitive judgements, or the knowledge of how to ride a bicycle. He terms the former implicit knowledge in contrast to the permanently uncodifiable tacit knowledge.

At the centre of the idea of knowledge management lies the key relationship between an individual's knowledge and their social and organizational contexts. The realization that people know things, and that this knowledge provides organizations with competitive advantage, has become widely expressed. However, this does not mean that managers should concentrate solely on accessing or somehow capturing existing knowledge. A core capability focuses on the ability to create new knowledge. Nonaka and Takeuchi's influential book *The Knowledge-Creating Company* has as its central theme the proposition that knowledge creation is the basis of competitive advantage (Nonaka and Takeuchi 1995). However, the authors do not propose that knowledge creation leads directly to competitive advantage. Rather, it is *mediated through innovation*. Although the application and integration of existing knowledge are also important for innovation, by definition, since innovation means 'new', it can only occur through, or concomitantly with, the creation of new knowledge. Knowledge creation is therefore closely linked to innovation.

We can see that a number of factors have come together to place knowledge on the top of the management agenda at this time:

- Wealth is increasingly perceived to be derived from knowledge and intangible assets. Company value in recent years has come to be increasingly dependent on intangible assets, knowledge assets, intellectual capital and intellectual property.
- People are seen as the locus of knowledge and thus also seen as the source of value creation. Following the downsizing, early redundancies and outsourcing of the 1980s, organizations re-discovered the importance of people. People own knowledge, create knowledge and value, and retain organizational memory. And they can leave.
- Endemic change and the need for organizational learning. The global pace of change requires continuous regeneration of organizational knowledge bases – organizations and the people within them must be continually learning.
- Advantage through innovation and knowledge creation. Competitive advantage is seen to be gained through innovation, which in turn depends on knowledge creation, knowledge sharing and knowledge application.
- Knowledge interdependence – the need for cross-boundary knowledge sharing. Organizations in all sectors have become more mutually dependent. Even the largest companies must collaborate in order to survive. Much new knowledge is created outside the corporate boundary, so organizations must develop absorptive capacity. This raises the reliance on cross-boundary knowledge inter-dependence between organizations.
- Technology limits and potential. The limits of traditional 'Information Systems' having been recognized, there are also the potentials of communications technologies and the internet, and for the emergence of knowledge technologies.

So much for the factors which have come together to place the issues of knowledge management and intellectual capital on the academic and the management agendas. Attempts to operationalize these ideas soon raise a raft of practical issues.

At the practical level, *knowledge management* focuses on a set of processes and practices. Some of these are supported by management tools or technologies. They address a wide range of knowledge processes that fall under five headings: creating, sharing, sourcing, mapping and measuring – see Figure 17.1.

A great deal of the debate to date as found in the literature and at the conferences on knowledge management has focused on these five sets of issues. Indeed, this is an optimistic assessment of the debate for too often it is much more restricted than Figure 17.1 suggests. The main preoccupations have been with the technological tools (most notably with information and communication technologies (ICT) including intranets and extranets). Beyond that predominant agenda there has also been

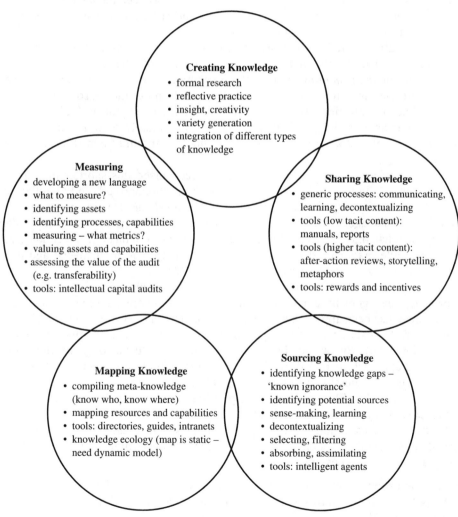

Figure 17.1 Key processes and tools

significant attention paid to issues relating to how to get employees to share knowledge, how to 'capture' employees' knowledge, and how to utilize the knowledge resources made available. The important issue of knowledge creation tends to be neglected by comparison. But there are, in addition we suggest, a whole set of management issues which go beyond these concerns, and of the more important of these are in fact HR issues.

KNOWLEDGE MANAGEMENT AND THE HR ISSUES

In the previous section we outlined the key features of knowledge management. Our aim in this section is to identify the *HR issues and problems* which need to be addressed as a result of this new perspective on organizational management. It is a paradox that while so many authorities and commentators on knowledge management have come to the conclusion that knowledge management ultimately depends upon people it is precisely the people (or HR) aspect which has been the most neglected in studies in this field. Moreover, HR practitioners and HR analysts have been slow in making their mark in this emerging domain.

An international study which examined the various issues and approaches to knowledge management found that three-quarters of the managers actually responsible for *implementing* such strategies thought that it was the people issues which were the most important and vital. But according to the person who led the study, while organizations recognize the importance of capturing and managing and transferring knowledge, they have so far been unable to translate the need into organizational strategies which draw out the human dimension (Pickard 1998: 38).

The high-priests of the movement have also recognized this shortcoming. Thus, Ikujiro Nonaka observes: 'despite all the talk about "brainpower" and "intellectual capital", few managers grasp the true nature of the knowledge-creating company – let alone how to manage it' (Nonaka 1991). And Thomas Davenport notes: 'Knowledge management has thus far been addressed at either a philosophical or a technological level with little pragmatic discussion of how knowledge can be managed and used more effectively on a daily basis' (Davenport 1997).

Likewise, one of the major literature reviews of the people management aspects of knowledge management emphasizes the point that, overwhelmingly, knowledge management has been approached with a technological bias (Scarbrough *et al.* 1999). The review 'reveals an alarming gap in the treatment of personnel management issues' (ibid.: 50). But as Scarbrough *et al.* also note, 'developing an alternative humanised approach to KM depends on more than simply criticising the IT-driven tendency currently dominant in the field' (ibid.: 51).

But *what are* the HR issues which are peculiar to organizations where knowledge has been recognized as a fundamental?

While, as we have noted above, the literature so far is thin in addressing this agenda, it is possible to identify some of the needs which seem to arise. These can be stated as a series of questions:

- To what extent is the concept of the 'knowledge worker' useful and sustainable?
- Who 'owns' and controls knowledge resources and capabilities and with what consequences?

- How will knowledge-generating workers in particular, and knowledge-workers in general, be managed and rewarded? How can organizations hold on to the valuable carriers of knowledge resources and capabilities?
- How can the communication of knowledge be facilitated? How can people be encouraged to share knowledge?
- Will new organizational forms be required and if so what form should they take?
- How can organizations access individuals' tacit and implicit knowledge? And what implications arise for handling motivation and commitment?
- In an age when knowledge resources are increasingly likely to lie outside the organizational boundary, how does an organization set about 'managing' workers who are not directly employed?

These are just some of the main questions and it will not be possible of course to provide full answers even to this selected list but it is important to identify them none the less. Underlying them all, when viewed from an employment relations perspective, is the wider issue concerning a possible shift in power between capital and 'labour'. If it really is the case that, increasingly, the source of value (and wealth) derives from 'knowledge', then workers who are the holders and generators of this vital resource would seem capable of exercising a degree of power which exceeds that traditionally associated with the idea of a 'mere' employee. If business organizations are fragmenting into smaller units and if key workers have unprecedented opportunities for mobility and even for launching their own enterprises then managers (as agents of organizations) would seem to be faced with a whole new set of problems and challenges. In other words, the idea of the 'knowledge economy' appears to place the fundamentals of human resource management onto an entirely new footing. A whole series of prior assumptions, the whole taken-for-granted nature of 'employment management' – including the basics of recruitment, selection, target-setting, discipline, reward, training and development and dismissal – may need to be opened up for questioning. The underlying assumption on which virtually all of the main techniques of 'personnel management' rest is that there is a hierarchical entity presided over by a top management group which is the repository and the fount of power and knowledge. If this assumption is opened up to challenge by the knowledge thesis then a whole set of issues would seem to require re-examination. We can only hope to make an initial start on such an agenda, and we begin with the concept of the 'knowledge worker'.

Who are the 'knowledge workers'?

Behind this question is implicitly another – i.e. are managers being asked to change their approaches to the management of all employees in the new knowledge age or just some of the staff? And if the latter, who is to be regarded as constituting this special category?

In some ways the answer to this question can be found in the seminal work of writers such as Peter Drucker who discussed the idea of 'knowledge work' (Drucker 1968), Daniel Bell who assessed the idea of the 'post industrial society' (Bell 1974), and Fritz Machlup (1962), who mapped and measured the knowledge economy, identifying the workers involved in the 'production of knowledge'. Ideas about the rise of knowledge work, the service society and the post-industrial society have been used by many others since. Often the assumption is that the increase in 'knowledge work' must also mean an increase in the number of 'knowledge workers' – that section of the workforce whose work predominantly entails handling information rather than material things. (On this basis, for example, Thomas Stewart (1997) claims that the proportion of the workforce meeting this criterion has risen during the course of the twentieth century from 17 per cent to 59 per cent.) But this kind of statistic while arguably interesting from the point of view of changes in the advanced economies is rather less helpful in understanding the actual nature of 'knowledge work'. It is highly questionable whether one can simply categorize people employed in non-material work as necessarily 'knowledge workers' and those engaged with 'things' as in a non-knowledge category.

In some instances we are witnessing merely a re-labelling of more familiar roles – see, for example, Sviokla (1996) who analyses the role of salespeople in these terms. In addition, re-conceptualizing sections of the workforce often results from 'political' manoeuvres to reposition them for status reasons – either up or down.

Attempts to demarcate 'knowledge workers' of any sort inevitably raise the question about who the 'non-knowledge workers' might be and what are the appropriate criteria to use in defining them. A case could be made that some forms of routine industrial assembly work have been systematically stripped of as much of their discretionary and knowledge content as possible and that these jobs at least can be excluded from the definitional category. Even here, however, there is scope for debate. The importance of 'know-how' among apparently 'unskilled' industrial workers has been demonstrated by Kusterer (1978), echoing Frederick Taylor's earlier conclusion that workers possess specialist knowledge based on their experience, and this knowledge may not be possessed by managers (Taylor 1911).

> Managers recognize frankly that the ... workmen, including the twenty or thirty trades, who are under them, possess this mass of traditional knowledge, a large part of which is not in the possession of management. The management, of course, includes foremen and superintendents, who themselves have been first-class workers at their trades. And yet these foremen and superintendents know, better than anyone else, that their own knowledge and personal skill falls far short of the combined knowledge and dexterity of the workmen under them.
>
> (Taylor 1911: 32)

There is, however, evidence that since the 1970s, much industrial work has become increasingly knowledge-intensive. For example, team leader roles at Ford in the engine and transmission plants are now predominantly staffed by graduate engineers as the roles have become more technically sophisticated and these graduates have increasingly displaced traditional foremen/supervisors (Storey 1992). Having reviewed the literature on knowledge work Choi (1995), comes to the conclusion that the term is usually narrowly reserved for professional and technical workers, and that, with the massive movement to empower workers at all levels, it is time to redefine the concept.

According to Daniel Bell, whereas industrial societies are goods-producing and involve a 'game against fabricated nature', in a post-industrial society it is a game between persons; information replaces energy and muscle power. As a game between persons, social life becomes more complicated, there is rapid social change and shifting fashions, and information becomes a central resource (Bell 1974). According to this interpretation, knowledge workers in the new post-industrial society are in the majority. The management requirements are now different but they are not esoteric. On the contrary they become the mainstream set of needs. This kind of argument enjoyed a resurgence in the 1990s and on the whole the message was again optimistic. But the interpretation did not go unchallenged. Other analyses have pointed to the increased precariousness, insecurity and fragmentation of work – see for example, Beck (1992) and Allen (1996).

The (new) knowledge workers are assumed to be characterized by higher levels of education and, it is assumed, greater needs for autonomy and self-actualization. This emphasis on autonomy and self-actualization begins to distance the notion of knowledge work from the assumption that workers' knowledge is a resource that is somehow amenable to 'capture' and codification, as many current knowledge management initiatives (in the spirit of Fredrick Taylor) would suggest.

> The mergers assume ... the burden of gathering together all of the traditional knowledge which in the past has been possessed by the workmen and then of classifying, tabulating, and reducing this knowledge to rules, laws, and formulae...
>
> (Taylor 1911: 36)

The more reflective current accounts of knowledge work see it as varied, non-repetitive and autonomous, and emphasize that one of the key activities of the knowledge worker is the process of creation of new knowledge on a continuing basis. Thus, knowledge work is characterized by variety rather than routine.

Key issues and problems in the management of knowledge workers

There are a number of fundamental issues which managers must confront if they are to engage with the knowledge worker problem. There are five in particular which deserve immediate attention. These are: first, the challenge of developing and sustaining an organizational culture that supports and promotes knowledge creation and thereby the ability to innovate; second the problem of gaining access to the form of knowledge (often highly tacit) which knowledge workers have and use; third, the problem of winning trust, motivation and commitment; fourth, the problem involved in managing workers who are often not conventional 'employees' – they may be contract workers and consultants; lastly, there are a set of problems which may be described as rendering the organization vulnerable because of its reliance on knowledge workers. We can briefly examine each of these in turn.

Organizational cultures for knowledge creation and innovation

While many current 'knowledge management' initiatives seek, with varying degrees of plausibility, to capture, codify, measure and utilize existing knowledge, organizations which aspire to be innovative need to consider what may be a more formidable challenge – the creation of new knowledge. Innovation depends on the ability to manage, as a dynamic process, the generation or creation of new knowledge, as well as the application, transformation and integration of existing knowledge. New knowledge is created during the innovation process, which is to say that learning has taken place – those involved have collectively or individually learned how to do something new.

Thus, a central knowledge management dilemma for organizations seeking to innovate stems from the need to build their knowledge bases cumulatively, share knowledge and learn from past experience, while at the same time they need to generate variety and untypicality in their knowledge base as the source of novel developments. For all organizations the knowledge management challenges presented by innovation focus on this tension between linear and non-linear processes – i.e. between the predictable and the unpredictable. Innovation therefore is far from safe and risk-free, and requires eclectic and diverse approaches to the types and sources of knowledge that might be relevant. Innovation is about diversity, untypicality and uncertainty, and it therefore carries a considerable degree of risk. Innovating organizations must expect, recognize and even encourage, failure. For most organizations, these requirements will imply a revision of the prevailing culture.

Accessing tacit and implicit knowledge

This issue is important because much of the important knowledge in contemporary post-industrial conditions resides in workers' heads; it may be implicit knowledge of the kind that can be articulated in the appropriate context, or tacit knowledge of the kind that must remain inexpressible (Baumard 1999). If the appropriate way to proceed is no longer to be reliably found in a manual or in the directions from a chief executive then the managerial problem shifts from the age-old one of instruct, supervise and monitor, to the new one of utilizing worker knowledge not only of *how* something might best be done but sometimes even ideas about *what* ought to be done. Workers long socialized into 'leaving their brains at the gatepost' can hardly be expected to make such a switch with ease. Likewise, their line managers – both supervisory first line and middle level managers whose roles depended upon such an expectation – are equally likely to find this change problematical.

Trust, motivation and commitment

Then there is the problem of trust, motivation and commitment. The literature on high commitment management suggests that its achievement is no easy thing. To what might the employee be committed: the task, the job, the workplace, the team, the business unit, the employer, or the profession? These and others are all possible. One of the most widely used definitions of commitment is that of March and Simon (1958) who saw it as 'identification with an organization and acceptance of its goals and values as one's own'. With the loosening of employment ties in the enterprise culture of the 1980s and 1990s the question about the precise identity of 'the organization' however becomes more problematic. The general idea is that workers who have a high commitment to the organization will have high morale, be less likely to leave, will have low absenteeism and will volunteer extra 'discretionary' effort and creative ideas.

Contract workers, consultants and cross-boundary relationships

A further problem is that increasingly the knowledge workers to be 'managed' are no longer employees of the organization – that is, they do not have an employment contract but a payment-for-services contract. Expertise is increasingly sought and required from beyond organizational boundaries from consultants and independent software houses and 'knowledge' itself is not some independent, objective 'thing' to be managed like money or a physical material asset. Knowledge comes in the form of ideas, data and information which are given meaning by, and open to interpretation and re-interpretation by, knowledgeable agents. In consequence, the managerial task may be to manage meanings.

Vulnerability of the organization

Organizations are vulnerable if irreplaceable or hard to replace knowledge workers occupy key positions (Willman 1996). Willman addresses the issue of what firms might do to protect their know-how in order to maintain competitive advantage. He suggests there is additionally a dilemma arising from the need for fluid internal dissemination of information and ideas on the one hand, and external vulnerability on the other.

Another kind of vulnerability is revealed by Robertson (1998) who examines the relationship between knowledge, power and organization within knowledge-intensive firms, such as consultancies in which reliance is placed on individual knowledge and expertise. He researched a UK consultancy over a twelve-year period from its start-up. He argues that the shifts in the relationships between knowledge and power are not necessarily in the direction predicted by most of the knowledge management literature which he views as rather sanguine. The consultancy did not develop a more flexible, networked form based on shared knowledge. Instead, individual analysts were able to employ their 'ego' power to maintain their autonomy. This created a new form of hierarchy.

So far then we have discussed the general idea of 'knowledge management' and we have drawn attention to a number of particular problems which arise for management where knowledge work becomes a central defining feature of an organization. In the next section we turn to an examination of what implications arise for human resource management.

HR PRACTICES FOR KNOWLEDGE MANAGEMENT

To some extent the lessons for good management of knowledge equate with good management of any workers. Indeed, most sets of prescriptions offered in recent conferences (and also in some influential texts such as Ulrich (1998)) imply that there are no differences at all. However, as we will see, there are some formulations which draw clear distinctions between the kind of HR strategy required for innovation and knowledge management in contrast to the HR strategies required for, say, a cost-minimization strategy. Likewise, drawing upon extensive research, Jeffrey Pfeffer has demonstrated how long term sustainable success based on differentiation which is hard to duplicate requires not only a particular HR strategy but, more importantly, careful implementation.

As a guide to the ordering of our material we will follow the framework as shown in Figure 17.2.

It should be noted that by the term 'HR strategy' in this chapter we refer to all three of the boxes in the lower part of the figure. That is, we regard HR strategy as constituted by: structural strategy, cultural strategy and HR practices. Moreover, it is contended that a coherent HR strategy only exists when each of these components is integrated in a mutually reinforcing manner. We will now examine each of these areas in turn.

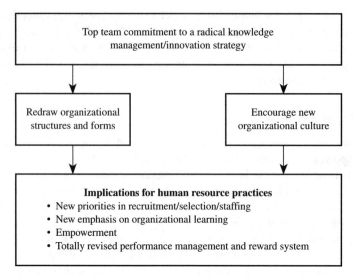

Figure 17.2 HR strategy for innovation and knowledge management

Designing appropriate organizational forms

It is widely held that while the spur to innovation may be the perception of competitive pressure, 'thereafter, success relies on *organisational features* such as cross-functional integration, flexibility, and the accumulation of firm specific skills' (Kay and Willman 1991: 2). In this section we will examine the way in which innovative behaviour can be encouraged through the redesign of organizational structures. The analysis is made at three levels – the team, the wider organization and the cross-organizational level.

Teams

Teams play a vital role in the knowledge creating company, claims Nonaka (1991: 104). In particular, it is suggested that teams can provide:

- a shared context in which individuals can interact with each other and engage in the constant dialogue on which effective reflection depends;
- new points of view through dialogue and discussion between team members;
- a pool of information which can be examined and drawn upon from various angles;
- a useful organizational axis because team leaders (middle managers) are at the intersection of the vertical and horizontal flows of information in the company. They serve as a bridge between the visionary ideals of the top and the often chaotic market reality of those at the front line of the business.

There have been many experiments with 'self-managing' teams working in production areas. Often these have been treated as separate islands with clearly defined boundaries and easily measured outcomes. However, it has been pointed out that unlike these situations, teams of knowledge workers can be successfully included in traditional organizational structures, providing that they have fluid and extensive links with the rest of the organization (Miner 1998). Failure to recognize this distinction has been seen as the principal reason for their limited success to date. Miner even suggests how the benefit of knowledge teams can be realized in a hierarchical structure, avoiding the necessity of embarking on widespread organizational change. He proposes a hybrid which locates the team in a central node in the larger knowledge work system.

Of course, much of the excitement (and possibly hype) concerning teams of knowledge workers has related to the notion of 'virtual teams'. For example, one recent commentator enthuses: 'Virtual teams, whose members are based at different locations, are the new production units of knowledge and are increasingly being recognised as a powerful way of working' (Young 1998). Some people even regard virtual cross functional teams as the new primary business units in knowledge intensive organizations. Their key winning attributes are said to be communication, collaboration and co-ordination.

But what is a virtual team? In one sense it could be the whole company – especially as information and communication technology allows the potential for effective communication across the whole organization. Not only do they allow for division of labour but it is suggested they can be powerful learning devices. Boland *et al*. (1995) refer to 'communities of knowing' while others draw attention to the importance of 'communities of practice' – informal communities that may cut across internal and external organizational boundaries (Brown 1991; Wenger 1998; Wenger and Synder 2000).

From an HR point of view, teams can be seen as important sources of learning and knowledge enhancement through knowledge sharing. They are regarded as fruitful working relationships which are formed when people who share a common purpose and experience similar problems come together to exchange ideas and information. By implication, the managerial lesson is that such communities should be safeguarded, facilitated and fostered.

Virtual teams operating across the globe in theory allow international organizations to work continuously on projects over 24 hours as different parts of the virtual team report for work in the different time zones.

Then there is the question about preferred modes of operation. One recommendation is that 'If you teach a team how to collaborate well, rather than continue to encourage individual 'stars', then the team's performance, its level of innovation and the quality of its organizational knowledge will improve dramatically' (Young 1998). And what of the team leader role? The virtual team leader, it has been suggested, should be coach, facilitator and knowledge manager: 'The role of the manager shifts from compiling information to debating with the team about the implications of the knowledge shared within it' (ibid.: 49). To develop and manage virtual teams would seem to require HR expertise in team development.

Organization-wide structures

Broadly speaking, firms can create one of two systems for 'organizing' knowledge work and innovation. One is the expert option which usually means the creation and maintenance of a distinct R&D department. The other is the wider empowerment system which seeks to extend responsibility more or less across the whole organization. Some would suggest that while the former option is more appropriate for high-tech product firms, the latter is more suitable for low-tech service firms.

In the main, the popular management books which herald the new age of competition based on knowledge tend to ignore this distinction and they proselytize a future pattern which they imply is universally applicable. Freeman's analysis of an extensive body of research on innovation suggests that R&D effort in reality has been predominantly located in larger firms (Freeman and Soete 1997). 'What is distinctive about modern industrial R&D is its scale, its scientific content and the extent of its professional specialisation. A much greater part of technological progress is now attributable to research and development work performed in specialised laboratories or pilot plants by full-time specialist staff' (Freeman, 1997: 9). In so far as this is the case, the HR task is twofold: first, to devise HR interventions appropriate for these elite groups and second, to manage the rest of these organizations in such a way as to maintain motivation, commitment and behaviour which allows timely implementation of the prototypes emerging from the specialists. There is also the further task of managing the interface between specialist R&D units and the main business.

Concerning the organizational design appropriate for organization-wide innovative performance, the modern literature offers a now broadly familiar formula (albeit labelled in various different ways). For example, Davidow and Malone (1992) urge the merits of *The Virtual Corporation*; while Ashkenus *et al.* (1995) explicate the features and the merits of *The Boundaryless Organization*. Meeting increasing customer demands in the face of competitors able to respond with speed means the necessity of breaking down internal and external boundaries; new types of employees will be needed – more educated, skilled and committed, adaptable to change and adept team-players. The name of the game will switch from asset management to 'resource leverage'. Information will be widely shared. Problems will be solved jointly. The management role will change dramatically: as work units become participative, managerial hierarchies become defunct. The implicit model appears to be the adaptable firms of Silicon Valley although Davidow and Malone also see merits in the German *Mittelstand* companies – global players in high-profit niche markets. There are echoes here of the flexible specialization thesis advanced by Piore and Sabel (1984). They used the term flexible specialization to refer to the efforts 'to convert the traditional highly integrated corporate structure into a more supple organizational form capable of responding quickly to shifting market conditions and product demand' (Piore 1986: 146). Piore and Sabel's economic models of flexible specialization were based on networks of small firms limited to regions such as the Veneto and Emilia Romagna in Italy.

The way in which larger firms have sought to respond to such lessons has frequently been to separate off multiple sub-units when they reach a certain size. One of the directors of BMT Group, a UK technical consultancy and R&D contractor, has described how they organize for knowledge work and innovation. Essentially, units ranging from as few as ten employees or as many as a hundred depending on the degree of coherence in the operation, are incorporated into separate subsidiary companies (Docherty 1993). In Hewlett-Packard in the UK we found that the practice was to create a separate division whenever an operation grew to a critical size. This type of splitting-off into sub-units with their own focus seems to be one of the more common organizational practices in the knowledge-intensive industries.

Inter-organizational arrangements/networks

Success in innovation would seem to require the ability not only to create new knowledge but also to access and assimilate knowledge across organizational boundaries. Organizations need to discern and adopt the best new technologies and know-how from a whole range of sources and many of these are likely to be outside the organization. The ability to assimilate new knowledge across organizational boundaries has been formalized as 'absorptive capacity' by Cohen and Levinthal (1990). These authors draw on research into how individuals deal with information and knowledge that is new to them – and, most notably, how they learn to draw upon and utilize the new knowledge.

An organization's absorptive capacity depends on the abilities of all the individuals in the organization to recognize what they know and the way(s) in which they know, the effectiveness with which decision-relevant and timely knowledge is available to whoever can use it, people's ability to make sense of and understand the ramifications of what is being presented to them, the scope for spotting unexpected significance in external signals and for encouraging novel linkages and interpretations to develop.

Since absorptive capacity is concerned with the assimilation of *new* knowledge (new to the organization), it depends on the diversity of existing knowledge and backgrounds and a group. Fundamentally, absorptive capacity depends on communication and learning.

However, the need for diversity must be balanced by the capability to communicate across organizational as well as disciplinary boundaries, i.e. knowledge sharing requires a shared language.

The practical implications of this are many but one structural device is to have 'boundary spanners' or 'gatekeepers', that is, employees who are active in various networks and who can therefore help to keep pace with the latest thinking and the latest developments. Gatekeepers must also communicate new information and knowledge in a form that can be understood by their colleagues, especially if it is complex or far removed from their experience. One specific indicator of the value of boundary spanners is the finding by Newell and Clark (1990) which reveals a statistical relationship between the extent of professional institute involvement by firm members and the degree of innovativeness in the organization.

Encouraging the emergence of an appropriate organizational culture

A whole body of influential work during the past couple of decades has emphasized the crucial significance of 'culture' in shaping behaviour patterns in organizations. Indeed, one of the most central tenets of the Human Resource Management school is that organizational culture is the key to organizational performance and that in consequence it is regarded as one of the priorities of top management (Storey 1992; Deal and Kennedy 1991; Legge 1989). Moreover, the exponents of this approach also suggest that organizational cultures can be re-designed so that employees take on new priorities, new values and new conventions. In a word, it is suggested that organizational cultures are not only critical but that they can be 'managed'. This is not of course an uncontested proposition.

From the work of Edgar Schein (1992), social scientists have adopted the idea that leadership and culture are intimately interrelated. The signals the chief executive and other senior managers send about priorities, appropriate behaviours, the kind of behaviours they reward, the things they pay attention to or ignore, the kind of people they recruit and promote (and those which they don't), the control systems and procedures they establish, the way they respond to crises and to mistakes – these, it is said, are the key ways in which organizational culture is shaped. The extent therefore to which innovative behaviour is encouraged or conversely discouraged will result from the various ways in which leaders of the organization create an environment which facilitates it or impedes it.

There is some evidence revealing how organizational culture can create barriers to innovation and thus knowledge creation. In particular an evaluation and reward structure which clearly gives priority to alternative behaviours such as conformance to procedure or to short-term profitability has been frequently noted. Likewise, the gap between what top managers espouse concerning the importance of innovation and knowledge creation – the necessity to take risks and the tolerance of failures – is adversely compared with what happens in practice and it is the practice which seems to set the tone for the shaping of culture rather than the corporate rhetoric.

Innovation can occur in a variety of organizational cultures. Pascale (1991) reveals how it can flourish in a context of constructive criticism and creative tensions. Other varied contexts where innovation is welcomed and encouraged have been noted – including organizations where there is a passion for learning, for curiosity, for quality enhancement, where individuals and groups have a sense of autonomy and independence. We found this to be so, for example, in our research at Hewlett-Packard, the BBC, Nortel, Psion, and in parts of Marconi Telecommunications.

A culture which is conducive to innovation is also likely to be one which is open to new ideas, to the creation of knowledge and to the free flow of ideas wherever these ideas may come from. Such cultures tend to be open to the flow of information across organizational boundaries both internal and external. This implies a culture where hierarchical distinctions are few, where cross-functional boundaries are low and where ideas matter more than title, status or position.

An idea underlying much of the work on innovation in corporations is that bureaucracies must rediscover 'entrepreneurship' (some writers have used the term 'intrapreneurship' in order to denote the specific deployment of entrepreneurial ideas in large corporate settings). This is usually taken to mean a customer focus, a willingness to take risks, 'ownership' of various business problems and so on. In other words, much of this programme is about undoing the characteristics of bureaucracies with their hierarchies, specialization and division of labour, their strict adherence to rule and procedure and their formalization (Kanter 1982, 1983).

Sharing knowledge should not be expected as necessarily a 'normal' thing in all cultures. Whereas in some cultures the notion that one would not share one's knowledge with work colleagues would be unthinkable, in western economies many people have a tendency to hoard knowledge and also to look with scepticism and even suspicion on knowledge derived from elsewhere. As has been noted, 'sharing and usage have to be motivated through time-honoured techniques – performance evaluation, and compensation for example' (Davenport 1997: 189). Hence, some firms evaluate and reward knowledge sharing; for example, Lotus Development (a division of IBM) allocates 25 per cent of its overall performance evaluation points among its customer support staff for knowledge sharing. Other organizations have introduced bonus schemes for rewarding knowledge sharers.

Resourcing

Where and how are the knowledge workers to be found? As noted earlier, there are two broad models: either a selective group of innovators and knowledge creators (usually R&D of some kind) or a more wide-ranging concept of an innovative culture where just about everyone is expected to be alert to the potentials of new ideas and the possibilities of innovation. Arguably it is possible to seek to operate both models simultaneously in that a specialist R&D facility might operate alongside a kaizen culture as in some Japanese companies. It is argued by some that the people closest to the customers are the ones in a prime position to evaluate the need for change.

It is reported in the American personnel literature that recruitment and retention of knowledge workers is being given high priority. An increasing number of US companies are recruiting engineers and scientists from overseas. Examples include Santa Clara (a manufacturer of semiconductors) and Texas Instruments. The argument is that in a global economy companies have to recruit the best people available, and that this means looking world-wide for the talents and skills needed (Greengard 1996).

In addition, human resource management practices in this regard also include more careful and sophisticated selection so that creative people are recruited. It also means attending to the issue of diversity in the composition of the workforce as a way of promoting alternative perspectives.

One argument suggests that it might be best to separate the people who need to ensure routine and continuity from those expected to break the usual routine because uncontrolled innovation risks disorganization and chaos (Peters 1989). But with the increased emphasis on process innovation (e.g. Davenport 1993) such a simple separation may be less easy to achieve in practice.

In dynamic sectors such as semiconductors and bioscience it is likely to be the creative and innovative individuals who are the carriers of the organization's core business competence. As such they are the critical resource. This raises a number of HR issues. First, they are likely to be highly coveted by competitors and therefore they need to be induced by a variety of methods to stay with the organization. Such measures might include profit sharing, the creation of a working environment which is attractive, challenging assignments and the space in which to pursue them, and a culture which is exciting but also seen as fair so that it is conducive to long-term commitment. Second, such people may need protecting even within the organization. Failure to conform may lead to pressure from certain quarters. Likewise it may be necessary to allow them to play to their strengths and not have these diluted by attempting to score widely across a wide span of conventional competency profiles. Third, the potential impact of such talent means that HR may be expected to take appropriate recruitment and selection measures which may break with agreed conventional procedures. Thus again, it is likely that HR will need to be innovative in its own methods.

Developing and learning

Learning and adaptation are arguably absolute necessities for organisms and systems to survive. From such a perspective, innovation and the dynamic creation of variety in the organizations knowledge bases are of paramount importance. But one does not necessarily need to adopt the 'organizations-as-organism' metaphor in order to accept that learning, development and innovation are of increasing importance in current circumstances and for the foreseeable future. To the extent that this is so, the development of the *capability* to innovate becomes a paramount concern for the HR agenda.

Leonard Barton stresses the link between learning, knowledge and innovation. The key elements she suggests are: shared problem solving; experimenting and prototyping; implementing new technical processes and tools; importing and absorbing technological knowledge from outside the firm; and learning from the market. These activities in turn require a fertile soil of growth and renewal if the innovative capacity is to be sustained and hence there is a strong message concerning continuous renewal. Part of this is the need for *higher-order learning*. Without higher-order learning managers will be absorbed by current problems. Engaging in higher-order learning means seeking to learn beyond immediate presenting problems. Managers who look for the meta-routines are constantly asking, 'Why are we doing this? Why are we doing it this way? These simple questions are profound. They also reach for the future; seeking answers to the simple questions will encourage long term thinking rather than reflex action' (Leonard Barton: 1995: 265).

Encouragement of learning for innovation may require, in turn, innovative approaches to learning. The idea of the learning organization has been widely promulgated. In part it means creating opportunities for learning in everyday working activities rather than learning being confined to off-the-job training. The operationalization of such a concept requires a substantial input from management at all levels. But it should not be assumed that people in organizations will adapt to learning unproblematically. As Schein (1992) has noted, even professionals 'avoid learning' and management consultants who evangelize the learning message are themselves typically unreflective about their own practices and unwilling to reflect critically upon their own performance.

Corporate memory

Part of the managerial agenda for learning and development in knowledge-work contexts ought to be the accumulation and preservation of knowledge by the 'organization' itself. This phenomenon is sometimes referred to as building 'corporate memory'. This topic has been examined by Van de Vliet (1997) who points out that departing employees take with them valuable knowledge and that little effort is usually made to store this corporate memory. The problem, it is suggested, is exacerbated by downsizing, re-engineering and outsourcing. Van de Vliet suggests ways of capturing a company's collective knowledge through: recording 'oral histories' at exit interviews and during important projects; conducting and using 'learning audits' which identify lessons to be applied in the future; constructing corporate histories in book form; archiving corporate memory via intranets.

Research at MIT in Boston (Dibella and Nevis, 1996) has helped to clarify and classify the ways in which organizations acquire and utilize knowledge. Three of their questions are especially pertinent here: (i) does important information tend to come from inside or outside the organization? (ii) is key knowledge personal and held by individuals or collective and available for shared use? (iii) is information normally communicated orally or written down and formalized? According to these researchers, the appropriate answers for organizations wishing to be innovative in their use of knowledge is to balance the two extremes in each case.

One problem to confront is that many companies conduct audits of new-product development projects but they do it in name only. As Leonard Barton (1995: 134) has observed,

> their reports moulder away in filing cabinets while the organization continues to make the same mistakes because the projects are not used as opportunities to learn about the developmental process. Failures that may have been intelligent the first time should have been avoidable the second and third time around.

Various steps designed to preserve corporate memory have been suggested. They include:

- Circulation of reports at the end of all projects
- Archiving of reports and related materials
- Exit interview
- Filing systems kept for five years
- Using senior managers as mentors to new recruits
- Active use of a corporate Intranet
- Mandatory completion of a one page 'Things we have learned' sheet at the end of every project
- Strong encouragement for people to record learning from 'failed' attempts
- Audits of 'knowledgeable people' across the organization.

Organizational learning

How does the concept of the Knowledge Organization differ from that of the Learning Organization (LO)? It can be seen to share many attributes. For example, both approaches contend that creating, disseminating and embodying knowledge both tacit and explicit is a key strategic resource. These capabilities hold the key for organizations hoping to unlock the organization's ability to learn faster than competitors and to adapt as the environment changes. However, there is evidently much ambiguity on this point in the literature and in the way practitioners view the issue. Some seem to see Knowledge Management as a development on from the Learning Organization. Thus a Business Intelligence report refers to Anglian Water as having 'broadened out' its Learning Organization initiative into knowledge management. On the other hand, others see Knowledge Management as one step towards the Learning Organization ideal. Glaxo Wellcome seemed to view their main initiative as the creation of a learning organization, knowledge management here being simply a component. Conversely, Monsanto saw them as balanced parts and Skandia seemed to prioritize intellectual capital and located learning as a support to this.

Whether the LO is a step towards a 'knowledge company' or vice versa, many recent commentators have emphasized how learning is critical for organizational success, particularly when it comes to knowledge work. Fisher (1998) identifies two types of obstacles to learning the first of which is described as 'skill impediments' and the second as 'will impediments'. Both of these can be tackled at the individual level. However, certain other impediments have to be overcome at the organizational level, which can be difficult in corporate cultures where open and honest dissemination of information is not encouraged. Fisher identifies four practices that can be employed to promote interaction in order to surmount these obstacles: organizing for socialization; creating cross-disciplinary learning experiences; promoting active experimentation (or 'mucking around'); and developing learning structures. Examples of their use, he maintains, include Thomas Edison's Menlo Park laboratories, Disney and Hewlett-Packard.

One of the most manifest signs of the new corporate attention to the importance of learning and knowledge is to be seen in the growth of 'corporate universities'. Perhaps the most famous are McDonald's and Disney but they have been joined by the high-tech companies such as Motorola and Microsoft. There are now more than 1,600 in the United States and the trend has developed also in Britain with key examples including Unipart University, British Telecom, British Aerospace and GEC. While some have grown out of pre-existing training centres others have been launched with much higher ambitions. BAe's is run in collaboration with Warwick Manufacturing Group and The Open University. Proponents argue that their recent growth is a response to the needs of a service economy wherein companies need to differentiate themselves through more capable staff.

Whichever learning initiative or medium is chosen it is worth bearing in mind that the way in which it is managed is likely to vary depending on which group is steering it. Is it, for example, the HR department, the strategic cluster or the technical experts (the R&D cluster)? The significance attached to who drives learning programmes is demonstrated by some research by Denton (1998). Using examples from 3M and Coca-Cola, Denton found that each of these interest groups adopt different approaches to learning and that these differences were related to the motives which each group had for championing that learning. Enhancing competitive capabilities and learning to cope with change were high on the agenda in each case but different priorities were revealed. Denton recommends that individuals from each group be involved at an early stage in the design of any learning initiative in order to ensure that all objectives are clearly defined and catered for.

Career development

When looking beyond formal training in order to facilitate learning, one of the most widely recognized approaches is to pay serious attention to staff career development. This can involve regular development reviews of individuals by key committees. Such senior committees not only ensure that line managers have to give attention to their people resources but they can also have the authority to ensure that internal movement and progression occurs for developmental purposes. One device worth trying is the use of staff secondments from one function and/or business area to another. For example this could involve R&D staff moving into product divisions or even into customer support and sales and marketing. It is known from previous detailed research that while wide functional experience is not uncommon in the UK, it tends to result from rather ad hoc decisions and unplanned opportunities. This has been shown to contrast with best practice in successful Japanese firms where job rotation between different functions, divisions and spin-out companies is far more systematic, regular and planned (Storey *et al.* 1997).

Involving and empowering

'Empowerment' has been regarded as such an important aspect of the management of knowledge workers that it deserves separate analysis. It is usually regarded as an alternative solution to command and control and rule-based regimes which stifle creativity and engender alienation and conflict. Although widely hailed and prescribed, there have been relatively few published details of the problems employers may experience in implementing such an approach or the conditions necessary to make the approach successful. This issue is examined in Marchington's chapter in this volume (Chapter 12).

Harnessing motivation

The success of all these kinds of steps hinge on the extent to which employees are *willing* to share their knowledge and expertise. If there is a sense of job insecurity staff may be reluctant to share in this way. Some commentators suggest that an answer can be found in the idea of 'employability' – that is, an expectation that an organization will play a part not in securing any job but in upgrading employee skills so that they remain in demand in the wider employment market. However, even this is questionable. If a characteristic of that employability resides in the individual's *distinctive knowledge*, this could conceivably act as a disincentive to sharing that knowledge. How can this dilemma be resolved? Elizabeth Lank (1997) of ICL offers four pieces of advice:

(i) Beware of individualistic performance measures and rewards. This prompt to individualization may produce counterproductive behaviours such as 'do what is measured' rather than doing what is required. If individualized measures and rewards are maintained, she suggests that these include measures of the contribution made by individuals to knowledge sharing and structural capital.

(ii) There needs to be adequate recognition given to those who do share professional knowledge. This could include a formal published directory of expertise and the public recognition which goes with this – possibly including 'appointments' to positions and some ceremony or reward. Knowledge sharers become the heroes.

(iii) Knowledge management must be built into key business processes, for example, making the production of a summary statement of new knowledge gained as part of the normal routine of project management.

(iv) Intranets and similar ICT tools can be used to make knowledge sharing as easy and routine as possible. Customer proposals, project summaries and so on can be deposited into a data archive or repository with just a few simple key strokes. Steps may also be needed to make ICT tools appealing and useful.

Overall, suggests Lank (1997: 412), the focus must be on the 'human factor' ensuring that KM processes give more than they take from employees. Whether the above set of interventions will be sufficient is, however, somewhat open to question.

It is important to recognize that there is not simply a *singular* 'motivational problem'. The issue of motivation occurs under different forms. Accordingly, the associated motivational methods are equally diverse. For example, to make partnering work effectively is likely to require a change of attitude and orientation among managers. Studies have found that a major reason for problems are the attitudes of middle managers who often display reluctance. Beecham and Cordey-Hayes (1998) report on a major study of partnering in the British car-components industry – a context in which partnering is especially critical. They found that a major reason for problems arising was the attitude of middle management in the traditional car plants, many of whom were suspicious of partnering. Firms tended to underestimate the amount of management effort required to make it work.

Motivating *creative* employees would seem to require rather different HR strategies from those devised with an almost opposite intent – that is to control passive and compliant employees. Caudron (1994) and Scott *et al.* (1994) suggest what some of these motivational devices for the creative employee might be. Scott for example, suggests that individual innovative behaviour is governed by perceptions of the 'climate for innovation' and that management style, group relations and so on are mediated through this directly or indirectly. The results also indicate that innovative behaviour is related to the quality of the supervisor–subordinate relationship. The importance accorded to motivating knowledge-sharing by the big accountancy firms such as KPMG and PricewaterhouseCoopers has been noted by Stokdyk (1998).

Reward strategies

There are some empirically-supported claims that companies in the US and Canada, whose success depends on innovation, are rewarding people for knowledge and skills (Covin and Stivers 1997). Reward strategies can cover a broad spectrum which extend beyond direct pay. There can be rewards for acquiring innovative capability and rewards for outputs such as achieving innovation targets. Reward might also take the form of recognition for achievement. This might mean applauding innovators more enthusiastically. It could also mean allowing space and time and resources for successful innovators to pursue their ideas.

The motivation to be innovative may be impeded if the traditional measure of short-term financial performance is given priority as is often the case. The adoption of a 'balanced scorecard' approach by some organizations may help to counter this one-dimensional measure by setting-out a broader range of objectives. Scorecards vary but innovation would nowadays usually be one of the target domains and this can help to motivate employees in this desired direction. 3M's well-known target to 'obtain at least 10 per cent of annual sales from products which did not exist a year ago' is one clear example. But the motivational aspect goes well beyond simply balancing the targets. A better example might be the vision expressed in the *Tomorrow's Company* report (RSA 1995). Such a company regards itself as having a collaborative, win-win mission with various stakeholders. This would seem to offer the potential for a high level of motivation for innovation. Some of the companies subscribing to this agenda have also sought to introduce 'fun' into the workplace through devices such as artists in residence and periodic surprises and other 'playful' interventions. AIT, a software company based in Henley-on-Thames is one such example. The managing director of AIT says that the creative success of the company depends on staff enjoying themselves at work.

But beyond such devices there may be more serious issues relating to change in the psychological contracts at work. Changes to the nature of the psychological contract are likely to require the driving of 'new deals' and Peter Herriott has suggested this process needs to be made far more explicit and open (Herriott and Pemberton 1997).

In line with this recommendation, Thomas Stewart (1998) argues that, in the knowledge economy, people should be treated as 'investors' in the companies where they work. He considers the implications for rewarding people who are treated in this way, and argues the importance of human capital. As a guiding principle, he suggests that the more human capital an employee puts at risk, the more he or she should be rewarded with equity. He points to professional firms as examples where 'human capitalists are king' and he suggests a formula by which the staff take more as the return on equity rises.

Others also advise particular reward systems for knowledge workers. For example, Despres and Hiltrop (1996) propose that reward systems for knowledge workers need to be externally effective (i.e. at least meet the market rate), and have an accepted internal equity. These writers place cultural, social and work challenge issues as more important than financial reward.

In line with these sorts of analyses it has often been assumed that if the expected contribution from knowledge workers is the delivery of innovation then some degree of long-term commitment from, and to, the organization will be a pre-requisite. Using different terminology, innovation has been said to be 'path dependent' (Freeman and Soete 1997; Teece et al. 1997; Rothwell 1992). Extrapolating from this it has been assumed that where innovation is wanted then a high commitment human resource strategy will be required. But recent work by Guest and Conway (2000) challenges this view. These researchers found that what mattered most was the clarity of the 'contract' not its type. In some circumstances, short-term contract workers whose contract clearly prioritizes innovation will be found to deliver on that expectation rather better than permanent employees whose psychological contract is clouded and confused by more diffuse expectations such as 'corporate citizenship'.

CONCLUSIONS

If we really are entering a knowledge economy wherein the expected contribution from 'labour' is of an entirely different kind than in the industrial past then there would appear to be significant implications for the management of these human resources. The true extent and nature of these implications have yet to be fully realized. Even if the economy as a whole is not undergoing a seismic shift the question concerning how to manage the knowledge workers, or knowledge work, in those companies which are mainly constituted by such workers remains a challenging one.

In this chapter we have sought to clarify the idea of 'knowledge management' and the implications of taking a 'knowledge management perspective' to the understanding of work in organizations. In particular, five elements were explained which were seen to constitute knowledge processes for an organization. These central organizational knowledge processes were: creating knowledge, sharing it, sourcing it, mapping it, and measuring it. The chapter also noted that despite the frequency with which HR issues have been said to constitute a crucial element in knowledge management success, the actual processes involved have so far not been examined in any depth. To help begin to correct for this the chapter moved on to clarify the meaning of the idea of 'knowledge work' and 'knowledge workers', and identified the sharing of tacit and implicit knowledge as a central issue.

A number of key problems which had a central bearing on HRM were examined. Five in particular were identified: the challenge of developing and sustaining a culture that supports knowledge creation and innovation; the problems organizations may have in accessing tacit and implicit knowledge; the problem of securing trust and commitment; the handling of 'atypical' contributors such as contract workers and consultants; and the problem of various vulnerabilities which organizations may face – not least being a potential shift in the balance of power whereby certain organizations may be heavily dependent on particular key workers.

The chapter then moved on to explore the HR practices which might be expected to be at the forefront in coping with this range of challenges. It was suggested that the agenda here was wide-ranging and included the need to re-examine the design of organizational forms, the role of organizational cultures, and the whole array of HR approaches including motivation and reward but with more than usual attention having to be paid to issues of learning and the safeguarding of organizational memory.

REFERENCES

Allen, J. and Henry N. (1996). 'Fragments of industry and employment: Contract service work and the shift towards precarious employment', in R.G. Crompton, D. Gallie and K. Purcell (eds) *Changing Forms of Employment*, London: Routledge.

Ashkenas, R., Ulrich, D. Tick, J. and Kerr, S. (1995) *The Boundaryless Organization: Breaking the Chains of Organizational Structure*, San Francisco: Jossey-Bass.

Baumard, P. (1999) *Tacit Knowledge in Organizations*, London: Sage.

Beecham, M.A. and Cordey-Hayes, M. (1998) 'Partnering and knowledge transfer in the UK motor industry', *Technovation*, **18**(3): 191–206.

Beck, U. (1992) *Risk Society*, London, Sage.

Bell, D. (1974) *The Coming of Post-Industrial Society: A Venture in Social Forecasting*, London: Heinemann.

Boland, R. and Tenkasi, R. (1995) 'Perspective making and perspective taking in communities of knowing', *Organization Science*, **6**(4): 350–73.

Brown, J.S. and Duguid P. (1991) 'Organizational learning and communities of practice', *Organization Science*, **2**(1): 40–57.

Caudron, S. (1994) 'Strategies for Managing Creative Workers', *Personnel Journal*, **73**(12); 103–7.

Choi, T.Y. and Varney G.H. (1995) 'Rethinking the knowledge workers: where have all the workers gone?' *Organization Development Journal*, **13**(2): 41–51.

Cohen, W.M. and Levinthal, D.A. (1990) 'Absorptive Capacity: a new perspective on learning and innovation', *Administrative Science Quarterly*, **35**: 128–52.

Covin, T.J. and Stivers, B.P. (1997) 'Knowledge management focus in US and Canadian firms'. *Creativity and Innovation Management*, **6**(3): 140–151.

Davenport, T.H. (1993) *Process Innovation*, Boston, MA: Harvard Business School.

Davenport, T.H. (1997) 'Ten principles of knowledge management and four case studies', *Knowledge & Process Management*, **4**(3): 187–208.

Davidow, W.H. and Malone, M.S. (1992) *The Virtual Corporation: Structuring and Revitalizing the Corporation for the 21st Century*, New York: Harper Business.

Deal, T.E. and Kennedy, A.A. (1991) *Corporate Cultures*, Reading, MA: Addison-Wesley.

Denton, J. (1998) 'Who is driving organizational learning?' *Professional Manager*, **7**(6): 33–36.

Despres, C. and Hiltrop J.-M. (1996) 'Compensation for technical professionals in the knowledge age', *Research Technology Management*, **39**(5): 48–57.

Dibella, A.J. and Nevis, E.C. (1996) 'Understanding organizational learning capabilities', *Journal of Management Studies*, **33**(3): 361–79.

Docherty, A. (1993) 'Getting the best out of "knowledge workers"', *Involvement*, Autumn: 6–12.

Drucker, P. (1968) *The Age of Discontinuity*, New York, Harper & Row.

Freeman, C. and Soete, L. (1997) *The Economics of Industrial Innovation*, London: Pinter.

Grant, R. (1991) 'The resource-based theory of competitive advantage: implications for strategy formation', *California Management Review*, **34**(Spring): 114–35.

Greengard, S. (1996) 'Gain the edge in the knowledge race', *Personnel Journal*, **75**(8): 52–56.

Guest, D. and Conway, N. (2000) 'Flexible employment contracts, innovation and learning', Working Paper, Birkbeck College.

Herriott, P. and Pemberton, C. (1997) 'Facilitating new deals', *Human Resource Management Journal*, **7**(1): 45–56.

Kanter, R.M. (1982) 'The middle manager as innovator', *Harvard Business Review*, **61**(July–August): 95–105.

Kanter, R.M. (1983) *The Changemasters: Corporate Entrepreneurs at Work*, New York: Routledge.

Kay, J. and William P. (1991) 'Managing technological innovation: architecture, trust and organizational relationships in the firm', Working Paper. London: London Business School.

Kusterer, K. (1978) *Know-how on the Job: The Important Working Knowledge of the Unskilled Worker*, Boulder, CO: Westview Press.

Lank, E. (1997) 'Leveraging invisible assets: the human factor', *Long Range Planning*, **30**(3): 406–12.

Legge, K. (1989) 'Human resource management: A critical analysis', in J. Storey (ed.) *New Perspectives on Human Resource Management*, London: Routledge.

Leonard-Barton, D. (1995) *Wellsprings of Knowledge: Building and Sustaining the Sources of Innovation*, Boston: Harvard Business School Press.

Machlup, F. (1962) *The Production and Distribution of Knowledge*, Princeton: Princeton University Press.

March, J.G. and Simon, H.A. (1958) *Organizations*, New York: Wiley.

Marshall, A. (1890) *Principles of Economics*, London: Macmillan.

Miner, D. and Beyerlein, M. (1998) 'Embedded knowledge teams: succeeding with hybrid organizational forms'. *Team Performance Management: An International Journal*, **4**(4): 116–21.

Newell, S. and Clark P.A. (1990) 'The importance of extra-organizational networks in the diffusion and appropriation of new technologies: the role of professional associations in the United States and Britain', *Knowledge: Creation, Diffusion, Utilization*, **12**(2): 199–211.

Nonaka, I. (1991) 'The knowledge creating company', *Harvard Business Review*, November–December: 96–104.

Nonaka, I. (1994) 'A dynamic theory of organizational knowledge creation', *Organization Science*, **5**(1): 14–36.

Nonaka, I. and Takeuchi, H. (1995) *The Knowledge-Creating Company: How Japanese Companies Create the Dynamics of Innovation*, Oxford: Oxford University Press.

O'Dell, C. and Grayson, C.J. (1998) 'If only we knew what we know: Identification and transfer on internal best practice', *California Management Review*, **40**(3): 154–74.

Pascale, R. (1991) *Managing on the Edge*, Harmondsworth: Penguin.

Pfeffer, J. (1998) *The Human Equation: Building profits by Putting People First*, Boston: Harvard Business School Press.

Piore, M and Sabel, C. (1984) *The Second Industrial Divide*, New York: Basic Books.

Prusack, L. (ed.) (1997) *Knowledge in Organizations*, Boston: Butterworth-Heinemann.

Robertson, M. and Swan, J. (1998) 'Modes of organizing in an expert consultancy: a case study of knowledge, power and egos', *Organization*, **5**(4): 543–65.

Rothwell, R. (1992) 'Successful industrial innovation: critical factors for the 1990s', *R&D Management*, **22**(3): 221–239.

RSA (1995) *Tomorrow's Company*, London: Royal Society of Arts.

Scarbrough, H., Swan, J. (1999) *Case Studies in Knowledge Management*, London: IPD.

Scarbrough, H., Swan, J. *et al.* (1999) *Knowledge Management: a Literature Review*, London, IPD.

Schein, E. (1992) *Organizational Culture and Leadership*, second edition, San Francisco: Jossey-Bass.

Scott, S.G. and Bruce, R. (1994) 'Determinants of innovative behavior: a path model of individual innovation in the workplace', *Academy of Management Journal*, **37**(3): 580–606.

Spender, J.C. (1996) 'Making knowledge the basis of a dynamic theory of the firm', *Strategic Management Journal*, **17**(Winter Special Issue): 45–62.

Stewart, T.A. (1997) *Intellectual Capital: The New Wealth of Organizations*, London: Nicholas Brealy.

Stewart, T.A. (1998) 'Will the real capitalist please stand up?' *Fortune*, **137**(9): 81–83.

Stokdyk, J. (1998) 'Doing the knowledge', *Accountancy Age*, **29**(Oct): 18–21.

Storey, J. (1992) *Developments in the Management of Human Resources*, Oxford: Blackwell.

Storey, J. and Barnett, E. (2000) 'Knowledge management initiatives: learning from failure', *Journal of Knowledge Management*, **4**(2): 145–57.

Storey, J., Edwards, P.K. and Sisson, K. (1997) *Managers in the Making*, London: Sage.

Sviokla, J.J. (1996) 'Knowledge workers and radically new technology', *Sloan Management Review*, **37**(4): 25–36.

Taylor, F.W. (1911) *Principles of Scientific Management*, New York: Harper.

Teece, D.J., Pisano, G. *et al.* (1997) 'Dynamic capabilities and strategic management', *Strategic Management Journal*, **18**(7): 509–533.

Ulrich, D. (1998) 'Intellectual capital = competence × commitment', *Sloan Management Review*, **39**(2): 15–27.

van de Vliet, A. (1997) 'Lest we forget', *Management Today*, January: 62–65.

Wenger, E. (1998) *Communities of Practice*, Cambridge: Cambridge University Press.

Wenger, E. and Snyder, W. (2000) 'Communities of practice: the organizational frontier', *Harvard Business Review*, January–February: 139–45.

Willman, P. (1996) 'Protecting know-how', *Business Strategy Review*, **7**(1): 9–14.

Young, R. (1998) 'Virtual teams: the wide awake club', *People Management*, **5** February: 46–49.

18 Looking to the Future

John Storey

The purpose of this final chapter is to take stock of some of the major points raised in the preceding chapters and to place this new knowledge alongside the introductory review conducted in Chapter 1. The intervening chapters have described and evaluated the nature and significance of the key developments in human resource management. The meanings, attributes, extent, advantages and disadvantages of innovations in this academic field and this realm of practice have been explored. But what, it might be asked, are the most important new issues and what of the future?

It should now be apparent enough that there is no single 'trend' in employment management towards (or even away from) one particular form of human resource management. The expectation previously held, by some, that a best practice mode of HRM would 'diffuse' across the economy (and indeed across different economies) now seems misplaced. There have certainly been forms of initiatives which have been widely adopted but the notion that a high-commitment management package would spread across different sectors until it became the dominant mode appears mistaken. Instead what we have witnessed, and continue to observe, is the playing-out of diverse tendencies. There are low-road as well as high-road paths to competitiveness.

Least-cost, lean production, and minimal investment types of organizations survive. Low-trust, high surveillance and control-based practices have flourished in certain employment growth areas of the economy – most notably in call centres. Likewise, various forms of labour flexibility have increased. Union membership and collective bargaining have continued to decline. New partnership arrangements have been tried and publicized but they have only affected a minority of organizations. So what is going on?

One of the most significant developments since the previous edition of this book has been the accumulation of an impressive array of studies which reveal how investment in HRM 'pays off' (see the discussion in Chapter 1). Yet despite such evidence, the task of 'persuading' employers of the wisdom of adopting such policies and practices appears to be as uphill as ever. Indeed, commenting on the WERS findings, Cully *et al.* (1999: 295) refer to the 'conundrum' of why high commitment management practices have not been more widespread given the 'compelling evidence' of their link with performance. It would seem that among the array of factors shaping and influencing the adoption of various employment practices the power of persuasion is somewhat limited when set alongside other factors.

What are these other factors? To answer this question we have to look to the raft of changes in the wider environment. A crucial one is the changing nature of product market competition which for a range of reasons has intensified. Markets have in many sectors become more open to global competition. Western companies are increasingly able and willing to locate manufacturing and service functions in low-wage countries. In the case of data handling services information and communication technology allows work to be allocated across the globe with the same immediacy as if it were located locally. Distance no longer presents a barrier. At the same time, the removal of exchange controls has intensified pressure on the trading sectors of the economy. Likewise, during the past 25 years the practice of furnishing state subsidies to ailing enterprises has drastically declined with direct consequences for traditional labour practices. European Union regulations serve to ensure that wavering member state governments avoid the temptation of electoral expedience in relation to this. At the same time, it has to be recognized that European directives have also resulted in an extensive range of new regulative requirements affecting employment practices. These include statutory restrictions on working time, part-time worker rights, and so on. Whether this platform of individual rights will serve to displace unions further or alternatively offer them an opportunity for enforcement remains open to question.

Such changes in product market conditions tend to impact on labour markets – but in diverse ways. While the bargaining power of unskilled and semi-skilled workers declines, the power exercised by those whose intellectual capital is in short supply can increase dramatically. Thus, investment bankers, for example, can attract very high bonuses even at a time when other bank staff jobs are being cut. To take just one example, early in the year 2000, Dresdner Bank paid £240 million in bonuses (a sum equivalent to nearly £32,000 per employee) in its investment banking business in an attempt to hold on to its talent during the failed merger talks with Deutsche Bank. The star performers whom the bank was especially anxious to retain were paid much higher sums. This emerging pattern of bifurcation, with some workers able to secure vast sums while others suffer poor rewards, reflects the hypothesis of those labour economists who argue that the economy is undergoing a shift to a state where certain holders of intellectual capital will reap extraordinary rewards (Albert and Bradley 1997; Stewart 1997). This contention is part of a wide-ranging thesis which holds that the key to competitiveness in the 'new economy' is fundamentally different from the mix of factors of production which predominated in the industrial age when economies of scale were crucial. Now, it is suggested, wealth-creation derives largely from 'intangible assets'. The argument has been summarized by Leadbeater (1999: 64) who writes 'This new economy will reward celebrities and stars, gamblers and entrepreneurs, but it offers less, at the moment, for the very large swathe of people who would have had stable jobs under the old order'. As characterized by Leadbeater, this is the phenomenon of the 'living on thin air economy'. Bill Gates' Microsoft is the most cited example. By the mid 1990s this company had stock worth $86 billion – only one billion of which was recordable as physical assets: 'the missing $85 billion of Microsoft's worth was entirely due to its intangible assets, its know-how, research capabilities, likely stream of new products, the Windows brand name and Gates himself' (ibid.: 98).

The argument is that intangible assets which largely derive from intellectual capital have become the crucial source of wealth-creation in the new economy. In so far as this is so, there would appear to be far-reaching implications for human resource management. There are two main strands to this. The first is predicated on the assumption that, in the main, the people who carry much of this intellectual capital around in their heads and who can 'walk out of the door each night' with these valuable assets, will still be employees of organizations and that, in consequence, employers will need to adjust their employment practices. This dimension was examined in Chapter 17.

A second strand, however, goes much further and posits a scenario where individual holders of intellectual capital become much more autonomous. Thus, for example Albert and Bradley (1997: 1) contend that work is being transformed in a way which means that 'the contemporary workforce is increasingly comprised of professional knowledge-based employees such as lawyers, accountants, managers, bankers, marketing and advertising executives, scientists, engineers, doctors, and computer programmers'. As a group these influential workers are labelled as experts – people whom Reich (1992) recognised as having 'the ability to manipulate intangible assets' and they also include journalists, musicians and film producers. The argument presented by Albert and Bradley is that much of the growth in 'atypical' work (i.e. away from conventional employment) has been driven not, as most of the literature implies, by organization strategy, but by these experts who are increasingly exercising their market power. This supply-side analysis has it that organizations have to respond to the increasing demands of such workers or risk losing them. Nor, in this analysis, is this group to be regarded as a numerically small elite. Albert and Bradley estimated that these knowledge workers would total 10.5 million by the year 2000 compared with only seven million manual workers. Such an analysis clearly shifts the ground of the conventional debate surrounding labour management.

But this predominantly optimistic interpretation is at odds with the more dominant analyses of flexible labour markets which detect not growing assertiveness, independence and confidence among the workforce but, on the contrary, increasing *insecurity* (Beck 1992; Heery and Salmon 2000). The 'insecurity thesis' as Heery and Salmon term it, is based on the premise that risk is being purposefully transferred by employers from organizations to workers through more contingent labour contracts. Thus while Albert and Bradley see many atypical workers opting for this work arrangement, others view this pattern of work as a consequence of employer initiative. The reality seems to be a complex mix of such forces. What can more safely be observed is that employment relations are fragmenting due to a variety of factors.

There are, it seems, a number of cross-cutting tendencies. Some of these lend support to the high commitment mode of HRM – for example, the idea of resource-based competition (Barney 1991, 1995), of core competences (Hamel and Prahalad 1994) and the importance of organizational learning (Argyris 1978; Senge 1990). But while this 'high road' approach to competitiveness may be of significance and can apparently be shown to result in positive outcomes (see, for example, Michie and Sheehan 1999 and the array of empirical studies cited in Chapter 1) there is none the less also evidence of much use of the 'low road' which heads off in a very different direction. The low road employer relies on a host of low-cost employment measures including a hire-and-fire pattern, low investment in training, low wages and low discretion jobs – all features inimical to high commitment employment policies.

This variety of practice has long been evident in British employment in particular and it seems likely that it will continue. Twenty years of experience with HRM suggest that the across-the-board diffusion thesis is unsupported. But on the other hand there are few signs of any other pattern assuming the mantle of orthodoxy. The adoption of new European-led social regulation suggests that American-style free-market policies will not be acceptable in an unbridled way; but neither does the adoption of a fully articulated European social model seem likely, despite the persuasive case mounted by its advocates (Sisson 2000). The most probable scenario is that some segments of the economy will persist along the low road – curbed from the worst excesses by a more comprehensive floor of legal rights; other segments will forge ahead based on the innovative uses of knowledge and intangible assets; while others will seek to compete in the global economy drawing upon the most judicious mixture of human resource policies and practices they can muster. And, given the current pace and extent of change in product and labour markets, one can also see why some organizations, such as British Telecom, which previously experienced relatively stable product and labour markets, now find themselves connecting with, and to some degree engaging as a player in, all three games at once. Arguably this is the real nature of the challenge facing managers of human resources in the future – the capability to manage diverse contributors, operating under diverse contracts in diverse ways.

REFERENCES

Albert, S. (1997), *Managing knowledge: experts, agencies and organizations*, Cambridge: Cambridge University Press.

Albert, S. and Bradley, K. (1997) *Managing Knowledge: Experts, Agencies and Organizations*, Cambridge: Cambridge University Press.

Argyris, C.A.S.D (1978) *Organizational Learning: A Theory of Action Perspective*, Reading MA: Addison-Wesley.

Barney, J. (1991) 'Firm resources and sustained competitive advantage', *Journal of Management*, **17**(1): 99–120.

Barney, J.B. (1995) 'Looking inside for competitive advantage', *Academy of Management Executive*, **9**(4): 49–61.

Beck, U. (1992) *Risk Society*, London: Sage.

Cully, M., Woodland, S. *et al.* (1999) *Britain at Work: As Depicted by the 1998 Workplace Employee Relations Survey*, London: Routledge.

Hamel, G. and Prahalad, C.K. (1994) *Competing for the Future*, Boston: Harvard Business School Press.

Heery, E. and Salmon, J. (2000) *The Insecure Workforce*, London: Routledge.

Leadbeater, C. (1999) *Living on Thin Air: The New Economy*, London: Viking.

Michie, J. and Sheehan, M. (1999) 'HRM practices, R&D expenditure and innovative investment: Evidence from the 1990 WIRS', *Industrial & Corporate Change*, **8**(2): 211–33.

Reich, R. (1992) *The Work of Nations*, New York: Vintage Press.

Senge, P. (1990) *The Fifth Discipline: The Art and Practice of the Learning Organization*, London: Century Business.

Sisson, K. (2000) 'The "new" European social model: the end of the search for an orthodoxy or another false dawn', *Employee Relations*, **21**(5): 445–62.

Stewart, T.A. (1997) *Intellectual capital: the new wealth of organizations*, London: Nicholas Brealy.

Index